Introduction to
Parallel Computing

We work with leading authors to develop the
strongest educational materials in computing,
bringing cutting-edge thinking and best
learning practice to a global market.

Under a range of well-known imprints, including
Addison-Wesley, we craft high-quality print and
electronic publications which help readers to understand
and apply their content, whether studying or at work.

To find out more about the complete range of our
publishing, please visit us on the World Wide Web at:
www.pearsoned.co.uk

ANANTH GRAMA • ANSHUL GUPTA

GEORGE KARYPIS • VIPIN KUMAR

Introduction to
Parallel Computing

Second Edition

PEARSON

Addison
Wesley

Harlow, England • London • New York • Boston • San Francisco • Toronto
Sydney • Tokyo • Singapore • Hong Kong • Seoul • Taipei • New Delhi
Cape Town • Madrid • Mexico City • Amsterdam • Munich • Paris • Milan

Pearson Education Limited
Edinburgh Gate
Harlow
Essex CM20 2JE
England

and Associated Companies throughout the world

Visit us on the World Wide Web at:
www.pearsoned.co.uk

First published by The Benjamin/Cummings Publishing Company, Inc. 1994
Second edition published 2003

ISBN-13: 978-0-201-64865-2

British Library Cataloguing-in-Publication Data
A catalogue record for this book is available from the British Library.

Library of Congress Cataloguing-in-Publication Data
Introduction to parallel computing / Ananth Grama [et al] – 2nd ed.
    p. cm.
    Includes bibliographical references and index.
    1. Parallel processing (Electronic computers) 2. Parallel algorithms. I. Grama, Ananth.

QA76.58 I578 2003
005.2—dc21

15
17

Printed and bound in Great Britain by Henry Ling limited, at the Dorset Press, Dorchester, DT1 1HD

To Joanna, Rinku, Krista, and Renu

Contents

Chapter 3

Principles of Parallel Algorithm Design   85

CHAPTER   4

Basic Communication Operations   147

Chapter 5

Analytical Modeling of Parallel Programs   195

Chapter 6

Programming Using the Message-Passing Paradigm   233

CHAPTER 7

Programming Shared Address Space Platforms   279

Chapter 8

Dense Matrix Algorithms   337

Chapter 9

Sorting   379

CHAPTER 10

Graph Algorithms   429

CHAPTER 11

Search Algorithms for Discrete Optimization Problems   469

CHAPTER 12

Dynamic Programming   515

CHAPTER 13

Fast Fourier Transform   537

APPENDIX A

Complexity of Functions and Order Analysis   565

Bibliography   569

Author Index   611

Subject Index   621

Preface

Since the 1994 release of the text "Introduction to Parallel Computing: Design and Analysis of Algorithms" by the same authors, the field of parallel computing has undergone significant changes. Whereas tightly coupled scalable message-passing platforms were the norm a decade ago, a significant portion of the current generation of platforms consists of inexpensive clusters of workstations, and multiprocessor workstations and servers. Programming models for these platforms have also evolved over this time. Whereas most machines a decade back relied on custom APIs for messaging and loop-based parallelism, current models standardize these APIs across platforms. Message passing libraries such as PVM and MPI, thread libraries such as POSIX threads, and directive based models such as OpenMP are widely accepted as standards, and have been ported to a variety of platforms.

With respect to applications, fluid dynamics, structural mechanics, and signal processing formed dominant applications a decade back. These applications continue to challenge the current generation of parallel platforms. However, a variety of new applications have also become important. These include data-intensive applications such as transaction processing and information retrieval, data mining and analysis, and multimedia services. Applications in emerging areas of computational biology and nanotechnology pose tremendous challenges for algorithms and systems development. Changes in architectures, programming models, and applications are also being accompanied by changes in how parallel platforms are made available to the users in the form of grid-based services.

This evolution has a profound impact on the process of design, analysis, and implementation of parallel algorithms. Whereas the emphasis of parallel algorithm design a decade back was on precise mapping of tasks to specific topologies such as meshes and hypercubes, current emphasis is on programmability and portability, both from points of view of algorithm design and implementation. To this effect, where possible, this book employs an architecture independent view of the underlying platforms and designs algorithms for an abstract model. With respect to programming models, Message Passing Interface (MPI), POSIX threads, and OpenMP have been selected. The evolving application mix for parallel computing is also reflected in various examples in the book.

This book forms the basis for a single concentrated course on parallel computing or a two-part sequence. Some suggestions for such a two-part sequence are:

1. Introduction to Parallel Computing: Chapters 1–6. This course would provide the basics of algorithm design and parallel programming.

2. Design and Analysis of Parallel Algorithms: Chapters 2 and 3 followed by Chapters 8–12. This course would provide an in-depth coverage of design and analysis of various parallel algorithms.

The material in this book has been tested in Parallel Algorithms and Parallel Computing courses at the University of Minnesota and Purdue University. These courses are taken primarily by graduate students and senior-level undergraduate students in Computer Science. In addition, related courses in Scientific Computation, for which this material has also been tested, are taken by graduate students in science and engineering, who are interested in solving computationally intensive problems.

Most chapters of the book include (i) examples and illustrations; (ii) problems that supplement the text and test students' understanding of the material; and (iii) bibliographic remarks to aid researchers and students interested in learning more about related and advanced topics. The comprehensive subject index helps the reader locate terms they might be interested in. The page number on which a term is defined is highlighted in boldface in the index. Furthermore, the term itself appears in bold italics where it is defined. The sections that deal with relatively complex material are preceded by a '*'. An instructors' manual containing slides of the figures and solutions to selected problems is also available from the publisher (`http://www.booksites.net/kumar`).

As with our previous book, we view this book as a continually evolving resource. We thank all the readers who have kindly shared critiques, opinions, problems, code, and other information relating to our first book. It is our sincere hope that we can continue this interaction centered around this new book. We encourage readers to address communication relating to this book to `book-vk@cs.umn.edu`. All relevant reader input will be added to the information archived at the site `http://www.cs.umn.edu/~parbook` with due credit to (and permission of) the sender(s). An on-line errata of the book will also be maintained at the site. We believe that in a highly dynamic field such as ours, a lot is to be gained from a healthy exchange of ideas and material in this manner.

Acknowledgments

We would like to begin by acknowledging our spouses, Joanna, Rinku, Krista, and Renu to whom this book is dedicated. Without their sacrifices this project would not have been seen completion. We also thank our parents, and family members, Akash, Avi, Chethan, Eleni, Larry, Mary-Jo, Naina, Petros, Samir, Subhasish, Varun, Vibhav, and Vipasha for their affectionate support and encouragement throughout this project.

Our respective institutions, Computer Sciences and Computing Research Institute (CRI) at Purdue University, Department of Computer Science & Engineering, the Army High Performance Computing Research Center (AHPCRC), and the Digital Technology Center (DTC) at the University of Minnesota, and the IBM T. J. Watson Research Center at Yorktown Heights, provided computing resources and active and nurturing environments for the completion of this project.

This project evolved from our first book. We would therefore like to acknowledge all of the people who helped us with both editions. Many people contributed to this project in different ways. We would like to thank Ahmed Sameh for his constant encouragement and support, and Dan Challou, Michael Heath, Dinesh Mehta, Tom Nurkkala, Paul Saylor, and Shang-Hua Teng for the valuable input they provided to the various versions of the book. We thank the students of the introduction to parallel computing classes at the University of Minnesota and Purdue university for identifying and working through the errors in the early drafts of the book. In particular, we acknowledge the patience and help of Jim Diehl and Rasit Eskicioglu, who worked through several early drafts of the manuscript to identify numerous errors. Ramesh Agarwal, David Bailey, Rupak Biswas, Jim Bottum, Thomas Downar, Rudolf Eigenmann, Sonia Fahmy, Greg Frederickson, John Gunnels, Fred Gustavson, Susanne Hambrusch, Bruce Hendrickson, Christoph Hoffmann, Kai Hwang, Ioannis Ioannidis, Chandrika Kamath, David Keyes, Mehmet Koyuturk, Piyush Mehrotra, Zhiyuan Li, Jens Palsberg, Voicu Popescu, Alex Pothen, Viktor Prasanna, Sanjay Ranka, Naren Ramakrishnan, Elisha Sacks, Vineet Singh, Sartaj Sahni, Vivek Sarin, Wojciech Szpankowski, Srikanth Thirumalai, Jan Vitek, and David Yau have been great technical resources. It was a pleasure working with the cooperative and helpful staff at Pearson Education. In particular, we would like to thank Keith Mansfield and Mary Lince for their professional handling of the project.

The Army Research Laboratory, ARO, DOE, NASA, and NSF provided parallel computing research support for Ananth Grama, George Karypis, and Vipin Kumar. In particular, Kamal Abdali, Michael Coyle, Jagdish Chandra, Frederica Darema, Stephen Davis, Wm Randolph Franklin, Richard Hirsch, Charles Koelbel, Raju Namburu, N. Radhakrishnan, John Van Rosendale, Subhash Saini, and Xiaodong Zhang have been supportive of our research programs in the area of parallel computing. Andrew Conn, Brenda Dietrich, John Forrest, David Jensen, and Bill Pulleyblank at IBM supported the work of Anshul Gupta over the years.

CHAPTER 1

Introduction to Parallel Computing

The past decade has seen tremendous advances in microprocessor technology. Clock rates of processors have increased from about 40 MHz (e.g., a MIPS R3000, circa 1988) to over 2.0 GHz (e.g., a Pentium 4, circa 2002). At the same time, processors are now capable of executing multiple instructions in the same cycle. The average number of cycles per instruction (CPI) of high end processors has improved by roughly an order of magnitude over the past 10 years. All this translates to an increase in the peak floating point operation execution rate (floating point operations per second, or FLOPS) of several orders of magnitude. A variety of other issues have also become important over the same period. Perhaps the most prominent of these is the ability (or lack thereof) of the memory system to feed data to the processor at the required rate. Significant innovations in architecture and software have addressed the alleviation of bottlenecks posed by the datapath and the memory.

The role of concurrency in accelerating computing elements has been recognized for several decades. However, their role in providing multiplicity of datapaths, increased access to storage elements (both memory and disk), scalable performance, and lower costs is reflected in the wide variety of applications of parallel computing. Desktop machines, engineering workstations, and compute servers with two, four, or even eight processors connected together are becoming common platforms for design applications. Large scale applications in science and engineering rely on larger configurations of parallel computers, often comprising hundreds of processors. Data intensive platforms such as database or web servers and applications such as transaction processing and data mining often use clusters of workstations that provide high aggregate disk bandwidth. Applications in graphics and visualization use multiple rendering pipes and processing elements to compute and render realistic environments with millions of polygons in real time. Applications requiring high availability rely on parallel and distributed platforms for redundancy. It is therefore extremely important, from the point of view of cost, performance, and application requirements, to understand the principles, tools, and techniques for programming the wide variety of parallel platforms currently available.

1.1   Motivating Parallelism

Development of parallel software has traditionally been thought of as time and effort intensive. This can be largely attributed to the inherent complexity of specifying and coordinating concurrent tasks, a lack of portable algorithms, standardized environments, and software development toolkits. When viewed in the context of the brisk rate of development of microprocessors, one is tempted to question the need for devoting significant effort towards exploiting parallelism as a means of accelerating applications. After all, if it takes two years to develop a parallel application, during which time the underlying hardware and/or software platform has become obsolete, the development effort is clearly wasted. However, there are some unmistakable trends in hardware design, which indicate that uniprocessor (or implicitly parallel) architectures may not be able to sustain the rate of *realizable* performance increments in the future. This is a result of lack of implicit parallelism as well as other bottlenecks such as the datapath and the memory. At the same time, standardized hardware interfaces have reduced the turnaround time from the development of a microprocessor to a parallel machine based on the microprocessor. Furthermore, considerable progress has been made in standardization of programming environments to ensure a longer life-cycle for parallel applications. All of these present compelling arguments in favor of parallel computing platforms.

1.1.1   The Computational Power Argument – from Transistors to FLOPS

In 1965, Gordon Moore made the following simple observation:

"The complexity for minimum component costs has increased at a rate of roughly a factor of two per year. Certainly over the short term this rate can be expected to continue, if not to increase. Over the longer term, the rate of increase is a bit more uncertain, although there is no reason to believe it will not remain nearly constant for at least 10 years. That means by 1975, the number of components per integrated circuit for minimum cost will be 65,000."

His reasoning was based on an empirical log-linear relationship between device complexity and time, observed over three data points. He used this to justify that by 1975, devices with as many as 65,000 components would become feasible on a single silicon chip occupying an area of only about one-fourth of a square inch. This projection turned out to be accurate with the fabrication of a 16K CCD memory with about 65,000 components in 1975. In a subsequent paper in 1975, Moore attributed the log-linear relationship to exponential behavior of die sizes, finer minimum dimensions, and "circuit and device cleverness". He went on to state that:

"There is no room left to squeeze anything out by being clever. Going forward from here we have to depend on the two size factors - bigger dies and finer dimensions."

He revised his rate of circuit complexity doubling to 18 months and projected from 1975 onwards at this reduced rate. This curve came to be known as "Moore's Law". Formally, Moore's Law states that circuit complexity doubles every eighteen months. This empirical relationship has been amazingly resilient over the years both for microprocessors as well as for DRAMs. By relating component density and increases in die-size to the computing power of a device, Moore's law has been extrapolated to state that the amount of computing power available at a given cost doubles approximately every 18 months.

The limits of Moore's law have been the subject of extensive debate in the past few years. Staying clear of this debate, the issue of translating transistors into useful OPS (operations per second) is the critical one. It is possible to fabricate devices with very large transistor counts. How we use these transistors to achieve increasing rates of computation is the key architectural challenge. A logical recourse to this is to rely on parallelism – both implicit and explicit. We will briefly discuss implicit parallelism in Section 2.1 and devote the rest of this book to exploiting explicit parallelism.

1.1.2   The Memory/Disk Speed Argument

The overall speed of computation is determined not just by the speed of the processor, but also by the ability of the memory system to feed data to it. While clock rates of high-end processors have increased at roughly 40% per year over the past decade, DRAM access times have only improved at the rate of roughly 10% per year over this interval. Coupled with increases in instructions executed per clock cycle, this gap between processor speed and memory presents a tremendous performance bottleneck. This growing mismatch between processor speed and DRAM latency is typically bridged by a hierarchy of successively faster memory devices called caches that rely on locality of data reference to deliver higher memory system performance. In addition to the latency, the net effective bandwidth between DRAM and the processor poses other problems for sustained computation rates.

The overall performance of the memory system is determined by the fraction of the total memory requests that can be satisfied from the cache. Memory system performance is addressed in greater detail in Section 2.2. Parallel platforms typically yield better memory system performance because they provide (i) larger aggregate caches, and (ii) higher aggregate bandwidth to the memory system (both typically linear in the number of processors). Furthermore, the principles that are at the heart of parallel algorithms, namely locality of data reference, also lend themselves to cache-friendly serial algorithms. This argument can be extended to disks where parallel platforms can be used to achieve high aggregate bandwidth to secondary storage. Here, parallel algorithms yield insights into the development of out-of-core computations. Indeed, some of the fastest growing application areas of parallel computing in data servers (database servers, web servers) rely not so much on their high aggregate computation rates but rather on the ability to pump data out at a faster rate.

1.1.3   The Data Communication Argument

As the networking infrastructure evolves, the vision of using the Internet as one large heterogeneous parallel/distributed computing environment has begun to take shape. Many applications lend themselves naturally to such computing paradigms. Some of the most impressive applications of massively parallel computing have been in the context of wide-area distributed platforms. The SETI (Search for Extra Terrestrial Intelligence) project utilizes the power of a large number of home computers to analyze electromagnetic signals from outer space. Other such efforts have attempted to factor extremely large integers and to solve large discrete optimization problems.

In many applications there are constraints on the location of data and/or resources across the Internet. An example of such an application is mining of large commercial datasets distributed over a relatively low bandwidth network. In such applications, even if the computing power is available to accomplish the required task without resorting to parallel computing, it is infeasible to collect the data at a central location. In these cases, the motivation for parallelism comes not just from the need for computing resources but also from the infeasibility or undesirability of alternate (centralized) approaches.

1.2   Scope of Parallel Computing

Parallel computing has made a tremendous impact on a variety of areas ranging from computational simulations for scientific and engineering applications to commercial applications in data mining and transaction processing. The cost benefits of parallelism coupled with the performance requirements of applications present compelling arguments in favor of parallel computing. We present a small sample of the diverse applications of parallel computing.

1.2.1   Applications in Engineering and Design

Parallel computing has traditionally been employed with great success in the design of airfoils (optimizing lift, drag, stability), internal combustion engines (optimizing charge distribution, burn), high-speed circuits (layouts for delays and capacitive and inductive effects), and structures (optimizing structural integrity, design parameters, cost, etc.), among others. More recently, design of microelectromechanical and nanoelectromechanical systems (MEMS and NEMS) has attracted significant attention. While most applications in engineering and design pose problems of multiple spatial and temporal scales and coupled physical phenomena, in the case of MEMS/NEMS design these problems are particularly acute. Here, we often deal with a mix of quantum phenomena, molecular dynamics, and stochastic and continuum models with physical processes such as conduction, convection, radiation, and structural mechanics, all in a single system. This presents formidable challenges for geometric modeling, mathematical modeling, and algorithm development, all in the context of parallel computers.

Other applications in engineering and design focus on optimization of a variety of processes. Parallel computers have been used to solve a variety of discrete and continuous optimization problems. Algorithms such as Simplex, Interior Point Method for linear optimization and Branch-and-bound, and Genetic programming for discrete optimization have been efficiently parallelized and are frequently used.

1.2.2 Scientific Applications

The past few years have seen a revolution in high performance scientific computing applications. The sequencing of the human genome by the International Human Genome Sequencing Consortium and Celera, Inc. has opened exciting new frontiers in bioinformatics. Functional and structural characterization of genes and proteins hold the promise of understanding and fundamentally influencing biological processes. Analyzing biological sequences with a view to developing new drugs and cures for diseases and medical conditions requires innovative algorithms as well as large-scale computational power. Indeed, some of the newest parallel computing technologies are targeted specifically towards applications in bioinformatics.

Advances in computational physics and chemistry have focused on understanding processes ranging in scale from quantum phenomena to macromolecular structures. These have resulted in design of new materials, understanding of chemical pathways, and more efficient processes. Applications in astrophysics have explored the evolution of galaxies, thermonuclear processes, and the analysis of extremely large datasets from telescopes. Weather modeling, mineral prospecting, flood prediction, etc., rely heavily on parallel computers and have very significant impact on day-to-day life.

Bioinformatics and astrophysics also present some of the most challenging problems with respect to analyzing extremely large datasets. Protein and gene databases (such as PDB, SwissProt, and ENTREZ and NDB) along with Sky Survey datasets (such as the Sloan Digital Sky Surveys) represent some of the largest scientific datasets. Effectively analyzing these datasets requires tremendous computational power and holds the key to significant scientific discoveries.

1.2.3 Commercial Applications

With the widespread use of the web and associated static and dynamic content, there is increasing emphasis on cost-effective servers capable of providing scalable performance. Parallel platforms ranging from multiprocessors to linux clusters are frequently used as web and database servers. For instance, on heavy volume days, large brokerage houses on Wall Street handle hundreds of thousands of simultaneous user sessions and millions of orders. Platforms such as IBMs SP supercomputers and Sun Ultra HPC servers power these business-critical sites. While not highly visible, some of the largest supercomputing networks are housed on Wall Street.

The availability of large-scale transaction data has also sparked considerable interest in data mining and analysis for optimizing business and marketing decisions. The sheer volume and geographically distributed nature of this data require the use of effective parallel algorithms for such problems as association rule mining, clustering, classification, and time-series analysis.

1.2.4   Applications in Computer Systems

As computer systems become more pervasive and computation spreads over the network, parallel processing issues become engrained into a variety of applications. In computer security, intrusion detection is an outstanding challenge. In the case of network intrusion detection, data is collected at distributed sites and must be analyzed rapidly for signaling intrusion. The infeasibility of collecting this data at a central location for analysis requires effective parallel and distributed algorithms. In the area of cryptography, some of the most spectacular applications of Internet-based parallel computing have focused on factoring extremely large integers.

Embedded systems increasingly rely on distributed control algorithms for accomplishing a variety of tasks. A modern automobile consists of tens of processors communicating to perform complex tasks for optimizing handling and performance. In such systems, traditional parallel and distributed algorithms for leader selection, maximal independent set, etc., are frequently used.

While parallel computing has traditionally confined itself to platforms with well behaved compute and network elements in which faults and errors do not play a significant role, there are valuable lessons that extend to computations on ad-hoc, mobile, or faulty environments.

1.3   Organization and Contents of the Text

This book provides a comprehensive and self-contained exposition of problem solving using parallel computers. Algorithms and metrics focus on practical and portable models of parallel machines. Principles of algorithm design focus on desirable attributes of parallel algorithms and techniques for achieving these in the contest of a large class of applications and architectures. Programming techniques cover standard paradigms such as MPI and POSIX threads that are available across a range of parallel platforms.

Chapters in this book can be grouped into four main parts as illustrated in Figure 1.1. These parts are as follows:

Fundamentals   This section spans Chapters 2 through 4 of the book. Chapter 2, Parallel Programming Platforms, discusses the physical organization of parallel platforms. It

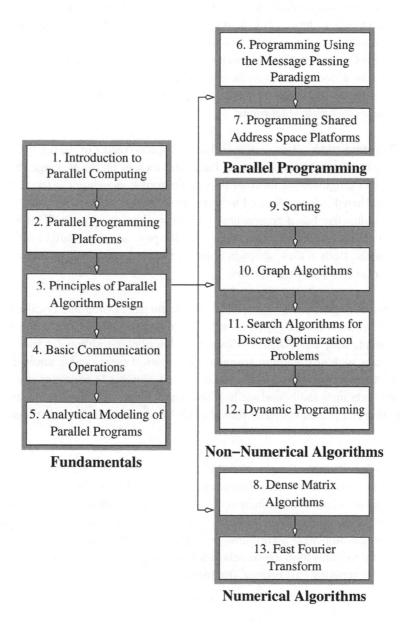

Figure 1.1   Recommended sequence for reading the chapters.

establishes cost metrics that can be used for algorithm design. The objective of this chapter is not to provide an exhaustive treatment of parallel architectures; rather, it aims to provide sufficient detail required to use these machines efficiently. Chapter 3, Principles of Parallel Algorithm Design, addresses key factors that contribute to efficient parallel algorithms and presents a suite of techniques that can be applied across a wide range of applications. Chapter 4, Basic Communication Operations, presents a core set of operations that are used throughout the book for facilitating efficient data transfer in parallel algorithms. Finally, Chapter 5, Analytical Modeling of Parallel Programs, deals with metrics for quantifying the performance of a parallel algorithm.

Parallel Programming This section includes Chapters 6 and 7 of the book. Chapter 6, Programming Using the Message-Passing Paradigm, focuses on the Message Passing Interface (MPI) for programming message passing platforms, including clusters. Chapter 7, Programming Shared Address Space Platforms, deals with programming paradigms such as threads and directive based approaches. Using paradigms such as POSIX threads and OpenMP, it describes various features necessary for programming shared-address-space parallel machines. Both of these chapters illustrate various programming concepts using a variety of examples of parallel programs.

Non-numerical Algorithms Chapters 9–12 present parallel non-numerical algorithms. Chapter 9 addresses sorting algorithms such as bitonic sort, bubble sort and its variants, quicksort, sample sort, and shellsort. Chapter 10 describes algorithms for various graph theory problems such as minimum spanning tree, shortest paths, and connected components. Algorithms for sparse graphs are also discussed. Chapter 11 addresses search-based methods such as branch-and-bound and heuristic search for combinatorial problems. Chapter 12 classifies and presents parallel formulations for a variety of dynamic programming algorithms.

Numerical Algorithms Chapters 8 and 13 present parallel numerical algorithms. Chapter 8 covers basic operations on dense matrices such as matrix multiplication, matrix-vector multiplication, and Gaussian elimination. This chapter is included before non-numerical algorithms, as the techniques for partitioning and assigning matrices to processors are common to many non-numerical algorithms. Furthermore, matrix-vector and matrix-matrix multiplication algorithms form the kernels of many graph algorithms. Chapter 13 describes algorithms for computing Fast Fourier Transforms.

1.4 Bibliographic Remarks

Many books discuss aspects of parallel processing at varying levels of detail. Hardware aspects of parallel computers have been discussed extensively in several textbooks and monographs [CSG98, LW95, HX98, AG94, Fly95, AG94, Sto93, DeC89, HB84, RF89,

Sie85, Tab90, Tab91, WF84, Woo86]. A number of texts discuss paradigms and languages for programming parallel computers [LB98, Pac98, GLS99, GSNL98, CDK$^+$00, WA98, And91, BA82, Bab88, Ble90, Con89, CT92, Les93, Per87, Wal91]. Akl [Akl97], Cole [Col89], Gibbons and Rytter [GR90], Foster [Fos95], Leighton [Lei92], Miller and Stout [MS96], and Quinn [Qui94] discuss various aspects of parallel algorithm design and analysis. Buyya (Editor) [Buy99] and Pfister [Pfi98] discuss various aspects of parallel computing using clusters. Jaja [Jaj92] covers parallel algorithms for the PRAM model of computation. Hillis [Hil85, HS86] and Hatcher and Quinn [HQ91] discuss data-parallel programming. Agha [Agh86] discusses a model of concurrent computation based on *actors*. Sharp [Sha85] addresses data-flow computing. Some books provide a general overview of topics in parallel computing [CL93, Fou94, Zom96, JGD87, LER92, Mol93, Qui94]. Many books address parallel processing applications in numerical analysis and scientific computing [DDSV99, FJDS96, GO93, Car89]. Fox *et al.* [FJL$^+$88] and Angus *et al.* [AFKW90] provide an application-oriented view of algorithm design for problems in scientific computing. Bertsekas and Tsitsiklis [BT97] discuss parallel algorithms, with emphasis on numerical applications.

Akl and Lyons [AL93] discuss parallel algorithms in computational geometry. Ranka and Sahni [RS90b] and Dew, Earnshaw, and Heywood [DEH89] address parallel algorithms for use in computer vision. Green [Gre91] covers parallel algorithms for graphics applications. Many books address the use of parallel processing in artificial intelligence applications [Gup87, HD89b, KGK90, KKKS94, Kow88, RZ89].

A useful collection of reviews, bibliographies and indexes has been put together by the Association for Computing Machinery [ACM91]. Messina and Murli [MM91] present a collection of papers on various aspects of the application and potential of parallel computing. The scope of parallel processing and various aspects of US government support have also been discussed in National Science Foundation reports [NSF91, GOV99].

A number of conferences address various aspects of parallel computing. A few important ones are the Supercomputing Conference, ACM Symposium on Parallel Algorithms and Architectures, the International Conference on Parallel Processing, the International Parallel and Distributed Processing Symposium, Parallel Computing, and the SIAM Conference on Parallel Processing. Important journals in parallel processing include IEEE Transactions on Parallel and Distributed Systems, International Journal of Parallel Programming, Journal of Parallel and Distributed Computing, Parallel Computing, IEEE Concurrency, and Parallel Processing Letters. These proceedings and journals provide a rich source of information on the state of the art in parallel processing.

Problems

1.1   Go to the Top 500 Supercomputers site (http://www.top500.org/) and list the five most powerful supercomputers along with their FLOPS rating.

1.2 List three major problems requiring the use of supercomputing in the following domains:

1. Structural Mechanics.

2. Computational Biology.

3. Commercial Applications.

1.3 Collect statistics on the number of components in state of the art integrated circuits over the years. Plot the number of components as a function of time and compare the growth rate to that dictated by Moore's law.

1.4 Repeat the above experiment for the peak FLOPS rate of processors and compare the speed to that inferred from Moore's law.

CHAPTER 2

Parallel Programming Platforms

The traditional logical view of a sequential computer consists of a memory connected to a processor via a datapath. All three components – processor, memory, and datapath – present bottlenecks to the overall processing rate of a computer system. A number of architectural innovations over the years have addressed these bottlenecks. One of the most important innovations is multiplicity – in processing units, datapaths, and memory units. This multiplicity is either entirely hidden from the programmer, as in the case of implicit parallelism, or exposed to the programmer in different forms. In this chapter, we present an overview of important architectural concepts as they relate to parallel processing. The objective is to provide sufficient detail for programmers to be able to write efficient code on a variety of platforms. We develop cost models and abstractions for quantifying the performance of various parallel algorithms, and identify bottlenecks resulting from various programming constructs.

We start our discussion of parallel platforms with an overview of serial and implicitly parallel architectures. This is necessitated by the fact that it is often possible to re-engineer codes to achieve significant speedups ($2\times$ to $5\times$ unoptimized speed) using simple program transformations. Parallelizing sub-optimal serial codes often has undesirable effects of un-reliable speedups and misleading runtimes. For this reason, we advocate optimizing serial performance of codes before attempting parallelization. As we shall demonstrate through this chapter, the tasks of serial and parallel optimization often have very similar characteristics. After discussing serial and implicitly parallel architectures, we devote the rest of this chapter to organization of parallel platforms, underlying cost models for algorithms, and platform abstractions for portable algorithm design. Readers wishing to delve directly into parallel architectures may choose to skip Sections 2.1 and 2.2.

2.1   Implicit Parallelism: Trends in Microprocessor Architectures*

While microprocessor technology has delivered significant improvements in clock speeds over the past decade, it has also exposed a variety of other performance bottlenecks. To alleviate these bottlenecks, microprocessor designers have explored alternate routes to cost-effective performance gains. In this section, we will outline some of these trends with a view to understanding their limitations and how they impact algorithm and code development. The objective here is not to provide a comprehensive description of processor architectures. There are several excellent texts referenced in the bibliography that address this topic.

Clock speeds of microprocessors have posted impressive gains - two to three orders of magnitude over the past 20 years. However, these increments in clock speed are severely diluted by the limitations of memory technology. At the same time, higher levels of device integration have also resulted in a very large transistor count, raising the obvious issue of how best to utilize them. Consequently, techniques that enable execution of multiple instructions in a single clock cycle have become popular. Indeed, this trend is evident in the current generation of microprocessors such as the Itanium, Sparc Ultra, MIPS, and Power4. In this section, we briefly explore mechanisms used by various processors for supporting multiple instruction execution.

2.1.1   Pipelining and Superscalar Execution

Processors have long relied on pipelines for improving execution rates. By overlapping various stages in instruction execution (fetch, schedule, decode, operand fetch, execute, store, among others), pipelining enables faster execution. The assembly-line analogy works well for understanding pipelines. If the assembly of a car, taking 100 time units, can be broken into 10 pipelined stages of 10 units each, a single assembly line can produce a car every 10 time units! This represents a 10-fold speedup over producing cars entirely serially, one after the other. It is also evident from this example that to increase the speed of a single pipeline, one would break down the tasks into smaller and smaller units, thus lengthening the pipeline and increasing overlap in execution. In the context of processors, this enables faster clock rates since the tasks are now smaller. For example, the Pentium 4, which operates at 2.0 GHz, has a 20 stage pipeline. Note that the speed of a single pipeline is ultimately limited by the largest atomic task in the pipeline. Furthermore, in typical instruction traces, every fifth to sixth instruction is a branch instruction. Long instruction pipelines therefore need effective techniques for predicting branch destinations so that pipelines can be speculatively filled. The penalty of a misprediction increases as the pipelines become deeper since a larger number of instructions need to be flushed. These factors place limitations on the depth of a processor pipeline and the resulting performance gains.

An obvious way to improve instruction execution rate beyond this level is to use multiple pipelines. During each clock cycle, multiple instructions are piped into the processor in parallel. These instructions are executed on multiple functional units. We illustrate this process with the help of an example.

Example 2.1 Superscalar execution

Consider a processor with two pipelines and the ability to simultaneously issue two instructions. These processors are sometimes also referred to as super-pipelined processors. The ability of a processor to issue multiple instructions in the same cycle is referred to as superscalar execution. Since the architecture illustrated in Figure 2.1 allows two issues per clock cycle, it is also referred to as two-way superscalar or dual issue execution.

```
1. load R1, @1000        1. load R1, @1000        1. load R1, @1000
2. load R2, @1008        2. add  R1, @1004        2. add  R1, @1004
3. add  R1, @1004        3. add  R1, @1008        3. load R2, @1008
4. add  R2, @100C        4. add  R1, @100C        4. add  R2, @100C
5. add  R1, R2           5. store R1, @2000       5. add  R1, R2
6. store R1, @2000                                6. store R1, @2000
```

       (i)   (ii)   (iii)

(a) Three different code fragments for adding a list of four numbers.

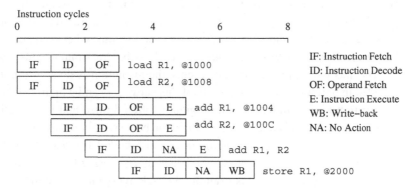

(b) Execution schedule for code fragment (i) above.

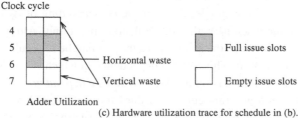

(c) Hardware utilization trace for schedule in (b).

Figure 2.1 Example of a two-way superscalar execution of instructions.

Consider the execution of the first code fragment in Figure 2.1 for adding four numbers. The first and second instructions are independent and therefore can be issued concurrently. This is illustrated in the simultaneous issue of the instructions load R1, @1000 and load R2, @1008 at $t = 0$. The instructions are fetched, decoded, and the operands are fetched. The next two instructions, add R1, @1004 and add R2, @100C are also mutually independent, although they must be executed after the first two instructions. Consequently, they can be issued concurrently at $t = 1$ since the processors are pipelined. These instructions terminate at $t = 5$. The next two instructions, add R1, R2 and store R1, @2000 cannot be executed concurrently since the result of the former (contents of register R1) is used by the latter. Therefore, only the add instruction is issued at $t = 2$ and the store instruction at $t = 3$. Note that the instruction add R1, R2 can be executed only after the previous two instructions have been executed. The instruction schedule is illustrated in Figure 2.1(b). The schedule assumes that each memory access takes a single cycle. In reality, this may not be the case. The implications of this assumption are discussed in Section 2.2 on memory system performance. ∎

In principle, superscalar execution seems natural, even simple. However, a number of issues need to be resolved. First, as illustrated in Example 2.1, instructions in a program may be related to each other. The results of an instruction may be required for subsequent instructions. This is referred to as **_true data dependency_**. For instance, consider the second code fragment in Figure 2.1 for adding four numbers. There is a true data dependency between load R1, @1000 and add R1, @1004, and similarly between subsequent instructions. Dependencies of this type must be resolved before simultaneous issue of instructions. This has two implications. First, since the resolution is done at runtime, it must be supported in hardware. The complexity of this hardware can be high. Second, the amount of instruction level parallelism in a program is often limited and is a function of coding technique. In the second code fragment, there can be no simultaneous issue, leading to poor resource utilization. The three code fragments in Figure 2.1(a) also illustrate that in many cases it is possible to extract more parallelism by reordering the instructions and by altering the code. Notice that in this example the code reorganization corresponds to exposing parallelism in a form that can be used by the instruction issue mechanism.

Another source of dependency between instructions results from the finite resources shared by various pipelines. As an example, consider the co-scheduling of two floating point operations on a dual issue machine with a single floating point unit. Although there might be no data dependencies between the instructions, they cannot be scheduled together since both need the floating point unit. This form of dependency in which two instructions compete for a single processor resource is referred to as **_resource dependency_**.

The flow of control through a program enforces a third form of dependency between instructions. Consider the execution of a conditional branch instruction. Since the branch destination is known only at the point of execution, scheduling instructions _a priori_ across branches may lead to errors. These dependencies are referred to as **_branch dependencies_** or *procedural dependencies* and are typically handled by speculatively scheduling across branches and rolling back in case of errors. Studies of typical traces have shown that on average, a branch instruction is encountered between every five to six instructions. Therefore, just as in populating instruction pipelines, accurate branch prediction is critical for efficient superscalar execution.

The ability of a processor to detect and schedule concurrent instructions is critical to superscalar performance. For instance, consider the third code fragment in Figure 2.1 which also computes the sum of four numbers. The reader will note that this is merely a semantically equivalent reordering of the first code fragment. However, in this case, there is a data dependency between the first two instructions – load R1, @1000 and add R1, @1004. Therefore, these instructions cannot be issued simultaneously. However, if the processor had the ability to look ahead, it would realize that it is possible to schedule the third instruction – load R2, @1008 – with the first instruction. In the next issue cycle, instructions two and four can be scheduled, and so on. In this way, the same execution schedule can be derived for the first and third code fragments. However, the processor needs the ability to issue instructions *out-of-order* to accomplish desired reordering. The parallelism available in *in-order* issue of instructions can be highly limited as illustrated by this example. Most current microprocessors are capable of out-of-order issue and completion. This model, also referred to as *dynamic instruction issue*, exploits maximum instruction level parallelism. The processor uses a window of instructions from which it selects instructions for simultaneous issue. This window corresponds to the look-ahead of the scheduler.

The performance of superscalar architectures is limited by the available instruction level parallelism. Consider the example in Figure 2.1. For simplicity of discussion, let us ignore the pipelining aspects of the example and focus on the execution aspects of the program. Assuming two execution units (multiply-add units), the figure illustrates that there are several zero-issue cycles (cycles in which the floating point unit is idle). These are essentially wasted cycles from the point of view of the execution unit. If, during a particular cycle, no instructions are issued on the execution units, it is referred to as *vertical waste*; if only part of the execution units are used during a cycle, it is termed *horizontal waste*. In the example, we have two cycles of vertical waste and one cycle with horizontal waste. In all, only three of the eight available cycles are used for computation. This implies that the code fragment will yield no more than three-eighths of the peak rated FLOP count of the processor. Often, due to limited parallelism, resource dependencies, or the inability of a processor to extract parallelism, the resources of superscalar processors are heavily under-utilized. Current microprocessors typically support up to four-issue superscalar execution.

2.1.2   Very Long Instruction Word Processors

The parallelism extracted by superscalar processors is often limited by the instruction look-ahead. The hardware logic for dynamic dependency analysis is typically in the range of 5-10% of the total logic on conventional microprocessors (about 5% on the four-way superscalar Sun UltraSPARC). This complexity grows roughly quadratically with the number of issues and can become a bottleneck. An alternate concept for exploiting instruction-level parallelism used in very long instruction word (VLIW) processors relies on the compiler to resolve dependencies and resource availability at compile time. Instructions that can be executed concurrently are packed into groups and parceled off to the processor as a single long instruction word (thus the name) to be executed on multiple functional units at the same time.

The VLIW concept, first used in Multiflow Trace (circa 1984) and subsequently as a variant in the Intel IA64 architecture, has both advantages and disadvantages compared to superscalar processors. Since scheduling is done in software, the decoding and instruction issue mechanisms are simpler in VLIW processors. The compiler has a larger context from which to select instructions and can use a variety of transformations to optimize parallelism when compared to a hardware issue unit. Additional parallel instructions are typically made available to the compiler to control parallel execution. However, compilers do not have the dynamic program state (e.g., the branch history buffer) available to make scheduling decisions. This reduces the accuracy of branch and memory prediction, but allows the use of more sophisticated static prediction schemes. Other runtime situations such as stalls on data fetch because of cache misses are extremely difficult to predict accurately. This limits the scope and performance of static compiler-based scheduling.

Finally, the performance of VLIW processors is very sensitive to the compilers' ability to detect data and resource dependencies and read and write hazards, and to schedule instructions for maximum parallelism. Loop unrolling, branch prediction and speculative execution all play important roles in the performance of VLIW processors. While superscalar and VLIW processors have been successful in exploiting implicit parallelism, they are generally limited to smaller scales of concurrency in the range of four- to eight-way parallelism.

2.2   Limitations of Memory System Performance*

The effective performance of a program on a computer relies not just on the speed of the processor but also on the ability of the memory system to feed data to the processor. At the logical level, a memory system, possibly consisting of multiple levels of caches, takes in a request for a memory word and returns a block of data of size b containing the requested word after l nanoseconds. Here, l is referred to as the *latency* of the memory. The rate at which data can be pumped from the memory to the processor determines the *bandwidth* of the memory system.

It is very important to understand the difference between latency and bandwidth since different, often competing, techniques are required for addressing these. As an analogy, if water comes out of the end of a fire hose 2 seconds after a hydrant is turned on, then the latency of the system is 2 seconds. Once the flow starts, if the hose pumps water at 1 gallon/second then the 'bandwidth' of the hose is 1 gallon/second. If we need to put out a fire immediately, we might desire a lower latency. This would typically require higher water pressure from the hydrant. On the other hand, if we wish to fight bigger fires, we might desire a higher flow rate, necessitating a wider hose and hydrant. As we shall see here, this analogy works well for memory systems as well. Latency and bandwidth both play critical roles in determining memory system performance. We examine these separately in greater detail using a few examples.

To study the effect of memory system latency, we assume in the following examples that a memory block consists of one word. We later relax this assumption while examining the role of memory bandwidth. Since we are primarily interested in maximum achievable performance, we also assume the best case cache-replacement policy. We refer the reader to the bibliography for a detailed discussion of memory system design.

Example 2.2   Effect of memory latency on performance
Consider a processor operating at 1 GHz (1 ns clock) connected to a DRAM with a latency of 100 ns (no caches). Assume that the processor has two multiply-add units and is capable of executing four instructions in each cycle of 1 ns. The peak processor rating is therefore 4 GFLOPS. Since the memory latency is equal to 100 cycles and block size is one word, every time a memory request is made, the processor must wait 100 cycles before it can process the data. Consider the problem of computing the dot-product of two vectors on such a platform. A dot-product computation performs one multiply-add on a single pair of vector elements, i.e., each floating point operation requires one data fetch. It is easy to see that the peak speed of this computation is limited to one floating point operation every 100 ns, or a speed of 10 MFLOPS, a very small fraction of the peak processor rating. This example highlights the need for effective memory system performance in achieving high computation rates. ∎

2.2.1   Improving Effective Memory Latency Using Caches

Handling the mismatch in processor and DRAM speeds has motivated a number of architectural innovations in memory system design. One such innovation addresses the speed mismatch by placing a smaller and faster memory between the processor and the DRAM. This memory, referred to as the cache, acts as a low-latency high-bandwidth storage. The data needed by the processor is first fetched into the cache. All subsequent accesses to data items residing in the cache are serviced by the cache. Thus, in principle, if a piece of data is repeatedly used, the effective latency of this memory system can be reduced by the cache. The fraction of data references satisfied by the cache is called the cache *hit ratio* of the computation on the system.   The effective computation rate of many applications is bounded not by the processing rate of the CPU, but by the rate at which data can be pumped into the CPU. Such computations are referred to as being *memory bound*. The performance of memory bound programs is critically impacted by the cache hit ratio.

Example 2.3   Impact of caches on memory system performance
As in the previous example, consider a 1 GHz processor with a 100 ns latency DRAM. In this case, we introduce a cache of size 32 KB with a latency of 1 ns or one cycle (typically on the processor itself). We use this setup to multiply two matrices A and B of dimensions 32×32. We have carefully chosen these numbers so that the cache is large enough to store matrices A and B, as well as the result matrix C. Once again, we assume an ideal cache placement strategy in which none of the data items are overwritten by others. Fetching the two matrices into the cache corresponds to fetching 2K words, which takes approximately 200 μs. We know from elementary algorithmics that multiplying two $n \times n$ matrices takes $2n^3$ operations. For our problem, this corresponds to 64K operations, which can be performed in 16K cycles (or 16 μs) at four instructions per cycle. The total time for the computation is therefore approximately the sum of time for load/store operations and the time for the computation itself, i.e., $200 + 16$ μs. This corresponds to a peak computation rate of 64K/216 or 303 MFLOPS. Note that this is a thirty-fold improvement over the previous example, although it is still less than 10% of the peak processor performance. We see in this example that by placing a small cache memory, we are able to improve processor utilization considerably.   ■

The improvement in performance resulting from the presence of the cache is based on the assumption that there is repeated reference to the same data item. This notion of repeated reference to a data item in a small time window is called *temporal locality* of reference. In our example, we had $O(n^2)$ data accesses and $O(n^3)$ computation. (See the Appendix for an explanation of the O notation.) Data reuse is critical for cache performance because if each data item is used only once, it would still have to be fetched once per use from the DRAM, and therefore the DRAM latency would be paid for each operation.

2.2.2   Impact of Memory Bandwidth

Memory bandwidth refers to the rate at which data can be moved between the processor and memory. It is determined by the bandwidth of the memory bus as well as the memory units. One commonly used technique to improve memory bandwidth is to increase the size of the memory blocks. For an illustration, let us relax our simplifying restriction on the size of the memory block and assume that a single memory request returns a contiguous block of four words. The single unit of four words in this case is also referred to as a *cache line*. Conventional computers typically fetch two to eight words together into the cache. We will see how this helps the performance of applications for which data reuse is limited.

Example 2.4   Effect of block size: dot-product of two vectors
Consider again a memory system with a single cycle cache and 100 cycle latency DRAM with the processor operating at 1 GHz. If the block size is one word, the pro-

cessor takes 100 cycles to fetch each word. For each pair of words, the dot-product performs one multiply-add, i.e., two FLOPs. Therefore, the algorithm performs one FLOP every 100 cycles for a peak speed of 10 MFLOPS as illustrated in Example 2.2.

Now let us consider what happens if the block size is increased to four words, i.e., the processor can fetch a four-word cache line every 100 cycles. Assuming that the vectors are laid out linearly in memory, eight FLOPs (four multiply-adds) can be performed in 200 cycles. This is because a single memory access fetches four consecutive words in the vector. Therefore, two accesses can fetch four elements of each of the vectors. This corresponds to a FLOP every 25 ns, for a peak speed of 40 MFLOPS. Note that increasing the block size from one to four words did not change the latency of the memory system. However, it increased the bandwidth four-fold. In this case, the increased bandwidth of the memory system enabled us to accelerate the dot-product algorithm which has no data reuse at all.

Another way of quickly estimating performance bounds is to estimate the cache hit ratio, using it to compute mean access time per word, and relating this to the FLOP rate via the underlying algorithm. For example, in this example, there are two DRAM accesses (cache misses) for every eight data accesses required by the algorithm. This corresponds to a cache hit ratio of 75%. Assuming that the dominant overhead is posed by the cache misses, the average memory access time contributed by the misses is 25% at 100 ns (or 25 ns/word). Since the dot-product has one operation/word, this corresponds to a computation rate of 40 MFLOPS as before. A more accurate estimate of this rate would compute the average memory access time as $0.75 \times 1 + 0.25 \times 100$ or 25.75 ns/word. The corresponding computation rate is 38.8 MFLOPS.   ■

Physically, the scenario illustrated in Example 2.4 corresponds to a wide data bus (4 words or 128 bits) connected to multiple memory banks. In practice, such wide buses are expensive to construct. In a more practical system, consecutive words are sent on the memory bus on subsequent bus cycles after the first word is retrieved. For example, with a 32 bit data bus, the first word is put on the bus after 100 ns (the associated latency) and one word is put on each subsequent bus cycle. This changes our calculations above slightly since the entire cache line becomes available only after $100 + 3 \times$ (memory bus cycle) ns. Assuming a data bus operating at 200 MHz, this adds 15 ns to the cache line access time. This does not change our bound on the execution rate significantly.

The above examples clearly illustrate how increased bandwidth results in higher peak computation rates. They also make certain assumptions that have significance for the programmer. The data layouts were assumed to be such that consecutive data words in memory were used by successive instructions. In other words, if we take a computation-centric view, there is a *spatial locality* of memory access. If we take a data-layout centric point of view, the computation is ordered so that successive computations require contiguous data. If the computation (or access pattern) does not have spatial locality, then effective bandwidth can be much smaller than the peak bandwidth.

An example of such an access pattern is in reading a dense matrix column-wise when the matrix has been stored in a row-major fashion in memory. Compilers can often be relied on to do a good job of restructuring computation to take advantage of spatial locality.

Example 2.5   Impact of strided access
Consider the following code fragment:

```
1    for (i = 0; i < 1000; i++)
2            column_sum[i] = 0.0;
3            for (j = 0; j < 1000; j++)
4                    column_sum[i] += b[j][i];
```

The code fragment sums columns of the matrix b into a vector column_sum. There are two observations that can be made: (i) the vector column_sum is small and easily fits into the cache; and (ii) the matrix b is accessed in a column order as illustrated in Figure 2.2(a). For a matrix of size 1000×1000, stored in a row-major order, this corresponds to accessing every 1000th entry. Therefore, it is likely that only one word in each cache line fetched from memory will be used. Consequently, the code fragment as written above is likely to yield poor performance.   ■

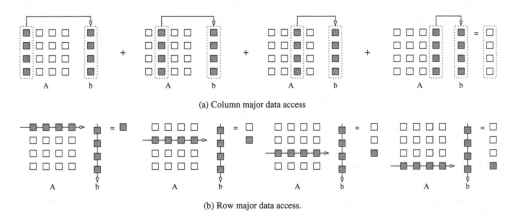

(a) Column major data access

(b) Row major data access.

Figure 2.2   Multiplying a matrix with a vector: (a) multiplying column-by-column, keeping a running sum; (b) computing each element of the result as a dot product of a row of the matrix with the vector.

The above example illustrates problems with strided access (with strides greater than one). The lack of spatial locality in computation causes poor memory system performance. Often it is possible to restructure the computation to remove strided access. In the case of our example, a simple rewrite of the loops is possible as follows:

Example 2.6 Eliminating strided access

Consider the following restructuring of the column-sum fragment:

```
1    for (i = 0; i < 1000; i++)
2            column_sum[i] = 0.0;
3    for (j = 0; j < 1000; j++)
4            for (i = 0; i < 1000; i++)
5                    column_sum[i] += b[j][i];
```

In this case, the matrix is traversed in a row-order as illustrated in Figure 2.2(b). However, the reader will note that this code fragment relies on the fact that the vector `column_sum` can be retained in the cache through the loops. Indeed, for this particular example, our assumption is reasonable. If the vector is larger, we would have to break the iteration space into blocks and compute the product one block at a time. This concept is also called *tiling* an iteration space. The improved performance of this loop is left as an exercise for the reader. ■

So the next question is whether we have effectively solved the problems posed by memory latency and bandwidth. While peak processor rates have grown significantly over the past decades, memory latency and bandwidth have not kept pace with this increase. Consequently, for typical computers, the ratio of peak FLOPS rate to peak memory bandwidth is anywhere between 1 MFLOPS/MBs (the ratio signifies FLOPS per megabyte/second of bandwidth) to 100 MFLOPS/MBs. The lower figure typically corresponds to large scale vector supercomputers and the higher figure to fast microprocessor based computers. This figure is very revealing in that it tells us that on average, a word must be reused 100 times after being fetched into the full bandwidth storage (typically L1 cache) to be able to achieve full processor utilization. Here, we define full-bandwidth as the rate of data transfer required by a computation to make it processor bound.

The series of examples presented in this section illustrate the following concepts:

- Exploiting spatial and temporal locality in applications is critical for amortizing memory latency and increasing effective memory bandwidth.

- Certain applications have inherently greater temporal locality than others, and thus have greater tolerance to low memory bandwidth. The ratio of the number of operations to number of memory accesses is a good indicator of anticipated tolerance to memory bandwidth.

- Memory layouts and organizing computation appropriately can make a significant impact on the spatial and temporal locality.

2.2.3 Alternate Approaches for Hiding Memory Latency

Imagine sitting at your computer browsing the web during peak network traffic hours. The lack of response from your browser can be alleviated using one of three simple approaches:

(i) we anticipate which pages we are going to browse ahead of time and issue requests for them in advance; (ii) we open multiple browsers and access different pages in each browser, thus while we are waiting for one page to load, we could be reading others; or (iii) we access a whole bunch of pages in one go – amortizing the latency across various accesses. The first approach is called *prefetching*, the second *multithreading*, and the third one corresponds to spatial locality in accessing memory words. Of these three approaches, spatial locality of memory accesses has been discussed before. We focus on prefetching and multithreading as techniques for latency hiding in this section.

Multithreading for Latency Hiding

A thread is a single stream of control in the flow of a program. We illustrate threads with a simple example:

Example 2.7   Threaded execution of matrix multiplication
Consider the following code segment for multiplying an $n \times n$ matrix a by a vector b to get vector c.

```
1    for (i = 0; i < n; i++)
2        c[i] = dot_product(get_row(a, i), b);
```

This code computes each element of c as the dot product of the corresponding row of a with the vector b. Notice that each dot-product is independent of the other, and therefore represents a concurrent unit of execution. We can safely rewrite the above code segment as:

```
1    for (i = 0; i < n; i++)
2        c[i] = create_thread(dot_product, get_row(a, i), b);
```

The only difference between the two code segments is that we have explicitly specified each instance of the dot-product computation as being a thread. (As we shall learn in Chapter 7, there are a number of APIs for specifying threads. We have simply chosen an intuitive name for a function to create threads.) Now, consider the execution of each instance of the function dot_product. The first instance of this function accesses a pair of vector elements and waits for them. In the meantime, the second instance of this function can access two other vector elements in the next cycle, and so on. After l units of time, where l is the latency of the memory system, the first function instance gets the requested data from memory and can perform the required computation. In the next cycle, the data items for the next function instance arrive, and so on. In this way, in every clock cycle, we can perform a computation. ■

The execution schedule in Example 2.7 is predicated upon two assumptions: the memory system is capable of servicing multiple outstanding requests, and the processor is capable of switching threads at every cycle. In addition, it also requires the program to have an explicit specification of concurrency in the form of threads. Multithreaded processors are capable of maintaining the context of a number of threads of computation with outstanding requests (memory accesses, I/O, or communication requests) and execute them as the requests are satisfied. Machines such as the HEP and Tera rely on multithreaded processors that can switch the context of execution in every cycle. Consequently, they are able to hide latency effectively, provided there is enough concurrency (threads) to keep the processor from idling. The tradeoffs between concurrency and latency will be a recurring theme through many chapters of this text.

Prefetching for Latency Hiding

In a typical program, a data item is loaded and used by a processor in a small time window. If the load results in a cache miss, then the use stalls. A simple solution to this problem is to advance the load operation so that even if there is a cache miss, the data is likely to have arrived by the time it is used. However, if the data item has been overwritten between load and use, a fresh load is issued. Note that this is no worse than the situation in which the load had not been advanced. A careful examination of this technique reveals that prefetching works for much the same reason as multithreading. In advancing the loads, we are trying to identify independent threads of execution that have no resource dependency (i.e., use the same registers) with respect to other threads. Many compilers aggressively try to advance loads to mask memory system latency.

> **Example 2.8**   Hiding latency by prefetching
> Consider the problem of adding two vectors a and b using a single for loop. In the first iteration of the loop, the processor requests a[0] and b[0]. Since these are not in the cache, the processor must pay the memory latency. While these requests are being serviced, the processor also requests a[1] and b[1]. Assuming that each request is generated in one cycle (1 ns) and memory requests are satisfied in 100 ns, after 100 such requests the first set of data items is returned by the memory system. Subsequently, one pair of vector components will be returned every cycle. In this way, in each subsequent cycle, one addition can be performed and processor cycles are not wasted. ∎

2.2.4   Tradeoffs of Multithreading and Prefetching

While it might seem that multithreading and prefetching solve all the problems related to memory system performance, they are critically impacted by the memory bandwidth.

> **Example 2.9**   Impact of bandwidth on multithreaded programs
> Consider a computation running on a machine with a 1 GHz clock, 4-word cache line, single cycle access to the cache, and 100 ns latency to DRAM. The computation has

a cache hit ratio at 1 KB of 25% and at 32 KB of 90%. Consider two cases: first, a single threaded execution in which the entire cache is available to the serial context, and second, a multithreaded execution with 32 threads where each thread has a cache residency of 1 KB. If the computation makes one data request in every cycle of 1 ns, in the first case the bandwidth requirement to DRAM is one word every 10 ns since the other words come from the cache (90% cache hit ratio). This corresponds to a bandwidth of 400 MB/s. In the second case, the bandwidth requirement to DRAM increases to three words every four cycles of each thread (25% cache hit ratio). Assuming that all threads exhibit similar cache behavior, this corresponds to 0.75 words/ns, or 3 GB/s. ∎

Example 2.9 illustrates a very important issue, namely that the bandwidth requirements of a multithreaded system may increase very significantly because of the smaller cache residency of each thread. In the example, while a sustained DRAM bandwidth of 400 MB/s is reasonable, 3.0 GB/s is more than most systems currently offer. At this point, multithreaded systems become bandwidth bound instead of latency bound. It is important to realize that multithreading and prefetching only address the latency problem and may often exacerbate the bandwidth problem.

Another issue relates to the additional hardware resources required to effectively use prefetching and multithreading. Consider a situation in which we have advanced 10 loads into registers. These loads require 10 registers to be free for the duration. If an intervening instruction overwrites the registers, we would have to load the data again. This would not increase the latency of the fetch any more than the case in which there was no prefetching. However, now we are fetching the same data item twice, resulting in doubling of the bandwidth requirement from the memory system. This situation is similar to the one due to cache constraints as illustrated in Example 2.9. It can be alleviated by supporting prefetching and multithreading with larger register files and caches.

2.3   Dichotomy of Parallel Computing Platforms

In the preceding sections, we pointed out various factors that impact the performance of a serial or implicitly parallel program. The increasing gap in peak and sustainable performance of current microprocessors, the impact of memory system performance, and the distributed nature of many problems present overarching motivations for parallelism. We now introduce, at a high level, the elements of parallel computing platforms that are critical for performance oriented and portable parallel programming. To facilitate our discussion of parallel platforms, we first explore a dichotomy based on the logical and physical organization of parallel platforms. The logical organization refers to a programmer's view of the platform while the physical organization refers to the actual hardware organization of the platform. The two critical components of parallel computing from a programmer's perspective are ways of expressing parallel tasks and mechanisms for specifying interaction between these tasks. The former is sometimes also referred to as the control structure and the latter as the communication model.

2.3.1 Control Structure of Parallel Platforms

Parallel tasks can be specified at various levels of granularity. At one extreme, each program in a set of programs can be viewed as one parallel task. At the other extreme, individual instructions within a program can be viewed as parallel tasks. Between these extremes lie a range of models for specifying the control structure of programs and the corresponding architectural support for them.

Example 2.10 Parallelism from single instruction on multiple processors
Consider the following code segment that adds two vectors:

```
1   for (i = 0; i < 1000; i++)
2           c[i] = a[i] + b[i];
```

In this example, various iterations of the loop are independent of each other; i.e., `c[0] = a[0] + b[0]; c[1] = a[1] + b[1];`, etc., can all be executed independently of each other. Consequently, if there is a mechanism for executing the same instruction, in this case `add` on all the processors with appropriate data, we could execute this loop much faster. ∎

Processing units in parallel computers cither operate under the centralized control of a single control unit or work independently. In architectures referred to as *single instruction stream, multiple data stream* (SIMD), a single control unit dispatches instructions to each processing unit. Figure 2.3(a) illustrates a typical SIMD architecture. In an SIMD parallel computer, the same instruction is executed synchronously by all processing units. In Example 2.10, the `add` instruction is dispatched to all processors and executed concurrently by them. Some of the earliest parallel computers such as the Illiac IV, MPP, DAP, CM-2, and MasPar MP-1 belonged to this class of machines. More recently, variants of this concept have found use in co-processing units such as the MMX units in Intel processors and DSP chips such as the Sharc. The Intel Pentium processor with its SSE (Streaming SIMD Extensions) provides a number of instructions that execute the same instruction on multiple data items. These architectural enhancements rely on the highly structured (regular) nature of the underlying computations, for example in image processing and graphics, to deliver improved performance.

While the SIMD concept works well for structured computations on parallel data structures such as arrays, often it is necessary to selectively turn off operations on certain data items. For this reason, most SIMD programming paradigms allow for an "activity mask". This is a binary mask associated with each data item and operation that specifies whether it should participate in the operation or not. Primitives such as `where (condition)`

PE: Processing Element

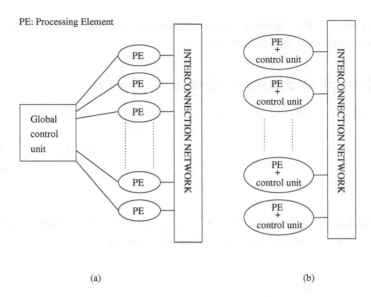

(a)   (b)

Figure 2.3   A typical SIMD architecture (a) and a typical MIMD architecture (b).

then `<stmnt>` `<elsewhere stmnt>` are used to support selective execution. Conditional execution can be detrimental to the performance of SIMD processors and therefore must be used with care.

In contrast to SIMD architectures, computers in which each processing element is capable of executing a different program independent of the other processing elements are called *multiple instruction stream, multiple data stream* (MIMD) computers. Figure 2.3(b) depicts a typical MIMD computer. A simple variant of this model, called the *single program multiple data* (SPMD) model, relies on multiple instances of the same program executing on different data. It is easy to see that the SPMD model has the same expressiveness as the MIMD model since each of the multiple programs can be inserted into one large `if-else` block with conditions specified by the task identifiers. The SPMD model is widely used by many parallel platforms and requires minimal architectural support. Examples of such platforms include the Sun Ultra Servers, multiprocessor PCs, workstation clusters, and the IBM SP.

SIMD computers require less hardware than MIMD computers because they have only one global control unit. Furthermore, SIMD computers require less memory because only one copy of the program needs to be stored. In contrast, MIMD computers store the program and operating system at each processor. However, the relative unpopularity of SIMD processors as general purpose compute engines can be attributed to their specialized hardware architectures, economic factors, design constraints, product life-cycle, and application characteristics. In contrast, platforms supporting the SPMD paradigm can be built from inexpensive off-the-shelf components with relatively little effort in a short amount of time. SIMD computers require extensive design effort resulting in longer product development times. Since the underlying serial processors change so rapidly, SIMD computers suffer from fast obsolescence. The irregular nature of many applications also makes SIMD architectures less suitable. Example 2.11 illustrates a case in which SIMD architectures yield poor resource utilization in the case of conditional execution.

> **Example 2.11**   Execution of conditional statements on a SIMD architecture
> Consider the execution of a conditional statement illustrated in Figure 2.4. The conditional statement in Figure 2.4(a) is executed in two steps. In the first step, all processors that have B equal to zero execute the instruction $C = A$. All other processors are idle. In the second step, the 'else' part of the instruction ($C = A/B$) is executed. The processors that were active in the first step now become idle. This illustrates one of the drawbacks of SIMD architectures.   ∎

2.3.2   Communication Model of Parallel Platforms

There are two primary forms of data exchange between parallel tasks – accessing a shared data space and exchanging messages.

Shared-Address-Space Platforms

The "shared-address-space" view of a parallel platform supports a common data space that is accessible to all processors. Processors interact by modifying data objects stored in this shared-address-space. Shared-address-space platforms supporting SPMD programming are also referred to as *multiprocessors*. Memory in shared-address-space platforms can be local (exclusive to a processor) or global (common to all processors). If the time taken by a processor to access any memory word in the system (global or local) is identical, the platform is classified as a *uniform memory access* (UMA) multicomputer. On the other hand, if the time taken to access certain memory words is longer than others, the platform is called a *non-uniform memory access* (NUMA) multicomputer. Figures 2.5(a) and (b) illustrate UMA platforms, whereas Figure 2.5(c) illustrates a NUMA platform. An interesting case is illustrated in Figure 2.5(b). Here, it is faster to access a memory word in cache than a location in memory. However, we still classify this as a UMA architecture. The reason for this is that all current microprocessors have cache hierarchies. Consequently, even a uniprocessor would not be termed UMA if cache access times are considered. For this reason, we define NUMA and UMA architectures only in terms of memory access times and not cache access times. Machines such as the SGI Origin 2000 and Sun Ultra HPC servers belong to the class of NUMA multiprocessors. The distinction between UMA and NUMA platforms is important. If accessing local memory is cheaper than accessing global memory, algorithms must build locality and structure data and computation accordingly.

The presence of a global memory space makes programming such platforms much easier. All read-only interactions are invisible to the programmer, as they are coded no differently than in a serial program. This greatly eases the burden of writing parallel programs.

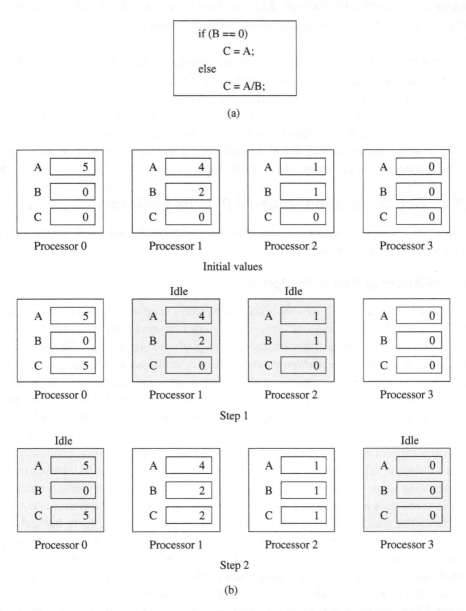

Figure 2.4 Executing a conditional statement on an SIMD computer with four processors: (a) the conditional statement; (b) the execution of the statement in two steps.

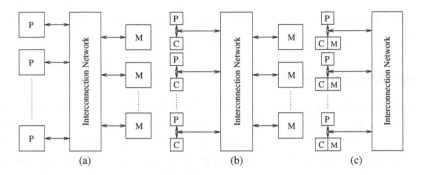

Figure 2.5 Typical shared-address-space architectures: (a) Uniform-memory-access shared-address-space computer; (b) Uniform-memory-access shared-address-space computer with caches and memories; (c) Non-uniform-memory-access shared-address-space computer with local memory only.

Read/write interactions are, however, harder to program than the read-only interactions, as these operations require mutual exclusion for concurrent accesses. Shared-address-space programming paradigms such as threads (POSIX, NT) and directives (OpenMP) therefore support synchronization using `locks` and related mechanisms.

The presence of caches on processors also raises the issue of multiple copies of a single memory word being manipulated by two or more processors at the same time. Supporting a shared-address-space in this context involves two major tasks: providing an address translation mechanism that locates a memory word in the system, and ensuring that concurrent operations on multiple copies of the same memory word have well-defined semantics. The latter is also referred to as the ***cache coherence*** mechanism. This mechanism and its implementation are discussed in greater detail in Section 2.4.6. Supporting cache coherence requires considerable hardware support. Consequently, some shared-address-space machines only support an address translation mechanism and leave the task of ensuring coherence to the programmer. The native programming model for such platforms consists of primitives such as `get` and `put`. These primitives allow a processor to get (and put) variables stored at a remote processor. However, if one of the copies of this variable is changed, the other copies are not automatically updated or invalidated.

It is important to note the difference between two commonly used and often misunderstood terms – shared-address-space and shared-memory computers. The term shared-memory computer is historically used for architectures in which the memory is physically shared among various processors, i.e., each processor has equal access to any memory segment. This is identical to the UMA model we just discussed. This is in contrast to a distributed-memory computer, in which different segments of the memory are physically associated with different processing elements. The dichotomy of shared- versus distributed-memory computers pertains to the physical organization of the machine and is discussed in greater detail in Section 2.4. Either of these physical models, shared or distributed memory, can present the logical view of a disjoint or shared-address-space platform. A distributed-memory shared-address-space computer is identical to a NUMA machine.

Message-Passing Platforms

The logical machine view of a message-passing platform consists of p processing nodes, each with its own exclusive address space. Each of these processing nodes can either be single processors or a shared-address-space multiprocessor – a trend that is fast gaining momentum in modern message-passing parallel computers. Instances of such a view come naturally from clustered workstations and non-shared-address-space multicomputers. On such platforms, interactions between processes running on different nodes must be accomplished using messages, hence the name *message passing*. This exchange of messages is used to transfer data, work, and to synchronize actions among the processes. In its most general form, message-passing paradigms support execution of a different program on each of the p nodes.

Since interactions are accomplished by sending and receiving messages, the basic operations in this programming paradigm are send and receive (the corresponding calls may differ across APIs but the semantics are largely identical). In addition, since the send and receive operations must specify target addresses, there must be a mechanism to assign a unique identification or ID to each of the multiple processes executing a parallel program. This ID is typically made available to the program using a function such as whoami, which returns to a calling process its ID. There is one other function that is typically needed to complete the basic set of message-passing operations – numprocs, which specifies the number of processes participating in the ensemble. With these four basic operations, it is possible to write any message-passing program. Different message-passing APIs, such as the Message Passing Interface (MPI) and Parallel Virtual Machine (PVM), support these basic operations and a variety of higher level functionality under different function names. Examples of parallel platforms that support the message-passing paradigm include the IBM SP, SGI Origin 2000, and workstation clusters.

It is easy to emulate a message-passing architecture containing p nodes on a shared-address-space computer with an identical number of nodes. Assuming uniprocessor nodes, this can be done by partitioning the shared-address-space into p disjoint parts and assigning one such partition exclusively to each processor. A processor can then "send" or "receive" messages by writing to or reading from another processor's partition while using appropriate synchronization primitives to inform its communication partner when it has finished reading or writing the data. However, emulating a shared-address-space architecture on a message-passing computer is costly, since accessing another node's memory requires sending and receiving messages.

2.4 Physical Organization of Parallel Platforms

In this section, we discuss the physical architecture of parallel machines. We start with an ideal architecture, outline practical difficulties associated with realizing this model, and discuss some conventional architectures.

2.4.1 Architecture of an Ideal Parallel Computer

A natural extension of the serial model of computation (the Random Access Machine, or RAM) consists of p processors and a global memory of unbounded size that is uniformly accessible to all processors. All processors access the same address space. Processors share a common clock but may execute different instructions in each cycle. This ideal model is also referred to as a *parallel random access machine (PRAM)*. Since PRAMs allow concurrent access to various memory locations, depending on how simultaneous memory accesses are handled, PRAMs can be divided into four subclasses.

1. *Exclusive-read, exclusive-write (EREW) PRAM.* In this class, access to a memory location is exclusive. No concurrent read or write operations are allowed. This is the weakest PRAM model, affording minimum concurrency in memory access.

2. *Concurrent-read, exclusive-write (CREW) PRAM.* In this class, multiple read accesses to a memory location are allowed. However, multiple write accesses to a memory location are serialized.

3. *Exclusive-read, concurrent-write (ERCW) PRAM.* Multiple write accesses are allowed to a memory location, but multiple read accesses are serialized.

4. *Concurrent-read, concurrent-write (CRCW) PRAM.* This class allows multiple read and write accesses to a common memory location. This is the most powerful PRAM model.

Allowing concurrent read access does not create any semantic discrepancies in the program. However, concurrent write access to a memory location requires arbitration. Several protocols are used to resolve concurrent writes. The most frequently used protocols are as follows:

- *Common*, in which the concurrent write is allowed if all the values that the processors are attempting to write are identical.

- *Arbitrary*, in which an arbitrary processor is allowed to proceed with the write operation and the rest fail.

- *Priority*, in which all processors are organized into a predefined prioritized list, and the processor with the highest priority succeeds and the rest fail.

- *Sum*, in which the sum of all the quantities is written (the sum-based write conflict resolution model can be extended to any associative operator defined on the quantities being written).

Architectural Complexity of the Ideal Model

Consider the implementation of an EREW PRAM as a shared-memory computer with p processors and a global memory of m words. The processors are connected to the memory through a set of switches. These switches determine the memory word being accessed by each processor. In an EREW PRAM, each of the p processors in the ensemble can access any of the memory words, provided that a word is not accessed by more than one processor simultaneously. To ensure such connectivity, the total number of switches must be $\Theta(mp)$. (See the Appendix for an explanation of the Θ notation.) For a reasonable memory size, constructing a switching network of this complexity is very expensive. Thus, PRAM models of computation are impossible to realize in practice.

2.4.2 Interconnection Networks for Parallel Computers

Interconnection networks provide mechanisms for data transfer between processing nodes or between processors and memory modules. A blackbox view of an interconnection network consists of n inputs and m outputs. The outputs may or may not be distinct from the inputs. Typical interconnection networks are built using links and switches. A link corresponds to physical media such as a set of wires or fibers capable of carrying information. A variety of factors influence link characteristics. For links based on conducting media, the capacitive coupling between wires limits the speed of signal propagation. This capacitive coupling and attenuation of signal strength are functions of the length of the link.

Interconnection networks can be classified as *static* or *dynamic*. Static networks consist of point-to-point communication links among processing nodes and are also referred to as *direct* networks. Dynamic networks, on the other hand, are built using switches and communication links. Communication links are connected to one another dynamically by the switches to establish paths among processing nodes and memory banks. Dynamic networks are also referred to as *indirect* networks. Figure 2.6(a) illustrates a simple static network of four processing elements or nodes. Each processing node is connected via a network interface to two other nodes in a mesh configuration. Figure 2.6(b) illustrates a dynamic network of four nodes connected via a network of switches to other nodes.

A single switch in an interconnection network consists of a set of input ports and a set of output ports. Switches provide a range of functionality. The minimal functionality provided by a switch is a mapping from the input to the output ports. The total number of ports on a switch is also called the *degree* of the switch. Switches may also provide support for internal buffering (when the requested output port is busy), routing (to alleviate congestion on the network), and multicast (same output on multiple ports). The mapping from input to output ports can be provided using a variety of mechanisms based on physical crossbars,

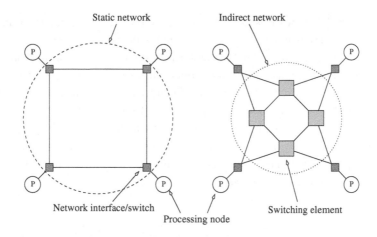

Figure 2.6 Classification of interconnection networks: (a) a static network; and (b) a dynamic network.

multi-ported memories, multiplexor-demultiplexors, and multiplexed buses. The cost of a switch is influenced by the cost of the mapping hardware, the peripheral hardware and packaging costs. The mapping hardware typically grows as the square of the degree of the switch, the peripheral hardware linearly as the degree, and the packaging costs linearly as the number of pins.

The connectivity between the nodes and the network is provided by a network interface. The network interface has input and output ports that pipe data into and out of the network. It typically has the responsibility of packetizing data, computing routing information, buffering incoming and outgoing data for matching speeds of network and processing elements, and error checking. The position of the interface between the processing element and the network is also important. While conventional network interfaces hang off the I/O buses, interfaces in tightly coupled parallel machines hang off the memory bus. Since I/O buses are typically slower than memory buses, the latter can support higher bandwidth.

2.4.3 Network Topologies

A wide variety of network topologies have been used in interconnection networks. These topologies try to trade off cost and scalability with performance. While pure topologies have attractive mathematical properties, in practice interconnection networks tend to be combinations or modifications of the pure topologies discussed in this section.

Bus-Based Networks

A bus-based network is perhaps the simplest network consisting of a shared medium that is common to all the nodes. A bus has the desirable property that the cost of the network scales linearly as the number of nodes, p. This cost is typically associated with bus interfaces. Furthermore, the distance between any two nodes in the network is constant ($O(1)$).

Buses are also ideal for broadcasting information among nodes. Since the transmission medium is shared, there is little overhead associated with broadcast compared to point-to-point message transfer. However, the bounded bandwidth of a bus places limitations on the overall performance of the network as the number of nodes increases. Typical bus based machines are limited to dozens of nodes. Sun Enterprise servers and Intel Pentium based shared-bus multiprocessors are examples of such architectures.

The demands on bus bandwidth can be reduced by making use of the property that in typical programs, a majority of the data accessed is local to the node. For such programs, it is possible to provide a cache for each node. Private data is cached at the node and only remote data is accessed through the bus.

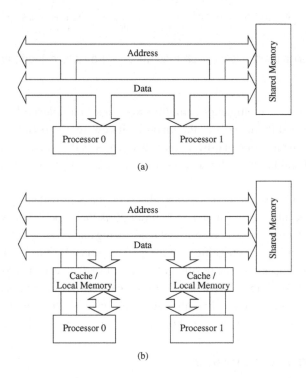

Figure 2.7 Bus-based interconnects (a) with no local caches; (b) with local memory/caches.

Example 2.12   Reducing shared-bus bandwidth using caches

Figure 2.7(a) illustrates p processors sharing a bus to the memory. Assuming that each processor accesses k data items, and each data access takes time t_{cycle}, the execution time is lower bounded by $t_{cycle} \times kp$ seconds. Now consider the hardware organization of Figure 2.7(b). Let us assume that 50% of the memory accesses ($0.5k$) are made to local data. This local data resides in the private memory of the processor. We assume that access time to the private memory is identical to the global memory, i.e., t_{cycle}. In this case, the total execution time is lower bounded by $0.5 \times t_{cycle} \times k + 0.5 \times t_{cycle} \times kp$. Here, the first term results from accesses to local data and the second term from access to shared data. It is easy to see that as p becomes large, the organization of Figure 2.7(b) results in a lower bound that approaches $0.5 \times t_{cycle} \times kp$. This time is a 50% improvement in lower bound on execution time compared to the organization of Figure 2.7(a). ■

In practice, shared and private data is handled in a more sophisticated manner. This is briefly addressed with cache coherence issues in Section 2.4.6.

Crossbar Networks

A simple way to connect p processors to b memory banks is to use a crossbar network. A crossbar network employs a grid of switches or switching nodes as shown in Figure 2.8. The crossbar network is a non-blocking network in the sense that the connection of a processing node to a memory bank does not block the connection of any other processing nodes to other memory banks.

The total number of switching nodes required to implement such a network is $\Theta(pb)$. It is reasonable to assume that the number of memory banks b is at least p; otherwise, at any given time, there will be some processing nodes that will be unable to access any memory

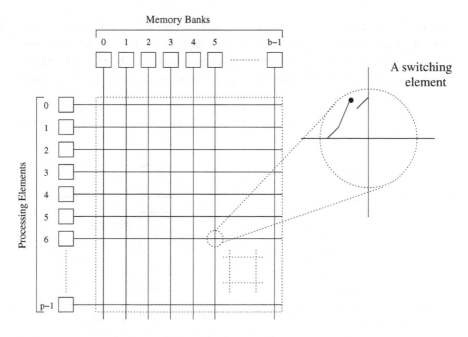

Figure 2.8 A completely non-blocking crossbar network connecting p processors to b memory banks.

banks. Therefore, as the value of p is increased, the complexity (component count) of the switching network grows as $\Omega(p^2)$. (See the Appendix for an explanation of the Ω notation.) As the number of processing nodes becomes large, this switch complexity is difficult to realize at high data rates. Consequently, crossbar networks are not very scalable in terms of cost.

Multistage Networks

The crossbar interconnection network is scalable in terms of performance but unscalable in terms of cost. Conversely, the shared bus network is scalable in terms of cost but unscalable in terms of performance. An intermediate class of networks called *multistage interconnection networks* lies between these two extremes. It is more scalable than the bus in terms of performance and more scalable than the crossbar in terms of cost.

The general schematic of a multistage network consisting of p processing nodes and b memory banks is shown in Figure 2.9. A commonly used multistage connection network is the *omega network*. This network consists of $\log p$ stages, where p is the number of inputs (processing nodes) and also the number of outputs (memory banks). Each stage of the omega network consists of an interconnection pattern that connects p inputs and p outputs; a link exists between input i and output j if the following is true:

$$j = \begin{cases} 2i, & 0 \le i \le p/2 - 1 \\ 2i + 1 - p, & p/2 \le i \le p - 1 \end{cases} \tag{2.1}$$

Equation 2.1 represents a left-rotation operation on the binary representation of i to obtain j. This interconnection pattern is called a *perfect shuffle*. Figure 2.10 shows a perfect shuffle interconnection pattern for eight inputs and outputs. At each stage of an omega network, a perfect shuffle interconnection pattern feeds into a set of $p/2$ switches

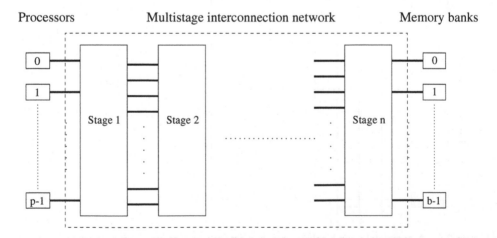

Figure 2.9   The schematic of a typical multistage interconnection network.

or switching nodes. Each switch is in one of two connection modes. In one mode, the inputs are sent straight through to the outputs, as shown in Figure 2.11(a). This is called the **pass-through** connection. In the other mode, the inputs to the switching node are crossed over and then sent out, as shown in Figure 2.11(b). This is called the **cross-over** connection.

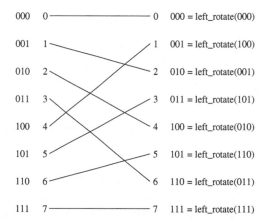

Figure 2.10 A perfect shuffle interconnection for eight inputs and outputs.

An omega network has $p/2 \times \log p$ switching nodes, and the cost of such a network grows as $\Theta(p \log p)$. Note that this cost is less than the $\Theta(p^2)$ cost of a complete crossbar network. Figure 2.12 shows an omega network for eight processors (denoted by the binary numbers on the left) and eight memory banks (denoted by the binary numbers on the right). Routing data in an omega network is accomplished using a simple scheme. Let s be the binary representation of a processor that needs to write some data into memory bank t. The data traverses the link to the first switching node. If the most significant bits of s and t are the same, then the data is routed in pass-through mode by the switch. If these bits are different, then the data is routed through in crossover mode. This scheme is repeated at the next switching stage using the next most significant bit. Traversing $\log p$ stages uses all $\log p$ bits in the binary representations of s and t.

(a)   (b)

Figure 2.11 Two switching configurations of the 2×2 switch: (a) Pass-through; (b) Cross-over.

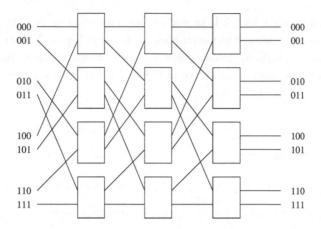

Figure 2.12   A complete omega network connecting eight inputs and eight outputs.

Figure 2.13 shows data routing over an omega network from processor two (010) to memory bank seven (111) and from processor six (110) to memory bank four (100). This figure also illustrates an important property of this network. When processor two (010) is communicating with memory bank seven (111), it blocks the path from processor six (110) to memory bank four (100). Communication link AB is used by both communication paths. Thus, in an omega network, access to a memory bank by a processor may disallow access to another memory bank by another processor. Networks with this property are referred to as ***blocking networks***.

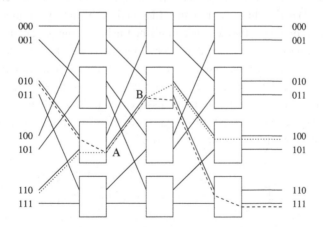

Figure 2.13   An example of blocking in omega network: one of the messages (010 to 111 or 110 to 100) is blocked at link AB.

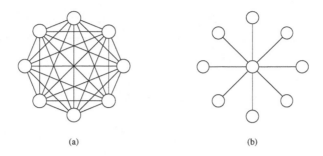

(a)   (b)

Figure 2.14   (a) A completely-connected network of eight nodes; (b) a star connected network of nine nodes.

Completely-Connected Network

In a *completely-connected network*, each node has a direct communication link to every other node in the network. Figure 2.14(a) illustrates a completely-connected network of eight nodes. This network is ideal in the sense that a node can send a message to another node in a single step, since a communication link exists between them. Completely-connected networks are the static counterparts of crossbar switching networks, since in both networks, the communication between any input/output pair does not block communication between any other pair.

Star-Connected Network

In a *star-connected network*, one processor acts as the central processor. Every other processor has a communication link connecting it to this processor. Figure 2.14(b) shows a star-connected network of nine processors. The star-connected network is similar to bus-based networks. Communication between any pair of processors is routed through the central processor, just as the shared bus forms the medium for all communication in a bus-based network. The central processor is the bottleneck in the star topology.

Linear Arrays, Meshes, and k-d Meshes

Due to the large number of links in completely connected networks, sparser networks are typically used to build parallel computers. A family of such networks spans the space of linear arrays and hypercubes. A linear array is a static network in which each node (except the two nodes at the ends) has two neighbors, one each to its left and right. A simple extension of the linear array (Figure 2.15(a)) is the ring or a 1-D torus (Figure 2.15(b)). The ring has a wraparound connection between the extremities of the linear array. In this case, each node has two neighbors.

A two-dimensional mesh illustrated in Figure 2.16(a) is an extension of the linear array to two-dimensions. Each dimension has $\sqrt{p}$ nodes with a node identified by a two-tuple (i, j). Every node (except those on the periphery) is connected to four other nodes whose

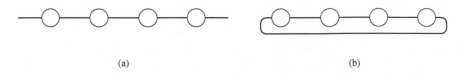

(a)   (b)

Figure 2.15 Linear arrays: (a) with no wraparound links; (b) with wraparound link.

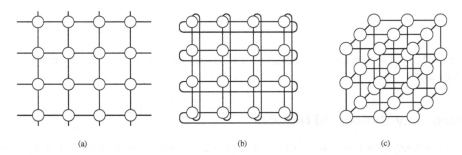

(a)   (b)   (c)

Figure 2.16 Two and three dimensional meshes: (a) 2-D mesh with no wraparound; (b) 2-D mesh with wraparound link (2-D torus); and (c) a 3-D mesh with no wraparound.

indices differ in any dimension by one. A 2-D mesh has the property that it can be laid out in 2-D space, making it attractive from a wiring standpoint. Furthermore, a variety of regularly structured computations map very naturally to a 2-D mesh. For this reason, 2-D meshes were often used as interconnects in parallel machines. Two dimensional meshes can be augmented with wraparound links to form two dimensional tori illustrated in Figure 2.16(b). The three-dimensional cube is a generalization of the 2-D mesh to three dimensions, as illustrated in Figure 2.16(c). Each node element in a 3-D cube, with the exception of those on the periphery, is connected to six other nodes, two along each of the three dimensions. A variety of physical simulations commonly executed on parallel computers (for example, 3-D weather modeling, structural modeling, etc.) can be mapped naturally to 3-D network topologies. For this reason, 3-D cubes are used commonly in interconnection networks for parallel computers (for example, in the Cray T3E).

The general class of k-d meshes refers to the class of topologies consisting of d dimensions with k nodes along each dimension. Just as a linear array forms one extreme of the k-d mesh family, the other extreme is formed by an interesting topology called the hypercube. The hypercube topology has two nodes along each dimension and $\log p$ dimensions. The construction of a hypercube is illustrated in Figure 2.17. A zero-dimensional hypercube consists of 2^0, i.e., one node. A one-dimensional hypercube is constructed from two zero-dimensional hypercubes by connecting them. A two-dimensional hypercube of four nodes is constructed from two one-dimensional hypercubes by connecting corresponding nodes. In general a d-dimensional hypercube is constructed by connecting corresponding nodes of two $(d-1)$ dimensional hypercubes. Figure 2.17 illustrates this for up to 16 nodes in a 4-D hypercube.

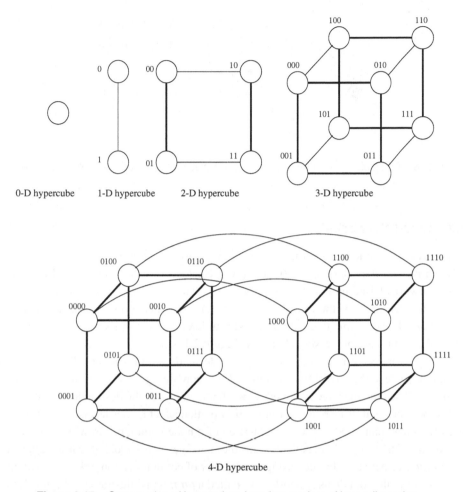

Figure 2.17   Construction of hypercubes from hypercubes of lower dimension.

It is useful to derive a numbering scheme for nodes in a hypercube. A simple numbering scheme can be derived from the construction of a hypercube. As illustrated in Figure 2.17, if we have a numbering of two subcubes of $p/2$ nodes, we can derive a numbering scheme for the cube of p nodes by prefixing the labels of one of the subcubes with a "0" and the labels of the other subcube with a "1". This numbering scheme has the useful property that the minimum distance between two nodes is given by the number of bits that are different in the two labels. For example, nodes labeled 0110 and 0101 are two links apart, since they differ at two bit positions. This property is useful for deriving a number of parallel algorithms for the hypercube architecture.

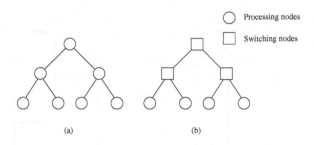

Figure 2.18   Complete binary tree networks: (a) a static tree network; and (b) a dynamic tree network.

Tree-Based Networks

A *tree network* is one in which there is only one path between any pair of nodes. Both linear arrays and star-connected networks are special cases of tree networks. Figure 2.18 shows networks based on complete binary trees. Static tree networks have a processing element at each node of the tree (Figure 2.18(a)). Tree networks also have a dynamic counterpart. In a dynamic tree network, nodes at intermediate levels are switching nodes and the leaf nodes are processing elements (Figure 2.18(b)).

To route a message in a tree, the source node sends the message up the tree until it reaches the node at the root of the smallest subtree containing both the source and destination nodes. Then the message is routed down the tree towards the destination node.

Tree networks suffer from a communication bottleneck at higher levels of the tree. For example, when many nodes in the left subtree of a node communicate with nodes in the right subtree, the root node must handle all the messages. This problem can be alleviated in dynamic tree networks by increasing the number of communication links and switching nodes closer to the root. This network, also called a *fat tree*, is illustrated in Figure 2.19.

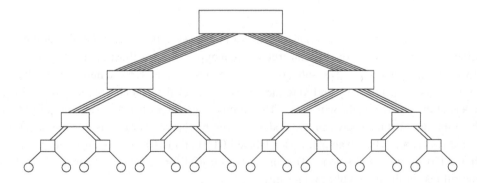

Figure 2.19   A fat tree network of 16 processing nodes.

2.4.4 Evaluating Static Interconnection Networks

We now discuss various criteria used to characterize the cost and performance of static interconnection networks. We use these criteria to evaluate static networks introduced in the previous subsection.

Diameter The *diameter* of a network is the maximum distance between any two processing nodes in the network. The distance between two processing nodes is defined as the shortest path (in terms of number of links) between them. The diameter of a completely-connected network is one, and that of a star-connected network is two. The diameter of a ring network is $\lfloor p/2 \rfloor$. The diameter of a two-dimensional mesh without wraparound connections is $2(\sqrt{p} - 1)$ for the two nodes at diagonally opposed corners, and that of a wraparound mesh is $2\lfloor \sqrt{p}/2 \rfloor$. The diameter of a hypercube-connected network is $\log p$ since two node labels can differ in at most $\log p$ positions. The diameter of a complete binary tree is $2\log((p + 1)/2)$ because the two communicating nodes may be in separate subtrees of the root node, and a message might have to travel all the way to the root and then down the other subtree.

Connectivity The *connectivity* of a network is a measure of the multiplicity of paths between any two processing nodes. A network with high connectivity is desirable, because it lowers contention for communication resources. One measure of connectivity is the minimum number of arcs that must be removed from the network to break it into two disconnected networks. This is called the *arc connectivity* of the network. The arc connectivity is one for linear arrays, as well as tree and star networks. It is two for rings and 2-D meshes without wraparound, four for 2-D wraparound meshes, and d for d-dimensional hypercubes.

Bisection Width and Bisection Bandwidth The *bisection width* of a network is defined as the minimum number of communication links that must be removed to partition the network into two equal halves. The bisection width of a ring is two, since any partition cuts across only two communication links. Similarly, the bisection width of a two-dimensional p-node mesh without wraparound connections is $\sqrt{p}$ and with wraparound connections is $2\sqrt{p}$. The bisection width of a tree and a star is one, and that of a completely-connected network of p nodes is $p^2/4$. The bisection width of a hypercube can be derived from its construction. We construct a d-dimensional hypercube by connecting corresponding links of two $(d - 1)$-dimensional hypercubes. Since each of these subcubes contains $2^{(d-1)}$ or $p/2$ nodes, at least $p/2$ communication links must cross any partition of a hypercube into two subcubes (Problem 2.15).

The number of bits that can be communicated simultaneously over a link connecting two nodes is called the *channel width*. Channel width is equal to the number of physical wires in each communication link. The peak rate at which a single physical wire can deliver bits is called the *channel rate*. The peak rate at which data can be communicated between

Table 2.1 A summary of the characteristics of various static network topologies connecting p nodes.

Network	Diameter	Bisection Width	Arc Connectivity	Cost (No. of links)
Completely-connected	1	$p^2/4$	$p-1$	$p(p-1)/2$
Star	2	1	1	$p-1$
Complete binary tree	$2\log((p+1)/2)$	1	1	$p-1$
Linear array	$p-1$	1	1	$p-1$
2-D mesh, no wraparound	$2(\sqrt{p}-1)$	$\sqrt{p}$	2	$2(p-\sqrt{p})$
2-D wraparound mesh	$2\lfloor\sqrt{p}/2\rfloor$	$2\sqrt{p}$	4	$2p$
Hypercube	$\log p$	$p/2$	$\log p$	$(p\log p)/2$
Wraparound k-ary d-cube	$d\lfloor k/2\rfloor$	$2k^{d-1}$	$2d$	dp

the ends of a communication link is called *channel bandwidth*. Channel bandwidth is the product of channel rate and channel width.

The *bisection bandwidth* of a network is defined as the minimum volume of communication allowed between any two halves of the network. It is the product of the bisection width and the channel bandwidth. Bisection bandwidth of a network is also sometimes referred to as *cross-section bandwidth*.

Cost Many criteria can be used to evaluate the cost of a network. One way of defining the cost of a network is in terms of the number of communication links or the number of wires required by the network. Linear arrays and trees use only $p-1$ links to connect p nodes. A d-dimensional wraparound mesh has dp links. A hypercube-connected network has $(p\log p)/2$ links.

The bisection bandwidth of a network can also be used as a measure of its cost, as it provides a lower bound on the area in a two-dimensional packaging or the volume in a three-dimensional packaging. If the bisection width of a network is w, the lower bound on the area in a two-dimensional packaging is $\Theta(w^2)$, and the lower bound on the volume in a three-dimensional packaging is $\Theta(w^{3/2})$. According to this criterion, hypercubes and completely connected networks are more expensive than the other networks.

We summarize the characteristics of various static networks in Table 2.1, which highlights the various cost-performance tradeoffs.

2.4.5 Evaluating Dynamic Interconnection Networks

A number of evaluation metrics for dynamic networks follow from the corresponding metrics for static networks. Since a message traversing a switch must pay an overhead, it is logical to think of each switch as a node in the network, in addition to the processing nodes. The diameter of the network can now be defined as the maximum distance between any two nodes in the network. This is indicative of the maximum delay that a message will encounter in being communicated between the selected pair of nodes. In reality, we would like the metric to be the maximum distance between any two processing nodes; however, for all networks of interest, this is equivalent to the maximum distance between any (processing or switching) pair of nodes.

The connectivity of a dynamic network can be defined in terms of node or edge connectivity. The node connectivity is the minimum number of nodes that must fail (be removed from the network) to fragment the network into two parts. As before, we should consider only switching nodes (as opposed to all nodes). However, considering all nodes gives a good approximation to the multiplicity of paths in a dynamic network. The arc connectivity of the network can be similarly defined as the minimum number of edges that must fail (be removed from the network) to fragment the network into two unreachable parts.

The bisection width of a dynamic network must be defined more precisely than diameter and connectivity. In the case of bisection width, we consider any possible partitioning of the p processing nodes into two equal parts. Note that this does not restrict the partitioning of the switching nodes. For each such partition, we select an induced partitioning of the switching nodes such that the number of edges crossing this partition is minimized. The minimum number of edges for any such partition is the bisection width of the dynamic network. Another intuitive way of thinking of bisection width is in terms of the minimum number of edges that must be removed from the network so as to partition the network into two halves with identical number of processing nodes. We illustrate this concept further in the following example:

Example 2.13 Bisection width of dynamic networks

Consider the network illustrated in Figure 2.20. We illustrate here three bisections, A, B, and C, each of which partitions the network into two groups of two processing nodes each. Notice that these partitions need not partition the network nodes equally. In the example, each partition results in an edge cut of four. We conclude that the bisection width of this graph is four. ∎

The cost of a dynamic network is determined by the link cost, as is the case with static networks, as well as the switch cost. In typical dynamic networks, the degree of a switch is constant. Therefore, the number of links and switches is asymptotically identical. Furthermore, in typical networks, switch cost exceeds link cost. For this reason, the cost of dynamic networks is often determined by the number of switching nodes in the network.

We summarize the characteristics of various dynamic networks in Table 2.2.

2.4.6 Cache Coherence in Multiprocessor Systems

While interconnection networks provide basic mechanisms for communicating messages (data), in the case of shared-address-space computers additional hardware is required to

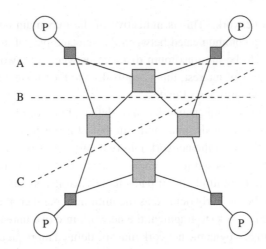

Figure 2.20 Bisection width of a dynamic network is computed by examining various equi-partitions of the processing nodes and selecting the minimum number of edges crossing the partition. In this case, each partition yields an edge cut of four. Therefore, the bisection width of this graph is four.

Table 2.2 A summary of the characteristics of various dynamic network topologies connecting p processing nodes.

Network	Diameter	Bisection Width	Arc Connectivity	Cost (No. of links)
Crossbar	1	p	1	p^2
Omega Network	$\log p$	$p/2$	2	$p/2$
Dynamic Tree	$2\log p$	1	2	$p - 1$

keep multiple copies of data consistent with each other. Specifically, if there exist two copies of the data (in different caches/memory elements), how do we ensure that different processors operate on these in a manner that follows predefined semantics?

The problem of keeping caches in multiprocessor systems coherent is significantly more complex than in uniprocessor systems. This is because in addition to multiple copies as in uniprocessor systems, there may also be multiple processors modifying these copies. Consider a simple scenario illustrated in Figure 2.21. Two processors P_0 and P_1 are connected over a shared bus to a globally accessible memory. Both processors load the same variable. There are now three copies of the variable. The coherence mechanism must now ensure that all operations performed on these copies are serializable (i.e., there exists some serial order of instruction execution that corresponds to the parallel schedule). When a processor changes the value of its copy of the variable, one of two things must happen: the other copies must be invalidated, or the other copies must be updated. Failing this, other processors may potentially work with incorrect (stale) values of the variable. These two protocols are referred to as *invalidate* and *update* protocols and are illustrated in Figure 2.21(a) and (b).

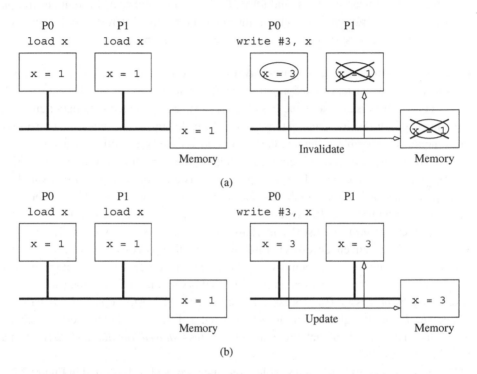

Figure 2.21   Cache coherence in multiprocessor systems: (a) Invalidate protocol; (b) Update protocol for shared variables.

In an update protocol, whenever a data item is written, all of its copies in the system are updated. For this reason, if a processor simply reads a data item once and never uses it, subsequent updates to this item at other processors cause excess overhead in terms of latency at source and bandwidth on the network. On the other hand, in this situation, an invalidate protocol invalidates the data item on the first update at a remote processor and subsequent updates need not be performed on this copy.

Another important factor affecting the performance of these protocols is *false sharing*. False sharing refers to the situation in which different processors update different parts of of the same cache-line. Thus, although the updates are not performed on shared variables, the system does not detect this. In an invalidate protocol, when a processor updates its part of the cache-line, the other copies of this line are invalidated. When other processors try to update their parts of the cache-line, the line must actually be fetched from the remote processor. It is easy to see that false-sharing can cause a cache-line to be ping-ponged between various processors. In an update protocol, this situation is slightly better since all reads can be performed locally and the writes must be updated. This saves an invalidate operation that is otherwise wasted.

The tradeoff between invalidate and update schemes is the classic tradeoff between communication overhead (updates) and idling (stalling in invalidates). Current generation cache coherent machines typically rely on invalidate protocols. The rest of our discussion of multiprocessor cache systems therefore assumes invalidate protocols.

Maintaining Coherence Using Invalidate Protocols   Multiple copies of a single data item are kept consistent by keeping track of the number of copies and the state of each of these copies. We discuss here one possible set of states associated with data items and events that trigger transitions among these states. Note that this set of states and transitions is not unique. It is possible to define other states and associated transitions as well.

Let us revisit the example in Figure 2.21. Initially the variable x resides in the global memory. The first step executed by both processors is a load operation on this variable. At this point, the state of the variable is said to be *shared*, since it is shared by multiple processors. When processor P_0 executes a store on this variable, it marks all other copies of this variable as *invalid*. It must also mark its own copy as modified or *dirty*. This is done to ensure that all subsequent accesses to this variable at other processors will be serviced by processor P_0 and not from the memory. At this point, say, processor P_1 executes another load operation on x. Processor P_1 attempts to fetch this variable and, since the variable was marked dirty by processor P_0, processor P_0 services the request. Copies of this variable at processor P_1 and the global memory are updated and the variable re-enters the shared state. Thus, in this simple model, there are three states - *shared*, *invalid*, and *dirty* - that a cache line goes through.

The complete state diagram of a simple three-state protocol is illustrated in Figure 2.22. The solid lines depict processor actions and the dashed lines coherence actions. For example, when a processor executes a read on an invalid block, the block is fetched and a transition is made from invalid to shared. Similarly, if a processor does a write on a shared block, the coherence protocol propagates a C_write (a coherence write) on the block. This triggers a transition from shared to invalid at all the other blocks.

Example 2.14   Maintaining coherence using a simple three-state protocol
Consider an example of two program segments being executed by processor P_0 and P_1 as illustrated in Figure 2.23. The system consists of local memories (or caches) at processors P_0 and P_1, and a global memory. The three-state protocol assumed in this example corresponds to the state diagram illustrated in Figure 2.22. Cache lines in this system can be either shared, invalid, or dirty. Each data item (variable) is assumed to be on a different cache line. Initially, the two variables x and y are tagged dirty and the only copies of these variables exist in the global memory. Figure 2.23 illustrates state transitions along with values of copies of the variables with each instruction execution. ∎

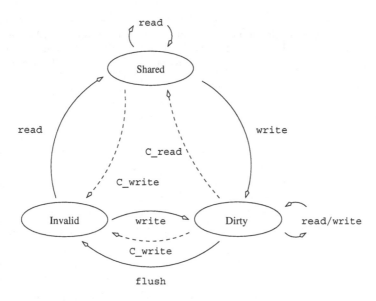

Figure 2.22 State diagram of a simple three-state coherence protocol.

The implementation of coherence protocols can be carried out using a variety of hardware mechanisms – snoopy systems, directory based systems, or combinations thereof.

Snoopy Cache Systems

Snoopy caches are typically associated with multiprocessor systems based on broadcast interconnection networks such as a bus or a ring. In such systems, all processors snoop on (monitor) the bus for transactions. This allows the processor to make state transitions for its cache-blocks. Figure 2.24 illustrates a typical snoopy bus based system. Each processor's cache has a set of tag bits associated with it that determine the state of the cache blocks. These tags are updated according to the state diagram associated with the coherence protocol. For instance, when the snoop hardware detects that a read has been issued to a cache block that it has a dirty copy of, it asserts control of the bus and puts the data out. Similarly, when the snoop hardware detects that a write operation has been issued on a cache block that it has a copy of, it invalidates the block. Other state transitions are made in this fashion locally.

Performance of Snoopy Caches Snoopy protocols have been extensively studied and used in commercial systems. This is largely because of their simplicity and the fact that existing bus based systems can be upgraded to accommodate snoopy protocols. The performance gains of snoopy systems are derived from the fact that if different processors operate on different data items, these items can be cached. Once these items are tagged dirty, all subsequent operations can be performed locally on the cache without generating external traffic. Similarly, if a data item is read by a number of processors, it transitions

Time	Instruction at Processor 0	Instruction at Processor 1	Variables and their states at Processor 0	Variables and their states at Processor 1	Variables and their states in Global mem.
					x = 5, D
					y = 12, D
	read x		x = 5, S		x = 5, S
		read y		y = 12, S	y = 12, S
	x = x + 1		x = 6, D		x = 5, I
		y = y + 1		y = 13, D	y = 12, I
	read y		y = 13, S	y = 13, S	y = 13, S
		read x	x = 6, S	x = 6, S	x = 6, S
	x = x + y		x = 19, D	x = 6, I	x = 6, I
		y = x + y	y = 13, I	y = 19, D	y = 13, I
	x = x + 1		x = 20, D		x = 6, I
		y = y + 1		y = 20, D	y = 13, I

Figure 2.23 Example of parallel program execution with the simple three-state coherence protocol discussed in Section 2.4.6.

to the shared state in the cache and all subsequent read operations become local. In both cases, the coherence protocol does not add any overhead. On the other hand, if multiple processors read and update the same data item, they generate coherence functions across processors. Since a shared bus has a finite bandwidth, only a constant number of such coherence operations can execute in unit time. This presents a fundamental bottleneck for snoopy bus based systems.

Snoopy protocols are intimately tied to multicomputers based on broadcast networks such as buses. This is because all processors must snoop all the messages. Clearly, broadcasting all of a processor's memory operations to all the processors is not a scalable solution. An obvious solution to this problem is to propagate coherence operations only to those processors that must participate in the operation (i.e., processors that have relevant copies of the data). This solution requires us to keep track of which processors have copies of various data items and also the relevant state information for these data items. This information is stored in a directory, and the coherence mechanism based on such information is called a directory-based system.

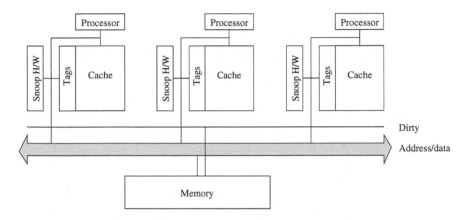

Figure 2.24   A simple snoopy bus based cache coherence system.

Directory Based Systems

Consider a simple system in which the global memory is augmented with a directory that maintains a bitmap representing cache-blocks and the processors at which they are cached (Figure 2.25). These bitmap entries are sometimes referred to as the ***presence bits***. As before, we assume a three-state protocol with the states labeled ***invalid***, ***dirty***, and ***shared***. The key to the performance of directory based schemes is the simple observation that only processors that hold a particular block (or are reading it) participate in the state transitions due to coherence operations. Note that there may be other state transitions triggered by processor read, write, or flush (retiring a line from cache) but these transitions can be handled locally with the operation reflected in the presence bits and state in the directory.

Revisiting the code segment in Figure 2.21, when processors P_0 and P_1 access the block corresponding to variable x, the state of the block is changed to shared, and the presence bits updated to indicate that processors P_0 and P_1 share the block. When P_0 executes a store on the variable, the state in the directory is changed to dirty and the presence bit of P_1 is reset. All subsequent operations on this variable performed at processor P_0 can proceed locally. If another processor reads the value, the directory notices the dirty tag and uses the presence bits to direct the request to the appropriate processor. Processor P_0 updates the block in the memory, and sends it to the requesting processor. The presence bits are modified to reflect this and the state transitions to shared.

Performance of Directory Based Schemes   As is the case with snoopy protocols, if different processors operate on distinct data blocks, these blocks become dirty in the respective caches and all operations after the first one can be performed locally. Furthermore, if multiple processors read (but do not update) a single data block, the data block gets replicated in the caches in the shared state and subsequent reads can happen without triggering any coherence overheads.

Coherence actions are initiated when multiple processors attempt to update the same

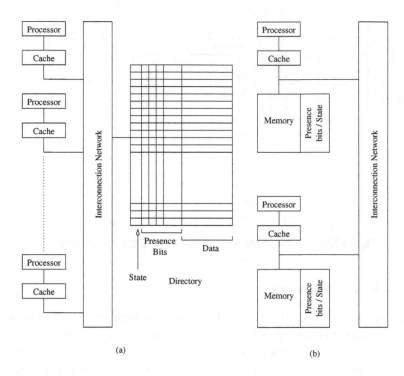

Figure 2.25   Architecture of typical directory based systems: (a) a centralized directory; and (b) a distributed directory.

data item. In this case, in addition to the necessary data movement, coherence operations add to the overhead in the form of propagation of state updates (invalidates or updates) and generation of state information from the directory. The former takes the form of communication overhead and the latter adds contention. The communication overhead is a function of the number of processors requiring state updates and the algorithm for propagating state information. The contention overhead is more fundamental in nature. Since the directory is in memory and the memory system can only service a bounded number of read/write operations in unit time, the number of state updates is ultimately bounded by the directory. If a parallel program requires a large number of coherence actions (large number of read/write shared data blocks) the directory will ultimately bound its parallel performance.

Finally, from the point of view of cost, the amount of memory required to store the directory may itself become a bottleneck as the number of processors increases. Recall that the directory size grows as $O(mp)$, where m is the number of memory blocks and p the number of processors. One solution would be to make the memory block larger (thus reducing m for a given memory size). However, this adds to other overheads such as false sharing, where two processors update distinct data items in a program but the data items happen to lie in the same memory block. This phenomenon is discussed in greater detail in Chapter 7.

Since the directory forms a central point of contention, it is natural to break up the task of maintaining coherence across multiple processors. The basic principle is to let each processor maintain coherence of its own memory blocks, assuming a physical (or logical) partitioning of the memory blocks across processors. This is the principle of a distributed directory system.

Distributed Directory Schemes   In scalable architectures, memory is physically distributed across processors. The corresponding presence bits of the blocks are also distributed. Each processor is responsible for maintaining the coherence of its own memory blocks. The architecture of such a system is illustrated in Figure 2.25(b). Since each memory block has an owner (which can typically be computed from the block address), its directory location is implicitly known to all processors. When a processor attempts to read a block for the first time, it requests the owner for the block. The owner suitably directs this request based on presence and state information locally available. Similarly, when a processor writes into a memory block, it propagates an invalidate to the owner, which in turn forwards the invalidate to all processors that have a cached copy of the block. In this way, the directory is decentralized and the contention associated with the central directory is alleviated. Note that the communication overhead associated with state update messages is not reduced.

Performance of Distributed Directory Schemes   As is evident, distributed directories permit $O(p)$ simultaneous coherence operations, provided the underlying network can sustain the associated state update messages. From this point of view, distributed directories are inherently more scalable than snoopy systems or centralized directory systems. The latency and bandwidth of the network become fundamental performance bottlenecks for such systems.

2.5   Communication Costs in Parallel Machines

One of the major overheads in the execution of parallel programs arises from communication of information between processing elements. The cost of communication is dependent on a variety of features including the programming model semantics, the network topology, data handling and routing, and associated software protocols. These issues form the focus of our discussion here.

2.5.1   Message Passing Costs in Parallel Computers

The time taken to communicate a message between two nodes in a network is the sum of the time to prepare a message for transmission and the time taken by the message to traverse the network to its destination. The principal parameters that determine the communication latency are as follows:

1. ***Startup time*** (t_s): The startup time is the time required to handle a message at the sending and receiving nodes. This includes the time to prepare the message (adding header, trailer, and error correction information), the time to execute the routing algorithm, and the time to establish an interface between the local node and the router. This delay is incurred only once for a single message transfer.

2. ***Per-hop time*** (t_h): After a message leaves a node, it takes a finite amount of time to reach the next node in its path. The time taken by the header of a message to travel between two directly-connected nodes in the network is called the per-hop time. It is also known as ***node latency***. The per-hop time is directly related to the latency within the routing switch for determining which output buffer or channel the message should be forwarded to.

3. ***Per-word transfer time*** (t_w): If the channel bandwidth is r words per second, then each word takes time $t_w = 1/r$ to traverse the link. This time is called the per-word transfer time. This time includes network as well as buffering overheads.

We now discuss two routing techniques that have been used in parallel computers – store-and-forward routing and cut-through routing.

Store-and-Forward Routing

In store-and-forward routing, when a message is traversing a path with multiple links, each intermediate node on the path forwards the message to the next node after it has received and stored the entire message. Figure 2.26(a) shows the communication of a message through a store-and-forward network.

Suppose that a message of size m is being transmitted through such a network. Assume that it traverses l links. At each link, the message incurs a cost t_h for the header and $t_w m$ for the rest of the message to traverse the link. Since there are l such links, the total time is $(t_h + t_w m)l$. Therefore, for store-and-forward routing, the total communication cost for a message of size m words to traverse l communication links is

$$t_{comm} = t_s + (mt_w + t_h)l. \tag{2.2}$$

In current parallel computers, the per-hop time t_h is quite small. For most parallel algorithms, it is less than $t_w m$ even for small values of m and thus can be ignored. For parallel platforms using store-and-forward routing, the time given by Equation 2.2 can be simplified to

$$t_{comm} = t_s + mlt_w.$$

Packet Routing

Store-and-forward routing makes poor use of communication resources. A message is sent from one node to the next only after the entire message has been received (Figure 2.26(a)).

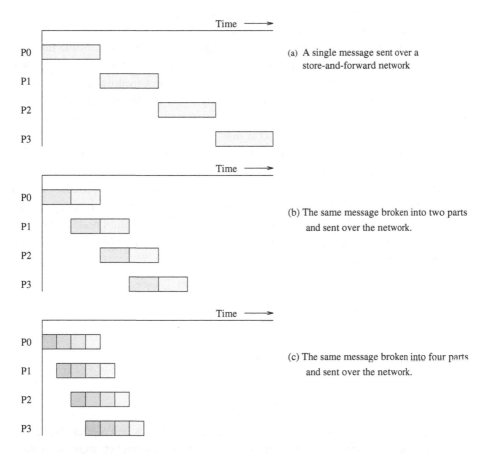

Figure 2.26 Passing a message from node P_0 to P_3 (a) through a store-and-forward communication network; (b) and (c) extending the concept to cut-through routing. The shaded regions represent the time that the message is in transit. The startup time associated with this message transfer is assumed to be zero.

Consider the scenario shown in Figure 2.26(b), in which the original message is broken into two equal sized parts before it is sent. In this case, an intermediate node waits for only half of the original message to arrive before passing it on. The increased utilization of communication resources and reduced communication time is apparent from Figure 2.26(b). Figure 2.26(c) goes a step further and breaks the message into four parts. In addition to better utilization of communication resources, this principle offers other advantages – lower overhead from packet loss (errors), possibility of packets taking different paths, and better error correction capability. For these reasons, this technique is the basis for long-haul communication networks such as the Internet, where error rates, number of hops, and variation in network state can be higher. Of course, the overhead here is that each packet must carry routing, error correction, and sequencing information.

Consider the transfer of an m word message through the network. The time taken for programming the network interfaces and computing the routing information, etc., is independent of the message length. This is aggregated into the startup time t_s of the message transfer. We assume a scenario in which routing tables are static over the time of message transfer (i.e., all packets traverse the same path). While this is not a valid assumption under all circumstances, it serves the purpose of motivating a cost model for message transfer. The message is broken into packets, and packets are assembled with their error, routing, and sequencing fields. The size of a packet is now given by $r + s$, where r is the original message and s is the additional information carried in the packet. The time for packetizing the message is proportional to the length of the message. We denote this time by mt_{w1}. If the network is capable of communicating one word every t_{w2} seconds, incurs a delay of t_h on each hop, and if the first packet traverses l hops, then this packet takes time $t_h l + t_{w2}(r + s)$ to reach the destination. After this time, the destination node receives an additional packet every $t_{w2}(r + s)$ seconds. Since there are $m/r - 1$ additional packets, the total communication time is given by:

$$t_{comm} = t_s + t_{w1}m + t_h l + t_{w2}(r + s) + \left(\frac{m}{r} - 1\right) t_{w2}(r + s)$$

$$= t_s + t_{w1}m + t_h l + t_{w2}m + t_{w2}\frac{s}{r}m$$

$$= t_s + t_h l + t_w m,$$

where

$$t_w = t_{w1} + t_{w2}\left(1 + \frac{s}{r}\right).$$

Packet routing is suited to networks with highly dynamic states and higher error rates, such as local- and wide-area networks. This is because individual packets may take different routes and retransmissions can be localized to lost packets.

Cut-Through Routing

In interconnection networks for parallel computers, additional restrictions can be imposed on message transfers to further reduce the overheads associated with packet switching. By forcing all packets to take the same path, we can eliminate the overhead of transmitting routing information with each packet. By forcing in-sequence delivery, sequencing information can be eliminated. By associating error information at message level rather than packet level, the overhead associated with error detection and correction can be reduced. Finally, since error rates in interconnection networks for parallel machines are extremely low, lean error detection mechanisms can be used instead of expensive error correction schemes.

The routing scheme resulting from these optimizations is called cut-through routing. In cut-through routing, a message is broken into fixed size units called *flow control digits* or *flits*. Since flits do not contain the overheads of packets, they can be much smaller than packets. A tracer is first sent from the source to the destination node to establish a connection. Once a connection has been established, the flits are sent one after the other. All flits follow the same path in a dovetailed fashion. An intermediate node does not wait for the entire message to arrive before forwarding it. As soon as a flit is received at an intermediate node, the flit is passed on to the next node. Unlike store-and-forward routing, it is no longer necessary to have buffer space at each intermediate node to store the entire message. Therefore, cut-through routing uses less memory and memory bandwidth at intermediate nodes, and is faster.

Consider a message that is traversing such a network. If the message traverses l links, and t_h is the per-hop time, then the header of the message takes time lt_h to reach the destination. If the message is m words long, then the entire message arrives in time $t_w m$ after the arrival of the header of the message. Therefore, the total communication time for cut-through routing is

$$t_{comm} = t_s + lt_h + t_w m. \tag{2.3}$$

This time is an improvement over store-and-forward routing since terms corresponding to number of hops and number of words are additive as opposed to multiplicative in the former. Note that if the communication is between nearest neighbors (that is, $l = 1$), or if the message size is small, then the communication time is similar for store-and-forward and cut-through routing schemes.

Most current parallel computers and many local area networks support cut-through routing. The size of a flit is determined by a variety of network parameters. The control circuitry must operate at the flit rate. Therefore, if we select a very small flit size, for a given link bandwidth, the required flit rate becomes large. This poses considerable challenges for designing routers as it requires the control circuitry to operate at a very high speed. On the other hand, as flit sizes become large, internal buffer sizes increase, so does the latency of message transfer. Both of these are undesirable. Flit sizes in recent cut-through interconnection networks range from four bits to 32 bytes. In many parallel programming paradigms that rely predominantly on short messages (such as cache lines), the latency of messages is critical. For these, it is unreasonable for a long message traversing a link to hold up a short message. Such scenarios are addressed in routers using multilane cut-through routing. In multilane cut-through routing, a single physical channel is split into a number of virtual channels.

Messaging constants t_s, t_w, and t_h are determined by hardware characteristics, software layers, and messaging semantics. Messaging semantics associated with paradigms such as message passing are best served by variable length messages, others by fixed length short messages. While effective bandwidth may be critical for the former, reducing latency is more important for the latter. Messaging layers for these paradigms are tuned to reflect these requirements.

While traversing the network, if a message needs to use a link that is currently in use, then the message is blocked. This may lead to deadlock. Figure 2.27 illustrates deadlock in a cut-through routing network. The destinations of messages 0, 1, 2, and 3 are A, B, C, and D, respectively. A flit from message 0 occupies the link CB (and the associated buffers).

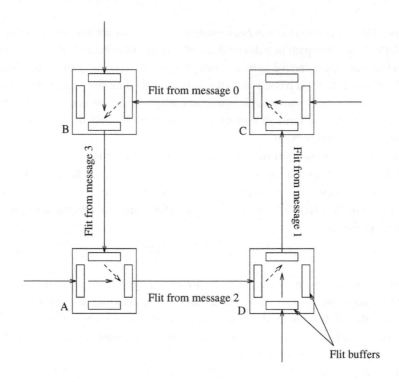

Flit from message 0

Flit from message 3

Flit from message 1

B

C

Flit from message 2

A   D

Flit buffers

----▶   Desired direction of message traversal

Figure 2.27   An example of deadlock in a cut-through routing network.

However, since link BA is occupied by a flit from message 3, the flit from message 0 is blocked. Similarly, the flit from message 3 is blocked since link AD is in use. We can see that no messages can progress in the network and the network is deadlocked. Deadlocks can be avoided in cut-through networks by using appropriate routing techniques and message buffers. These are discussed in Section 2.6.

A Simplified Cost Model for Communicating Messages

As we have just seen in Section 2.5.1, the cost of communicating a message between two nodes l hops away using cut-through routing is given by

$$t_{comm} = t_s + lt_h + t_w m.$$

This equation implies that in order to optimize the cost of message transfers, we would need to:

1. **Communicate in bulk.** That is, instead of sending small messages and paying a startup cost t_s for each, we want to aggregate small messages into a single large

message and amortize the startup latency across a larger message. This is because on typical platforms such as clusters and message-passing machines, the value of t_s is much larger than those of t_h or t_w.

2. **Minimize the volume of data.** To minimize the overhead paid in terms of per-word transfer time t_w, it is desirable to reduce the volume of data communicated as much as possible.

3. **Minimize distance of data transfer.** Minimize the number of hops l that a message must traverse.

While the first two objectives are relatively easy to achieve, the task of minimizing distance of communicating nodes is difficult, and in many cases an unnecessary burden on the algorithm designer. This is a direct consequence of the following characteristics of parallel platforms and paradigms:

- In many message-passing libraries such as MPI, the programmer has little control on the mapping of processes onto physical processors. In such paradigms, while tasks might have well defined topologies and may communicate only among neighbors in the task topology, the mapping of processes to nodes might destroy this structure.

- Many architectures rely on randomized (two-step) routing, in which a message is first sent to a random node from source and from this intermediate node to the destination. This alleviates hot-spots and contention on the network. Minimizing number of hops in a randomized routing network yields no benefits.

- The per-hop time (t_h) is typically dominated either by the startup latency (t_s) for small messages or by per-word component $(t_w m)$ for large messages. Since the maximum number of hops (l) in most networks is relatively small, the per-hop time can be ignored with little loss in accuracy.

All of these point to a simpler cost model in which the cost of transferring a message between two nodes on a network is given by:

$$t_{comm} = t_s + t_w m \qquad (2.4)$$

This expression has significant implications for architecture-independent algorithm design as well as for the accuracy of runtime predictions. Since this cost model implies that it takes the same amount of time to communicate between any pair of nodes, it corresponds to a completely connected network. Instead of designing algorithms for each specific architecture (for example, a mesh, hypercube, or tree), we can design algorithms with this cost model in mind and port it to any target parallel computer.

This raises the important issue of loss of accuracy (or fidelity) of prediction when the algorithm is ported from our simplified model (which assumes a completely connected network) to an actual machine architecture. If our initial assumption that the t_h term is typically dominated by the t_s or t_w terms is valid, then the loss in accuracy should be minimal.

However, it is important to note that our basic cost model is valid only for uncongested networks. Architectures have varying thresholds for when they get congested; i.e., a linear array has a much lower threshold for congestion than a hypercube. Furthermore, different communication patterns congest a given network to different extents. Consequently, our simplified cost model is valid only as long as the underlying communication pattern does not congest the network.

Example 2.15   Effect of congestion on communication cost

Consider a $\sqrt{p} \times \sqrt{p}$ mesh in which each node is only communicating with its nearest neighbor. Since no links in the network are used for more than one communication, the time for this operation is $t_s + t_w m$, where m is the number of words communicated. This time is consistent with our simplified model.

Consider an alternate scenario in which each node is communicating with a randomly selected node. This randomness implies that there are $p/2$ communications (or $p/4$ bi-directional communications) occurring across any equi-partition of the machine (since the node being communicated with could be in either half with equal probability). From our discussion of bisection width, we know that a 2-D mesh has a bisection width of $\sqrt{p}$. From these two, we can infer that some links would now have to carry at least $\frac{p/4}{\sqrt{p}} = \sqrt{p}/4$ messages, assuming bi-directional communication channels. These messages must be serialized over the link. If each message is of size m, the time for this operation is at least $t_s + t_w m \times \sqrt{p}/4$. This time is not in conformity with our simplified model.   ■

The above example illustrates that for a given architecture, some communication patterns can be non-congesting and others may be congesting. This makes the task of modeling communication costs dependent not just on the architecture, but also on the communication pattern. To address this, we introduce the notion of **effective bandwidth**. For communication patterns that do not congest the network, the effective bandwidth is identical to the link bandwidth. However, for communication operations that congest the network, the effective bandwidth is the link bandwidth scaled down by the degree of congestion on the most congested link. This is often difficult to estimate since it is a function of process to node mapping, routing algorithms, and communication schedule. Therefore, we use a lower bound on the message communication time. The associated link bandwidth is scaled down by a factor p/b, where b is the bisection width of the network.

In the rest of this text, we will work with the simplified communication model for message passing with effective per-word time t_w because it allows us to design algorithms in an architecture-independent manner. We will also make specific notes on when a communication operation within an algorithm congests the network and how its impact is factored into parallel runtime. The communication times in the book apply to the general class of k-d meshes. While these times may be realizable on other architectures as well, this is a function of the underlying architecture.

2.5.2 Communication Costs in Shared-Address-Space Machines

The primary goal of associating communication costs with parallel programs is to associate a figure of merit with a program to guide program development. This task is much more difficult for cache-coherent shared-address-space machines than for message-passing or non-cache-coherent architectures. The reasons for this are as follows:

- Memory layout is typically determined by the system. The programmer has minimal control on the location of specific data items over and above permuting data structures to optimize access. This is particularly important in distributed memory shared-address-space architectures because it is difficult to identify local and remote accesses. If the access times for local and remote data items are significantly different, then the cost of communication can vary greatly depending on the data layout.

- Finite cache sizes can result in cache thrashing. Consider a scenario in which a node needs a certain fraction of the total data to compute its results. If this fraction is smaller than locally available cache, the data can be fetched on first access and computed on. However, if the fraction exceeds available cache, then certain portions of this data might get overwritten, and consequently accessed several times. This overhead can cause sharp degradation in program performance as the problem size is increased. To remedy this, the programmer must alter execution schedules (e.g., blocking loops as illustrated in serial matrix multiplication in Problem 2.5) for minimizing working set size. While this problem is common to both serial and multiprocessor platforms, the penalty is much higher in the case of multiprocessors since each miss might now involve coherence operations and interprocessor communication.

- Overheads associated with invalidate and update operations are difficult to quantify. After a data item has been fetched by a processor into cache, it may be subject to a variety of operations at another processor. For example, in an invalidate protocol, the cache line might be invalidated by a write operation at a remote processor. In this case, the next read operation on the data item must pay a remote access latency cost again. Similarly, the overhead associated with an update protocol might vary significantly depending on the number of copies of a data item. The number of concurrent copies of a data item and the schedule of instruction execution are typically beyond the control of the programmer.

- Spatial locality is difficult to model. Since cache lines are generally longer than one word (anywhere from four to 128 words), different words might have different access latencies associated with them even for the first access. Accessing a neighbor of a previously fetched word might be extremely fast, if the cache line has not yet been overwritten. Once again, the programmer has minimal control over this, other than to permute data structures to maximize spatial locality of data reference.

- Prefetching can play a role in reducing the overhead associated with data access. Compilers can advance loads and, if sufficient resources exist, the overhead associated with these loads may be completely masked. Since this is a function of the compiler, the underlying program, and availability of resources (registers/cache), it is very difficult to model accurately.

- False sharing is often an important overhead in many programs. Two words used by (threads executing on) different processor may reside on the same cache line. This may cause coherence actions and communication overheads, even though none of the data might be shared. The programmer must adequately pad data structures used by various processors to minimize false sharing.

- Contention in shared accesses is often a major contributing overhead in shared address space machines. Unfortunately, contention is a function of execution schedule and consequently very difficult to model accurately (independent of the scheduling algorithm). While it is possible to get loose asymptotic estimates by counting the number of shared accesses, such a bound is often not very meaningful.

Any cost model for shared-address-space machines must account for all of these overheads. Building these into a single cost model results in a model that is too cumbersome to design programs for and too specific to individual machines to be generally applicable.

As a first-order model, it is easy to see that accessing a remote word results in a cache line being fetched into the local cache. The time associated with this includes the coherence overheads, network overheads, and memory overheads. The coherence and network overheads are functions of the underlying interconnect (since a coherence operation must be potentially propagated to remote processors and the data item must be fetched). In the absence of knowledge of what coherence operations are associated with a specific access and where the word is coming from, we associate a constant overhead to accessing a cache line of the shared data. For the sake of uniformity with the message-passing model, we refer to this cost as t_s. Because of various latency-hiding protocols, such as prefetching, implemented in modern processor architectures, we assume that a constant cost of t_s is associated with initiating access to a contiguous chunk of m words of shared data, even if m is greater than the cache line size. We further assume that accessing shared data is costlier than accessing local data (for instance, on a NUMA machine, local data is likely to reside in a local memory module, while data shared by p processors will need to be fetched from a nonlocal module for at least $p - 1$ processors). Therefore, we assign a per-word access cost of t_w to shared data.

From the above discussion, it follows that we can use the same expression $t_s + t_w m$ to account for the cost of sharing a single chunk of m words between a pair of processors in both shared-memory and message-passing paradigms (Equation 2.4) with the difference that the value of the constant t_s relative to t_w is likely to be much smaller on a shared-memory machine than on a distributed memory machine (t_w is likely to be near zero for a UMA machine). Note that the cost $t_s + t_w m$ assumes read-only access without contention.

If multiple processes access the same data, then the cost is multiplied by the number of processes, just as in the message-passing where the process that owns the data will need to send a message to each receiving process. If the access is read-write, then the cost will be incurred again for subsequent access by processors other than the one writing. Once again, there is an equivalence with the message-passing model. If a process modifies the contents of a message that it receives, then it must send it back to processes that subsequently need access to the refreshed data. While this model seems overly simplified in the context of shared-address-space machines, we note that the model provides a good estimate of the cost of sharing an array of m words between a pair of processors.

The simplified model presented above accounts primarily for remote data access but does not model a variety of other overheads. Contention for shared data access must be explicitly accounted for by counting the number of accesses to shared data between co-scheduled tasks. The model does not explicitly include many of the other overheads. Since different machines have caches of varying sizes, it is difficult to identify the point at which working set size exceeds the cache size resulting in cache thrashing, in an architecture independent manner. For this reason, effects arising from finite caches are ignored in this cost model. Maximizing spatial locality (cache line effects) is not explicitly included in the cost. False sharing is a function of the instruction schedules as well as data layouts. The cost model assumes that shared data structures are suitably padded and, therefore, does not include false sharing costs. Finally, the cost model does not account for overlapping communication and computation. Other models have been proposed to model overlapped communication. However, designing even simple algorithms for these models is cumbersome. The related issue of multiple concurrent computations (threads) on a single processor is not modeled in the expression. Instead, each processor is assumed to execute a single concurrent unit of computation.

2.6   Routing Mechanisms for Interconnection Networks

Efficient algorithms for routing a message to its destination are critical to the performance of parallel computers. A *routing mechanism* determines the path a message takes through the network to get from the source to the destination node. It takes as input a message's source and destination nodes. It may also use information about the state of the network. It returns one or more paths through the network from the source to the destination node.

Routing mechanisms can be classified as *minimal* or *non-minimal*. A minimal routing mechanism always selects one of the shortest paths between the source and the destination. In a minimal routing scheme, each link brings a message closer to its destination, but the scheme can lead to congestion in parts of the network. A non-minimal routing scheme, in contrast, may route the message along a longer path to avoid network congestion.

Routing mechanisms can also be classified on the basis of how they use information regarding the state of the network. A *deterministic routing* scheme determines a unique path for a message, based on its source and destination. It does not use any information regarding the state of the network. Deterministic schemes may result in uneven use of the communication resources in a network. In contrast, an *adaptive routing* scheme uses information regarding the current state of the network to determine the path of the message. Adaptive routing detects congestion in the network and routes messages around it.

One commonly used deterministic minimal routing technique is called *dimension-ordered routing*. Dimension-ordered routing assigns successive channels for traversal by a message based on a numbering scheme determined by the dimension of the channel. The dimension-ordered routing technique for a two-dimensional mesh is called *XY-routing* and that for a hypercube is called *E-cube routing*.

Consider a two-dimensional mesh without wraparound connections. In the XY-routing scheme, a message is sent first along the X dimension until it reaches the column of the destination node and then along the Y dimension until it reaches its destination. Let $P_{Sy,Sx}$ represent the position of the source node and $P_{Dy,Dx}$ represent that of the destination node. Any minimal routing scheme should return a path of length $|Sx - Dx| + |Sy - Dy|$. Assume that $Dx \geq Sx$ and $Dy \geq Sy$. In the XY-routing scheme, the message is passed through intermediate nodes $P_{Sy,Sx+1}, P_{Sy,Sx+2}, \ldots, P_{Sy,Dx}$ along the X dimension and then through nodes $P_{Sy+1,Dx}, P_{Sy+2,Dx}, \ldots, P_{Dy,Dx}$ along the Y dimension to reach the destination. Note that the length of this path is indeed $|Sx - Dx| + |Sy - Dy|$.

E-cube routing for hypercube-connected networks works similarly. Consider a d-dimensional hypercube of p nodes. Let P_s and P_d be the labels of the source and destination nodes. We know from Section 2.4.3 that the binary representations of these labels are d bits long. Furthermore, the minimum distance between these nodes is given by the number of ones in $P_s \oplus P_d$ (where $\oplus$ represents the bitwise exclusive-OR operation). In the E-cube algorithm, node P_s computes $P_s \oplus P_d$ and sends the message along dimension k, where k is the position of the least significant nonzero bit in $P_s \oplus P_d$. At each intermediate step, node P_i, which receives the message, computes $P_i \oplus P_d$ and forwards the message along the dimension corresponding to the least significant nonzero bit. This process continues until the message reaches its destination. Example 2.16 illustrates E-cube routing in a three-dimensional hypercube network.

Example 2.16   E-cube routing in a hypercube network
Consider the three-dimensional hypercube shown in Figure 2.28. Let $P_s = 010$ and $P_d = 111$ represent the source and destination nodes for a message. Node P_s computes $010 \oplus 111 = 101$. In the first step, P_s forwards the message along the dimension corresponding to the least significant bit to node 011. Node 011 sends the message along the dimension corresponding to the most significant bit ($011 \oplus 111 = 100$). The message reaches node 111, which is the destination of the message.   ∎

In the rest of this book we assume deterministic and minimal message routing for analyzing parallel algorithms.

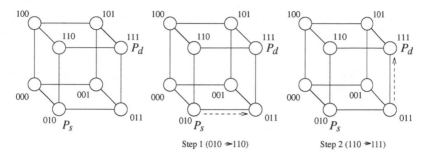

Figure 2.28 Routing a message from node P_s (010) to node P_d (111) in a three-dimensional hypercube using E-cube routing.

2.7 Impact of Process-Processor Mapping and Mapping Techniques

As we have discussed in Section 2.5.1, a programmer often does not have control over how logical processes are mapped to physical nodes in a network. For this reason, even communication patterns that are not inherently congesting may congest the network. We illustrate this with the following example:

Example 2.17   Impact of process mapping
Consider the scenario illustrated in Figure 2.29. The underlying architecture is a 16-node mesh with nodes labeled from 1 to 16 (Figure 2.29(a)) and the algorithm has been implemented as 16 processes, labeled 'a' through 'p' (Figure 2.29(b)). The algorithm has been tuned for execution on a mesh in such a way that there are no congesting communication operations. We now consider two mappings of the processes to nodes as illustrated in Figures 2.29(c) and (d). Figure 2.29(c) is an intuitive mapping and is such that a single link in the underlying architecture only carries data corresponding to a single communication channel between processes. Figure 2.29(d), on the other hand, corresponds to a situation in which processes have been mapped randomly to processing nodes. In this case, it is easy to see that each link in the machine carries up to six channels of data between processes. This may potentially result in considerably larger communication times if the required data rates on communication channels between processes is high.

∎

It is evident from the above example that while an algorithm may be fashioned out of non-congesting communication operations, the mapping of processes to nodes may in fact induce congestion on the network and cause degradation in performance.

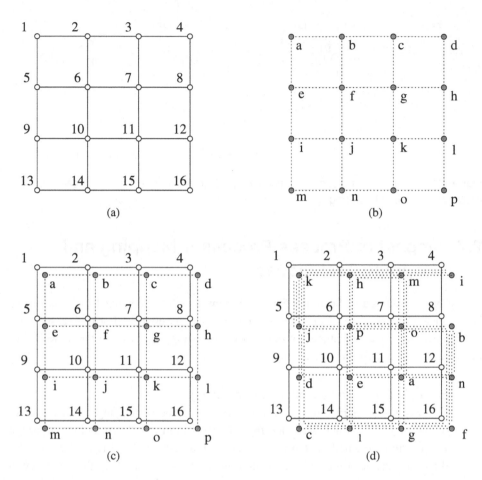

Figure 2.29 Impact of process mapping on performance: (a) underlying architecture; (b) processes and their interactions; (c) an intuitive mapping of processes to nodes; and (d) a random mapping of processes to nodes.

2.7.1 Mapping Techniques for Graphs

While the programmer generally does not have control over process-processor mapping, it is important to understand algorithms for such mappings. This is because these mappings can be used to determine degradation in the performance of an algorithm. Given two graphs, $G(V, E)$ and $G'(V', E')$, mapping graph G into graph G' maps each vertex in the set V onto a vertex (or a set of vertices) in set V' and each edge in the set E onto an edge (or a set of edges) in E'. When mapping graph $G(V, E)$ into $G'(V', E')$, three parameters are important. First, it is possible that more than one edge in E is mapped onto a single edge in E'. The maximum number of edges mapped onto any edge in E' is called the ***congestion*** of the mapping. In Example 2.17, the mapping in Figure 2.29(c) has a congestion of one and that in Figure 2.29(d) has a congestion of six. Second, an edge in E may be mapped onto multiple contiguous edges in E'. This is significant because traffic on the corresponding communication link must traverse more than one link, possibly contributing to congestion on the network. The maximum number of links in E' that any edge in E is mapped onto is called the **dilation** of the mapping. Third, the sets V and V' may contain different numbers of vertices. In this case, a node in V corresponds to more than one node in V'. The ratio of the number of nodes in the set V' to that in set V is called the **expansion** of the mapping. In the context of process-processor mapping, we want the expansion of the mapping to be identical to the ratio of virtual and physical processors.

In this section, we discuss embeddings of some commonly encountered graphs such as 2-D meshes (matrix operations illustrated in Chapter 8), hypercubes (sorting and FFT algorithms in Chapters 9 and 13, respectively), and trees (broadcast, barriers in Chapter 4). We limit the scope of the discussion to cases in which sets V and V' contain an equal number of nodes (i.e., an expansion of one).

Embedding a Linear Array into a Hypercube

A linear array (or a ring) composed of 2^d nodes (labeled 0 through $2^d - 1$) can be embedded into a d-dimensional hypercube by mapping node i of the linear array onto node $G(i, d)$ of the hypercube. The function $G(i, x)$ is defined as follows:

$$G(0, 1) = 0$$
$$G(1, 1) = 1$$
$$G(i, x + 1) = \begin{cases} G(i, x), & i < 2^x \\ 2^x + G(2^{x+1} - 1 - i, x), & i \geq 2^x \end{cases}$$

The function G is called the **binary reflected Gray code** (RGC). The entry $G(i, d)$ denotes the ith entry in the sequence of Gray codes of d bits. Gray codes of $d + 1$ bits are derived from a table of Gray codes of d bits by reflecting the table and prefixing the reflected entries with a 1 and the original entries with a 0. This process is illustrated in Figure 2.30(a).

A careful look at the Gray code table reveals that two adjoining entries ($G(i, d)$ and $G(i + 1, d)$) differ from each other at only one bit position. Since node i in the linear array is mapped to node $G(i, d)$, and node $i + 1$ is mapped to $G(i + 1, d)$, there is a direct link in the hypercube that corresponds to each direct link in the linear array. (Recall that two nodes whose labels differ at only one bit position have a direct link in a hypercube.) Therefore, the mapping specified by the function G has a dilation of one and a congestion of one. Figure 2.30(b) illustrates the embedding of an eight-node ring into a three-dimensional hypercube.

Embedding a Mesh into a Hypercube

Embedding a mesh into a hypercube is a natural extension of embedding a ring into a hypercube. We can embed a $2^r \times 2^s$ wraparound mesh into a 2^{r+s}-node hypercube by

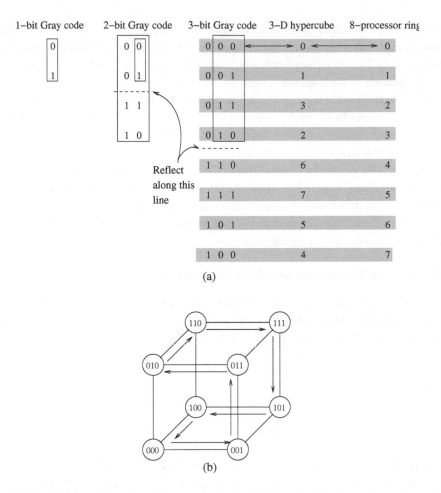

Figure 2.30   (a) A three-bit reflected Gray code ring; and (b) its embedding into a three-dimensional hypercube.

mapping node (i, j) of the mesh onto node $G(i, r - 1)\|G(j, s - 1)$ of the hypercube (where $\|$ denotes concatenation of the two Gray codes). Note that immediate neighbors in the mesh are mapped to hypercube nodes whose labels differ in exactly one bit position. Therefore, this mapping has a dilation of one and a congestion of one.

For example, consider embedding a 2×4 mesh into an eight-node hypercube. The values of r and s are 1 and 2, respectively. Node (i, j) of the mesh is mapped to node $G(i, 1)\|G(j, 2)$ of the hypercube. Therefore, node $(0, 0)$ of the mesh is mapped to node 000 of the hypercube, because $G(0, 1)$ is 0 and $G(0, 2)$ is 00; concatenating the two yields the label 000 for the hypercube node. Similarly, node $(0, 1)$ of the mesh is mapped to node 001 of the hypercube, and so on. Figure 2.31 illustrates embedding meshes into hypercubes.

This mapping of a mesh into a hypercube has certain useful properties. All nodes in

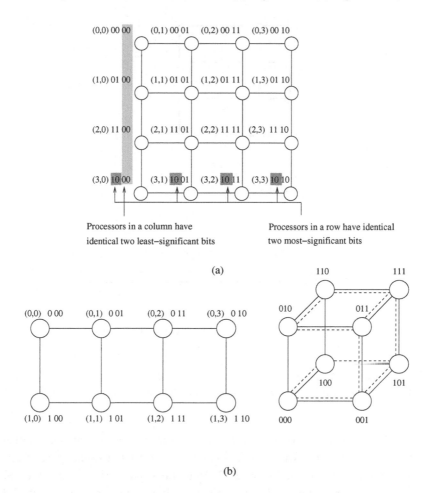

Figure 2.31   (a) A 4 × 4 mesh illustrating the mapping of mesh nodes to the nodes in a four-dimensional hypercube; and (b) a 2 × 4 mesh embedded into a three-dimensional hypercube.

the same row of the mesh are mapped to hypercube nodes whose labels have r identical most significant bits. We know from Section 2.4.3 that fixing any r bits in the node label of an $(r + s)$-dimensional hypercube yields a subcube of dimension s with 2^s nodes. Since each mesh node is mapped onto a unique node in the hypercube, and each row in the mesh has 2^s nodes, every row in the mesh is mapped to a distinct subcube in the hypercube. Similarly, each column in the mesh is mapped to a distinct subcube in the hypercube.

Embedding a Mesh into a Linear Array

We have, up until this point, considered embeddings of sparser networks into denser networks. A 2-D mesh has $2 \times p$ links. In contrast, a p-node linear array has p links. Consequently, there must be a congestion associated with this mapping.

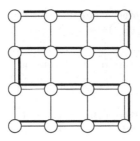

(a) Mapping a linear array into a
2D mesh (congestion 1).

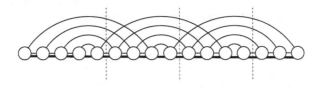

(b) Inverting the mapping – mapping a 2D mesh into a
linear array (congestion 5)

Figure 2.32   (a) Embedding a 16 node linear array into a 2-D mesh; and (b) the inverse of the mapping. Solid lines correspond to links in the linear array and normal lines to links in the mesh.

Consider first the mapping of a linear array into a mesh. We assume that neither the mesh nor the linear array has wraparound connections. An intuitive mapping of a linear array into a mesh is illustrated in Figure 2.32. Here, the solid lines correspond to links in the linear array and normal lines to links in the mesh. It is easy to see from Figure 2.32(a) that a congestion-one, dilation-one mapping of a linear array to a mesh is possible.

Consider now the inverse of this mapping, i.e., we are given a mesh and we map vertices of the mesh to those in a linear array using the inverse of the same mapping function. This mapping is illustrated in Figure 2.32(b). As before, the solid lines correspond to edges in the linear array and normal lines to edges in the mesh. As is evident from the figure, the congestion of the mapping in this case is five – i.e., no solid line carries more than five normal lines. In general, it is easy to show that the congestion of this (inverse) mapping is $\sqrt{p} + 1$ for a general p-node mapping (one for each of the $\sqrt{p}$ edges to the next row, and one additional edge).

While this is a simple mapping, the question at this point is whether we can do better. To answer this question, we use the bisection width of the two networks. We know that the bisection width of a 2-D mesh without wraparound links is $\sqrt{p}$, and that of a linear array is 1. Assume that the best mapping of a 2-D mesh into a linear array has a congestion of r. This implies that if we take the linear array and cut it in half (at the middle), we will cut only one linear array link, or no more than r mesh links. We claim that r must be at least equal to the bisection width of the mesh. This follows from the fact that an equi-partition of the linear array into two also partitions the mesh into two. Therefore, at least $\sqrt{p}$ mesh links must cross the partition, by definition of bisection width. Consequently, the one linear array link connecting the two halves must carry at least $\sqrt{p}$ mesh links. Therefore, the congestion of any mapping is lower bounded by $\sqrt{p}$. This is almost identical to the simple (inverse) mapping we have illustrated in Figure 2.32(b).

The lower bound established above has a more general applicability when mapping denser networks to sparser ones. One may reasonably believe that the lower bound on congestion of a mapping of network S with x links into network Q with y links is x/y. In the case of the mapping from a mesh to a linear array, this would be $2p/p$, or 2. However, this lower bound is overly conservative. A tighter lower bound is in fact possible by examining the bisection width of the two networks. We illustrate this further in the next section.

Embedding a Hypercube into a 2-D Mesh

Consider the embedding of a p-node hypercube into a p-node 2-D mesh. For the sake of convenience, we assume that p is an even power of two. In this scenario, it is possible to visualize the hypercube as $\sqrt{p}$ subcubes, each with $\sqrt{p}$ nodes. We do this as follows: let $d = \log p$ be the dimension of the hypercube. From our assumption, we know that d is even. We take the $d/2$ least significant bits and use them to define individual subcubes of $\sqrt{p}$ nodes. For example, in the case of a 4D hypercube, we use the lower two bits to define the subcubes as (0000, 0001, 0011, 0010), (0100, 0101, 0111, 0110), (1100, 1101, 1111, 1110), and (1000, 1001, 1011, 1010). Note at this point that if we fix the $d/2$ least significant bits across all of these subcubes, we will have another subcube as defined by the $d/2$ most significant bits. For example, if we fix the lower two bits across the subcubes to 10, we get the nodes (0010, 0110, 1110, 1010). The reader can verify that this corresponds to a 2-D subcube.

The mapping from a hypercube to a mesh can now be defined as follows: each $\sqrt{p}$ node subcube is mapped to a $\sqrt{p}$ node row of the mesh. We do this by simply inverting the linear-array to hypercube mapping. The bisection width of the $\sqrt{p}$ node hypercube is $\sqrt{p}/2$. The corresponding bisection width of a $\sqrt{p}$ node row is 1. Therefore the congestion of this subcube-to-row mapping is $\sqrt{p}/2$ (at the edge that connects the two halves of the row). This is illustrated for the cases of $p = 16$ and $p = 32$ in Figure 2.33(a) and (b). In this fashion, we can map each subcube to a different row in the mesh. Note that while we have computed the congestion resulting from the subcube-to-row mapping, we have not addressed the congestion resulting from the column mapping. We map the hypercube nodes into the mesh in such a way that nodes with identical $d/2$ least significant bits in the hypercube are mapped to the same column. This results in a subcube-to-column mapping, where each subcube/column has $\sqrt{p}$ nodes. Using the same argument as in the case of subcube-to-row mapping, this results in a congestion of $\sqrt{p}/2$. Since the congestion from the row and column mappings affects disjoint sets of edges, the total congestion of this mapping is $\sqrt{p}/2$.

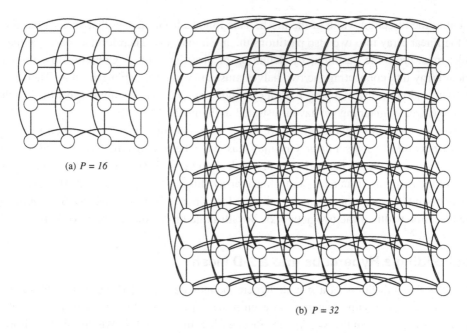

(a) *P = 16*

(b) *P = 32*

Figure 2.33   Embedding a hypercube into a 2-D mesh.

To establish a lower bound on the congestion, we follow the same argument as in Section 2.7.1. Since the bisection width of a hypercube is $p/2$ and that of a mesh is $\sqrt{p}$, the lower bound on congestion is the ratio of these, i.e., $\sqrt{p}/2$. We notice that our mapping yields this lower bound on congestion.

Process-Processor Mapping and Design of Interconnection Networks

Our analysis in previous sections reveals that it is possible to map denser networks into sparser networks with associated congestion overheads. This implies that a sparser network whose link bandwidth is increased to compensate for the congestion can be expected to perform as well as the denser network (modulo dilation effects). For example, a mesh whose links are faster by a factor of $\sqrt{p}/2$ will yield comparable performance to a hypercube. We call such a mesh a fat-mesh. A fat-mesh has the same bisection-bandwidth as a hypercube; however it has a higher diameter. As we have seen in Section 2.5.1, by using appropriate message routing techniques, the effect of node distance can be minimized. It is important to note that higher dimensional networks involve more complicated layouts, wire crossings, and variable wire-lengths. For these reasons, fattened lower dimensional networks provide attractive alternate approaches to designing interconnects. We now do a more formal examination of the cost-performance tradeoffs of parallel architectures.

2.7.2 Cost-Performance Tradeoffs

We now examine how various cost metrics can be used to investigate cost-performance tradeoffs in interconnection networks. We illustrate this by analyzing the performance of a mesh and a hypercube network with identical costs.

If the cost of a network is proportional to the number of wires, then a square p-node wraparound mesh with $(\log p)/4$ wires per channel costs as much as a p-node hypercube with one wire per channel. Let us compare the average communication times of these two networks. The average distance l_{av} between any two nodes in a two-dimensional wraparound mesh is $\sqrt{p}/2$ and that in a hypercube is $(\log p)/2$. The time for sending a message of size m between nodes that are l_{av} hops apart is given by $t_s + t_h l_{av} + t_w m$ in networks that use cut-through routing. Since the channel width of the mesh is scaled up by a factor of $(\log p)/4$, the per-word transfer time is reduced by the same factor. Hence, if the per-word transfer time on the hypercube is t_w, then the same time on a mesh with fattened channels is given by $4t_w/(\log p)$. Hence, the average communication latency for a hypercube is given by $t_s + t_h(\log p)/2 + t_w m$ and that for a wraparound mesh of the same cost is $t_s + t_h\sqrt{p}/2 + 4t_w m/(\log p)$.

Let us now investigate the behavior of these expressions. For a fixed number of nodes, as the message size is increased, the communication term due to t_w dominates. Comparing t_w for the two networks, we see that the time for a wraparound mesh $(4t_w m/(\log p))$ is less than the time for a hypercube $(t_w m)$ if p is greater than 16 and the message size m is sufficiently large. Under these circumstances, point-to-point communication of large messages between random pairs of nodes takes less time on a wraparound mesh with cut-through routing than on a hypercube of the same cost. Furthermore, for algorithms in which communication is suited to a mesh, the extra bandwidth of each channel results in better performance. Note that, with store-and-forward routing, the mesh is no longer more cost-efficient than a hypercube. Similar cost-performance tradeoffs can be analyzed for the general case of k-ary d-cubes (Problems 2.25–2.29).

The communication times above are computed under light load conditions in the network. As the number of messages increases, there is contention on the network. Contention affects the mesh network more adversely than the hypercube network. Therefore, if the network is heavily loaded, the hypercube will outperform the mesh.

If the cost of a network is proportional to its bisection width, then a p-node wraparound mesh with $\sqrt{p}/4$ wires per channel has a cost equal to a p-node hypercube with one wire per channel. Let us perform an analysis similar to the one above to investigate cost-performance tradeoffs using this cost metric. Since the mesh channels are wider by a factor of $\sqrt{p}/4$, the per-word transfer time will be lower by an identical factor. Therefore, the communication times for the hypercube and the mesh networks of the same cost are given by $t_s + t_h(\log p)/2 + t_w m$ and $t_s + t_h\sqrt{p}/2 + 4t_w m/\sqrt{p}$, respectively. Once again, as the message size m becomes large for a given number of nodes, the t_w term dominates. Comparing this term for the two networks, we see that for $p > 16$ and sufficiently large message sizes, a mesh outperforms a hypercube of the same cost. Therefore, for large enough messages, a mesh is always better than a hypercube of the same cost, provided the network is lightly loaded. Even when the network is heavily loaded, the performance of a mesh is similar to that of a hypercube of the same cost.

2.8 Bibliographic Remarks

Several textbooks discuss various aspects of high-performance architectures [PH90, PH96, Sto93]. Parallel architectures and interconnection networks have been well described [CSG98, LW95, HX98, Fly95, AG94, DeC89, HB84, Lil92, Sie85, Sto93]. Historically, the classification of parallel computers as SISD, SIMD, and MIMD was introduced by Flynn [Fly72]. He also proposed the MISD (multiple instruction stream, single data stream) model. MISD is less natural than the other classes, although it can be viewed as a model for pipelining. Darema [DRGNP] introduced the Single Program Multiple Data (SPMD) paradigm. Ni [Ni91] provides a layered classification of parallel computers based on hardware architecture, address space, communication model, language, programming environment, and applications.

Interconnection networks have been an area of active interest for decades. Feng [Fen81] provides a tutorial on static and dynamic interconnection networks. The perfect shuffle interconnection pattern was introduced by Stone [Sto71]. Omega networks were introduced by Lawrie [Law75]. Other multistage networks have also been proposed. These include the Flip network [Bat76] and the Baseline network [WF80]. Mesh of trees and pyramidal mesh are discussed by Leighton [Lei92]. Leighton [Lei92] also provides a detailed discussion of many related networks.

The C.mmp was an early research prototype MIMD shared-address-space parallel computer based on the Crossbar switch [WB72]. The Sun Ultra HPC Server and Fujitsu VPP 500 are examples of crossbar-based parallel computers or their variants. Several parallel computers were based on multistage interconnection networks including the BBN Butterfly [BBN89], the NYU Ultracomputer [GGK+83], and the IBM RP-3 [PBG+85]. The SGI Origin 2000, Stanford Dash [LLG+92] and the KSR-1 [Ken90] are NUMA shared-address-space computers.

The Cosmic Cube [Sei85] was among the first message-passing parallel computers based on a hypercube-connected network. These were followed by the nCUBE 2 [nCU90] and the Intel iPSC-1, iPSC-2, and iPSC/860. More recently, the SGI Origin 2000 uses a network similar to a hypercube. Saad and Shultz [SS88, SS89a] derive interesting properties of the hypercube-connected network and a variety of other static networks [SS89b]. Many parallel computers, such as the Cray T3E, are based on the mesh network. The Intel Paragon XP/S [Sup91] and the Mosaic C [Sei92] are earlier examples of two-dimensional mesh-based computers. The MIT J-Machine [D+92] was based on a three-dimensional mesh network. The performance of mesh-connected computers can be improved by augmenting the mesh network with broadcast buses [KR87a]. The reconfigurable mesh architecture (Figure 2.35 in Problem 2.16) was introduced by Miller et al. [MKRS88]. Other examples of reconfigurable meshes include the TRAC and PCHIP.

The DADO parallel computer was based on a tree network [SM86]. It used a complete binary tree of depth 10. Leiserson [Lei85b] introduced the fat-tree interconnection network and proved several interesting characteristics of it. He showed that for a given volume of hardware, no network has much better performance than a fat tree. The Thinking Machines CM-5 [Thi91] parallel computer was based on a fat tree interconnection network.

The Illiac IV [Bar68] was among the first SIMD parallel computers. Other SIMD computers include the Goodyear MPP [Bat80], the DAP 610, and the CM-2 [Thi90], MasPar MP-1, and MasPar MP-2 [Nic90]. The CM-5 and DADO incorporate both SIMD and MIMD features. Both are MIMD computers but have extra hardware for fast synchronization, which enables them to operate in SIMD mode. The CM-5 had a control network to augment the data network. The control network provides such functions as broadcast, reduction, combining, and other global operations.

Leighton [Lei92] and Ranka and Sahni [RS90b] discuss embedding one interconnection network into another. Gray codes, used in embedding linear array and mesh topologies, are discussed by Reingold [RND77]. Ranka and Sahni [RS90b] discuss the concepts of congestion, dilation, and expansion.

A comprehensive survey of cut-through routing techniques is provided by Ni and McKinley [NM93]. The wormhole routing technique was proposed by Dally and Seitz [DS86]. A related technique called *virtual cut-through*, in which communication buffers are provided at intermediate nodes, was described by Kermani and Kleinrock [KK79]. Dally and Seitz [DS87] discuss deadlock-free wormhole routing based on channel dependence graphs. Deterministic routing schemes based on dimension ordering are often used to avoid deadlocks. Cut-through routing has been used in several parallel computers. The E-cube routing scheme for hypercubes was proposed by [SB77].

Dally [Dal90b] discusses cost-performance tradeoffs of networks for message-passing computers. Using the bisection bandwidth of a network as a measure of the cost of the network, he shows that low-dimensional networks (such as two-dimensional meshes) are more cost-effective than high-dimensional networks (such as hypercubes) [Dal87, Dal90b, Dal90a]. Kreeger and Vempaty [KV92] derive the bandwidth equalization factor for a mesh with respect to a hypercube-connected computer for all-to-all personalized communication (Section 4.5). Gupta and Kumar [GK93b] analyze the cost-performance tradeoffs of FFT computations on mesh and hypercube networks.

The properties of PRAMs have been studied extensively [FW78, KR88, LY86, Sni82, Sni85]. Books by Akl [Akl89], Gibbons [GR90], and Jaja [Jaj92] address PRAM algorithms. Our discussion of PRAM is based upon the book by Jaja [Jaj92]. A number of processor networks have been proposed to simulate PRAM models [AHMP87, HP89, LPP88, LPP89, MV84, Upf84, UW84]. Mehlhorn and Vishkin [MV84] propose the *module parallel computer* (MPC) to simulate PRAM models. The MPC is a message-passing parallel computer composed of p processors, each with a fixed amount of memory and connected by a completely-connected network. The MPC is capable of probabilistically simulating T steps of a PRAM in $T \log p$ steps if the total memory is increased by a factor of log p. The main drawback of the MPC model is that a completely-connected network is difficult to construct for a large number of processors. Alt *et al.* [AHMP87] propose another model called the ***bounded-degree network*** (BDN). In this network, each processor is connected to a fixed number of other processors. Karlin and Upfal [KU86] describe an $O(T \log p)$ time probabilistic simulation of a PRAM on a BDN. Hornick and Preparata [HP89] propose a bipartite network that connects sets of processors and memory pools. They investigate both the message-passing MPC and BDN based on a mesh of trees.

Many modifications of the PRAM model have been proposed that attempt to bring it closer to practical parallel computers. Aggarwal, Chandra, and Snir [ACS89b] propose the LPRAM (local-memory PRAM) model and the BPRAM (block PRAM) model [ACS89b]. They also introduce a hierarchical memory model of computation [ACS89a]. In this model, memory units at different levels are accessed in different times. Parallel algorithms for this model induce locality by bringing data into faster memory units before using them and returning them to the slower memory units. Other PRAM models such as phase PRAM [Gib89], XPRAM [Val90b], and the delay model [PY88] have also been proposed. Many researchers have investigated abstract universal models for parallel computers [CKP+93a, Sny86, Val90a]. Models such as BSP [Val90a], Postal model [BNK92], LogP [CKP+93b], A^3 [GKRS96], C^3 [HK96], CGM [DFRC96], and QSM [Ram97] have been proposed with similar objectives.

Problems

2.1 Design an experiment (i.e., design and write programs and take measurements) to determine the memory bandwidth of your computer and to estimate the caches at various levels of the hierarchy. Use this experiment to estimate the bandwidth and L1 cache of your computer. Justify your answer. (Hint: To test bandwidth, you do not want reuse. To test cache size, you want reuse to see the effect of the cache and to increase this size until the reuse decreases sharply.)

2.2 Consider a memory system with a level 1 cache of 32 KB and DRAM of 512 MB with the processor operating at 1 GHz. The latency to L1 cache is one cycle and the latency to DRAM is 100 cycles. In each memory cycle, the processor fetches four words (cache line size is four words). What is the peak achievable performance of a dot product of two vectors? Note: Where necessary, assume an optimal cache placement policy.

```
1           /* dot product loop */
2           for (i = 0; i < dim; i++)
3                   dot_prod += a[i] * b[i];
```

2.3 Now consider the problem of multiplying a dense matrix with a vector using a two-loop dot-product formulation. The matrix is of dimension $4K \times 4K$. (Each row of the matrix takes 16 KB of storage.) What is the peak achievable performance of this technique using a two-loop dot-product based matrix-vector product?

```
1              /* matrix-vector product loop */
2              for (i = 0; i < dim; i++)
3                    for (j = 0; i < dim; j++)
4                          c[i] += a[i][j] * b[j];
```

2.4 Extending this further, consider the problem of multiplying two dense matrices of dimension $4K \times 4K$. What is the peak achievable performance using a three-loop dot-product based formulation? (Assume that matrices are laid out in a row-major fashion.)

```
1              /* matrix-matrix product loop */
2              for (i = 0; i < dim; i++)
3                    for (j = 0; i < dim; j++)
4                          for (k = 0; k < dim; k++)
5                                c[i][j] += a[i][k] * b[k][j];
```

2.5 Restructure the matrix multiplication algorithm to achieve better cache performance. The most obvious cause of the poor performance of matrix multiplication was the absence of spatial locality. In some cases, we were wasting three of the four words fetched from memory. To fix this problem, we compute the elements of the result matrix four at a time. Using this approach, we can increase our FLOP count with a simple restructuring of the program. However, it is possible to achieve much higher performance from this problem. This is possible by viewing the matrix multiplication problem as a cube in which each internal grid point corresponds to a multiply-add operation. Matrix multiplication algorithms traverse this cube in different ways, which induce different partitions of the cube. The data required for computing a partition grows as the surface area of the input faces of the partition and the computation as the volume of the partition. For the algorithms discussed above, we were slicing thin partitions of the cube for which the area and volume were comparable (thus achieving poor cache performance). To remedy this, we restructure the computation by partitioning the cube into subcubes of size $k \times k \times k$. The data associated with this is $3 \times k^2$ (k^2 data for each of the three matrices) and the computation is k^3. To maximize performance, we would like $3 \times k^2$ to be equal to $8K$ since that is the amount of cache available (assuming the same machine parameters as in Problem 2.2). This corresponds to $k = 51$. The computation associated with a cube of this dimension is 132651 multiply-add operations or 265302 FLOPs. To perform this computation, we needed to fetch two submatrices of size 51×51. This corresponds to 5202 words or 1301 cache lines. Accessing these cache lines takes 130100 ns. Since 265302 FLOPs are performed in 130100 ns, the peak computation rate of this formulation is 2.04 GFLOPS. Code this example and plot the performance as a function of k. (Code on any conventional microprocessor. Make sure you note the clock speed, the microprocessor and the cache available at each level.)

2.6 Consider an SMP with a distributed shared-address-space. Consider a simple cost model in which it takes 10 ns to access local cache, 100 ns to access local memory, and 400 ns to access remote memory. A parallel program is running on this machine. The program is perfectly load balanced with 80% of all accesses going to local cache, 10% to local memory, and 10% to remote memory. What is the effective memory access time for this computation? If the computation is memory bound, what is the peak computation rate?

Now consider the same computation running on one processor. Here, the processor hits the cache 70% of the time and local memory 30% of the time. What is the effective peak computation rate for one processor? What is the fractional computation rate of a processor in a parallel configuration as compared to the serial configuration?

Hint: Notice that the cache hit for multiple processors is higher than that for one processor. This is typically because the aggregate cache available on multiprocessors is larger than on single processor systems.

2.7 What are the major differences between message-passing and shared-address-space computers? Also outline the advantages and disadvantages of the two.

2.8 Why is it difficult to construct a true shared-memory computer? What is the minimum number of switches for connecting p processors to a shared memory with b words (where each word can be accessed independently)?

2.9 Of the four PRAM models (EREW, CREW, ERCW, and CRCW), which model is the most powerful? Why?

2.10 **[Lei92]** The *Butterfly network* is an interconnection network composed of $\log p$ levels (as the omega network). In a Butterfly network, each switching node i at a level l is connected to the identically numbered element at level $l + 1$ and to a switching node whose number differs from itself only at the lth most significant bit. Therefore, switching node S_i is connected to element S_j at level l if $j = i$ or $j = i \oplus (2^{\log p - l})$.

Figure 2.34 illustrates a Butterfly network with eight processing nodes. Show the equivalence of a Butterfly network and an omega network.

Hint: Rearrange the switches of an omega network so that it looks like a Butterfly network.

2.11 Consider the omega network described in Section 2.4.3. As shown there, this network is a blocking network (that is, a processor that uses the network to access a memory location might prevent another processor from accessing another memory location). Consider an omega network that connects p processors. Define a function f that maps $P = [0, 1, \ldots, p - 1]$ onto a permutation P' of P (that is, $P'[i] = f(P[i])$ and $P'[i] \in P$ for all $0 \le i < p$). Think of this function as mapping communication requests by the processors so that processor $P[i]$ requests communication with processor $P'[i]$.

1. How many distinct permutation functions exist?

2. How many of these functions result in non-blocking communication?

3. What is the probability that an arbitrary function will result in non-blocking

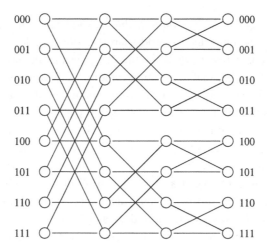

000
001
010
011
100
101
110
111

000
001
010
011
100
101
110
111

Figure 2.34   A Butterfly network with eight processing nodes.

communication?

2.12   A cycle in a graph is defined as a path originating and terminating at the same node. The length of a cycle is the number of edges in the cycle. Show that there are no odd-length cycles in a d-dimensional hypercube.

2.13   The labels in a d-dimensional hypercube use d bits. Fixing any k of these bits, show that the nodes whose labels differ in the remaining $d - k$ bit positions form a $(d - k)$-dimensional subcube composed of $2^{(d-k)}$ nodes.

2.14   Let A and B be two nodes in a d-dimensional hypercube. Define $H(A, B)$ to be the Hamming distance between A and B, and $P(A, B)$ to be the number of distinct paths connecting A and B. These paths are called *parallel paths* and have no common nodes other than A and B. Prove the following:

1. The minimum distance in terms of communication links between A and B is given by $H(A, B)$.

2. The total number of parallel paths between any two nodes is $P(A, B) = d$.

3. The number of parallel paths between A and B of length $H(A, B)$ is $P_{length=H(A,B)}(A, B) = H(A, B)$.

4. The length of the remaining $d - H(A, B)$ parallel paths is $H(A, B) + 2$.

2.15   In the informal derivation of the bisection width of a hypercube, we used the construction of a hypercube to show that a d-dimensional hypercube is formed from two $(d-1)$-dimensional hypercubes. We argued that because corresponding nodes in each of these subcubes have a direct communication link, there are $2^d - 1$ links across the partition. However, it is possible to partition a hypercube into two parts such that neither of the partitions is a hypercube. Show that any such partitions will have more than $2^d - 1$ direct links between them.

2.16   **[MKRS88]** A $\sqrt{p} \times \sqrt{p}$ *reconfigurable mesh* consists of a $\sqrt{p} \times \sqrt{p}$ array of processing nodes connected to a grid-shaped reconfigurable broadcast bus. A 4×4 reconfigurable mesh is shown in Figure 2.35. Each node has locally-controllable bus switches. The internal connections among the four ports, north (N), east (E), west (W), and south (S), of a node can be configured during the execution of an algorithm. Note that there are 15 connection patterns. For example, {SW, EN} represents the configuration in which port S is connected to port W and port N is connected to port E. Each bit of the bus carries one of *1-signal* or *0-signal* at any time. The switches allow the broadcast bus to be divided into subbuses, providing smaller reconfigurable meshes. For a given set of switch settings, a *subbus* is a maximally-connected subset of the nodes. Other than the buses and the switches, the reconfigurable mesh is similar to the standard two-dimensional mesh. Assume that only one node is allowed to broadcast on a *subbus* shared by multiple nodes at any time.

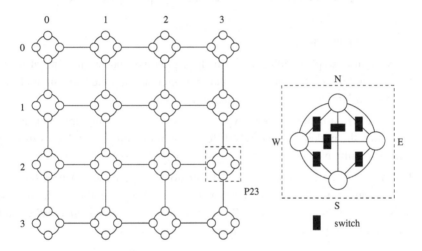

Figure 2.35   Switch connection patterns in a reconfigurable mesh.

Determine the bisection width, the diameter, and the number of switching nodes and communication links for a reconfigurable mesh of $\sqrt{p} \times \sqrt{p}$ processing nodes. What are the advantages and disadvantages of a reconfigurable mesh as compared to a wraparound mesh?

2.17   **[Lei92]** A *mesh of trees* is a network that imposes a tree interconnection on a grid of processing nodes. A $\sqrt{p} \times \sqrt{p}$ mesh of trees is constructed as follows. Starting with a $\sqrt{p} \times \sqrt{p}$ grid, a complete binary tree is imposed on each row of the grid. Then a complete binary tree is imposed on each column of the grid. Figure 2.36 illustrates the construction of a 4×4 mesh of trees. Assume that the nodes at intermediate levels are switching nodes. Determine the bisection width, diameter, and total number of switching nodes in a $\sqrt{p} \times \sqrt{p}$ mesh.

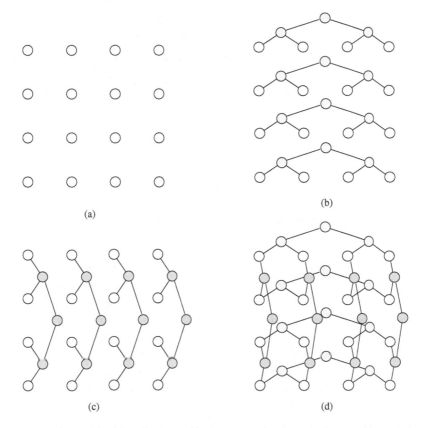

Figure 2.36 The construction of a 4 × 4 mesh of trees: (a) a 4 × 4 grid, (b) complete binary trees imposed over individual rows, (c) complete binary trees imposed over each column, and (d) the complete 4 × 4 mesh of trees.

2.18 **[Lei92]** Extend the two-dimensional mesh of trees (Problem 2.17) to d dimensions to construct a $p^{1/d} \times p^{1/d} \times \cdots \times p^{1/d}$ mesh of trees. We can do this by fixing grid positions in all dimensions to different values and imposing a complete binary tree on the one dimension that is being varied.

Derive the total number of switching nodes in a $p^{1/d} \times p^{1/d} \times \cdots \times p^{1/d}$ mesh of trees. Calculate the diameter, bisection width, and wiring cost in terms of the total number of wires. What are the advantages and disadvantages of a mesh of trees as compared to a wraparound mesh?

2.19 **[Lei92]** A network related to the mesh of trees is the d-dimensional **pyramidal mesh**. A d-dimensional pyramidal mesh imposes a pyramid on the underlying grid of processing nodes (as opposed to a complete tree in the mesh of trees). The generalization is as follows. In the mesh of trees, all dimensions except one are fixed and a tree is imposed on the remaining dimension. In a pyramid, all but two dimensions are fixed and a pyramid is imposed on the mesh formed by these two

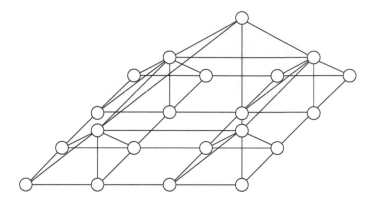

Figure 2.37 A 4 × 4 pyramidal mesh.

dimensions. In a tree, each node i at level k is connected to node $i/2$ at level $k - 1$. Similarly, in a pyramid, a node (i, j) at level k is connected to a node $(i/2, j/2)$ at level $k - 1$. Furthermore, the nodes at each level are connected in a mesh. A two-dimensional pyramidal mesh is illustrated in Figure 2.37.

For a $\sqrt{p} \times \sqrt{p}$ pyramidal mesh, assume that the intermediate nodes are switching nodes, and derive the diameter, bisection width, arc connectivity, and cost in terms of the number of communication links and switching nodes. What are the advantages and disadvantages of a pyramidal mesh as compared to a mesh of trees?

2.20 **[Lei92]** One of the drawbacks of a hypercube-connected network is that different wires in the network are of different lengths. This implies that data takes different times to traverse different communication links. It appears that two-dimensional mesh networks with wraparound connections suffer from this drawback too. However, it is possible to fabricate a two-dimensional wraparound mesh using wires of fixed length. Illustrate this layout by drawing such a 4 × 4 wraparound mesh.

2.21 Show how to embed a p-node three-dimensional mesh into a p-node hypercube. What are the allowable values of p for your embedding?

2.22 Show how to embed a p-node mesh of trees into a p-node hypercube.

2.23 Consider a complete binary tree of $2^d - 1$ nodes in which each node is a processing node. What is the minimum-dilation mapping of such a tree onto a d-dimensional hypercube?

2.24 The concept of a *minimum congestion mapping* is very useful. Consider two parallel computers with different interconnection networks such that a congestion-r mapping of the first into the second exists. Ignoring the dilation of the mapping, if each communication link in the second computer is more than r times faster than the first computer, the second computer is strictly superior to the first.

Now consider mapping a d-dimensional hypercube onto a 2^d-node mesh. Ignoring the dilation of the mapping, what is the minimum-congestion mapping of the hypercube onto the mesh? Use this result to determine whether a 1024-node mesh with communication links operating at 25 million bytes per second is strictly better than a 1024-node hypercube (whose nodes are identical to those used in the mesh) with communication links operating at two million bytes per second.

2.25 Derive the diameter, number of links, and bisection width of a k-ary d-cube with p nodes. Define l_{av} to be the average distance between any two nodes in the network. Derive l_{av} for a k-ary d-cube.

2.26 Consider the routing of messages in a parallel computer that uses store-and-forward routing. In such a network, the cost of sending a single message of size m from P_{source} to $P_{destination}$ via a path of length d is $t_s + t_w \times d \times m$. An alternate way of sending a message of size m is as follows. The user breaks the message into k parts each of size m/k, and then sends these k distinct messages one by one from P_{source} to $P_{destination}$. For this new method, derive the expression for time to transfer a message of size m to a node d hops away under the following two cases:

1. Assume that another message can be sent from P_{source} as soon as the previous message has reached the next node in the path.

2. Assume that another message can be sent from P_{source} only after the previous message has reached $P_{destination}$.

For each case, comment on the value of this expression as the value of k varies between 1 and m. Also, what is the optimal value of k if t_s is very large, or if $t_s = 0$?

2.27 Consider a hypercube network of p nodes. Assume that the channel width of each communication link is one. The channel width of the links in a k-ary d-cube (for $d < \log p$) can be increased by equating the cost of this network with that of a hypercube. Two distinct measures can be used to evaluate the cost of a network.

1. The cost can be expressed in terms of the total number of wires in the network (the total number of wires is a product of the number of communication links and the channel width).

2. The bisection bandwidth can be used as a measure of cost.

Using each of these cost metrics and equating the cost of a k-ary d-cube with a hypercube, what is the channel width of a k-ary d-cube with an identical number of nodes, channel rate, and cost?

2.28 The results from Problems 2.25 and 2.27 can be used in a cost-performance analysis of static interconnection networks. Consider a k-ary d-cube network of p nodes with cut-through routing. Assume a hypercube-connected network of p nodes with channel width one. The channel width of other networks in the family is scaled up so that their cost is identical to that of the hypercube. Let s and s' be the scaling factors for the channel width derived by equating the costs specified by the two cost metrics in Problem 2.27.

For each of the two scaling factors s and s', express the average communication time between any two nodes as a function of the dimensionality (d) of a k-ary d-cube and the number of nodes. Plot the communication time as a function of the dimensionality for $p = 256, 512$, and 1024, message size $m = 512$ bytes, $t_s = 50.0\mu s$, and $t_h = t_w = 0.5\mu s$ (for the hypercube). For these values of p and m, what is the dimensionality of the network that yields the best performance for a given cost?

2.29 Repeat Problem 2.28 for a k-ary d-cube with store-and-forward routing.

CHAPTER 3

Principles of Parallel Algorithm Design

Algorithm development is a critical component of problem solving using computers. A sequential algorithm is essentially a recipe or a sequence of basic steps for solving a given problem using a serial computer. Similarly, a parallel algorithm is a recipe that tells us how to solve a given problem using multiple processors. However, specifying a parallel algorithm involves more than just specifying the steps. At the very least, a parallel algorithm has the added dimension of concurrency and the algorithm designer must specify sets of steps that can be executed simultaneously. This is essential for obtaining any performance benefit from the use of a parallel computer. In practice, specifying a nontrivial parallel algorithm may include some or all of the following:

- Identifying portions of the work that can be performed concurrently.

- Mapping the concurrent pieces of work onto multiple processes running in parallel.

- Distributing the input, output, and intermediate data associated with the program.

- Managing accesses to data shared by multiple processors.

- Synchronizing the processors at various stages of the parallel program execution.

Typically, there are several choices for each of the above steps, but usually, relatively few combinations of choices lead to a parallel algorithm that yields performance commensurate with the computational and storage resources employed to solve the problem. Often, different choices yield the best performance on different parallel architectures or under different parallel programming paradigms.

In this chapter, we methodically discuss the process of designing and implementing parallel algorithms. We shall assume that the onus of providing a complete description of a parallel algorithm or program lies on the programmer or the algorithm designer. Tools and compilers for automatic parallelization at the current state of the art seem to work well only for highly structured programs or portions of programs. Therefore, we do not consider these in this chapter or elsewhere in this book.

3.1 Preliminaries

Dividing a computation into smaller computations and assigning them to different processors for parallel execution are the two key steps in the design of parallel algorithms. In this section, we present some basic terminology and introduce these two key steps in parallel algorithm design using matrix-vector multiplication and database query processing as examples.

3.1.1 Decomposition, Tasks, and Dependency Graphs

The process of dividing a computation into smaller parts, some or all of which may potentially be executed in parallel, is called *decomposition*. *Tasks* are programmer-defined units of computation into which the main computation is subdivided by means of decomposition. Simultaneous execution of multiple tasks is the key to reducing the time required to solve the entire problem. Tasks can be of arbitrary size, but once defined, they are regarded as indivisible units of computation. The tasks into which a problem is decomposed may not all be of the same size.

> **Example 3.1** Dense matrix-vector multiplication
> Consider the multiplication of a dense $n \times n$ matrix A with a vector b to yield another vector y. The ith element $y[i]$ of the product vector is the dot-product of the ith row of A with the input vector b; i.e., $y[i] = \sum_{j=1}^{n} A[i, j].b[j]$. As shown later in Figure 3.1, the computation of each $y[i]$ can be regarded as a task. Alternatively, as shown later in Figure 3.4, the computation could be decomposed into fewer, say four, tasks where each task computes roughly $n/4$ of the entries of the vector y. ∎

Note that all tasks in Figure 3.1 are independent and can be performed all together or in any sequence. However, in general, some tasks may use data produced by other tasks and thus may need to wait for these tasks to finish execution. An abstraction used to express such dependencies among tasks and their relative order of execution is known as a *task-dependency graph*. A task-dependency graph is a directed acyclic graph in which the nodes represent tasks and the directed edges indicate the dependencies amongst them. The task corresponding to a node can be executed when all tasks connected to this node by incoming edges have completed. Note that task-dependency graphs can be disconnected and the edge-set of a task-dependency graph can be empty. This is the case for matrix-vector multiplication, where each task computes a subset of the entries of the product

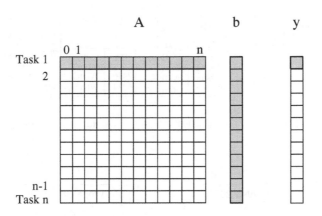

Figure 3.1 Decomposition of dense matrix-vector multiplication into n tasks, where n is the number of rows in the matrix. The portions of the matrix and the input and output vectors accessed by Task 1 are highlighted.

vector. To see a more interesting task-dependency graph, consider the following database query processing example.

Example 3.2 Database query processing

Table 3.1 shows a relational database of vehicles. Each row of the table is a record that contains data corresponding to a particular vehicle, such as its ID, model, year, color, etc. in various fields. Consider the computations performed in processing the following query:

MODEL="Civic" AND YEAR="2001" AND (COLOR="Green" OR COLOR="White")

This query looks for all 2001 Civics whose color is either Green or White. On a relational database, this query is processed by creating a number of intermediate

ID#	Model	Year	Color	Dealer	Price
4523	Civic	2002	Blue	MN	$18,000
3476	Corolla	1999	White	IL	$15,000
7623	Camry	2001	Green	NY	$21,000
9834	Prius	2001	Green	CA	$18,000
6734	Civic	2001	White	OR	$17,000
5342	Altima	2001	Green	FL	$19,000
3845	Maxima	2001	Blue	NY	$22,000
8354	Accord	2000	Green	VT	$18,000
4395	Civic	2001	Red	CA	$17,000
7352	Civic	2002	Red	WA	$18,000

Table 3.1 A database storing information about used vehicles.

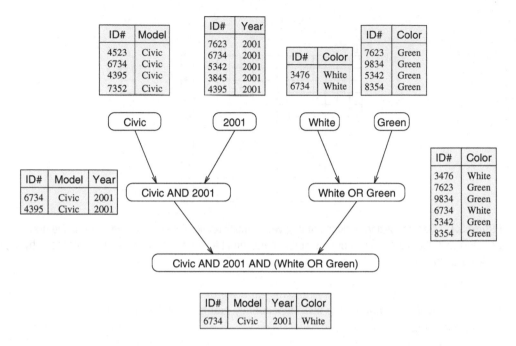

Figure 3.2 The different tables and their dependencies in a query processing operation.

tables. One possible way is to first create the following four tables: a table containing all Civics, a table containing all 2001-model cars, a table containing all green-colored cars, and a table containing all white-colored cars. Next, the computation proceeds by combining these tables by computing their pairwise intersections or unions. In particular, it computes the intersection of the Civic-table with the 2001-model year table, to construct a table of all 2001-model Civics. Similarly, it computes the union of the green- and white-colored tables to compute a table storing all cars whose color is either green or white. Finally, it computes the intersection of the table containing all the 2001 Civics with the table containing all the green or white vehicles, and returns the desired list. ∎

The various computations involved in processing the query in Example 3.2 can be visualized by the task-dependency graph shown in Figure 3.2. Each node in this figure is a task that corresponds to an intermediate table that needs to be computed and the arrows between nodes indicate dependencies between the tasks. For example, before we can compute the table that corresponds to the 2001 Civics, we must first compute the table of all the Civics and a table of all the 2001-model cars.

Note that often there are multiple ways of expressing certain computations, especially those involving associative operators such as addition, multiplication, and logical AND or OR. Different ways of arranging computations can lead to different task-dependency

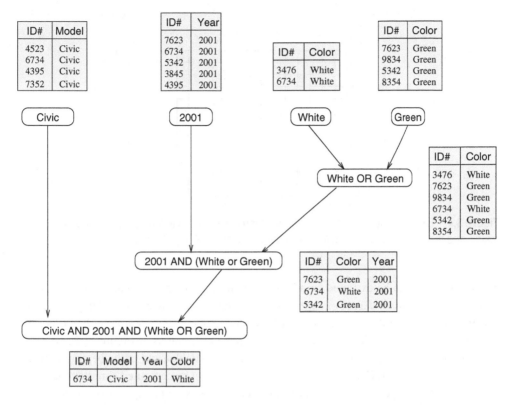

Figure 3.3 An alternate data-dependency graph for the query processing operation.

graphs with different characteristics. For instance, the database query in Example 3.2 can be solved by first computing a table of all green or white cars, then performing an intersection with a table of all 2001 model cars, and finally combining the results with the table of all Civics. This sequence of computation results in the task-dependency graph shown in Figure 3.3.

3.1.2 Granularity, Concurrency, and Task-Interaction

The number and size of tasks into which a problem is decomposed determines the *granularity* of the decomposition. A decomposition into a large number of small tasks is called *fine-grained* and a decomposition into a small number of large tasks is called *coarse-grained*. For example, the decomposition for matrix-vector multiplication shown in Figure 3.1 would usually be considered fine-grained because each of a large number of tasks performs a single dot-product. Figure 3.4 shows a coarse-grained decomposition of the same problem into four tasks, where each tasks computes $n/4$ of the entries of the output vector of length n.

A concept related to granularity is that of *degree of concurrency*. The maximum num-

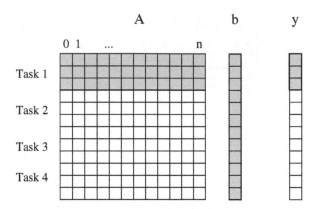

Figure 3.4 Decomposition of dense matrix-vector multiplication into four tasks. The portions of the matrix and the input and output vectors accessed by Task 1 are highlighted.

ber of tasks that can be executed simultaneously in a parallel program at any given time is known as its *maximum degree of concurrency*. In most cases, the maximum degree of concurrency is less than the total number of tasks due to dependencies among the tasks. For example, the maximum degree of concurrency in the task-graphs of Figures 3.2 and 3.3 is four. In these task-graphs, maximum concurrency is available right at the beginning when tables for Model, Year, Color Green, and Color White can be computed simultaneously. In general, for task-dependency graphs that are trees, the maximum degree of concurrency is always equal to the number of leaves in the tree.

A more useful indicator of a parallel program's performance is the *average degree of concurrency*, which is the average number of tasks that can run concurrently over the entire duration of execution of the program.

Both the maximum and the average degrees of concurrency usually increase as the granularity of tasks becomes smaller (finer). For example, the decomposition of matrix-vector multiplication shown in Figure 3.1 has a fairly small granularity and a large degree of concurrency. The decomposition for the same problem shown in Figure 3.4 has a larger granularity and a smaller degree of concurrency.

The degree of concurrency also depends on the shape of the task-dependency graph and the same granularity, in general, does not guarantee the same degree of concurrency. For example, consider the two task graphs in Figure 3.5, which are abstractions of the task graphs of Figures 3.2 and 3.3, respectively (Problem 3.1). The number inside each node represents the amount of work required to complete the task corresponding to that node. The average degree of concurrency of the task graph in Figure 3.5(a) is 2.33 and that of the task graph in Figure 3.5(b) is 1.88 (Problem 3.1), although both task-dependency graphs are based on the same decomposition.

A feature of a task-dependency graph that determines the average degree of concurrency for a given granularity is its **critical path**. In a task-dependency graph, let us refer to the nodes with no incoming edges by *start nodes* and the nodes with no outgoing edges

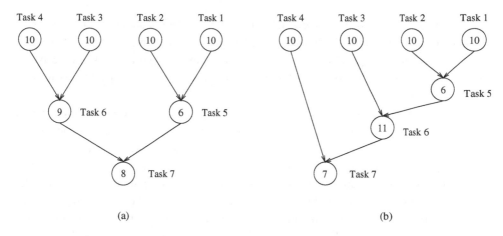

Figure 3.5 Abstractions of the task graphs of Figures 3.2 and 3.3, respectively.

by *finish nodes*. The longest directed path between any pair of start and finish nodes is known as the critical path. The sum of the weights of nodes along this path is known as the ***critical path length***, where the weight of a node is the size or the amount of work associated with the corresponding task. The ratio of the total amount of work to the critical-path length is the average degree of concurrency. Therefore, a shorter critical path favors a higher degree of concurrency. For example, the critical path length is 27 in the task-dependency graph shown in Figure 3.5(a) and is 34 in the task-dependency graph shown in Figure 3.5(b). Since the total amount of work required to solve the problems using the two decompositions is 63 and 64, respectively, the average degree of concurrency of the two task-dependency graphs is 2.33 and 1.88, respectively.

Although it may appear that the time required to solve a problem can be reduced simply by increasing the granularity of decomposition and utilizing the resulting concurrency to perform more and more tasks in parallel, this is not the case in most practical scenarios. Usually, there is an inherent bound on how fine-grained a decomposition a problem permits. For instance, there are n^2 multiplications and additions in matrix-vector multiplication considered in Example 3.1 and the problem cannot be decomposed into more than $O(n^2)$ tasks even by using the most fine-grained decomposition.

Other than limited granularity and degree of concurrency, there is another important practical factor that limits our ability to obtain unbounded speedup (ratio of serial to parallel execution time) from parallelization. This factor is the ***interaction*** among tasks running on different physical processors. The tasks that a problem is decomposed into often share input, output, or intermediate data. The dependencies in a task-dependency graph usually result from the fact that the output of one task is the input for another. For example, in the database query example, tasks share intermediate data; the table generated by one task is often used by another task as input. Depending on the definition of the tasks and the parallel programming paradigm, there may be interactions among tasks that appear to be independent in a task-dependency graph. For example, in the decomposition for matrix-vector multiplication, although all tasks are independent, they all need access to the entire input vector b. Since originally there is only one copy of the vector b, tasks may have to send and receive messages for all of them to access the entire vector in the distributed-memory paradigm.

The pattern of interaction among tasks is captured by what is known as a *task-interaction graph*. The nodes in a task-interaction graph represent tasks and the edges connect tasks that interact with each other. The nodes and edges of a task-interaction graph can be assigned weights proportional to the amount of computation a task performs and the amount of interaction that occurs along an edge, if this information is known. The edges in a task-interaction graph are usually undirected, but directed edges can be used to indicate the direction of flow of data, if it is unidirectional. The edge-set of a task-interaction graph is usually a superset of the edge-set of the task-dependency graph. In the database query example discussed earlier, the task-interaction graph is the same as the task-dependency graph. We now give an example of a more interesting task-interaction graph that results from the problem of sparse matrix-vector multiplication.

Example 3.3   Sparse matrix-vector multiplication

Consider the problem of computing the product $y = Ab$ of a sparse $n \times n$ matrix A with a dense $n \times 1$ vector b. A matrix is considered sparse when a significant number of entries in it are zero and the locations of the non-zero entries do not conform to a predefined structure or pattern. Arithmetic operations involving sparse matrices can often be optimized significantly by avoiding computations involving the zeros. For instance, while computing the ith entry $y[i] = \sum_{j=1}^{n} (A[i, j] \times b[j])$ of the product vector, we need to compute the products $A[i, j] \times b[j]$ for only those values of j for which $A[i, j] \neq 0$. For example, $y[0] = A[0, 0].b[0] + A[0, 1].b[1] + A[0, 4].b[4] + A[0, 8].b[8]$.

One possible way of decomposing this computation is to partition the output vector y and have each task compute an entry in it. Figure 3.6(a) illustrates this decomposition. In addition to assigning the computation of the element $y[i]$ of the output vector to Task i, we also make it the "owner" of row $A[i, *]$ of the matrix and the element $b[i]$ of the input vector. Note that the computation of $y[i]$ requires access to many elements of b that are owned by other tasks. So Task i must get these elements from the appropriate locations. In the message-passing paradigm, with the ownership of $b[i]$, Task i also inherits the responsibility of sending $b[i]$ to all the other tasks that need it for their computation. For example, Task 4 must send $b[4]$ to Tasks 0, 5, 8, and 9 and must get $b[0]$, $b[5]$, $b[8]$, and $b[9]$ to perform its own computation. The resulting task-interaction graph is shown in Figure 3.6(b).   ∎

Chapter 5 contains detailed quantitative analysis of overheads due to interaction and limited concurrency and their effect on the performance and scalability of parallel

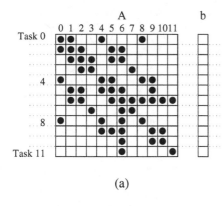
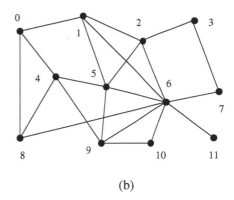

(a)   (b)

Figure 3.6   A decomposition for sparse matrix-vector multiplication and the corresponding task-interaction graph. In the decomposition Task i computes $\sum_{0 \le j \le 11, A[i,j] \ne 0} A[i, j].b[j]$.

algorithm-architecture combinations. In this section, we have provided a basic introduction to these factors because they require important consideration in designing parallel algorithms.

3.1.3   Processes and Mapping

The tasks, into which a problem is decomposed, run on physical processors. However, for reasons that we shall soon discuss, we will use the term *process* in this chapter to refer to a processing or computing agent that performs tasks. In this context, the term process does not adhere to the rigorous operating system definition of a process. Instead, it is an abstract entity that uses the code and data corresponding to a task to produce the output of that task within a finite amount of time after the task is activated by the parallel program. During this time, in addition to performing computations, a process may synchronize or communicate with other processes, if needed. In order to obtain any speedup over a sequential implementation, a parallel program must have several processes active simultaneously, working on different tasks. The mechanism by which tasks are assigned to processes for execution is called *mapping*. For example, four processes could be assigned the task of computing one submatrix of C each in the matrix-multiplication computation of Example 3.5.

The task-dependency and task-interaction graphs that result from a choice of decomposition play an important role in the selection of a good mapping for a parallel algorithm. A good mapping should seek to maximize the use of concurrency by mapping independent tasks onto different processes, it should seek to minimize the total completion time by ensuring that processes are available to execute the tasks on the critical path as soon as such tasks become executable, and it should seek to minimize interaction among processes by mapping tasks with a high degree of mutual interaction onto the same process. In most nontrivial parallel algorithms, these tend to be conflicting goals. For instance, the most efficient decomposition-mapping combination is a single task mapped onto a single

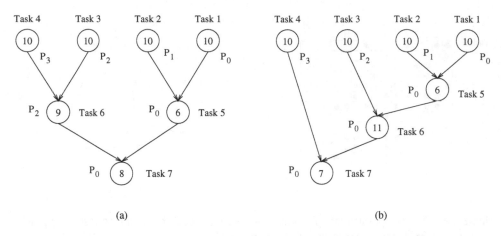

Figure 3.7 Mappings of the task graphs of Figure 3.5 onto four processes.

process. It wastes no time in idling or interacting, but achieves no speedup either. Finding a balance that optimizes the overall parallel performance is the key to a successful parallel algorithm. Therefore, mapping of tasks onto processes plays an important role in determining how efficient the resulting parallel algorithm is. Even though the degree of concurrency is determined by the decomposition, it is the mapping that determines how much of that concurrency is actually utilized, and how efficiently.

For example, Figure 3.7 shows efficient mappings for the decompositions and the task-interaction graphs of Figure 3.5 onto four processes. Note that, in this case, a maximum of four processes can be employed usefully, although the total number of tasks is seven. This is because the maximum degree of concurrency is only four. The last three tasks can be mapped arbitrarily among the processes to satisfy the constraints of the task-dependency graph. However, it makes more sense to map the tasks connected by an edge onto the same process because this prevents an inter-task interaction from becoming an inter-processes interaction. For example, in Figure 3.7(b), if Task 5 is mapped onto process P_2, then both processes P_0 and P_1 will need to interact with P_2. In the current mapping, only a single interaction between P_0 and P_1 suffices.

3.1.4 Processes versus Processors

In the context of parallel algorithm design, processes are logical computing agents that perform tasks. Processors are the hardware units that physically perform computations. In this text, we choose to express parallel algorithms and programs in terms of processes. In most cases, when we refer to processes in the context of a parallel algorithm, there is a one-to-one correspondence between processes and processors and it is appropriate to assume that there are as many processes as the number of physical CPUs on the parallel computer. However, sometimes a higher level of abstraction may be required to express a parallel algorithm, especially if it is a complex algorithm with multiple stages or with different forms of parallelism.

Treating processes and processors separately is also useful when designing parallel programs for hardware that supports multiple programming paradigms. For instance, consider a parallel computer that consists of multiple computing nodes that communicate with each other via message passing. Now each of these nodes could be a shared-address-space module with multiple CPUs. Consider implementing matrix multiplication on such a parallel computer. The best way to design a parallel algorithm is to do so in two stages. First, develop a decomposition and mapping strategy suitable for the message-passing paradigm and use this to exploit parallelism among the nodes. Each task that the original matrix multiplication problem decomposes into is a matrix multiplication computation itself. The next step is to develop a decomposition and mapping strategy suitable for the shared-memory paradigm and use this to implement each task on the multiple CPUs of a node.

3.2 Decomposition Techniques

As mentioned earlier, one of the fundamental steps that we need to undertake to solve a problem in parallel is to split the computations to be performed into a set of tasks for concurrent execution defined by the task-dependency graph. In this section, we describe some commonly used decomposition techniques for achieving concurrency. This is not an exhaustive set of possible decomposition techniques. Also, a given decomposition is not always guaranteed to lead to the best parallel algorithm for a given problem. Despite these shortcomings, the decomposition techniques described in this section often provide a good starting point for many problems and one or a combination of these techniques can be used to obtain effective decompositions for a large variety of problems.

These techniques are broadly classified as *recursive decomposition*, *data-decomposition*, *exploratory decomposition*, and *speculative decomposition*. The recursive- and data-decomposition techniques are relatively *general purpose* as they can be used to decompose a wide variety of problems. On the other hand, speculative- and exploratory-decomposition techniques are more of a *special purpose* nature because they apply to specific classes of problems.

3.2.1 Recursive Decomposition

Recursive decomposition is a method for inducing concurrency in problems that can be solved using the divide-and-conquer strategy. In this technique, a problem is solved by first dividing it into a set of independent subproblems. Each one of these subproblems is solved by recursively applying a similar division into smaller subproblems followed by a combination of their results. The divide-and-conquer strategy results in natural concurrency, as different subproblems can be solved concurrently.

Example 3.4   Quicksort
Consider the problem of sorting a sequence A of n elements using the commonly

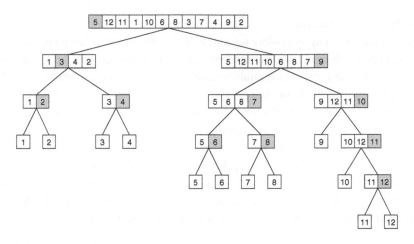

Figure 3.8 The quicksort task-dependency graph based on recursive decomposition for sorting a sequence of 12 numbers.

used quicksort algorithm. Quicksort is a divide and conquer algorithm that starts by selecting a pivot element x and then partitions the sequence A into two subsequences A_0 and A_1 such that all the elements in A_0 are smaller than x and all the elements in A_1 are greater than or equal to x. This partitioning step forms the *divide* step of the algorithm. Each one of the subsequences A_0 and A_1 is sorted by recursively calling quicksort. Each one of these recursive calls further partitions the sequences. This is illustrated in Figure 3.8 for a sequence of 12 numbers. The recursion terminates when each subsequence contains only a single element.   ■

In Figure 3.8, we define a task as the work of partitioning a given subsequence. Therefore, Figure 3.8 also represents the task graph for the problem. Initially, there is only one sequence (i.e., the root of the tree), and we can use only a single process to partition it. The completion of the root task results in two subsequences (A_0 and A_1, corresponding to the two nodes at the first level of the tree) and each one can be partitioned in parallel. Similarly, the concurrency continues to increase as we move down the tree.

Sometimes, it is possible to restructure a computation to make it amenable to recursive decomposition even if the commonly used algorithm for the problem is not based on the divide-and-conquer strategy. For example, consider the problem of finding the minimum element in an unordered sequence A of n elements. The serial algorithm for solving this problem scans the entire sequence A, recording at each step the minimum element found so far as illustrated in Algorithm 3.1. It is easy to see that this serial algorithm exhibits no concurrency.

Once we restructure this computation as a divide-and-conquer algorithm, we can use recursive decomposition to extract concurrency. Algorithm 3.2 is a divide-and-conquer algorithm for finding the minimum element in an array. In this algorithm, we split the

---

```
1.    procedure SERIAL_MIN (A, n)
2.    begin
3.       min = A[0];
4.       for i := 1 to n - 1 do
5.          if (A[i] < min) min := A[i];
6.       endfor;
7.       return min;
8.    end SERIAL_MIN
```

Algorithm 3.1   A serial program for finding the minimum in an array of numbers A of length n.

```
1.    procedure RECURSIVE_MIN (A, n)
2.    begin
3.       if (n = 1) then
4.          min := A[0];
5.       else
6.          lmin := RECURSIVE_MIN (A, n/2);
7.          rmin := RECURSIVE_MIN (&(A[n/2]), n - n/2);
8.          if (lmin < rmin) then
9.             min := lmin;
10.         else
11.            min := rmin;
12.         endelse;
13.      endelse;
14.      return min;
15.   end RECURSIVE_MIN
```

Algorithm 3.2   A recursive program for finding the minimum in an array of numbers A of length n.

sequence A into two subsequences, each of size $n/2$, and we find the minimum for each of these subsequences by performing a recursive call. Now the overall minimum element is found by selecting the minimum of these two subsequences. The recursion terminates when there is only one element left in each subsequence. Having restructured the serial computation in this manner, it is easy to construct a task-dependency graph for this problem. Figure 3.9 illustrates such a task-dependency graph for finding the minimum of eight numbers where each task is assigned the work of finding the minimum of two numbers.

3.2.2 Data Decomposition

Data decomposition is a powerful and commonly used method for deriving concurrency in algorithms that operate on large data structures. In this method, the decomposition of computations is done in two steps. In the first step, the data on which the computations

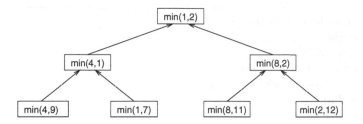

Figure 3.9   The task-dependency graph for finding the minimum number in the sequence {4, 9, 1, 7, 8, 11, 2, 12}. Each node in the tree represents the task of finding the minimum of a pair of numbers.

are performed is partitioned, and in the second step, this data partitioning is used to induce a partitioning of the computations into tasks. The operations that these tasks perform on different data partitions are usually similar (e.g., matrix multiplication introduced in Example 3.5) or are chosen from a small set of operations (e.g., LU factorization introduced in Example 3.10).

The partitioning of data can be performed in many possible ways as discussed next. In general, one must explore and evaluate all possible ways of partitioning the data and determine which one yields a natural and efficient computational decomposition.

Partitioning Output Data   In many computations, each element of the output can be computed independently of others as a function of the input. In such computations, a partitioning of the output data automatically induces a decomposition of the problems into tasks, where each task is assigned the work of computing a portion of the output. We introduce the problem of matrix-multiplication in Example 3.5 to illustrate a decomposition based on partitioning output data.

Example 3.5   Matrix multiplication

Consider the problem of multiplying two $n \times n$ matrices A and B to yield a matrix C. Figure 3.10 shows a decomposition of this problem into four tasks. Each matrix is considered to be composed of four blocks or submatrices defined by splitting each dimension of the matrix into half. The four submatrices of C, roughly of size $n/2 \times n/2$ each, are then independently computed by four tasks as the sums of the appropriate products of submatrices of A and B.   ■

Most matrix algorithms, including matrix-vector and matrix-matrix multiplication, can be formulated in terms of block matrix operations. In such a formulation, the matrix is viewed as composed of blocks or submatrices and the scalar arithmetic operations on its elements are replaced by the equivalent matrix operations on the blocks. The results of the element and the block versions of the algorithm are mathematically equivalent (Problem 3.10). Block versions of matrix algorithms are often used to aid decomposition.

$$\begin{pmatrix} A_{1,1} & A_{1,2} \\ A_{2,1} & A_{2,2} \end{pmatrix} \cdot \begin{pmatrix} B_{1,1} & B_{1,2} \\ B_{2,1} & B_{2,2} \end{pmatrix} \rightarrow \begin{pmatrix} C_{1,1} & C_{1,2} \\ C_{2,1} & C_{2,2} \end{pmatrix}$$

(a)

Task 1: $C_{1,1} = A_{1,1}B_{1,1} + A_{1,2}B_{2,1}$
Task 2: $C_{1,2} = A_{1,1}B_{1,2} + A_{1,2}B_{2,2}$
Task 3: $C_{2,1} = A_{2,1}B_{1,1} + A_{2,2}B_{2,1}$
Task 4: $C_{2,2} = A_{2,1}B_{1,2} + A_{2,2}B_{2,2}$

(b)

Figure 3.10   (a) Partitioning of input and output matrices into 2×2 submatrices. (b) A decomposition of matrix multiplication into four tasks based on the partitioning of the matrices in (a).

The decomposition shown in Figure 3.10 is based on partitioning the output matrix C into four submatrices and each of the four tasks computes one of these submatrices. The reader must note that data-decomposition is distinct from the decomposition of the computation into tasks. Although the two are often related and the former often aids the latter, a given data-decomposition does not result in a unique decomposition into tasks. For example, Figure 3.11 shows two other decompositions of matrix multiplication, each into eight tasks, corresponding to the same data-decomposition as used in Figure 3.10(a).

We now introduce another example to illustrate decompositions based on data partitioning. Example 3.6 describes the problem of computing the frequency of a set of itemsets in a transaction database, which can be decomposed based on the partitioning of output data.

Decomposition I	**Decomposition II**
Task 1: $C_{1,1} = A_{1,1}B_{1,1}$	Task 1: $C_{1,1} = A_{1,1}B_{1,1}$
Task 2: $C_{1,1} = C_{1,1} + A_{1,2}B_{2,1}$	Task 2: $C_{1,1} = C_{1,1} + A_{1,2}B_{2,1}$
Task 3: $C_{1,2} = A_{1,1}B_{1,2}$	Task 3: $C_{1,2} = A_{1,2}B_{2,2}$
Task 4: $C_{1,2} = C_{1,2} + A_{1,2}B_{2,2}$	Task 4: $C_{1,2} = C_{1,2} + A_{1,1}B_{1,2}$
Task 5: $C_{2,1} = A_{2,1}B_{1,1}$	Task 5: $C_{2,1} = A_{2,2}B_{2,1}$
Task 6: $C_{2,1} = C_{2,1} + A_{2,2}B_{2,1}$	Task 6: $C_{2,1} = C_{2,1} + A_{2,1}B_{1,1}$
Task 7: $C_{2,2} = A_{2,1}B_{1,2}$	Task 7: $C_{2,2} = A_{2,1}B_{1,2}$
Task 8: $C_{2,2} = C_{2,2} + A_{2,2}B_{2,2}$	Task 8: $C_{2,2} = C_{2,2} + A_{2,2}B_{2,2}$

Figure 3.11   Two examples of decomposition of matrix multiplication into eight tasks.

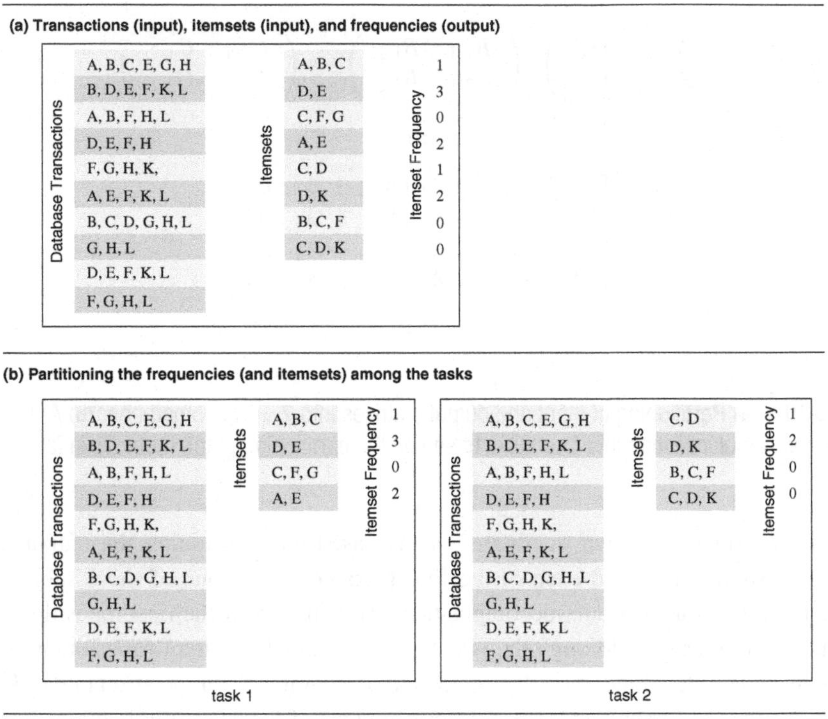

(a) Transactions (input), itemsets (input), and frequencies (output)

Database Transactions	Itemsets	Itemset Frequency
A, B, C, E, G, H	A, B, C	1
B, D, E, F, K, L	D, E	3
A, B, F, H, L	C, F, G	0
D, E, F, H	A, E	2
F, G, H, K,	C, D	1
A, E, F, K, L	D, K	2
B, C, D, G, H, L	B, C, F	0
G, H, L	C, D, K	0
D, E, F, K, L		
F, G, H, L		

(b) Partitioning the frequencies (and itemsets) among the tasks

Database Transactions	Itemsets	Itemset Frequency
A, B, C, E, G, H	A, B, C	1
B, D, E, F, K, L	D, E	3
A, B, F, H, L	C, F, G	0
D, E, F, H	A, E	2
F, G, H, K,		
A, E, F, K, L		
B, C, D, G, H, L		
G, H, L		
D, E, F, K, L		
F, G, H, L		

task 1

Database Transactions	Itemsets	Itemset Frequency
A, B, C, E, G, H	C, D	1
B, D, E, F, K, L	D, K	2
A, B, F, H, L	B, C, F	0
D, E, F, H	C, D, K	0
F, G, H, K,		
A, E, F, K, L		
B, C, D, G, H, L		
G, H, L		
D, E, F, K, L		
F, G, H, L		

task 2

Figure 3.12   Computing itemset frequencies in a transaction database.

Example 3.6   Computing frequencies of itemsets in a transaction database
Consider the problem of computing the frequency of a set of itemsets in a transaction database. In this problem we are given a set T containing n transactions and a set I containing m itemsets. Each transaction and itemset contains a small number of items, out of a possible set of items. For example, T could be a grocery stores database of customer sales with each transaction being an individual grocery list of a shopper and each itemset could be a group of items in the store. If the store desires to find out how many customers bought each of the designated groups of items, then it would need to find the number of times that each itemset in I appears in all the transactions; i.e., the number of transactions of which each itemset is a subset of. Figure 3.12(a) shows an example of this type of computation. The database shown in Figure 3.12 consists of 10 transactions, and we are interested in computing the frequency of the eight itemsets shown in the second column. The actual frequencies of these itemsets in the database, which are the output of the frequency-computing program, are shown in the third column. For instance, itemset {D, K} appears twice, once in the second and once in the ninth transaction.   ∎

Figure 3.12(b) shows how the computation of frequencies of the itemsets can be decomposed into two tasks by partitioning the output into two parts and having each task compute its half of the frequencies. Note that, in the process, the itemsets input has also been partitioned, but the primary motivation for the decomposition of Figure 3.12(b) is to have each task independently compute the subset of frequencies assigned to it.

Partitioning Input Data Partitioning of output data can be performed only if each output can be naturally computed as a function of the input. In many algorithms, it is not possible or desirable to partition the output data. For example, while finding the minimum, maximum, or the sum of a set of numbers, the output is a single unknown value. In a sorting algorithm, the individual elements of the output cannot be efficiently determined in isolation. In such cases, it is sometimes possible to partition the input data, and then use this partitioning to induce concurrency. A task is created for each partition of the input data and this task performs as much computation as possible using these local data. Note that the solutions to tasks induced by input partitions may not directly solve the original problem. In such cases, a follow-up computation is needed to combine the results. For example, while finding the sum of a sequence of N numbers using p processes ($N > p$), we can partition the input into p subsets of nearly equal sizes. Each task then computes the sum of the numbers in one of the subsets. Finally, the p partial results can be added up to yield the final result.

The problem of computing the frequency of a set of itemsets in a transaction database described in Example 3.6 can also be decomposed based on a partitioning of input data. Figure 3.13(a) shows a decomposition based on a partitioning of the input set of transactions. Each of the two tasks computes the frequencies of all the itemsets in its respective subset of transactions. The two sets of frequencies, which are the independent outputs of the two tasks, represent intermediate results. Combining the intermediate results by pairwise addition yields the final result.

Partitioning both Input and Output Data In some cases, in which it is possible to partition the output data, partitioning of input data can offer additional concurrency. For example, consider the 4-way decomposition shown in Figure 3.13(b) for computing itemset frequencies. Here, both the transaction set and the frequencies are divided into two parts and a different one of the four possible combinations is assigned to each of the four tasks. Each task then computes a local set of frequencies. Finally, the outputs of Tasks 1 and 3 are added together, as are the outputs of Tasks 2 and 4.

Partitioning Intermediate Data Algorithms are often structured as multi-stage computations such that the output of one stage is the input to the subsequent stage. A decomposition of such an algorithm can be derived by partitioning the input or the output data of an intermediate stage of the algorithm. Partitioning intermediate data can sometimes lead to higher concurrency than partitioning input or output data. Often, the intermediate data are not generated explicitly in the serial algorithm for solving the problem and some re-

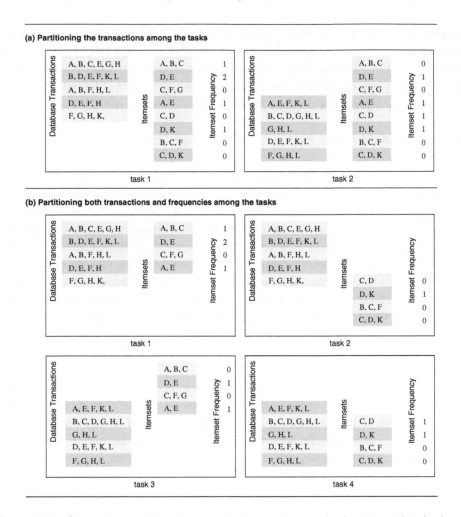

Figure 3.13 Some decompositions for computing itemset frequencies in a transaction database.

structuring of the original algorithm may be required to use intermediate data partitioning to induce a decomposition.

Let us revisit matrix multiplication to illustrate a decomposition based on partitioning intermediate data. Recall that the decompositions induced by a 2×2 partitioning of the output matrix C, as shown in Figures 3.10 and 3.11, have a maximum degree of concurrency of four. We can increase the degree of concurrency by introducing an intermediate stage in which eight tasks compute their respective product submatrices and store the results in a temporary three-dimensional matrix D, as shown in Figure 3.14. The submatrix $D_{k,i,j}$ is the product of $A_{i,k}$ and $B_{k,j}$.

A partitioning of the intermediate matrix D induces a decomposition into eight tasks. Figure 3.15 shows this decomposition. After the multiplication phase, a relatively inexpen-

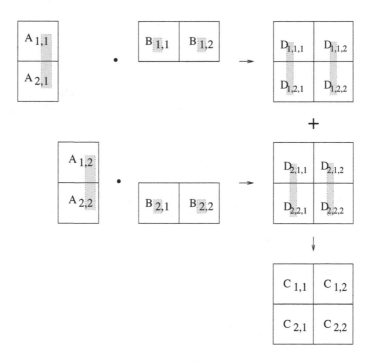

Figure 3.14 Multiplication of matrices A and B with partitioning of the three-dimensional intermediate matrix D.

sive matrix addition step can compute the result matrix C. All submatrices $D_{*,i,j}$ with the same second and third dimensions i and j are added to yield $C_{i,j}$. The eight tasks numbered 1 through 8 in Figure 3.15 perform $O(n^3/8)$ work each in multiplying $n/2 \times n/2$ submatrices of A and B. Then, four tasks numbered 9 through 12 spend $O(n^2/4)$ time each in adding the appropriate $n/2 \times n/2$ submatrices of the intermediate matrix D to yield the final result matrix C. Figure 3.16 shows the task-dependency graph corresponding to the decomposition shown in Figure 3.15.

Note that all elements of D are computed implicitly in the original decomposition shown in Figure 3.11, but are not explicitly stored. By restructuring the original algorithm and by explicitly storing D, we have been able to devise a decomposition with higher concurrency. This, however, has been achieved at the cost of extra aggregate memory usage.

The Owner-Computes Rule   A decomposition based on partitioning output or input data is also widely referred to as the *owner-computes* rule. The idea behind this rule is that each partition performs all the computations involving data that it owns. Depending on the nature of the data or the type of data-partitioning, the owner-computes rule may mean different things. For instance, when we assign partitions of the input data to tasks, then the owner-computes rule means that a task performs all the computations that can be done using these data. On the other hand, if we partition the output data, then the owner-

Stage I

$$\left(\begin{array}{cc} A_{1,1} & A_{1,2} \\ A_{2,1} & A_{2,2} \end{array}\right) \cdot \left(\begin{array}{cc} B_{1,1} & B_{1,2} \\ B_{2,1} & B_{2,2} \end{array}\right) \rightarrow \left(\left\{\begin{array}{cc} D_{1,1,1} & D_{1,1,2} \\ D_{1,2,2} & D_{1,2,2} \\ D_{2,1,1} & D_{2,1,2} \\ D_{2,2,2} & D_{2,2,2} \end{array}\right\}\right)$$

Stage II

$$\left(\begin{array}{cc} D_{1,1,1} & D_{1,1,2} \\ D_{1,2,2} & D_{1,2,2} \end{array}\right) + \left(\begin{array}{cc} D_{2,1,1} & D_{2,1,2} \\ D_{2,2,2} & D_{2,2,2} \end{array}\right) \rightarrow \left(\begin{array}{cc} C_{1,1} & C_{1,2} \\ C_{2,1} & C_{2,2} \end{array}\right)$$

A decomposition induced by a partitioning of D

$$
\begin{array}{lll}
\text{Task 01:} & D_{1,1,1} = A_{1,1}B_{1,1} \\
\text{Task 02:} & D_{2,1,1} = A_{1,2}B_{2,1} \\
\text{Task 03:} & D_{1,1,2} = A_{1,1}B_{1,2} \\
\text{Task 04:} & D_{2,1,2} = A_{1,2}B_{2,2} \\
\text{Task 05:} & D_{1,2,1} = A_{2,1}B_{1,1} \\
\text{Task 06:} & D_{2,2,1} = A_{2,2}B_{2,1} \\
\text{Task 07:} & D_{1,2,2} = A_{2,1}B_{1,2} \\
\text{Task 08:} & D_{2,2,2} = A_{2,2}B_{2,2} \\
\text{Task 09:} & C_{1,1} = D_{1,1,1} + D_{2,1,1} \\
\text{Task 10:} & C_{1,2} = D_{1,1,2} + D_{2,1,2} \\
\text{Task 11:} & C_{2,1} = D_{1,2,1} + D_{2,2,1} \\
\text{Task 12:} & C_{2,2} = D_{1,2,2} + D_{2,2,2}
\end{array}
$$

Figure 3.15   A decomposition of matrix multiplication based on partitioning the intermediate three-dimensional matrix.

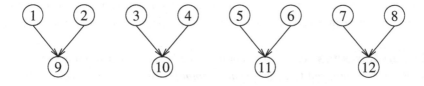

Figure 3.16   The task-dependency graph of the decomposition shown in Figure 3.15.

computes rule means that a task computes all the data in the partition assigned to it.

3.2.3 Exploratory Decomposition

Exploratory decomposition is used to decompose problems whose underlying computations correspond to a search of a space for solutions. In exploratory decomposition, we partition the search space into smaller parts, and search each one of these parts concurrently, until the desired solutions are found. For an example of exploratory decomposition, consider the 15-puzzle problem.

> **Example 3.7** The 15-puzzle problem
> The 15-puzzle consists of 15 tiles numbered 1 through 15 and one blank tile placed in a 4×4 grid. A tile can be moved into the blank position from a position adjacent to it, thus creating a blank in the tile's original position. Depending on the configuration of the grid, up to four moves are possible: up, down, left, and right. The initial and final configurations of the tiles are specified. The objective is to determine any sequence or a shortest sequence of moves that transforms the initial configuration to the final configuration. Figure 3.17 illustrates sample initial and final configurations and a sequence of moves leading from the initial configuration to the final configuration. ∎

The 15-puzzle is typically solved using tree-search techniques. Starting from the initial configuration, all possible successor configurations are generated. A configuration may have 2, 3, or 4 possible successor configurations, each corresponding to the occupation of the empty slot by one of its neighbors. The task of finding a path from initial to final configuration now translates to finding a path from one of these newly generated configurations to the final configuration. Since one of these newly generated configurations must be closer to the solution by one move (if a solution exists), we have made some progress towards finding the solution. The configuration space generated by the tree search is often referred to as a state space graph. Each node of the graph is a configuration and each edge of the graph connects configurations that can be reached from one another by a single move of a tile.

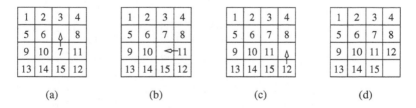

Figure 3.17 A 15-puzzle problem instance showing the initial configuration (a), the final configuration (d), and a sequence of moves leading from the initial to the final configuration.

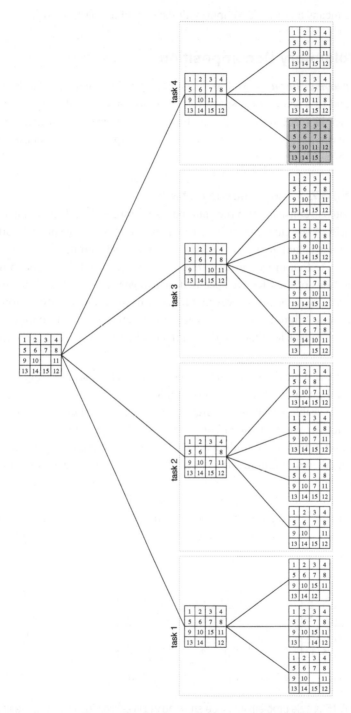

Figure 3.18   The states generated by an instance of the 15-puzzle problem.

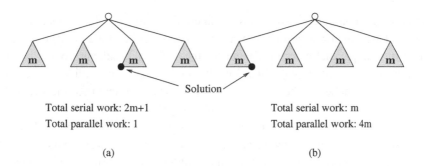

Figure 3.19 An illustration of anomalous speedups resulting from exploratory decomposition.

One method for solving this problem in parallel is as follows. First, a few levels of configurations starting from the initial configuration are generated serially until the search tree has a sufficient number of leaf nodes (i.e., configurations of the 15-puzzle). Now each node is assigned to a task to explore further until at least one of them finds a solution. As soon as one of the concurrent tasks finds a solution it can inform the others to terminate their searches. Figure 3.18 illustrates one such decomposition into four tasks in which task 4 finds the solution.

Note that even though exploratory decomposition may appear similar to data-decomposition (the search space can be thought of as being the data that get partitioned) it is fundamentally different in the following way. The tasks induced by data-decomposition are performed in their entirety and each task performs useful computations towards the solution of the problem. On the other hand, in exploratory decomposition, unfinished tasks can be terminated as soon as an overall solution is found. Hence, the portion of the search space searched (and the aggregate amount of work performed) by a parallel formulation can be very different from that searched by a serial algorithm. The work performed by the parallel formulation can be either smaller or greater than that performed by the serial algorithm. For example, consider a search space that has been partitioned into four concurrent tasks as shown in Figure 3.19. If the solution lies right at the beginning of the search space corresponding to task 3 (Figure 3.19(a)), then it will be found almost immediately by the parallel formulation. The serial algorithm would have found the solution only after performing work equivalent to searching the entire space corresponding to tasks 1 and 2. On the other hand, if the solution lies towards the end of the search space corresponding to task 1 (Figure 3.19(b)), then the parallel formulation will perform almost four times the work of the serial algorithm and will yield no speedup.

3.2.4 Speculative Decomposition

Speculative decomposition is used when a program may take one of many possible computationally significant branches depending on the output of other computations that precede it. In this situation, while one task is performing the computation whose output is used in deciding the next computation, other tasks can concurrently start the computations of the next stage. This scenario is similar to evaluating one or more of the branches of a *switch* statement in C in parallel before the input for the *switch* is available. While one task is performing the computation that will eventually resolve the switch, other tasks could pick up the multiple branches of the switch in parallel. When the input for the *switch* has finally been computed, the computation corresponding to the correct branch would be used while that corresponding to the other branches would be discarded. The parallel run time is smaller than the serial run time by the amount of time required to evaluate the condition on which the next task depends because this time is utilized to perform a useful computation for the next stage in parallel. However, this parallel formulation of a switch guarantees at least some wasteful computation. In order to minimize the wasted computation, a slightly different formulation of speculative decomposition could be used, especially in situations where one of the outcomes of the switch is more likely than the others. In this case, only the most promising branch is taken up a task in parallel with the preceding computation. In case the outcome of the switch is different from what was anticipated, the computation is rolled back and the correct branch of the switch is taken.

The speedup due to speculative decomposition can add up if there are multiple speculative stages. An example of an application in which speculative decomposition is useful is ***discrete event simulation***. A detailed description of discrete event simulation is beyond the scope of this chapter; however, we give a simplified description of the problem.

Example 3.8   Parallel discrete event simulation
Consider the simulation of a system that is represented as a network or a directed graph. The nodes of this network represent components. Each component has an input buffer of jobs. The initial state of each component or node is idle. An idle component picks up a job from its input queue, if there is one, processes that job in some finite amount of time, and puts it in the input buffer of the components which are connected to it by outgoing edges. A component has to wait if the input buffer of one of its outgoing neighbors if full, until that neighbor picks up a job to create space in the buffer. There is a finite number of input job types. The output of a component (and hence the input to the components connected to it) and the time it takes to process a job is a function of the input job. The problem is to simulate the functioning of the network for a given sequence or a set of sequences of input jobs and compute the total completion time and possibly other aspects of system behavior. Figure 3.20 shows a simple network for a discrete event solution problem.   ■

The problem of simulating a sequence of input jobs on the network described in Example 3.8 appears inherently sequential because the input of a typical component is the output of another. However, we can define speculative tasks that start simulating a subpart of the network, each assuming one of several possible inputs to that stage. When an actual input to a certain stage becomes available (as a result of the completion of another selector task

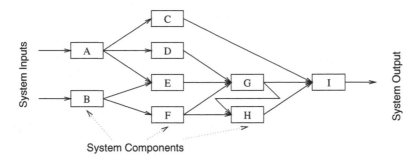

Figure 3.20 A simple network for discrete event simulation.

from a previous stage), then all or part of the work required to simulate this input would have already been finished if the speculation was correct, or the simulation of this stage is restarted with the most recent correct input if the speculation was incorrect.

Speculative decomposition is different from exploratory decomposition in the following way. In speculative decomposition, the input at a branch leading to multiple parallel tasks is unknown, whereas in exploratory decomposition, the output of the multiple tasks originating at a branch is unknown. In speculative decomposition, the serial algorithm would strictly perform only one of the tasks at a speculative stage because when it reaches the beginning of that stage, it knows exactly which branch to take. Therefore, by preemptively computing for multiple possibilities out of which only one materializes, a parallel program employing speculative decomposition performs more aggregate work than its serial counterpart. Even if only one of the possibilities is explored speculatively, the parallel algorithm may perform more or the same amount of work as the serial algorithm. On the other hand, in exploratory decomposition, the serial algorithm too may explore different alternatives one after the other, because the branch that may lead to the solution is not known beforehand. Therefore, the parallel program may perform more, less, or the same amount of aggregate work compared to the serial algorithm depending on the location of the solution in the search space.

3.2.5 Hybrid Decompositions

So far we have discussed a number of decomposition methods that can be used to derive concurrent formulations of many algorithms. These decomposition techniques are not exclusive, and can often be combined together. Often, a computation is structured into multiple stages and it is sometimes necessary to apply different types of decomposition in different stages. For example, while finding the minimum of a large set of n numbers, a purely recursive decomposition may result in far more tasks than the number of processes, P, available. An efficient decomposition would partition the input into P roughly equal parts and have each task compute the minimum of the sequence assigned to it. The final result can be obtained by finding the minimum of the P intermediate results by using the

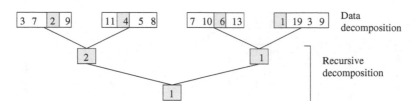

Figure 3.21 Hybrid decomposition for finding the minimum of an array of size 16 using four tasks.

recursive decomposition shown in Figure 3.21.

As another example of an application of hybrid decomposition, consider performing quicksort in parallel. In Example 3.4, we used a recursive decomposition to derive a concurrent formulation of quicksort. This formulation results in $O(n)$ tasks for the problem of sorting a sequence of size n. But due to the dependencies among these tasks and due to uneven sizes of the tasks, the effective concurrency is quite limited. For example, the first task for splitting the input list into two parts takes $O(n)$ time, which puts an upper limit on the performance gain possible via parallelization. But the step of splitting lists performed by tasks in parallel quicksort can also be decomposed using the input decomposition technique discussed in Section 9.4.1. The resulting hybrid decomposition that combines recursive decomposition and the input data-decomposition leads to a highly concurrent formulation of quicksort.

3.3 Characteristics of Tasks and Interactions

The various decomposition techniques described in the previous section allow us to identify the concurrency that is available in a problem and decompose it into tasks that can be executed in parallel. The next step in the process of designing a parallel algorithm is to take these tasks and assign (i.e., map) them onto the available processes. While devising a mapping scheme to construct a good parallel algorithm, we often take a cue from the decomposition. The nature of the tasks and the interactions among them has a bearing on the mapping. In this section, we shall discuss the various properties of tasks and inter-task interactions that affect the choice of a good mapping.

3.3.1 Characteristics of Tasks

The following four characteristics of the tasks have a large influence on the suitability of a mapping scheme.

Task Generation The tasks that constitute a parallel algorithm may be generated either statically or dynamically. *Static task generation* refers to the scenario where all the tasks are known before the algorithm starts execution. Data decomposition usually leads to static task generation. Examples of data-decomposition leading to a static task generation include matrix-multiplication and LU factorization (Problem 3.5). Recursive decomposition can also lead to a static task-dependency graph. Finding the minimum of a list of numbers (Figure 3.9) is an example of a static recursive task-dependency graph.

Certain decompositions lead to a ***dynamic task generation*** during the execution of the algorithm. In such decompositions, the actual tasks and the task-dependency graph are not explicitly available *a priori*, although the high level rules or guidelines governing task generation are known as a part of the algorithm. Recursive decomposition can lead to dynamic task generation. For example, consider the recursive decomposition in quicksort (Figure 3.8). The tasks are generated dynamically, and the size and shape of the task tree is determined by the values in the input array to be sorted. An array of the same size can lead to task-dependency graphs of different shapes and with a different total number of tasks.

Exploratory decomposition can be formulated to generate tasks either statically or dynamically. For example, consider the 15-puzzle problem discussed in Section 3.2.3. One way to generate a static task-dependency graph using exploratory decomposition is as follows. First, a preprocessing task starts with the initial configuration and expands the search tree in a breadth-first manner until a predefined number of configurations are generated. These configuration now represent independent tasks, which can be mapped onto different processes and run independently. A different decomposition that generates tasks dynamically would be one in which a task takes a state as input, expands it through a predefined number of steps of breadth-first search and spawns new tasks to perform the same computation on each of the resulting states (unless it has found the solution, in which case the algorithm terminates).

Task Sizes   The size of a task is the relative amount of time required to complete it. The complexity of mapping schemes often depends on whether or not the tasks are ***uniform***; i.e., whether or not they require roughly the same amount of time. If the amount of time required by the tasks varies significantly, then they are said to be ***non-uniform***. For example, the tasks in the decompositions for matrix multiplication shown in Figures 3.10 and 3.11 would be considered uniform. On the other hand, the tasks in quicksort in Figure 3.8 are non-uniform.

Knowledge of Task Sizes   The third characteristic that influences the choice of mapping scheme is knowledge of the task size. If the size of all the tasks is known, then this information can often be used in mapping of tasks to processes. For example, in the various decompositions for matrix multiplication discussed so far, the computation time for each task is known before the parallel program starts. On the other hand, the size of a typical task in the 15-puzzle problem is unknown. We do not know *a priori* how many moves will lead to the solution from a given state.

Size of Data Associated with Tasks   Another important characteristic of a task is the size of data associated with it. The reason this is an important consideration for mapping is that the data associated with a task must be available to the process performing that task, and the size and the location of these data may determine the process that can perform the task without incurring excessive data-movement overheads.

Different types of data associated with a task may have different sizes. For instance, the input data may be small but the output may be large, or vice versa. For example, the input to a task in the 15-puzzle problem may be just one state of the puzzle. This is a small input relative to the amount of computation that may be required to find a sequence of moves from this state to a solution state. In the problem of computing the minimum of a sequence, the size of the input is proportional to the amount of computation, but the output is just one number. In the parallel formulation of the quick sort, the size of both the input and the output data is of the same order as the sequential time needed to solve the task.

3.3.2   Characteristics of Inter-Task Interactions

In any nontrivial parallel algorithm, tasks need to interact with each other to share data, work, or synchronization information. Different parallel algorithms require different types of interactions among concurrent tasks. The nature of these interactions makes them more suitable for certain programming paradigms and mapping schemes, and less suitable for others. The types of inter-task interactions can be described along different dimensions, each corresponding to a distinct characteristic of the underlying computations.

Static versus Dynamic   One way of classifying the type of interactions that take place among concurrent tasks is to consider whether or not these interactions have a *static* or *dynamic* pattern. An interaction pattern is static if for each task, the interactions happen at predetermined times, and if the set of tasks to interact with at these times is known prior to the execution of the algorithm. In other words, in a static interaction pattern, not only is the task-interaction graph known *a priori*, but the stage of the computation at which each interaction occurs is also known. An interaction pattern is dynamic if the timing of interactions or the set of tasks to interact with cannot be determined prior to the execution of the algorithm.

Static interactions can be programmed easily in the message-passing paradigm, but dynamic interactions are harder to program. The reason is that interactions in message-passing require active involvement of both interacting tasks – the sender and the receiver of information. The unpredictable nature of dynamic iterations makes it hard for both the sender and the receiver to participate in the interaction at the same time. Therefore, when implementing a parallel algorithm with dynamic interactions in the message-passing paradigm, the tasks must be assigned additional synchronization or polling responsibility. Shared-address space programming can code both types of interactions equally easily.

The decompositions for parallel matrix multiplication presented earlier in this chapter exhibit static inter-task interactions. For an example of dynamic interactions, consider solving the 15-puzzle problem in which tasks are assigned different states to explore after an initial step that generates the desirable number of states by applying breadth-first search on the initial state. It is possible that a certain state leads to all dead ends and a task exhausts its search space without reaching the goal state, while other tasks are still busy trying to find a solution. The task that has exhausted its work can pick up an unexplored state from the queue of another busy task and start exploring it. The interactions involved in such a transfer of work from one task to another are dynamic.

Regular versus Irregular   Another way of classifying the interactions is based upon their spatial structure. An interaction pattern is considered to be *regular* if it has some structure that can be exploited for efficient implementation. On the other hand, an inter-action pattern is called *irregular* if no such regular pattern exists. Irregular and dynamic communications are harder to handle, particularly in the message-passing programming paradigm. An example of a decomposition with a regular interaction pattern is the prob-lem of image dithering.

Example 3.9   Image dithering
In image dithering, the color of each pixel in the image is determined as the weighted average of its original value and the values of its neighboring pixels. We can easily decompose this computation, by breaking the image into square regions and using a different task to dither each one of these regions. Note that each task needs to access the pixel values of the region assigned to it as well as the values of the image surrounding its region. Thus, if we regard the tasks as nodes of a graph with an edge linking a pair of interacting tasks, the resulting pattern is a two-dimensional mesh, as shown in Figure 3.22.   ∎

Sparse matrix-vector multiplication discussed in Section 3.1.2 provides a good example of irregular interaction, which is shown in Figure 3.6. In this decomposition, even though each task, by virtue of the decomposition, knows *a priori* which rows of matrix A it needs to access, without scanning the row(s) of A assigned to it, a task cannot know which entries of vector b it requires. The reason is that the access pattern for b depends on the structure of the sparse matrix A.

Read-only versus Read-Write   We have already learned that sharing of data among tasks leads to inter-task interaction. However, the type of sharing may impact the choice of the mapping. Data sharing interactions can be categorized as either *read-only* or *read-write* interactions. As the name suggests, in read-only interactions, tasks require only a read-access to the data shared among many concurrent tasks. For example, in the decomposition for parallel matrix multiplication shown in Figure 3.10, the tasks only need to read the shared input matrices A and B. In read-write interactions, multiple tasks need to read and write on some shared data. For example, consider the problem of solving the 15-puzzle. The parallel formulation method proposed in Section 3.2.3 uses an exhaustive search to find a solution. In this formulation, each state is considered an equally suitable candidate for further expansion. The search can be made more efficient if the states that appear to

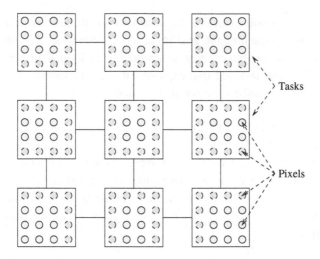

Figure 3.22   The regular two-dimensional task-interaction graph for image dithering. The pixels with dotted outline require color values from the boundary pixels of the neighboring tasks.

be closer to the solution are given a priority for further exploration. An alternative search technique known as heuristic search implements such a strategy. In heuristic search, we use a heuristic to provide a relative approximate indication of the distance of each state from the solution (i.e. the potential number of moves required to reach the solution). In the case of the 15-puzzle, the number of tiles that are out of place in a given state could serve as such a heuristic. The states that need to be expanded further are stored in a priority queue based on the value of this heuristic. While choosing the states to expand, we give preference to more promising states, i.e. the ones that have fewer out-of-place tiles and hence, are more likely to lead to a quick solution. In this situation, the priority queue constitutes shared data and tasks need both read and write access to it; they need to put the states resulting from an expansion into the queue and they need to pick up the next most promising state for the next expansion.

One-way versus Two-way   In some interactions, the data or work needed by a task or a subset of tasks is explicitly supplied by another task or subset of tasks. Such interactions are called *two-way* interactions and usually involve predefined producer and consumer tasks. In other interactions, only one of a pair of communicating tasks initiates the interaction and completes it without interrupting the other one. Such an interaction is called a *one-way* interaction. All read-only interactions can be formulated as one-way interactions. Read-write interactions can be either one-way or two-way.

The shared-address-space programming paradigms can handle both one-way and two-way interactions equally easily. However, one-way interactions cannot be directly programmed in the message-passing paradigm because the source of the data to be transferred must explicitly send the data to the recipient. In the message-passing paradigm, all one-way interactions must be converted to two-way interactions via program restructuring. Static one-way interactions can be easily converted to two-way communications. Since the time and the location in the program of a static one-way interaction is known *a priori*, introducing a matching interaction operation in the partner task is enough to convert a one-way static interaction to a two-way static interaction. On the other hand, dynamic one-way interactions can require some nontrivial program restructuring to be converted to two-way interactions. The most common such restructuring involves polling. Each task checks for pending requests from other tasks after regular intervals, and services such requests, if any.

3.4 Mapping Techniques for Load Balancing

Once a computation has been decomposed into tasks, these tasks are mapped onto processes with the objective that all tasks complete in the shortest amount of elapsed time. In order to achieve a small execution time, the **overheads** of executing the tasks in parallel must be minimized. For a given decomposition, there are two key sources of overhead. The time spent in inter-process interaction is one source of overhead. Another important source of overhead is the time that some processes may spend being idle. Some processes can be idle even before the overall computation is finished for a variety of reasons. Uneven load distribution may cause some processes to finish earlier than others. At times, all the unfinished tasks mapped onto a process may be waiting for tasks mapped onto other processes to finish in order to satisfy the constraints imposed by the task-dependency graph. Both interaction and idling are often a function of mapping. Therefore, a good mapping of tasks onto processes must strive to achieve the twin objectives of (1) reducing the amount of time processes spend in interacting with each other, and (2) reducing the total amount of time some processes are idle while the others are engaged in performing some tasks.

These two objectives often conflict with each other. For example, the objective of minimizing the interactions can be easily achieved by assigning sets of tasks that need to interact with each other onto the same process. In most cases, such a mapping will result in a highly unbalanced workload among the processes. In fact, following this strategy to the limit will often map all tasks onto a single process. As a result, the processes with a lighter load will be idle when those with a heavier load are trying to finish their tasks. Similarly, to balance the load among processes, it may be necessary to assign tasks that interact heavily to different processes. Due to the conflicts between these objectives, finding a good mapping is a nontrivial problem.

In this section, we will discuss various schemes for mapping tasks onto processes with the primary view of balancing the task workload of processes and minimizing their idle time. Reducing inter-process interaction is the topic of Section 3.5. The reader should be aware that assigning a balanced aggregate load of tasks to each process is a necessary but not sufficient condition for reducing process idling. Recall that the tasks resulting from a decomposition are not all ready for execution at the same time. A task-dependency graph determines which tasks can execute in parallel and which must wait for some others to

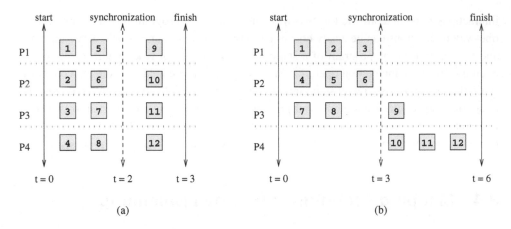

Figure 3.23   Two mappings of a hypothetical decomposition with a synchronization.

finish at a given stage in the execution of a parallel algorithm. Therefore, it is possible in a certain parallel formulation that although all processes perform the same aggregate amount of work, at different times, only a fraction of the processes are active while the remainder contain tasks that must wait for other tasks to finish. Similarly, poor synchronization among interacting tasks can lead to idling if one of the tasks has to wait to send or receive data from another task. A good mapping must ensure that the computations and interactions among processes at each stage of the execution of the parallel algorithm are well balanced. Figure 3.23 shows two mappings of 12-task decomposition in which the last four tasks can be started only after the first eight are finished due to dependencies among tasks. As the figure shows, two mappings, each with an overall balanced workload, can result in different completion times.

Mapping techniques used in parallel algorithms can be broadly classified into two categories: *static* and *dynamic*. The parallel programming paradigm and the characteristics of tasks and the interactions among them determine whether a static or a dynamic mapping is more suitable.

- **Static Mapping:** Static mapping techniques distribute the tasks among processes prior to the execution of the algorithm. For statically generated tasks, either static or dynamic mapping can be used. The choice of a good mapping in this case depends on several factors, including the knowledge of task sizes, the size of data associated with tasks, the characteristics of inter-task interactions, and even the parallel programming paradigm. Even when task sizes are known, in general, the problem of obtaining an optimal mapping is an NP-complete problem for non-uniform tasks. However, for many practical cases, relatively inexpensive heuristics provide fairly acceptable approximate solutions to the optimal static mapping problem.

  Algorithms that make use of static mapping are in general easier to design and program.

- **Dynamic Mapping:** Dynamic mapping techniques distribute the work among processes during the execution of the algorithm. If tasks are generated dynamically, then they must be mapped dynamically too. If task sizes are unknown, then a static mapping can potentially lead to serious load-imbalances and dynamic mappings are usually more effective. If the amount of data associated with tasks is large relative to the computation, then a dynamic mapping may entail moving this data among processes. The cost of this data movement may outweigh some other advantages of dynamic mapping and may render a static mapping more suitable. However, in a shared-address-space paradigm, dynamic mapping may work well even with large data associated with tasks if the interaction is read-only. The reader should be aware that the shared-address-space programming paradigm does not automatically provide immunity against data-movement costs. If the underlying hardware is NUMA (Section 2.3.2), then the data may physically move from a distant memory. Even in a cc-UMA architecture, the data may have to move from one cache to another.

  Algorithms that require dynamic mapping are usually more complicated, particularly in the message-passing programming paradigm.

Having discussed the guidelines for choosing between static and dynamic mappings, we now describe various schemes of these two types of mappings in detail.

3.4.1   Schemes for Static Mapping

Static mapping is often, though not exclusively, used in conjunction with a decomposition based on data partitioning. Static mapping is also used for mapping certain problems that are expressed naturally by a static task-dependency graph. In the following subsections, we will discuss mapping schemes based on data partitioning and task partitioning.

Mappings Based on Data Partitioning

In this section, we will discuss mappings based on partitioning two of the most common ways of representing data in algorithms, namely, arrays and graphs. The data-partitioning actually induces a decomposition, but the partitioning or the decomposition is selected with the final mapping in mind.

Array Distribution Schemes   In a decomposition based on partitioning data, the tasks are closely associated with portions of data by the owner-computes rule. Therefore, mapping the relevant data onto the processes is equivalent to mapping tasks onto processes. We now study some commonly used techniques of distributing arrays or matrices among processes.

Block Distributions

Block distributions are some of the simplest ways to distribute an array and assign uniform contiguous portions of the array to different processes. In these distributions, a

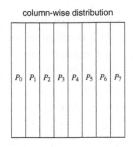

Figure 3.24   Examples of one-dimensional partitioning of an array among eight processes.

d-dimensional array is distributed among the processes such that each process receives a contiguous block of array entries along a specified subset of array dimensions. Block distributions of arrays are particularly suitable when there is a locality of interaction, i.e., computation of an element of an array requires other nearby elements in the array.

For example, consider an $n \times n$ two-dimensional array A with n rows and n columns. We can now select one of these dimensions, e.g., the first dimension, and partition the array into p parts such that the kth part contains rows $kn/p \ldots (k + 1)n/p - 1$, where $0 \leq k < p$. That is, each partition contains a block of n/p consecutive rows of A. Similarly, if we partition A along the second dimension, then each partition contains a block of n/p consecutive columns. These row- and column-wise array distributions are illustrated in Figure 3.24.

Similarly, instead of selecting a single dimension, we can select multiple dimensions to partition. For instance, in the case of array A we can select both dimensions and partition the matrix into blocks such that each block corresponds to a $n/p_1 \times n/p_2$ section of the matrix, with $p = p_1 \times p_2$ being the number of processes. Figure 3.25 illustrates two different two-dimensional distributions, on a 4×4 and 2×8 process grid, respectively. In general, given a d-dimensional array, we can distribute it using up to a d-dimensional block distribution.

Using these block distributions we can load-balance a variety of parallel computations

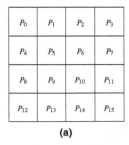

(a)

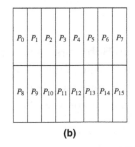

(b)

Figure 3.25   Examples of two-dimensional distributions of an array, (a) on a 4×4 process grid, and (b) on a 2×8 process grid.

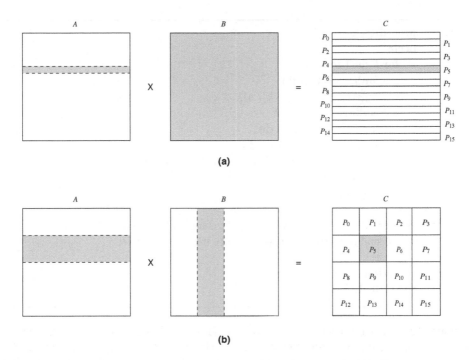

Figure 3.26 Data sharing needed for matrix multiplication with (a) one-dimensional and (b) two-dimensional partitioning of the output matrix. Shaded portions of the input matrices A and B are required by the process that computes the shaded portion of the output matrix C.

that operate on multi-dimensional arrays. For example, consider the $n \times n$ matrix multiplication $C = A \times B$, as discussed in Section 3.2.2. One way of decomposing this computation is to partition the output matrix C. Since each entry of C requires the same amount of computation, we can balance the computations by using either a one- or two-dimensional block distribution to partition C uniformly among the p available processes. In the first case, each process will get a block of n/p rows (or columns) of C, whereas in the second case, each process will get a block of size $n/\sqrt{p} \times n/\sqrt{p}$. In either case, the process will be responsible for computing the entries of the partition of C assigned to it.

As the matrix-multiplication example illustrates, quite often we have the choice of mapping the computations using either a one- or a two-dimensional distribution (and even more choices in the case of higher dimensional arrays). In general, higher dimensional distributions allow us to use more processes. For example, in the case of matrix-matrix multiplication, a one-dimensional distribution will allow us to use up to n processes by assigning a single row of C to each process. On the other hand, a two-dimensional distribution will allow us to use up to n^2 processes by assigning a single element of C to each process.

In addition to allowing a higher degree of concurrency, higher dimensional distributions also sometimes help in reducing the amount of interactions among the different processes for many problems. Figure 3.26 illustrates this in the case of dense matrix-multiplication.

```
1.    procedure COL_LU (A)
2.    begin
3.        for k := 1 to n do
4.            for j := k to n do
5.                A[j, k] := A[j, k]/A[k, k];
6.            endfor;
7.            for j := k + 1 to n do
8.                for i := k + 1 to n do
9.                    A[i, j] := A[i, j] − A[i, k] × A[k, j];
10.               endfor;
11.           endfor;
      /*
After this iteration, column A[k + 1 : n, k] is logically the kth
column of L and row A[k, k : n] is logically the kth row of U.
      */
12.       endfor;
13.   end COL_LU
```

Algorithm 3.3   A serial column-based algorithm to factor a nonsingular matrix A into a lower-triangular matrix L and an upper-triangular matrix U. Matrices L and U share space with A. On Line 9, $A[i, j]$ on the left side of the assignment is equivalent to $L[i, j]$ if $i > j$; otherwise, it is equivalent to $U[i, j]$.

With a one-dimensional partitioning along the rows, each process needs to access the corresponding n/p rows of matrix A and the entire matrix B, as shown in Figure 3.26(a) for process P_5. Thus the total amount of data that needs to be accessed is $n^2/p + n^2$. However, with a two-dimensional distribution, each process needs to access $n/\sqrt{p}$ rows of matrix A and $n/\sqrt{p}$ columns of matrix B, as shown in Figure 3.26(b) for process P_5. In the two-dimensional case, the total amount of shared data that each process needs to access is $O(n^2/\sqrt{p})$, which is significantly smaller compared to $O(n^2)$ shared data in the one-dimensional case.

Cyclic and Block-Cyclic Distributions

If the amount of work differs for different elements of a matrix, a block distribution can potentially lead to load imbalances. A classic example of this phenomenon is LU factorization of a matrix, in which the amount of computation increases from the top left to the bottom right of the matrix.

Example 3.10   Dense LU factorization

In its simplest form, the LU factorization algorithm factors a nonsingular square matrix A into the product of a lower triangular matrix L with a unit diagonal and an upper triangular matrix U. Algorithm 3.3 shows the serial algorithm. Let A be an

$$
\begin{pmatrix} A_{1,1} & A_{1,2} & A_{1,3} \\ A_{2,1} & A_{2,2} & A_{2,3} \\ A_{3,1} & A_{3,2} & A_{3,3} \end{pmatrix} \rightarrow \begin{pmatrix} L_{1,1} & 0 & 0 \\ L_{2,1} & L_{2,2} & 0 \\ L_{3,1} & L_{3,2} & L_{3,3} \end{pmatrix} \cdot \begin{pmatrix} U_{1,1} & U_{1,2} & U_{1,3} \\ 0 & U_{2,2} & U_{2,3} \\ 0 & 0 & U_{3,3} \end{pmatrix}
$$

1: $A_{1,1} \rightarrow L_{1,1}U_{1,1}$

2: $L_{2,1} = A_{2,1}U_{1,1}^{-1}$

3: $L_{3,1} = A_{3,1}U_{1,1}^{-1}$

4: $U_{1,2} = L_{1,1}^{-1}A_{1,2}$

5: $U_{1,3} = L_{1,1}^{-1}A_{1,3}$

6: $A_{2,2} = A_{2,2} - L_{2,1}U_{1,2}$

7: $A_{3,2} = A_{3,2} - L_{3,1}U_{1,2}$

8: $A_{2,3} = A_{2,3} - L_{2,1}U_{1,3}$

9: $A_{3,3} = A_{3,3} - L_{3,1}U_{1,3}$

10: $A_{2,2} \rightarrow L_{2,2}U_{2,2}$

11: $L_{3,2} = A_{3,2}U_{2,2}^{-1}$

12: $U_{2,3} = L_{2,2}^{-1}A_{2,3}$

13: $A_{3,3} = A_{3,3} - L_{3,2}U_{2,3}$

14: $A_{3,3} \rightarrow L_{3,3}U_{3,3}$

Figure 3.27 A decomposition of LU factorization into 14 tasks.

$n \times n$ matrix with rows and columns numbered from 1 to n. The factorization process consists of n major steps – each consisting of an iteration of the outer loop starting at Line 3 in Algorithm 3.3. In step k, first, the partial column $A[k + 1 : n, k]$ is divided by $A[k, k]$. Then, the outer product $A[k + 1 : n, k] \times A[k, k + 1 : n]$ is subtracted from the $(n - k) \times (n - k)$ submatrix $A[k + 1 : n, k + 1 : n]$. In a practical implementation of LU factorization, separate arrays are not used for L and U and A is modified to store L and U in its lower and upper triangular parts, respectively. The 1's on the principal diagonal of L are implicit and the diagonal entries actually belong to U after factorization.

Figure 3.27 shows a possible decomposition of LU factorization into 14 tasks using a 3 × 3 block partitioning of the matrix and using a block version of Algorithm 3.3. ∎

For each iteration of the outer loop $k := 1$ to n, the next nested loop in Algorithm 3.3 goes from $k + 1$ to n. In other words, the active part of the matrix, as shown in Figure 3.28, shrinks towards the bottom right corner of the matrix as the computation proceeds. Therefore, in a block distribution, the processes assigned to the beginning rows and columns (i.e., left rows and top columns) would perform far less work than those assigned to the later rows and columns. For example, consider the decomposition for LU factorization shown in Figure 3.27 with a 3 × 3 two-dimensional block partitioning of the matrix. If we map all tasks associated with a certain block onto a process in a 9-process ensemble, then a significant amount of idle time will result. First, computing different blocks of the matrix requires different amounts of work. This is illustrated in Figure 3.29. For example, computing the final value of $A_{1,1}$ (which is actually $L_{1,1}U_{1,1}$) requires only one task – Task 1. On the other hand, computing the final value of $A_{3,3}$ requires three tasks – Task 9, Task 13, and Task 14. Secondly, the process working on a block may idle even when there are unfinished tasks associated with that block. This idling can occur if the constraints imposed by the task-dependency graph do not allow the remaining tasks on this process to

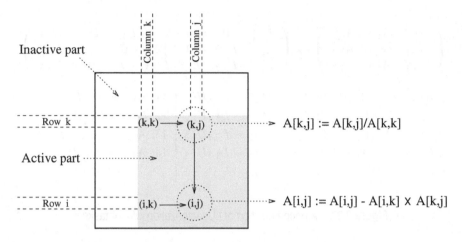

Figure 3.28 A typical computation in Gaussian elimination and the active part of the coefficient matrix during the kth iteration of the outer loop.

proceed until one or more tasks mapped onto other processes are completed.

The ***block-cyclic distribution*** is a variation of the block distribution scheme that can be used to alleviate the load-imbalance and idling problems. A detailed description of LU factorization with block-cyclic mapping is covered in Chapter 8, where it is shown how a block-cyclic mapping leads to a substantially more balanced work distribution than in Figure 3.29. The central idea behind a block-cyclic distribution is to partition an array into many more blocks than the number of available processes. Then we assign the partitions (and the associated tasks) to processes in a round-robin manner so that each process gets several non-adjacent blocks. More precisely, in a one-dimensional block-cyclic distribution of a matrix among p processes, the rows (columns) of an $n \times n$ matrix are divided into αp groups of $n/(\alpha p)$ consecutive rows (columns), where $1 \leq \alpha \leq n/p$. Now, these

P_0 T_1	P_3 T_4	P_6 T_5
P_1 T_2	P_4 T_6 T_{10}	P_7 T_8 T_{12}
P_2 T_3	P_5 T_7 T_{11}	P_8 T_9 T_{13} T_{14}

Figure 3.29 A naive mapping of LU factorization tasks onto processes based on a two-dimensional block distribution.

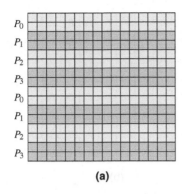

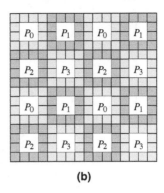

(a) **(b)**

Figure 3.30 Examples of one- and two-dimensional block-cyclic distributions among four processes. (a) The rows of the array are grouped into blocks each consisting of two rows, resulting in eight blocks of rows. These blocks are distributed to four processes in a wraparound fashion. (b) The matrix is blocked into 16 blocks each of size 4×4, and it is mapped onto a 2×2 grid of processes in a wraparound fashion.

blocks are distributed among the p processes in a wraparound fashion such that block b_i is assigned to process $P_{i\%p}$ ('%' is the modulo operator). This distribution assigns α blocks of the matrix to each process, but each subsequent block that gets assigned to the same process is p blocks away. We can obtain a two-dimensional block-cyclic distribution of an $n \times n$ array by partitioning it into square blocks of size $\alpha\sqrt{p} \times \alpha\sqrt{p}$ and distributing them on a hypothetical $\sqrt{p} \times \sqrt{p}$ array of processes in a wraparound fashion. Similarly, the block-cyclic distribution can be extended to arrays of higher dimensions. Figure 3.30 illustrates one- and two-dimensional block cyclic distributions of a two-dimensional array.

The reason why a block-cyclic distribution is able to significantly reduce the amount of idling is that all processes have a sampling of tasks from all parts of the matrix. As a result, even if different parts of the matrix require different amounts of work, the overall work on each process balances out. Also, since the tasks assigned to a process belong to different parts of the matrix, there is a good chance that at least some of them are ready for execution at any given time.

Note that if we increase α to its upper limit of n/p, then each block is a single row (column) of the matrix in a one-dimensional block-cyclic distribution and a single element of the matrix in a two-dimensional block-cyclic distribution. Such a distribution is known as a *cyclic distribution*. A cyclic distribution is an extreme case of a block-cyclic distribution and can result in an almost perfect load balance due to the extreme fine-grained underlying decomposition. However, since a process does not have any contiguous data to work on, the resulting lack of locality may result in serious performance penalties. Additionally, such a decomposition usually leads to a high degree of interaction relative to the amount computation in each task. The lower limit of 1 for the value of α results in maximum locality and interaction optimality, but the distribution degenerates to a block distribution. Therefore, an appropriate value of α must be used to strike a balance between interaction

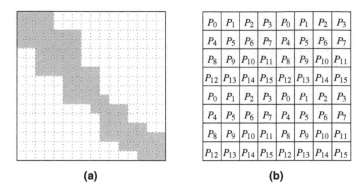

P_0	P_1	P_2	P_3	P_0	P_1	P_2	P_3
P_4	P_5	P_6	P_7	P_4	P_5	P_6	P_7
P_8	P_9	P_{10}	P_{11}	P_8	P_9	P_{10}	P_{11}
P_{12}	P_{13}	P_{14}	P_{15}	P_{12}	P_{13}	P_{14}	P_{15}
P_0	P_1	P_2	P_3	P_0	P_1	P_2	P_3
P_4	P_5	P_6	P_7	P_4	P_5	P_6	P_7
P_8	P_9	P_{10}	P_{11}	P_8	P_9	P_{10}	P_{11}
P_{12}	P_{13}	P_{14}	P_{15}	P_{12}	P_{13}	P_{14}	P_{15}

(a)   (b)

Figure 3.31   Using the block-cyclic distribution shown in (b) to distribute the computations performed in array (a) will lead to load imbalances.

conservation and load balance.

As in the case of block-distributions, higher dimensional block-cyclic distributions are usually preferable as they tend to incur a lower volume of inter-task interaction.

Randomized Block Distributions

A block-cyclic distribution may not always be able to balance computations when the distribution of work has some special patterns. For example, consider the sparse matrix shown in Figure 3.31(a) in which the shaded areas correspond to regions containing non-zero elements. If this matrix is distributed using a two-dimensional block-cyclic distribution, as illustrated in Figure 3.31(b), then we will end up assigning more non-zero blocks to the diagonal processes P_0, P_5, P_{10}, and P_{15} than on any other processes. In fact some processes, like P_{12}, will not get any work.

Randomized block distribution, a more general form of the block distribution, can be used in situations illustrated in Figure 3.31. Just like a block-cyclic distribution, load balance is sought by partitioning the array into many more blocks than the number of available processes. However, the blocks are uniformly and randomly distributed among the processes. A one-dimensional randomized block distribution can be achieved as follows. A vector V of length αp (which is equal to the number of blocks) is used and $V[j]$ is set to j for $0 \le j < \alpha p$. Now, V is randomly permuted, and process P_i is assigned the blocks stored in $V[i\alpha \ldots (i + 1)\alpha - 1]$. Figure 3.32 illustrates this for $p = 4$ and $\alpha = 3$. A two-dimensional randomized block distribution of an $n \times n$ array can be computed similarly by randomly permuting two vectors of length $\alpha\sqrt{p}$ each and using them to choose the row and column indices of the blocks to be assigned to each process. As illustrated in Figure 3.33, the random block distribution is more effective in load balancing the computations performed in Figure 3.31.

Graph Partitioning   The array-based distribution schemes that we described so far are quite effective in balancing the computations and minimizing the interactions for a wide

$$V = [0, 1, 2, 3, 4, 5, 6, 7, 8, 9, 10, 11]$$

$$\text{random}(V) = [8, 2, 6, 0, 3, 7, 11, 1, 9, 5, 4, 10]$$

$$\text{mapping} = 8 \ 2 \ 6 \ 0 \ 3 \ 7 \ 11 \ 1 \ 9 \ 5 \ 4 \ 10$$

$$P_0 \quad P_1 \quad P_2 \quad P_3$$

Figure 3.32   A one-dimensional randomized block mapping of 12 blocks onto four process (i.e., $\alpha = 3$).

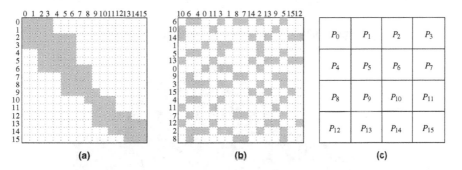

(a)   (b)   (c)

Figure 3.33   Using a two-dimensional random block distribution shown in (b) to distribute the computations performed in array (a), as shown in (c).

range of algorithms that use dense matrices and have structured and regular interaction patterns. However, there are many algorithms that operate on sparse data structures and for which the pattern of interaction among data elements is data dependent and highly irregular. Numerical simulations of physical phenomena provide a large source of such type of computations. In these computations, the physical domain is discretized and represented by a mesh of elements. The simulation of the physical phenomenon being modeled then involves computing the values of certain physical quantities at each mesh point. The computation at a mesh point usually requires data corresponding to that mesh point and to the points that are adjacent to it in the mesh. For example, Figure 3.34 shows a mesh imposed on Lake Superior. The simulation of a physical phenomenon such the dispersion of a water contaminant in the lake would now involve computing the level of contamination at each vertex of this mesh at various intervals of time.

Since, in general, the amount of computation at each point is the same, the load can be easily balanced by simply assigning the same number of mesh points to each process. However, if a distribution of the mesh points to processes does not strive to keep nearby mesh points together, then it may lead to high interaction overheads due to excessive data sharing. For example, if each process receives a random set of points as illustrated in Figure 3.35, then each process will need to access a large set of points belonging to other

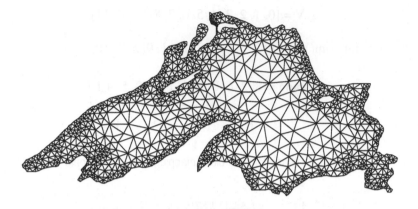

Figure 3.34 A mesh used to model Lake Superior.

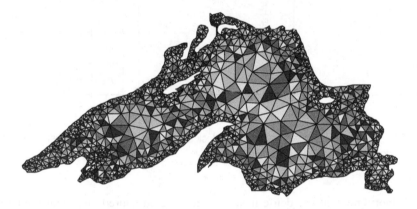

Figure 3.35 A random distribution of the mesh elements to eight processes.

processes to complete computations for its assigned portion of the mesh.

Ideally, we would like to distribute the mesh points in a way that balances the load and at the same time minimizes the amount of data that each process needs to access in order to complete its computations. Therefore, we need to partition the mesh into p parts such that each part contains roughly the same number of mesh-points or vertices, and the number of edges that cross partition boundaries (i.e., those edges that connect points belonging to two different partitions) is minimized. Finding an exact optimal partition is an NP-complete problem. However, algorithms that employ powerful heuristics are available to compute reasonable partitions. After partitioning the mesh in this manner, each one of these p partitions is assigned to one of the p processes. As a result, each process is assigned a contiguous region of the mesh such that the total number of mesh points that needs to be accessed across partition boundaries is minimized. Figure 3.36 shows a good partitioning of the Lake Superior mesh – the kind that a typical graph partitioning software would generate.

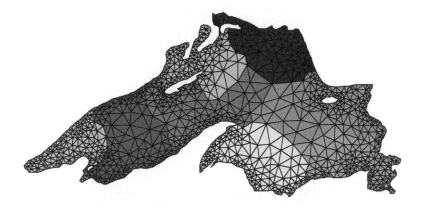

Figure 3.36 A distribution of the mesh elements to eight processes, by using a graph-partitioning algorithm.

Mappings Based on Task Partitioning

A mapping based on partitioning a task-dependency graph and mapping its nodes onto processes can be used when the computation is naturally expressible in the form of a static task-dependency graph with tasks of known sizes. As usual, this mapping must seek to achieve the often conflicting objectives of minimizing idle time and minimizing the interaction time of the parallel algorithm. Determining an optimal mapping for a general task-dependency graph is an NP-complete problem. However, specific situations often lend themselves to a simpler optimal or acceptable approximate solution.

As a simple example of a mapping based on task partitioning, consider a task-dependency graph that is a perfect binary tree. Such a task-dependency graph can occur in practical problems with recursive decomposition, such as the decomposition for finding the minimum of a list of numbers (Figure 3.9). Figure 3.37 shows a mapping of this task-dependency graph onto eight processes. It is easy to see that this mapping minimizes the interaction overhead by mapping many interdependent tasks onto the same process (i.e., the tasks along a straight branch of the tree) and others on processes only one communication link away from each other. Although there is some inevitable idling (e.g., when process 0 works on the root task, all other processes are idle), this idling is inherent in the task-dependency graph. The mapping shown in Figure 3.37 does not introduce any further idling and all tasks that are permitted to be concurrently active by the task-dependency graph are mapped onto different processes for parallel execution.

For some problems, an approximate solution to the problem of finding a good mapping can be obtained by partitioning the task-interaction graph. In the problem of modeling contaminant dispersion in Lake Superior discussed earlier in the context of data partitioning, we can define tasks such that each one of them is responsible for the computations associated with a certain mesh point. Now the mesh used to discretize the lake also acts as a task-interaction graph. Therefore, for this problem, using graph-partitioning to find a

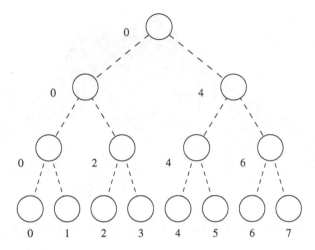

Figure 3.37 Mapping of a binary tree task-dependency graph onto a hypercube of processes.

good mapping can also be viewed as task partitioning.

Another similar problem where task partitioning is applicable is that of sparse matrix-vector multiplication discussed in Section 3.1.2. A simple mapping of the task-interaction graph of Figure 3.6 is shown in Figure 3.38. This mapping assigns tasks corresponding to four consecutive entries of b to each process. Figure 3.39 shows another partitioning for the task-interaction graph of the sparse matrix vector multiplication problem shown in Figure 3.6 for three processes. The list Ci contains the indices of b that the tasks on Process i need to access from tasks mapped onto other processes. A quick comparison of the lists $C0$, $C1$, and $C2$ in the two cases readily reveals that the mapping based on partitioning the task interaction graph entails fewer exchanges of elements of b between processes than the naive mapping.

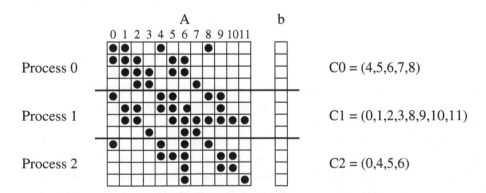

Figure 3.38 A mapping for sparse matrix-vector multiplication onto three processes. The list Ci contains the indices of b that Process i needs to access from other processes.

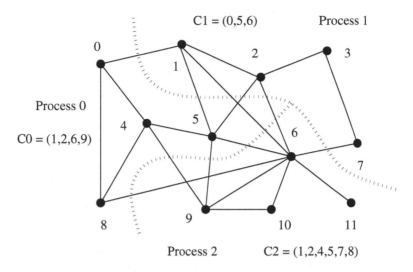

Figure 3.39 Reducing interaction overhead in sparse matrix-vector multiplication by partitioning the task-interaction graph.

Hierarchical Mappings

Certain algorithms are naturally expressed as task-dependency graphs; however, a mapping based solely on the task-dependency graph may suffer from load-imbalance or inadequate concurrency. For example, in the binary-tree task-dependency graph of Figure 3.37, only a few tasks are available for concurrent execution in the top part of the tree. If the tasks are large enough, then a better mapping can be obtained by a further decomposition of the tasks into smaller subtasks. In the case where the task-dependency graph is a binary tree with four levels, the root task can be partitioned among eight processes, the tasks at the next level can be partitioned among four processes each, followed by tasks partitioned among two processes each at the next level. The eight leaf tasks can have a one-to-one mapping onto the processes. Figure 3.40 illustrates such a hierarchical mapping. Parallel quicksort introduced in Example 3.4 has a task-dependency graph similar to the one shown in Figure 3.37, and hence is an ideal candidate for a hierarchical mapping of the type shown in Figure 3.40.

An important practical problem to which the hierarchical mapping example discussed above applies directly is that of sparse matrix factorization. The high-level computations in sparse matrix factorization are guided by a task-dependency graph which is known as an *elimination graph* (*elimination tree* if the matrix is symmetric). However, the tasks in the elimination graph (especially the ones closer to the root) usually involve substantial computations and are further decomposed into subtasks using data-decomposition. A hierarchical mapping, using task partitioning at the top layer and array partitioning at the bottom layer, is then applied to this hybrid decomposition. In general, a hierarchical mapping can have many layers and different decomposition and mapping techniques may be

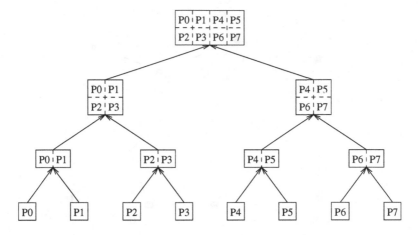

Figure 3.40 An example of hierarchical mapping of a task-dependency graph. Each node represented by an array is a supertask. The partitioning of the arrays represents subtasks, which are mapped onto eight processes.

suitable for different layers.

3.4.2   Schemes for Dynamic Mapping

Dynamic mapping is necessary in situations where a static mapping may result in a highly imbalanced distribution of work among processes or where the task-dependency graph itself if dynamic, thus precluding a static mapping. Since the primary reason for using a dynamic mapping is balancing the workload among processes, dynamic mapping is often referred to as dynamic load-balancing. Dynamic mapping techniques are usually classified as either *centralized* or *distributed*.

Centralized Schemes

In a centralized dynamic load balancing scheme, all executable tasks are maintained in a common central data structure or they are maintained by a special process or a subset of processes. If a special process is designated to manage the pool of available tasks, then it is often referred to as the *master* and the other processes that depend on the master to obtain work are referred to as *slaves*. Whenever a process has no work, it takes a portion of available work from the central data structure or the master process. Whenever a new task is generated, it is added to this centralized data structure or reported to the master process. Centralized load-balancing schemes are usually easier to implement than distributed schemes, but may have limited scalability. As more and more processes are used, the large number of accesses to the common data structure or the master process tends to become a bottleneck.

As an example of a scenario where centralized mapping may be applicable, consider the problem of sorting the entries in each row of an $n \times n$ matrix A. Serially, this can be accomplished by the following simple program segment:

```
1       for (i=1; i<n; i++)
2           sort(A[i],n);
```

Recall that the time to sort an array using some of the commonly used sorting algorithms, such as quicksort, can vary significantly depending on the initial order of the elements to be sorted. Therefore, each iteration of the loop in the program shown above can take different amounts of time. A naive mapping of the task of sorting an equal number of rows to each process may lead to load-imbalance. A possible solution to the potential load-imbalance problem in this case would be to maintain a central pool of indices of the rows that have yet to be sorted. Whenever a process is idle, it picks up an available index, deletes it, and sorts the row with that index, as long as the pool of indices is not empty. This method of scheduling the independent iterations of a loop among parallel processes is known as *self scheduling*.

The assignment of a single task to a process at a time is quite effective in balancing the computation; however, it may lead to bottlenecks in accessing the shared work queue, especially if each task (i.e., each loop iteration in this case) does not require a large enough amount of computation. If the average size of each task is M, and it takes Δ time to assign work to a process, then at most M/Δ processes can be kept busy effectively. The bottleneck can be eased by getting more than one task at a time. In *chunk scheduling*, every time a process runs out of work it gets a group of tasks. The potential problem with such a scheme is that it may lead to load-imbalances if the number of tasks (i.e., chunk) assigned in a single step is large. The danger of load-imbalance due to large chunk sizes can be reduced by decreasing the chunk-size as the program progresses. That is, initially the chunk size is large, but as the number of iterations left to be executed decreases, the chunk size also decreases. A variety of schemes have been developed for gradually adjusting the chunk size, that decrease the chunk size either linearly or non-linearly.

Distributed Schemes

In a distributed dynamic load balancing scheme, the set of executable tasks are distributed among processes which exchange tasks at run time to balance work. Each process can send work to or receive work from any other process. These methods do not suffer from the bottleneck associated with the centralized schemes. Some of the critical parameters of a distributed load balancing scheme are as follows:

- How are the sending and receiving processes paired together?

- Is the work transfer initiated by the sender or the receiver?

- How much work is transferred in each exchange? If too little work is transferred, then the receiver may not receive enough work and frequent transfers resulting in excessive interaction may be required. If too much work is transferred, then the sender may be out of work soon, again resulting in frequent transfers.

- When is the work transfer performed? For example, in receiver initiated load balancing, work may be requested when the process has actually run out of work or when the receiver has too little work left and anticipates being out of work soon.

A detailed study of each of these parameters is beyond the scope of this chapter. These load balancing schemes will be revisited in the context of parallel algorithms to which they apply when we discuss these algorithms in the later chapters – in particular, Chapter 11 in the context of parallel search algorithms.

Suitability to Parallel Architectures

Note that, in principle, both centralized and distributed mapping schemes can be implemented in both message-passing and shared-address-space paradigms. However, by its very nature any dynamic load balancing scheme requires movement of tasks from one process to another. Hence, for such schemes to be effective on message-passing computers, the size of the tasks in terms of computation should be much higher than the size of the data associated with the tasks. In a shared-address-space paradigm, the tasks don't need to be moved explicitly, although there is some implied movement of data to local caches or memory banks of processes. In general, the computational granularity of tasks to be moved can be much smaller on shared-address architecture than on message-passing architectures.

3.5 Methods for Containing Interaction Overheads

As noted earlier, reducing the interaction overhead among concurrent tasks is important for an efficient parallel program. The overhead that a parallel program incurs due to interaction among its processes depends on many factors, such as the volume of data exchanged during interactions, the frequency of interaction, the spatial and temporal pattern of interactions, etc.

In this section, we will discuss some general techniques that can be used to reduce the interaction overheads incurred by parallel programs. These techniques manipulate one or more of the three factors above in order to reduce the interaction overhead. Some of these are applicable while devising the decomposition and mapping schemes for the algorithms and some are applicable while programming the algorithm in a given paradigm. All techniques may not be applicable in all parallel programming paradigms and some of them may require support from the underlying hardware.

3.5.1 Maximizing Data Locality

In most nontrivial parallel programs, the tasks executed by different processes require access to some common data. For example, in sparse matrix-vector multiplication $y = Ab$, in which tasks correspond to computing individual elements of vector y (Figure 3.6), all elements of the input vector b need to be accessed by multiple tasks. In addition to sharing the original input data, interaction may result if processes require data generated by other processes. The interaction overheads can be reduced by using techniques that promote the use of local data or data that have been recently fetched. Data locality enhancing techniques encompass a wide range of schemes that try to minimize the volume of nonlocal data that are accessed, maximize the reuse of recently accessed data, and minimize the frequency of accesses. In many cases, these schemes are similar in nature to the data reuse optimizations often performed in modern cache based microprocessors.

Minimize Volume of Data-Exchange   A fundamental technique for reducing the interaction overhead is to minimize the overall volume of shared data that needs to be accessed by concurrent processes. This is akin to maximizing the temporal data locality, i.e., making as many of the consecutive references to the same data as possible. Clearly, performing as much of the computation as possible using locally available data obviates the need for bringing in more data into local memory or cache for a process to perform its tasks. As discussed previously, one way of achieving this is by using appropriate decomposition and mapping schemes. For example, in the case of matrix multiplication, we saw that by using a two-dimensional mapping of the computations to the processes we were able to reduce the amount of shared data (i.e., matrices A and B) that needs to be accessed by each task to $2n^2/\sqrt{p}$ as opposed to $n^2/p + n^2$ required by a one-dimensional mapping (Figure 3.26). In general, using higher dimensional distribution often helps in reducing the volume of nonlocal data that needs to be accessed.

Another way of decreasing the amount of shared data that are accessed by multiple processes is to use local data to store intermediate results, and perform the shared data access to only place the final results of the computation. For example, consider computing the dot product of two vectors of length n in parallel such that each of the p tasks multiplies n/p pairs of elements. Rather than adding each individual product of a pair of numbers to the final result, each task can first create a partial dot product of its assigned portion of the vectors of length n/p in its own local location, and only access the final shared location once to add this partial result. This will reduce the number of accesses to the shared location where the result is stored to p from n.

Minimize Frequency of Interactions   Minimizing interaction frequency is important in reducing the interaction overheads in parallel programs because there is a relatively high startup cost associated with each interaction on many architectures. Interaction frequency can be reduced by restructuring the algorithm such that shared data are accessed and used in large pieces. Thus, by amortizing the startup cost over large accesses, we can reduce the overall interaction overhead, even if such restructuring does not necessarily reduce the overall volume of shared data that need to be accessed. This is akin to increasing the spatial locality of data access, i.e., ensuring the proximity of consecutively accessed data locations. On a shared-address-space architecture, each time a word is accessed, an entire cache line containing many words is fetched. If the program is structured to have spatial locality, then fewer cache lines are accessed. On a message-passing system, spatial locality leads to fewer message-transfers over the network because each message can transfer larger amounts of useful data. The number of messages can sometimes be reduced further on a message-passing system by combining messages between the same source-destination pair into larger messages if the interaction pattern permits and if the data for multiple messages are available at the same time, albeit in separate data structures.

Sparse matrix-vector multiplication is a problem whose parallel formulation can use this technique to reduce interaction overhead. In typical applications, repeated sparse matrix-vector multiplication is performed with matrices of the same nonzero pattern but different numerical nonzero values. While solving this problem in parallel, a process interacts with others to access elements of the input vector that it may need for its local computation. Through a one-time scanning of the nonzero pattern of the rows of the sparse matrix that a process is responsible for, it can determine exactly which elements of the input vector it needs and from which processes. Then, before starting each multiplication, a process can first collect all the nonlocal entries of the input vector that it requires, and then perform an interaction-free multiplication. This strategy is far superior than trying to access a nonlocal element of the input vector as and when required in the computation.

3.5.2   Minimizing Contention and Hot Spots

Our discussion so far has been largely focused on reducing interaction overheads by directly or indirectly reducing the frequency and volume of data transfers. However, the data-access and inter-task interaction patterns can often lead to contention that can increase the overall interaction overhead. In general, contention occurs when multiple tasks try to access the same resources concurrently. Multiple simultaneous transmissions of data over the same interconnection link, multiple simultaneous accesses to the same memory block, or multiple processes sending messages to the same process at the same time, can all lead to contention. This is because only one of the multiple operations can proceed at a time and the others are queued and proceed sequentially.

Consider the problem of multiplying two matrices $C = AB$, using the two-dimensional partitioning shown in Figure 3.26(b). Let p be the number of tasks with a one-to-one mapping of tasks onto processes. Let each task be responsible for computing a unique $C_{i,j}$, for $0 \le i, j < \sqrt{p}$. The straightforward way of performing this computation is for $C_{i,j}$ to be computed according to the following formula (written in matrix-block notation):

$$C_{i,j} = \sum_{k=0}^{\sqrt{p}-1} A_{i,k} * B_{k,j} \tag{3.1}$$

Looking at the memory access patterns of the above equation, we see that at any one of the $\sqrt{p}$ steps, $\sqrt{p}$ tasks will be accessing the same block of A and B. In particular, all the tasks that work on the same row of C will be accessing the same block of A. For example, all $\sqrt{p}$

processes computing $C_{0,0}, C_{0,1}, \ldots, C_{0,\sqrt{p}-1}$ will attempt to read $A_{0,0}$ at once. Similarly, all the tasks working on the same column of C will be accessing the same block of B. The need to concurrently access these blocks of matrices A and B will create contention on both NUMA shared-address-space and message-passing parallel architectures.

One way of reducing contention is to redesign the parallel algorithm to access data in contention-free patterns. For the matrix multiplication algorithm, this contention can be eliminated by modifying the order in which the block multiplications are performed in Equation 3.1. A contention-free way of performing these block-multiplications is to compute $C_{i,j}$ by using the formula

$$C_{i,j} = \sum_{k=0}^{\sqrt{p}-1} A_{i,(i+j+k)\%\sqrt{p}} * B_{(i+j+k)\%\sqrt{p},j} \tag{3.2}$$

where '%' denotes the modulo operation. By using this formula, all the tasks $P_{*,j}$ that work on the same row of C will be accessing block $A_{*,(*+j+k)\%\sqrt{p}}$, which is different for each task. Similarly, all the tasks $P_{i,*}$ that work on the same column of C will be accessing block $B_{(i+*+k)\%\sqrt{p},*}$, which is also different for each task. Thus, by simply rearranging the order in which the block-multiplications are performed, we can completely eliminate the contention. For example, among the processes computing the first block row of C, the process computing $C_{0,j}$ will access $A_{0,j}$ from the first block row of A instead of $A_{0,0}$.

Centralized schemes for dynamic mapping (Section 3.4.2) are a frequent source of contention for shared data structures or communication channels leading to the master process. The contention may be reduced by choosing a distributed mapping scheme over a centralized one, even though the former may be harder to implement.

3.5.3 Overlapping Computations with Interactions

The amount of time that processes spend waiting for shared data to arrive or to receive additional work after an interaction has been initiated can be reduced, often substantially, by doing some useful computations during this waiting time. There are a number of techniques that can be used to overlap computations with interactions.

A simple way of overlapping is to initiate an interaction early enough so that it is completed before it is needed for computation. To achieve this, we must be able to identify computations that can be performed before the interaction and do not depend on it. Then the parallel program must be structured to initiate the interaction at an earlier point in the execution than it is needed in the original algorithm. Typically, this is possible if the interaction pattern is spatially and temporally static (and therefore, predictable) or if multiple tasks that are ready for execution are available on the same process so that if one blocks to wait for an interaction to complete, the process can work on another task. The reader should note that by increasing the number of parallel tasks to promote computation-interaction overlap, we are reducing the granularity of the tasks, which in general tends to increase overheads. Therefore, this technique must be used judiciously.

In certain dynamic mapping schemes, as soon as a process runs out of work, it requests and gets additional work from another process. It then waits for the request to be serviced. If the process can anticipate that it is going to run out of work and initiate a work transfer interaction in advance, then it may continue towards finishing the tasks at hand while the request for more work is being serviced. Depending on the problem, estimating the amount of remaining work may be easy or hard.

In most cases, overlapping computations with interaction requires support from the programming paradigm, the operating system, and the hardware. The programming paradigm must provide a mechanism to allow interactions and computations to proceed concurrently. This mechanism should be supported by the underlying hardware. Disjoint address-space paradigms and architectures usually provide this support via non-blocking message passing primitives. The programming paradigm provides functions for sending and receiving messages that return control to the user's program before they have actually completed. Thus, the program can use these primitives to initiate the interactions, and then proceed with the computations. If the hardware permits computation to proceed concurrently with message transfers, then the interaction overhead can be reduced significantly.

On a shared-address-space architecture, the overlapping of computations and interaction is often assisted by prefetching hardware. In this case, an access to shared data is nothing more than a regular load or store instruction. The prefetch hardware can anticipate the memory addresses that will need to be accessed in the immediate future, and can initiate the access in advance of when they are needed. In the absence of prefetching hardware, the same effect can be achieved by a compiler that detects the access pattern and places pseudo-references to certain key memory locations before these locations are actually utilized by the computation. The degree of success of this scheme is dependent upon the available structure in the program that can be inferred by the prefetch hardware and by the degree of independence with which the prefetch hardware can function while computation is in progress.

3.5.4 Replicating Data or Computations

Replication of data or computations is another technique that may be useful in reducing interaction overheads.

In some parallel algorithms, multiple processes may require frequent read-only access to shared data structure, such as a hash-table, in an irregular pattern. Unless the additional memory requirements are prohibitive, it may be best in a situation like this to replicate a copy of the shared data structure on each process so that after the initial interaction during replication, all subsequent accesses to this data structure are free of any interaction overhead.

In the shared-address-space paradigm, replication of frequently accessed read-only data is often affected by the caches without explicit programmer intervention. Explicit data replication is particularly suited for architectures and programming paradigms in which read-only access to shared data is significantly more expensive or harder to express than local data accesses. Therefore, the message-passing programming paradigm benefits the most from data replication, which may reduce interaction overhead and also significantly simplify the writing of the parallel program.

Data replication, however, does not come without its own cost. Data replication increases the memory requirements of a parallel program. The aggregate amount of memory required to store the replicated data increases linearly with the number of concurrent processes. This may limit the size of the problem that can be solved on a given parallel computer. For this reason, data replication must be used selectively to replicate relatively small amounts of data.

In addition to input data, the processes in a parallel program often share intermediate results. In some situations, it may be more cost-effective for a process to compute these intermediate results than to get them from another process that generates them. In such situations, interaction overhead can be traded for replicated computation. For example, while performing the Fast Fourier Transform (see Section 13.2.3 for more details), on an N-point series, N distinct powers of ω or "twiddle factors" are computed and used at various points in the computation. In a parallel implementation of FFT, different processes require overlapping subsets of these N twiddle factors. In a message-passing paradigm, it is best for each process to locally compute all the twiddle factors it needs. Although the parallel algorithm may perform many more twiddle factor computations than the serial algorithm, it may still be faster than sharing the twiddle factors.

3.5.5 Using Optimized Collective Interaction Operations

As discussed in Section 3.3.2, often the interaction patterns among concurrent activities are static and regular. A class of such static and regular interaction patterns are those that are performed by groups of tasks, and they are used to achieve regular data accesses or to perform certain type of computations on distributed data. A number of key such *collective* interaction operations have been identified that appear frequently in many parallel algorithms. Broadcasting some data to all the processes or adding up numbers, each belonging to a different process, are examples of such collective operations. The collective data-sharing operations can be classified into three categories. The first category contains operations that are used by the tasks to access data, the second category of operations are used to perform some communication-intensive computations, and finally, the third category is used for synchronization.

Highly optimized implementations of these collective operations have been developed that minimize the overheads due to data transfer as well as contention. Chapter 4 describes algorithms for implementing some of the commonly used collective interaction operations. Optimized implementations of these operations are available in library form from the vendors of most parallel computers, e.g., MPI (message passing interface). As a result, the algorithm designer does not need to think about how these operations are implemented and needs to focus only on the functionality achieved by these operations. However, as discussed in Section 3.5.6, sometimes the interaction pattern may make it worthwhile for

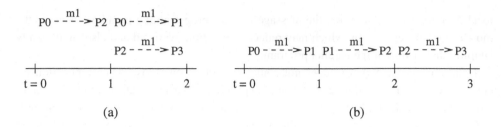

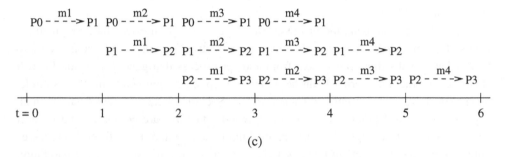

Figure 3.41   Illustration of overlapping interactions in broadcasting data from one to four processes.

the parallel programmer to implement one's own collective communication procedure.

3.5.6   Overlapping Interactions with Other Interactions

If the data-transfer capacity of the underlying hardware permits, then overlapping interactions between multiple pairs of processes can reduce the effective volume of communication. As an example of overlapping interactions, consider the commonly used collective communication operation of one-to-all broadcast in a message-passing paradigm with four processes P_0, P_1, P_2, and P_3. A commonly used algorithm to broadcast some data from P_0 to all other processes works as follows. In the first step, P_0 sends the data to P_2. In the second step, P_0 sends the data to P_1, and concurrently, P_2 sends the same data that it had received from P_0 to P_3. The entire operation is thus complete in two steps because the two interactions of the second step require only one time step. This operation is illustrated in Figure 3.41(a). On the other hand, a naive broadcast algorithm would send the data from P_0 to P_1 to P_2 to P_3, thereby consuming three steps as illustrated in Figure 3.41(b).

Interestingly, however, there are situations when the naive broadcast algorithm shown in Figure 3.41(b) may be adapted to actually increase the amount of overlap. Assume that a parallel algorithm needs to broadcast four data structures one after the other. The entire interaction would require eight steps using the first two-step broadcast algorithm. However, using the naive algorithm accomplishes the interaction in only six steps as shown in Figure 3.41(c). In the first step, P_0 sends the first message to P_1. In the second step P_0 sends the second message to P_1 while P_1 simultaneously sends the first message to P_2. In the third step, P_0 sends the third message to P_1, P_1 sends the second message to P_2, and P_2 sends the first message to P_3. Proceeding similarly in a pipelined fashion, the last of the four messages is sent out of P_0 after four steps and reaches P_3 in six. Since this method is rather expensive for a single broadcast operation, it is unlikely to be included in a collective communication library. However, the programmer must infer from the interaction pattern of the algorithm that in this scenario, it is better to make an exception to the suggestion of Section 3.5.5 and write your own collective communication function.

3.6 Parallel Algorithm Models

Having discussed the techniques for decomposition, mapping, and minimizing interaction overheads, we now present some of the commonly used parallel algorithm models. An algorithm model is typically a way of structuring a parallel algorithm by selecting a decomposition and mapping technique and applying the appropriate strategy to minimize interactions.

3.6.1 The Data-Parallel Model

The *data-parallel model* is one of the simplest algorithm models. In this model, the tasks are statically or semi-statically mapped onto processes and each task performs similar operations on different data. This type of parallelism that is a result of identical operations being applied concurrently on different data items is called **data parallelism**. The work may be done in phases and the data operated upon in different phases may be different. Typically, data-parallel computation phases are interspersed with interactions to synchronize the tasks or to get fresh data to the tasks. Since all tasks perform similar computations, the decomposition of the problem into tasks is usually based on data partitioning because a uniform partitioning of data followed by a static mapping is sufficient to guarantee load balance.

Data-parallel algorithms can be implemented in both shared-address-space and message-passing paradigms. However, the partitioned address-space in a message-passing paradigm may allow better control of placement, and thus may offer a better handle on locality. On the other hand, shared-address space can ease the programming effort, especially if the distribution of data is different in different phases of the algorithm.

Interaction overheads in the data-parallel model can be minimized by choosing a locality preserving decomposition and, if applicable, by overlapping computation and interaction and by using optimized collective interaction routines. A key characteristic of data-parallel problems is that for most problems, the degree of data parallelism increases with the size of the problem, making it possible to use more processes to effectively solve larger problems.

An example of a data-parallel algorithm is dense matrix multiplication described in Section 3.1.1. In the decomposition shown in Figure 3.10, all tasks are identical; they are applied to different data.

3.6.2 The Task Graph Model

As discussed in Section 3.1, the computations in any parallel algorithm can be viewed as a task-dependency graph. The task-dependency graph may be either trivial, as in the case of matrix multiplication, or nontrivial (Problem 3.5). However, in certain parallel algorithms, the task-dependency graph is explicitly used in mapping. In the *task graph model*, the interrelationships among the tasks are utilized to promote locality or to reduce interaction costs. This model is typically employed to solve problems in which the amount of data associated with the tasks is large relative to the amount of computation associated with them. Usually, tasks are mapped statically to help optimize the cost of data movement among tasks. Sometimes a decentralized dynamic mapping may be used, but even then, the mapping uses the information about the task-dependency graph structure and the interaction pattern of tasks to minimize interaction overhead. Work is more easily shared in paradigms with globally addressable space, but mechanisms are available to share work in disjoint address space.

Typical interaction-reducing techniques applicable to this model include reducing the volume and frequency of interaction by promoting locality while mapping the tasks based on the interaction pattern of tasks, and using asynchronous interaction methods to overlap the interaction with computation.

Examples of algorithms based on the task graph model include parallel quicksort (Section 9.4.1), sparse matrix factorization, and many parallel algorithms derived via divide-and-conquer decomposition. This type of parallelism that is naturally expressed by independent tasks in a task-dependency graph is called *task parallelism*.

3.6.3 The Work Pool Model

The *work pool* or the *task pool* model is characterized by a dynamic mapping of tasks onto processes for load balancing in which any task may potentially be performed by any process. There is no desired premapping of tasks onto processes. The mapping may be centralized or decentralized. Pointers to the tasks may be stored in a physically shared list, priority queue, hash table, or tree, or they could be stored in a physically distributed data structure. The work may be statically available in the beginning, or could be dynamically generated; i.e., the processes may generate work and add it to the global (possibly distributed) work pool. If the work is generated dynamically and a decentralized mapping is used, then a termination detection algorithm (Section 11.4.4) would be required so that all processes can actually detect the completion of the entire program (i.e., exhaustion of all potential tasks) and stop looking for more work.

In the message-passing paradigm, the work pool model is typically used when the amount of data associated with tasks is relatively small compared to the computation associated with the tasks. As a result, tasks can be readily moved around without causing too much data interaction overhead. The granularity of the tasks can be adjusted to attain the desired level of tradeoff between load-imbalance and the overhead of accessing the work pool for adding and extracting tasks.

Parallelization of loops by chunk scheduling (Section 3.4.2) or related methods is an example of the use of the work pool model with centralized mapping when the tasks are statically available. Parallel tree search where the work is represented by a centralized or distributed data structure is an example of the use of the work pool model where the tasks are generated dynamically.

3.6.4 The Master-Slave Model

In the *master-slave* or the *manager-worker* model, one or more master processes generate work and allocate it to worker processes. The tasks may be allocated *a priori* if the manager can estimate the size of the tasks or if a random mapping can do an adequate job of load balancing. In another scenario, workers are assigned smaller pieces of work at different times. The latter scheme is preferred if it is time consuming for the master to generate work and hence it is not desirable to make all workers wait until the master has generated all work pieces. In some cases, work may need to be performed in phases, and work in each phase must finish before work in the next phases can be generated. In this case, the manager may cause all workers to synchronize after each phase. Usually, there is no desired premapping of work to processes, and any worker can do any job assigned to it. The manager-worker model can be generalized to the hierarchical or multi-level manager-worker model in which the top-level manager feeds large chunks of tasks to second-level managers, who further subdivide the tasks among their own workers and may perform part of the work themselves. This model is generally equally suitable to shared-address-space or message-passing paradigms since the interaction is naturally two-way; i.e., the manager knows that it needs to give out work and workers know that they need to get work from the manager.

While using the master-slave model, care should be taken to ensure that the master does not become a bottleneck, which may happen if the tasks are too small (or the workers are relatively fast). The granularity of tasks should be chosen such that the cost of doing work dominates the cost of transferring work and the cost of synchronization. Asynchronous interaction may help overlap interaction and the computation associated with work genera-tion by the master. It may also reduce waiting times if the nature of requests from workers is non-deterministic.

3.6.5 The Pipeline or Producer-Consumer Model

In the *pipeline model*, a stream of data is passed on through a succession of processes, each of which perform some task on it. This simultaneous execution of different programs on a data stream is called **stream parallelism**. With the exception of the process initiating the pipeline, the arrival of new data triggers the execution of a new task by a process in the pipeline. The processes could form such pipelines in the shape of linear or multidi-mensional arrays, trees, or general graphs with or without cycles. A pipeline is a chain of producers and consumers. Each process in the pipeline can be viewed as a consumer of a sequence of data items for the process preceding it in the pipeline and as a producer of data for the process following it in the pipeline. The pipeline does not need to be a linear chain; it can be a directed graph. The pipeline model usually involves a static mapping of tasks onto processes.

Load balancing is a function of task granularity. The larger the granularity, the longer it takes to fill up the pipeline, i.e. for the trigger produced by the first process in the chain to propagate to the last process, thereby keeping some of the processes waiting. However, too fine a granularity may increase interaction overheads because processes will need to inter-act to receive fresh data after smaller pieces of computation. The most common interaction reduction technique applicable to this model is overlapping interaction with computation.

An example of a two-dimensional pipeline is the parallel LU factorization algorithm, which is discussed in detail in Section 8.3.1.

3.6.6 Hybrid Models

In some cases, more than one model may be applicable to the problem at hand, resulting in a hybrid algorithm model. A hybrid model may be composed either of multiple mod-els applied hierarchically or multiple models applied sequentially to different phases of a parallel algorithm. In some cases, an algorithm formulation may have characteristics of more than one algorithm model. For instance, data may flow in a pipelined manner in a pattern guided by a task-dependency graph. In another scenario, the major computation may be described by a task-dependency graph, but each node of the graph may represent a supertask comprising multiple subtasks that may be suitable for data-parallel or pipelined parallelism. Parallel quicksort (Sections 3.2.5 and 9.4.1) is one of the applications for which a hybrid model is ideally suited.

3.7 Bibliographic Remarks

Various texts, such as those by Wilson [Wil95], Akl [Akl97], Hwang and Xu [HX98], Wilkinson and Allen [WA99], and Culler and Singh [CSG98], among others, present sim-ilar or slightly varying models for parallel programs and steps in developing parallel algo-rithms. The book by Goedecker and Hoisie [GH01] is among the relatively few textbooks that focus on the practical aspects of writing high-performance parallel programs. Kwok and Ahmad [KA99a, KA99b] present comprehensive surveys of techniques for mapping tasks onto processes.

Most of the algorithms used in this chapter as examples are discussed in detail in other chapters in this book dedicated to the respective class of problems. Please refer to the bibliographic remarks in those chapters for further references on these algorithms.

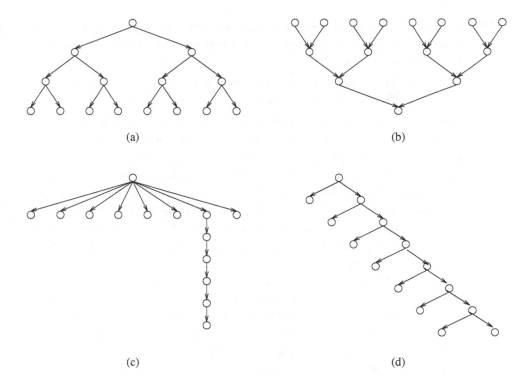

Figure 3.42   Task-dependency graphs for Problem 3.2.

Problems

3.1   In Example 3.2, each union and intersection operation can be performed in time proportional to the sum of the number of records in the two input tables. Based on this, construct the weighted task-dependency graphs corresponding to Figures 3.2 and 3.3, where the weight of each node is equivalent to the amount of work required by the corresponding task. What is the average degree of concurrency of each graph?

3.2   For the task graphs given in Figure 3.42, determine the following:

1.   Maximum degree of concurrency.

2.   Critical path length.

3.   Maximum achievable speedup over one process assuming that an arbitrarily large number of processes is available.

4.   The minimum number of processes needed to obtain the maximum possible speedup.

5.   The maximum achievable speedup if the number of processes is limited to (a) 2, (b) 4, and (c) 8.

3.3 What are the average degrees of concurrency and critical-path lengths of task-dependency graphs corresponding to the decompositions for matrix multiplication shown in Figures 3.10 and 3.11?

3.4 Let d be the maximum degree of concurrency in a task-dependency graph with t tasks and a critical-path length l. Prove that $\lceil \frac{t}{l} \rceil \leq d \leq t - l + 1$.

3.5 Consider LU factorization of a dense matrix shown in Algorithm 3.3. Figure 3.27 shows the decomposition of LU factorization into 14 tasks based on a two-dimensional partitioning of the matrix A into nine blocks $A_{i,j}$, $1 \leq i, j \leq 3$. The blocks of A are modified into corresponding blocks of L and U as a result of factorization. The diagonal blocks of L are lower triangular submatrices with unit diagonals and the diagonal blocks of U are upper triangular submatrices. Task 1 factors the submatrix $A_{1,1}$ using Algorithm 3.3. Tasks 2 and 3 implement the block versions of the loop on Lines 4–6 of Algorithm 3.3. Tasks 4 and 5 are the upper-triangular counterparts of tasks 2 and 3. The element version of LU factorization in Algorithm 3.3 does not show these steps because the diagonal entries of L are 1; however, a block version must compute a block-row of U as a product of the inverse of the corresponding diagonal block of L with the block-row of A. Tasks 6–9 implement the block version of the loops on Lines 7–11 of Algorithm 3.3. Thus, Tasks 1–9 correspond to the block version of the first iteration of the outermost loop of Algorithm 3.3. The remainder of the tasks complete the factorization of A. Draw a task-dependency graph corresponding to the decomposition shown in Figure 3.27.

3.6 Enumerate the critical paths in the decomposition of LU factorization shown in Figure 3.27.

3.7 Show an efficient mapping of the task-dependency graph of the decomposition shown in Figure 3.27 onto three processes. Prove informally that your mapping is the best possible mapping for three processes.

3.8 Describe and draw an efficient mapping of the task-dependency graph of the decomposition shown in Figure 3.27 onto four processes and prove that your mapping is the best possible mapping for four processes.

3.9 Assuming that each task takes a unit amount of time,[1] which of the two mappings – the one onto three processes or the one onto four processes – solves the problem faster?

3.10 Prove that block steps 1 through 14 in Figure 3.27 with block size b (i.e., each $A_{i,j}$, $L_{i,j}$, and $U_{i,j}$ is a $b \times b$ submatrix) are mathematically equivalent to running the algorithm of Algorithm 3.3 on an $n \times n$ matrix A, where $n = 3b$.
Hint: Using induction on b is one possible approach.

---

[1] In practice, for a block size $b \gg 1$, Tasks 1, 10, and 14 require about $2/3b^3$ arithmetic operations; Tasks 2, 3, 4, 5, 11, and 12 require about b^3 operations; and Tasks 6, 7, 8, 9, and 13 require about $2b^3$ operations.

```
1.    procedure FFT_like_pattern(A, n)
2.    begin
3.        m := log₂ n;
4.        for j := 0 to m − 1 do
5.            k := 2ʲ;
6.            for i := 0 to n − 1 do
7.                A[i] := A[i] + A[i XOR 2ʲ];
8.        endfor
9.    end FFT_like_pattern
```

Algorithm 3.4   A sample serial program to be parallelized.

3.11   Figure 3.27 shows the decomposition into 14 tasks of LU factorization of a matrix split into blocks using a 3×3 two-dimensional partitioning. If an $m \times m$ partitioning is used, derive an expression for the number of tasks $t(m)$ as a function of m in a decomposition along similar lines.
Hint: Show that $t(m) = t(m − 1) + m^2$.

3.12   In the context of Problem 3.11, derive an expression for the maximum degree of concurrency $d(m)$ as a function of m.

3.13   In the context of Problem 3.11, derive an expression for the critical-path length $l(m)$ as a function of m.

3.14   Show efficient mappings for the decompositions for the database query problem shown in Figures 3.2 and 3.3. What is the maximum number of processes that you would use in each case?

3.15   In the algorithm shown in Algorithm 3.4, assume a decomposition such that each execution of Line 7 is a task. Draw a task-dependency graph and a task-interaction graph.

3.16   In Algorithm 3.4, if $n = 16$, devise a good mapping for 16 processes.

3.17   In Algorithm 3.4, if $n = 16$, devise a good mapping for 8 processes.

3.18   Repeat Problems 3.15, 3.16, and 3.17 if the statement of Line 3 in Algorithm 3.4 is changed to $m = (\log_2 n) − 1$.

3.19   Consider a simplified version of bucket-sort. You are given an array A of n random integers in the range $[1 \ldots r]$ as input. The output data consist of r buckets, such that at the end of the algorithm, Bucket i contains indices of all the elements in A that are equal to i.

   • Describe a decomposition based on partitioning the input data (i.e., the array A) and an appropriate mapping onto p processes. Describe briefly how the resulting parallel algorithm would work.

   • Describe a decomposition based on partitioning the output data (i.e., the set of r buckets) and an appropriate mapping onto p processes. Describe briefly how the resulting parallel algorithm would work.

3.20 In the context of Problem 3.19, which of the two decompositions leads to a better parallel algorithm? Should the relative values of n and r have a bearing on the selection of one of the two decomposition schemes?

3.21 Consider seven tasks with running times of 1, 2, 3, 4, 5, 5, and 10 units, respectively. Assuming that it does not take any time to assign work to a process, compute the best- and worst-case speedup for a centralized scheme for dynamic mapping with two processes.

3.22 Suppose there are M tasks that are being mapped using a centralized dynamic load balancing scheme and we have the following information about these tasks:

- Average task size is 1.
- Minimum task size is 0.
- Maximum task size is m.
- It takes a process Δ time to pick up a task.

Compute the best- and worst-case speedups for self-scheduling and chunk-scheduling assuming that tasks are available in batches of l ($l < M$). What are the actual values of the best- and worst-case speedups for the two scheduling methods when $p = 10$, $\Delta = 0.2$, $m = 20$, $M = 100$, and $l = 2$?

CHAPTER **4**

Basic Communication Operations

In most parallel algorithms, processes need to exchange data with other processes. This exchange of data can significantly impact the efficiency of parallel programs by introducing interaction delays during their execution. For instance, recall from Section 2.5 that it takes roughly $t_s + mt_w$ time for a simple exchange of an m-word message between two processes running on different nodes of an interconnection network with cut-through routing. Here t_s is the latency or the startup time for the data transfer and t_w is the per-word transfer time, which is inversely proportional to the available bandwidth between the nodes. Many interactions in practical parallel programs occur in well-defined patterns involving more than two processes. Often either all processes participate together in a single global interaction operation, or subsets of processes participate in interactions local to each subset. These common basic patterns of interprocess interaction or communication are frequently used as building blocks in a variety of parallel algorithms. Proper implementation of these basic communication operations on various parallel architectures is a key to the efficient execution of the parallel algorithms that use them.

In this chapter, we present algorithms to implement some commonly used communication patterns on simple interconnection networks, such as the linear array, two-dimensional mesh, and the hypercube. The choice of these interconnection networks is motivated primarily by pedagogical reasons. For instance, although it is unlikely that large scale parallel computers will be based on the linear array or ring topology, it is important to understand various communication operations in the context of linear arrays because the rows and columns of meshes are linear arrays. Parallel algorithms that perform rowwise or column-wise communication on meshes use linear array algorithms. The algorithms for a number of communication operations on a mesh are simple extensions of the corresponding linear array algorithms to two dimensions. Furthermore, parallel algorithms using regular data structures such as arrays often map naturally onto one- or two-dimensional arrays of processes. This too makes it important to study interprocess interaction on a linear array or mesh interconnection network. The hypercube architecture, on the other hand, is interesting because many algorithms with recursive interaction patterns map naturally onto a hypercube topology. Most of these algorithms may perform equally well on interconnection networks other than the hypercube, but it is simpler to visualize their communication patterns on a hypercube.

The algorithms presented in this chapter in the context of simple network topologies are practical and are highly suitable for modern parallel computers, even though most such computers are unlikely to have an interconnection network that exactly matches one of the networks considered in this chapter. The reason is that on a modern parallel computer, the time to transfer data of a certain size between two nodes is often independent of the relative location of the nodes in the interconnection network. This homogeneity is afforded by a variety of firmware and hardware features such as randomized routing algorithms and cut-through routing, etc. Furthermore, the end user usually does not have explicit control over mapping processes onto physical processors. Therefore, we assume that the transfer of m words of data between *any* pair of nodes in an interconnection network incurs a cost of $t_s + mt_w$. On most architectures, this assumption is reasonably accurate as long as a free link is available between the source and destination nodes for the data to traverse. However, if many pairs of nodes are communicating simultaneously, then the messages may take longer. This can happen if the number of messages passing through a cross-section of the network exceeds the cross-section bandwidth (Section 2.4.4) of the network. In such situations, we need to adjust the value of t_w to reflect the slowdown due to congestion. As discussed in Section 2.5.1, we refer to the adjusted value of t_w as effective t_w. We will make a note in the text when we come across communication operations that may cause congestion on certain networks.

As discussed in Section 2.5.2, the cost of data-sharing among processors in the shared-address-space paradigm can be modeled using the same expression $t_s + mt_w$, usually with different values of t_s and t_w relative to each other as well as relative to the computation speed of the processors of the parallel computer. Therefore, parallel algorithms requiring one or more of the interaction patterns discussed in this chapter can be assumed to incur costs whose expression is close to one derived in the context of message-passing.

In the following sections we describe various communication operations and derive expressions for their time complexity. We assume that the interconnection network supports cut-through routing (Section 2.5.1) and that the communication time between any pair of nodes is practically independent of of the number of intermediate nodes along the paths between them. We also assume that the communication links are bidirectional; that is, two directly-connected nodes can send messages of size m to each other simultaneously in time $t_s + t_w m$. We assume a single-port communication model, in which a node can send a message on only one of its links at a time. Similarly, it can receive a message on only one link at a time. However, a node can receive a message while sending another message at the same time on the same or a different link.

Many of the operations described here have duals and other related operations that we can perform by using procedures very similar to those for the original operations. The *dual* of a communication operation is the opposite of the original operation and can be performed by reversing the direction and sequence of messages in the original operation. We will mention such operations wherever applicable.

4.1   One-to-All Broadcast and All-to-One Reduction

Parallel algorithms often require a single process to send identical data to all other processes or to a subset of them. This operation is known as *one-to-all broadcast*. Initially, only the source process has the data of size m that needs to be broadcast. At the termination of the procedure, there are p copies of the initial data – one belonging to each process. The dual of one-to-all broadcast is *all-to-one reduction*. In an all-to-one reduction operation, each of the p participating processes starts with a buffer M containing m words. The data from all processes are combined through an associative operator and accumulated at a single destination process into one buffer of size m. Reduction can be used to find the sum, product, maximum, or minimum of sets of numbers – the ith word of the accumulated M is the sum, product, maximum, or minimum of the ith words of each of the original buffers. Figure 4.1 shows one-to-all broadcast and all-to-one reduction among p processes.

One-to-all broadcast and all-to-one reduction are used in several important parallel algorithms including matrix-vector multiplication, Gaussian elimination, shortest paths, and vector inner product. In the following subsections, we consider the implementation of one-to-all broadcast in detail on a variety of interconnection topologies.

4.1.1   Ring or Linear Array

A naive way to perform one-to-all broadcast is to sequentially send $p - 1$ messages from the source to the other $p - 1$ processes. However, this is inefficient because the source process becomes a bottleneck. Moreover, the communication network is underutilized because only the connection between a single pair of nodes is used at a time. A better broadcast algorithm can be devised using a technique commonly known as *recursive doubling*. The source process first sends the message to another process. Now both these processes can simultaneously send the message to two other processes that are still waiting for the

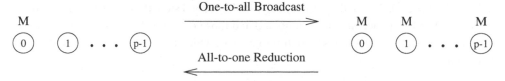

Figure 4.1   One-to-all broadcast and all-to-one reduction.

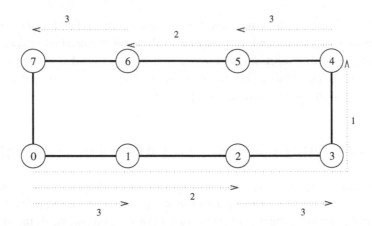

Figure 4.2   One-to-all broadcast on an eight-node ring. Node 0 is the source of the broadcast. Each message transfer step is shown by a numbered, dotted arrow from the source of the message to its destination. The number on an arrow indicates the time step during which the message is transferred.

message. By continuing this procedure until all the processes have received the data, the message can be broadcast in log p steps.

The steps in a one-to-all broadcast on an eight-node linear array or ring are shown in Figure 4.2. The nodes are labeled from 0 to 7. Each message transmission step is shown by a numbered, dotted arrow from the source of the message to its destination. Arrows indicating messages sent during the same time step have the same number.

Note that on a linear array, the destination node to which the message is sent in each step must be carefully chosen. In Figure 4.2, the message is first sent to the farthest node (4) from the source (0). In the second step, the distance between the sending and receiving nodes is halved, and so on. The message recipients are selected in this manner at each step to avoid congestion on the network. For example, if node 0 sent the message to node 1 in the first step and then nodes 0 and 1 attempted to send messages to nodes 2 and 3, respectively, in the second step, the link between nodes 1 and 2 would be congested as it would be a part of the shortest route for both the messages in the second step.

Reduction on a linear array can be performed by simply reversing the direction and the sequence of communication, as shown in Figure 4.3. In the first step, each odd numbered node sends its buffer to the even numbered node just before itself, where the contents of the two buffers are combined into one. After the first step, there are four buffers left to be reduced on nodes 0, 2, 4, and 6, respectively. In the second step, the contents of the buffers on nodes 0 and 2 are accumulated on node 0 and those on nodes 6 and 4 are accumulated on node 4. Finally, node 4 sends its buffer to node 0, which computes the final result of the reduction.

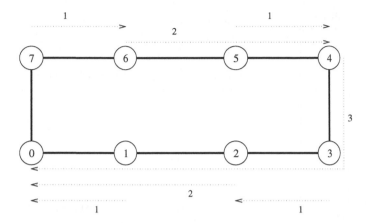

Figure 4.3   Reduction on an eight-node ring with node 0 as the destination of the reduction.

Example 4.1   Matrix-vector multiplication

Consider the problem of multiplying an $n \times n$ matrix A with an $n \times 1$ vector x on an $n \times n$ mesh of nodes to yield an $n \times 1$ result vector y. Algorithm 8.1 shows a serial algorithm for this problem. Figure 4.4 shows one possible mapping of the matrix and the vectors in which each element of the matrix belongs to a different process, and the vector is distributed among the processes in the topmost row of the mesh and the result vector is generated on the leftmost column of processes.

Since all the rows of the matrix must be multiplied with the vector, each process needs the element of the vector residing in the topmost process of its column. Hence, before computing the matrix-vector product, each column of nodes performs a one-to-all broadcast of the vector elements with the topmost process of the column as the source. This is done by treating each column of the $n \times n$ mesh as an n-node linear array, and simultaneously applying the linear array broadcast procedure described previously to all columns.

After the broadcast, each process multiplies its matrix element with the result of the broadcast. Now, each row of processes needs to add its result to generate the corresponding element of the product vector. This is accomplished by performing all-to-one reduction on each row of the process mesh with the first process of each row as the destination of the reduction operation.

For example, P_9 will receive $x[1]$ from P_1 as a result of the broadcast, will multiply it with $A[2, 1]$ and will participate in an all-to-one reduction with P_8, P_{10}, and P_{11} to accumulate $y[2]$ on P_8. ■

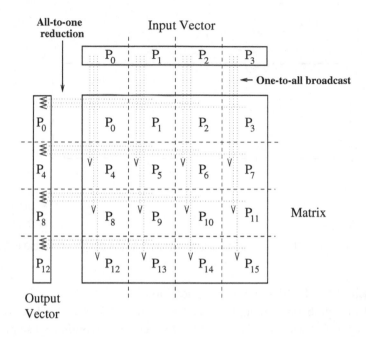

Figure 4.4 One-to-all broadcast and all-to-one reduction in the multiplication of a 4×4 matrix with a 4×1 vector.

4.1.2 Mesh

We can regard each row and column of a square mesh of p nodes as a linear array of $\sqrt{p}$ nodes. So a number of communication algorithms on the mesh are simple extensions of their linear array counterparts. A linear array communication operation can be performed in two phases on a mesh. In the first phase, the operation is performed along one or all rows by treating the rows as linear arrays. In the second phase, the columns are treated similarly.

Consider the problem of one-to-all broadcast on a two-dimensional square mesh with $\sqrt{p}$ rows and $\sqrt{p}$ columns. First, a one-to-all broadcast is performed from the source to the remaining ($\sqrt{p} - 1$) nodes of the same row. Once all the nodes in a row of the mesh have acquired the data, they initiate a one-to-all broadcast in their respective columns. At the end of the second phase, every node in the mesh has a copy of the initial message. The communication steps for one-to-all broadcast on a mesh are illustrated in Figure 4.5 for $p = 16$, with node 0 at the bottom-left corner as the source. Steps 1 and 2 correspond to the first phase, and steps 3 and 4 correspond to the second phase.

We can use a similar procedure for one-to-all broadcast on a three-dimensional mesh as well. In this case, rows of $p^{1/3}$ nodes in each of the three dimensions of the mesh would be treated as linear arrays. As in the case of a linear array, reduction can be performed on two- and three-dimensional meshes by simply reversing the direction and the order of messages.

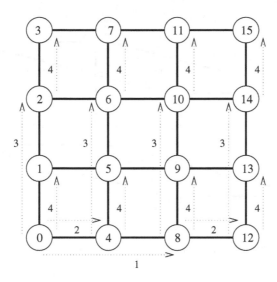

Figure 4.5   One-to-all broadcast on a 16-node mesh.

4.1.3   Hypercube

The previous subsection showed that one-to-all broadcast is performed in two phases on a two-dimensional mesh, with the communication taking place along a different dimension in each phase. Similarly, the process is carried out in three phases on a three-dimensional mesh. A hypercube with 2^d nodes can be regarded as a d-dimensional mesh with two nodes in each dimension. Hence, the mesh algorithm can be extended to the hypercube, except that the process is now carried out in d steps – one in each dimension.

Figure 4.6 shows a one-to-all broadcast on an eight-node (three-dimensional) hypercube with node 0 as the source. In this figure, communication starts along the highest dimension (that is, the dimension specified by the most significant bit of the binary representation of a node label) and proceeds along successively lower dimensions in subsequent steps. Note that the source and the destination nodes in three communication steps of the algorithm shown in Figure 4.6 are identical to the ones in the broadcast algorithm on a linear array shown in Figure 4.2. However, on a hypercube, the order in which the dimensions are chosen for communication does not affect the outcome of the procedure. Figure 4.6 shows only one such order. Unlike a linear array, the hypercube broadcast would not suffer from congestion if node 0 started out by sending the message to node 1 in the first step, followed by nodes 0 and 1 sending messages to nodes 2 and 3, respectively, and finally nodes 0, 1, 2, and 3 sending messages to nodes 4, 5, 6, and 7, respectively.

4.1.4   Balanced Binary Tree

The hypercube algorithm for one-to-all broadcast maps naturally onto a balanced binary tree in which each leaf is a processing node and intermediate nodes serve only as switching

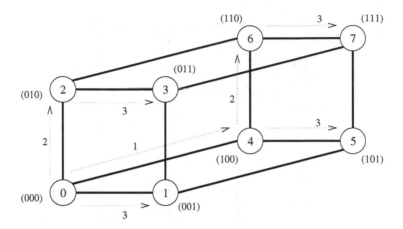

Figure 4.6   One-to-all broadcast on a three-dimensional hypercube. The binary representations of node labels are shown in parentheses.

units. This is illustrated in Figure 4.7 for eight nodes. In this figure, the communicating nodes have the same labels as in the hypercube algorithm illustrated in Figure 4.6. Figure 4.7 shows that there is no congestion on any of the communication links at any time. The difference between the communication on a hypercube and the tree shown in Figure 4.7 is that there is a different number of switching nodes along different paths on the tree.

4.1.5   Detailed Algorithms

A careful look at Figures 4.2, 4.5, 4.6, and 4.7 would reveal that the basic communication pattern for one-to-all broadcast is identical on all the four interconnection networks considered in this section. We now describe procedures to implement the broadcast and reduction operations. For the sake of simplicity, the algorithms are described here in the context of a hypercube and assume that the number of communicating processes is a power of 2. However, they apply to any network topology, and can be easily extended to work for any number of processes (Problem 4.1).

Algorithm 4.1 shows a one-to-all broadcast procedure on a 2^d-node network when node 0 is the source of the broadcast. The procedure is executed at all the nodes. At any node, the value of my_id is the label of that node. Let X be the message to be broadcast, which initially resides at the source node 0. The procedure performs d communication steps, one along each dimension of a hypothetical hypercube. In Algorithm 4.1, communication proceeds from the highest to the lowest dimension (although the order in which dimensions are chosen does not matter). The loop counter i indicates the current dimension of the hypercube in which communication is taking place. Only the nodes with zero in the i least significant bits of their labels participate in communication along dimension i. For instance, on the three-dimensional hypercube shown in Figure 4.6, i is equal to 2 in the

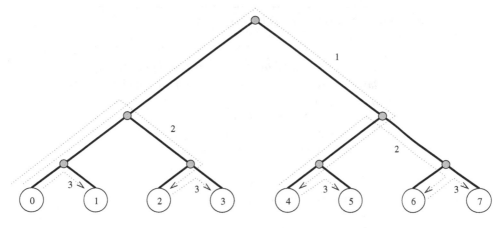

Figure 4.7 One-to-all broadcast on an eight-node tree.

first time step. Therefore, only nodes 0 and 4 communicate, since their two least significant bits are zero. In the next time step, when $i = 1$, all nodes (that is, 0, 2, 4, and 6) with zero in their least significant bits participate in communication. The procedure terminates after communication has taken place along all dimensions.

The variable *mask* helps determine which nodes communicate in a particular iteration of the loop. The variable *mask* has d (= log p) bits, all of which are initially set to one (Line 3). At the beginning of each iteration, the most significant nonzero bit of *mask* is reset to zero (Line 5). Line 6 determines which nodes communicate in the current iteration of the outer loop. For instance, for the hypercube of Figure 4.6, *mask* is initially set to 111, and it would be 011 during the iteration corresponding to $i = 2$ (the i least significant bits of *mask* are ones). The AND operation on Line 6 selects only those nodes that have zeros in their i least significant bits.

Among the nodes selected for communication along dimension i, the nodes with a zero at bit position i send the data, and the nodes with a one at bit position i receive it. The test to determine the sending and receiving nodes is performed on Line 7. For example, in Figure 4.6, node 0 (000) is the sender and node 4 (100) is the receiver in the iteration corresponding to $i = 2$. Similarly, for $i = 1$, nodes 0 (000) and 4 (100) are senders while nodes 2 (010) and 6 (110) are receivers.

Algorithm 4.1 works only if node 0 is the source of the broadcast. For an arbitrary source, we must relabel the nodes of the hypothetical hypercube by XORing the label of each node with the label of the source node before we apply this procedure. A modified one-to-all broadcast procedure that works for any value of *source* between 0 and $p - 1$ is shown in Algorithm 4.2. By performing the XOR operation at Line 3, Algorithm 4.2 relabels the source node to 0, and relabels the other nodes relative to the source. After this relabeling, the algorithm of Algorithm 4.1 can be applied to perform the broadcast.

Algorithm 4.3 gives a procedure to perform an all-to-one reduction on a hypothetical

---

```
1.    procedure ONE_TO_ALL_BC(d, my_id, X)
2.    begin
3.        mask := 2^d − 1;                    /* Set all d bits of mask to 1 */
4.        for i := d − 1 downto 0 do          /* Outer loop */
5.            mask := mask XOR 2^i;           /* Set bit i of mask to 0 */
6.            if (my_id AND mask) = 0 then    /* If lower i bits of my_id are 0 */
7.                if (my_id AND 2^i) = 0 then
8.                    msg_destination := my_id XOR 2^i;
9.                    send X to msg_destination;
10.               else
11.                   msg_source := my_id XOR 2^i;
12.                   receive X from msg_source;
13.               endelse;
14.           endif;
15.       endfor;
16.   end ONE_TO_ALL_BC
```

Algorithm 4.1   One-to-all broadcast of a message X from node 0 of a d-dimensional p-node hypercube ($d = \log p$). AND and XOR are bitwise logical-and and exclusive-or operations, respectively.

d-dimensional hypercube such that the final result is accumulated on node 0. Single node-accumulation is the dual of one-to-all broadcast. Therefore, we obtain the communication pattern required to implement reduction by reversing the order and the direction of messages in one-to-all broadcast. Procedure ALL_TO_ONE_REDUCE(d, my_id, m, X, sum) shown in Algorithm 4.3 is very similar to procedure ONE_TO_ALL_BC(d, my_id, X) shown in Algorithm 4.1. One difference is that the communication in all-to-one reduction proceeds from the lowest to the highest dimension. This change is reflected in the way that variables $mask$ and i are manipulated in Algorithm 4.3. The criterion for determining the source and the destination among a pair of communicating nodes is also reversed (Line 7). Apart from these differences, procedure ALL_TO_ONE_REDUCE has extra instructions (Lines 13 and 14) to add the contents of the messages received by a node in each iteration (any associative operation can be used in place of addition).

4.1.6   Cost Analysis

Analyzing the cost of one-to-all broadcast and all-to-one reduction is fairly straightforward. Assume that p processes participate in the operation and the data to be broadcast or reduced contains m words. The broadcast or reduction procedure involves $\log p$ point-to-point simple message transfers, each at a time cost of $t_s + t_w m$. Therefore, the total time taken by the procedure is

$$T = (t_s + t_w m) \log p. \tag{4.1}$$

```
1.     procedure GENERAL_ONE_TO_ALL_BC(d, my_id, source, X)
2.     begin
3.         my_virtual_id := my_id XOR source;
4.         mask := 2^d − 1;
5.         for i := d − 1 downto 0 do      /* Outer loop */
6.             mask := mask XOR 2^i;   /* Set bit i of mask to 0 */
7.             if (my_virtual_id AND mask) = 0 then
8.                 if (my_virtual_id AND 2^i) = 0 then
9.                     virtual_dest := my_virtual_id XOR 2^i;
10.                    send X to (virtual_dest XOR source);
               /* Convert virtual_dest to the label of the physical destination */
11.                else
12.                    virtual_source := my_virtual_id XOR 2^i;
13.                    receive X from (virtual_source XOR source);
               /* Convert virtual_source to the label of the physical source */
14.                endelse;
15.        endfor;
16.    end GENERAL_ONE_TO_ALL_BC
```

Algorithm 4.2 One-to-all broadcast of a message X initiated by $source$ on a d-dimensional hypothetical hyporoube. The AND and XOR operations are bitwise logical operations.

4.2 All-to-All Broadcast and Reduction

All-to-all broadcast is a generalization of one-to-all broadcast in which all p nodes simultaneously initiate a broadcast. A process sends the same m-word message to every other process, but different processes may broadcast different messages. All-to-all broadcast is used in matrix operations, including matrix multiplication and matrix-vector multiplication. The dual of all-to-all broadcast is *all-to-all reduction*, in which every node is the destination of an all-to-one reduction (Problem 4.8). Figure 4.8 illustrates all-to-all broadcast and all-to-all reduction.

One way to perform an all-to-all broadcast is to perform p one-to-all broadcasts, one

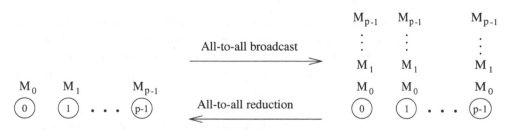

Figure 4.8 All-to-all broadcast and all-to-all reduction.

---

1.   **procedure** ALL_TO_ONE_REDUCE(d, my_id, m, X, sum)
2.   **begin**
3.   **for** $j := 0$ **to** $m - 1$ **do** $sum[j] := X[j]$;
4. $mask := 0$;
5. .   **for** $i := 0$ **to** $d - 1$ **do**
                   /* Select nodes whose lower i bits are 0 */
6.   **if** (my_id AND $mask$) = 0 **then**
7.   **if** (my_id AND 2^i) $\neq 0$ **then**
8. $msg\_destination := my\_id$ XOR 2^i;
9.   **send** sum to $msg\_destination$;
10.   **else**
11. $msg\_source := my\_id$ XOR 2^i;
12.   **receive** X from msg_source;
13.   **for** $j := 0$ **to** $m - 1$ **do**
14. $sum[j] := sum[j] + X[j]$;
15.   **endelse**;
16. $mask := mask$ XOR 2^i;   /* Set bit i of $mask$ to 1 */
17.   **endfor**;
18.   **end** ALL_TO_ONE_REDUCE

Algorithm 4.3 Single-node accumulation on a d-dimensional hypercube. Each node contributes a message X containing m words, and node 0 is the destination of the sum. The AND and XOR operations are bitwise logical operations.

starting at each node. If performed naively, on some architectures this approach may take up to p times as long as a one-to-all broadcast. It is possible to use the communication links in the interconnection network more efficiently by performing all p one-to-all broadcasts simultaneously so that all messages traversing the same path at the same time are concatenated into a single message whose size is the sum of the sizes of individual messages.

The following sections describe all-to-all broadcast on linear array, mesh, and hypercube topologies.

4.2.1 Linear Array and Ring

While performing all-to-all broadcast on a linear array or a ring, all communication links can be kept busy simultaneously until the operation is complete because each node always has some information that it can pass along to its neighbor. Each node first sends to one of its neighbors the data it needs to broadcast. In subsequent steps, it forwards the data received from one of its neighbors to its other neighbor.

Figure 4.9 illustrates all-to-all broadcast for an eight-node ring. The same procedure would also work on a linear array with bidirectional links. As with the previous figures, the integer label of an arrow indicates the time step during which the message is sent. In all-to-all broadcast, p different messages circulate in the p-node ensemble. In Figure 4.9,

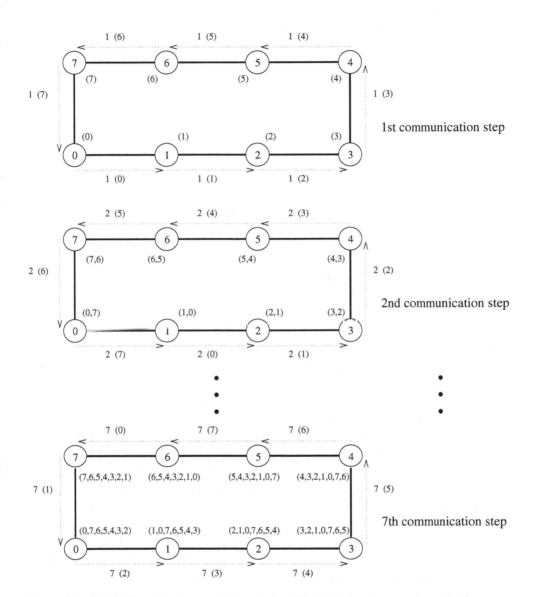

Figure 4.9   All-to-all broadcast on an eight-node ring. The label of each arrow shows the time step and, within parentheses, the label of the node that owned the current message being transferred before the beginning of the broadcast. The number(s) in parentheses next to each node are the labels of nodes from which data has been received prior to the current communication step. Only the first, second, and last communication steps are shown.

---

1.   **procedure** ALL_TO_ALL_BC_RING(my_id, my_msg, p, $result$)
2.   **begin**
3. $left := (my\_id - 1) \bmod p$;
4. $right := (my\_id + 1) \bmod p$;
5. $result := my\_msg$;
6. $msg := result$;
7.   **for** $i := 1$ **to** $p - 1$ **do**
8.   **send** msg to $right$;
9.   **receive** msg from $left$;
10. $result := result \cup msg$;
11.   **endfor**;
12.   **end** ALL_TO_ALL_BC_RING

Algorithm 4.4   All-to-all broadcast on a p-node ring.

each message is identified by its initial source, whose label appears in parentheses along with the time step. For instance, the arc labeled 2 (7) between nodes 0 and 1 represents the data communicated in time step 2 that node 0 received from node 7 in the preceding step. As Figure 4.9 shows, if communication is performed circularly in a single direction, then each node receives all $(p - 1)$ pieces of information from all other nodes in $(p - 1)$ steps.

Algorithm 4.4 gives a procedure for all-to-all broadcast on a p-node ring. The initial message to be broadcast is known locally as my_msg at each node. At the end of the procedure, each node stores the collection of all p messages in $result$. As the program shows, all-to-all broadcast on a mesh applies the linear array procedure twice, once along the rows and once along the columns.

In all-to-all reduction, the dual of all-to-all broadcast, each node starts with p messages, each one destined to be accumulated at a distinct node. All-to-all reduction can be performed by reversing the direction and sequence of the messages. For example, the first communication step for all-to-all reduction on an 8-node ring would correspond to the last step of Figure 4.9 with node 0 sending $msg[1]$ to 7 instead of receiving it. The only additional step required is that upon receiving a message, a node must combine it with the local copy of the message that has the same destination as the received message before forwarding the combined message to the next neighbor. Algorithm 4.5 gives a procedure for all-to-all reduction on a p-node ring.

4.2.2 Mesh

Just like one-to-all broadcast, the all-to-all broadcast algorithm for the 2-D mesh is based on the linear array algorithm, treating rows and columns of the mesh as linear arrays. Once again, communication takes place in two phases. In the first phase, each row of the mesh performs an all-to-all broadcast using the procedure for the linear array. In this phase, all nodes collect $\sqrt{p}$ messages corresponding to the $\sqrt{p}$ nodes of their respective rows. Each

---

```
1.    procedure ALL_TO_ALL_RED_RING(my_id, my_msg, p, result)
2.    begin
3.        left := (my_id − 1) mod p;
4.        right := (my_id + 1) mod p;
5.        recv := 0;
6.        for i := 1 to p − 1 do
7.            j := (my_id + i) mod p;
8.            temp := msg[j] + recv;
9.            send temp to left;
10.           receive recv from right;
11.       endfor;
12.       result := msg[my_id] + recv;
13.   end ALL_TO_ALL_RED_RING
```

Algorithm 4.5   All-to-all reduction on a p-node ring.

node consolidates this information into a single message of size $m\sqrt{p}$, and proceeds to the second communication phase of the algorithm. The second communication phase is a columnwise all-to-all broadcast of the consolidated messages. By the end of this phase, each node obtains all p pieces of m-word data that originally resided on different nodes. The distribution of data among the nodes of a 3×3 mesh at the beginning of the first and the second phases of the algorithm is shown in Figure 4.10.

Algorithm 4.6 gives a procedure for all-to-all broadcast on a $\sqrt{p} \times \sqrt{p}$ mesh. The mesh procedure for all-to-all reduction is left as an exercise for the reader (Problem 4.4).

4.2.3 Hypercube

The hypercube algorithm for all-to-all broadcast is an extension of the mesh algorithm to log p dimensions. The procedure requires log p steps. Communication takes place along a different dimension of the p-node hypercube in each step. In every step, pairs of nodes exchange their data and double the size of the message to be transmitted in the next step by concatenating the received message with their current data. Figure 4.11 shows these steps for an eight-node hypercube with bidirectional communication channels.

Algorithm 4.7 gives a procedure for implementing all-to-all broadcast on a d-dimensional hypercube. Communication starts from the lowest dimension of the hypercube and then proceeds along successively higher dimensions (Line 4). In each iteration, nodes communicate in pairs so that the labels of the nodes communicating with each other in the ith iteration differ in the ith least significant bit of their binary representations (Line 5). After an iteration's communication steps, each node concatenates the data it receives during that iteration with its resident data (Line 8). This concatenated message is transmitted in the following iteration.

As usual, the algorithm for all-to-all reduction can be derived by reversing the order

```
1.    procedure ALL_TO_ALL_BC_MESH(my_id, my_msg, p, result)
2.    begin

/* Communication along rows */
3.        left := my_id − (my_id mod √p) + (my_id − 1) mod √p;
4.        right := my_id − (my_id mod √p) + (my_id + 1) mod √p;
5.        result := my_msg;
6.        msg := result;
7.        for i := 1 to √p − 1 do
8.            send msg to right;
9.            receive msg from left;
10.           result := result ∪ msg;
11.       endfor;

/* Communication along columns */
12.       up := (my_id − √p) mod p;
13.       down := (my_id + √p) mod p;
14.       msg := result;
15.       for i := 1 to √p − 1 do
16.           send msg to down;
17.           receive msg from up;
18.           result := result ∪ msg;
19.       endfor;
20.   end ALL_TO_ALL_BC_MESH
```

Algorithm 4.6   All-to-all broadcast on a square mesh of p nodes.

```
1.    procedure ALL_TO_ALL_BC_HCUBE(my_id, my_msg, d, result)
2.    begin
3.        result := my_msg;
4.        for i := 0 to d − 1 do
5.            partner := my_id XOR 2^i;
6.            send result to partner;
7.            receive msg from partner;
8.            result := result ∪ msg;
9.        endfor;
10.   end ALL_TO_ALL_BC_HCUBE
```

Algorithm 4.7   All-to-all broadcast on a d-dimensional hypercube.

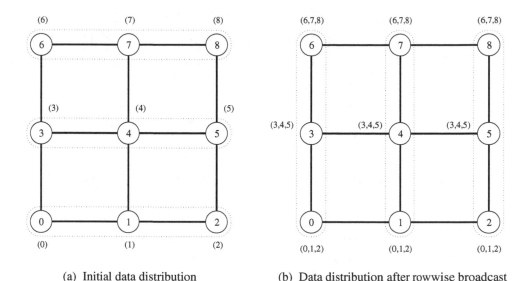

(a) Initial data distribution   (b) Data distribution after rowwise broadcast

Figure 4.10 All-to-all broadcast on a 3 × 3 mesh. The groups of nodes communicating with each other in each phase are enclosed by dotted boundaries. By the end of the second phase, all nodes get (0,1,2,3,4,5,6,7) (that is, a message from each node).

```
1.    procedure ALL_TO_ALL_RED_HCUBE(my_id, msg, d, result)
2.    begin
3.        recloc := 0;
4.        for i := d − 1 to 0 do
5.            partner := my_id XOR 2^i;
6.            j := my_id AND 2^i;
7.            k := (my_id XOR 2^i) AND 2^i;
8.            senloc := recloc + k;
9.            recloc := recloc + j;
10.           send msg[senloc .. senloc + 2^i − 1] to partner;
11.           receive temp[0 .. 2^i − 1] from partner;
12.           for j := 0 to 2^i − 1 do
13.               msg[recloc + j] := msg[recloc + j] + temp[j];
14.           endfor;
15.       endfor;
16.       result := msg[my_id];
17.   end ALL_TO_ALL_RED_HCUBE
```

Algorithm 4.8 All-to-all broadcast on a *d*-dimensional hypercube. AND and XOR are bitwise logical-and and exclusive-or operations, respectively.

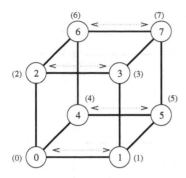

(a) Initial distribution of messages

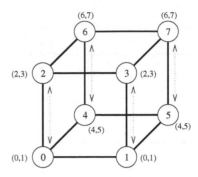

(b) Distribution before the second step

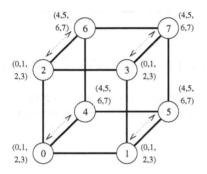

(c) Distribution before the third step

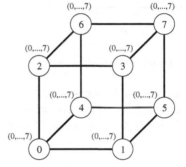

(d) Final distribution of messages

Figure 4.11   All-to-all broadcast on an eight-node hypercube.

and direction of messages in all-to-all broadcast. Furthermore, instead of concatenating the messages, the reduction operation needs to select the appropriate subsets of the buffer to send out and accumulate received messages in each iteration. Algorithm 4.8 gives a procedure for all-to-all reduction on a d-dimensional hypercube. It uses *senloc* to index into the starting location of the outgoing message and *recloc* to index into the location where the incoming message is added in each iteration.

4.2.4   Cost Analysis

On a ring or a linear array, all-to-all broadcast involves $p - 1$ steps of communication between nearest neighbors. Each step, involving a message of size m, takes time $t_s + t_w m$. Therefore, the time taken by the entire operation is

$$T = (t_s + t_w m)(p - 1). \tag{4.2}$$

Similarly, on a mesh, the first phase of $\sqrt{p}$ simultaneous all-to-all broadcasts (each among $\sqrt{p}$ nodes) concludes in time $(t_s + t_w m)(\sqrt{p} - 1)$. The number of nodes participating in each all-to-all broadcast in the second phase is also $\sqrt{p}$, but the size of each message is now $m\sqrt{p}$. Therefore, this phase takes time $(t_s + t_w m\sqrt{p})(\sqrt{p} - 1)$ to complete. The time for the entire all-to-all broadcast on a p-node two-dimensional square mesh is the sum of the times spent in the individual phases, which is

$$T = 2t_s(\sqrt{p} - 1) + t_w m(p - 1). \tag{4.3}$$

On a p-node hypercube, the size of each message exchanged in the ith of the $\log p$ steps is $2^{i-1}m$. It takes a pair of nodes time $t_s + 2^{i-1}t_w m$ to send and receive messages from each other during the ith step. Hence, the time to complete the entire procedure is

$$\begin{aligned} T &= \sum_{i=1}^{\log p}(t_s + 2^{i-1}t_w m) \\ &= t_s \log p + t_w m(p - 1). \end{aligned} \tag{4.4}$$

Equations 4.2, 4.3, and 4.4 show that the term associated with t_w in the expressions for the communication time of all-to-all broadcast is $t_w m(p - 1)$ for all the architectures. This term also serves as a lower bound for the communication time of all-to-all broadcast for parallel computers on which a node can communicate on only one of its ports at a time. This is because each node receives at least $m(p - 1)$ words of data, regardless of the architecture. Thus, for large messages, a highly connected network like a hypercube is no better than a simple ring in performing all-to-all broadcast or all-to-all reduction. In fact, the straightforward all-to-all broadcast algorithm for a simple architecture like a ring has great practical importance. A close look at the algorithm reveals that it is a sequence of p one-to-all broadcasts, each with a different source. These broadcasts are pipelined so that all of them are complete in a total of p nearest-neighbor communication steps. Many parallel algorithms involve a series of one-to-all broadcasts with different sources, often interspersed with some computation. If each one-to-all broadcast is performed using the hypercube algorithm of Section 4.1.3, then n broadcasts would require time $n(t_s + t_w m) \log p$. On the other hand, by pipelining the broadcasts as shown in Figure 4.9, all of them can be performed spending no more than time $(t_s + t_w m)(p - 1)$ in communication, provided that the sources of all broadcasts are different and $n \leq p$. In later chapters, we show how such pipelined broadcast improves the performance of some parallel algorithms such as Gaussian elimination (Section 8.3.1), back substitution (Section 8.3.3), and Floyd's algorithm for finding the shortest paths in a graph (Section 10.4.2).

Another noteworthy property of all-to-all broadcast is that, unlike one-to-all broadcast, the hypercube algorithm cannot be applied unaltered to mesh and ring architectures. The reason is that the hypercube procedure for all-to-all broadcast would cause congestion on the communication channels of a smaller-dimensional network with the same number of nodes. For instance, Figure 4.12 shows the result of performing the third step (Figure 4.11(c)) of the hypercube all-to-all broadcast procedure on a ring. One of the links of the ring is traversed by all four messages and would take four times as much time to complete the communication step.

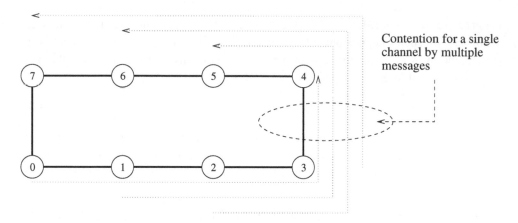

Figure 4.12   Contention for a channel when the communication step of Figure 4.11(c) for the hypercube is mapped onto a ring.

4.3   All-Reduce and Prefix-Sum Operations

The communication pattern of all-to-all broadcast can be used to perform some other operations as well. One of these operations is a third variation of reduction, in which each node starts with a buffer of size m and the final results of the operation are identical buffers of size m on each node that are formed by combining the original p buffers using an associative operator. Semantically, this operation, often referred to as the **all-reduce** operation, is identical to performing an all-to-one reduction followed by a one-to-all broadcast of the result. This operation is different from all-to-all reduction, in which p simultaneous all-to-one reductions take place, each with a different destination for the result.

An all-reduce operation with a single-word message on each node is often used to implement barrier synchronization on a message-passing computer. The semantics of the reduction operation are such that, while executing a parallel program, no node can finish the reduction before each node has contributed a value.

A simple method to perform all-reduce is to perform an all-to-one reduction followed by a one-to-all broadcast. However, there is a faster way to perform all-reduce by using the communication pattern of all-to-all broadcast. Figure 4.11 illustrates this algorithm for an eight-node hypercube. Assume that each integer in parentheses in the figure, instead of denoting a message, denotes a number to be added that originally resided at the node with that integer label. To perform reduction, we follow the communication steps of the all-to-all broadcast procedure, but at the end of each step, add two numbers instead of concatenating two messages. At the termination of the reduction procedure, each node holds the sum $(0 + 1 + 2 + \cdots + 7)$ (rather than eight messages numbered from 0 to 7, as in the case of all-to-all broadcast). Unlike all-to-all broadcast, each message transferred in the reduction operation has only one word. The size of the messages does not double in each step because the numbers are added instead of being concatenated. Therefore, the total communication time for all log p steps is

$$T = (t_s + t_w m) \log p. \tag{4.5}$$

Algorithm 4.7 can be used to perform a sum of p numbers if *my_msg*, *msg*, and *result* are numbers (rather than messages), and the union operation ('$\cup$') on Line 8 is replaced by addition.

Finding **prefix sums** (also known as the **scan** operation) is another important problem that can be solved by using a communication pattern similar to that used in all-to-all broadcast and all-reduce operations. Given p numbers $n_0, n_1, \ldots, n_{p-1}$ (one on each node), the problem is to compute the sums $s_k = \Sigma_{i=0}^{k} n_i$ for all k between 0 and $p - 1$. For example, if the original sequence of numbers is $\langle 3, 1, 4, 0, 2 \rangle$, then the sequence of prefix sums is $\langle 3, 4, 8, 8, 10 \rangle$. Initially, n_k resides on the node labeled k, and at the end of the procedure, the same node holds s_k. Instead of starting with a single numbers, each node could start with a buffer or vector of size m and the m-word result would be the sum of the corresponding elements of buffers.

Figure 4.13 illustrates the prefix sums procedure for an eight-node hypercube. This figure is a modification of Figure 4.11. The modification is required to accommodate the fact that in prefix sums the node with label k uses information from only the k-node subset of those nodes whose labels are less than or equal to k. To accumulate the correct prefix sum, every node maintains an additional result buffer. This buffer is denoted by square brackets in Figure 4.13. At the end of a communication step, the content of an incoming message is added to the result buffer only if the message comes from a node with a smaller label than that of the recipient node. The contents of the outgoing message (denoted by parentheses in the figure) are updated with every incoming message, just as in the case of the all-reduce operation. For instance, after the first communication step, nodes 0, 2, and 4 do not add the data received from nodes 1, 3, and 5 to their result buffers. However, the contents of the outgoing messages for the next step are updated.

Since not all of the messages received by a node contribute to its final result, some of the messages it receives may be redundant. We have omitted these steps of the standard all-to-all broadcast communication pattern from Figure 4.13, although the presence or absence of these messages does not affect the results of the algorithm. Algorithm 4.9 gives a procedure to solve the prefix sums problem on a d-dimensional hypercube.

4.4 Scatter and Gather

In the **scatter** operation, a single node sends a unique message of size m to every other node. This operation is also known as **one-to-all personalized communication**. One-to-all personalized communication is different from one-to-all broadcast in that the source node starts with p unique messages, one destined for each node. Unlike one-to-all broadcast, one-to-all personalized communication does not involve any duplication of data. The dual of one-to-all personalized communication or the scatter operation is the **gather** operation,

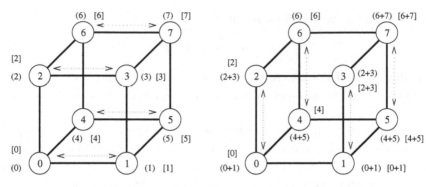

(a) Initial distribution of values   (b) Distribution of sums before second step

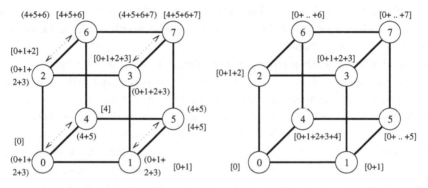

(c) Distribution of sums before third step   (d) Final distribution of prefix sums

Figure 4.13 Computing prefix sums on an eight-node hypercube. At each node, square brackets show the local prefix sum accumulated in the result buffer and parentheses enclose the contents of the outgoing message buffer for the next step.

```
1.    procedure PREFIX_SUMS_HCUBE(my_id, my_number, d, result)
2.    begin
3.        result := my_number;
4.        msg := result;
5.        for i := 0 to d − 1 do
6.            partner := my_id XOR 2^i;
7.            send msg to partner;
8.            receive number from partner;
9.            msg := msg + number;
10.           if (partner < my_id) then result := result + number;
11.       endfor;
12.   end PREFIX_SUMS_HCUBE
```

Algorithm 4.9 Prefix sums on a d-dimensional hypercube.

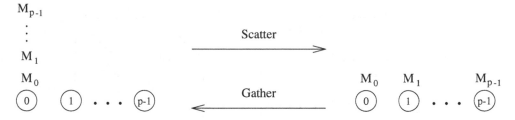

Figure 4.14 Scatter and gather operations.

or *concatenation*, in which a single node collects a unique message from each node. A gather operation is different from an all-to-one reduce operation in that it does not involve any combination or reduction of data. Figure 4.14 illustrates the scatter and gather operations.

Although the scatter operation is semantically different from one-to-all broadcast, the scatter algorithm is quite similar to that of the broadcast. Figure 4.15 shows the communication steps for the scatter operation on an eight-node hypercube. The communication patterns of one-to-all broadcast (Figure 4.6) and scatter (Figure 4.15) are identical. Only the size and the contents of messages are different. In Figure 4.15, the source node (node 0) contains all the messages. The messages are identified by the labels of their destination nodes. In the first communication step, the source transfers half of the messages to one of its neighbors. In subsequent steps, each node that has some data transfers half of it to a neighbor that has yet to receive any data. There is a total of log p communication steps corresponding to the log p dimensions of the hypercube.

The gather operation is simply the reverse of scatter. Each node starts with an m word message. In the first step, every odd numbered node sends its buffer to an even numbered neighbor behind it, which concatenates the received message with its own buffer. Only the even numbered nodes participate in the next communication step which results in nodes with multiples of four labels gathering more data and doubling the sizes of their data. The process continues similarly, until node 0 has gathered the entire data.

Just like one-to-all broadcast and all-to-one reduction, the hypercube algorithms for scatter and gather can be applied unaltered to linear array and mesh interconnection topologies without any increase in the communication time.

Cost Analysis All links of a p-node hypercube along a certain dimension join two $p/2$-node subcubes (Section 2.4.3). As Figure 4.15 illustrates, in each communication step of the scatter operations, data flow from one subcube to another. The data that a node owns before starting communication in a certain dimension are such that half of them need to be sent to a node in the other subcube. In every step, a communicating node keeps half of its data, meant for the nodes in its subcube, and sends the other half to its neighbor in the other subcube. The time in which all data are distributed to their respective destinations is

$$T = t_s \log p + t_w m(p - 1). \tag{4.6}$$

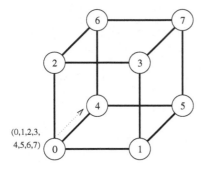

(a) Initial distribution of messages

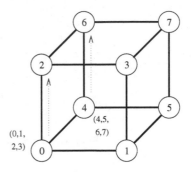

(b) Distribution before the second step

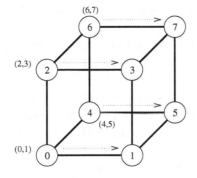

(c) Distribution before the third step

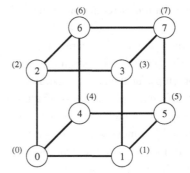

(d) Final distribution of messages

Figure 4.15   The scatter operation on an eight-node hypercube.

The scatter and gather operations can also be performed on a linear array and on a 2-D square mesh in time $t_s \log p + t_w m(p - 1)$ (Problem 4.7). Note that disregarding the term due to message-startup time, the cost of scatter and gather operations for large messages on any k-d mesh interconnection network (Section 2.4.3) is similar. In the scatter operation, at least $m(p - 1)$ words of data must be transmitted out of the source node, and in the gather operation, at least $m(p - 1)$ words of data must be received by the destination node. Therefore, as in the case of all-to-all broadcast, $t_w m(p - 1)$ is a lower bound on the communication time of scatter and gather operations. This lower bound is independent of the interconnection network.

4.5   All-to-All Personalized Communication

In *all-to-all personalized communication*, each node sends a distinct message of size m to every other node. Each node sends different messages to different nodes, unlike all-to-all broadcast, in which each node sends the same message to all other nodes. Figure 4.16

Figure 4.16   All-to-all personalized communication.

illustrates the all-to-all personalized communication operation. A careful observation of this figure would reveal that this operation is equivalent to transposing a two-dimensional array of data distributed among p processes using one-dimensional array partitioning (Figure 3.24). All-to-all personalized communication is also known as ***total exchange***. This operation is used in a variety of parallel algorithms such as fast Fourier transform, matrix transpose, sample sort, and some parallel database join operations.

Example 4.2   Matrix transposition

The transpose of an $n \times n$ matrix A is a matrix A^T of the same size, such that $A^T[i, j] = A[j, i]$ for $0 \le i, j < n$. Consider an $n \times n$ matrix mapped onto n processors such that each processor contains one full row of the matrix. With this mapping, processor P_i initially contains the elements of the matrix with indices $[i, 0], [i, 1], \ldots, [i, n - 1]$. After the transposition, element $[i, 0]$ belongs to P_0, element $[i, 1]$ belongs to P_1, and so on. In general, element $[i, j]$ initially resides on P_i, but moves to P_j during the transposition. The data-communication pattern of this procedure is shown in Figure 4.17 for a 4×4 matrix mapped onto four processes using one-dimensional rowwise partitioning. Note that in this figure every processor sends a distinct element of the matrix to every other processor. This is an example of all-to-all personalized communication.

In general, if we use p processes such that $p \le n$, then each process initially holds n/p rows (that is, n^2/p elements) of the matrix. Performing the transposition now involves an all-to-all personalized communication of matrix blocks of size $n/p \times n/p$, instead of individual elements.   ∎

We now discuss the implementation of all-to-all personalized communication on parallel computers with linear array, mesh, and hypercube interconnection networks. The communication patterns of all-to-all personalized communication are identical to those of all-to-all broadcast on all three architectures. Only the size and the contents of messages are different.

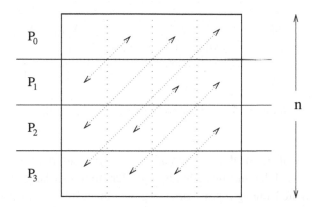

Figure 4.17   All-to-all personalized communication in transposing a 4 × 4 matrix using four processes.

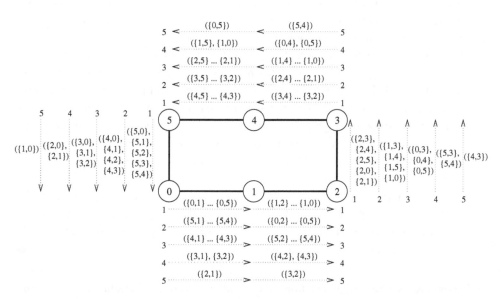

Figure 4.18   All-to-all personalized communication on a six-node ring. The label of each message is of the form {x, y}, where x is the label of the node that originally owned the message, and y is the label of the node that is the final destination of the message. The label ({x_1, y_1}, {x_2, y_2}, ..., {x_n, y_n}) indicates a message that is formed by concatenating n individual messages.

4.5.1 Ring

Figure 4.18 shows the steps in an all-to-all personalized communication on a six-node linear array. To perform this operation, every node sends $p - 1$ pieces of data, each of size m. In the figure, these pieces of data are identified by pairs of integers of the form $\{i, j\}$, where i is the source of the message and j is its final destination. First, each node sends all pieces of data as one consolidated message of size $m(p - 1)$ to one of its neighbors (all nodes communicate in the same direction). Of the $m(p - 1)$ words of data received by a node in this step, one m-word packet belongs to it. Therefore, each node extracts the information meant for it from the data received, and forwards the remaining $(p - 2)$ pieces of size m each to the next node. This process continues for $p - 1$ steps. The total size of data being transferred between nodes decreases by m words in each successive step. In every step, each node adds to its collection one m-word packet originating from a different node. Hence, in $p - 1$ steps, every node receives the information from all other nodes in the ensemble.

In the above procedure, all messages are sent in the same direction. If half of the messages are sent in one direction and the remaining half are sent in the other direction, then the communication cost due to the t_w can be reduced by a factor of two. For the sake of simplicity, we ignore this constant-factor improvement.

Cost Analysis On a ring or a bidirectional linear array, all-to-all personalized communication involves $p - 1$ communication steps. Since the size of the messages transferred in the ith step is $m(p - i)$, the total time taken by this operation is

$$
\begin{aligned}
T &= \sum_{i=1}^{p-1}(t_s + t_w m(p - i)) \\
&= t_s(p - 1) + \sum_{i=1}^{p-1} i t_w m \\
&= (t_s + t_w m p/2)(p - 1).
\end{aligned} \tag{4.7}
$$

In the all-to-all personalized communication procedure described above, each node sends $m(p - 1)$ words of data because it has an m-word packet for every other node. Assume that all messages are sent either clockwise or counterclockwise. The average distance that an m-word packet travels is $(\Sigma_{i=1}^{p-1} i)/(p - 1)$, which is equal to $p/2$. Since there are p nodes, each performing the same type of communication, the total traffic (the total number of data words transferred between directly-connected nodes) on the network is $m(p - 1) \times p/2 \times p$. The total number of inter-node links in the network to share this load is p. Hence, the communication time for this operation is at least $(t_w \times m(p - 1)p^2/2)/p$, which is equal to $t_w m(p - 1)p/2$. Disregarding the message startup time t_s, this is exactly the time taken by the linear array procedure. Therefore, the all-to-all personalized communication algorithm described in this section is optimal.

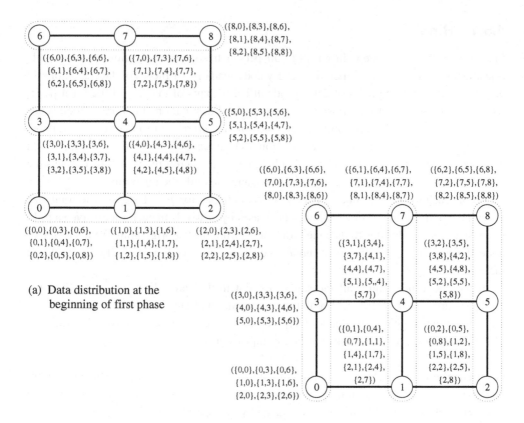

(a) Data distribution at the beginning of first phase

(b) Data distribution at the beginning of second phase

Figure 4.19 The distribution of messages at the beginning of each phase of all-to-all personalized communication on a 3×3 mesh. At the end of the second phase, node i has messages ($\{0,i\}$, $\ldots,\{8,i\}$), where $0 \leq i \leq 8$. The groups of nodes communicating together in each phase are enclosed in dotted boundaries.

4.5.2 Mesh

In all-to-all personalized communication on a $\sqrt{p} \times \sqrt{p}$ mesh, each node first groups its p messages according to the columns of their destination nodes. Figure 4.19 shows a 3×3 mesh, in which every node initially has nine m-word messages, one meant for each node. Each node assembles its data into three groups of three messages each (in general, $\sqrt{p}$ groups of $\sqrt{p}$ messages each). The first group contains the messages destined for nodes labeled 0, 3, and 6; the second group contains the messages for nodes labeled 1, 4, and 7; and the last group has messages for nodes labeled 2, 5, and 8.

After the messages are grouped, all-to-all personalized communication is performed independently in each row with clustered messages of size $m\sqrt{p}$. One cluster contains the information for all $\sqrt{p}$ nodes of a particular column. Figure 4.19(b) shows the distribution of data among the nodes at the end of this phase of communication.

Before the second communication phase, the messages in each node are sorted again, this time according to the rows of their destination nodes; then communication similar to the first phase takes place in all the columns of the mesh. By the end of this phase, each node receives a message from every other node.

Cost Analysis   We can compute the time spent in the first phase by substituting $\sqrt{p}$ for the number of nodes, and $m\sqrt{p}$ for the message size in Equation 4.7. The result of this substitution is $(t_s + t_w mp/2)(\sqrt{p} - 1)$. The time spent in the second phase is the same as that in the first phase. Therefore, the total time for all-to-all personalized communication of messages of size m on a p-node two-dimensional square mesh is

$$T = (2t_s + t_w mp)(\sqrt{p} - 1). \tag{4.8}$$

The expression for the communication time of all-to-all personalized communication in Equation 4.8 does not take into account the time required for the local rearrangement of data (that is, sorting the messages by rows or columns). Assuming that initially the data is ready for the first communication phase, the second communication phase requires the rearrangement of mp words of data. If t_r is the time to perform a read and a write operation on a single word of data in a node's local memory, then the total time spent in data rearrangement by a node during the entire procedure is $t_r mp$ (Problem 4.21). This time is much smaller than the time spent by each node in communication.

An analysis along the lines of that for the linear array would show that the communication time given by Equation 4.8 for all-to-all personalized communication on a square mesh is optimal within a small constant factor (Problem 4.11).

4.5.3 Hypercube

One way of performing all-to-all personalized communication on a p-node hypercube is to simply extend the two-dimensional mesh algorithm to $\log p$ dimensions. Figure 4.20 shows the communication steps required to perform this operation on a three-dimensional hypercube. As shown in the figure, communication takes place in $\log p$ steps. Pairs of nodes exchange data in a different dimension in each step. Recall that in a p-node hypercube, a set of $p/2$ links in the same dimension connects two subcubes of $p/2$ nodes each (Section 2.4.3). At any stage in all-to-all personalized communication, every node holds p packets of size m each. While communicating in a particular dimension, every node sends $p/2$ of these packets (consolidated as one message). The destinations of these packets are the nodes of the other subcube connected by the links in current dimension.

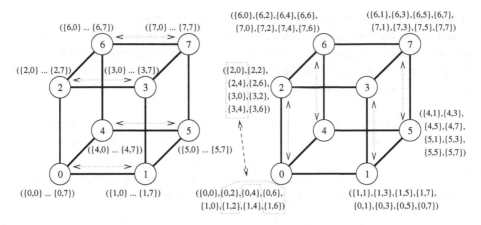

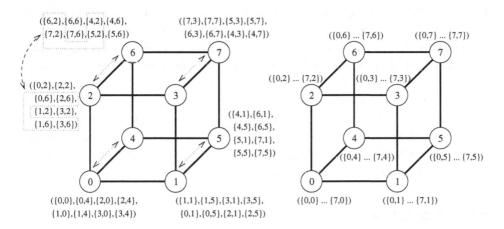

Figure 4.20   An all-to-all personalized communication algorithm on a three-dimensional hypercube.

In the preceding procedure, a node must rearrange its messages locally before each of the log p communication steps. This is necessary to make sure that all $p/2$ messages destined for the same node in a communication step occupy contiguous memory locations so that they can be transmitted as a single consolidated message.

Cost Analysis   In the above hypercube algorithm for all-to-all personalized communication, $mp/2$ words of data are exchanged along the bidirectional channels in each of the log p iterations. The resulting total communication time is

$$T = (t_s + t_w mp/2) \log p. \tag{4.9}$$

Before each of the $\log p$ communication steps, a node rearranges mp words of data. Hence, a total time of $t_r mp \log p$ is spent by each node in local rearrangement of data during the entire procedure. Here t_r is the time needed to perform a read and a write operation on a single word of data in a node's local memory. For most practical computers, t_r is much smaller than t_w; hence, the time to perform an all-to-all personalized communication is dominated by the communication time.

Interestingly, unlike the linear array and mesh algorithms described in this section, the hypercube algorithm is not optimal. Each of the p nodes sends and receives $m(p-1)$ words of data and the average distance between any two nodes on a hypercube is $(\log p)/2$. Therefore, the total data traffic on the network is $p \times m(p-1) \times (\log p)/2$. Since there is a total of $(p \log p)/2$ links in the hypercube network, the lower bound on the all-to-all personalized communication time is

$$\begin{aligned} T &= \frac{t_w pm(p-1)(\log p)/2}{(p \log p)/2} \\ &= t_w m(p-1). \end{aligned}$$

An Optimal Algorithm

An all-to-all personalized communication effectively results in all pairs of nodes exchanging some data. On a hypercube, the best way to perform this exchange is to have every pair of nodes communicate directly with each other. Thus, each node simply performs $p-1$ communication steps, exchanging m words of data with a different node in every step. A node must choose its communication partner in each step so that the hypercube links do not suffer congestion. Figure 4.21 shows one such congestion-free schedule for pairwise exchange of data in a three-dimensional hypercube. As the figure shows, in the jth communication step, node i exchanges data with node (i XOR j). For example, in part (a) of the figure (step 1), the labels of communicating partners differ in the least significant bit. In part (g) (step 7), the labels of communicating partners differ in all the bits, as the binary representation of seven is 111. In this figure, all the paths in every communication step are congestion-free, and none of the bidirectional links carry more than one message in the same direction. This is true in general for a hypercube of any dimension. If the messages are routed appropriately, a congestion-free schedule exists for the $p-1$ communication steps of all-to-all personalized communication on a p-node hypercube. Recall from Section 2.4.3 that a message traveling from node i to node j on a hypercube must pass through at least l links, where l is the Hamming distance between i and j (that is, the number of nonzero bits in the binary representation of (i XOR j)). A message traveling from node i to node j traverses links in l dimensions (corresponding to the nonzero bits in the binary representation of (i XOR j)). Although the message can follow one of the several paths of length l that exist between i and j (assuming $l > 1$), a distinct path is obtained by sorting the dimensions along which the message travels in ascending order. According to this strategy, the first link is chosen in the dimension corresponding to the least significant nonzero bit of (i XOR j), and so on. This routing scheme is known as **E-cube routing**.

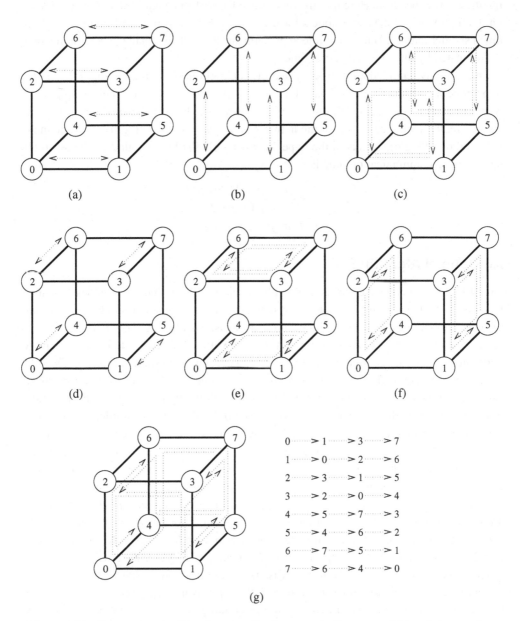

Figure 4.21 Seven steps in all-to-all personalized communication on an eight-node hypercube.

```
1.    procedure ALL_TO_ALL_PERSONAL(d, my_id)
2.    begin
3.       for i := 1 to 2^d − 1 do
4.       begin
5.          partner := my_id XOR i;
6.          send M_{my_id,partner} to partner;
7.          receive M_{partner,my_id} from partner;
8.       endfor;
9.    end ALL_TO_ALL_PERSONAL
```

Algorithm 4.10   A procedure to perform all-to-all personalized communication on a d-dimensional hypercube. The message $M_{i,j}$ initially resides on node i and is destined for node j.

Algorithm 4.10 for all-to-all personalized communication on a d-dimensional hypercube is based on this strategy.

Cost Analysis   E-cube routing ensures that by choosing communication pairs according to Algorithm 4.10, a communication time of $t_s + t_w m$ is guaranteed for a message transfer between node i and node j because there is no contention with any other message traveling in the same direction along the link between nodes i and j. The total communication time for the entire operation is

$$T = (t_s + t_w m)(p − 1). \tag{4.10}$$

A comparison of Equations 4.9 and 4.10 shows the term associated with t_s is higher for the second hypercube algorithm, while the term associated with t_w is higher for the first algorithm. Therefore, for small messages, the startup time may dominate, and the first algorithm may still be useful.

4.6   Circular Shift

Circular shift is a member of a broader class of global communication operations known as *permutation*. A permutation is a simultaneous, one-to-one data redistribution operation in which each node sends a packet of m words to a unique node. We define a *circular q-shift* as the operation in which node i sends a data packet to node $(i + q)$ mod p in a p-node ensemble ($0 < q < p$). The shift operation finds application in some matrix computations and in string and image pattern matching.

4.6.1   Mesh

The implementation of a circular q-shift is fairly intuitive on a ring or a bidirectional linear array. It can be performed by $\min\{q, p − q\}$ neighbor-to-neighbor communications in one direction. Mesh algorithms for circular shift can be derived by using the ring algorithm.

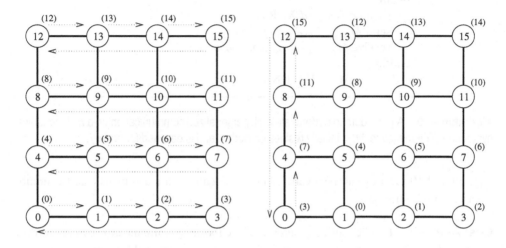

(a) Initial data distribution and the first communication step

(b) Step to compensate for backward row shifts

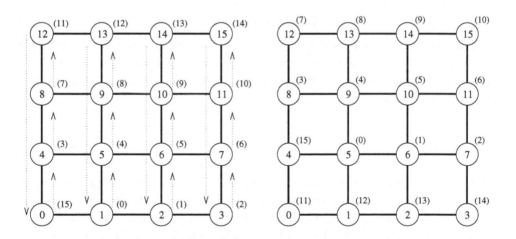

(c) Column shifts in the third communication step

(d) Final distribution of the data

Figure 4.22   The communication steps in a circular 5-shift on a 4 × 4 mesh.

If the nodes of the mesh have row-major labels, a circular q-shift can be performed on a p-node square wraparound mesh in two stages. This is illustrated in Figure 4.22 for a circular 5-shift on a 4×4 mesh. First, the entire set of data is shifted simultaneously by $(q \bmod \sqrt{p})$ steps along the rows. Then it is shifted by $\lfloor q/\sqrt{p} \rfloor$ steps along the columns. During the circular row shifts, some of the data traverse the wraparound connection from the highest to the lowest labeled nodes of the rows. All such data packets must shift an additional step forward along the columns to compensate for the $\sqrt{p}$ distance that they lost while traversing the backward edge in their respective rows. For example, the 5-shift in Figure 4.22 requires one row shift, a compensatory column shift, and finally one column shift.

In practice, we can choose the direction of the shifts in both the rows and the columns to minimize the number of steps in a circular shift. For instance, a 3-shift on a 4×4 mesh can be performed by a single backward row shift. Using this strategy, the number of unit shifts in a direction cannot exceed $\lfloor \sqrt{p}/2 \rfloor$.

Cost Analysis   Taking into account the compensating column shift for some packets, the total time for any circular q-shift on a p-node mesh using packets of size m has an upper bound of

$$T = (t_s + t_w m)(\sqrt{p} + 1).$$

4.6.2 Hypercube

In developing a hypercube algorithm for the shift operation, we map a linear array with 2^d nodes onto a d-dimensional hypercube. We do this by assigning node i of the linear array to node j of the hypercube such that j is the d-bit binary reflected Gray code (RGC) of i. Figure 4.23 illustrates this mapping for eight nodes. A property of this mapping is that any two nodes at a distance of 2^i on the linear array are separated by exactly two links on the hypercube. An exception is $i = 0$ (that is, directly-connected nodes on the linear array) when only one hypercube link separates the two nodes.

To perform a q-shift, we expand q as a sum of distinct powers of 2. The number of terms in the sum is the same as the number of ones in the binary representation of q. For example, the number 5 can be expressed as $2^2 + 2^0$. These two terms correspond to bit positions 0 and 2 in the binary representation of 5, which is 101. If q is the sum of s distinct powers of 2, then the circular q-shift on a hypercube is performed in s phases.

In each phase of communication, all data packets move closer to their respective destinations by short cutting the linear array (mapped onto the hypercube) in leaps of the powers of 2. For example, as Figure 4.23 shows, a 5-shift is performed by a 4-shift followed by a 1-shift. The number of communication phases in a q-shift is exactly equal to the number of ones in the binary representation of q. Each phase consists of two communication steps, except the 1-shift, which, if required (that is, if the least significant bit of q is 1), consists of a single step. For example, in a 5-shift, the first phase of a 4-shift (Figure 4.23(a)) consists

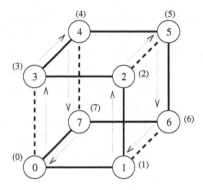

First communication step of the 4-shift

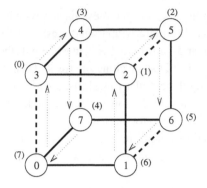

Second communication step of the 4-shift

(a) The first phase (a 4-shift)

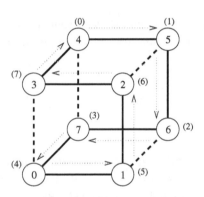

(b) The second phase (a 1-shift)

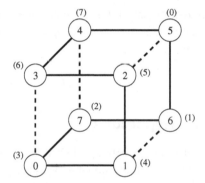

(c) Final data distribution after the 5-shift

Figure 4.23 The mapping of an eight-node linear array onto a three-dimensional hypercube to perform a circular 5-shift as a combination of a 4-shift and a 1-shift.

of two steps and the second phase of a 1-shift (Figure 4.23(b)) consists of one step. Thus, the total number of steps for any q in a p-node hypercube is at most $2 \log p - 1$.

All communications in a given time step are congestion-free. This is ensured by the property of the linear array mapping that all nodes whose mutual distance on the linear array is a power of 2 are arranged in disjoint subarrays on the hypercube. Thus, all nodes can freely communicate in a circular fashion in their respective subarrays. This is shown in Figure 4.23(a), in which nodes labeled 0, 3, 4, and 7 form one subarray and nodes labeled 1, 2, 5, and 6 form another subarray.

The upper bound on the total communication time for any shift of m-word packets on a p-node hypercube is

$$T = (t_s + t_w m)(2 \log p - 1). \tag{4.11}$$

We can reduce this upper bound to $(t_s + t_w m) \log p$ by performing both forward and backward shifts. For example, on eight nodes, a 6-shift can be performed by a single backward 2-shift instead of a forward 4-shift followed by a forward 2-shift.

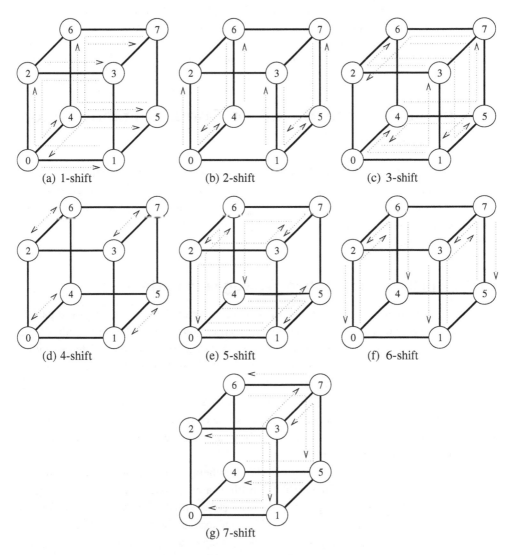

Figure 4.24 Circular q-shifts on an 8-node hypercube for $1 \le q < 8$.

We now show that if the E-cube routing introduced in Section 4.5 is used, then the time for circular shift on a hypercube can be improved by almost a factor of $\log p$ for large messages. This is because with E-cube routing, each pair of nodes with a constant distance l ($i \leq l < p$) has a congestion-free path (Problem 4.22) in a p-node hypercube with bidirectional channels. Figure 4.24 illustrates the non-conflicting paths of all the messages in circular q-shift operations for $1 \leq q < 8$ on an eight-node hypercube. In a circular q-shift on a p-node hypercube, the longest path contains $\log p - \gamma(q)$ links, where $\gamma(q)$ is the highest integer j such that q is divisible by 2^j (Problem 4.23). Thus, the total communication time for messages of length m is

$$T = t_s + t_w m. \tag{4.12}$$

4.7   Improving the Speed of Some Communication Operations

So far in this chapter, we have derived procedures for various communication operations and their communication times under the assumptions that the original messages could not be split into smaller parts and that each node had a single port for sending and receiving data. In this section, we briefly discuss the impact of relaxing these assumptions on some of the communication operations.

4.7.1   Splitting and Routing Messages in Parts

In the procedures described in Sections 4.1–4.6, we assumed that an entire m-word packet of data travels between the source and the destination nodes along the same path. If we split large messages into smaller parts and then route these parts through different paths, we can sometimes utilize the communication network better. We have already shown that, with a few exceptions like one-to-all broadcast, all-to-one reduction, all-reduce, etc., the communication operations discussed in this chapter are asymptotically optimal for large messages; that is, the terms associated with t_w in the costs of these operations cannot be reduced asymptotically. In this section, we present asymptotically optimal algorithms for three global communication operations.

Note that the algorithms of this section rely on m being large enough to be split into p roughly equal parts. Therefore, the earlier algorithms are still useful for shorter messages. A comparison of the cost of the algorithms in this section with those presented earlier in this chapter for the same operations would reveal that the term associated with t_s increases and the term associated with t_w decreases when the messages are split. Therefore, depending on the actual values of t_s, t_w, and p, there is a cut-off value for the message size m and only the messages longer than the cut-off would benefit from the algorithms in this section.

One-to-All Broadcast

Consider broadcasting a single message M of size m from one source node to all the nodes in a p-node ensemble. If m is large enough so that M can be split into p parts $M_0, M_1, \ldots, M_{p-1}$ of size m/p each, then a scatter operation (Section 4.4) can place M_i on node i in time $t_s \log p + t_w(m/p)(p-1)$. Note that the desired result of the one-to-all broadcast is to place $M = M_0 \cup M_1 \cup \cdots \cup M_{p-1}$ on all nodes. This can be accomplished by an all-to-all broadcast of the messages of size m/p residing on each node after the scatter operation. This all-to-all broadcast can be completed in time $t_s \log p + t_w(m/p)(p-1)$ on a hypercube. Thus, on a hypercube, one-to-all broadcast can be performed in time

$$
\begin{aligned}
T &= 2 \times (t_s \log p + t_w(p-1)\frac{m}{p}) \\
&\approx 2 \times (t_s \log p + t_w m).
\end{aligned}
\tag{4.13}
$$

Compared to Equation 4.1, this algorithm has double the startup cost, but the cost due to the t_w term has been reduced by a factor of $(\log p)/2$. Similarly, one-to-all broadcast can be improved on linear array and mesh interconnection networks as well.

All-to-One Reduction

All-to-one reduction is a dual of one-to-all broadcast. Therefore, an algorithm for all-to-one reduction can be obtained by reversing the direction and the sequence of communication in one-to-all broadcast. We showed above how an optimal one-to-all broadcast algorithm can be obtained by performing a scatter operation followed by an all-to-all broadcast. Therefore, using the notion of duality, we should be able to perform an all-to-one reduction by performing all-to-all reduction (dual of all-to-all broadcast) followed by a gather operation (dual of scatter). We leave the details of such an algorithm as an exercise for the reader (Problem 4.17).

All-Reduce

Since an all-reduce operation is semantically equivalent to an all-to-one reduction followed by a one-to-all broadcast, the asymptotically optimal algorithms for these two operations presented above can be used to construct a similar algorithm for the all-reduce operation. Breaking all-to-one reduction and one-to-all broadcast into their component operations, it can be shown that an all-reduce operation can be accomplished by an all-to-all reduction followed by a gather followed by a scatter followed by an all-to-all broadcast. Since the intermediate gather and scatter would simply nullify each other's effect, all-reduce just requires an all-to-all reduction and an all-to-all broadcast. First, the m-word messages on each of the p nodes are logically split into p components of size roughly m/p words. Then, an all-to-all reduction combines all the ith components on p_i. After this step, each node is left with a distinct m/p-word component of the final result. An all-to-all broadcast can construct the concatenation of these components on each node.

A p-node hypercube interconnection network allows all-to-one reduction and one-to-all broadcast involving messages of size m/p in time $t_s \log p + t_w(m/p)(p-1)$ each. Therefore, the all-reduce operation can be completed in time

$$
\begin{aligned}
T &= 2 \times (t_s \log p + t_w(p-1)\frac{m}{p}) \\
&\approx 2 \times (t_s \log p + t_w m).
\end{aligned}
\tag{4.14}
$$

4.7.2 All-Port Communication

In a parallel architecture, a single node may have multiple communication ports with links to other nodes in the ensemble. For example, each node in a two-dimensional wraparound mesh has four ports, and each node in a d-dimensional hypercube has d ports. In this book, we generally assume what is known as the *single-port communication* model. In single-port communication, a node can send data on only one of its ports at a time. Similarly, a node can receive data on only one port at a time. However, a node can send and receive data simultaneously, either on the same port or on separate ports. In contrast to the single-port model, an *all-port communication* model permits simultaneous communication on all the channels connected to a node.

On a p-node hypercube with all-port communication, the coefficients of t_w in the expressions for the communication times of one-to-all and all-to-all broadcast and personalized communication are all smaller than their single-port counterparts by a factor of $\log p$. Since the number of channels per node for a linear array or a mesh is constant, all-port communication does not provide any asymptotic improvement in communication time on these architectures.

Despite the apparent speedup, the all-port communication model has certain limitations. For instance, not only is it difficult to program, but it requires that the messages are large enough to be split efficiently among different channels. In several parallel algorithms, an increase in the size of messages means a corresponding increase in the granularity of computation at the nodes. When the nodes are working with large data sets, the internode communication time is dominated by the computation time if the computational complexity of the algorithm is higher than the communication complexity. For example, in the case of matrix multiplication, there are n^3 computations for n^2 words of data transferred among the nodes. If the communication time is a small fraction of the total parallel run time, then improving the communication by using sophisticated techniques is not very advantageous in terms of the overall run time of the parallel algorithm.

Another limitation of all-port communication is that it can be effective only if data can be fetched and stored in memory at a rate sufficient to sustain all the parallel communication. For example, to utilize all-port communication effectively on a p-node hypercube, the memory bandwidth must be greater than the communication bandwidth of a single channel by a factor of at least $\log p$; that is, the memory bandwidth must increase with the number of nodes to support simultaneous communication on all ports. Some modern parallel computers, like the IBM SP, have a very natural solution for this problem. Each

Table 4.1 Summary of communication times of various operations discussed in Sections 4.1–4.7 on a hypercube interconnection network. The message size for each operation is m and the number of nodes is p.

Operation	Hypercube Time	B/W Requirement
One-to-all broadcast, All-to-one reduction	$\min((t_s + t_w m) \log p, 2(t_s \log p + t_w m))$	$\Theta(1)$
All-to-all broadcast, All-to-all reduction	$t_s \log p + t_w m (p - 1)$	$\Theta(1)$
All-reduce	$\min((t_s + t_w m) \log p, 2(t_s \log p + t_w m))$	$\Theta(1)$
Scatter, Gather	$t_s \log p + t_w m (p - 1)$	$\Theta(1)$
All-to-all personalized	$(t_s + t_w m)(p - 1)$	$\Theta(p)$
Circular shift	$t_s + t_w m$	$\Theta(p)$

node of the distributed-memory parallel computer is a NUMA shared-memory multiprocessor. Multiple ports are then served by separate memory banks and full memory and communication bandwidth can be utilized if the buffers for sending and receiving data are placed appropriately across different memory banks.

4.8 Summary

Table 4.1 summarizes the communication times for various collective communications operations discussed in this chapter. The time for one-to-all broadcast, all-to-one reduction, and the all-reduce operations is the minimum of two expressions. This is because, depending on the message size m, either the algorithms described in Sections 4.1 and 4.3 or the ones described in Section 4.7 are faster. Table 4.1 assumes that the algorithm most suitable for the given message size is chosen. The communication-time expressions in Table 4.1 have been derived in the earlier sections of this chapter in the context of a hypercube interconnection network with cut-through routing. However, these expressions and the corresponding algorithms are valid for any architecture with a $\Theta(p)$ cross-section bandwidth (Section 2.4.4). In fact, the terms associated with t_w for the expressions for all operations listed in Table 4.1, except all-to-all personalized communication and circular shift, would remain unchanged even on ring and mesh networks (or any k-d mesh network) provided that the logical processes are mapped onto the physical nodes of the network appropriately. The last column of Table 4.1 gives the asymptotic cross-section bandwidth required to perform an operation in the time given by the second column of the table, assuming an optimal mapping of processes to nodes. For large messages, only all-to-all personalized communication and circular shift require the full $\Theta(p)$ cross-section bandwidth. Therefore, as

Table 4.2   MPI names of the various operations discussed in this chapter.

Operation	MPI Name
One-to-all broadcast	MPI_Bcast
All-to-one reduction	MPI_Reduce
All-to-all broadcast	MPI_Allgather
All-to-all reduction	MPI_Reduce_scatter
All-reduce	MPI_Allreduce
Gather	MPI_Gather
Scatter	MPI_Scatter
All-to-all personalized	MPI_Alltoall

discussed in Section 2.5.1, when applying the expressions for the time of these operations on a network with a smaller cross-section bandwidth, the t_w term must reflect the effective bandwidth. For example, the bisection width of a p-node square mesh is $\Theta(\sqrt{p})$ and that of a p-node ring is $\Theta(1)$. Therefore, while performing all-to-all personalized communication on a square mesh, the effective per-word transfer time would be $\Theta(\sqrt{p})$ times the t_w of individual links, and on a ring, it would be $\Theta(p)$ times the t_w of individual links.

The collective communications operations discussed in this chapter occur frequently in many parallel algorithms. In order to facilitate speedy and portable design of efficient parallel programs, most parallel computer vendors provide pre-packaged software for performing these collective communications operations. The most commonly used standard API for these operations is known as the Message Passing Interface, or MPI. Table 4.2 gives the names of the MPI functions that correspond to the communications operations described in this chapter.

4.9   Bibliographic Remarks

In this chapter, we studied a variety of data communication operations for the linear array, mesh, and hypercube interconnection topologies. Saad and Schultz [SS89b] discuss implementation issues for these operations on these and other architectures, such as shared-memory and a switch or bus interconnect. Most parallel computer vendors provide standard APIs for inter-process communications via message-passing. Two of the most common APIs are the message passing interface (MPI) [SOHL+96] and the parallel virtual machine (PVM) [GBD+94].

The hypercube algorithm for a certain communication operation is often the best algorithm for other less-connected architectures too, if they support cut-through routing. Due to the versatility of the hypercube architecture and the wide applicability of its algorithms, extensive work has been done on implementing various communication operations on hypercubes [BOS+91, BR90, BT97, FF86, JH89, Joh90, MdV87, RS90b, SS89a, SW87].

The properties of a hypercube network that are used in deriving the algorithms for various communication operations on it are described by Saad and Schultz [SS88].

The all-to-all personalized communication problem in particular has been analyzed for the hypercube architecture by Boppana and Raghavendra [BR90], Johnsson and Ho [JH91], Seidel [Sei89], and Take [Tak87]. E-cube routing that guarantees congestion-free communication in Algorithm 4.10 for all-to-all personalized communication is described by Nugent [Nug88].

The all-reduce and the prefix sums algorithms of Section 4.3 are described by Ranka and Sahni [RS90b]. Our discussion of the circular shift operation is adapted from Bertsekas and Tsitsiklis [BT97]. A generalized form of prefix sums, often referred to as *scan*, has been used by some researchers as a basic primitive in data-parallel programming. Blelloch [Ble90] defines a *scan vector model*, and describes how a wide variety of parallel programs can be expressed in terms of the scan primitive and its variations.

The hypercube algorithm for one-to-all broadcast using spanning binomial trees is described by Bertsekas and Tsitsiklis [BT97] and Johnsson and Ho [JH89]. In the spanning tree algorithm described in Section 4.7.1, we split the m-word message to be broadcast into $\log p$ parts of size $m/\log p$ for ease of presenting the algorithm. Johnsson and Ho [JH89] show that the optimal size of the parts is $\lceil (\sqrt{t_s m/t_w \log p}) \rceil$. In this case, the number of messages may be greater than $\log p$. These smaller messages are sent from the root of the spanning binomial tree to its $\log p$ subtrees in a circular fashion. With this strategy, one-to-all broadcast on a p-node hypercube can be performed in time $t_s \log p + t_w m + 2t_w \lceil (\sqrt{t_s m/t_w \log p}) \rceil \log p$.

Algorithms using the all-port communication model have been described for a variety of communication operations on the hypercube architecture by Bertsekas and Tsitsiklis [BT97], Johnsson and Ho [JH89], Ho and Johnsson [HJ87], Saad and Schultz [SS89a], and Stout and Wagar [SW87]. Johnsson and Ho [JH89] show that on a p-node hypercube with all-port communication, the coefficients of t_w in the expressions for the communication times of one-to-all and all-to-all broadcast and personalized communication are all smaller than those of their single-port counterparts by a factor of $\log p$. Gupta and Kumar [GK91] show that all-port communication may not improve the scalability of an algorithm on a parallel architecture over single-port communication.

The elementary operations described in this chapter are not the only ones used in parallel applications. A variety of other useful operations for parallel computers have been described in literature, including selection [Akl89], pointer jumping [HS86, Jaj92], BPC permutations [Joh90, RS90b], fetch-and-op [GGK$^+$83], packing [Lev87, Sch80], bit reversal [Loa92], and keyed-scan or multi-prefix [Ble90, Ran89].

Sometimes data communication does not follow any predefined pattern, but is arbitrary, depending on the application. In such cases, a simplistic approach of routing the messages along the shortest data paths between their respective sources and destinations leads to contention and imbalanced communication. Leighton, Maggs, and Rao [LMR88], Valiant [Val82], and Valiant and Brebner [VB81] discuss efficient routing methods for arbitrary permutations of messages.

Problems

4.1 Modify Algorithms 4.1, 4.2, and 4.3 so that they work for any number of processes, not just the powers of 2.

4.2 Section 4.1 presents the recursive doubling algorithm for one-to-all broadcast, for all three networks (ring, mesh, hypercube). Note that in the hypercube algorithm of Figure 4.6, a message is sent along the highest dimension first, and then sent to lower dimensions (in Algorithm 4.1, line 4, i goes down from $d - 1$ to 0). The same algorithm can be used for mesh and ring and ensures that messages sent in different time steps do not interfere with each other.

Let's now change the algorithm so that the message is sent along the lowest dimension first (i.e., in Algorithm 3.1, line 4, i goes up from 0 to $d - 1$). So in the first time step, processor 0 will communicate with processor 1; in the second time step, processors 0 and 1 will communicate with 2 and 3, respectively; and so on.

1. What is the run time of this revised algorithm on hypercube?

2. What is the run time of this revised algorithm on ring?

For these derivations, if k messages have to traverse the same link at the same time, then assume that the effective per-word-transfer time for these messages is kt_w.

4.3 On a ring, all-to-all broadcast can be implemented in two different ways: (a) the standard ring algorithm as shown in Figure 4.9 and (b) the hypercube algorithm as shown in Figure 4.11.

1. What is the run time for case (a)?

2. What is the run time for case (b)?

If k messages have to traverse the same link at the same time, then assume that the effective per-word-transfer time for these messages is kt_w. Also assume that $t_s = 100 \times t_w$.

1. Which of the two methods, (a) or (b), above is better if the message size m is very large?

2. Which method is better if m is very small (may be one word)?

4.4 Write a procedure along the lines of Algorithm 4.6 for performing all-to-all reduction on a mesh.

4.5 **(All-to-all broadcast on a tree)** Given a balanced binary tree as shown in Figure 4.7, describe a procedure to perform all-to-all broadcast that takes time $(t_s + t_w mp/2) \log p$ for m-word messages on p nodes. Assume that only the leaves of the tree contain nodes, and that an exchange of two m-word messages between any two nodes connected by bidirectional channels takes time $t_s + t_w mk$ if the communication channel (or a part of it) is shared by k simultaneous messages.

4.6   Consider the all-reduce operation in which each processor starts with an array of m words, and needs to get the global sum of the respective words in the array at each processor. This operation can be implemented on a ring using one of the following three alternatives:

(i) All-to-all broadcast of all the arrays followed by a local computation of the sum of the respective elements of the array.

(ii) Single node accumulation of the elements of the array, followed by a one-to-all broadcast of the result array.

(iii) An algorithm that uses the pattern of the all-to-all broadcast, but simply adds numbers rather than concatenating messages.

1.   For each of the above cases, compute the run time in terms of m, t_s, and t_w.

2.   Assume that $t_s = 100$, $t_w = 1$, and m is very large. Which of the three alternatives (among (i), (ii) or (iii)) is better?

3.   Assume that $t_s = 100$, $t_w = 1$, and m is very small (say 1). Which of the three alternatives (among (i), (ii) or (iii)) is better?

4.7   (**One-to-all personalized communication on a linear array and a mesh**) Give the procedures and their communication times for one-to-all personalized communication of m-word messages on p nodes for the linear array and the mesh architectures.

Hint: For the mesh, the algorithm proceeds in two phases as usual and starts with the source distributing pieces of $m\sqrt{p}$ words among the $\sqrt{p}$ nodes in its row such that each of these nodes receives the data meant for all the $\sqrt{p}$ nodes in its column.

4.8   (**All-to-all reduction**) The dual of all-to-all broadcast is all-to-all reduction, in which each node is the destination of an all-to-one reduction. For example, consider the scenario where p nodes have a vector of p elements each, and the ith node (for all i such that $0 \leq i < p$) gets the sum of the ith elements of all the vectors. Describe an algorithm to perform all-to-all reduction on a hypercube with addition as the associative operator. If each message contains m words and t_{add} is the time to perform one addition, how much time does your algorithm take (in terms of m, p, t_{add}, t_s and t_w)?

Hint: In all-to-all broadcast, each node starts with a single message and collects p such messages by the end of the operation. In all-to-all reduction, each node starts with p distinct messages (one meant for each node) but ends up with a single message.

4.9   Parts (c), (e), and (f) of Figure 4.21 show that for any node in a three-dimensional hypercube, there are exactly three nodes whose shortest distance from the node is two links. Derive an exact expression for the number of nodes (in terms of p and l) whose shortest distance from any given node in a p-node hypercube is l.

4.10   Give a hypercube algorithm to compute prefix sums of n numbers if p is the number of nodes and n/p is an integer greater than 1. Assuming that it takes time

t_{add} to add two numbers and time t_s to send a message of unit length between two directly-connected nodes, give an exact expression for the total time taken by the algorithm.

4.11 Show that if the message startup time t_s is zero, then the expression $t_w m p(\sqrt{p} - 1)$ for the time taken by all-to-all personalized communication on a $\sqrt{p} \times \sqrt{p}$ mesh is optimal within a small (≤ 4) constant factor.

4.12 Modify the linear array and the mesh algorithms in Sections 4.1–4.5 to work without the end-to-end wraparound connections. Compare the new communication times with those of the unmodified procedures. What is the maximum factor by which the time for any of the operations increases on either the linear array or the mesh?

4.13 (**3-D mesh**) Give optimal (within a small constant) algorithms for one-to-all and all-to-all broadcasts and personalized communications on a $p^{1/3} \times p^{1/3} \times p^{1/3}$ three-dimensional mesh of p nodes with store-and-forward routing. Derive expressions for the total communication times of these procedures.

4.14 Assume that the cost of building a parallel computer with p nodes is proportional to the total number of communication links within it. Let the cost effectiveness of an architecture be inversely proportional to the product of the cost of a p-node ensemble of this architecture and the communication time of a certain operation on it. Assuming t_s to be zero, which architecture is more cost effective for each of the operations discussed in this chapter – a standard 3-D mesh or a sparse 3-D mesh?

4.15 Repeat Problem 4.14 when t_s is a nonzero constant but $t_w = 0$. Under this model of communication, the message transfer time between two directly-connected nodes is fixed, regardless of the size of the message. Also, if two packets are combined and transmitted as one message, the communication latency is still t_s.

4.16 (**k-to-all broadcast**) Let k-to-all broadcast be an operation in which k nodes simultaneously perform a one-to-all broadcast of m-word messages. Give an algorithm for this operation that has a total communication time of $t_s \log p + t_w m(k \log(p/k) + k - 1)$ on a p-node hypercube. Assume that the m-word messages cannot be split, k is a power of 2, and $1 \leq k \leq p$.

4.17 Give a detailed description of an algorithm for performing all-to-one reduction in time $2(t_s \log p + t_w m(p-1)/p)$ on a p-node hypercube by splitting the original messages of size m into p nearly equal parts of size m/p each.

4.18 If messages can be split and their parts can be routed independently, then derive an algorithm for k-to-all broadcast such that its communication time is less than that of the algorithm in Problem 4.16 for a p-node hypercube.

4.19 Show that, if $m \geq p$, then all-to-one reduction with message size m can be performed on a p-node hypercube spending time $2(t_s \log p + t_w m)$ in communication. *Hint:* Express all-to-one reduction as a combination of all-to-all reduction and gather.

4.20 (**k-to-all personalized communication**) In k-to-all personalized communication, k nodes simultaneously perform a one-to-all personalized communication ($1 \leq k \leq p$) in a p-node ensemble with individual packets of size m. Show that, if k is a power of 2, then this operation can be performed on a hypercube in time $t_s(\log(p/k) + k - 1) + t_w m(p - 1)$.

4.21 Assuming that it takes time t_r to perform a read and a write operation on a single word of data in a node's local memory, show that all-to-all personalized communication on a p-node mesh (Section 4.5.2) spends a total of time $t_r m p$ in internal data movement on the nodes, where m is the size of an individual message.
Hint: The internal data movement is equivalent to transposing a $\sqrt{p} \times \sqrt{p}$ array of messages of size m.

4.22 Show that in a p-node hypercube, all the p data paths in a circular q-shift are congestion-free if E-cube routing (Section 4.5) is used.
Hint: (1) If $q > p/2$, then a q-shift is isomorphic to a $(p - q)$-shift on a p-node hypercube. (2) Prove by induction on hypercube dimension. If all paths are congestion-free for a q-shift ($1 \leq q < p$) on a p-node hypercube, then all these paths are congestion-free on a $2p$-node hypercube also.

4.23 Show that the length of the longest path of any message in a circular q-shift on a p-node hypercube is $\log p - \gamma(q)$, where $\gamma(q)$ is the highest integer j such that q is divisible by 2^j.
Hint: (1) If $q = p/2$, then $\gamma(q) = \log p - 1$ on a p-node hypercube. (2) Prove by induction on hypercube dimension. For a given q, $\gamma(q)$ increases by one each time the number of nodes is doubled.

4.24 Derive an expression for the parallel run time of the hypercube algorithms for one-to-all broadcast, all-to-all broadcast, one-to-all personalized communication, and all-to-all personalized communication adapted unaltered for a mesh with identical communication links (same channel width and channel rate). Compare the performance of these adaptations with that of the best mesh algorithms.

4.25 As discussed in Section 2.4.4, two common measures of the cost of a network are (1) the total number of wires in a parallel computer (which is a product of number of communication links and channel width); and (2) the bisection bandwidth. Consider a hypercube in which the channel width of each link is one, that is $t_w = 1$. The channel width of a mesh-connected computer with equal number of nodes and identical cost is higher, and is determined by the cost metric used. Let s and s' represent the factors by which the channel width of the mesh is increased in accordance with the two cost metrics. Derive the values of s and s'. Using these, derive the communication time of the following operations on a mesh:

1. One-to-all broadcast

2. All-to-all broadcast

3. One-to-all personalized communication

    4.   All-to-all personalized communication

Compare these times with the time taken by the same operations on a hypercube with equal cost.

4.26 Consider a completely-connected network of p nodes. For the four communication operations in Problem 4.25 derive an expression for the parallel run time of the hypercube algorithms on the completely-connected network. Comment on whether the added connectivity of the network yields improved performance for these operations.

CHAPTER 5

Analytical Modeling of Parallel Programs

A sequential algorithm is usually evaluated in terms of its execution time, expressed as a function of the size of its input. The execution time of a parallel algorithm depends not only on input size but also on the number of processing elements used, and their relative computation and interprocess communication speeds. Hence, a parallel algorithm cannot be evaluated in isolation from a parallel architecture without some loss in accuracy. A *parallel system* is the combination of an algorithm and the parallel architecture on which it is implemented. In this chapter, we study various metrics for evaluating the performance of parallel systems.

A number of measures of performance are intuitive. Perhaps the simplest of these is the wall-clock time taken to solve a given problem on a given parallel platform. However, as we shall see, a single figure of merit of this nature cannot be extrapolated to other problem instances or larger machine configurations. Other intuitive measures quantify the benefit of parallelism, i.e., how much faster the parallel program runs with respect to the serial program. However, this characterization suffers from other drawbacks, in addition to those mentioned above. For instance, what is the impact of using a poorer serial algorithm that is more amenable to parallel processing? For these reasons, more complex measures for extrapolating performance to larger machine configurations or problems are often necessary. With these objectives in mind, this chapter focuses on metrics for quantifying the performance of parallel programs.

5.1 Sources of Overhead in Parallel Programs

Using twice as many hardware resources, one can reasonably expect a program to run twice as fast. However, in typical parallel programs, this is rarely the case, due to a variety

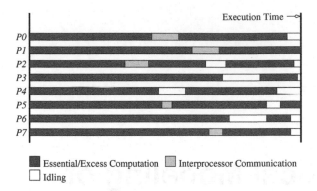

Essential/Excess Computation ◼ Interprocessor Communication
☐ Idling

Figure 5.1   The execution profile of a hypothetical parallel program executing on eight process-ing elements. Profile indicates times spent performing computation (both essential and excess), communication, and idling.

of overheads associated with parallelism. An accurate quantification of these overheads is critical to the understanding of parallel program performance.

A typical execution profile of a parallel program is illustrated in Figure 5.1. In addi-tion to performing essential computation (i.e., computation that would be performed by the serial program for solving the same problem instance), a parallel program may also spend time in interprocess communication, idling, and excess computation (computation not performed by the serial formulation).

Interprocess Interaction   Any nontrivial parallel system requires its processing ele-ments to interact and communicate data (e.g., intermediate results). The time spent com-municating data between processing elements is usually the most significant source of parallel processing overhead.

Idling   Processing elements in a parallel system may become idle due to many reasons such as load imbalance, synchronization, and presence of serial components in a program. In many parallel applications (for example, when task generation is dynamic), it is impos-sible (or at least difficult) to predict the size of the subtasks assigned to various processing elements. Hence, the problem cannot be subdivided statically among the processing ele-ments while maintaining uniform workload. If different processing elements have different workloads, some processing elements may be idle during part of the time that others are working on the problem. In some parallel programs, processing elements must synchro-nize at certain points during parallel program execution. If all processing elements are not ready for synchronization at the same time, then the ones that are ready sooner will be idle until all the rest are ready. Parts of an algorithm may be unparallelizable, allowing only a single processing element to work on it. While one processing element works on the serial part, all the other processing elements must wait.

Excess Computation The fastest known sequential algorithm for a problem may be difficult or impossible to parallelize, forcing us to use a parallel algorithm based on a poorer but easily parallelizable (that is, one with a higher degree of concurrency) sequential algorithm. The difference in computation performed by the parallel program and the best serial program is the excess computation overhead incurred by the parallel program.

A parallel algorithm based on the best serial algorithm may still perform more aggregate computation than the serial algorithm. An example of such a computation is the Fast Fourier Transform algorithm. In its serial version, the results of certain computations can be reused. However, in the parallel version, these results cannot be reused because they are generated by different processing elements. Therefore, some computations are performed multiple times on different processing elements. Chapter 13 discusses these algorithms in detail.

Since different parallel algorithms for solving the same problem incur varying overheads, it is important to quantify these overheads with a view to establishing a figure of merit for each algorithm.

5.2 Performance Metrics for Parallel Systems

It is important to study the performance of parallel programs with a view to determining the best algorithm, evaluating hardware platforms, and examining the benefits from parallelism. A number of metrics have been used based on the desired outcome of performance analysis.

5.2.1 Execution Time

The serial runtime of a program is the time elapsed between the beginning and the end of its execution on a sequential computer. The *parallel runtime* is the time that elapses from the moment a parallel computation starts to the moment the last processing element finishes execution. We denote the serial runtime by T_S and the parallel runtime by T_P.

5.2.2 Total Parallel Overhead

The overheads incurred by a parallel program are encapsulated into a single expression referred to as the *overhead function*. We define overhead function or *total overhead* of a parallel system as the total time collectively spent by all the processing elements over and above that required by the fastest known sequential algorithm for solving the same problem on a single processing element. We denote the overhead function of a parallel system by the symbol T_o.

The total time spent in solving a problem summed over all processing elements is pT_P. T_S units of this time are spent performing useful work, and the remainder is overhead. Therefore, the overhead function (T_o) is given by

$$T_o = pT_P - T_S. \tag{5.1}$$

5.2.3 Speedup

When evaluating a parallel system, we are often interested in knowing how much performance gain is achieved by parallelizing a given application over a sequential implementation. Speedup is a measure that captures the relative benefit of solving a problem in parallel. It is defined as the ratio of the time taken to solve a problem on a single processing element to the time required to solve the same problem on a parallel computer with p identical processing elements. We denote speedup by the symbol S.

Example 5.1   Adding n numbers using n processing elements

Consider the problem of adding n numbers by using n processing elements. Initially, each processing element is assigned one of the numbers to be added and, at the end of the computation, one of the processing elements stores the sum of all the numbers. Assuming that n is a power of two, we can perform this operation in $\log n$ steps by propagating partial sums up a logical binary tree of processing elements. Figure 5.2 illustrates the procedure for $n = 16$. The processing elements are labeled from 0 to 15. Similarly, the 16 numbers to be added are labeled from 0 to 15. The sum of the numbers with consecutive labels from i to j is denoted by Σ_i^j.

Each step shown in Figure 5.2 consists of one addition and the communication of a single word. The addition can be performed in some constant time, say t_c, and the communication of a single word can be performed in time $t_s + t_w$. Therefore, the addition and communication operations take a constant amount of time. Thus,

$$T_P = \Theta(\log n). \tag{5.2}$$

Since the problem can be solved in $\Theta(n)$ time on a single processing element, its speedup is

$$S = \Theta\left(\frac{n}{\log n}\right). \tag{5.3}$$

∎

For a given problem, more than one sequential algorithm may be available, but all of these may not be equally suitable for parallelization. When a serial computer is used, it is natural to use the sequential algorithm that solves the problem in the least amount of time. Given a parallel algorithm, it is fair to judge its performance with respect to the fastest sequential algorithm for solving the same problem on a single processing element. Sometimes, the asymptotically fastest sequential algorithm to solve a problem is not known, or its runtime has a large constant that makes it impractical to implement. In such cases, we take the fastest known algorithm that would be a practical choice for a serial computer to be the best sequential algorithm. We compare the performance of a parallel algorithm to solve a problem with that of the best sequential algorithm to solve the same problem. We formally define the *speedup* S as the ratio of the serial runtime of the best sequential

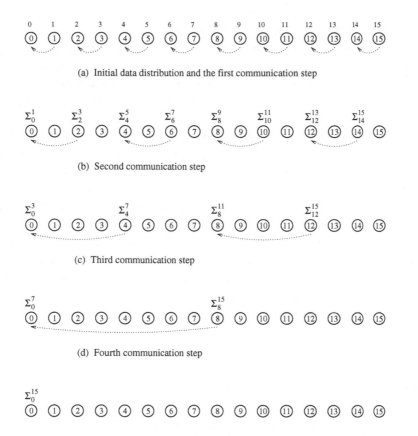

Figure 5.2 Computing the globalsum of 16 partial sums using 16 processing elements. Σ_i^j denotes the sum of numbers with consecutive labels from i to j.

algorithm for solving a problem to the time taken by the parallel algorithm to solve the same problem on p processing elements. The p processing elements used by the parallel algorithm are assumed to be identical to the one used by the sequential algorithm.

Example 5.2 Computing speedups of parallel programs

Consider the example of parallelizing bubble sort (Section 9.3.1). Assume that a serial version of bubble sort of 10^5 records takes 150 seconds and a serial quicksort can sort the same list in 30 seconds. If a parallel version of bubble sort, also called odd-even sort, takes 40 seconds on four processing elements, it would appear that the parallel odd-even sort algorithm results in a speedup of 150/40 or 3.75. However, this conclusion is misleading, as in reality the parallel algorithm results in a speedup of 30/40 or 0.75 with respect to the best serial algorithm. ∎

Theoretically, speedup can never exceed the number of processing elements, p. If the best sequential algorithm takes T_S units of time to solve a given problem on a single processing element, then a speedup of p can be obtained on p processing elements if none of the processing elements spends more than time T_S/p. A speedup greater than p is possible only if each processing element spends less than time T_S/p solving the problem. In this case, a single processing element could emulate the p processing elements and solve the problem in fewer than T_S units of time. This is a contradiction because speedup, by definition, is computed with respect to the best sequential algorithm. If T_S is the serial runtime of the algorithm, then the problem cannot be solved in less than time T_S on a single processing element.

In practice, a speedup greater than p is sometimes observed (a phenomenon known as *superlinear speedup*). This usually happens when the work performed by a serial algorithm is greater than its parallel formulation or due to hardware features that put the serial implementation at a disadvantage. For example, the data for a problem might be too large to fit into the cache of a single processing element, thereby degrading its performance due to the use of slower memory elements. But when partitioned among several processing elements, the individual data-partitions would be small enough to fit into their respective processing elements' caches. In the remainder of this book, we disregard superlinear speedup due to hierarchical memory.

Example 5.3   Superlinearity effects from caches
Consider the execution of a parallel program on a two-processor parallel system. The program attempts to solve a problem instance of size W. With this size and available cache of 64 KB on one processor, the program has a cache hit rate of 80%. Assuming the latency to cache of 2 ns and latency to DRAM of 100 ns, the effective memory access time is $2 \times 0.8 + 100 \times 0.2$, or 21.6 ns. If the computation is memory bound and performs one FLOP/memory access, this corresponds to a processing rate of 46.3 MFLOPS. Now consider a situation when each of the two processors is effectively executing half of the problem instance (i.e., size $W/2$). At this problem size, the cache hit ratio is expected to be higher, since the effective problem size is smaller. Let us assume that the cache hit ratio is 90%, 8% of the remaining data comes from local DRAM, and the other 2% comes from the remote DRAM (communication overhead). Assuming that remote data access takes 400 ns, this corresponds to an overall access time of $2 \times 0.9 + 100 \times 0.08 + 400 \times 0.02$, or 17.8 ns. The corresponding execution rate at each processor is therefore 56.18, for a total execution rate of 112.36 MFLOPS. The speedup in this case is given by the increase in speed over serial formulation, i.e., 112.36/46.3 or 2.43! Here, because of increased cache hit ratio resulting from lower problem size per processor, we notice superlinear speedup.   ∎

Example 5.4 Superlinearity effects due to exploratory decomposition

Consider an algorithm for exploring leaf nodes of an unstructured tree. Each leaf has a label associated with it and the objective is to find a node with a specified label, in this case 'S'. Such computations are often used to solve combinatorial problems, where the label 'S' could imply the solution to the problem (Section 11.6). In Figure 5.3, we illustrate such a tree. The solution node is the rightmost leaf in the tree. A serial formulation of this problem based on depth-first tree traversal explores the entire tree, i.e., all 14 nodes. If it takes time t_c to visit a node, the time for this traversal is $14t_c$. Now consider a parallel formulation in which the left subtree is explored by processing element 0 and the right subtree by processing element 1. If both processing elements explore the tree at the same speed, the parallel formulation explores only the shaded nodes before the solution is found. Notice that the total work done by the parallel algorithm is only nine node expansions, i.e., $9t_c$. The corresponding parallel time, assuming the root node expansion is serial, is $5t_c$ (one root node expansion, followed by four node expansions by each processing element). The speedup of this two-processor execution is therefore $14t_c/5t_c$, or 2.8!

The cause for this superlinearity is that the work performed by parallel and serial algorithms is different. Indeed, if the two-processor algorithm was implemented as two processes on the same processing element, the algorithmic superlinearity would disappear for this problem instance. Note that when exploratory decomposition is used, the relative amount of work performed by serial and parallel algorithms is dependent upon the location of the solution, and it is often not possible to find a serial algorithm that is optimal for all instances. Such effects are further analyzed in greater detail in Chapter 11. ∎

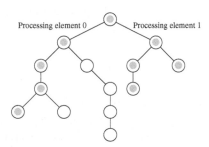

Figure 5.3 Searching an unstructured tree for a node with a given label, 'S', on two processing elements using depth-first traversal. The two-processor version with processor 0 searching the left subtree and processor 1 searching the right subtree expands only the shaded nodes before the solution is found. The corresponding serial formulation expands the entire tree. It is clear that the serial algorithm does more work than the parallel algorithm.

5.2.4 Efficiency

Only an ideal parallel system containing p processing elements can deliver a speedup equal to p. In practice, ideal behavior is not achieved because while executing a parallel algorithm, the processing elements cannot devote 100% of their time to the computations of the algorithm. As we saw in Example 5.1, part of the time required by the processing elements to compute the sum of n numbers is spent idling (and communicating in real systems). *Efficiency* is a measure of the fraction of time for which a processing element is usefully employed; it is defined as the ratio of speedup to the number of processing elements. In an ideal parallel system, speedup is equal to p and efficiency is equal to one. In practice, speedup is less than p and efficiency is between zero and one, depending on the effectiveness with which the processing elements are utilized. We denote efficiency by the symbol E. Mathematically, it is given by

$$E = \frac{S}{p}. \tag{5.4}$$

Example 5.5   Efficiency of adding n numbers on n processing elements
From Equation 5.3 and the preceding definition, the efficiency of the algorithm for adding n numbers on n processing elements is

$$
\begin{aligned}
E &= \frac{\Theta\left(\frac{n}{\log n}\right)}{n} \\
&= \Theta\left(\frac{1}{\log n}\right)
\end{aligned}
$$

∎

We also illustrate the process of deriving the parallel runtime, speedup, and efficiency while preserving various constants associated with the parallel platform.

Example 5.6   Edge detection on images
Given an $n \times n$ pixel image, the problem of detecting edges corresponds to applying a 3×3 template to each pixel. The process of applying the template corresponds to multiplying pixel values with corresponding template values and summing across the template (a convolution operation). This process is illustrated in Figure 5.4(a) along with typical templates (Figure 5.4(b)). Since we have nine multiply-add operations for each pixel, if each multiply-add takes time t_c, the entire operation takes time $9t_c n^2$ on a serial computer.

A simple parallel algorithm for this problem partitions the image equally across the processing elements and each processing element applies the template to its own subimage. Note that for applying the template to the boundary pixels, a processing element must get data that is assigned to the adjoining processing element. Specifically, if a processing element is assigned a vertically sliced subimage of dimension

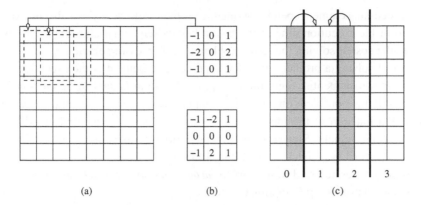

Figure 5.4 Example of edge detection: (a) an 8 × 8 image; (b) typical templates for detecting edges; and (c) partitioning of the image across four processors with shaded regions indicating image data that must be communicated from neighboring processors to processor 1.

$n \times (n/p)$, it must access a single layer of n pixels from the processing element to the left and a single layer of n pixels from the processing element to the right (note that one of these accesses is redundant for the two processing elements assigned the subimages at the extremities). This is illustrated in Figure 5.4(c).

On a message passing machine, the algorithm executes in two steps: (i) exchange a layer of n pixels with each of the two adjoining processing elements; and (ii) apply template on local subimage. The first step involves two n-word messages (assuming each pixel takes a word to communicate RGB data). This takes time $2(t_s + t_w n)$. The second step takes time $9t_c n^2/p$. The total time for the algorithm is therefore given by:

$$T_P = 9t_c \frac{n^2}{p} + 2(t_s + t_w n)$$

The corresponding values of speedup and efficiency are given by:

$$S = \frac{9t_c n^2}{9t_c \frac{n^2}{p} + 2(t_s + t_w n)}$$

and

$$E = \frac{1}{1 + \frac{2p(t_s + t_w n)}{9t_c n^2}}.$$

■

5.2.5 Cost

We define the *cost* of solving a problem on a parallel system as the product of parallel runtime and the number of processing elements used. Cost reflects the sum of the time that each processing element spends solving the problem. Efficiency can also be expressed as the ratio of the execution time of the fastest known sequential algorithm for solving a problem to the cost of solving the same problem on p processing elements.

The cost of solving a problem on a single processing element is the execution time of the fastest known sequential algorithm. A parallel system is said to be *cost-optimal* if the cost of solving a problem on a parallel computer has the same asymptotic growth (in Θ terms) as a function of the input size as the fastest-known sequential algorithm on a single processing element. Since efficiency is the ratio of sequential cost to parallel cost, a cost-optimal parallel system has an efficiency of $\Theta(1)$.

Cost is sometimes referred to as **work** or **processor-time product**, and a cost-optimal system is also known as a pT_P-optimal system.

Example 5.7 Cost of adding n numbers on n processing elements

The algorithm given in Example 5.1 for adding n numbers on n processing elements has a processor-time product of $\Theta(n \log n)$. Since the serial runtime of this operation is $\Theta(n)$, the algorithm is not cost optimal. ∎

Cost optimality is a very important practical concept although it is defined in terms of asymptotics. We illustrate this using the following example.

Example 5.8 Performance of non-cost optimal algorithms

Consider a sorting algorithm that uses n processing elements to sort the list in time $(\log n)^2$. Since the serial runtime of a (comparison-based) sort is $n \log n$, the speedup and efficiency of this algorithm are given by $n/\log n$ and $1/\log n$, respectively. The pT_P product of this algorithm is $n(\log n)^2$. Therefore, this algorithm is not cost optimal but only by a factor of $\log n$. Let us consider a realistic scenario in which the number of processing elements p is much less than n. An assignment of these n tasks to $p < n$ processing elements gives us a parallel time less than $n(\log n)^2/p$. This follows from the fact that if n processing elements take time $(\log n)^2$, then one processing element would take time $n(\log n)^2$; and p processing elements would take time $n(\log n)^2/p$. The corresponding speedup of this formulation is $p/\log n$. Consider the problem of sorting 1024 numbers ($n = 1024$, $\log n = 10$) on 32 processing elements. The speedup expected is only $p/\log n$ or 3.2. This number gets worse as n increases. For $n = 10^6$, $\log n = 20$ and the speedup is only 1.6. Clearly, there is a significant cost associated with not being cost-optimal even by a very small factor (note that a factor of $\log p$ is smaller than even $\sqrt{p}$). This emphasizes the practical importance of cost-optimality. ∎

5.3 The Effect of Granularity on Performance

Example 5.7 illustrated an instance of an algorithm that is not cost-optimal. The algorithm discussed in this example uses as many processing elements as the number of inputs, which is excessive in terms of the number of processing elements. In practice, we assign larger pieces of input data to processing elements. This corresponds to increasing the granularity of computation on the processing elements. Using fewer than the maximum possible number of processing elements to execute a parallel algorithm is called *scaling down* a parallel system in terms of the number of processing elements. A naive way to scale down a parallel system is to design a parallel algorithm for one input element per processing element, and then use fewer processing elements to simulate a large number of processing elements. If there are n inputs and only p processing elements ($p < n$), we can use the parallel algorithm designed for n processing elements by assuming n virtual processing elements and having each of the p physical processing elements simulate n/p virtual processing elements.

As the number of processing elements decreases by a factor of n/p, the computation at each processing element increases by a factor of n/p because each processing element now performs the work of n/p processing elements. If virtual processing elements are mapped appropriately onto physical processing elements, the overall communication time does not grow by more than a factor of n/p. The total parallel runtime increases, at most, by a factor of n/p, and the processor-time product does not increase. Therefore, if a parallel system with n processing elements is cost-optimal, using p processing elements (where $p < n$) to simulate n processing elements preserves cost-optimality.

A drawback of this naive method of increasing computational granularity is that if a parallel system is not cost-optimal to begin with, it may still not be cost-optimal after the granularity of computation increases. This is illustrated by the following example for the problem of adding n numbers.

Example 5.9 Adding n numbers on p processing elements

Consider the problem of adding n numbers on p processing elements such that $p < n$ and both n and p are powers of 2. We use the same algorithm as in Example 5.1 and simulate n processing elements on p processing elements. The steps leading to the solution are shown in Figure 5.5 for $n = 16$ and $p = 4$. Virtual processing element i is simulated by the physical processing element labeled i mod p; the numbers to be added are distributed similarly. The first $\log p$ of the $\log n$ steps of the original algorithm are simulated in $(n/p) \log p$ steps on p processing elements. In the remaining steps, no communication is required because the processing elements that communicate in the original algorithm are simulated by the same processing element; hence, the remaining numbers are added locally. The algorithm takes $\Theta((n/p) \log p)$ time in the steps that require communication, after which a single processing element is left with n/p numbers to add, taking time $\Theta(n/p)$. Thus, the overall parallel execution time of this parallel system is $\Theta((n/p) \log p)$. Consequently, its cost is

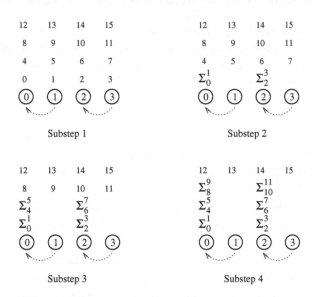

(a) Four processors simulating the first communication step of 16 processors

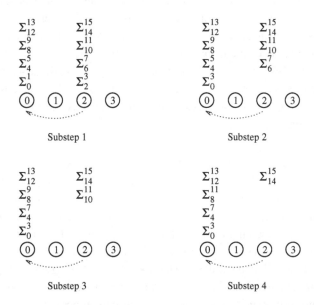

(b) Four processors simulating the second communication step of 16 processors

Figure 5.5 Four processing elements simulating 16 processing elements to compute the sum of 16 numbers (first two steps). Σ_i^j denotes the sum of numbers with consecutive labels from i to j.

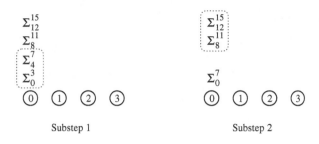

Substep 1   Substep 2

(c) Simulation of the third step in two substeps

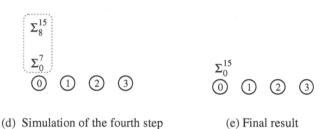

(d) Simulation of the fourth step   (e) Final result

Figure 5.5 (continued)   Four processing elements simulating 16 processing elements to compute the sum of 16 numbers (last three steps).

$\Theta(n \log p)$, which is asymptotically higher than the $\Theta(n)$ cost of adding n numbers sequentially. Therefore, the parallel system is not cost-optimal. ∎

Example 5.1 showed that n numbers can be added on an n-processor machine in time $\Theta(\log n)$. When using p processing elements to simulate n virtual processing elements $(p < n)$, the expected parallel runtime is $\Theta((n/p) \log n)$. However, in Example 5.9 this task was performed in time $\Theta((n/p) \log p)$ instead. The reason is that every communication step of the original algorithm does not have to be simulated; at times, communication takes place between virtual processing elements that are simulated by the same physical processing element. For these operations, there is no associated overhead. For example, the simulation of the third and fourth steps (Figure 5.5(c) and (d)) did not require any communication. However, this reduction in communication was not enough to make the algorithm cost-optimal. Example 5.10 illustrates that the same problem (adding n numbers on p processing elements) can be performed cost-optimally with a smarter assignment of data to processing elements.

Example 5.10   Adding n numbers cost-optimally
An alternate method for adding n numbers using p processing elements is illustrated in Figure 5.6 for $n = 16$ and $p = 4$. In the first step of this algorithm, each processing element locally adds its n/p numbers in time $\Theta(n/p)$. Now the problem is reduced

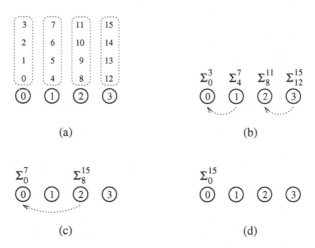

Figure 5.6   A cost-optimal way of computing the sum of 16 numbers using four processing elements.

to adding the p partial sums on p processing elements, which can be done in time $\Theta(\log p)$ by the method described in Example 5.1. The parallel runtime of this algorithm is

$$T_P = \Theta(n/p + \log p), \tag{5.5}$$

and its cost is $\Theta(n + p \log p)$. As long as $n = \Omega(p \log p)$, the cost is $\Theta(n)$, which is the same as the serial runtime. Hence, this parallel system is cost-optimal.   ∎

These simple examples demonstrate that the manner in which the computation is mapped onto processing elements may determine whether a parallel system is cost-optimal. Note, however, that we cannot make all non-cost-optimal systems cost-optimal by scaling down the number of processing elements.

5.4   Scalability of Parallel Systems

Very often, programs are designed and tested for smaller problems on fewer processing elements. However, the real problems these programs are intended to solve are much larger, and the machines contain larger number of processing elements. Whereas code development is simplified by using scaled-down versions of the machine and the problem, their performance and correctness (of programs) is much more difficult to establish based on scaled-down systems. In this section, we will investigate techniques for evaluating the scalability of parallel programs using analytical tools.

Example 5.11   Why is performance extrapolation so difficult?
Consider three parallel algorithms for computing an n-point Fast Fourier Transform

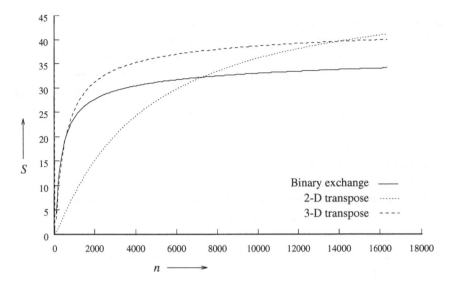

Figure 5.7 A comparison of the speedups obtained by the binary-exchange, 2-D transpose and 3-D transpose algorithms on 64 processing elements with $t_c = 2$, $t_w = 4$, $t_s = 25$, and $t_h = 2$ (see Chapter 13 for details).

(FFT) on 64 processing elements. Figure 5.7 illustrates speedup as the value of n is increased to 18 K. Keeping the number of processing elements constant, at smaller values of n, one would infer from observed speedups that binary exchange and 3-D transpose algorithms are the best. However, as the problem is scaled up to 18 K points or more, it is evident from Figure 5.7 that the 2-D transpose algorithm yields best speedup. (These algorithms are discussed in greater detail in Chapter 13.) ■

Similar results can be shown relating to the variation in number of processing elements as the problem size is held constant. Unfortunately, such parallel performance traces are the norm as opposed to the exception, making performance prediction based on limited observed data very difficult.

5.4.1 Scaling Characteristics of Parallel Programs

The efficiency of a parallel program can be written as:

$$E = \frac{S}{p} = \frac{T_S}{pT_P}$$

Using the expression for parallel overhead (Equation 5.1), we can rewrite this expression as

$$E = \frac{1}{1 + \frac{T_o}{T_S}}. \tag{5.6}$$

The total overhead function T_o is an increasing function of p. This is because every program must contain some serial component. If this serial component of the program takes time t_{serial}, then during this time all the other processing elements must be idle. This corresponds to a total overhead function of $(p - 1) \times t_{serial}$. Therefore, the total overhead function T_o grows at least linearly with p. In addition, due to communication, idling, and excess computation, this function may grow superlinearly in the number of processing elements. Equation 5.6 gives us several interesting insights into the scaling of parallel programs. First, for a given problem size (i.e. the value of T_S remains constant), as we increase the number of processing elements, T_o increases. In such a scenario, it is clear from Equation 5.6 that the overall efficiency of the parallel program goes down. This characteristic of decreasing efficiency with increasing number of processing elements for a given problem size is common to all parallel programs.

Example 5.12   Speedup and efficiency as functions of the number of processing elements
Consider the problem of adding n numbers on p processing elements. We use the same algorithm as in Example 5.10. However, to illustrate actual speedups, we work with constants here instead of asymptotics. Assuming unit time for adding two numbers, the first phase (local summations) of the algorithm takes roughly n/p time. The second phase involves $\log p$ steps with a communication and an addition at each step. If a single communication takes unit time as well, the time for this phase is $2 \log p$. Therefore, we can derive parallel time, speedup, and efficiency as:

$$T_P = \frac{n}{p} + 2 \log p \tag{5.7}$$

$$S = \frac{n}{\frac{n}{p} + 2 \log p} \tag{5.8}$$

$$E = \frac{1}{1 + \frac{2p \log p}{n}} \tag{5.9}$$

These expressions can be used to calculate the speedup and efficiency for any pair of n and p. Figure 5.8 shows the S versus p curves for a few different values of n and p. Table 5.1 shows the corresponding efficiencies.

Figure 5.8 and Table 5.1 illustrate that the speedup tends to saturate and efficiency drops as a consequence of *Amdahl's law* (Problem 5.1). Furthermore, a larger instance of the same problem yields higher speedup and efficiency for the same number of processing elements, although both speedup and efficiency continue to drop with increasing p.   ■

Let us investigate the effect of increasing the problem size keeping the number of processing elements constant. We know that the total overhead function T_o is a function of both problem size T_S and the number of processing elements p. In many cases, T_o grows sublinearly with respect to T_S. In such cases, we can see that efficiency increases if the

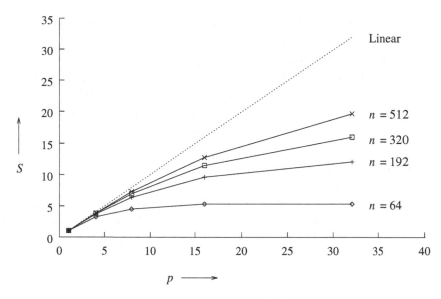

Figure 5.8   Speedup versus the number of processing elements for adding a list of numbers.

problem size is increased keeping the number of processing elements constant. For such algorithms, it should be possible to keep the efficiency fixed by increasing both the size of the problem and the number of processing elements simultaneously. For instance, in Table 5.1, the efficiency of adding 64 numbers using four processing elements is 0.80. If the number of processing elements is increased to 8 and the size of the problem is scaled up to add 192 numbers, the efficiency remains 0.80. Increasing p to 16 and n to 512 results in the same efficiency. This ability to maintain efficiency at a fixed value by simultaneously increasing the number of processing elements and the size of the problem is exhibited by many parallel systems. We call such systems *scalable* parallel systems. The *scalability* of a parallel system is a measure of its capacity to increase speedup in proportion to the number of processing elements. It reflects a parallel system's ability to utilize increasing processing resources effectively.

Table 5.1   Efficiency as a function of n and p for adding n numbers on p processing elements.

n	$p = 1$	$p = 4$	$p = 8$	$p = 16$	$p = 32$
64	1.0	*0.80*	0.57	0.33	0.17
192	1.0	0.92	*0.80*	0.60	0.38
320	1.0	0.95	0.87	0.71	0.50
512	1.0	0.97	0.91	*0.80*	0.62

Recall from Section 5.2.5 that a cost-optimal parallel system has an efficiency of $\Theta(1)$. Therefore, scalability and cost-optimality of parallel systems are related. A scalable parallel system can always be made cost-optimal if the number of processing elements and the size of the computation are chosen appropriately. For instance, Example 5.10 shows that the parallel system for adding n numbers on p processing elements is cost-optimal when $n = \Omega(p \log p)$. Example 5.13 shows that the same parallel system is scalable if n is increased in proportion to $\Theta(p \log p)$ as p is increased.

Example 5.13   Scalability of adding n numbers

For the cost-optimal addition of n numbers on p processing elements $n = \Omega(p \log p)$. As shown in Table 5.1, the efficiency is 0.80 for $n = 64$ and $p = 4$. At this point, the relation between n and p is $n = 8p \log p$. If the number of processing elements is increased to eight, then $8p \log p = 192$. Table 5.1 shows that the efficiency is indeed 0.80 with $n = 192$ for eight processing elements. Similarly, for $p = 16$, the efficiency is 0.80 for $n = 8p \log p = 512$. Thus, this parallel system remains cost-optimal at an efficiency of 0.80 if n is increased as $8p \log p$.   ■

5.4.2   The Isoefficiency Metric of Scalability

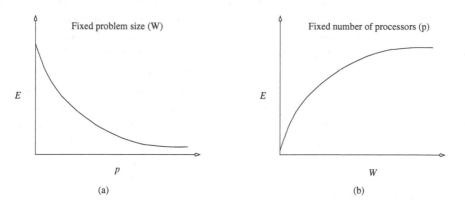

Figure 5.9   Variation of efficiency: (a) as the number of processing elements is increased for a given problem size; and (b) as the problem size is increased for a given number of processing elements. The phenomenon illustrated in graph (b) is not common to all parallel systems.

We summarize the discussion in the section above with the following two observations:

1. For a given problem size, as we increase the number of processing elements, the overall efficiency of the parallel system goes down. This phenomenon is common to all parallel systems.

2. In many cases, the efficiency of a parallel system increases if the problem size is increased while keeping the number of processing elements constant.

These two phenomena are illustrated in Figure 5.9(a) and (b), respectively. Following from these two observations, we define a scalable parallel system as one in which the efficiency can be kept constant as the number of processing elements is increased, provided that the problem size is also increased. It is useful to determine the rate at which the problem size must increase with respect to the number of processing elements to keep the efficiency fixed. For different parallel systems, the problem size must increase at different rates in order to maintain a fixed efficiency as the number of processing elements is increased. This rate determines the degree of scalability of the parallel system. As we shall show, a lower rate is more desirable than a higher growth rate in problem size. Let us now investigate metrics for quantitatively determining the degree of scalability of a parallel system. However, before we do that, we must define the notion of *problem size* precisely.

Problem Size   When analyzing parallel systems, we frequently encounter the notion of the size of the problem being solved. Thus far, we have used the term *problem size* informally, without giving a precise definition. A naive way to express problem size is as a parameter of the input size; for instance, n in case of a matrix operation involving $n \times n$ matrices. A drawback of this definition is that the interpretation of problem size changes from one problem to another. For example, doubling the input size results in an eight-fold increase in the execution time for matrix multiplication and a four-fold increase for matrix addition (assuming that the conventional $\Theta(n^3)$ algorithm is the best matrix multiplication algorithm, and disregarding more complicated algorithms with better asymptotic complexities).

A consistent definition of the size or the magnitude of the problem should be such that, regardless of the problem, doubling the problem size always means performing twice the amount of computation. Therefore, we choose to express problem size in terms of the total number of basic operations required to solve the problem. By this definition, the problem size is $\Theta(n^3)$ for $n \times n$ matrix multiplication (assuming the conventional algorithm) and $\Theta(n^2)$ for $n \times n$ matrix addition. In order to keep it unique for a given problem, we define *problem size* as the number of basic computation steps in the best sequential algorithm to solve the problem on a single processing element, where the best sequential algorithm is defined as in Section 5.2.3. Because it is defined in terms of sequential time complexity, the problem size is a function of the size of the input. The symbol we use to denote problem size is W.

In the remainder of this chapter, we assume that it takes unit time to perform one basic computation step of an algorithm. This assumption does not impact the analysis of any parallel system because the other hardware-related constants, such as message startup time, per-word transfer time, and per-hop time, can be normalized with respect to the time taken by a basic computation step. With this assumption, the problem size W is equal to the serial runtime T_S of the fastest known algorithm to solve the problem on a sequential computer.

The Isoefficiency Function

Parallel execution time can be expressed as a function of problem size, overhead function, and the number of processing elements. We can write parallel runtime as:

$$T_P = \frac{W + T_o(W, p)}{p} \tag{5.10}$$

The resulting expression for speedup is

$$S = \frac{W}{T_P}$$

$$= \frac{Wp}{W + T_o(W, p)}. \tag{5.11}$$

Finally, we write the expression for efficiency as

$$E = \frac{S}{p}$$

$$= \frac{W}{W + T_o(W, p)}$$

$$= \frac{1}{1 + T_o(W, p)/W}. \tag{5.12}$$

In Equation 5.12, if the problem size is kept constant and p is increased, the efficiency decreases because the total overhead T_o increases with p. If W is increased keeping the number of processing elements fixed, then for scalable parallel systems, the efficiency increases. This is because T_o grows slower than $\Theta(W)$ for a fixed p. For these parallel systems, efficiency can be maintained at a desired value (between 0 and 1) for increasing p, provided W is also increased.

For different parallel systems, W must be increased at different rates with respect to p in order to maintain a fixed efficiency. For instance, in some cases, W might need to grow as an exponential function of p to keep the efficiency from dropping as p increases. Such parallel systems are poorly scalable. The reason is that on these parallel systems it is difficult to obtain good speedups for a large number of processing elements unless the problem size is enormous. On the other hand, if W needs to grow only linearly with respect to p, then the parallel system is highly scalable. That is because it can easily deliver speedups proportional to the number of processing elements for reasonable problem sizes.

For scalable parallel systems, efficiency can be maintained at a fixed value (between 0 and 1) if the ratio T_o/W in Equation 5.12 is maintained at a constant value. For a desired value E of efficiency,

$$E = \frac{1}{1 + T_o(W, p)/W},$$

$$\frac{T_o(W, p)}{W} = \frac{1 - E}{E},$$

$$W = \frac{E}{1 - E} T_o(W, p). \tag{5.13}$$

Let $K = E/(1 - E)$ be a constant depending on the efficiency to be maintained. Since T_o is a function of W and p, Equation 5.13 can be rewritten as

$$W = KT_o(W, p). \tag{5.14}$$

From Equation 5.14, the problem size W can usually be obtained as a function of p by algebraic manipulations. This function dictates the growth rate of W required to keep the efficiency fixed as p increases. We call this function the *isoefficiency function* of the parallel system. The isoefficiency function determines the ease with which a parallel system can maintain a constant efficiency and hence achieve speedups increasing in proportion to the number of processing elements. A small isoefficiency function means that small increments in the problem size are sufficient for the efficient utilization of an increasing number of processing elements, indicating that the parallel system is highly scalable. However, a large isoefficiency function indicates a poorly scalable parallel system. The isoefficiency function does not exist for unscalable parallel systems, because in such systems the efficiency cannot be kept at any constant value as p increases, no matter how fast the problem size is increased.

Example 5.14   Isoefficiency function of adding numbers
The overhead function for the problem of adding n numbers on p processing elements is approximately $2p \log p$, as given by Equations 5.9 and 5.1. Substituting T_o by $2p \log p$ in Equation 5.14, we get

$$W = K2p \log p. \tag{5.15}$$

Thus, the asymptotic isoefficiency function for this parallel system is $\Theta(p \log p)$. This means that, if the number of processing elements is increased from p to p', the problem size (in this case, n) must be increased by a factor of $(p' \log p')/(p \log p)$ to get the same efficiency as on p processing elements. In other words, increasing the number of processing elements by a factor of p'/p requires that n be increased by a factor of $(p' \log p')/(p \log p)$ to increase the speedup by a factor of p'/p.   ∎

In the simple example of adding n numbers, the overhead due to communication (hereafter referred to as the *communication overhead*) is a function of p only. In general, communication overhead can depend on both the problem size and the number of processing elements. A typical overhead function can have several distinct terms of different orders of magnitude with respect to p and W. In such a case, it can be cumbersome (or even impossible) to obtain the isoefficiency function as a closed function of p. For example, consider a hypothetical parallel system for which $T_o = p^{3/2} + p^{3/4}W^{3/4}$. For this overhead function, Equation 5.14 can be rewritten as $W = Kp^{3/2} + Kp^{3/4}W^{3/4}$. It is hard to solve this equation for W in terms of p.

Recall that the condition for constant efficiency is that the ratio T_o/W remains fixed. As p and W increase, the efficiency is nondecreasing as long as none of the terms of T_o

grow faster than W. If T_o has multiple terms, we balance W against each term of T_o and compute the respective isoefficiency functions for individual terms. The component of T_o that requires the problem size to grow at the highest rate with respect to p determines the overall asymptotic isoefficiency function of the parallel system. Example 5.15 further illustrates this technique of isoefficiency analysis.

Example 5.15   Isoefficiency function of a parallel system with a complex overhead function

Consider a parallel system for which $T_o = p^{3/2} + p^{3/4} W^{3/4}$. Using only the first term of T_o in Equation 5.14, we get

$$W = K p^{3/2}. \tag{5.16}$$

Using only the second term, Equation 5.14 yields the following relation between W and p:

$$
\begin{aligned}
W &= K p^{3/4} W^{3/4} \\
W^{1/4} &= K p^{3/4} \\
W &= K^4 p^3
\end{aligned}
\tag{5.17}
$$

To ensure that the efficiency does not decrease as the number of processing elements increases, the first and second terms of the overhead function require the problem size to grow as $\Theta(p^{3/2})$ and $\Theta(p^3)$, respectively. The asymptotically higher of the two rates, $\Theta(p^3)$, gives the overall asymptotic isoefficiency function of this parallel system, since it subsumes the rate dictated by the other term. The reader may indeed verify that if the problem size is increased at this rate, the efficiency is $\Theta(1)$ and that any rate lower than this causes the efficiency to fall with increasing p.   ∎

In a single expression, the isoefficiency function captures the characteristics of a parallel algorithm as well as the parallel architecture on which it is implemented. After performing isoefficiency analysis, we can test the performance of a parallel program on a few processing elements and then predict its performance on a larger number of processing elements. However, the utility of isoefficiency analysis is not limited to predicting the impact on performance of an increasing number of processing elements. Section 5.4.5 shows how the isoefficiency function characterizes the amount of parallelism inherent in a parallel algorithm. We will see in Chapter 13 that isoefficiency analysis can also be used to study the behavior of a parallel system with respect to changes in hardware parameters such as the speed of processing elements and communication channels. Chapter 11 illustrates how isoefficiency analysis can be used even for parallel algorithms for which we cannot derive a value of parallel runtime.

5.4.3 Cost-Optimality and the Isoefficiency Function

In Section 5.2.5, we stated that a parallel system is cost-optimal if the product of the number of processing elements and the parallel execution time is proportional to the execution time of the fastest known sequential algorithm on a single processing element. In other words, a parallel system is cost-optimal if and only if

$$pT_P = \Theta(W). \tag{5.18}$$

Substituting the expression for T_P from the right-hand side of Equation 5.10, we get the following:

$$W + T_o(W, p) = \Theta(W)$$
$$T_o(W, p) = O(W) \tag{5.19}$$
$$W = \Omega(T_o(W, p)) \tag{5.20}$$

Equations 5.19 and 5.20 suggest that a parallel system is cost-optimal if and only if its overhead function does not asymptotically exceed the problem size. This is very similar to the condition given by Equation 5.14 for maintaining a fixed efficiency while increasing the number of processing elements in a parallel system. If Equation 5.14 yields an isoefficiency function $f(p)$, then it follows from Equation 5.20 that the relation $W = \Omega(f(p))$ must be satisfied to ensure the cost-optimality of a parallel system as it is scaled up. The following example further illustrates the relationship between cost-optimality and the isoefficiency function.

Example 5.16 Relationship between cost-optimality and isoefficiency
Consider the cost-optimal solution to the problem of adding n numbers on p processing elements, presented in Example 5.10. For this parallel system, $W \approx n$, and $T_o = \Theta(p \log p)$. From Equation 5.14, its isoefficiency function is $\Theta(p \log p)$; that is, the problem size must increase as $\Theta(p \log p)$ to maintain a constant efficiency. In Example 5.10 we also derived the condition for cost-optimality as $W = \Omega(p \log p)$.
■

5.4.4 A Lower Bound on the Isoefficiency Function

We discussed earlier that a smaller isoefficiency function indicates higher scalability. Accordingly, an ideally-scalable parallel system must have the lowest possible isoefficiency function. For a problem consisting of W units of work, no more than W processing elements can be used cost-optimally; additional processing elements will be idle. If the problem size grows at a rate slower than $\Theta(p)$ as the number of processing elements increases, then the number of processing elements will eventually exceed W. Even for an ideal parallel system with no communication, or other overhead, the efficiency will drop because processing elements added beyond $p = W$ will be idle. Thus, asymptotically, the problem size must increase at least as fast as $\Theta(p)$ to maintain fixed efficiency; hence, $\Omega(p)$ is the asymptotic lower bound on the isoefficiency function. It follows that the isoefficiency function of an ideally scalable parallel system is $\Theta(p)$.

5.4.5 The Degree of Concurrency and the Isoefficiency Function

A lower bound of $\Omega(p)$ is imposed on the isoefficiency function of a parallel system by the number of operations that can be performed concurrently. The maximum number of tasks that can be executed simultaneously at any time in a parallel algorithm is called its **degree of concurrency**. The degree of concurrency is a measure of the number of operations that an algorithm can perform in parallel for a problem of size W; it is independent of the parallel architecture. If $C(W)$ is the degree of concurrency of a parallel algorithm, then for a problem of size W, no more than $C(W)$ processing elements can be employed effectively.

> **Example 5.17**   Effect of concurrency on isoefficiency function
> Consider solving a system of n equations in n variables by using Gaussian elimination (Section 8.3.1). The total amount of computation is $\Theta(n^3)$. But the n variables must be eliminated one after the other, and eliminating each variable requires $\Theta(n^2)$ computations. Thus, at most $\Theta(n^2)$ processing elements can be kept busy at any time. Since $W = \Theta(n^3)$ for this problem, the degree of concurrency $C(W)$ is $\Theta(W^{2/3})$ and at most $\Theta(W^{2/3})$ processing elements can be used efficiently. On the other hand, given p processing elements, the problem size should be at least $\Omega(p^{3/2})$ to use them all. Thus, the isoefficiency function of this computation due to concurrency is $\Theta(p^{3/2})$.
>
> ■

The isoefficiency function due to concurrency is optimal (that is, $\Theta(p)$) only if the degree of concurrency of the parallel algorithm is $\Theta(W)$. If the degree of concurrency of an algorithm is less than $\Theta(W)$, then the isoefficiency function due to concurrency is worse (that is, greater) than $\Theta(p)$. In such cases, the overall isoefficiency function of a parallel system is given by the maximum of the isoefficiency functions due to concurrency, communication, and other overheads.

5.5 Minimum Execution Time and Minimum Cost-Optimal Execution Time

We are often interested in knowing how fast a problem can be solved, or what the minimum possible execution time of a parallel algorithm is, provided that the number of processing elements is not a constraint. As we increase the number of processing elements for a given problem size, either the parallel runtime continues to decrease and asymptotically approaches a minimum value, or it starts rising after attaining a minimum value (Problem 5.12). We can determine the minimum parallel runtime T_P^{min} for a given W by differentiating the expression for T_P with respect to p and equating the derivative to zero (assuming that the function $T_P(W, p)$ is differentiable with respect to p). The number of processing elements for which T_P is minimum is determined by the following equation:

$$\frac{d}{dp}T_P = 0 \qquad (5.21)$$

Let p_0 be the value of the number of processing elements that satisfies Equation 5.21. The value of T_P^{min} can be determined by substituting p_0 for p in the expression for T_P. In the following example, we derive the expression for T_P^{min} for the problem of adding n numbers.

Example 5.18   Minimum execution time for adding n numbers
Under the assumptions of Example 5.12, the parallel run time for the problem of adding n numbers on p processing elements can be approximated by

$$T_P = \frac{n}{p} + 2\log p. \qquad (5.22)$$

Equating the derivative with respect to p of the right-hand side of Equation 5.22 to zero we get the solutions for p as follows:

$$-\frac{n}{p^2} + \frac{2}{p} = 0$$
$$-n + 2p = 0$$
$$p = \frac{n}{2} \qquad (5.23)$$

Substituting $p = n/2$ in Equation 5.22, we get

$$T_P^{min} = 2\log n. \qquad (5.24)$$

∎

In Example 5.18, the processor-time product for $p = p_0$ is $\Theta(n \log n)$, which is higher than the $\Theta(n)$ serial complexity of the problem. Hence, the parallel system is not cost-optimal for the value of p that yields minimum parallel runtime. We now derive an important result that gives a lower bound on parallel runtime if the problem is solved cost-optimally.

Let $T_P^{cost-opt}$ be the minimum time in which a problem can be solved by a cost-optimal parallel system. From the discussion regarding the equivalence of cost-optimality and the isoefficiency function in Section 5.4.3, we conclude that if the isoefficiency function of a parallel system is $\Theta(f(p))$, then a problem of size W can be solved cost-optimally if and only if $W = \Omega(f(p))$. In other words, given a problem of size W, a cost-optimal solution requires that $p = O(f^{-1}(W))$. Since the parallel runtime is $\Theta(W/p)$ for a cost-optimal parallel system (Equation 5.18), the lower bound on the parallel runtime for solving a problem of size W cost-optimally is

$$T_P^{cost\_opt} = \Omega\left(\frac{W}{f^{-1}(W)}\right). \tag{5.25}$$

Example 5.19 Minimum cost-optimal execution time for adding n numbers
As derived in Example 5.14, the isoefficiency function $f(p)$ of this parallel system is $\Theta(p \log p)$. If $W = n = f(p) = p \log p$, then $\log n = \log p + \log \log p$. Ignoring the double logarithmic term, $\log n \approx \log p$. If $n = f(p) = p \log p$, then $p = f^{-1}(n) = n/\log p \approx n/\log n$. Hence, $f^{-1}(W) = \Theta(n/\log n)$. As a consequence of the relation between cost-optimality and the isoefficiency function, the maximum number of processing elements that can be used to solve this problem cost-optimally is $\Theta(n/\log n)$. Using $p = n/\log n$ in Equation 5.2, we get

$$\begin{aligned} T_P^{cost\_opt} &= \log n + \log\left(\frac{n}{\log n}\right) \\ &= 2\log n - \log\log n. \end{aligned} \tag{5.26}$$

■

It is interesting to observe that both T_P^{min} and $T_P^{cost\_opt}$ for adding n numbers are $\Theta(\log n)$ (Equations 5.24 and 5.26). Thus, for this problem, a cost-optimal solution is also the asymptotically fastest solution. The parallel execution time cannot be reduced asymptotically by using a value of p greater than that suggested by the isoefficiency function for a given problem size (due to the equivalence between cost-optimality and the isoefficiency function). This is not true for parallel systems in general, however, and it is quite possible that $T_P^{cost\_opt} > \Theta(T_P^{min})$. The following example illustrates such a parallel system.

Example 5.20 A parallel system with $T_P^{cost\_opt} > \Theta(T_P^{min})$
Consider the hypothetical parallel system of Example 5.15, for which

$$T_o = p^{3/2} + p^{3/4}W^{3/4}. \tag{5.27}$$

From Equation 5.10, the parallel runtime for this system is

$$T_P = \frac{W}{p} + p^{1/2} + \frac{W^{3/4}}{p^{1/4}}. \tag{5.28}$$

Using the methodology of Example 5.18,

$$\frac{d}{dp}T_P = -\frac{W}{p^2} + \frac{1}{2p^{1/2}} - \frac{W^{3/4}}{4p^{5/4}} = 0,$$

$$-W + \frac{1}{2}p^{3/2} - \frac{1}{4}W^{3/4}p^{3/4} = 0,$$

$$p^{3/4} = \frac{1}{4}W^{3/4} \pm (\frac{1}{16}W^{3/2} + 2W)^{1/2}$$

$$= \Theta(W^{3/4}),$$

$$p = \Theta(W).$$

From the preceding analysis, $p_0 = \Theta(W)$. Substituting p by the value of p_0 in Equation 5.28, we get

$$T_P^{min} = \Theta(W^{1/2}). \tag{5.29}$$

According to Example 5.15, the overall isoefficiency function for this parallel system is $\Theta(p^3)$, which implies that the maximum number of processing elements that can be used cost-optimally is $\Theta(W^{1/3})$. Substituting $p = \Theta(W^{1/3})$ in Equation 5.28, we get

$$T_P^{cost\_opt} = \Theta(W^{2/3}). \tag{5.30}$$

A comparison of Equations 5.29 and 5.30 shows that $T_P^{cost\_opt}$ is asymptotically greater than T_P^{min}. ∎

In this section, we have seen examples of both types of parallel systems: those for which $T_P^{cost\_opt}$ is asymptotically equal to T_P^{min}, and those for which $T_P^{cost\_opt}$ is asymptotically greater than T_P^{min}. Most parallel systems presented in this book are of the first type. Parallel systems for which the runtime can be reduced by an order of magnitude by using an asymptotically higher number of processing elements than indicated by the isoefficiency function are rare.

While deriving the minimum execution time for any parallel system, it is important to be aware that the maximum number of processing elements that can be utilized is bounded by the degree of concurrency $C(W)$ of the parallel algorithm. It is quite possible that p_0 is greater than $C(W)$ for a parallel system (Problems 5.13 and 5.14). In such cases, the value of p_0 is meaningless, and T_P^{min} is given by

$$T_P^{min} = \frac{W + T_o(W, C(W))}{C(W)}. \tag{5.31}$$

5.6 Asymptotic Analysis of Parallel Programs

At this point, we have accumulated an arsenal of powerful tools for quantifying the performance and scalability of an algorithm. Let us illustrate the use of these tools for evaluating a set of parallel programs for solving a given problem. Often, we ignore constants and concern ourselves with the asymptotic behavior of quantities. In many cases, this can yield a clearer picture of relative merits and demerits of various parallel programs.

Table 5.2 Comparison of four different algorithms for sorting a given list of numbers. The table shows number of processing elements, parallel runtime, speedup, efficiency and the pT_P product.

Algorithm	A1	A2	A3	A4
p	n^2	$\log n$	n	$\sqrt{n}$
T_P	1	n	$\sqrt{n}$	$\sqrt{n}\log n$
S	$n\log n$	$\log n$	$\sqrt{n}\log n$	$\sqrt{n}$
E	$\frac{\log n}{n}$	1	$\frac{\log n}{\sqrt{n}}$	1
pT_P	n^2	$n\log n$	$n^{1.5}$	$n\log n$

Consider the problem of sorting a list of n numbers. The fastest serial programs for this problem run in time $O(n\log n)$. Let us look at four different parallel algorithms A1, A2, A3, and A4, for sorting a given list. The parallel runtime of the four algorithms along with the number of processing elements they can use is given in Table 5.2. The objective of this exercise is to determine which of these four algorithms is the best. Perhaps the simplest metric is one of speed; the algorithm with the lowest T_P is the best. By this metric, algorithm A1 is the best, followed by A3, A4, and A2. This is also reflected in the fact that the speedups of the set of algorithms are also in this order.

However, in practical situations, we will rarely have n^2 processing elements as are required by algorithm A1. Furthermore, resource utilization is an important aspect of practical program design. So let us look at how efficient each of these algorithms are. This metric of evaluating the algorithm presents a starkly different image. Algorithms A2 and A4 are the best, followed by A3 and A1. The last row of Table 5.2 presents the cost of the four algorithms. From this row, it is evident that the costs of algorithms A1 and A3 are higher than the serial runtime of $n\log n$ and therefore neither of these algorithms is cost optimal. However, algorithms A2 and A4 are cost optimal.

This set of algorithms illustrate that it is important to first understand the objectives of parallel algorithm analysis and to use appropriate metrics. This is because use of different metrics may often result in contradictory outcomes.

5.7 Other Scalability Metrics

A number of other metrics of scalability of parallel systems have been proposed. These metrics are specifically suited to different system requirements. For example, in real time applications, the objective is to scale up a system to accomplish a task in a specified time bound. One such application is multimedia decompression, where MPEG streams must be decompressed at the rate of 25 frames/second. Consequently, a parallel system must decode a single frame in 40 ms (or with buffering, at an average of 1 frame in 40 ms over the buffered frames). Other such applications arise in real-time control, where a control vector must be generated in real-time. Several scalability metrics consider constraints on physical architectures. In many applications, the maximum size of a problem is constrained not by time, efficiency, or underlying models, but by the memory available on the machine. In such cases, metrics make assumptions on the growth function of available memory (with number of processing elements) and estimate how the performance of the parallel system changes with such scaling. In this section, we examine some of the related metrics and how they can be used in various parallel applications.

Scaled Speedup   This metric is defined as the speedup obtained when the problem size is increased linearly with the number of processing elements. If the scaled-speedup curve is close to linear with respect to the number of processing elements, then the parallel system is considered scalable. This metric is related to isoefficiency if the parallel algorithm under consideration has linear or near-linear isoefficiency function. In this case the scaled-speedup metric provides results very close to those of isoefficiency analysis, and the scaled-speedup is linear or near-linear with respect to the number of processing elements. For parallel systems with much worse isoefficiencies, the results provided by the two metrics may be quite different. In this case, the scaled-speedup versus number of processing elements curve is sublinear.

Two generalized notions of scaled speedup have been examined. They differ in the methods by which the problem size is scaled up with the number of processing elements. In one method, the size of the problem is increased to fill the available memory on the parallel computer. The assumption here is that aggregate memory of the system increases with the number of processing elements. In the other method, the size of the problem grows with p subject to an upper-bound on execution time.

Example 5.21   Memory and time-constrained scaled speedup for matrix-vector products
The serial runtime of multiplying a matrix of dimension $n \times n$ with a vector is $t_c n^2$, where t_c is the time for a single multiply-add operation. The corresponding parallel runtime using a simple parallel algorithm is given by:

$$T_P = t_c \frac{n^2}{p} + t_s \log p + t_w n$$

and the speedup S is given by:

$$S = \frac{t_c n^2}{t_c \frac{n^2}{p} + t_s \log p + t_w n} \tag{5.32}$$

The total memory requirement of the algorithm is $\Theta(n^2)$. Let us consider the two cases of problem scaling. In the case of memory constrained scaling, we assume that the memory of the parallel system grows linearly with the number of processing elements, i.e., $m = \Theta(p)$. This is a reasonable assumption for most current parallel platforms. Since $m = \Theta(n^2)$, we have $n^2 = c \times p$, for some constant c. Therefore, the scaled speedup S' is given by:

$$S' = \frac{t_c c \times p}{t_c \frac{c \times p}{p} + t_s \log p + t_w \sqrt{c \times p}}$$

or

$$S' = \frac{c_1 p}{c_2 + c_3 \log p + c_4 \sqrt{p}}.$$

In the limiting case, $S' = O(\sqrt{p})$.

In the case of time constrained scaling, we have $T_P = O(n^2/p)$. Since this is constrained to be constant, $n^2 = O(p)$. We notice that this case is identical to the memory constrained case. This happened because the memory and runtime of the algorithm are asymptotically identical.   ∎

Example 5.22   Memory and time-constrained scaled speedup for matrix-matrix products

The serial runtime of multiplying two matrices of dimension $n \times n$ is $t_c n^3$, where t_c, as before, is the time for a single multiply-add operation. The corresponding parallel runtime using a simple parallel algorithm is given by:

$$T_P = t_c \frac{n^3}{p} + t_s \log p + 2t_w \frac{n^2}{\sqrt{p}}$$

and the speedup S is given by:

$$S = \frac{t_c n^3}{t_c \frac{n^3}{p} + t_s \log p + 2t_w \frac{n^2}{\sqrt{p}}} \tag{5.33}$$

The total memory requirement of the algorithm is $\Theta(n^2)$. Let us consider the two cases of problem scaling. In the case of memory constrained scaling, as before, we assume that the memory of the parallel system grows linearly with the number of processing elements, i.e., $m = \Theta(p)$. Since $m = \Theta(n^2)$, we have $n^2 = c \times p$, for some constant c. Therefore, the scaled speedup S' is given by:

$$S' = \frac{t_c(c \times p)^{1.5}}{t_c \frac{(c \times p)^{1.5}}{p} + t_s \log p + 2t_w \frac{c \times p}{\sqrt{p}}} = O(p)$$

In the case of time constrained scaling, we have $T_P = O(n^3/p)$. Since this is constrained to be constant, $n^3 = O(p)$, or $n^3 = c \times p$ (for some constant c).

Therefore, the time-constrained speedup S'' is given by:

$$S'' = \frac{t_c c \times p}{t_c \frac{c \times p}{p} + t_s \log p + 2t_w \frac{(c \times p)^{2/3}}{\sqrt{p}}} = O(p^{5/6})$$

This example illustrates that memory-constrained scaling yields linear speedup, whereas time-constrained speedup yields sublinear speedup in the case of matrix multiplication. ■

Serial Fraction f The experimentally determined serial fraction f can be used to quantify the performance of a parallel system on a fixed-size problem. Consider a case when the serial runtime of a computation can be divided into a totally parallel and a totally serial component, i.e.,

$$W = T_{ser} + T_{par}.$$

Here, T_{ser} and T_{par} correspond to totally serial and totally parallel components. From this, we can write:

$$T_P = T_{ser} + \frac{T_{par}}{p}.$$

Here, we have assumed that all of the other parallel overheads such as excess computation and communication are captured in the serial component T_{ser}. From these equations, it follows that:

$$T_P = T_{ser} + \frac{W - T_{ser}}{p} \tag{5.34}$$

The serial fraction f of a parallel program is defined as:

$$f = \frac{T_{ser}}{W}.$$

Therefore, from Equation 5.34, we have:

$$T_P = f \times W + \frac{W - f \times W}{p}$$

$$\frac{T_P}{W} = f + \frac{1 - f}{p}$$

Since $S = W/T_P$, we have

$$\frac{1}{S} = f + \frac{1 - f}{p}.$$

Solving for f, we get:

$$f = \frac{1/S - 1/p}{1 - 1/p}. \tag{5.35}$$

It is easy to see that smaller values of f are better since they result in higher efficiencies. If f increases with the number of processing elements, then it is considered as an indicator of rising communication overhead, and thus an indicator of poor scalability.

Example 5.23 Serial component of the matrix-vector product

From Equations 5.35 and 5.32, we have

$$f = \frac{\frac{t_c \frac{n^2}{p} + t_s \log p + t_w n}{t_c n^2}}{1 - 1/p} \tag{5.36}$$

Simplifying the above expression, we get

$$f = \frac{t_s p \log p + t_w n p}{t_c n^2} \times \frac{1}{p - 1}$$

$$f \approx \frac{t_s \log p + t_w n}{t_c n^2}$$

It is useful to note that the denominator of this equation is the serial runtime of the algorithm and the numerator corresponds to the overhead in parallel execution. ∎

In addition to these metrics, a number of other metrics of performance have been proposed in the literature. We refer interested readers to the bibliography for references to these.

5.8 Bibliographic Remarks

To use today's massively parallel computers effectively, larger problems must be solved as more processing elements are added. However, when the problem size is fixed, the objective is to attain the best compromise between efficiency and parallel runtime. Performance issues for fixed-size problems have been addressed by several researchers [FK89, GK93a, KF90, NW88, TL90, Wor90]. In most situations, additional computing power derived from increasing the number of processing elements can be used to solve bigger problems. In some situations, however, different ways of increasing the problem size may apply, and a variety of constraints may guide the scaling up of the workload with respect to the number of processing elements [SHG93]. Time-constrained scaling and memory-constrained scaling have been explored by Gustafson *et al.* [GMB88, Gus88, Gus92], Sun and Ni [SN90, SN93], and Worley [Wor90, Wor88, Wor91] (Problem 5.9).

An important scenario is one in which we want to make the most efficient use of the parallel system; in other words, we want the overall performance of the parallel system to increase linearly with p. This is possible only for scalable parallel systems, which are exactly those for which a fixed efficiency can be maintained for arbitrarily large p by simply increasing the problem size. For such systems, it is natural to use the isoefficiency function or related metrics [GGK93, CD87, KR87b, KRS88]. Isoefficiency analysis has been found to be very useful in characterizing the scalability of a variety of parallel algorithms [GK91, GK93b, GKS92, HX98, KN91, KR87b, KR89, KS91b, RS90b, SKAT91b, TL90, WS89, WS91]. Gupta and Kumar [GK93a, KG94] have demonstrated the relevance of the isoefficiency function in the fixed time case as well. They have shown that if the iso-efficiency function is greater than $\Theta(p)$, then the problem size cannot be increased indefinitely while maintaining a fixed execution time, no matter how many processing elements are used. A number of other researchers have analyzed the performance of parallel systems with concern for overall efficiency [EZL89, FK89, MS88, NW88, TL90, Zho89, ZRV89].

Kruskal, Rudolph, and Snir [KRS88] define the concept of *parallel efficient (PE)* problems. Their definition is related to the concept of isoefficiency function. Problems in the class PE have algorithms with a polynomial isoefficiency function at some efficiency. The class PE makes an important distinction between algorithms with polynomial isoefficiency functions and those with worse isoefficiency functions. Kruskal *et al.* proved the invariance of the class PE over a variety of parallel computational models and interconnection schemes. An important consequence of this result is that an algorithm with a polynomial isoefficiency on one architecture will have a polynomial isoefficiency on many other architectures as well. There can be exceptions, however; for instance, Gupta and Kumar [GK93b] show that the fast Fourier transform algorithm has a polynomial isoefficiency on a hypercube but an exponential isoefficiency on a mesh.

Vitter and Simons [VS86] define a class of problems called *PC**. PC* includes problems with efficient parallel algorithms on a PRAM. A problem in class *P* (the polynomial-time class) is in PC* if it has a parallel algorithm on a PRAM that can use a polynomial (in terms of input size) number of processing elements and achieve a minimal efficiency ϵ. Any problem in PC* has at least one parallel algorithm such that, for an efficiency ϵ, its isoefficiency function exists and is a polynomial.

A discussion of various scalability and performance measures can be found in the survey by Kumar and Gupta [KG94]. Besides the ones cited so far, a number of other metrics of performance and scalability of parallel systems have been proposed [BW89, CR89, CR91, Fla90, Hil90, Kun86, Mol87, MR, NA91, SG91, SR91, SZ96, VC89].

Flatt and Kennedy [FK89, Fla90] show that if the overhead function satisfies certain mathematical properties, then there exists a unique value p_0 of the number of processing elements for which T_P is minimum for a given W. A property of T_o on which their analysis depends heavily is that $T_o > \Theta(p)$. Gupta and Kumar [GK93a] show that there exist parallel systems that do not obey this condition, and in such cases the point of peak performance is determined by the degree of concurrency of the algorithm being used.

Marinescu and Rice [MR] develop a model to describe and analyze a parallel computation on an MIMD computer in terms of the number of threads of control p into which the computation is divided and the number of events $g(p)$ as a function of p. They consider the case where each event is of a fixed duration θ and hence $T_o = \theta g(p)$. Under these assumptions on T_o, they conclude that with increasing number of processing elements, the speedup saturates at some value if $T_o = \Theta(p)$, and it asymptotically approaches zero if $T_o = \Theta(p^m)$, where $m \geq 2$. Gupta and Kumar [GK93a] generalize these results for a wider class of overhead functions. They show that the speedup saturates at some maximum value if $T_o \leq \Theta(p)$, and the speedup attains a maximum value and then drops monotonically with p if $T_o > \Theta(p)$.

Eager *et al.* [EZL89] and Tang and Li [TL90] have proposed a criterion of optimality of a parallel system so that a balance is struck between efficiency and speedup. They propose that a good choice of operating point on the execution time versus efficiency curve is that where the incremental benefit of adding processing elements is roughly $\frac{1}{2}$ per processing element or, in other words, efficiency is 0.5. They conclude that for $T_o = \Theta(p)$, this is also equivalent to operating at a point where the ES product is maximum or $p(T_P)^2$ is minimum. This conclusion is a special case of the more general case presented by Gupta and Kumar [GK93a].

Belkhale and Banerjee [BB90], Leuze *et al.* [LDP89], Ma and Shea [MS88], and Park and Dowdy [PD89] address the important problem of optimal partitioning of the processing elements of a parallel computer among several applications of different scalabilities executing simultaneously.

Problems

5.1 **(Amdahl's law [Amd67])** If a problem of size W has a serial component W_S, prove that W/W_S is an upper bound on its speedup, no matter how many processing elements are used.

5.2 **(Superlinear speedup)** Consider the search tree shown in Figure 5.10(a), in which the dark node represents the solution.
(a) If a sequential search of the tree is performed using the standard depth-first search (DFS) algorithm (Section 11.2.1), how much time does it take to find the solution if traversing each arc of the tree takes one unit of time?
(b) Assume that the tree is partitioned between two processing elements that are assigned to do the search job, as shown in Figure 5.10(b). If both processing elements perform a DFS on their respective halves of the tree, how much time does it take for the solution to be found? What is the speedup? Is there a speedup anomaly? If so, can you explain the anomaly?

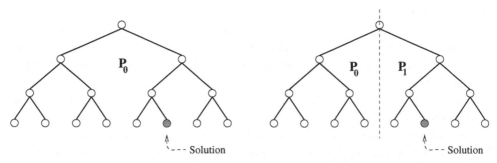

(a) DFS with one processing element   (b) DFS with two processing elements

Figure 5.10   Superlinear(?) speedup in parallel depth first search.

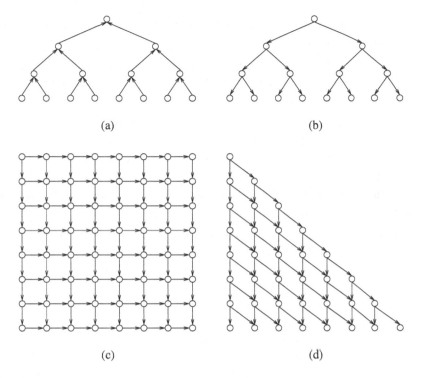

Figure 5.11   Dependency graphs for Problem 5.3.

5.3   (**The DAG model of parallel computation**) Parallel algorithms can often be represented by dependency graphs. Four such dependency graphs are shown in Figure 5.11. If a program can be broken into several tasks, then each node of the graph represents one task. The directed edges of the graph represent the dependencies between the tasks or the order in which they must be performed to yield correct results. A node of the dependency graph can be scheduled for execution as soon as the tasks at all the nodes that have incoming edges to that node have finished execution. For example, in Figure 5.11(b), the nodes on the second level from the root can begin execution only after the task at the root is finished. Any deadlock-free dependency graph must be a *directed acyclic graph* (DAG); that is, it is devoid of any cycles. All the nodes that are scheduled for execution can be worked on in parallel provided enough processing elements are available. If N is the number of nodes in a graph, and n is an integer, then $N = 2^n - 1$ for graphs (a) and (b), $N = n^2$ for graph (c), and $N = n(n + 1)/2$ for graph (d) (graphs (a) and (b) are drawn for $n = 4$ and graphs (c) and (d) are drawn for $n = 8$). Assuming that each task takes one unit of time and that interprocessor communication time is zero, for the algorithms represented by each of these graphs:

1.   Compute the degree of concurrency.

2. Compute the maximum possible speedup if an unlimited number of processing elements is available.

3. Compute the values of speedup, efficiency, and the overhead function if the number of processing elements is (i) the same as the degree of concurrency and (ii) equal to half of the degree of concurrency.

5.4 Consider a parallel system containing p processing elements solving a problem consisting of W units of work. Prove that if the isoefficiency function of the system is worse (greater) than $\Theta(p)$, then the problem cannot be solved cost-optimally with $p = \Theta(W)$. Also prove the converse that if the problem can be solved cost-optimally only for $p < \Theta(W)$, then the isoefficiency function of the parallel system is worse than linear.

5.5 **(Scaled speedup)** *Scaled speedup* is defined as the speedup obtained when the problem size is increased linearly with the number of processing elements; that is, if W is chosen as a base problem size for a single processing element, then

$$Scaled\ speedup = \frac{pW}{T_P(pW, p)}. \tag{5.37}$$

For the problem of adding n numbers on p processing elements (Example 5.1), plot the speedup curves, assuming that the base problem for $p = 1$ is that of adding 256 numbers. Use $p = 1$, 4, 16, 64, and 256. Assume that it takes 10 time units to communicate a number between two processing elements, and that it takes one unit of time to add two numbers. Now plot the standard speedup curve for the base problem size and compare it with the scaled speedup curve.
Hint: The parallel runtime is $(n/p - 1) + 11 \log p$.

5.6 Plot a third speedup curve for Problem 5.5, in which the problem size is scaled up according to the isoefficiency function, which is $\Theta(p \log p)$. Use the same expression for T_P.
Hint: The scaled speedup under this method of scaling is given by the following equation:

$$Isoefficient\ scaled\ speedup = \frac{pW \log p}{T_P(pW \log p, p)}$$

5.7 Plot the efficiency curves for the problem of adding n numbers on p processing elements corresponding to the standard speedup curve (Problem 5.5), the scaled speedup curve (Problem 5.5), and the speedup curve when the problem size is increased according to the isoefficiency function (Problem 5.6).

5.8 A drawback of increasing the number of processing elements without increasing the total workload is that the speedup does not increase linearly with the number of processing elements, and the efficiency drops monotonically. Based on your experience with Problems 5.5 and 5.7, discuss whether or not scaled speedup increases linearly with the number of processing elements in general. What can you say about the isoefficiency function of a parallel system whose scaled speedup curve matches the speedup curve determined by increasing the problem size according to the isoefficiency function?

5.9 **(Time-constrained scaling)** Using the expression for T_P from Problem 5.5 for p = 1, 4, 16, 64, 256, 1024, and 4096, what is the largest problem that can be solved if the total execution time is not to exceed 512 time units? In general, is it possible to solve an arbitrarily large problem in a fixed amount of time, provided that an unlimited number of processing elements is available? Why?

5.10 **(Prefix sums)** Consider the problem of computing the prefix sums (Example 5.1) of n numbers on n processing elements. What is the parallel runtime, speedup, and efficiency of this algorithm? Assume that adding two numbers takes one unit of time and that communicating one number between two processing elements takes 10 units of time. Is the algorithm cost-optimal?

5.11 Design a cost-optimal version of the prefix sums algorithm (Problem 5.10) for computing all prefix-sums of n numbers on p processing elements where $p < n$. Assuming that adding two numbers takes one unit of time and that communicating one number between two processing elements takes 10 units of time, derive expressions for T_P, S, E, cost, and the isoefficiency function.

5.12 **[GK93a]** Prove that if $T_o \leq \Theta(p)$ for a given problem size, then the parallel execution time will continue to decrease as p is increased and will asymptotically approach a constant value. Also prove that if $T_o > \Theta(p)$, then T_P first decreases and then increases with p; hence, it has a distinct minimum.

5.13 The parallel runtime of a parallel implementation of the FFT algorithm with p processing elements is given by $T_P = (n/p) \log n + t_w(n/p) \log p$ for an input sequence of length n (Equation 13.4 with $t_s = 0$). The maximum number of processing elements that the algorithm can use for an n-point FFT is n. What are the values of p_0 (the value of p that satisfies Equation 5.21) and T_P^{min} for $t_w = 10$?

5.14 **[GK93a]** Consider two parallel systems with the same overhead function, but with different degrees of concurrency. Let the overhead function of both parallel systems be $W^{1/3}p^{3/2} + 0.1W^{2/3}p$. Plot the T_P versus p curve for $W = 10^6$, and $1 \leq p \leq 2048$. If the degree of concurrency is $W^{1/3}$ for the first algorithm and $W^{2/3}$ for the second algorithm, compute the values of T_P^{min} for both parallel systems. Also compute the cost and efficiency for both the parallel systems at the point on the T_P versus p curve where their respective minimum runtimes are achieved.

CHAPTER 6

Programming Using the Message-Passing Paradigm

Numerous programming languages and libraries have been developed for explicit parallel programming. These differ in their view of the address space that they make available to the programmer, the degree of synchronization imposed on concurrent activities, and the multiplicity of programs. The *message-passing programming paradigm* is one of the oldest and most widely used approaches for programming parallel computers. Its roots can be traced back in the early days of parallel processing and its wide-spread adoption can be attributed to the fact that it imposes minimal requirements on the underlying hardware.

In this chapter, we first describe some of the basic concepts of the message-passing programming paradigm and then explore various message-passing programming techniques using the standard and widely-used Message Passing Interface.

6.1 Principles of Message-Passing Programming

There are two key attributes that characterize the message-passing programming paradigm. The first is that it assumes a partitioned address space and the second is that it supports only explicit parallelization.

The logical view of a machine supporting the message-passing paradigm consists of p processes, each with its own exclusive address space. Instances of such a view come naturally from clustered workstations and non-shared address space multicomputers. There are two immediate implications of a partitioned address space. First, each data element must belong to one of the partitions of the space; hence, data must be explicitly partitioned and placed. This adds complexity to programming, but encourages locality of access that is critical for achieving high performance on non-UMA architecture, since a processor can access its local data much faster than non-local data on such architectures. The second implication is that all interactions (read-only or read/write) require cooperation of two processes – the process that has the data and the process that wants to access the data. This requirement for cooperation adds a great deal of complexity for a number of reasons. The process that has the data must participate in the interaction even if it has no logical connection to the events at the requesting process. In certain circumstances, this requirement leads to unnatural programs. In particular, for dynamic and/or unstructured interactions the complexity of the code written for this type of paradigm can be very high for this reason. However, a primary advantage of explicit two-way interactions is that the programmer is fully aware of all the costs of non-local interactions, and is more likely to think about algorithms (and mappings) that minimize interactions. Another major advantage of this type of programming paradigm is that it can be efficiently implemented on a wide variety of architectures.

The message-passing programming paradigm requires that the parallelism is coded explicitly by the programmer. That is, the programmer is responsible for analyzing the underlying serial algorithm/application and identifying ways by which he or she can decompose the computations and extract concurrency. As a result, programming using the message-passing paradigm tends to be hard and intellectually demanding. However, on the other hand, properly written message-passing programs can often achieve very high performance and scale to a very large number of processes.

Structure of Message-Passing Programs   Message-passing programs are often written using the *asynchronous* or *loosely synchronous* paradigms. In the asynchronous paradigm, all concurrent tasks execute asynchronously. This makes it possible to implement any parallel algorithm. However, such programs can be harder to reason about, and can have non-deterministic behavior due to race conditions. Loosely synchronous programs are a good compromise between these two extremes. In such programs, tasks or subsets of tasks synchronize to perform interactions. However, between these interactions, tasks execute completely asynchronously. Since the interaction happens synchronously, it is still quite easy to reason about the program. Many of the known parallel algorithms can be naturally implemented using loosely synchronous programs.

In its most general form, the message-passing paradigm supports execution of a different program on each of the p processes. This provides the ultimate flexibility in parallel programming, but makes the job of writing parallel programs effectively unscalable. For this reason, most message-passing programs are written using the *single program multiple data* (SPMD) approach. In SPMD programs the code executed by different processes is identical except for a small number of processes (e.g., the "root" process). This does not mean that the processes work in lock-step. In an extreme case, even in an SPMD program, each process could execute a different code (the program contains a large case statement with code for each process). But except for this degenerate case, most processes execute the same code. SPMD programs can be loosely synchronous or completely asynchronous.

6.2   The Building Blocks: Send and Receive Operations

Since interactions are accomplished by sending and receiving messages, the basic operations in the message-passing programming paradigm are send and receive. In their simplest form, the prototypes of these operations are defined as follows:

```
send(void *sendbuf, int nelems, int dest)
receive(void *recvbuf, int nelems, int source)
```

The sendbuf points to a buffer that stores the data to be sent, recvbuf points to a buffer that stores the data to be received, nelems is the number of data units to be sent and received, dest is the identifier of the process that receives the data, and source is the identifier of the process that sends the data.

However, to stop at this point would be grossly simplifying the programming and performance ramifications of how these functions are implemented. To motivate the need for further investigation, let us start with a simple example of a process sending a piece of data to another process as illustrated in the following code-fragment:

```
1       P0                              P1
2
3       a = 100;                        receive(&a, 1, 0)
4       send(&a, 1, 1);                 printf("%d\n", a);
5       a = 0;
```

In this simple example, process P0 sends a message to process P1 which receives and prints the message. The important thing to note is that process P0 changes the value of a to 0 immediately following the send. The semantics of the send operation require that the value received by process P1 must be 100 as opposed to 0. That is, the value of a at the time of the send operation must be the value that is received by process P1.

It may seem that it is quite straightforward to ensure the semantics of the send and receive operations. However, based on how the send and receive operations are implemented this may not be the case. Most message passing platforms have additional hardware support for sending and receiving messages. They may support DMA (direct memory access) and asynchronous message transfer using network interface hardware. Network interfaces allow the transfer of messages from buffer memory to desired location without CPU intervention. Similarly, DMA allows copying of data from one memory location to another (e.g., communication buffers) without CPU support (once they have been programmed). As a result, if the send operation programs the communication hardware and returns before the communication operation has been accomplished, process P1 might receive the value 0 in a instead of 100!

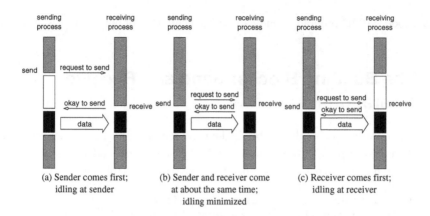

Figure 6.1 Handshake for a blocking non-buffered send/receive operation. It is easy to see that in cases where sender and receiver do not reach communication point at similar times, there can be considerable idling overheads.

While this is undesirable, there are in fact reasons for supporting such send operations for performance reasons. In the rest of this section, we will discuss send and receive operations in the context of such a hardware environment, and motivate various implementation details and message-passing protocols that help in ensuring the semantics of the send and receive operations.

6.2.1   Blocking Message Passing Operations

A simple solution to the dilemma presented in the code fragment above is for the send operation to return only when it is semantically safe to do so. Note that this is not the same as saying that the send operation returns only after the receiver has received the data. It simply means that the sending operation blocks until it can guarantee that the semantics will not be violated on return irrespective of what happens in the program subsequently. There are two mechanisms by which this can be achieved.

Blocking Non-Buffered Send/Receive

In the first case, the send operation does not return until the matching receive has been encountered at the receiving process. When this happens, the message is sent and the send operation returns upon completion of the communication operation. Typically, this process involves a handshake between the sending and receiving processes. The sending process sends a request to communicate to the receiving process. When the receiving process encounters the target receive, it responds to the request. The sending process upon receiving this response initiates a transfer operation. The operation is illustrated in Figure 6.1. Since there are no buffers used at either sending or receiving ends, this is also referred to as a ***non-buffered blocking operation***.

Idling Overheads in Blocking Non-Buffered Operations   In Figure 6.1, we illustrate three scenarios in which the send is reached before the receive is posted, the send and receive are posted around the same time, and the receive is posted before the send is reached. In cases (a) and (c), we notice that there is considerable idling at the sending and receiving process. It is also clear from the figures that a blocking non-buffered protocol is suitable when the send and receive are posted at roughly the same time. However, in an asynchronous environment, this may be impossible to predict. This idling overhead is one of the major drawbacks of this protocol.

Deadlocks in Blocking Non-Buffered Operations   Consider the following simple exchange of messages that can lead to a deadlock:

```
1       P0                              P1
2
3       send(&a, 1, 1);                 send(&a, 1, 0);
4       receive(&b, 1, 1);              receive(&b, 1, 0);
```

The code fragment makes the values of a available to both processes P0 and P1. However, if the send and receive operations are implemented using a blocking non-buffered protocol, the send at P0 waits for the matching receive at P1 whereas the send at process P1 waits for the corresponding receive at P0, resulting in an infinite wait.

As can be inferred, deadlocks are very easy in blocking protocols and care must be taken to break cyclic waits of the nature outlined. In the above example, this can be corrected by replacing the operation sequence of one of the processes by a `receive` and a `send` as opposed to the other way around. This often makes the code more cumbersome and buggy.

Blocking Buffered Send/Receive

A simple solution to the idling and deadlocking problem outlined above is to rely on buffers at the sending and receiving ends. We start with a simple case in which the sender has a buffer pre-allocated for communicating messages. On encountering a send operation, the sender simply copies the data into the designated buffer and returns after the copy operation has been completed. The sender process can now continue with the program knowing that any changes to the data will not impact program semantics. The actual communication can be accomplished in many ways depending on the available hardware resources. If the hardware supports asynchronous communication (independent of the CPU), then a network transfer can be initiated after the message has been copied into the buffer. Note that at the receiving end, the data cannot be stored directly at the target location since this would violate program semantics. Instead, the data is copied into a buffer at the receiver as well. When the receiving process encounters a receive operation, it checks to see if the message is available in its receive buffer. If so, the data is copied into the target location. This operation is illustrated in Figure 6.2(a).

In the protocol illustrated above, buffers are used at both sender and receiver and communication is handled by dedicated hardware. Sometimes machines do not have such

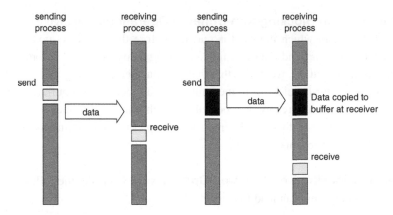

Figure 6.2 Blocking buffered transfer protocols: (a) in the presence of communication hardware with buffers at send and receive ends; and (b) in the absence of communication hardware, sender interrupts receiver and deposits data in buffer at receiver end.

communication hardware. In this case, some of the overhead can be saved by buffering only on one side. For example, on encountering a send operation, the sender interrupts the receiver, both processes participate in a communication operation and the message is deposited in a buffer at the receiver end. When the receiver eventually encounters a receive operation, the message is copied from the buffer into the target location. This protocol is illustrated in Figure 6.2(b). It is not difficult to conceive a protocol in which the buffering is done only at the sender and the receiver initiates a transfer by interrupting the sender.

It is easy to see that buffered protocols alleviate idling overheads at the cost of adding buffer management overheads. In general, if the parallel program is highly synchronous (i.e., sends and receives are posted around the same time), non-buffered sends may perform better than buffered sends. However, in general applications, this is not the case and buffered sends are desirable unless buffer capacity becomes an issue.

Example 6.1 Impact of finite buffers in message passing
Consider the following code fragment:

```
1       P0                                P1
2
3       for (i = 0; i < 1000; i++) {      for (i = 0; i < 1000; i++) {
4          produce_data(&a);                 receive(&a, 1, 0);
5          send(&a, 1, 1);                   consume_data(&a);
6       }                                 }
```

In this code fragment, process P0 produces 1000 data items and process P1 consumes them. However, if process P1 was slow getting to this loop, process P0 might have sent all of its data. If there is enough buffer space, then both processes can proceed; however, if the buffer is not sufficient (i.e., buffer overflow), the sender would have to be blocked until some of the corresponding receive operations had been posted, thus freeing up buffer space. This can often lead to unforeseen overheads and performance degradation. In general, it is a good idea to write programs that have bounded buffer requirements.   ■

Deadlocks in Buffered Send and Receive Operations   While buffering alleviates many of the deadlock situations, it is still possible to write code that deadlocks. This is due to the fact that as in the non-buffered case, receive calls are always blocking (to ensure semantic consistency). Thus, a simple code fragment such as the following deadlocks since both processes wait to receive data but nobody sends it.

```
1       P0                              P1
2
3       receive(&a, 1, 1);              receive(&a, 1, 0);
4       send(&b, 1, 1);                 send(&b, 1, 0);
```

Once again, such circular waits have to be broken. However, deadlocks are caused only by waits on receive operations in this case.

6.2.2   Non-Blocking Message Passing Operations

In blocking protocols, the overhead of guaranteeing semantic correctness was paid in the form of idling (non-buffered) or buffer management (buffered). Often, it is possible to require the programmer to ensure semantic correctness and provide a fast send/receive operation that incurs little overhead. This class of non-blocking protocols returns from the send or receive operation before it is semantically safe to do so. Consequently, the user must be careful not to alter data that may be potentially participating in a communication operation. Non-blocking operations are generally accompanied by a check-status operation, which indicates whether the semantics of a previously initiated transfer may be violated or not. Upon return from a non-blocking send or receive operation, the process is free to perform any computation that does not depend upon the completion of the operation. Later in the program, the process can check whether or not the non-blocking operation has completed, and, if necessary, wait for its completion.

As illustrated in Figure 6.3, non-blocking operations can themselves be buffered or non-buffered. In the non-buffered case, a process wishing to send data to another simply posts a pending message and returns to the user program. The program can then do other useful work. At some point in the future, when the corresponding receive is posted, the communication operation is initiated. When this operation is completed, the check-status operation indicates that it is safe for the programmer to touch this data. This transfer is indicated in Figure 6.4(a).

Comparing Figures 6.4(a) and 6.1(a), it is easy to see that the idling time when the process is waiting for the corresponding receive in a blocking operation can now be utilized for computation, provided it does not update the data being sent. This alleviates the major bottleneck associated with the former at the expense of some program restructuring.

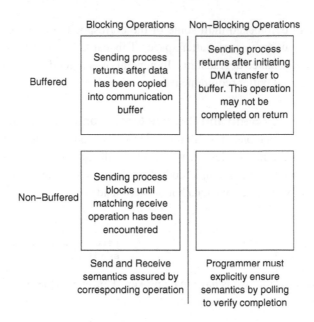

Figure 6.3   Space of possible protocols for send and receive operations.

The benefits of non-blocking operations are further enhanced by the presence of dedicated communication hardware. This is illustrated in Figure 6.4(b). In this case, the communication overhead can be almost entirely masked by non-blocking operations. In this case, however, the data being received is unsafe for the duration of the receive operation.

Non-blocking operations can also be used with a buffered protocol. In this case, the sender initiates a DMA operation and returns immediately. The data becomes safe the moment the DMA operation has been completed. At the receiving end, the receive operation initiates a transfer from the sender's buffer to the receiver's target location. Using buffers with non-blocking operation has the effect of reducing the time during which the data is unsafe.

Typical message-passing libraries such as Message Passing Interface (MPI) and Parallel Virtual Machine (PVM) implement both blocking and non-blocking operations. Blocking operations facilitate safe and easier programming and non-blocking operations are useful for performance optimization by masking communication overhead. One must, however, be careful using non-blocking protocols since errors can result from unsafe access to data that is in the process of being communicated.

6.3   MPI: the Message Passing Interface

Many early generation commercial parallel computers were based on the message-passing architecture due to its lower cost relative to shared-address-space architectures. Since

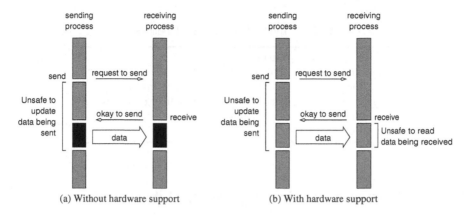

Figure 6.4 Non-blocking non-buffered send and receive operations (a) in absence of communication hardware; (b) in presence of communication hardware.

message-passing is the natural programming paradigm for these machines, this resulted in the development of many different message-passing libraries. In fact, message-passing became the modern-age form of assembly language, in which every hardware vendor provided its own library, that performed very well on its own hardware, but was incompatible with the parallel computers offered by other vendors. Many of the differences between the various vendor-specific message-passing libraries were only syntactic; however, often enough there were some serious semantic differences that required significant re-engineering to port a message-passing program from one library to another.

The message-passing interface, or MPI as it is commonly known, was created to essentially solve this problem. MPI defines a standard library for message-passing that can be used to develop portable message-passing programs using either C or Fortran. The MPI standard defines both the syntax as well as the semantics of a core set of library routines that are very useful in writing message-passing programs. MPI was developed by a group of researchers from academia and industry, and has enjoyed wide support by almost all the hardware vendors. Vendor implementations of MPI are available on almost all commercial parallel computers.

The MPI library contains over 125 routines, but the number of key concepts is much smaller. In fact, it is possible to write fully-functional message-passing programs by using only the six routines shown in Table 6.1. These routines are used to initialize and terminate the MPI library, to get information about the parallel computing environment, and to send and receive messages.

In this section we describe these routines as well as some basic concepts that are essential in writing correct and efficient message-passing programs using MPI.

Table 6.1   The minimal set of MPI routines.

`MPI_Init`	Initializes MPI.
`MPI_Finalize`	Terminates MPI.
`MPI_Comm_size`	Determines the number of processes.
`MPI_Comm_rank`	Determines the label of the calling process.
`MPI_Send`	Sends a message.
`MPI_Recv`	Receives a message.

6.3.1   Starting and Terminating the MPI Library

`MPI_Init` is called prior to any calls to other MPI routines. Its purpose is to initialize the MPI environment. Calling `MPI_Init` more than once during the execution of a program will lead to an error. `MPI_Finalize` is called at the end of the computation, and it performs various clean-up tasks to terminate the MPI environment. No MPI calls may be performed after `MPI_Finalize` has been called, not even `MPI_Init`. Both `MPI_Init` and `MPI_Finalize` must be called by all the processes, otherwise MPI's behavior will be undefined. The exact calling sequences of these two routines for C are as follows:

```
int MPI_Init(int *argc, char ***argv)
int MPI_Finalize()
```

The arguments `argc` and `argv` of `MPI_Init` are the command-line arguments of the C program. An MPI implementation is expected to remove from the `argv` array any command-line arguments that should be processed by the implementation before returning back to the program, and to decrement `argc` accordingly. Thus, command-line processing should be performed only after `MPI_Init` has been called. Upon successful execution, `MPI_Init` and `MPI_Finalize` return `MPI_SUCCESS`; otherwise they return an implementation-defined error code.

The bindings and calling sequences of these two functions are illustrative of the naming practices and argument conventions followed by MPI. All MPI routines, data-types, and constants are prefixed by "`MPI_`". The return code for successful completion is `MPI_SUCCESS`. This and other MPI constants and data-structures are defined for C in the file `"mpi.h"`. This header file must be included in each MPI program.

6.3.2   Communicators

A key concept used throughout MPI is that of the *communication domain*. A communication domain is a set of processes that are allowed to communicate with each other. Information about communication domains is stored in variables of type `MPI_Comm`, that are called ***communicators***. These communicators are used as arguments to all message transfer MPI routines and they uniquely identify the processes participating in the message transfer operation. Note that each process can belong to many different (possibly overlapping) communication domains.

The communicator is used to define a set of processes that can communicate with each other. This set of processes form a ***communication domain***. In general, all the processes may need to communicate with each other. For this reason, MPI defines a default communicator called MPI_COMM_WORLD which includes all the processes involved in the parallel execution. However, in many cases we want to perform communication only within (possibly overlapping) groups of processes. By using a different communicator for each such group, we can ensure that no messages will ever interfere with messages destined to any other group. How to create and use such communicators is described at a later point in this chapter. For now, it suffices to use MPI_COMM_WORLD as the communicator argument to all the MPI functions that require a communicator.

6.3.3 Getting Information

The MPI_Comm_size and MPI_Comm_rank functions are used to determine the number of processes and the label of the calling process, respectively. The calling sequences of these routines are as follows:

```
int MPI_Comm_size(MPI_Comm comm, int *size)
int MPI_Comm_rank(MPI_Comm comm, int *rank)
```

The function MPI_Comm_size returns in the variable size the number of processes that belong to the communicator comm. So, when there is a single process per processor, the call MPI_Comm_size(MPI_COMM_WORLD, &size) will return in size the number of processors used by the program. Every process that belongs to a communicator is uniquely identified by its ***rank***. The rank of a process is an integer that ranges from zero up to the size of the communicator minus one. A process can determine its rank in a communicator by using the MPI_Comm_rank function that takes two arguments: the communicator and an integer variable rank. Up on return, the variable rank stores the rank of the process. Note that each process that calls either one of these functions must belong in the supplied communicator, otherwise an error will occur.

Example 6.2 Hello World
We can use the four MPI functions just described to write a program that prints out a "Hello World" message from each processor.

```
1   #include <mpi.h>
2
3   main(int argc, char *argv[])
4   {
5     int npes, myrank;
6
7     MPI_Init(&argc, &argv);
8     MPI_Comm_size(MPI_COMM_WORLD, &npes);
```

```
9     MPI_Comm_rank(MPI_COMM_WORLD, &myrank);
10    printf("From process %d out of %d, Hello World!\n",
11            myrank, npes);
12    MPI_Finalize();
13  }
```

■

6.3.4 Sending and Receiving Messages

The basic functions for sending and receiving messages in MPI are the MPI_Send and MPI_Recv, respectively. The calling sequences of these routines are as follows:

```
int MPI_Send(void *buf, int count, MPI_Datatype datatype,
        int dest, int tag, MPI_Comm comm)
int MPI_Recv(void *buf, int count, MPI_Datatype datatype,
        int source, int tag, MPI_Comm comm, MPI_Status *status)
```

MPI_Send sends the data stored in the buffer pointed by buf. This buffer consists of consecutive entries of the type specified by the parameter datatype. The number of entries in the buffer is given by the parameter count. The correspondence between MPI datatypes and those provided by C is shown in Table 6.2. Note that for all C datatypes, an equivalent MPI datatype is provided. However, MPI allows two additional datatypes that are not part of the C language. These are MPI_BYTE and MPI_PACKED.

MPI_BYTE corresponds to a byte (8 bits) and MPI_PACKED corresponds to a collection of data items that has been created by packing non-contiguous data. Note that the length of the message in MPI_Send, as well as in other MPI routines, is specified in terms of the number of entries being sent and not in terms of the number of bytes. Specifying the length in terms of the number of entries has the advantage of making the MPI code portable, since the number of bytes used to store various datatypes can be different for different architectures.

The destination of the message sent by MPI_Send is uniquely specified by the dest and comm arguments. The dest argument is the rank of the destination process in the communication domain specified by the communicator comm. Each message has an integer-valued tag associated with it. This is used to distinguish different types of messages. The message-tag can take values ranging from zero up to the MPI defined constant MPI_TAG_UB. Even though the value of MPI_TAG_UB is implementation specific, it is at least 32,767.

MPI_Recv receives a message sent by a process whose rank is given by the source in the communication domain specified by the comm argument. The tag of the sent message must be that specified by the tag argument. If there are many messages with identical tag from the same process, then any one of these messages is received. MPI allows specification of wildcard arguments for both source and tag. If source is set to MPI_ANY_SOURCE, then any process of the communication domain can be the source

Table 6.2   Correspondence between the datatypes supported by MPI and those supported by C.

MPI Datatype	C Datatype
MPI_CHAR	signed char
MPI_SHORT	signed short int
MPI_INT	signed int
MPI_LONG	signed long int
MPI_UNSIGNED_CHAR	unsigned char
MPI_UNSIGNED_SHORT	unsigned short int
MPI_UNSIGNED	unsigned int
MPI_UNSIGNED_LONG	unsigned long int
MPI_FLOAT	float
MPI_DOUBLE	double
MPI_LONG_DOUBLE	long double
MPI_BYTE	
MPI_PACKED	

of the message. Similarly, if `tag` is set to `MPI_ANY_TAG`, then messages with any tag are accepted. The received message is stored in continuous locations in the buffer pointed to by `buf`. The `count` and `datatype` arguments of `MPI_Recv` are used to specify the length of the supplied buffer. The received message should be of length equal to or less than this length. This allows the receiving process to not know the exact size of the message being sent. If the received message is larger than the supplied buffer, then an overflow error will occur, and the routine will return the error `MPI_ERR_TRUNCATE`.

After a message has been received, the `status` variable can be used to get information about the `MPI_Recv` operation. In C, `status` is stored using the `MPI_Status` data-structure. This is implemented as a structure with three fields, as follows:

```
typedef struct MPI_Status {
  int MPI_SOURCE;
  int MPI_TAG;
  int MPI_ERROR;
};
```

`MPI_SOURCE` and `MPI_TAG` store the source and the tag of the received message. They are particularly useful when `MPI_ANY_SOURCE` and `MPI_ANY_TAG` are used for the `source` and `tag` arguments. `MPI_ERROR` stores the error-code of the received message.

The status argument also returns information about the length of the received message. This information is not directly accessible from the `status` variable, but it can be retrieved by calling the `MPI_Get_count` function. The calling sequence of this function is as follows:

```
int MPI_Get_count(MPI_Status *status, MPI_Datatype datatype,
        int *count)
```

MPI_Get_count takes as arguments the status returned by MPI_Recv and the type of the received data in datatype, and returns the number of entries that were actually received in the count variable.

The MPI_Recv returns only after the requested message has been received and copied into the buffer. That is, MPI_Recv is a blocking receive operation. However, MPI allows two different implementations for MPI_Send. In the first implementation, MPI_Send returns only after the corresponding MPI_Recv have been issued and the message has been sent to the receiver. In the second implementation, MPI_Send first copies the message into a buffer and then returns, without waiting for the corresponding MPI_Recv to be executed. In either implementation, the buffer that is pointed by the buf argument of MPI_Send can be safely reused and overwritten. MPI programs must be able to run correctly regardless of which of the two methods is used for implementing MPI_Send. Such programs are called *safe*. In writing safe MPI programs, sometimes it is helpful to forget about the alternate implementation of MPI_Send and just think of it as being a blocking send operation.

Avoiding Deadlocks   The semantics of MPI_Send and MPI_Recv place some restrictions on how we can mix and match send and receive operations. For example, consider the following piece of code in which process 0 sends two messages with different tags to process 1, and process 1 receives them in the reverse order.

```
1   int a[10], b[10], myrank;
2   MPI_Status status;
3   ...
4   MPI_Comm_rank(MPI_COMM_WORLD, &myrank);
5   if (myrank == 0) {
6     MPI_Send(a, 10, MPI_INT, 1, 1, MPI_COMM_WORLD);
7     MPI_Send(b, 10, MPI_INT, 1, 2, MPI_COMM_WORLD);
8   }
9   else if (myrank == 1) {
10    MPI_Recv(b, 10, MPI_INT, 0, 2, MPI_COMM_WORLD);
11    MPI_Recv(a, 10, MPI_INT, 0, 1, MPI_COMM_WORLD);
12  }
13  ...
```

If MPI_Send is implemented using buffering, then this code will run correctly provided that sufficient buffer space is available. However, if MPI_Send is implemented by blocking until the matching receive has been issued, then neither of the two processes will be able to proceed. This is because process zero (i.e., myrank == 0) will wait until process one issues the matching MPI_Recv (i.e., the one with tag equal to 1), and at the same time process one will wait until process zero performs the matching MPI_Send (i.e., the one with tag equal to 2). This code fragment is not safe, as its behavior is implementation dependent. It is up to the programmer to ensure that his or her program will run correctly on any MPI implementation. The problem in this program can be corrected by *matching the order in which the send and receive operations are issued*. Similar deadlock situations can also occur when a process sends a message to itself. Even though this is legal, its behavior is implementation dependent and must be avoided.

Improper use of `MPI_Send` and `MPI_Recv` can also lead to deadlocks in situations when each processor needs to send and receive a message in a circular fashion. Consider the following piece of code, in which process i sends a message to process $i + 1$ (modulo the number of processes) and receives a message from process $i - 1$ (module the number of processes).

```
1   int a[10], b[10], npes, myrank;
2   MPI_Status status;
3   ...
4   MPI_Comm_size(MPI_COMM_WORLD, &npes);
5   MPI_Comm_rank(MPI_COMM_WORLD, &myrank);
6   MPI_Send(a, 10, MPI_INT, (myrank+1)%npes, 1, MPI_COMM_WORLD);
7   MPI_Recv(b, 10, MPI_INT, (myrank-1+npes)%npes, 1, MPI_COMM_WORLD);
8   ...
```

When `MPI_Send` is implemented using buffering, the program will work correctly, since every call to `MPI_Send` will get buffered, allowing the call of the `MPI_Recv` to be performed, which will transfer the required data. However, if `MPI_Send` blocks until the matching receive has been issued, all processes will enter an infinite wait state, waiting for the neighboring process to issue a `MPI_Recv` operation. Note that the deadlock still remains even when we have only two processes. Thus, when pairs of processes need to exchange data, the above method leads to an unsafe program. The above example can be made safe, by rewriting it as follows:

```
1   int a[10], b[10], npes, myrank;
2   MPI_Status status;
3   ...
4   MPI_Comm_size(MPI_COMM_WORLD, &npes);
5   MPI_Comm_rank(MPI_COMM_WORLD, &myrank);
6   if (myrank%2 == 1) {
7     MPI_Send(a, 10, MPI_INT, (myrank+1)%npes, 1, MPI_COMM_WORLD);
8     MPI_Recv(b, 10, MPI_INT, (myrank-1+npes)%npes, 1, MPI_COMM_WORLD);
9   }
10  else {
11    MPI_Recv(b, 10, MPI_INT, (myrank-1+npes)%npes, 1, MPI_COMM_WORLD);
12    MPI_Send(a, 10, MPI_INT, (myrank+1)%npes, 1, MPI_COMM_WORLD);
13  }
14  ...
```

This new implementation partitions the processes into two groups. One consists of the odd-numbered processes and the other of the even-numbered processes. The odd-numbered processes perform a send followed by a receive, and the even-numbered processes perform a receive followed by a send. Thus, when an odd-numbered process calls `MPI_Send`, the target process (which has an even number) will call `MPI_Recv` to receive that message, before attempting to send its own message.

Sending and Receiving Messages Simultaneously   The above communication pattern appears frequently in many message-passing programs, and for this reason MPI provides the `MPI_Sendrecv` function that both sends and receives a message.

MPI_Sendrecv does not suffer from the circular deadlock problems of MPI_Send and MPI_Recv. You can think of MPI_Sendrecv as allowing data to travel for both send and receive simultaneously. The calling sequence of MPI_Sendrecv is the following:

```
int MPI_Sendrecv(void *sendbuf, int sendcount,
         MPI_Datatype senddatatype, int dest, int sendtag,
         void *recvbuf, int recvcount, MPI_Datatype recvdatatype,
         int source, int recvtag, MPI_Comm comm,
         MPI_Status *status)
```

The arguments of MPI_Sendrecv are essentially the combination of the arguments of MPI_Send and MPI_Recv. The send and receive buffers must be disjoint, and the source and destination of the messages can be the same or different. The safe version of our earlier example using MPI_Sendrecv is as follows.

```
1   int a[10], b[10], npes, myrank;
2   MPI_Status status;
3   ...
4   MPI_Comm_size(MPI_COMM_WORLD, &npes);
5   MPI_Comm_rank(MPI_COMM_WORLD, &myrank);
6   MPI_SendRecv(a, 10, MPI_INT, (myrank+1)%npes, 1,
7                b, 10, MPI_INT, (myrank-1+npes)%npes, 1,
8                MPI_COMM_WORLD, &status);
9   ...
```

In many programs, the requirement for the send and receive buffers of MPI_Sendrecv be disjoint may force us to use a temporary buffer. This increases the amount of memory required by the program and also increases the overall run time due to the extra copy. This problem can be solved by using that MPI_Sendrecv_replace MPI function. This function performs a blocking send and receive, but it uses a single buffer for both the send and receive operation. That is, the received data replaces the data that was sent out of the buffer. The calling sequence of this function is the following:

```
int MPI_Sendrecv_replace(void *buf, int count,
         MPI_Datatype datatype, int dest, int sendtag,
         int source, int recvtag, MPI_Comm comm,
         MPI_Status *status)
```

Note that both the send and receive operations must transfer data of the same datatype.

6.3.5   Example: Odd-Even Sort

We will now use the MPI functions described in the previous sections to write a complete message-passing program that will sort a list of numbers using the odd-even sorting algorithm. Recall from Section 9.3.1 that the odd-even sorting algorithm sorts a sequence of n elements using p processes in a total of p phases. During each of these phases, the odd- or even-numbered processes perform a compare-split step with their right neighbors. The MPI program for performing the odd-even sort in parallel is shown in Program 6.1. To simplify the presentation, this program assumes that n is divisible by p.

Program 6.1   Odd-Even Sorting

```
1   #include <stdlib.h>
2   #include <mpi.h> /* Include MPI's header file */
3
4   main(int argc, char *argv[])
5   {
6     int n;          /* The total number of elements to be sorted */
7     int npes;       /* The total number of processes */
8     int myrank;     /* The rank of the calling process */
9     int nlocal;     /* The local number of elements, and the array that stores them */
10    int *elmnts;    /* The array that stores the local elements */
11    int *relmnts;   /* The array that stores the received elements */
12    int oddrank;    /* The rank of the process during odd-phase communication */
13    int evenrank;   /* The rank of the process during even-phase communication */
14    int *wspace;    /* Working space during the compare-split operation */
15    int i;
16    MPI_Status status;
17
18    /* Initialize MPI and get system information */
19    MPI_Init(&argc, &argv);
20    MPI_Comm_size(MPI_COMM_WORLD, &npes);
21    MPI_Comm_rank(MPI_COMM_WORLD, &myrank);
22
23    n = atoi(argv[1]);
24    nlocal = n/npes; /* Compute the number of elements to be stored locally. */
25
26    /* Allocate memory for the various arrays */
27    elmnts  = (int *)malloc(nlocal*sizeof(int));
28    relmnts = (int *)malloc(nlocal*sizeof(int));
29    wspace  = (int *)malloc(nlocal*sizeof(int));
30
31    /* Fill-in the elmnts array with random elements */
32    srandom(myrank);
33    for (i=0; i<nlocal; i++)
34      elmnts[i] = random();
35
36    /* Sort the local elements using the built-in quicksort routine */
37    qsort(elmnts, nlocal, sizeof(int), IncOrder);
38
39    /* Determine the rank of the processors that myrank needs to communicate during the */
40    /* odd and even phases of the algorithm */
41    if (myrank%2 == 0) {
42      oddrank  = myrank-1;
43      evenrank = myrank+1;
44    }
45    else {
46      oddrank  = myrank+1;
47      evenrank = myrank-1;
48    }
49
50    /* Set the ranks of the processors at the end of the linear */
51    if (oddrank == -1 || oddrank == npes)
52      oddrank = MPI_PROC_NULL;
53    if (evenrank == -1 || evenrank == npes)
54      evenrank = MPI_PROC_NULL;
55
56    /* Get into the main loop of the odd-even sorting algorithm */
57    for (i=0; i<npes-1; i++) {
58      if (i%2 == 1) /* Odd phase */
59        MPI_Sendrecv(elmnts, nlocal, MPI_INT, oddrank, 1, relmnts,
```

```
60                nlocal, MPI_INT, oddrank, 1, MPI_COMM_WORLD, &status);
61        else /* Even phase */
62          MPI_Sendrecv(elmnts, nlocal, MPI_INT, evenrank, 1, relmnts,
63                nlocal, MPI_INT, evenrank, 1, MPI_COMM_WORLD, &status);
64
65        CompareSplit(nlocal, elmnts, relmnts, wspace,
66                        myrank < status.MPI_SOURCE);
67      }
68
69      free(elmnts); free(relmnts); free(wspace);
70      MPI_Finalize();
71  }
72
73  /* This is the CompareSplit function */
74  CompareSplit(int nlocal, int *elmnts, int *relmnts, int *wspace,
75                  int keepsmall)
76  {
77      int i, j, k;
78
79      for (i=0; i<nlocal; i++)
80        wspace[i] = elmnts[i];   /* Copy the elmnts array into the wspace array */
81
82      if (keepsmall) { /* Keep the nlocal smaller elements */
83        for (i=j=k=0; k<nlocal; k++) {
84          if (j == nlocal || (i < nlocal && wspace[i] < relmnts[j]))
85            elmnts[k] = wspace[i++];
86          else
87            elmnts[k] = relmnts[j++];
88        }
89      }
90      else { /* Keep the nlocal larger elements */
91        for (i=k=nlocal-1, j=nlocal-1; k>=0; k--) {
92          if (j == 0 || (i >= 0 && wspace[i] >= relmnts[j]))
93            elmnts[k] = wspace[i--];
94          else
95            elmnts[k] = relmnts[j--];
96        }
97      }
98  }
99
100 /* The IncOrder function that is called by qsort is defined as follows */
101 int IncOrder(const void *e1, const void *e2)
102 {
103     return (*((int *)e1) - *((int *)e2));
104 }
```

6.4 Topologies and Embedding

MPI views the processes as being arranged in a one-dimensional topology and uses a linear ordering to number the processes. However, in many parallel programs, processes are naturally arranged in higher-dimensional topologies (e.g., two- or three-dimensional). In such programs, both the computation and the set of interacting processes are naturally identified by their coordinates in that topology. For example, in a parallel program in which the processes are arranged in a two-dimensional topology, process (i, j) may need to send message to (or receive message from) process (k, l). To implement these programs

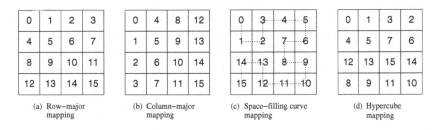

Figure 6.5 Different ways to map a set of processes to a two-dimensional grid. (a) and (b) show a row- and column-wise mapping of these processes, (c) shows a mapping that follows a space-filling curve (dotted line), and (d) shows a mapping in which neighboring processes are directly connected in a hypercube.

in MPI, we need to map each MPI process to a process in that higher-dimensional topology.

Many such mappings are possible. Figure 6.5 illustrates some possible mappings of eight MPI processes onto a 4×4 two-dimensional topology. For example, for the mapping shown in Figure 6.5(a), an MPI process with rank *rank* corresponds to process (*row*, *col*) in the grid such that *row* = *rank/4* and *col* = *rank%4* (where '%' is C's module operator). As an illustration, the process with rank 7 is mapped to process (1, 3) in the grid.

In general, the goodness of a mapping is determined by the pattern of interaction among the processes in the higher-dimensional topology, the connectivity of physical processors, and the mapping of MPI processes to physical processors. For example, consider a program that uses a two-dimensional topology and each process needs to communicate with its neighboring processes along the x and y directions of this topology. Now, if the processors of the underlying parallel system are connected using a hypercube interconnection network, then the mapping shown in Figure 6.5(d) is better, since neighboring processes in the grid are also neighboring processors in the hypercube topology.

However, the mechanism used by MPI to assign ranks to the processes in a communication domain does not use any information about the interconnection network, making it impossible to perform topology embeddings in an intelligent manner. Furthermore, even if we had that information, we will need to specify different mappings for different interconnection networks, diminishing the architecture independent advantages of MPI. A better approach is to let the library itself compute the most appropriate embedding of a given topology to the processors of the underlying parallel computer. This is exactly the approach facilitated by MPI. MPI provides a set of routines that allows the programmer to arrange the processes in different topologies without having to explicitly specify how these processes are mapped onto the processors. It is up to the MPI library to find the most appropriate mapping that reduces the cost of sending and receiving messages.

6.4.1 Creating and Using Cartesian Topologies

MPI provides routines that allow the specification of virtual process topologies of arbitrary connectivity in terms of a graph. Each node in the graph corresponds to a process and two nodes are connected if they communicate with each other. Graphs of processes can be used to specify any desired topology. However, most commonly used topologies in message-passing programs are one-, two-, or higher-dimensional grids, that are also referred to as *Cartesian topologies*. For this reason, MPI provides a set of specialized routines for specifying and manipulating this type of multi-dimensional grid topologies.

MPI's function for describing Cartesian topologies is called `MPI_Cart_create`. Its calling sequence is as follows.

```
int MPI_Cart_create(MPI_Comm comm_old, int ndims, int *dims,
        int *periods, int reorder, MPI_Comm *comm_cart)
```

This function takes the group of processes that belong to the communicator `comm_old` and creates a virtual process topology. The topology information is attached to a new communicator `comm_cart` that is created by `MPI_Cart_create`. Any subsequent MPI routines that want to take advantage of this new Cartesian topology must use `comm_cart` as the communicator argument. Note that all the processes that belong to the `comm_old` communicator must call this function. The shape and properties of the topology are specified by the arguments `ndims`, `dims`, and `periods`. The argument `ndims` specifies the number of dimensions of the topology. The array `dims` specify the size along each dimension of the topology. The ith element of this array stores the size of the ith dimension of the topology. The array `periods` is used to specify whether or not the topology has wraparound connections. In particular, if `periods[i]` is true (non-zero in C), then the topology has wraparound connections along dimension i, otherwise it does not. Finally, the argument `reorder` is used to determine if the processes in the new group (i.e., communicator) are to be reordered or not. If `reorder` is false, then the rank of each process in the new group is identical to its rank in the old group. Otherwise, `MPI_Cart_create` may reorder the processes if that leads to a better embedding of the virtual topology onto the parallel computer. If the total number of processes specified in the `dims` array is smaller than the number of processes in the communicator specified by `comm_old`, then some processes will not be part of the Cartesian topology. For this set of processes, the value of `comm_cart` will be set to `MPI_COMM_NULL` (an MPI defined constant). Note that it will result in an error if the total number of processes specified by `dims` is greater than the number of processes in the `comm_old` communicator.

Process Naming   When a Cartesian topology is used, each process is better identified by its coordinates in this topology. However, all MPI functions that we described for sending and receiving messages require that the source and the destination of each message be specified using the rank of the process. For this reason, MPI provides two functions, `MPI_Cart_rank` and `MPI_Cart_coord`, for performing coordinate-to-rank and rank-to-coordinate translations, respectively. The calling sequences of these routines are the following:

```
int MPI_Cart_rank(MPI_Comm comm_cart, int *coords, int *rank)
int MPI_Cart_coord(MPI_Comm comm_cart, int rank, int maxdims,
        int *coords)
```

The `MPI_Cart_rank` takes the coordinates of the process as argument in the `coords` array and returns its rank in `rank`. The `MPI_Cart_coords` takes the rank of the process `rank` and returns its Cartesian coordinates in the array `coords`, of length `maxdims`. Note that `maxdims` should be at least as large as the number of dimensions in the Cartesian topology specified by the communicator `comm_cart`.

Frequently, the communication performed among processes in a Cartesian topology is that of shifting data along a dimension of the topology. MPI provides the function `MPI_Cart_shift`, that can be used to compute the rank of the source and destination processes for such operation. The calling sequence of this function is the following:

```
int MPI_Cart_shift(MPI_Comm comm_cart, int dir, int s_step,
        int *rank_source, int *rank_dest)
```

The direction of the shift is specified in the `dir` argument, and is one of the dimensions of the topology. The size of the shift step is specified in the `s_step` argument. The computed ranks are returned in `rank_source` and `rank_dest`. If the Cartesian topology was created with wraparound connections (i.e., the `periods[dir]` entry was set to true), then the shift wraps around. Otherwise, a `MPI_PROC_NULL` value is returned for `rank_source` and/or `rank_dest` for those processes that are outside the topology.

6.4.2 Example: Cannon's Matrix-Matrix Multiplication

To illustrate how the various topology functions are used we will implement Cannon's algorithm for multiplying two matrices A and B, described in Section 8.2.2. Cannon's algorithm views the processes as being arranged in a virtual two-dimensional square array. It uses this array to distribute the matrices A, B, and the result matrix C in a block fashion. That is, if $n \times n$ is the size of each matrix and p is the total number of process, then each matrix is divided into square blocks of size $n/\sqrt{p} \times n/\sqrt{p}$ (assuming that p is a perfect square). Now, process $P_{i,j}$ in the grid is assigned the $A_{i,j}$, $B_{i,j}$, and $C_{i,j}$ blocks of each matrix. After an initial data alignment phase, the algorithm proceeds in $\sqrt{p}$ steps. In each step, every process multiplies the locally available blocks of matrices A and B, and then sends the block of A to the leftward process, and the block of B to the upward process.

Program 6.2 shows the MPI function that implements Cannon's algorithm. The dimension of the matrices is supplied in the parameter n. The parameters a, b, and c point to the locally stored portions of the matrices A, B, and C, respectively. The size of these arrays is $n/\sqrt{p} \times n/\sqrt{p}$, where p is the number of processes. This routine assumes that p is a perfect square and that n is a multiple of $\sqrt{p}$. The parameter comm stores the communicator describing the processes that call the `MatrixMatrixMultiply` function. Note that the remaining programs in this chapter will be provided in the form of a function, as opposed to complete stand-alone programs.

Program 6.2 Cannon's Matrix-Matrix Multiplication with MPI's Topologies

---

```
1   MatrixMatrixMultiply(int n, double *a, double *b, double *c,
2                        MPI_Comm comm)
3   {
4     int i;
5     int nlocal;
6     int npes, dims[2], periods[2];
7     int myrank, my2drank, mycoords[2];
8     int uprank, downrank, leftrank, rightrank, coords[2];
9     int shiftsource, shiftdest;
10    MPI_Status status;
11    MPI_Comm comm_2d;
12
13    /* Get the communicator related information */
14    MPI_Comm_size(comm, &npes);
15    MPI_Comm_rank(comm, &myrank);
16
17    /* Set up the Cartesian topology */
18    dims[0] = dims[1] = sqrt(npes);
19
20    /* Set the periods for wraparound connections */
21    periods[0] = periods[1] = 1;
22
23    /* Create the Cartesian topology, with rank reordering */
24    MPI_Cart_create(comm, 2, dims, periods, 1, &comm_2d);
25
26    /* Get the rank and coordinates with respect to the new topology */
27    MPI_Comm_rank(comm_2d, &my2drank);
28    MPI_Cart_coords(comm_2d, my2drank, 2, mycoords);
29
30    /* Compute ranks of the up and left shifts */
31    MPI_Cart_shift(comm_2d, 0, -1, &rightrank, &leftrank);
32    MPI_Cart_shift(comm_2d, 1, -1, &downrank, &uprank);
33
34    /* Determine the dimension of the local matrix block */
35    nlocal = n/dims[0];
36
37    /* Perform the initial matrix alignment. First for A and then for B */
38    MPI_Cart_shift(comm_2d, 0, -mycoords[0], &shiftsource, &shiftdest);
39    MPI_Sendrecv_replace(a, nlocal*nlocal, MPI_DOUBLE, shiftdest,
40        1, shiftsource, 1, comm_2d, &status);
41
42    MPI_Cart_shift(comm_2d, 1, -mycoords[1], &shiftsource, &shiftdest);
43    MPI_Sendrecv_replace(b, nlocal*nlocal, MPI_DOUBLE,
44        shiftdest, 1, shiftsource, 1, comm_2d, &status);
45
46    /* Get into the main computation loop */
47    for (i=0; i<dims[0]; i++) {
48      MatrixMultiply(nlocal, a, b, c); /* c = c + a*b */
49
50      /* Shift matrix a left by one */
51      MPI_Sendrecv_replace(a, nlocal*nlocal, MPI_DOUBLE,
52          leftrank, 1, rightrank, 1, comm_2d, &status);
53
54      /* Shift matrix b up by one */
55      MPI_Sendrecv_replace(b, nlocal*nlocal, MPI_DOUBLE,
56          uprank, 1, downrank, 1, comm_2d, &status);
57    }
58
59    /* Restore the original distribution of a and b */
```

```
60    MPI_Cart_shift(comm_2d, 0, +mycoords[0], &shiftsource, &shiftdest);
61    MPI_Sendrecv_replace(a, nlocal*nlocal, MPI_DOUBLE,
62        shiftdest, 1, shiftsource, 1, comm_2d, &status);
63
64    MPI_Cart_shift(comm_2d, 1, +mycoords[1], &shiftsource, &shiftdest);
65    MPI_Sendrecv_replace(b, nlocal*nlocal, MPI_DOUBLE,
66        shiftdest, 1, shiftsource, 1, comm_2d, &status);
67
68    MPI_Comm_free(&comm_2d);    /* Free up communicator */
69  }
70
71  /* This function performs a serial matrix-matrix multiplication c = a*b */
72  MatrixMultiply(int n, double *a, double *b, double *c)
73  {
74    int i, j, k;
75
76    for (i=0; i<n; i++)
77      for (j=0; j<n; j++)
78        for (k=0; k<n; k++)
79          c[i*n+j] += a[i*n+k]*b[k*n+j];
80  }
```

6.5 Overlapping Communication with Computation

The MPI programs we developed so far used blocking send and receive operations whenever they needed to perform point-to-point communication. Recall that a blocking send operation remains blocked until the message has been copied out of the send buffer (either into a system buffer at the source process or sent to the destination process). Similarly, a blocking receive operation returns only after the message has been received and copied into the receive buffer. For example, consider Cannon's matrix-matrix multiplication program described in Program 6.2. During each iteration of its main computational loop (lines 47–57), it first computes the matrix multiplication of the sub-matrices stored in a and b, and then shifts the blocks of a and b, using `MPI_Sendrecv_replace` which blocks until the specified matrix block has been sent and received by the corresponding processes. In each iteration, each process spends $O(n^3/p^{1.5})$ time for performing the matrix-matrix multiplication and $O(n^2/p)$ time for shifting the blocks of matrices A and B. Now, since the blocks of matrices A and B do not change as they are shifted among the processors, it will be preferable if we can overlap the transmission of these blocks with the computation for the matrix-matrix multiplication, as many recent distributed-memory parallel computers have dedicated communication controllers that can perform the transmission of messages without interrupting the CPUs.

6.5.1 Non-Blocking Communication Operations

In order to overlap communication with computation, MPI provides a pair of functions for performing non-blocking send and receive operations. These functions are `MPI_Isend` and `MPI_Irecv`. `MPI_Isend` starts a send operation but does not complete, that is, it returns before the data is copied out of the buffer. Similarly, MPI_Irecv starts a receive operation but returns before the data has been received and copied into the buffer. With the support of appropriate hardware, the transmission and reception of messages can proceed concurrently with the computations performed by the program upon the return of the above functions.

However, at a later point in the program, a process that has started a non-blocking send or receive operation must make sure that this operation has completed before it proceeds with its computations. This is because a process that has started a non-blocking send operation may want to overwrite the buffer that stores the data that are being sent, or a process that has started a non-blocking receive operation may want to use the data it requested. To check the completion of non-blocking send and receive operations, MPI provides a pair of functions MPI_Test and MPI_Wait. The first tests whether or not a non-blocking operation has finished and the second waits (i.e., gets blocked) until a non-blocking operation actually finishes.

The calling sequences of MPI_Isend and MPI_Irecv are the following:

```
int MPI_Isend(void *buf, int count, MPI_Datatype datatype,
          int dest, int tag, MPI_Comm comm, MPI_Request *request)
int MPI_Irecv(void *buf, int count, MPI_Datatype datatype,
          int source, int tag, MPI_Comm comm, MPI_Request *request)
```

Note that these functions have similar arguments as the corresponding blocking send and receive functions. The main difference is that they take an additional argument request. MPI_Isend and MPI_Irecv functions allocate a *request object* and return a pointer to it in the request variable. This request object is used as an argument in the MPI_Test and MPI_Wait functions to identify the operation whose status we want to query or to wait for its completion.

Note that the MPI_Irecv function does not take a status argument similar to the blocking receive function, but the status information associated with the receive operation is returned by the MPI_Test and MPI_Wait functions.

```
int MPI_Test(MPI_Request *request, int *flag, MPI_Status *status)
int MPI_Wait(MPI_Request *request, MPI_Status *status)
```

MPI_Test tests whether or not the non-blocking send or receive operation identified by its request has finished. It returns flag = {true} (non-zero value in C) if it completed, otherwise it returns {false} (a zero value in C). In the case that the non-blocking operation has finished, the request object pointed to by request is deallocated and request is set to MPI_REQUEST_NULL. Also the status object is set to contain information about the operation. If the operation has not finished, request is not modified and the value of the status object is undefined. The MPI_Wait function blocks until the non-blocking operation identified by request completes. In that case it deallocates the request object, sets it to MPI_REQUEST_NULL, and returns information about the completed operation in the status object.

For the cases that the programmer wants to explicitly deallocate a request object, MPI provides the following function.

```
int MPI_Request_free(MPI_Request *request)
```

Note that the deallocation of the request object does not have any effect on the associated non-blocking send or receive operation. That is, if it has not yet completed it will proceed until its completion. Hence, one must be careful before explicitly deallocating a request object, since without it, we cannot check whether or not the non-blocking operation has completed.

A non-blocking communication operation can be matched with a corresponding blocking operation. For example, a process can send a message using a non-blocking send operation and this message can be received by the other process using a blocking receive operation.

Avoiding Deadlocks By using non-blocking communication operations we can remove most of the deadlocks associated with their blocking counterparts. For example, as we discussed in Section 6.3 the following piece of code is not safe.

```
1   int a[10], b[10], myrank;
2   MPI_Status status;
3   ...
4   MPI_Comm_rank(MPI_COMM_WORLD, &myrank);
5   if (myrank == 0) {
6     MPI_Send(a, 10, MPI_INT, 1, 1, MPI_COMM_WORLD);
7     MPI_Send(b, 10, MPI_INT, 1, 2, MPI_COMM_WORLD);
8   }
9   else if (myrank == 1) {
10    MPI_Recv(b, 10, MPI_INT, 0, 2, &status, MPI_COMM_WORLD);
11    MPI_Recv(a, 10, MPI_INT, 0, 1, &status, MPI_COMM_WORLD);
12  }
13  ...
```

However, if we replace either the send or receive operations with their non-blocking counterparts, then the code will be safe, and will correctly run on any MPI implementation.

```
1   int a[10], b[10], myrank;
2   MPI_Status status;
3   MPI_Request requests[2];
4   ...
5   MPI_Comm_rank(MPI_COMM_WORLD, &myrank);
6   if (myrank == 0) {
7     MPI_Send(a, 10, MPI_INT, 1, 1, MPI_COMM_WORLD);
8     MPI_Send(b, 10, MPI_INT, 1, 2, MPI_COMM_WORLD);
9   }
10  else if (myrank == 1) {
11    MPI_Irecv(b, 10, MPI_INT, 0, 2, &requests[0], MPI_COMM_WORLD);
12    MPI_Irecv(a, 10, MPI_INT, 0, 1, &requests[1], MPI_COMM_WORLD);
13  }
14  ...
```

This example also illustrates that the non-blocking operations started by any process can finish in any order depending on the transmission or reception of the corresponding messages. For example, the second receive operation will finish before the first does.

Example: Cannon's Matrix-Matrix Multiplication (Using Non-Blocking Operations)

Program 6.3 shows the MPI program that implements Cannon's algorithm using non-blocking send and receive operations. The various parameters are identical to those of Program 6.2.

Program 6.3   Non-Blocking Cannon's Matrix-Matrix Multiplication

```
1  MatrixMatrixMultiply_NonBlocking(int n, double *a, double *b,
2                                   double *c, MPI_Comm comm)
3  {
4    int i, j, nlocal;
5    double *a_buffers[2], *b_buffers[2];
6    int npes, dims[2], periods[2];
7    int myrank, my2drank, mycoords[2];
8    int uprank, downrank, leftrank, rightrank, coords[2];
9    int shiftsource, shiftdest;
10   MPI_Status status;
11   MPI_Comm comm_2d;
12   MPI_Request reqs[4];
13
14   /* Get the communicator related information */
15   MPI_Comm_size(comm, &npes);
16   MPI_Comm_rank(comm, &myrank);
17
18   /* Set up the Cartesian topology */
19   dims[0] = dims[1] = sqrt(npes);
20
21   /* Set the periods for wraparound connections */
22   periods[0] = periods[1] = 1;
23
24   /* Create the Cartesian topology, with rank reordering */
25   MPI_Cart_create(comm, 2, dims, periods, 1, &comm_2d);
26
27   /* Get the rank and coordinates with respect to the new topology */
28   MPI_Comm_rank(comm_2d, &my2drank);
29   MPI_Cart_coords(comm_2d, my2drank, 2, mycoords);
30
31   /* Compute ranks of the up and left shifts */
32   MPI_Cart_shift(comm_2d, 0, -1, &rightrank, &leftrank);
33   MPI_Cart_shift(comm_2d, 1, -1, &downrank, &uprank);
34
35   /* Determine the dimension of the local matrix block */
36   nlocal = n/dims[0];
37
38   /* Setup the a_buffers and b_buffers arrays */
39   a_buffers[0] = a;
40   a_buffers[1] = (double *)malloc(nlocal*nlocal*sizeof(double));
41   b_buffers[0] = b;
42   b_buffers[1] = (double *)malloc(nlocal*nlocal*sizeof(double));
43
44   /* Perform the initial matrix alignment. First for A and then for B */
```

```
45      MPI_Cart_shift(comm_2d, 0, -mycoords[0], &shiftsource, &shiftdest);
46      MPI_Sendrecv_replace(a_buffers[0], nlocal*nlocal, MPI_DOUBLE,
47         shiftdest, 1, shiftsource, 1, comm_2d, &status);
48
49      MPI_Cart_shift(comm_2d, 1, -mycoords[1], &shiftsource, &shiftdest);
50      MPI_Sendrecv_replace(b_buffers[0], nlocal*nlocal, MPI_DOUBLE,
51         shiftdest, 1, shiftsource, 1, comm_2d, &status);
52
53      /* Get into the main computation loop */
54      for (i=0; i<dims[0]; i++) {
55        MPI_Isend(a_buffers[i%2], nlocal*nlocal, MPI_DOUBLE,
56           leftrank, 1, comm_2d, &reqs[0]);
57        MPI_Isend(b_buffers[i%2], nlocal*nlocal, MPI_DOUBLE,
58           uprank, 1, comm_2d, &reqs[1]);
59        MPI_Irecv(a_buffers[(i+1)%2], nlocal*nlocal, MPI_DOUBLE,
60           rightrank, 1, comm_2d, &reqs[2]);
61        MPI_Irecv(b_buffers[(i+1)%2], nlocal*nlocal, MPI_DOUBLE,
62           downrank, 1, comm_2d, &reqs[3]);
63
64        /* c = c + a*b */
65        MatrixMultiply(nlocal, a_buffers[i%2], b_buffers[i%2], c);
66
67        for (j=0; j<4; j++)
68          MPI_Wait(&reqs[j], &status);
69      }
70
71      /* Restore the original distribution of a and b */
72      MPI_Cart_shift(comm_2d, 0, +mycoords[0], &shiftsource, &shiftdest);
73      MPI_Sendrecv_replace(a_buffers[i%2], nlocal*nlocal, MPI_DOUBLE,
74         shiftdest, 1, shiftsource, 1, comm_2d, &status);
75
76      MPI_Cart_shift(comm_2d, 1, +mycoords[1], &shiftsource, &shiftdest);
77      MPI_Sendrecv_replace(b_buffers[i%2], nlocal*nlocal, MPI_DOUBLE,
78         shiftdest, 1, shiftsource, 1, comm_2d, &status);
79
80      MPI_Comm_free(&comm_2d);   /* Free up communicator */
81
82      free(a_buffers[1]);
83      free(b_buffers[1]);
84    }
```

There are two main differences between the blocking program (Program 6.2) and this non-blocking one. The first difference is that the non-blocking program requires the use of the additional arrays *a_buffers* and *b_buffers*, that are used as the buffer of the blocks of *A* and *B* that are being received while the computation involving the previous blocks is performed. The second difference is that in the main computational loop, it first starts the non-blocking send operations to send the locally stored blocks of *A* and *B* to the processes left and up the grid, and then starts the non-blocking receive operations to receive the blocks for the next iteration from the processes right and down the grid. Having initiated these four non-blocking operations, it proceeds to perform the matrix-matrix multiplication of the blocks it currently stores. Finally, before it proceeds to the next iteration, it uses MPI_Wait to wait for the send and receive operations to complete.

Note that in order to overlap communication with computation we have to use two auxiliary arrays – one for *A* and one for *B*. This is to ensure that incoming messages never overwrite the blocks of *A* and *B* that are used in the computation, which proceeds concurrently with the data transfer. Thus, increased performance (by overlapping communication with computation) comes at the expense of increased memory requirements. This is a trade-off that is often made in message-passing programs, since communication overheads can be quite high for loosely coupled distributed memory parallel computers.

6.6   Collective Communication and Computation Operations

MPI provides an extensive set of functions for performing many commonly used collective communication operations. In particular, the majority of the basic communication operations described in Chapter 4 are supported by MPI. All of the collective communication functions provided by MPI take as an argument a communicator that defines the group of processes that participate in the collective operation. All the processes that belong to this communicator participate in the operation, and all of them must call the collective communication function. Even though collective communication operations do not act like barriers (i.e., it is possible for a processor to go past its call for the collective communication operation even before other processes have reached it), it acts like a *virtual* synchronization step in the following sense: the parallel program should be written such that it behaves correctly even if a global synchronization is performed before and after the collective call. Since the operations are virtually synchronous, they do not require tags. In some of the collective functions data is required to be sent from a single process (source-process) or to be received by a single process (target-process). In these functions, the source- or target-process is one of the arguments supplied to the routines. All the processes in the group (i.e., communicator) must specify the same source- or target-process. For most collective communication operations, MPI provides two different variants. The first transfers equal-size data to or from each process, and the second transfers data that can be of different sizes.

6.6.1   Barrier

The barrier synchronization operation is performed in MPI using the `MPI_Barrier` function.

```
int MPI_Barrier(MPI_Comm comm)
```

The only argument of `MPI_Barrier` is the communicator that defines the group of processes that are synchronized. The call to `MPI_Barrier` returns only after all the processes in the group have called this function.

6.6.2   Broadcast

The one-to-all broadcast operation described in Section 4.1 is performed in MPI using the `MPI_Bcast` function.

Table 6.3   Predefined reduction operations.

Operation	Meaning	Datatypes
MPI_MAX	Maximum	C integers and floating point
MPI_MIN	Minimum	C integers and floating point
MPI_SUM	Sum	C integers and floating point
MPI_PROD	Product	C integers and floating point
MPI_LAND	Logical AND	C integers
MPI_BAND	Bit-wise AND	C integers and byte
MPI_LOR	Logical OR	C integers
MPI_BOR	Bit-wise OR	C integers and byte
MPI_LXOR	Logical XOR	C integers
MPI_BXOR	Bit-wise XOR	C integers and byte
MPI_MAXLOC	max-min value-location	Data-pairs
MPI_MINLOC	min-min value-location	Data-pairs

```
int MPI_Bcast(void *buf, int count, MPI_Datatype datatype,
        int source, MPI_Comm comm)
```

MPI_Bcast sends the data stored in the buffer buf of process source to all the other processes in the group. The data received by each process is stored in the buffer buf. The data that is broadcast consist of count entries of type datatype. The amount of data sent by the source process must be equal to the amount of data that is being received by each process; i.e., the count and datatype fields must match on all processes.

6.6.3   Reduction

The all-to-one reduction operation described in Section 4.1 is performed in MPI using the MPI_Reduce function.

```
int MPI_Reduce(void *sendbuf, void *recvbuf, int count,
        MPI_Datatype datatype, MPI_Op op, int target,
        MPI_Comm comm)
```

MPI_Reduce combines the elements stored in the buffer sendbuf of each process in the group, using the operation specified in op, and returns the combined values in the buffer recvbuf of the process with rank target. Both the sendbuf and recvbuf must have the same number of count items of type datatype. Note that all processes must provide a recvbuf array, even if they are not the *target* of the reduction operation. When count is more than one, then the combine operation is applied element-wise on each entry of the sequence. All the processes must call MPI_Reduce with the same value for count, datatype, op, target, and comm.

MPI provides a list of predefined operations that can be used to combine the elements stored in sendbuf. MPI also allows programmers to define their own operations, which is

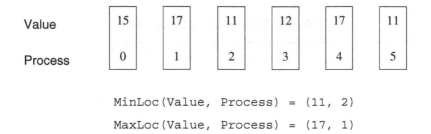

$$\text{MinLoc(Value, Process)} = (11, 2)$$
$$\text{MaxLoc(Value, Process)} = (17, 1)$$

Figure 6.6   An example use of the MPI_MINLOC and MPI_MAXLOC operators.

not covered in this book. The predefined operations are shown in Table 6.3. For example, in order to compute the maximum of the elements stored in sendbuf, the MPI_MAX value must be used for the op argument. Not all of these operations can be applied to all possible data-types supported by MPI. For example, a bit-wise OR operation (i.e., $op = $ MPI_BOR) is not defined for real-valued data-types such as MPI_FLOAT and MPI_REAL. The last column of Table 6.3 shows the various data-types that can be used with each operation.

The operation MPI_MAXLOC combines pairs of values (v_i, l_i) and returns the pair (v, l) such that v is the maximum among all v_i's and l is the smallest among all l_i's such that $v = v_i$. Similarly, MPI_MINLOC combines pairs of values and returns the pair (v, l) such that v is the minimum among all v_i's and l is the smallest among all l_i's such that $v = v_i$. One possible application of MPI_MAXLOC or MPI_MINLOC is to compute the maximum or minimum of a list of numbers each residing on a different process and also the rank of the first process that stores this maximum or minimum, as illustrated in Figure 6.6. Since both MPI_MAXLOC and MPI_MINLOC require datatypes that correspond to pairs of values, a new set of MPI datatypes have been defined as shown in Table 6.4. In C, these datatypes are implemented as structures containing the corresponding types.

When the result of the reduction operation is needed by all the processes, MPI provides the MPI_Allreduce operation that returns the result to all the processes. This function provides the functionality of the all-reduce operation described in Section 4.3.

Table 6.4   MPI datatypes for data-pairs used with the MPI_MAXLOC and MPI_MINLOC reduction operations.

MPI Datatype	C Datatype
MPI_2INT	pair of ints
MPI_SHORT_INT	short and int
MPI_LONG_INT	long and int
MPI_LONG_DOUBLE_INT	long double and int
MPI_FLOAT_INT	float and int
MPI_DOUBLE_INT	double and int

```
int MPI_Allreduce(void *sendbuf, void *recvbuf, int count,
        MPI_Datatype datatype, MPI_Op op, MPI_Comm comm)
```

Note that there is no target argument since all processes receive the result of the operation.

6.6.4   Prefix

The prefix-sum operation described in Section 4.3 is performed in MPI using the MPI_Scan function.

```
int MPI_Scan(void *sendbuf, void *recvbuf, int count,
        MPI_Datatype datatype, MPI_Op op, MPI_Comm comm)
```

MPI_Scan performs a prefix reduction of the data stored in the buffer sendbuf at each process and returns the result in the buffer recvbuf. The receive buffer of the process with rank i will store, at the end of the operation, the reduction of the send buffers of the processes whose ranks range from 0 up to and including i. The type of supported operations (i.e., op) as well as the restrictions on the various arguments of MPI_Scan are the same as those for the reduction operation MPI_Reduce.

6.6.5   Gather

The gather operation described in Section 4.4 is performed in MPI using the MPI_Gather function.

```
int MPI_Gather(void *sendbuf, int sendcount,
        MPI_Datatype senddatatype, void *recvbuf, int recvcount,
        MPI_Datatype recvdatatype, int target, MPI_Comm comm)
```

Each process, including the target process, sends the data stored in the array sendbuf to the target process. As a result, if p is the number of processors in the communication comm, the target process receives a total of p buffers. The data is stored in the array recvbuf of the target process, in a rank order. That is, the data from process with rank i are stored in the recvbuf starting at location $i *$ sendcount (assuming that the array recvbuf is of the same type as recvdatatype).

The data sent by each process must be of the same size and type. That is, MPI_Gather must be called with the sendcount and senddatatype arguments having the same values at each process. The information about the receive buffer, its length and type applies only for the target process and is ignored for all the other processes. The argument recvcount specifies the number of elements received by each process and not the total number of elements it receives. So, recvcount must be the same as sendcount and their datatypes must be matching.

MPI also provides the MPI_Allgather function in which the data are gathered to all the processes and not only at the target process.

```
int MPI_Allgather(void *sendbuf, int sendcount,
        MPI_Datatype senddatatype, void *recvbuf, int recvcount,
        MPI_Datatype recvdatatype, MPI_Comm comm)
```

The meanings of the various parameters are similar to those for `MPI_Gather`; however, each process must now supply a `recvbuf` array that will store the gathered data.

In addition to the above versions of the gather operation, in which the sizes of the arrays sent by each process are the same, MPI also provides versions in which the size of the arrays can be different. MPI refers to these operations as the *vector* variants. The vector variants of the `MPI_Gather` and `MPI_Allgather` operations are provided by the functions `MPI_Gatherv` and `MPI_Allgatherv`, respectively.

```
int MPI_Gatherv(void *sendbuf, int sendcount,
        MPI_Datatype senddatatype, void *recvbuf,
        int *recvcounts, int *displs,
        MPI_Datatype recvdatatype, int target, MPI_Comm comm)

int MPI_Allgatherv(void *sendbuf, int sendcount,
        MPI_Datatype senddatatype, void *recvbuf,
        int *recvcounts, int *displs, MPI_Datatype recvdatatype,
        MPI_Comm comm)
```

These functions allow a different number of data elements to be sent by each process by replacing the `recvcount` parameter with the array `recvcounts`. The amount of data sent by process i is equal to `recvcounts[i]`. Note that the size of `recvcounts` is equal to the size of the communicator `comm`. The array parameter `displs`, which is also of the same size, is used to determine where in `recvbuf` the data sent by each process will be stored. In particular, the data sent by process i are stored in `recvbuf` starting at location `displs[i]`. Note that, as opposed to the non-vector variants, the `sendcount` parameter can be different for different processes.

6.6.6   Scatter

The scatter operation described in Section 4.4 is performed in MPI using the `MPI_Scatter` function.

```
int MPI_Scatter(void *sendbuf, int sendcount,
        MPI_Datatype senddatatype, void *recvbuf, int recvcount,
        MPI_Datatype recvdatatype, int source, MPI_Comm comm)
```

The `source` process sends a different part of the send buffer `sendbuf` to each processes, including itself. The data that are received are stored in `recvbuf`. Process i receives `sendcount` contiguous elements of type `senddatatype` starting from the $i * $ `sendcount` location of the `sendbuf` of the source process (assuming that `sendbuf` is of the same type as `senddatatype`). `MPI_Scatter` must be called by all the processes with the same values for the `sendcount`, `senddatatype`, `recvcount`, recvdatatype, source, and comm arguments. Note again that sendcount is the number of elements sent to each individual process.

Similarly to the gather operation, MPI provides a vector variant of the scatter operation, called MPI_Scatterv, that allows different amounts of data to be sent to different processes.

```
int MPI_Scatterv(void *sendbuf, int *sendcounts, int *displs,
        MPI_Datatype senddatatype, void *recvbuf, int recvcount,
        MPI_Datatype recvdatatype, int source, MPI_Comm comm)
```

As we can see, the parameter sendcount has been replaced by the array sendcounts that determines the number of elements to be sent to each process. In particular, the target process sends sendcounts[i] elements to process i. Also, the array displs is used to determine where in sendbuf these elements will be sent from. In particular, if sendbuf is of the same type is senddatatype, the data sent to process i start at location displs[i] of array sendbuf. Both the sendcounts and displs arrays are of size equal to the number of processes in the communicator. Note that by appropriately setting the displs array we can use MPI_Scatterv to send overlapping regions of sendbuf.

6.6.7   All-to-All

The all-to-all personalized communication operation described in Section 4.5 is performed in MPI by using the MPI_Alltoall function.

```
int MPI_Alltoall(void *sendbuf, int sendcount,
        MPI_Datatype senddatatype, void *recvbuf, int recvcount,
        MPI_Datatype recvdatatype, MPI_Comm comm)
```

Each process sends a different portion of the sendbuf array to each other process, including itself. Each process sends to process i sendcount contiguous elements of type senddatatype starting from the $i * $ sendcount location of its sendbuf array. The data that are received are stored in the recvbuf array. Each process receives from process i recvcount elements of type recvdatatype and stores them in its recvbuf array starting at location $i * $ recvcount. MPI_Alltoall must be called by all the processes with the same values for the sendcount, senddatatype, recvcount, recvdatatype, and comm arguments. Note that sendcount and recvcount are the number of elements sent to, and received from, each individual process.

MPI also provides a vector variant of the all-to-all personalized communication operation called MPI_Alltoallv that allows different amounts of data to be sent to and received from each process.

```
int MPI_Alltoallv(void *sendbuf, int *sendcounts, int *sdispls
        MPI_Datatype senddatatype, void *recvbuf, int *recvcounts,
        int *rdispls, MPI_Datatype recvdatatype, MPI_Comm comm)
```

The parameter `sendcounts` is used to specify the number of elements sent to each process, and the parameter `sdispls` is used to specify the location in `sendbuf` in which these elements are stored. In particular, each process sends to process i, starting at location `sdispls[i]` of the array `sendbuf`, `sendcounts[i]` contiguous elements. The parameter `recvcounts` is used to specify the number of elements received by each process, and the parameter `rdispls` is used to specify the location in `recvbuf` in which these elements are stored. In particular, each process receives from process i `recvcounts[i]` elements that are stored in contiguous locations of `recvbuf` starting at location `rdispls[i]`. `MPI_Alltoallv` must be called by all the processes with the same values for the `senddatatype`, `recvdatatype`, and `comm` arguments.

6.6.8 Example: One-Dimensional Matrix-Vector Multiplication

Our first message-passing program using collective communications will be to multiply a dense $n \times n$ matrix A with a vector b, i.e., $x = Ab$. As discussed in Section 8.1, one way of performing this multiplication in parallel is to have each process compute different portions of the product-vector x. In particular, each one of the p processes is responsible for computing n/p consecutive elements of x. This algorithm can be implemented in MPI by distributing the matrix A in a row-wise fashion, such that each process receives the n/p rows that correspond to the portion of the product-vector x it computes. Vector b is distributed in a fashion similar to x.

Program 6.4 shows the MPI program that uses a row-wise distribution of matrix A. The dimension of the matrices is supplied in the parameter n, the parameters a and b point to the locally stored portions of matrix A and vector b, respectively, and the parameter x points to the local portion of the output matrix-vector product. This program assumes that n is a multiple of the number of processors.

Program 6.4 Row-wise Matrix-Vector Multiplication

```
1   RowMatrixVectorMultiply(int n, double *a, double *b, double *x,
2                           MPI_Comm comm)
3   {
4     int i, j;
5     int nlocal;           /* Number of locally stored rows of A */
6     double *fb;           /* Will point to a buffer that stores the entire vector b */
7     int npes, myrank;
8     MPI_Status status;
9
10    /* Get information about the communicator */
11    MPI_Comm_size(comm, &npes);
12    MPI_Comm_rank(comm, &myrank);
13
14    /* Allocate the memory that will store the entire vector b */
15    fb = (double *)malloc(n*sizeof(double));
16
17    nlocal = n/npes;
18
19    /* Gather the entire vector b on each processor using MPI's ALLGATHER operation */
20    MPI_Allgather(b, nlocal, MPI_DOUBLE, fb, nlocal, MPI_DOUBLE,
```

```
21          comm);
22
23      /* Perform the matrix-vector multiplication involving the locally stored submatrix */
24      for (i=0; i<nlocal; i++) {
25        x[i] = 0.0;
26        for (j=0; j<n; j++)
27          x[i] += a[i*n+j]*fb[j];
28      }
29
30      free(fb);
31  }
```

An alternate way of computing x is to parallelize the task of performing the dot-product for each element of x. That is, for each element x_i, of vector x, all the processes will compute a part of it, and the result will be obtained by adding up these partial dot-products. This algorithm can be implemented in MPI by distributing matrix A in a column-wise fashion. Each process gets n/p consecutive columns of A, and the elements of vector b that correspond to these columns. Furthermore, at the end of the computation we want the product-vector x to be distributed in a fashion similar to vector b. Program 6.5 shows the MPI program that implements this column-wise distribution of the matrix.

Program 6.5   Column-wise Matrix-Vector Multiplication

```
1   ColMatrixVectorMultiply(int n, double *a, double *b, double *x,
2                           MPI_Comm comm)
3   {
4     int i, j;
5     int nlocal;
6     double *px;
7     double *fx;
8     int npes, myrank;
9     MPI_Status status;
10
11    /* Get identity and size information from the communicator */
12    MPI_Comm_size(comm, &npes);
13    MPI_Comm_rank(comm, &myrank);
14
15    nlocal = n/npes;
16
17    /* Allocate memory for arrays storing intermediate results. */
18    px = (double *)malloc(n*sizeof(double));
19    fx = (double *)malloc(n*sizeof(double));
20
21    /* Compute the partial-dot products that correspond to the local columns of A. */
22    for (i=0; i<n; i++) {
23      px[i] = 0.0;
24      for (j=0; j<nlocal; j++)
25        px[i] += a[i*nlocal+j]*b[j];
26    }
27
28    /* Sum-up the results by performing an element-wise reduction operation */
29    MPI_Reduce(px, fx, n, MPI_DOUBLE, MPI_SUM, 0, comm);
30
31    /* Redistribute fx in a fashion similar to that of vector b */
32    MPI_Scatter(fx, nlocal, MPI_DOUBLE, x, nlocal, MPI_DOUBLE, 0,
33        comm);
34
```

```
35    free(px); free(fx);
36  }
```

Comparing these two programs for performing matrix-vector multiplication we see that the row-wise version needs to perform only a `MPI_Allgather` operation whereas the column-wise program needs to perform a `MPI_Reduce` and a `MPI_Scatter` operation. In general, a row-wise distribution is preferable as it leads to small communication overhead (see Problem 6.6). However, many times, an application needs to compute not only Ax but also $A^T x$. In that case, the row-wise distribution can be used to compute Ax, but the computation of $A^T x$ requires the column-wise distribution (a row-wise distribution of A is a column-wise distribution of its transpose A^T). It is much cheaper to use the program for the column-wise distribution than to transpose the matrix and then use the row-wise program. We must also note that using a dual of the all-gather operation, it is possible to develop a parallel formulation for column-wise distribution that is as fast as the program using row-wise distribution (see Problem 6.7). However, this dual operation is not available in MPI.

6.6.9   Example: Single-Source Shortest-Path

Our second message-passing program that uses collective communication operations computes the shortest paths from a source-vertex s to all the other vertices in a graph using Dijkstra's single-source shortest-path algorithm described in Section 10.3. This program is shown in Program 6.6.

The parameter n stores the total number of vertices in the graph, and the parameter source stores the vertex from which we want to compute the single-source shortest path. The parameter wgt points to the locally stored portion of the weighted adjacency matrix of the graph. The parameter lengths points to a vector that will store the length of the shortest paths from source to the locally stored vertices. Finally, the parameter comm is the communicator to be used by the MPI routines. Note that this routine assumes that the number of vertices is a multiple of the number of processors.

Program 6.6   Dijkstra's Single-Source Shortest-Path

```
 1  SingleSource(int n, int source, int *wgt, int *lengths, MPI_Comm comm)
 2  {
 3    int i, j;
 4    int nlocal;    /* The number of vertices stored locally */
 5    int *marker;   /* Used to mark the vertices belonging to Vₒ */
 6    int firstvtx;  /* The index number of the first vertex that is stored locally */
 7    int lastvtx;   /* The index number of the last vertex that is stored locally */
 8    int u, udist;
 9    int lminpair[2], gminpair[2];
10    int npes, myrank;
11    MPI_Status status;
12
13    MPI_Comm_size(comm, &npes);
14    MPI_Comm_rank(comm, &myrank);
```

```
15
16    nlocal   = n/npes;
17    firstvtx = myrank*nlocal;
18    lastvtx  = firstvtx+nlocal-1;
19
20    /* Set the initial distances from source to all the other vertices */
21    for (j=0; j<nlocal; j++)
22       lengths[j] = wgt[source*nlocal + j];
23
24    /* This array is used to indicate if the shortest part to a vertex has been found or not. */
25    /* if marker[v] is one, then the shortest path to v has been found, otherwise it has not. */
26    marker = (int *)malloc(nlocal*sizeof(int));
27    for (j=0; j<nlocal; j++)
28       marker[j] = 1;
29
30    /* The process that stores the source vertex, marks it as being seen */
31    if (source >= firstvtx && source <= lastvtx)
32       marker[source-firstvtx] = 0;
33
34    /* The main loop of Dijkstra's algorithm */
35    for (i=1; i<n; i++) {
36       /* Step 1: Find the local vertex that is at the smallest distance from source */
37       lminpair[0] = MAXINT; /* set it to an architecture dependent large number */
38       lminpair[1] = -1;
39       for (j=0; j<nlocal; j++) {
40          if (marker[j] && lengths[j] < lminpair[0]) {
41             lminpair[0] = lengths[j];
42             lminpair[1] = firstvtx+j;
43          }
44       }
45
46       /* Step 2: Compute the global minimum vertex, and insert it into Vc */
47       MPI_Allreduce(lminpair, gminpair, 1, MPI_2INT, MPI_MINLOC,
48             comm);
49       udist = gminpair[0];
50       u = gminpair[1];
51
52       /* The process that stores the minimum vertex, marks it as being seen */
53       if (u == lminpair[1])
54          marker[u-firstvtx] = 0;
55
56       /* Step 3: Update the distances given that u got inserted */
57       for (j=0; j<nlocal; j++) {
58          if (marker[j] && udist + wgt[u*nlocal+j] < lengths[j])
59             lengths[j] = udist + wgt[u*nlocal+j];
60       }
61    }
62
63    free(marker);
64 }
```

The main computational loop of Dijkstra's parallel single-source shortest path algorithm performs three steps. First, each process finds the locally stored vertex in V_o that has the smallest distance from the source. Second, the vertex that has the smallest distance over all processes is determined, and it is included in V_c. Third, all processes update their distance arrays to reflect the inclusion of the new vertex in V_c.

The first step is performed by scanning the locally stored vertices in V_o and determining the one vertex v with the smaller *lengths*[v] value. The result of this computation is stored in the array *lminpair*. In particular, *lminpair*[0] stores the distance of the vertex, and *lminpair*[1] stores the vertex itself. The reason for using this storage scheme will become clear when we consider the next step, in which we must compute the vertex that has the smallest overall distance from the source. We can find the overall shortest distance by performing a min-reduction on the distance values stored in *lminpair*[0]. However, in addition to the shortest distance, we also need to know the vertex that is at that shortest distance. For this reason, the appropriate reduction operation is the MPI_MINLOC which returns both the minimum as well as an index value associated with that minimum. Because of MPI_MINLOC we use the two-element array *lminpair* to store the distance as well as the vertex that achieves this distance. Also, because the result of the reduction operation is needed by all the processes to perform the third step, we use the MPI_Allreduce operation to perform the reduction. The result of the reduction operation is returned in the *gminpair* array. The third and final step during each iteration is performed by scanning the local vertices that belong in V_o and updating their shortest distances from the source vertex.

Avoiding Load Imbalances   Program 6.6 assigns n/p consecutive columns of W to each processor and in each iteration it uses the MPI_MINLOC reduction operation to select the vertex v to be included in V_c. Recall that the MPI_MINLOC operation for the pairs (a, i) and (a, j) will return the one that has the smaller index (since both of them have the same value). Consequently, among the vertices that are equally close to the source vertex, it favors the smaller numbered vertices. This may lead to load imbalances, because vertices stored in lower-ranked processes will tend to be included in V_c faster than vertices in higher-ranked processes (especially when many vertices in V_o are at the same minimum distance from the source). Consequently, the size of the set V_o will be larger in higher-ranked processes, dominating the overall runtime.

One way of correcting this problem is to distribute the columns of W using a cyclic distribution. In this distribution process i gets every pth vertex starting from vertex i. This scheme also assigns n/p vertices to each process but these vertices have indices that span almost the entire graph. Consequently, the preference given to lower-numbered vertices by MPI_MINLOC does not lead to load-imbalance problems.

6.6.10   Example: Sample Sort

The last problem requiring collective communications that we will consider is that of sorting a sequence A of n elements using the sample sort algorithm described in Section 9.5. The program is shown in Program 6.7.

The SampleSort function takes as input the sequence of elements stored at each process and returns a pointer to an array that stores the sorted sequence as well as the number of elements in this sequence. The elements of this SampleSort function are integers and they are sorted in increasing order. The total number of elements to be sorted is specified by the parameter n and a pointer to the array that stores the local portion of these elements is specified by elmnts. On return, the parameter nsorted will store the number of elements in the returned sorted array. This routine assumes that n is a multiple of the number of processes.

Program 6.7   Samplesort
_____

```
1   int *SampleSort(int n, int *elmnts, int *nsorted, MPI_Comm comm)
2   {
3       int i, j, nlocal, npes, myrank;
4       int *sorted_elmnts, *splitters, *allpicks;
5       int *scounts, *sdispls, *rcounts, *rdispls;
6
7       /* Get communicator-related information */
8       MPI_Comm_size(comm, &npes);
9       MPI_Comm_rank(comm, &myrank);
10
11      nlocal = n/npes;
12
13      /* Allocate memory for the arrays that will store the splitters */
14      splitters = (int *)malloc(npes*sizeof(int));
15      allpicks = (int *)malloc(npes*(npes-1)*sizeof(int));
16
17      /* Sort local array */
18      qsort(elmnts, nlocal, sizeof(int), IncOrder);
19
20      /* Select local npes-1 equally spaced elements */
21      for (i=1; i<npes, i++)
22          splitters[i-1] = elmnts[i*nlocal/npes];
23
24      /* Gather the samples in the processors */
25      MPI_Allgather(splitters, npes-1, MPI_INT, allpicks, npes-1,
26          MPI_INT, comm);
27
28      /* sort these samples */
29      qsort(allpicks, npes*(npes-1), sizeof(int), IncOrder);
30
31      /* Select splitters */
32      for (i=1; i<npes; i++)
33          splitters[i-1] = allpicks[i*npes];
34      splitters[npes-1] = MAXINT;
35
36      /* Compute the number of elements that belong to each bucket */
37      scounts = (int *)malloc(npes*sizeof(int));
38      for (i=0; i<npes; i++)
39          scounts[i] = 0;
40
41      for (j=i=0; i<nlocal; i++) {
42          if (elmnts[i] < splitters[j])
43              scounts[j]++;
44          else
45              scounts[++j]++;
46      }
47
48      /* Determine the starting location of each bucket's elements in the elmnts array */
49      sdispls = (int *)malloc(npes*sizeof(int));
50      sdispls[0] = 0;
51      for (i=1; i<npes; i++)
52          sdispls[i] = sdispls[i-1]+scounts[i-1];
53
54      /* Perform an all-to-all to inform the corresponding processes of the number of elements */
```

```
55      /* they are going to receive. This information is stored in rcounts array */
56      rcounts = (int *)malloc(npes*sizeof(int));
57      MPI_Alltoall(scounts, 1, MPI_INT, rcounts, 1, MPI_INT, comm);
58
59      /* Based on rcounts determine where in the local array the data from each processor */
60      /* will be stored. This array will store the received elements as well as the final */
61      /* sorted sequence */
62      rdispls = (int *)malloc(npes*sizeof(int));
63      rdispls[0] = 0;
64      for (i=1; i<npes; i++)
65        rdispls[i] = rdispls[i-1]+rcounts[i-1];
66
67      *nsorted = rdispls[npes-1]+rcounts[i-1];
68      sorted_elmnts = (int *)malloc((*nsorted)*sizeof(int));
69
70      /* Each process sends and receives the corresponding elements, using the MPI_Alltoallv */
71      /* operation. The arrays scounts and sdispls are used to specify the number of elements */
72      /* to be sent and where these elements are stored, respectively. The arrays rcounts */
73      /* and rdispls are used to specify the number of elements to be received, and where these */
74      /* elements will be stored, respectively. */
75      MPI_Alltoallv(elmnts, scounts, sdispls, MPI_INT, sorted_elmnts,
76          rcounts, rdispls, MPI_INT, comm);
77
78      /* Perform the final local sort */
79      qsort(sorted_elmnts, *nsorted, sizeof(int), IncOrder);
80
81      free(splitters); free(allpicks); free(scounts); free(sdispls);
82      free(rcounts);  free(rdispls);
83
84      return sorted_elmnts;
85    }
```

6.7   Groups and Communicators

In many parallel algorithms, communication operations need to be restricted to certain subsets of processes. MPI provides several mechanisms for partitioning the group of processes
that belong to a communicator into subgroups each corresponding to a different communicator. A general method for partitioning a graph of processes is to use MPI_Comm_split
that is defined as follows:

```
int MPI_Comm_split(MPI_Comm comm, int color, int key,
        MPI_Comm *newcomm)
```

This function is a collective operation, and thus needs to be called by all the processes in the
communicator comm. The function takes color and key as input parameters in addition
to the communicator, and partitions the group of processes in the communicator comm
into disjoint subgroups. Each subgroup contains all processes that have supplied the same
value for the color parameter. Within each subgroup, the processes are ranked in the
order defined by the value of the key parameter, with ties broken according to their rank in
the old communicator (i.e., comm). A new communicator for each subgroup is returned in
the newcomm parameter. Figure 6.7 shows an example of splitting a communicator using
the MPI_Comm_split function. If each process called MPI_Comm_split using the

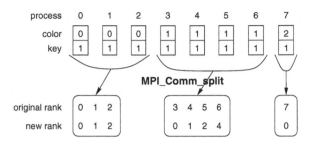

Figure 6.7   Using `MPI_Comm_split` to split a group of processes in a communicator into sub-groups.

values of parameters `color` and `key` as shown in Figure 6.7, then three communicators will be created, containing processes {0, 1, 2}, {3, 4, 5, 6}, and {7}, respectively.

Splitting Cartesian Topologies   In many parallel algorithms, processes are arranged in a virtual grid, and in different steps of the algorithm, communication needs to be restricted to a different subset of the grid. MPI provides a convenient way to partition a Cartesian topology to form lower-dimensional grids.

MPI provides the `MPI_Cart_sub` function that allows us to partition a Cartesian topology into sub-topologies that form lower-dimensional grids. For example, we can partition a two-dimensional topology into groups, each consisting of the processes along the row or column of the topology. The calling sequence of `MPI_Cart_sub` is the following:

```
int MPI_Cart_sub(MPI_Comm comm_cart, int *keep_dims,
        MPI_Comm *comm_subcart)
```

The array `keep_dims` is used to specify how the Cartesian topology is partitioned. In particular, if `keep_dims[i]` is true (non-zero value in C) then the `i`th dimension is retained in the new sub-topology. For example, consider a three-dimensional topology of size $2 \times 4 \times 7$. If `keep_dims` is {true, false, true}, then the original topology is split into four two-dimensional sub-topologies of size 2×7, as illustrated in Figure 6.8(a). If `keep_dims` is {false, false, true}, then the original topology is split into eight one-dimensional topologies of size seven, illustrated in Figure 6.8(b). Note that the number of sub-topologies created is equal to the product of the number of processes along the dimensions that are not being retained. The original topology is specified by the communicator `comm_cart`, and the returned communicator `comm_subcart` stores information about the created sub-topology. Only a single communicator is returned to each process, and for processes that do not belong to the same sub-topology, the group specified by the returned communicator is different.

The processes belonging to a given sub-topology can be determined as follows. Consider a three-dimensional topology of size $d_1 \times d_2 \times d_3$, and assume that `keep_dims` is set to {true, false, true}. The group of processes that belong to the same sub-topology as the

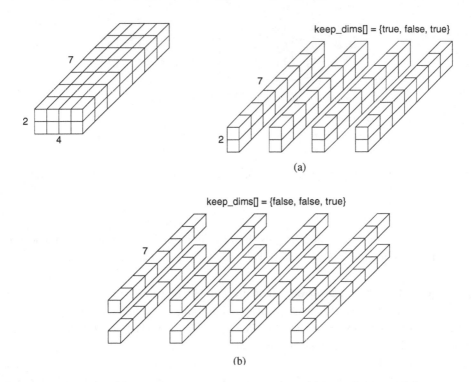

Figure 6.8 Splitting a Cartesian topology of size $2 \times 4 \times 7$ into (a) four subgroups of size $2 \times 1 \times 7$, and (b) eight subgroups of size $1 \times 1 \times 7$.

process with coordinates (x, y, z) is given by $(*, y, *)$, where a '*' in a coordinate denotes all the possible values for this coordinate. Note also that since the second coordinate can take d_2 values, a total of d_2 sub-topologies are created.

Also, the coordinate of a process in a sub-topology created by `MPI_Cart_sub` can be obtained from its coordinate in the original topology by disregarding the coordinates that correspond to the dimensions that were not retained. For example, the coordinate of a process in the column-based sub-topology is equal to its row-coordinate in the two-dimensional topology. For instance, the process with coordinates $(2, 3)$ has a coordinate of (2) in the sub-topology that corresponds to the third column of the grid.

6.7.1 Example: Two-Dimensional Matrix-Vector Multiplication

In Section 6.6.8, we presented two programs for performing the matrix-vector multiplication $x = Ab$ using a row- and column-wise distribution of the matrix. As discussed in Section 8.1.2, an alternative way of distributing matrix A is to use a two-dimensional distribution, giving rise to the two-dimensional parallel formulations of the matrix-vector multiplication algorithm.

Program 6.8 shows how these topologies and their partitioning are used to implement the two-dimensional matrix-vector multiplication. The dimension of the matrix is supplied in the parameter n, the parameters a and b point to the locally stored portions of matrix A and vector b, respectively, and the parameter x points to the local portion of the output matrix-vector product. Note that only the processes along the first column of the process grid will store b initially, and that upon return, the same set of processes will store the result x. For simplicity, the program assumes that the number of processes p is a perfect square and that n is a multiple of $\sqrt{p}$.

Program 6.8   Two-Dimensional Matrix-Vector Multiplication

```
1   MatrixVectorMultiply_2D(int n, double *a, double *b, double *x,
2                           MPI_Comm comm)
3   {
4     int ROW=0, COL=1;   /* Improve readability */
5     int i, j, nlocal;
6     double *px;   /* Will store partial dot products */
7     int npes, dims[2], periods[2], keep_dims[2];
8     int myrank, my2drank, mycoords[2];
9     int other_rank, coords[2];
10    MPI_Status status;
11    MPI_Comm comm_2d, comm_row, comm_col;
12
13    /* Get information about the communicator */
14    MPI_Comm_size(comm, &npes);
15    MPI_Comm_rank(comm, &myrank);
16
17    /* Compute the size of the square grid */
18    dims[ROW] = dims[COL] = sqrt(npes);
19
20    nlocal = n/dims[ROW];
21
22    /* Allocate memory for the array that will hold the partial dot-products */
23    px = malloc(nlocal*sizeof(double));
24
25    /* Set up the Cartesian topology and get the rank & coordinates of the process in this topology */
26    periods[ROW] = periods[COL] = 1;  /* Set the periods for wrap-around connections */
27
28    MPI_Cart_create(MPI_COMM_WORLD, 2, dims, periods, 1, &comm_2d);
29
30    MPI_Comm_rank(comm_2d, &my2drank);  /* Get my rank in the new topology */
31    MPI_Cart_coords(comm_2d, my2drank, 2, mycoords);   /* Get my coordinates */
32
33    /* Create the row-based sub-topology */
34    keep_dims[ROW] = 0;
35    keep_dims[COL] = 1;
36    MPI_Cart_sub(comm_2d, keep_dims, &comm_row);
37
38    /* Create the column-based sub-topology */
39    keep_dims[ROW] = 1;
40    keep_dims[COL] = 0;
41    MPI_Cart_sub(comm_2d, keep_dims, &comm_col);
42
43    /* Redistribute the b vector. */
44    /* Step 1. The processors along the 0th column send their data to the diagonal processors */
45    if (mycoords[COL] == 0 && mycoords[ROW] != 0) { /* I'm in the first column */
46      coords[ROW] = mycoords[ROW];
47      coords[COL] = mycoords[ROW];
48      MPI_Cart_rank(comm_2d, coords, &other_rank);
```

```
49        MPI_Send(b, nlocal, MPI_DOUBLE, other_rank, 1, comm_2d);
50      }
51      if (mycoords[ROW] == mycoords[COL] && mycoords[ROW] != 0) {
52        coords[ROW] = mycoords[ROW];
53        coords[COL] = 0;
54        MPI_Cart_rank(comm_2d, coords, &other_rank);
55        MPI_Recv(b, nlocal, MPI_DOUBLE, other_rank, 1, comm_2d,
56            &status);
57      }
58
59      /* Step 2. The diagonal processors perform a column-wise broadcast */
60      coords[0] = mycoords[COL];
61      MPI_Cart_rank(comm_col, coords, &other_rank);
62      MPI_Bcast(b, nlocal, MPI_DOUBLE, other_rank, comm_col);
63
64      /* Get into the main computational loop */
65      for (i=0; i<nlocal; i++) {
66        px[i] = 0.0;
67        for (j=0; j<nlocal; j++)
68          px[i] += a[i*nlocal+j]*b[j];
69      }
70
71      /* Perform the sum-reduction along the rows to add up the partial dot-products */
72      coords[0] = 0;
73      MPI_Cart_rank(comm_row, coords, &other_rank);
74      MPI_Reduce(px, x, nlocal, MPI_DOUBLE, MPI_SUM, other_rank,
75          comm_row);
76
77      MPI_Comm_free(&comm_2d);   /* Free up communicator */
78      MPI_Comm_free(&comm_row);  /* Free up communicator */
79      MPI_Comm_free(&comm_col);  /* Free up communicator */
80
81      free(px);
82    }
```

6.8   Bibliographic Remarks

The best source for information about MPI is the actual reference of the library itself [Mes94]. At the time of writing of this book, there have been two major releases of the MPI standard. The first release, version 1.0, was released in 1994 and its most recent revision, version 1.2, has been implemented by the majority of hardware vendors. The second release of the MPI standard, version 2.0 [Mes97], contains numerous significant enhancements over version 1.x, such as one-sided communication, dynamic process creation, and extended collective operations. However, despite the fact that the standard was voted in 1997, there are no widely available MPI-2 implementations that support the entire set of features specified in that standard. In addition to the above reference manuals, a number of books have been written that focus on parallel programming using MPI [Pac98, GSNL98, GLS99].

In addition to MPI implementations provided by various hardware vendors, there are a number of publicly available MPI implementations that were developed by various government research laboratories and universities. Among them, the MPICH [GLDS96, GL96b] (available at http://www-unix.mcs.anl.gov/mpi/mpich) distributed by Argonne National

Laboratories and the LAM-MPI (available at http://www.lam-mpi.org) distributed by Indiana University are widely used and are portable to a number of different architectures. In fact, these implementations of MPI have been used as the starting point for a number of specialized MPI implementations that are suitable for off-the-shelf high-speed interconnection networks such as those based on gigabit Ethernet and Myrinet networks.

Problems

6.1 Describe a message-transfer protocol for buffered sends and receives in which the buffering is performed only by the sending process. What kind of additional hardware support is needed to make these types of protocols practical?

6.2 One of the advantages of non-blocking communication operations is that they allow the transmission of the data to be done concurrently with computations. Discuss the type of restructuring that needs to be performed on a program to allow for the maximal overlap of computation with communication. Is the sending process in a better position to benefit from this overlap than the receiving process?

6.3 As discussed in Section 6.3.4 the MPI standard allows for two different implementations of the MPI_Send operation – one using buffered-sends and the other using blocked-sends. Discuss some of the potential reasons why MPI allows these two different implementations. In particular, consider the cases of different message-sizes and/or different architectural characteristics.

6.4 Consider the various mappings of 16 processors on a 4×4 two-dimensional grid shown in Figure 6.5. Show how $n = \sqrt{p} \times \sqrt{p}$ processors will be mapped using each one of these four schemes.

6.5 Consider Cannon's matrix-matrix multiplication algorithm. Our discussion of Cannon's algorithm has been limited to cases in which A and B are square matrices, mapped onto a square grid of processes. However, Cannon's algorithm can be extended for cases in which A, B, and the process grid are not square. In particular, let matrix A be of size $n \times k$ and matrix B be of size $k \times m$. The matrix C obtained by multiplying A and B is of size $n \times m$. Also, let $q \times r$ be the number of processes in the grid arranged in q rows and r columns. Develop an MPI program for multiplying two such matrices on a $q \times r$ process grid using Cannon's algorithm.

6.6 Show how the row-wise matrix-vector multiplication program (Program 6.4) needs to be changed so that it will work correctly in cases in which the dimension of the matrix does not have to be a multiple of the number of processes.

6.7 Consider the column-wise implementation of matrix-vector product (Program 6.5). An alternate implementation will be to use MPI_Allreduce to perform the required reduction operation and then have each process copy the locally stored elements of vector x from the vector fx. What will be the cost of this implementation? Another implementation can be to perform p single-node reduction operations using a different process as the root. What will be the cost of this implementation?

6.8   Consider Dijkstra's single-source shortest-path algorithm described in Section 6.6.9. Describe why a column-wise distribution is preferable to a row-wise distribution of the weighted adjacency matrix.

6.9   Show how the two-dimensional matrix-vector multiplication program (Program 6.8) needs to be changed so that it will work correctly for a matrix of size $n \times m$ on a $q \times r$ process grid.

CHAPTER 7

Programming Shared Address Space Platforms

Explicit parallel programming requires specification of parallel tasks along with their interactions. These interactions may be in the form of synchronization between concurrent tasks or communication of intermediate results. In shared address space architectures, communication is implicitly specified since some (or all) of the memory is accessible to all the processors. Consequently, programming paradigms for shared address space machines focus on constructs for expressing concurrency and synchronization along with techniques for minimizing associated overheads. In this chapter, we discuss shared-address-space programming paradigms along with their performance issues and related extensions to directive-based paradigms.

Shared address space programming paradigms can vary on mechanisms for data sharing, concurrency models, and support for synchronization. Process based models assume that all data associated with a process is private, by default, unless otherwise specified (using UNIX system calls such as shmget and shmat). While this is important for ensuring protection in multiuser systems, it is not necessary when multiple concurrent aggregates are cooperating to solve the same problem. The overheads associated with enforcing protection domains make processes less suitable for parallel programming. In contrast, lightweight processes and threads assume that all memory is global. By relaxing the protection domain, lightweight processes and threads support much faster manipulation. As a result, this is the preferred model for parallel programming and forms the focus of this chapter. Directive based programming models extend the threaded model by facilitating creation and synchronization of threads. In this chapter, we study various aspects of programming using threads and parallel directives.

7.1 Thread Basics

A *thread* is a single stream of control in the flow of a program. We initiate threads with a simple example:

Example 7.1   What are threads?
Consider the following code segment that computes the product of two dense matrices of size $n \times n$.

```
1   for (row = 0; row < n; row++)
2       for (column = 0; column < n; column++)
3           c[row][column] =
4               dot_product(get_row(a, row),
5                               get_col(b, col));
```

The for loop in this code fragment has n^2 iterations, each of which can be executed independently. Such an independent sequence of instructions is referred to as a thread. In the example presented above, there are n^2 threads, one for each iteration of the for-loop. Since each of these threads can be executed independently of the others, they can be scheduled concurrently on multiple processors. We can transform the above code segment as follows:

```
1   for (row = 0; row < n; row++)
2       for (column = 0; column < n; column++)
3           c[row][column] =
4               create_thread(dot_product(get_row(a, row),
5                                   get_col(b, col)));
```

Here, we use a function, create_thread, to provide a mechanism for specifying a C function as a thread. The underlying system can then schedule these threads on multiple processors. ∎

Logical Memory Model of a Thread   To execute the code fragment in Example 7.1 on multiple processors, each processor must have access to matrices *a*, *b*, and *c*. This is accomplished via a shared address space (described in Chapter 2). All memory in the logical machine model of a thread is globally accessible to every thread as illustrated in Figure 7.1(a). However, since threads are invoked as function calls, the stack corresponding to the function call is generally treated as being local to the thread. This is due to the liveness considerations of the stack. Since threads are scheduled at runtime (and no *a priori* schedule of their execution can be safely assumed), it is not possible to determine which stacks are live. Therefore, it is considered poor programming practice to treat stacks (thread-local variables) as global data. This implies a logical machine model illustrated in Figure 7.1(b), where memory modules *M* hold thread-local (stack allocated) data.
    While this logical machine model gives the view of an equally accessible address space,

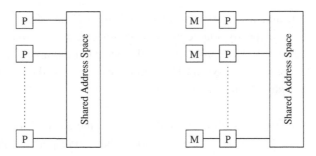

Figure 7.1   The logical machine model of a thread-based programming paradigm.

physical realizations of this model deviate from this assumption. In distributed shared address space machines such as the Origin 2000, the cost to access a physically local memory may be an order of magnitude less than that of accessing remote memory. Even in architectures where the memory is truly equally accessible to all processors (such as shared bus architectures with global shared memory), the presence of caches with processors skews memory access time. Issues of locality of memory reference become important for extracting performance from such architectures.

7.2   Why Threads?

Threaded programming models offer significant advantages over message-passing programming models along with some disadvantages as well. Before we discuss threading APIs, let us briefly look at some of these.

Software Portability   Threaded applications can be developed on serial machines and run on parallel machines without any changes. This ability to migrate programs between diverse architectural platforms is a very significant advantage of threaded APIs. It has implications not just for software utilization but also for application development since supercomputer time is often scarce and expensive.

Latency Hiding   One of the major overheads in programs (both serial and parallel) is the access latency for memory access, I/O, and communication. By allowing multiple threads to execute on the same processor, threaded APIs enable this latency to be hidden (as seen in Chapter 2). In effect, while one thread is waiting for a communication operation, other threads can utilize the CPU, thus masking associated overhead.

Scheduling and Load Balancing   While writing shared address space parallel programs, a programmer must express concurrency in a way that minimizes overheads of remote interaction and idling. While in many structured applications the task of allocating equal work to processors is easily accomplished, in unstructured and dynamic applications (such as game playing and discrete optimization) this task is more difficult. Threaded APIs allow the programmer to specify a large number of concurrent tasks and support system-level dynamic mapping of tasks to processors with a view to minimizing idling overheads. By providing this support at the system level, threaded APIs rid the programmer of the burden of explicit scheduling and load balancing.

Ease of Programming, Widespread Use   Due to the aforementioned advantages, threaded programs are significantly easier to write than corresponding programs using message passing APIs. Achieving identical levels of performance for the two programs may require additional effort, however. With widespread acceptance of the POSIX thread API, development tools for POSIX threads are more widely available and stable. These issues are important from the program development and software engineering aspects.

7.3   The POSIX Thread API

A number of vendors provide vendor-specific thread APIs. The IEEE specifies a standard 1003.1c-1995, POSIX API. Also referred to as Pthreads, POSIX has emerged as the standard threads API, supported by most vendors. We will use the Pthreads API for introducing multithreading concepts. The concepts themselves are largely independent of the API and can be used for programming with other thread APIs (NT threads, Solaris threads, Java threads, etc.) as well. All the illustrative programs presented in this chapter can be executed on workstations as well as parallel computers that support Pthreads.

7.4   Thread Basics: Creation and Termination

Let us start our discussion with a simple threaded program for computing the value of π.

Example 7.2   Threaded program for computing π
The method we use here is based on generating random numbers in a unit length square and counting the number of points that fall within the largest circle inscribed in the square. Since the area of the circle (πr^2) is equal to $\pi/4$, and the area of the square is 1×1, the fraction of random points that fall in the circle should approach $\pi/4$.

A simple threaded strategy for generating the value of π assigns a fixed number of points to each thread. Each thread generates these random points and keeps track of the number of points that land in the circle locally. After all threads finish execution, their counts are combined to compute the value of π (by calculating the fraction over all threads and multiplying by 4).

To implement this threaded program, we need a function for creating threads and waiting for all threads to finish execution (so we can accrue count). Threads can be created in the Pthreads API using the function `pthread_create`. The prototype of this function is:

```
1   #include <pthread.h>
2   int
3   pthread_create (
4       pthread_t   *thread_handle,
5       const pthread_attr_t   *attribute,
6       void *   (*thread_function)(void *),
7       void   *arg);
```

The `pthread_create` function creates a single thread that corresponds to the invocation of the function `thread_function` (and any other functions called by `thread_function`). On successful creation of a thread, a unique identifier is associated with the thread and assigned to the location pointed to by `thread_handle`. The thread has the attributes described by the `attribute` argument. When this argument is NULL, a thread with default attributes is created. We will discuss the `attribute` parameter in detail in Section 7.6. The `arg` field specifies a pointer to the argument to function `thread_function`. This argument is typically used to pass the workspace and other thread-specific data to a thread. In the `compute_pi` example, it is used to pass an integer id that is used as a seed for randomization. The `thread_handle` variable is written before the the function `pthread_create` returns; and the new thread is ready for execution as soon as it is created. If the thread is scheduled on the same processor, the new thread may, in fact, preempt its creator. This is important to note because all thread initialization procedures must be completed before creating the thread. Otherwise, errors may result based on thread scheduling. This is a very common class of errors caused by race conditions for data access that shows itself in some execution instances, but not in others. On successful creation of a thread, `pthread_create` returns 0; else it returns an error code. The reader is referred to the Pthreads specification for a detailed description of the error-codes.

In our program for computing the value of π, we first read in the desired number of threads, `num_threads`, and the desired number of sample points, `sample_points`. These points are divided equally among the threads. The program uses an array, `hits`, for assigning an integer id to each thread (this id is used as a seed for randomizing the random number generator). The same array is used to keep track of the number of hits (points inside the circle) encountered by each thread upon return. The program creates `num_threads` threads, each invoking the function `compute_pi`, using the `pthread_create` function.

Once the respective `compute_pi` threads have generated assigned number of random points and computed their hit ratios, the results must be combined to determine π. The main program must wait for the threads to run to completion. This is done using the function `pthread_join` which suspends execution of the calling thread until the specified thread terminates. The prototype of the `pthread_join` function is as follows:

```
1   int
2   pthread_join (
3       pthread_t    thread,
4       void    **ptr);
```

A call to this function waits for the termination of the thread whose id is given by `thread`. On a successful call to `pthread_join`, the value passed to `pthread_exit` is returned in the location pointed to by `ptr`. On successful completion, `pthread_join` returns 0, else it returns an error-code.

Once all threads have joined, the value of π is computed by multiplying the combined hit ratio by 4.0. The complete program is as follows:

```
1   #include <pthread.h>
2   #include <stdlib.h>
3
4   #define MAX_THREADS    512
5   void *compute_pi (void *);
6
7   int total_hits, total_misses, hits[MAX_THREADS],
8       sample_points, sample_points_per_thread, num_threads;
9
10  main() {
11      int i;
12      pthread_t p_threads[MAX_THREADS];
13      pthread_attr_t   attr;
14      double computed_pi;
15      double time_start, time_end;
16      struct timeval tv;
17      struct timezone tz;
18
19      pthread_attr_init (&attr);
20      pthread_attr_setscope (&attr,PTHREAD_SCOPE_SYSTEM);
21      printf("Enter number of sample points: ");
22      scanf("%d", &sample_points);
23      printf("Enter number of threads: ");
24      scanf("%d", &num_threads);
25
26      gettimeofday(&tv, &tz);
27      time_start = (double)tv.tv_sec +
28                  (double)tv.tv_usec / 1000000.0;
29
30      total_hits = 0;
31      sample_points_per_thread = sample_points / num_threads;
32      for (i=0; i< num_threads; i++) {
33          hits[i] = i;
34          pthread_create(&p_threads[i], &attr, compute_pi,
35              (void *) &hits[i]);
36      }
37      for (i=0; i< num_threads; i++) {
38          pthread_join(p_threads[i], NULL);
```

```
39              total_hits += hits[i];
40          }
41      computed_pi = 4.0*(double) total_hits /
42          ((double)(sample_points));
43      gettimeofday(&tv, &tz);
44      time_end = (double)tv.tv_sec +
45                 (double)tv.tv_usec / 1000000.0;
46
47      printf("Computed PI = %lf\n", computed_pi);
48      printf(" %lf\n", time_end - time_start);
49  }
50
51  void *compute_pi (void *s) {
52      int seed, i, *hit_pointer;
53      double rand_no_x, rand_no_y;
54      int local_hits;
55
56      hit_pointer = (int *) s;
57      seed = *hit_pointer;
58      local_hits = 0;
59      for (i = 0; i < sample_points_per_thread; i++) {
60          rand_no_x =(double)(rand_r(&seed))/(double)((2<<14)-1);
61          rand_no_y =(double)(rand_r(&seed))/(double)((2<<14)-1);
62          if (((rand_no_x - 0.5) * (rand_no_x - 0.5) +
63              (rand_no_y - 0.5) * (rand_no_y - 0.5)) < 0.25)
64              local_hits ++;
65          seed *= i;
66      }
67      *hit_pointer = local_hits;
68      pthread_exit(0);
69  }
```

Programming Notes   The reader must note, in the above example, the use of the function `rand_r` (instead of superior random number generators such as `drand48`). The reason for this is that many functions (including `rand` and `drand48`) are not *reentrant*.   Reentrant functions are those that can be safely called when another instance has been suspended in the middle of its invocation. It is easy to see why all thread functions must be reentrant because a thread can be preempted in the middle of its execution. If another thread starts executing the same function at this point, a non-reentrant function might not work as desired.

Performance Notes   We execute this program on a four-processor SGI Origin 2000. The logarithm of the number of threads and execution time are illustrated in Figure 7.2 (the curve labeled "local"). We can see that at 32 threads, the runtime of the program is roughly 3.91 times less than the corresponding time for one thread. On a four-processor machine, this corresponds to a parallel efficiency of 0.98.

The other curves in Figure 7.2 illustrate an important performance overhead called *false sharing*. Consider the following change to the program: instead of incrementing a local variable, `local_hits`, and assigning it to the array entry outside the loop, we now directly increment the corresponding entry in the `hits` array. This

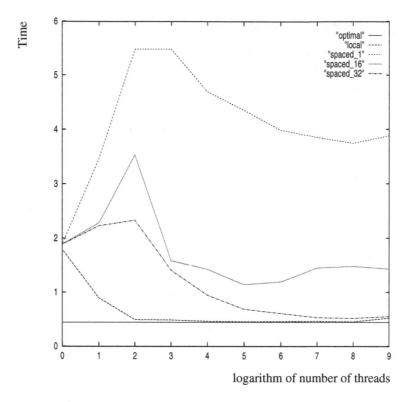

Figure 7.2   Execution time of the `compute_pi` program as a function of number of threads.

can be done by changing line 64 to `* (hit_pointer) ++;`, and deleting line 67. It is easy to verify that the program is semantically identical to the one before. However, on executing this modified program the observed performance is illustrated in the curve labeled "spaced_1" in Figure 7.2. This represents a significant slowdown instead of a speedup!

The drastic impact of this seemingly innocuous change is explained by a phenomenon called **false sharing**. In this example, two adjoining data items (which likely reside on the same cache line) are being continually written to by threads that might be scheduled on different processors. From our discussion in Chapter 2, we know that a write to a shared cache line results in an invalidate and a subsequent read must fetch the cache line from the most recent write location. With this in mind, we can see that the cache lines corresponding to the `hits` array generate a large number of invalidates and reads because of repeated increment operations. This situation, in which two threads 'falsely' share data because it happens to be on the same cache line, is called false sharing.

It is in fact possible to use this simple example to estimate the cache line size of the system. We change `hits` to a two-dimensional array and use only the first column of the array to store counts. By changing the size of the second dimension, we can force entries in the first column of the `hits` array to lie on different cache lines (since arrays in C are stored row-major). The results of this experiment are illustrated in Figure 7.2 by curves labeled "spaced_16" and "spaced_32", in which the second dimension of the `hits` array is 16 and 32 integers, respectively. It is evident from the figure that as the entries are spaced apart, the performance improves. This is consistent with our understanding that spacing the entries out pushes them into different cache lines, thereby reducing the false sharing overhead.   ■

Having understood how to create and join threads, let us now explore mechanisms in Pthreads for synchronizing threads.

7.5   Synchronization Primitives in Pthreads

While communication is implicit in shared-address-space programming, much of the effort associated with writing correct threaded programs is spent on synchronizing concurrent threads with respect to their data accesses or scheduling.

7.5.1   Mutual Exclusion for Shared Variables

Using `pthread_create` and `pthread_join` calls, we can create concurrent tasks. These tasks work together to manipulate data and accomplish a given task. When multiple threads attempt to manipulate the same data item, the results can often be incoherent if proper care is not taken to synchronize them. Consider the following code fragment being executed by multiple threads. The variable `my_cost` is thread-local and `best_cost` is a global variable shared by all threads.

```
1   /* each thread tries to update variable best_cost as follows */
2   if (my_cost < best_cost)
3       best_cost = my_cost;
```

To understand the problem with shared data access, let us examine one execution instance of the above code fragment. Assume that there are two threads, the initial value of `best_cost` is 100, and the values of `my_cost` are 50 and 75 at threads t1 and t2, respectively. If both threads execute the condition inside the `if` statement concurrently, then both threads enter the `then` part of the statement. Depending on which thread executes first, the value of `best_cost` at the end could be either 50 or 75. There are two problems here: the first is the non-deterministic nature of the result; second, and more importantly, the value 75 of `best_cost` is inconsistent in the sense that no serialization of the two threads can possibly yield this result. This is an undesirable situation, sometimes also referred to as a race condition (so called because the result of the computation depends on the race between competing threads).

The aforementioned situation occurred because the test-and-update operation illustrated above is an atomic operation; i.e., the operation should not be broken into sub-operations. Furthermore, the code corresponds to a critical segment; i.e., a segment that must be executed by only one thread at any time. Many statements that seem atomic in higher level languages such as C may in fact be non-atomic; for example, a statement of the form global_count += 5 may comprise several assembler instructions and therefore must be handled carefully.

Threaded APIs provide support for implementing critical sections and atomic operations using **mutex-locks** (mutual exclusion locks). Mutex-locks have two states: locked and unlocked. At any point of time, only one thread can lock a mutex lock. A lock is an atomic operation generally associated with a piece of code that manipulates shared data. To access the shared data, a thread must first try to acquire a mutex-lock. If the mutex-lock is already locked, the process trying to acquire the lock is blocked. This is because a locked mutex-lock implies that there is another thread currently in the critical section and that no other thread must be allowed in. When a thread leaves a critical section, it must unlock the mutex-lock so that other threads can enter the critical section. All mutex-locks must be initialized to the unlocked state at the beginning of the program.

The Pthreads API provides a number of functions for handling mutex-locks. The function pthread_mutex_lock can be used to attempt a lock on a mutex-lock. The prototype of the function is:

```
1   int
2   pthread_mutex_lock (
3        pthread_mutex_t    *mutex_lock);
```

A call to this function attempts a lock on the mutex-lock mutex_lock. (The data type of a mutex_lock is predefined to be pthread_mutex_t.) If the mutex-lock is already locked, the calling thread blocks; otherwise the mutex-lock is locked and the calling thread returns. A successful return from the function returns a value 0. Other values indicate error conditions such as deadlocks.

On leaving a critical section, a thread must unlock the mutex-lock associated with the section. If it does not do so, no other thread will be able to enter this section, typically resulting in a deadlock. The Pthreads function pthread_mutex_unlock is used to unlock a mutex-lock. The prototype of this function is:

```
1   int
2   pthread_mutex_unlock (
3        pthread_mutex_t *mutex_lock);
```

On calling this function, in the case of a normal mutex-lock, the lock is relinquished and one of the blocked threads is scheduled to enter the critical section. The specific thread is determined by the scheduling policy. There are other types of locks (other than normal locks), which are discussed in Section 7.6 along with the associated semantics of the function pthread_mutex_unlock. If a programmer attempts a pthread_mutex_unlock on a previously unlocked mutex or one that is locked by another thread, the effect is undefined.

We need one more function before we can start using mutex-locks, namely, a function to initialize a mutex-lock to its unlocked state. The Pthreads function for this is pthread_mutex_init. The prototype of this function is as follows:

```
1   int
2   pthread_mutex_init (
3       pthread_mutex_t    *mutex_lock,
4       const pthread_mutexattr_t   *lock_attr);
```

This function initializes the mutex-lock mutex_lock to an unlocked state. The attributes of the mutex-lock are specified by lock_attr. If this argument is set to NULL, the default mutex-lock attributes are used (normal mutex-lock). Attributes objects for threads are discussed in greater detail in Section 7.6.

Example 7.3   Computing the minimum entry in a list of integers
Armed with basic mutex-lock functions, let us write a simple threaded program to compute the minimum of a list of integers. The list is partitioned equally among the threads. The size of each thread's partition is stored in the variable partial_list_size and the pointer to the start of each thread's partial list is passed to it as the pointer list_ptr. The threaded program for accomplishing this is as follows:

```
1   #include <pthread.h>
2   void *find_min(void *list_ptr);
3   pthread_mutex_t minimum_value_lock;
4   int minimum_value, partial_list_size;
5
6   main() {
7       /* declare and initialize data structures and list */
8       minimum_value = MIN_INT;
9       pthread_init();
10      pthread_mutex_init(&minimum_value_lock, NULL);
11
12      /* initialize lists, list_ptr, and partial_list_size */
13      /* create and join threads here */
14  }
15
16  void *find_min(void *list_ptr) {
17      int *partial_list_pointer, my_min, i;
18      my_min = MIN_INT;
19      partial_list_pointer = (int *) list_ptr;
20      for (i = 0; i < partial_list_size; i++)
21          if (partial_list_pointer[i] < my_min)
22              my_min = partial_list_pointer[i];
23      /* lock the mutex associated with minimum_value and
24      update the variable as required */
25      pthread_mutex_lock(&minimum_value_lock);
26      if (my_min < minimum_value)
27          minimum_value = my_min;
```

```
28      /* and unlock the mutex */
29      pthread_mutex_unlock(&minimum_value_lock);
30      pthread_exit(0);
31  }
```

Programming Notes In this example, the test-update operation for minimum_value is protected by the mutex-lock minimum_value_lock. Threads execute pthread_mutex_lock to gain exclusive access to the variable minimum_value. Once this access is gained, the value is updated as required, and the lock subsequently released. Since at any point of time, only one thread can hold a lock, only one thread can test-update the variable. ∎

Example 7.4   Producer-consumer work queues

A common use of mutex-locks is in establishing a producer-consumer relationship between threads. The producer creates tasks and inserts them into a work-queue. The consumer threads pick up tasks from the task queue and execute them. Let us consider a simple instance of this paradigm in which the task queue can hold only one task (in a general case, the task queue may be longer but is typically of bounded size). Producer-consumer relations are ubiquitous. See Exercise 7.4 for an example application in multimedia processing. A simple (and incorrect) threaded program would associate a producer thread with creating a task and placing it in a shared data structure and the consumer threads with picking up tasks from this shared data structure and executing them. However, this simple version does not account for the following possibilities:

- The producer thread must not overwrite the shared buffer when the previous task has not been picked up by a consumer thread.

- The consumer threads must not pick up tasks until there is something present in the shared data structure.

- Individual consumer threads should pick up tasks one at a time.

To implement this, we can use a variable called task_available. If this variable is 0, consumer threads must wait, but the producer thread can insert tasks into the shared data structure task_queue. If task_available is equal to 1, the producer thread must wait to insert the task into the shared data structure but one of the consumer threads can pick up the task available. All of these operations on the variable task_available should be protected by mutex-locks to ensure that only one thread is executing test-update on it. The threaded version of this program is as follows:

```
1   pthread_mutex_t task_queue_lock;
2   int task_available;
3
4   /* other shared data structures here */
```

```
5
6   main() {
7       /* declarations and initializations */
8       task_available = 0;
9       pthread_init();
10      pthread_mutex_init(&task_queue_lock, NULL);
11      /* create and join producer and consumer threads */
12  }
13
14  void *producer(void *producer_thread_data) {
15      int inserted;
16      struct task my_task;
17      while (!done()) {
18          inserted = 0;
19          create_task(&my_task);
20          while (inserted == 0) {
21              pthread_mutex_lock(&task_queue_lock);
22              if (task_available == 0) {
23                  insert_into_queue(my_task);
24                  task_available = 1;
25                  inserted = 1;
26              }
27              pthread_mutex_unlock(&task_queue_lock);
28          }
29      }
30  }
31
32  void *consumer(void *consumer_thread_data) {
33      int extracted;
34      struct task my_task;
35      /* local data structure declarations */
36      while (!done()) {
37          extracted = 0;
38          while (extracted == 0) {
39              pthread_mutex_lock(&task_queue_lock);
40              if (task_available == 1) {
41                  extract_from_queue(&my_task);
42                  task_available = 0;
43                  extracted = 1;
44              }
45              pthread_mutex_unlock(&task_queue_lock);
46          }
47          process_task(my_task);
48      }
49  }
```

Programming Notes   In this example, the producer thread creates a task and waits for space on the queue. This is indicated by the variable task_available being 0. The test and update of this variable as well as insertion and extraction from the shared queue are protected by a mutex called task_queue_lock. Once space is available on the task queue, the recently created task is inserted into the task queue and the availability of the task is signaled by setting task_available to 1. Within the producer thread, the fact that the recently created task has been inserted into the queue is signaled by the variable inserted being set to 1, which allows the producer to produce the next task. Irrespective of whether a recently created task is successfully inserted into the queue or not, the lock is relinquished. This allows consumer threads to pick up work from the queue in case there is work on the queue to begin with. If the lock is not relinquished, threads would deadlock since a consumer would not be able to get the lock to pick up the task and the producer would not be able to insert its task into the task queue. The consumer thread waits for a task to become available and executes it when available. As was the case with the producer thread, the consumer relinquishes the lock in each iteration of the `while` loop to allow the producer to insert work into the queue if there was none.   ■

Overheads of Locking

Locks represent serialization points since critical sections must be executed by threads one after the other. Encapsulating large segments of the program within locks can, therefore, lead to significant performance degradation. It is important to minimize the size of critical sections. For instance, in the above example, the `create_task` and `process_task` functions are left outside the critical region, but `insert_into_queue` and `extract_from_queue` functions are left inside the critical region. The former is left out in the interest of making the critical section as small as possible. The `insert_into_queue` and `extract_from_queue` functions are left inside because if the lock is relinquished after updating `task_available` but not inserting or extracting the task, other threads may gain access to the shared data structure while the insertion or extraction is in progress, resulting in errors. It is therefore important to handle critical sections and shared data structures with extreme care.

Alleviating Locking Overheads

It is often possible to reduce the idling overhead associated with locks using an alternate function, `pthread_mutex_trylock`. This function attempts a lock on `mutex_lock`. If the lock is successful, the function returns a zero. If it is already locked by another thread, instead of blocking the thread execution, it returns a value `EBUSY`. This allows the thread to do other work and to poll the mutex for a lock. Furthermore, `pthread_mutex_trylock` is typically much faster than `pthread_mutex_lock` on typical systems since it does not have to deal with queues associated with locks for multiple threads waiting on the lock. The prototype of `pthread_mutex_trylock` is:

```
1   int
2   pthread_mutex_trylock (
3       pthread_mutex_t *mutex_lock);
```

We illustrate the use of this function using the following example:

Example 7.5   Finding k matches in a list
We consider the example of finding k matches to a query item in a given list. The

list is partitioned equally among the threads. Assuming that the list has n entries, each of the p threads is responsible for searching n/p entries of the list. The program segment for computing this using the `pthread_mutex_lock` function is as follows:

```
1  void *find_entries(void *start_pointer) {
2
3      /* This is the thread function */
4
5      struct database_record *next_record;
6      int count;
7      current_pointer = start_pointer;
8      do {
9          next_record = find_next_entry(current_pointer);
10         count = output_record(next_record);
11     } while (count < requested_number_of_records);
12  }
13
14  int output_record(struct database_record *record_ptr) {
15      int count;
16      pthread_mutex_lock(&output_count_lock);
17      output_count ++;
18      count = output_count;
19      pthread_mutex_unlock(&output_count_lock);
20
21      if (count <= requested_number_of_records)
22          print_record(record_ptr);
23      return (count);
24  }
```

This program segment finds an entry in its part of the database, updates the global count and then finds the next entry. If the time for a lock-update count-unlock cycle is t_1 and the time to find an entry is t_2, then the total time for satisfying the query is $(t_1 + t_2) \times n_{max}$, where n_{max} is the maximum number of entries found by any thread. If t_1 and t_2 are comparable, then locking leads to considerable overhead.

This locking overhead can be alleviated by using the function `pthread_mutex_trylock`. Each thread now finds the next entry and tries to acquire the lock and update count. If another thread already has the lock, the record is inserted into a local list and the thread proceeds to find other matches. When it finally gets the lock, it inserts all entries found locally thus far into the list (provided the number does not exceed the desired number of entries). The corresponding `output_record` function is as follows:

```
1  int output_record(struct database_record *record_ptr) {
2      int count;
3      int lock_status;
4      lock_status = pthread_mutex_trylock(&output_count_lock);
5      if (lock_status == EBUSY) {
6          insert_into_local_list(record_ptr);
7          return(0);
```

```
8       }
9       else {
10          count = output_count;
11          output_count += number_on_local_list + 1;
12          pthread_mutex_unlock(&output_count_lock);
13          print_records(record_ptr, local_list,
14              requested_number_of_records - count);
15          return(count + number_on_local_list + 1);
16      }
17  }
```

Programming Notes   Examining this function closely, we notice that if the lock for updating the global count is not available, the function inserts the current record into a local list and returns. If the lock is available, it increments the global count by the number of records on the local list, and then by one (for the current record). It then unlocks the associated lock and proceeds to print as many records as are required using the function print_records.

Performance Notes   The time for execution of this version is less than the time for the first one on two counts: first, as mentioned, the time for executing a pthread_mutex_trylock is typically much smaller than that for a pthread_mutex_lock. Second, since multiple records may be inserted on each lock, the number of locking operations is also reduced. The number of records actually searched (across all threads) may be slightly larger than the number of records actually desired (since there may be entries in the local lists that may never be printed). However, since this time would otherwise have been spent idling for the lock anyway, this overhead does not cause a slowdown.

■

The above example illustrates the use of the function pthread_mutex_trylock instead of pthread_mutex_lock. The general use of the function is in reducing idling overheads associated with mutex-locks. If the computation is such that the critical section can be delayed and other computations can be performed in the interim, pthread_mutex_trylock is the function of choice. Another determining factor, as has been mentioned, is the fact that for most implementations pthread_mutex_trylock is a much cheaper function than pthread_mutex_lock. In fact, for highly optimized codes, even when a pthread_mutex_lock is required, a pthread_mutex_trylock inside a loop may often be desirable, since if the lock is acquired within the first few calls, it would be cheaper than a pthread_mutex_lock.

7.5.2   Condition Variables for Synchronization

As we noted in the previous section, indiscriminate use of locks can result in idling overhead from blocked threads. While the function pthread_mutex_trylock alleviates this overhead, it introduces the overhead of polling for availability of locks. For example, if the producer-consumer example is rewritten using `pthread_mutex_trylock` instead of `pthread_mutex_lock`, the producer and consumer threads would have to periodically poll for availability of lock (and subsequently availability of buffer space or tasks on queue). A natural solution to this problem is to suspend the execution of the producer until space becomes available (an interrupt driven mechanism as opposed to a polled mechanism). The availability of space is signaled by the consumer thread that consumes the task. The functionality to accomplish this is provided by a *condition variable*.

A condition variable is a data object used for synchronizing threads. This variable allows a thread to block itself until specified data reaches a predefined state. In the producer-consumer case, the shared variable `task_available` must become 1 before the consumer threads can be signaled. The boolean condition `task_available == 1` is referred to as a predicate. A condition variable is associated with this predicate. When the predicate becomes true, the condition variable is used to signal one or more threads waiting on the condition. A single condition variable may be associated with more than one predicate. However, this is strongly discouraged since it makes the program difficult to debug.

A condition variable always has a mutex associated with it. A thread locks this mutex and tests the predicate defined on the shared variable (in this case `task_available`); if the predicate is not true, the thread waits on the condition variable associated with the predicate using the function `pthread_cond_wait`. The prototype of this function is:

```
1    int pthread_cond_wait(pthread_cond_t *cond,
2          pthread_mutex_t *mutex);
```

A call to this function blocks the execution of the thread until it receives a signal from another thread or is interrupted by an OS signal. In addition to blocking the thread, the `pthread_cond_wait` function releases the lock on `mutex`. This is important because otherwise no other thread will be able to work on the shared variable `task_available` and the predicate would never be satisfied. When the thread is released on a signal, it waits to reacquire the lock on `mutex` before resuming execution. It is convenient to think of each condition variable as being associated with a queue. Threads performing a condition wait on the variable relinquish their lock and enter the queue. When the condition is signaled (using `pthread_cond_signal`), one of these threads in the queue is unblocked, and when the mutex becomes available, it is handed to this thread (and the thread becomes runnable).

In the context of our producer-consumer example, the producer thread produces the task and, since the lock on `mutex` has been relinquished (by waiting consumers), it can insert its task on the queue and set `task_available` to 1 after locking `mutex`. Since the predicate has now been satisfied, the producer must wake up one of the consumer threads by signaling it. This is done using the function `pthread_cond_signal`, whose prototype is as follows:

```
1       int pthread_cond_signal(pthread_cond_t *cond);
```

The function unblocks at least one thread that is currently waiting on the condition variable cond. The producer then relinquishes its lock on mutex by explicitly calling pthread_mutex_unlock, allowing one of the blocked consumer threads to consume the task.

Before we rewrite our producer-consumer example using condition variables, we need to introduce two more function calls for initializing and destroying condition variables, pthread_cond_init and pthread_cond_destroy respectively. The prototypes of these calls are as follows:

```
1   int pthread_cond_init(pthread_cond_t *cond,
2       const pthread_condattr_t *attr);
3   int pthread_cond_destroy(pthread_cond_t *cond);
```

The function pthread_cond_init initializes a condition variable (pointed to by cond) whose attributes are defined in the attribute object attr. Setting this pointer to NULL assigns default attributes for condition variables. If at some point in a program a condition variable is no longer required, it can be discarded using the function pthread_cond_destroy. These functions for manipulating condition variables enable us to rewrite our producer-consumer segment as follows:

Example 7.6   Producer-consumer using condition variables

Condition variables can be used to block execution of the producer thread when the work queue is full and the consumer thread when the work queue is empty. We use two condition variables cond_queue_empty and cond_queue_full for specifying empty and full queues respectively. The predicate associated with cond_queue_empty is task_available == 0, and cond_queue_full is asserted when task_available == 1.

The producer queue locks the mutex task_queue_cond_lock associated with the shared variable task_available. It checks to see if task_available is 0 (i.e., queue is empty). If this is the case, the producer inserts the task into the work queue and signals any waiting consumer threads to wake up by signaling the condition variable cond_queue_full. It subsequently proceeds to create additional tasks. If task_available is 1 (i.e., queue is full), the producer performs a condition wait on the condition variable cond_queue_empty (i.e., it waits for the queue to become empty). The reason for implicitly releasing the lock on task_queue_cond_lock becomes clear at this point. If the lock is not released, no consumer will be able to consume the task and the queue would never be empty. At this point, the producer thread is blocked. Since the lock is available to the consumer, the thread can consume the task and signal the condition variable cond_queue_empty when the task has been taken off the work queue.

The consumer thread locks the mutex task_queue_cond_lock to check if the shared variable task_available is 1. If not, it performs a condition wait on cond_queue_full. (Note that this signal is generated from the producer when a task is inserted into the work queue.) If there is a task available, the consumer takes it off the work queue and signals the producer. In this way, the producer and consumer threads operate by signaling each other. It is easy to see that this mode of operation is similar to an interrupt-based operation as opposed to a polling-based operation of `pthread_mutex_trylock`. The program segment for accomplishing this producer-consumer behavior is as follows:

```
1   pthread_cond_t cond_queue_empty, cond_queue_full;
2   pthread_mutex_t task_queue_cond_lock;
3   int task_available;
4
5   /* other data structures here */
6
7   main() {
8       /* declarations and initializations */
9       task_available = 0;
10      pthread_init();
11      pthread_cond_init(&cond_queue_empty, NULL);
12      pthread_cond_init(&cond_queue_full, NULL);
13      pthread_mutex_init(&task_queue_cond_lock, NULL);
14      /* create and join producer and consumer threads */
15  }
16
17  void *producer(void *producer_thread_data) {
18      int inserted;
19      while (!done()) {
20          create_task();
21          pthread_mutex_lock(&task_queue_cond_lock);
22          while (task_available == 1)
23              pthread_cond_wait(&cond_queue_empty,
24                  &task_queue_cond_lock);
25          insert_into_queue();
26          task_available = 1;
27          pthread_cond_signal(&cond_queue_full);
28          pthread_mutex_unlock(&task_queue_cond_lock);
29      }
30  }
31
32  void *consumer(void *consumer_thread_data) {
33      while (!done()) {
34          pthread_mutex_lock(&task_queue_cond_lock);
35          while (task_available == 0)
36              pthread_cond_wait(&cond_queue_full,
37                  &task_queue_cond_lock);
38          my_task = extract_from_queue();
39          task_available = 0;
40          pthread_cond_signal(&cond_queue_empty);
41          pthread_mutex_unlock(&task_queue_cond_lock);
42          process_task(my_task);
43      }
44  }
```

Programming Notes An important point to note about this program segment is that the predicate associated with a condition variable is checked in a loop. One might expect that when `cond_queue_full` is asserted, the value of `task_available` must be 1. However, it is a good practice to check for the condition in a loop because the thread might be woken up due to other reasons (such as an OS signal). In other cases, when the condition variable is signaled using a condition broadcast (signaling all waiting threads instead of just one), one of the threads that got the lock earlier might invalidate the condition. In the example of multiple producers and multiple consumers, a task available on the work queue might be consumed by one of the other consumers.

Performance Notes   When a thread performs a condition wait, it takes itself off the runnable list – consequently, it does not use any CPU cycles until it is woken up. This is in contrast to a mutex lock which consumes CPU cycles as it polls for the lock.

∎

In the above example, each task could be consumed by only one consumer thread. Therefore, we choose to signal one blocked thread at a time. In some other computations, it may be beneficial to wake all threads that are waiting on the condition variable as opposed to a single thread. This can be done using the function `pthread_cond_broadcast`.

```
1   int pthread_cond_broadcast(pthread_cond_t *cond);
```

An example of this is in the producer-consumer scenario with large work queues and multiple tasks being inserted into the work queue on each insertion cycle. This is left as an exercise for the reader (Exercise 7.2). Another example of the use of `pthread_cond_broadcast` is in the implementation of barriers illustrated in Section 7.8.2.

It is often useful to build time-outs into condition waits. Using the function `pthread_cond_timedwait`, a thread can perform a wait on a condition variable until a specified time expires. At this point, the thread wakes up by itself if it does not receive a signal or a broadcast. The prototype for this function is:

```
1   int pthread_cond_timedwait(pthread_cond_t *cond,
2       pthread_mutex_t *mutex,
3       const struct timespec *abstime);
```

If the absolute time `abstime` specified expires before a signal or broadcast is received, the function returns an error message. It also reacquires the lock on `mutex` when it becomes available.

7.6   Controlling Thread and Synchronization Attributes

In our discussion thus far, we have noted that entities such as threads and synchronization variables can have several attributes associated with them. For example, different threads may be scheduled differently (round-robin, prioritized, etc.), they may have different stack sizes, and so on. Similarly, a synchronization variable such as a mutex-lock may be of different types. The Pthreads API allows a programmer to change the default attributes of entities using *attributes objects*.

An attributes object is a data-structure that describes entity (thread, mutex, condition variable) properties. When creating a thread or a synchronization variable, we can specify the attributes object that determines the properties of the entity. Once created, the thread or synchronization variable's properties are largely fixed (Pthreads allows the user to change the priority of the thread). Subsequent changes to attributes objects do not change the properties of entities created using the attributes object prior to the change. There are several advantages of using attributes objects. First, it separates the issues of program semantics and implementation. Thread properties are specified by the user. How these are implemented at the system level is transparent to the user. This allows for greater portability across operating systems. Second, using attributes objects improves modularity and readability of the programs. Third, it allows the user to modify the program easily. For instance, if the user wanted to change the scheduling from round robin to time-sliced for all threads, they would only need to change the specific attribute in the attributes object.

To create an attributes object with the desired properties, we must first create an object with default properties and then modify the object as required. We look at Pthreads functions for accomplishing this for threads and synchronization variables.

7.6.1 Attributes Objects for Threads

The function `pthread_attr_init` lets us create an attributes object for threads. The prototype of this function is

```
1   int
2   pthread_attr_init (
3       pthread_attr_t    *attr);
```

This function initializes the attributes object `attr` to the default values. Upon successful completion, the function returns a 0, otherwise it returns an error code. The attributes object may be destroyed using the function `pthread_attr_destroy`. The prototype of this function is:

```
1   int
2   pthread_attr_destroy (
3       pthread_attr_t    *attr);
```

The call returns a 0 on successful removal of the attributes object `attr`. Individual properties associated with the attributes object can be changed using the following functions: `pthread_attr_setdetachstate`, `pthread_attr_setguardsize_np`, `pthread_attr_setstacksize`, `pthread_attr_setinheritsched`, `pthread_attr_setschedpolicy`, and `pthread_attr_setschedparam`. These functions can be used to set the detach state in a thread attributes object, the stack guard size, the stack size, whether scheduling policy is inherited from the creating thread, the scheduling policy (in case it is not inherited), and scheduling parameters, respectively. We refer the reader to the Pthreads manuals for a detailed description of these functions. For most parallel programs, default thread properties are generally adequate.

7.6.2   Attributes Objects for Mutexes

The Pthreads API supports three different kinds of locks. All of these locks use the same functions for locking and unlocking; however, the type of lock is determined by the lock attribute. The mutex lock used in examples thus far is called a ***normal mutex***. This is the default type of lock. Only a single thread is allowed to lock a normal mutex once at any point in time. If a thread with a lock attempts to lock it again, the second locking call results in a deadlock.

Consider the following example of a thread searching for an element in a binary tree. To ensure that other threads are not changing the tree during the search process, the thread locks the tree with a single mutex `tree_lock`. The search function is as follows:

```
1   search_tree(void *tree_ptr)
2   {
3       struct node *node_pointer;
4       node_pointer = (struct node *) tree_ptr;
5       pthread_mutex_lock(&tree_lock);
6       if (is_search_node(node_pointer) == 1) {
7           /* solution is found here */
8           print_node(node_pointer);
9           pthread_mutex_unlock(&tree_lock);
10          return(1);
11      }
12      else {
13          if (tree_ptr -> left != NULL)
14              search_tree((void *) tree_ptr -> left);
15          if (tree_ptr -> right != NULL)
16              search_tree((void *) tree_ptr -> right);
17      }
18      printf("Search unsuccessful\n");
19      pthread_mutex_unlock(&tree_lock);
20  }
```

If `tree_lock` is a normal mutex, the first recursive call to the function `search_tree` ends in a deadlock since a thread attempts to lock a mutex that it holds a lock on. For addressing such situations, the Pthreads API supports a ***recursive mutex***. A recursive mutex allows a single thread to lock a mutex multiple times. Each time a thread locks the mutex, a lock counter is incremented. Each unlock decrements the counter. For any other thread to be able to successfully lock a recursive mutex, the lock counter must be zero (i.e., each lock by another thread must have a corresponding unlock). A recursive mutex is useful when a thread function needs to call itself recursively.

In addition to normal and recursive mutexes, a third kind of mutex called an ***errorcheck mutex*** is also supported. The operation of an errorcheck mutex is similar to a normal mutex in that a thread can lock a mutex only once. However, unlike a normal mutex, when a thread attempts a lock on a mutex it has already locked, instead of deadlocking it returns an error. Therefore, an errorcheck mutex is more useful for debugging purposes.

The type of mutex can be specified using a mutex attribute object. To create and initialize a mutex attribute object to default values, Pthreads provides the function `pthread_mutexattr_init`. The prototype of the function is:

```
1   int
2   pthread_mutexattr_init (
3        pthread_mutexattr_t    *attr);
```

This creates and initializes a mutex attributes object `attr`. The default type of mutex is a normal mutex. Pthreads provides the function `pthread_mutexattr_settype_np` for setting the type of mutex specified by the mutex attributes object. The prototype for this function is:

```
1   int
2   pthread_mutexattr_settype_np (
3        pthread_mutexattr_t    *attr,
4        int    type);
```

Here, `type` specifies the type of the mutex and can take one of the following values corresponding to the three mutex types – normal, recursive, or errorcheck:

- PTHREAD_MUTEX_NORMAL_NP

- PTHREAD_MUTEX_RECURSIVE_NP

- PTHREAD_MUTEX_ERRORCHECK_NP

A mutex-attributes object can be destroyed using the `pthread_attr_destroy` that takes the mutex attributes object `attr` as its only argument.

7.7 Thread Cancellation

Consider a simple program to evaluate a set of positions in a chess game. Assume that there are k moves, each being evaluated by an independent thread. If at any point of time, a position is established to be of a certain quality, the other positions that are known to be of worse quality must stop being evaluated. In other words, the threads evaluating the corresponding board positions must be canceled. Posix threads provide this cancellation feature in the function `pthread_cancel`. The prototype of this function is:

```
1   int
2   pthread_cancel (
3        pthread_t    thread);
```

Here, `thread` is the handle to the thread to be canceled. A thread may cancel itself or cancel other threads. When a call to this function is made, a cancellation is sent to the specified thread. It is not guaranteed that the specified thread will receive or act on the cancellation. Threads can protect themselves against cancellation. When a cancellation is actually performed, cleanup functions are invoked for reclaiming the thread data structures. After this the thread is canceled. This process is similar to termination of a thread using the `pthread_exit` call. This is performed independently of the thread that made the original request for cancellation. The `pthread_cancel` function returns after a cancellation has been sent. The cancellation may itself be performed later. The function returns a 0 on successful completion. This does not imply that the requested thread has been canceled; it implies that the specified thread is a valid thread for cancellation.

7.8 Composite Synchronization Constructs

While the Pthreads API provides a basic set of synchronization constructs, often, there is a need for higher level constructs. These higher level constructs can be built using basic synchronization constructs. In this section, we look at some of these constructs along with their performance aspects and applications.

7.8.1 Read-Write Locks

In many applications, a data structure is read frequently but written infrequently. For such scenarios, it is useful to note that multiple reads can proceed without any coherence problems. However, writes must be serialized. This points to an alternate structure called a read-write lock. A thread reading a shared data item acquires a read lock on the variable. A read lock is granted when there are other threads that may already have read locks. If there is a write lock on the data (or if there are queued write locks), the thread performs a condition wait. Similarly, if there are multiple threads requesting a write lock, they must perform a condition wait. Using this principle, we design functions for read locks `mylib_rwlock_rlock`, write locks `mylib_rwlock_wlock`, and unlocking `mylib_rwlock_unlock`.

The read-write locks illustrated are based on a data structure called `mylib_rwlock_t`. This structure maintains a count of the number of readers, the writer (a 0/1 integer specifying whether a writer is present), a condition variable `readers_proceed` that is signaled when readers can proceed, a condition variable `writer_proceed` that is signaled when one of the writers can proceed, a count `pending_writers` of pending writers, and a mutex `read_write_lock` associated with the shared data structure. The function `mylib_rwlock_init` is used to initialize various components of this data structure.

The function `mylib_rwlock_rlock` attempts a read lock on the data structure. It checks to see if there is a write lock or pending writers. If so, it performs a condition wait on the condition variable `readers_proceed`, otherwise it increments the count of readers and proceeds to grant a read lock. The function my1ib_rwlock_wlock attempts a write lock on the data structure. It checks to see if there are readers or writers; if so, it increments the count of pending writers and performs a condition wait on the condition variable writer_proceed. If there are no readers or writer, it grants a write lock and proceeds.

The function my1ib_rwlock_unlock unlocks a read or write lock. It checks to see if there is a write lock, and if so, it unlocks the data structure by setting the writer field to 0. If there are readers, it decrements the number of readers readers. If there are no readers left and there are pending writers, it signals one of the writers to proceed (by signaling writer_proceed). If there are no pending writers but there are pending readers, it signals all the reader threads to proceed. The code for initializing and locking/unlocking is as follows:

```
1   typedef struct {
2       int readers;
3       int writer;
4       pthread_cond_t readers_proceed;
5       pthread_cond_t writer_proceed;
6       int pending_writers;
7       pthread_mutex_t read_write_lock;
8   } mylib_rwlock_t;
9
10
11  void mylib_rwlock_init (mylib_rwlock_t *l) {
12      l -> readers = l -> writer = l -> pending_writers = 0;
13      pthread_mutex_init(&(l -> read_write_lock), NULL);
14      pthread_cond_init(&(l -> readers_proceed), NULL);
15      pthread_cond_init(&(l -> writer_proceed), NULL);
16  }
17
18  void mylib_rwlock_rlock(mylib_rwlock_t *l) {
19      /* if there is a write lock or pending writers, perform condition
20      wait.. else increment count of readers and grant read lock */
21
22      pthread_mutex_lock(&(l -> read_write_lock));
23      while ((l -> pending_writers > 0) || (l -> writer > 0))
24          pthread_cond_wait(&(l -> readers_proceed),
25              &(l -> read_write_lock));
26      l -> readers ++;
27      pthread_mutex_unlock(&(l -> read_write_lock));
28  }
29
30
31  void mylib_rwlock_wlock(mylib_rwlock_t *l) {
32      /* if there are readers or writers, increment pending writers
33      count and wait. On being woken, decrement pending writers
34      count and increment writer count */
35
36      pthread_mutex_lock(&(l -> read_write_lock));
37      while ((l -> writer > 0) || (l -> readers > 0))  {
38          l -> pending_writers ++;
39          pthread_cond_wait(&(l -> writer_proceed),
40              &(l -> read_write_lock));
41      }
```

```
42        l -> pending_writers --;
43        l -> writer ++
44        pthread_mutex_unlock(&(l -> read_write_lock));
45    }
46
47
48    void mylib_rwlock_unlock(mylib_rwlock_t *l) {
49        /* if there is a write lock then unlock, else if there are
50        read locks, decrement count of read locks. If the count
51        is 0 and there is a pending writer, let it through, else
52        if there are pending readers, let them all go through */
53
54        pthread_mutex_lock(&(l -> read_write_lock));
55        if (l -> writer > 0)
56            l -> writer = 0;
57        else if (l -> readers > 0)
58            l -> readers --;
59        pthread_mutex_unlock(&(l -> read_write_lock));
60        if ((l -> readers == 0) && (l -> pending_writers > 0))
61            pthread_cond_signal(&(l -> writer_proceed));
62        else if (l -> readers > 0)
63            pthread_cond_broadcast(&(l -> readers_proceed));
64    }
```

We now illustrate the use of read-write locks with some examples.

Example 7.7   Using read-write locks for computing the minimum of a list of numbers

A simple use of read-write locks is in computing the minimum of a list of numbers. In our earlier implementation, we associated a lock with the minimum value. Each thread locked this object and updated the minimum value, if necessary. In general, the number of times the value is examined is greater than the number of times it is updated. Therefore, it is beneficial to allow multiple reads using a read lock and write after a write lock only if needed. The corresponding program segment is as follows:

```
1    void *find_min_rw(void *list_ptr) {
2        int *partial_list_pointer, my_min, i;
3        my_min = MIN_INT;
4        partial_list_pointer = (int *) list_ptr;
5        for (i = 0; i < partial_list_size; i++)
6            if (partial_list_pointer[i] < my_min)
7                my_min = partial_list_pointer[i];
8        /* lock the mutex associated with minimum_value and
9        update the variable as required */
10        mylib_rwlock_rlock(&read_write_lock);
11        if (my_min < minimum_value) {
12            mylib_rwlock_unlock(&read_write_lock);
13            mylib_rwlock_wlock(&read_write_lock);
14            minimum_value = my_min;
15        }
16        /* and unlock the mutex */
17        mylib_rwlock_unlock(&read_write_lock);
```

```
18      pthread_exit(0);
19  }
```

Programming Notes In this example, each thread computes the minimum element in its partial list. It then attempts a read lock on the lock associated with the global minimum value. If the global minimum value is greater than the locally minimum value (thus requiring an update), the read lock is relinquished and a write lock is sought. Once the write lock has been obtained, the global minimum can be updated. The performance gain obtained from read-write locks is influenced by the number of threads and the number of updates (write locks) required. In the extreme case when the first value of the global minimum is also the true minimum value, no write locks are subsequently sought. In this case, the version using read-write locks performs better. In contrast, if each thread must update the global minimum, the read locks are superfluous and add overhead to the program.   ∎

Example 7.8   Using read-write locks for implementing hash tables
A commonly used operation in applications ranging from database query to state space search is the search of a key in a database. The database is organized as a hash table. In our example, we assume that collisions are handled by chaining colliding entries into linked lists. Each list has a lock associated with it. This lock ensures that lists are not being updated and searched at the same time. We consider two versions of this program: one using mutex locks and one using read-write locks developed in this section.

The mutex lock version of the program hashes the key into the table, locks the mutex associated with the table index, and proceeds to search/update within the linked list. The thread function for doing this is as follows:

```
1   manipulate_hash_table(int entry) {
2       int table_index, found;
3       struct list_entry *node, *new_node;
4
5       table_index = hash(entry);
6       pthread_mutex_lock(&hash_table[table_index].list_lock);
7       found = 0;
8       node = hash_table[table_index].next;
9       while ((node != NULL) && (!found)) {
10          if (node -> value == entry)
11              found = 1;
12          else
13              node = node -> next;
14      }
15      pthread_mutex_unlock(&hash_table[table_index].list_lock);
16      if (found)
17          return(1);
18      else
19          insert_into_hash_table(entry);
20  }
```

Here, the function `insert_into_hash_table` must lock `hash_table[table_index].list_lock` before performing the actual insertion. When a large fraction of the queries are found in the hash table (i.e., they do not need to be inserted), these searches are serialized. It is easy to see that multiple threads can be safely allowed to search the hash table and only updates to the table must be serialized. This can be accomplished using read-write locks. We can rewrite the `manipulate_hash_table` function as follows:

```
1   manipulate_hash_table(int entry)
2   {
3        int table_index, found;
4        struct list_entry *node, *new_node;
5
6        table_index = hash(entry);
7        mylib_rwlock_rlock(&hash_table[table_index].list_lock);
8        found = 0;
9        node = hash_table[table_index].next;
10       while ((node != NULL) && (!found)) {
11           if (node -> value == entry)
12               found = 1;
13           else
14               node = node -> next;
15       }
16       mylib_rwlock_rlock(&hash_table[table_index].list_lock);
17       if (found)
18           return(1);
19       else
20           insert_into_hash_table(entry);
21   }
```

Here, the function `insert_into_hash_table` must first get a write lock on `hash_table[table_index].list_lock` before performing actual insertion.

Programming Notes   In this example, we assume that the `list_lock` field has been defined to be of type `mylib_rwlock_t` and all read-write locks associated with the hash tables have been initialized using the function `mylib_rwlock_init`. Using `mylib_rwlock_rlock` instead of a mutex lock allows multiple threads to search respective entries concurrently. Thus, if the number of successful searches outnumber insertions, this formulation is likely to yield better performance. Note that the `insert_into_hash_table` function must be suitably modified to use write locks (instead of mutex locks as before).   ∎

It is important to identify situations where read-write locks offer advantages over normal locks. Since read-write locks offer no advantage over normal mutexes for writes, they are beneficial only when there are a significant number of read operations. Furthermore, as the critical section becomes larger, read-write locks offer more advantages. This is because the serialization overhead paid by normal mutexes is higher. Finally, since read-write locks rely on condition variables, the underlying thread system must provide fast condition wait, signal, and broadcast functions. It is possible to do a simple analysis to understand the relative merits of read-write locks (Exercise 7.7).

7.8.2 Barriers

An important and often used construct in threaded (as well as other parallel) programs is a barrier. A barrier call is used to hold a thread until all other threads participating in the barrier have reached the barrier. Barriers can be implemented using a counter, a mutex and a condition variable. (They can also be implemented simply using mutexes; however, such implementations suffer from the overhead of busy-wait.) A single integer is used to keep track of the number of threads that have reached the barrier. If the count is less than the total number of threads, the threads execute a condition wait. The last thread entering (and setting the count to the number of threads) wakes up all the threads using a condition broadcast. The code for accomplishing this is as follows:

```
1   typedef struct {
2       pthread_mutex_t count_lock;
3       pthread_cond_t ok_to_proceed;
4       int count;
5   } mylib_barrier_t;
6
7   void mylib_init_barrier(mylib_barrier_t *b) {
8       b -> count = 0;
9       pthread_mutex_init(&(b -> count_lock), NULL);
10      pthread_cond_init(&(b -> ok_to_proceed), NULL);
11  }
12
13  void mylib_barrier (mylib_barrier_t *b, int num_threads) {
14      pthread_mutex_lock(&(b -> count_lock));
15      b -> count ++;
16      if (b -> count == num_threads) {
17          b -> count = 0;
18          pthread_cond_broadcast(&(b -> ok_to_proceed));
19      }
20      else
21          while (pthread_cond_wait(&(b -> ok_to_proceed),
22              &(b -> count_lock)) != 0);
23      pthread_mutex_unlock(&(b -> count_lock));
24  }
```

In the above implementation of a barrier, threads enter the barrier and stay until the broadcast signal releases them. The threads are released one by one since the mutex count_lock is passed among them one after the other. The trivial lower bound on execution time of this function is therefore $O(n)$ for n threads. This implementation of a barrier can be speeded up using multiple barrier variables.

Let us consider an alternate barrier implementation in which there are $n/2$ condition variable-mutex pairs for implementing a barrier for n threads. The barrier works as follows: at the first level, threads are paired up and each pair of threads shares a single condition variable-mutex pair. A designated member of the pair waits for both threads to arrive at the pairwise barrier. Once this happens, all the designated members are organized into pairs, and this process continues until there is only one thread. At this point, we know that all threads have reached the barrier point. We must release all threads at this point. However, releasing them requires signaling all $n/2$ condition variables. We use the same hierarchical strategy for doing this. The designated thread in a pair signals the respective condition variables.

```
1    typedef struct barrier_node {
2         pthread_mutex_t count_lock;
3         pthread_cond_t ok_to_proceed_up;
4         pthread_cond_t ok_to_proceed_down;
5         int count;
6    } mylib_barrier_t_internal;
7
8    typedef struct barrier_node mylog_logbarrier_t[MAX_THREADS];
9    pthread_t p_threads[MAX_THREADS];
10   pthread_attr_t attr;
11
12   void mylib_init_barrier(mylog_logbarrier_t b) {
13        int i;
14        for (i = 0; i < MAX_THREADS; i++) {
15             b[i].count = 0;
16             pthread_mutex_init(&(b[i].count_lock), NULL);
17             pthread_cond_init(&(b[i].ok_to_proceed_up), NULL);
18             pthread_cond_init(&(b[i].ok_to_proceed_down), NULL);
19        }
20   }
21
22   void mylib_logbarrier (mylog_logbarrier_t b, int num_threads,
23              int thread_id) {
24        int i, base, index;
25        i = 2;
26        base = 0;
27
28        do {
29             index = base + thread_id / i;
30             if (thread_id % i == 0) {
31                  pthread_mutex_lock(&(b[index].count_lock));
32                  b[index].count ++;
33                  while (b[index].count < 2)
34                       pthread_cond_wait(&(b[index].ok_to_proceed_up),
35                            &(b[index].count_lock));
36                       pthread_mutex_unlock(&(b[index].count_lock));
37             }
38             else {
39                  pthread_mutex_lock(&(b[index].count_lock));
40                  b[index].count ++;
41                  if (b[index].count == 2)
42                       pthread_cond_signal(&(b[index].ok_to_proceed_up));
43                  while (pthread_cond_wait(&(b[index].ok_to_proceed_down),
44                       &(b[index].count_lock)) != 0);
45                  pthread_mutex_unlock(&(b[index].count_lock));
46                  break;
47             }
48             base = base + num_threads/i;
49             i = i * 2;
```

```
50          } while (i <= num_threads);
51          i = i / 2;
52          for (; i > 1; i = i / 2) {
53              base = base - num_threads/i;
54              index = base + thread_id / i;
55              pthread_mutex_lock(&(b[index].count_lock));
56              b[index].count = 0;
57              pthread_cond_signal(&(b[index].ok_to_proceed_down));
58              pthread_mutex_unlock(&(b[index].count_lock));
59          }
60  }
```

In this implementation of a barrier, we visualize the barrier as a binary tree. Threads arrive at the leaf nodes of this tree. Consider an instance of a barrier with eight threads. Threads 0 and 1 are paired up on a single leaf node. One of these threads is designated as the representative of the pair at the next level in the tree. In the above example, thread 0 is considered the representative and it waits on the condition variable ok_to_proceed_up for thread 1 to catch up. All even numbered threads proceed to the next level in the tree. Now thread 0 is paired up with thread 2 and thread 4 with thread 6. Finally thread 0 and 4 are paired. At this point, thread 0 realizes that all threads have reached the desired barrier point and releases threads by signaling the condition ok_to_proceed_down. When all threads are released, the barrier is complete.

It is easy to see that there are $n - 1$ nodes in the tree for an n thread barrier. Each node corresponds to two condition variables, one for releasing the thread up and one for releasing it down, one lock, and a count of number of threads reaching the node. The tree nodes are linearly laid out in the array mylog_logbarrier_t with the $n/2$ leaf nodes taking the first $n/2$ elements, the $n/4$ tree nodes at the next higher level taking the next $n/4$ nodes and so on.

It is interesting to study the performance of this program. Since threads in the linear barrier are released one after the other, it is reasonable to expect runtime to be linear in the number of threads even on multiple processors. In Figure 7.3, we plot the runtime of 1000 barriers in a sequence on a 32 processor SGI Origin 2000. The linear runtime of the sequential barrier is clearly reflected in the runtime. The logarithmic barrier executing on a single processor does just as much work asymptotically as a sequential barrier (albeit with a higher constant). However, on a parallel machine, in an ideal case when threads are assigned so that subtrees of the binary barrier tree are assigned to different processors, the time grows as $O(n/p + \log p)$. While this is difficult to achieve without being able to examine or assign blocks of threads corresponding to subtrees to individual processors, the logarithmic barrier displays significantly better performance than the serial barrier. Its performance tends to be linear in n as n becomes large for a given number of processors. This is because the n/p term starts to dominate the $\log p$ term in the execution time. This is observed both from observations as well as from analytical intuition.

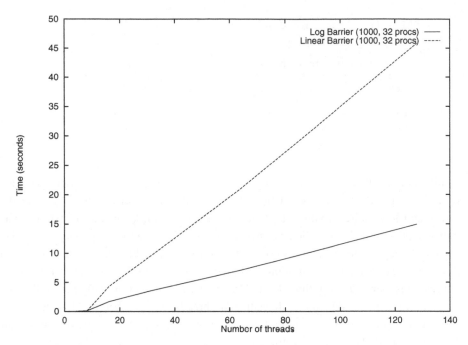

Figure 7.3   Execution time of 1000 sequential and logarithmic barriers as a function of number of threads on a 32 processor SGI Origin 2000.

7.9   Tips for Designing Asynchronous Programs

When designing multithreaded applications, it is important to remember that one cannot assume any order of execution with respect to other threads. Any such order must be explicitly established using the synchronization mechanisms discussed above: mutexes, condition variables, and joins. In addition, the system may provide other means of synchronization. However, for portability reasons, we discourage the use of these mechanisms.

In many thread libraries, threads are switched at semi-deterministic intervals. Such libraries are more forgiving of synchronization errors in programs. These libraries are called *slightly asynchronous* libraries. On the other hand, kernel threads (threads supported by the kernel) and threads scheduled on multiple processors are less forgiving. The programmer must therefore not make any assumptions regarding the level of asynchrony in the threads library.

Let us look at some common errors that arise from incorrect assumptions on relative execution times of threads:

- Say, a thread T1 creates another thread T2. T2 requires some data from thread T1. This data is transferred using a global memory location. However, thread T1 places the data in the location after creating thread T2. The implicit assumption here is that T1 will not be switched until it blocks; or that T2 will get to the point at which it uses the data only after T1 has stored it there. Such assumptions may lead to errors since it is possible that T1 gets switched as soon as it creates T2. In such a situation, T1 will receive uninitialized data.

- Assume, as before, that thread T1 creates T2 and that it needs to pass data to thread T2 which resides on its stack. It passes this data by passing a pointer to the stack location to thread T2. Consider the scenario in which T1 runs to completion before T2 gets scheduled. In this case, the stack frame is released and some other thread may overwrite the space pointed to formerly by the stack frame. In this case, what thread T2 reads from the location may be invalid data. Similar problems may exist with global variables.

- We strongly discourage the use of scheduling techniques as means of synchronization. It is especially difficult to keep track of scheduling decisions on parallel machines. Further, as the number of processors change, these issues may change depending on the thread scheduling policy. It may happen that higher priority threads are actually waiting while lower priority threads are running.

We recommend the following rules of thumb which help minimize the errors in threaded programs.

- Set up all the requirements for a thread before actually creating the thread. This includes initializing the data, setting thread attributes, thread priorities, mutex-attributes, etc. Once you create a thread, it is possible that the newly created thread actually runs to completion before the creating thread gets scheduled again.

- When there is a producer-consumer relation between two threads for certain data items, make sure the producer thread places the data before it is consumed and that intermediate buffers are guaranteed to not overflow.

- At the consumer end, make sure that the data lasts at least until all potential consumers have consumed the data. This is particularly relevant for stack variables.

- Where possible, define and use group synchronizations and data replication. This can improve program performance significantly.

While these simple tips provide guidelines for writing error-free threaded programs, extreme caution must be taken to avoid race conditions and parallel overheads associated with synchronization.

7.10 OpenMP: a Standard for Directive Based Parallel Programming

In the first part of this chapter, we studied the use of threaded APIs for programming shared address space machines. While standardization and support for these APIs has come a long way, their use is still predominantly restricted to system programmers as opposed to application programmers. One of the reasons for this is that APIs such as Pthreads are considered to be low-level primitives. Conventional wisdom indicates that a large class of applications can be efficiently supported by higher level constructs (or directives) which rid the programmer of the mechanics of manipulating threads. Such directive-based languages have existed for a long time, but only recently have standardization efforts succeeded in the form of OpenMP. OpenMP is an API that can be used with FORTRAN, C, and C++ for programming shared address space machines. OpenMP directives provide support for concurrency, synchronization, and data handling while obviating the need for explicitly setting up mutexes, condition variables, data scope, and initialization. We use the OpenMP C API in the rest of this chapter.

7.10.1   The OpenMP Programming Model

We initiate the OpenMP programming model with the aid of a simple program. OpenMP directives in C and C++ are based on the `#pragma` compiler directives. The directive itself consists of a directive name followed by clauses.

```
1   #pragma omp directive [clause list]
```

OpenMP programs execute serially until they encounter the `parallel` directive. This directive is responsible for creating a group of threads. The exact number of threads can be specified in the directive, set using an environment variable, or at runtime using OpenMP functions. The main thread that encounters the `parallel` directive becomes the *master* of this group of threads and is assigned the thread id 0 within the group. The `parallel` directive has the following prototype:

```
1   #pragma omp parallel [clause list]
2   /* structured block */
3
```

Each thread created by this directive executes the `structured block` specified by the parallel directive. The clause list is used to specify conditional parallelization, number of threads, and data handling.

- **Conditional Parallelization:** The clause `if (scalar expression)` determines whether the parallel construct results in creation of threads. Only one `if` clause can be used with a parallel directive.

- **Degree of Concurrency:** The clause `num_threads (integer expression)` specifies the number of threads that are created by the `parallel` directive.

- **Data Handling:** The clause `private (variable list)` indicates that the set of variables specified is local to each thread – i.e., each thread has its own copy of each variable in the list. The clause `firstprivate (variable list)` is similar to the `private` clause, except the values of variables on entering the threads are initialized to corresponding values before the parallel directive. The clause `shared (variable list)` indicates that all variables in the list are shared across all the threads, i.e., there is only one copy. Special care must be taken while handling these variables by threads to ensure serializability.

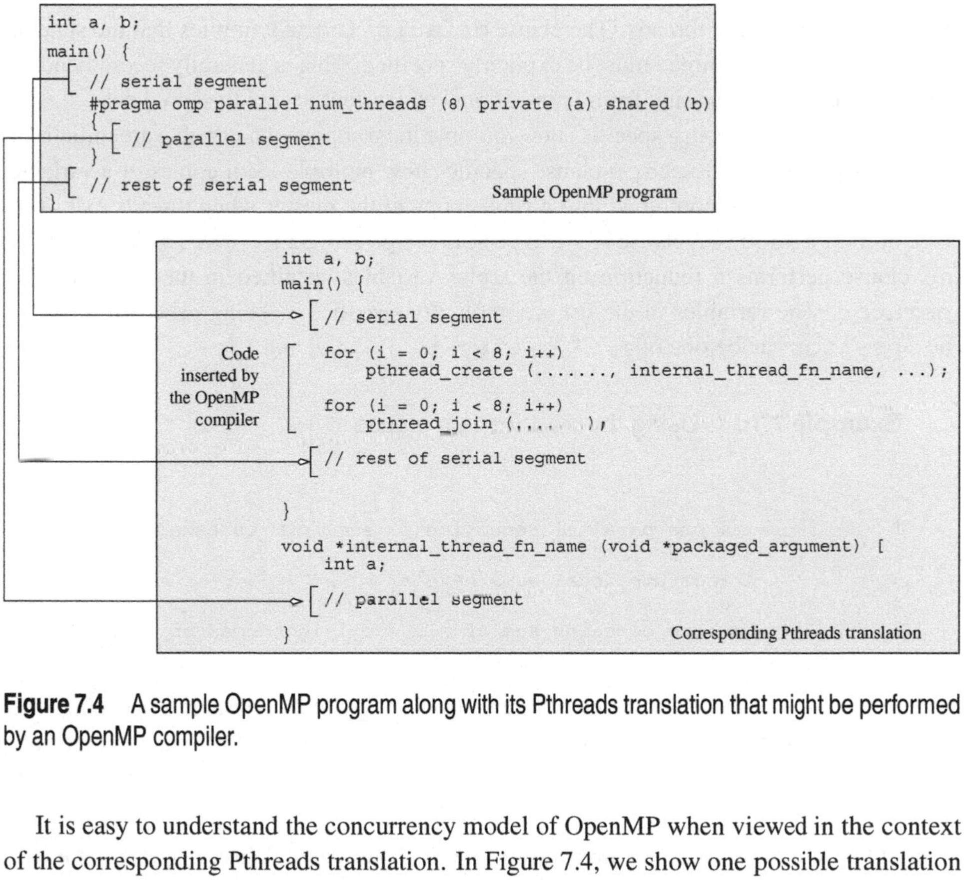

```
int a, b;
main() {
    // serial segment
    #pragma omp parallel num_threads (8) private (a) shared (b)
    {
        // parallel segment
    }
    // rest of serial segment
}
```
Sample OpenMP program

```
int a, b;
main() {
    // serial segment
```
Code inserted by the OpenMP compiler
```
    for (i = 0; i < 8; i++)
        pthread_create (......., internal_thread_fn_name, ...);
    for (i = 0; i < 8; i++)
        pthread_join (,... );
    // rest of serial segment

}
void *internal_thread_fn_name (void *packaged_argument) {
    int a;
    // parallel segment
}
```
Corresponding Pthreads translation

Figure 7.4 A sample OpenMP program along with its Pthreads translation that might be performed by an OpenMP compiler.

It is easy to understand the concurrency model of OpenMP when viewed in the context of the corresponding Pthreads translation. In Figure 7.4, we show one possible translation of an OpenMP program to a Pthreads program. The interested reader may note that such a translation can easily be automated through a Yacc or CUP script.

Example 7.9 Using the `parallel` directive

```
1   #pragma omp parallel if (is_parallel == 1) num_threads(8) \
2                       private (a) shared (b) firstprivate(c)
3   {
4       /* structured block */
5   }
```

Here, if the value of the variable is_parallel equals one, eight threads are created. Each of these threads gets private copies of variables a and c, and shares a single value of variable b. Furthermore, the value of each copy of c is initialized to the value of c before the parallel directive.   ∎

The default state of a variable is specified by the clause default (shared) or default (none). The clause default (shared) implies that, by default, a variable is shared by all the threads. The clause default (none) implies that the state of each variable used in a thread must be explicitly specified. This is generally recommended, to guard against errors arising from unintentional concurrent access to shared data.

Just as firstprivate specifies how multiple local copies of a variable are initialized inside a thread, the reduction clause specifies how multiple local copies of a variable at different threads are combined into a single copy at the master when threads exit. The usage of the reduction clause is reduction (operator: variable list). This clause performs a reduction on the scalar variables specified in the list using the operator. The variables in the list are implicitly specified as being private to threads. The operator can be one of +, *, -, &, |, ^, &&, and ||.

Example 7.10   Using the reduction clause

```
1    #pragma omp parallel reduction(+: sum) num_threads(8)
2    {
3        /* compute local sums here */
4    }
5    /* sum here contains sum of all local instances of sums */
```

In this example, each of the eight threads gets a copy of the variable sum. When the threads exit, the sum of all of these local copies is stored in the single copy of the variable (at the master thread).   ∎

In addition to these data handling clauses, there is one other clause, copyin. We will describe this clause in Section 7.10.4 after we discuss data scope in greater detail.

We can now use the parallel directive along with the clauses to write our first OpenMP program. We introduce two functions to facilitate this. The omp_get_num_threads () function returns the number of threads in the parallel region and the omp_get_thread_num () function returns the integer i.d. of each thread (recall that the master thread has an i.d. 0).

Example 7.11   Computing PI using OpenMP directives
Our first OpenMP example follows from Example 7.2, which presented a Pthreads program for the same problem. The parallel directive specifies that all variables

except `npoints`, the total number of random points in two dimensions across all threads, are local. Furthermore, the directive specifies that there are eight threads, and the value of `sum` after all threads complete execution is the sum of local values at each thread. The function `omp_get_num_threads` is used to determine the total number of threads. As in Example 7.2, a `for` loop generates the required number of random points (in two dimensions) and determines how many of them are within the prescribed circle of unit diameter.

```
1    /* ************************************************************
2        An OpenMP version of a threaded program to compute PI.
3        ******************************************************** */
4
5        #pragma omp parallel default(private) shared (npoints) \
6                            reduction(+: sum) num_threads(8)
7        {
8          num_threads = omp_get_num_threads();
9          sample_points_per_thread = npoints / num_threads;
10         sum = 0;
11         for (i = 0; i < sample_points_per_thread; i++) {
12           rand_no_x =(double)(rand_r(&seed))/(double)((2<<14)-1);
13           rand_no_y =(double)(rand_r(&seed))/(double)((2<<14)-1);
14           if (((rand_no_x - 0.5) * (rand_no_x - 0.5) +
15               (rand_no_y - 0.5) * (rand_no_y - 0.5)) < 0.25)
16               sum ++;
17         }
18       }
```

■

Note that this program is much easier to write in terms of specifying creation and termination of threads compared to the corresponding POSIX threaded program.

7.10.2 Specifying Concurrent Tasks in OpenMP

The `parallel` directive can be used in conjunction with other directives to specify concurrency across iterations and tasks. OpenMP provides two directives – `for` and `sections` – to specify concurrent iterations and tasks.

The `for` Directive

The `for` directive is used to split parallel iteration spaces across threads. The general form of a `for` directive is as follows:

```
1        #pragma omp for [clause list]
2            /* for loop */
3
```

The clauses that can be used in this context are: `private`, `firstprivate`, `lastprivate`, `reduction`, `schedule`, `nowait`, and `ordered`. The first four clauses deal with data handling and have identical semantics as in the case of the parallel directive. The lastprivate clause deals with how multiple local copies of a variable are written back into a single copy at the end of the parallel for loop. When using a for loop (or sections directive as we shall see) for farming work to threads, it is sometimes desired that the last iteration (as defined by serial execution) of the for loop update the value of a variable. This is accomplished using the lastprivate directive.

Example 7.12   Using the for directive for computing π

Recall from Example 7.11 that each iteration of the for loop is independent, and can be executed concurrently. In such situations, we can simplify the program using the for directive. The modified code segment is as follows:

```
1     #pragma omp parallel default(private) shared (npoints) \
2                          reduction(+: sum) num_threads(8)
3     {
4       sum = 0;
5       #pragma omp for
6       for (i = 0; i < npoints; i++) {
7         rand_no_x =(double)(rand_r(&seed))/(double)((2<<14)-1);
8         rand_no_y =(double)(rand_r(&seed))/(double)((2<<14)-1);
9         if (((rand_no_x - 0.5) * (rand_no_x - 0.5) +
10            (rand_no_y - 0.5) * (rand_no_y - 0.5)) < 0.25)
11            sum ++;
12      }
13    }
```

The for directive in this example specifies that the for loop immediately following the directive must be executed in parallel, i.e., split across various threads. Notice that the loop index goes from 0 to npoints in this case, as opposed to sample_points_per_thread in Example 7.11. The loop index for the for directive is assumed to be private, by default. It is interesting to note that the only difference between this OpenMP segment and the corresponding serial code is the two directives. This example illustrates how simple it is to convert many serial programs into OpenMP-based threaded programs. ∎

Assigning Iterations to Threads

The schedule clause of the for directive deals with the assignment of iterations to threads. The general form of the schedule directive is schedule(scheduling_class[, parameter]). OpenMP supports four scheduling classes: static, dynamic, guided, and runtime.

Example 7.13   Scheduling classes in OpenMP – matrix multiplication.

We explore various scheduling classes in the context of dense matrix multiplication. The code for multiplying two matrices a and b to yield matrix c is as follows:

```
1       for (i = 0; i < dim; i++) {
2           for (j = 0; j < dim; j++) {
3               c(i,j) = 0;
4               for (k = 0; k < dim; k++) {
5                   c(i,j) += a(i, k) * b(k, j);
6               }
7           }
8       }
```

The code segment above specifies a three-dimensional iteration space providing us with an ideal example for studying various scheduling classes in OpenMP.
■

Static The general form of the static scheduling class is schedule (static [, chunk-size]). This technique splits the iteration space into equal chunks of size chunk-size and assigns them to threads in a round-robin fashion. When no chunk-size is specified, the iteration space is split into as many chunks as there are threads and one chunk is assigned to each thread.

Example 7.14 Static scheduling of loops in matrix multiplication
The following modification of the matrix-multiplication program causes the outermost iteration to be split statically across threads as illustrated in Figure 7.5(a).

```
1   #pragma omp parallel default(private) shared (a, b, c, dim) \
2                         num_threads(4)
3       #pragma omp for schedule(static)
4       for (i = 0; i < dim; i++) {
5           for (j = 0; j < dim; j++) {
6               c(i,j) = 0;
7               for (k = 0; k < dim; k++) {
8                   c(i,j) += a(i, k) * b(k, j);
9               }
10          }
11      }
```

Since there are four threads in all, if dim = 128, the size of each partition is 32 columns, since we have not specified the chunk size. Using schedule(static, 16) results in the partitioning of the iteration space illustrated in Figure 7.5(b). Another example of the split illustrated in Figure 7.5(c) results when each for loop in the program in Example 7.13 is parallelized across threads with a schedule(static) and nested parallelism is enabled (see Section 7.10.6). ■

Dynamic Often, because of a number of reasons, ranging from heterogeneous computing resources to non-uniform processor loads, equally partitioned workloads take widely varying execution times. For this reason, OpenMP has a dynamic scheduling class. The

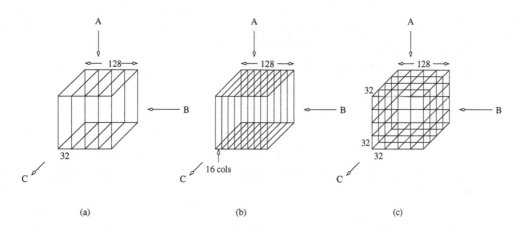

Figure 7.5 Three different schedules using the static scheduling class of OpenMP.

general form of this class is schedule(dynamic[, chunk-size]). The iteration space is partitioned into chunks given by chunk-size. However, these are assigned to threads as they become idle. This takes care of the temporal imbalances resulting from static scheduling. If no chunk-size is specified, it defaults to a single iteration per chunk.

Guided Consider the partitioning of an iteration space of 100 iterations with a chunk size of 5. This corresponds to 20 chunks. If there are 16 threads, in the best case, 12 threads get one chunk each and the remaining four threads get two chunks. Consequently, if there are as many processors as threads, this assignment results in considerable idling. The solution to this problem (also referred to as an ***edge effect***) is to reduce the chunk size as we proceed through the computation. This is the principle of the guided scheduling class. The general form of this class is schedule(guided[, chunk-size]). In this class, the chunk size is reduced exponentially as each chunk is dispatched to a thread. The chunk-size refers to the smallest chunk that should be dispatched. Therefore, when the number of iterations left is less than chunk-size, the entire set of iterations is dispatched at once. The value of chunk-size defaults to one if none is specified.

Runtime Often it is desirable to delay scheduling decisions until runtime. For example, if one would like to see the impact of various scheduling strategies to select the best one, the scheduling can be set to runtime. In this case the environment variable OMP_SCHEDULE determines the scheduling class and the chunk size.

When no scheduling class is specified with the omp for directive, the actual scheduling technique is not specified and is implementation dependent. The for directive places additional restrictions on the for loop that follows. For example, it must not have a break statement, the loop control variable must be an integer, the initialization expression of the for loop must be an integer assignment, the logical expression must be one of <, ≤, >, or $\geq$, and the increment expression must have integer increments or decrements only. For more details on these restrictions, we refer the reader to the OpenMP manuals.

Synchronization Across Multiple `for` Directives

Often, it is desirable to have a sequence of `for`-directives within a parallel construct that do not execute an implicit barrier at the end of each `for` directive. OpenMP provides a clause – `nowait`, which can be used with a `for` directive to indicate that the threads can proceed to the next statement without waiting for all other threads to complete the `for` loop execution. This is illustrated in the following example:

Example 7.15   Using the `nowait` clause

Consider the following example in which variable `name` needs to be looked up in two lists – `current_list` and `past_list`. If the name exists in a list, it must be processed accordingly. The name might exist in both lists. In this case, there is no need to wait for all threads to complete execution of the first loop before proceeding to the second loop. Consequently, we can use the `nowait` clause to save idling and synchronization overheads as follows:

```
1       #pragma omp parallel
2       {
3           #pragma omp for nowait
4               for (i = 0; i < nmax; i++)
5                   if (isEqual(name, current_list[i])
6                       processCurrentName(name);
7           #pragma omp for
8               for (i = 0; i < mmax; i++)
9                   if (isEqual(name, past_list[i])
10                      processPastName(name);
11      }
```

■

The `sections` Directive

The `for` directive is suited to partitioning iteration spaces across threads. Consider now a scenario in which there are three tasks (`taskA`, `taskB`, and `taskC`) that need to be executed. Assume that these tasks are independent of each other and therefore can be assigned to different threads. OpenMP supports such non-iterative parallel task assignment using the `sections` directive. The general form of the `sections` directive is as follows:

```
1   #pragma omp sections [clause list]
2   {
3       [#pragma omp section
4           /* structured block */
5       ]
6       [#pragma omp section
```

```
7              /* structured block */
8       ]
9       ...
10   }
```

This sections directive assigns the structured block corresponding to each section to one thread (indeed more than one section can be assigned to a single thread). The clause list may include the following clauses – private, firstprivate, lastprivate, reduction, and nowait. The syntax and semantics of these clauses are identical to those in the case of the for directive. The lastprivate clause, in this case, specifies that the last section (lexically) of the sections directive updates the value of the variable. The nowait clause specifies that there is no implicit synchronization among all threads at the end of the sections directive.

For executing the three concurrent tasks taskA, taskB, and taskC, the corresponding sections directive is as follows:

```
1        #pragma omp parallel
2        {
3            #pragma omp sections
4            {
5                #pragma omp section
6                {
7                    taskA();
8                }
9                #pragma omp section
10               {
11                   taskB();
12               }
13               #pragma omp section
14               {
15                   taskC();
16               }
17           }
18       }
```

If there are three threads, each section (in this case, the associated task) is assigned to one thread. At the end of execution of the assigned section, the threads synchronize (unless the nowait clause is used). Note that it is illegal to branch in and out of section blocks.

Merging Directives

In our discussion thus far, we use the directive parallel to create concurrent threads, and for and sections to farm out work to threads. If there was no parallel directive specified, the for and sections directives would execute serially (all work is farmed to a single thread, the master thread). Consequently, for and sections directives are generally preceded by the parallel directive. OpenMP allows the programmer to merge the parallel directives to parallel for and parallel sections, respectively. The clause list for the merged directive can be from the clause lists of either the parallel or for / sections directives.
For example:

```
1        #pragma omp parallel default (private) shared (n)
2        {
3            #pragma omp for
4            for (i = 0 < i < n; i++) {
5            /* body of parallel for loop */
6            }
7        }
```

is identical to:

```
1        #pragma omp parallel for default (private) shared (n)
2        {
3            for (i = 0 < i < n; i++) {
4            /* body of parallel for loop */
5            }
6        }
7
```

and:

```
1        #pragma omp parallel
2        {
3            #pragma omp sections
4            {
5                #pragma omp section
6                {
7                   taskA();
8                }
9                #pragma omp section
10               {
11                  taskB();
12               }
13               /* other sections here */
14           }
15       }
```

is identical to:

```
1        #pragma omp parallel sections
2        {
3            #pragma omp section
4            {
5                taskA();
6            }
7            #pragma omp section
8            {
9                taskB();
10           }
11           /* other sections here */
12       }
```

Nesting `parallel` Directives

Let us revisit Program 7.13. To split each of the `for` loops across various threads, we would modify the program as follows:

```
1    #pragma omp parallel for default(private) shared (a, b, c, dim) \
2                        num_threads(2)
3        for (i = 0; i < dim; i++) {
4        #pragma omp parallel for default(private) shared (a, b, c, dim) \
5                        num_threads(2)
6            for (j = 0; j < dim; j++) {
7                c(i,j) = 0;
8                #pragma omp parallel for default(private) \
9                        shared (a, b, c, dim) num_threads(2)
10               for (k = 0; k < dim; k++) {
11                   c(i,j) += a(i, k) * b(k, j);
12               }
13           }
14       }
```

We start by making a few observations about how this segment is written. Instead of nesting three for directives inside a single parallel directive, we have used three parallel for directives. This is because OpenMP does not allow for, sections, and single directives that bind to the same parallel directive to be nested. Furthermore, the code as written only generates a logical team of threads on encountering a nested parallel directive. The newly generated logical team is still executed by the same thread corresponding to the outer parallel directive. To generate a new set of threads, nested parallelism must be enabled using the OMP_NESTED environment variable. If the OMP_NESTED environment variable is set to FALSE, then the inner parallel region is serialized and executed by a single thread. If the OMP_NESTED environment variable is set to TRUE, nested parallelism is enabled. The default state of this environment variable is FALSE, i.e., nested parallelism is disabled. OpenMP environment variables are discussed in greater detail in Section 7.10.6.

There are a number of other restrictions associated with the use of synchronization constructs in nested parallelism. We refer the reader to the OpenMP manual for a discussion of these restrictions.

7.10.3   Synchronization Constructs in OpenMP

In Section 7.5, we described the need for coordinating the execution of multiple threads. This may be the result of a desired execution order, the atomicity of a set of instructions, or the need for serial execution of code segments. The Pthreads API supports mutexes and condition variables. Using these we implemented a range of higher level functionality in the form of read-write locks, barriers, monitors, etc. The OpenMP standard provides this high-level functionality in an easy-to-use API. In this section, we will explore these directives and their use.

Synchronization Point: The barrier Directive

A barrier is one of the most frequently used synchronization primitives. OpenMP provides a barrier directive, whose syntax is as follows:

```
1       #pragma omp barrier
```

On encountering this directive, all threads in a team wait until others have caught up, and then release. When used with nested `parallel` directives, the `barrier` directive binds to the closest `parallel` directive. For executing barriers conditionally, it is important to note that a `barrier` directive must be enclosed in a compound statement that is conditionally executed. This is because pragmas are compiler directives and not a part of the language. Barriers can also be effected by ending and restarting `parallel` regions. However, there is usually a higher overhead associated with this. Consequently, it is not the method of choice for implementing barriers.

Single Thread Executions: The `single` and `master` Directives

Often, a computation within a parallel section needs to be performed by just one thread. A simple example of this is the computation of the mean of a list of numbers. Each thread can compute a local sum of partial lists, add these local sums to a shared global sum, and have one thread compute the mean by dividing this global sum by the number of entries in the list. The last step can be accomplished using a `single` directive.

A `single` directive specifies a structured block that is executed by a single (arbitrary) thread. The syntax of the `single` directive is as follows:

```
1   #pragma omp single [clause list]
2           structured block
```

The clause list can take clauses `private`, `firstprivate`, and `nowait`. These clauses have the same semantics as before. On encountering the `single` block, the first thread enters the block. All the other threads proceed to the end of the block. If the `nowait` clause has been specified at the end of the block, then the other threads proceed; otherwise they wait at the end of the `single` block for the thread to finish executing the block. This directive is useful for computing global data as well as performing I/O.

The `master` directive is a specialization of the `single` directive in which only the master thread executes the structured block. The syntax of the `master` directive is as follows:

```
1   #pragma omp master
2           structured block
```

In contrast to the `single` directive, there is no implicit barrier associated with the `master` directive.

Critical Sections: The `critical` and `atomic` Directives

In our discussion of Pthreads, we had examined the use of locks to protect critical regions – regions that must be executed serially, one thread at a time. In addition to explicit lock management (Section 7.10.5), OpenMP provides a `critical` directive for implementing critical regions. The syntax of a `critical` directive is:

```
1  #pragma omp critical [(name)]
2              structured block
```

Here, the optional identifier name can be used to identify a critical region. The use of name allows different threads to execute different code while being protected from each other.

Example 7.16   Using the `critical` directive for producer-consumer threads

Consider a producer-consumer scenario in which a producer thread generates a task and inserts it into a task-queue. The consumer thread extracts tasks from the queue and executes them one at a time. Since there is concurrent access to the task-queue, these accesses must be serialized using critical blocks. Specifically, the tasks of inserting and extracting from the task-queue must be serialized. This can be implemented as follows:

```
1      #pragma omp parallel sections
2      {
3          #pragma parallel section
4          {
5              /* producer thread */
6              task = produce_task();
7              #pragma omp critical ( task_queue)
8              {
9                  insert_into_queue(task);
10             }
11         }
12         #pragma parallel section
13         {
14             /* consumer thread */
15             #pragma omp critical ( task_queue)
16             {
17                 task = extract_from_queue(task);
18             }
19             consume_task(task);
20         }
21     }
```

Note that queue full and queue empty conditions must be explicitly handled here in functions insert_into_queue and extract_from_queue.

■

The `critical` directive ensures that at any point in the execution of the program, only one thread is within a critical section specified by a certain name. If a thread is already inside a critical section (with a name), all others must wait until it is done before entering the named critical section. The name field is optional. If no name is specified, the critical section maps to a default name that is the same for all unnamed critical sections. The names of critical sections are global across the program.

It is easy to see that the `critical` directive is a direct application of the corresponding `mutex` function in Pthreads. The name field maps to the name of the mutex on which the lock is performed. As is the case with Pthreads, it is important to remember that `critical` sections represent serialization points in the program and therefore we must reduce the size of the critical sections as much as possible (in terms of execution time) to get good performance.

There are some obvious safeguards that must be noted while using the `critical` directive. The `block` of instructions must represent a structured block, i.e., no jumps are permitted into or out of the block. It is easy to see that the former would result in non-critical access and the latter in an unreleased lock, which could cause the threads to wait indefinitely.

Often, a critical section consists simply of an update to a single memory location, for example, incrementing or adding to an integer. OpenMP provides another directive, `atomic`, for such atomic updates to memory locations. The `atomic` directive specifies that the memory location update in the following instruction should be performed as an atomic operation. The update instruction can be one of the following forms:

```
1   x binary_operation = expr
2    x++
3    ++x
4    x--
5    --x
```

Here, `expr` is a scalar expression that does not include a reference to x, x itself is an lvalue of scalar type, and `binary_operation` is one of $\{+, *, -, /, \&, \| , \ll, \gg\}$. It is important to note that the `atomic` directive only atomizes the load and store of the scalar variable. The evaluation of the expression is not atomic. Care must be taken to ensure that there are no race conditions hidden therein. This also explains why the `expr` term in the `atomic` directive cannot contain the updated variable itself. All `atomic` directives can be replaced by `critical` directives provided they have the same name. However, the availability of atomic hardware instructions may optimize the performance of the program, compared to translation to `critical` directives.

In-Order Execution: The `ordered` Directive

In many circumstances, it is necessary to execute a segment of a parallel loop in the order in which the serial version would execute it. For example, consider a `for` loop in which, at some point, we compute the cumulative sum in array `cumul_sum` of a list stored in array `list`. The array `cumul_sum` can be computed using a `for` loop over index i serially by executing `cumul_sum[i] = cumul_sum[i-1] + list[i]`. When executing this `for` loop across threads, it is important to note that `cumul_sum[i]` can be computed only after `cumul_sum[i-1]` has been computed. Therefore, the statement would have to executed within an `ordered` block.

The syntax of the `ordered` directive is as follows:

```
1   #pragma omp ordered
2        structured block
```

Since the ordered directive refers to the in-order execution of a for loop, it must be within the scope of a for or parallel for directive. Furthermore, the for or parallel for directive must have the ordered clause specified to indicate that the loop contains an ordered block.

Example 7.17   Computing the cumulative sum of a list using the ordered directive

As we have just seen, to compute the cumulative sum of i numbers of a list, we can add the current number to the cumulative sum of i-1 numbers of the list. This loop must, however, be executed in order. Furthermore, the cumulative sum of the first element is simply the element itself. We can therefore write the following code segment using the ordered directive.

```
1        cumul_sum[0] = list[0];
2        #pragma omp parallel for private (i) \
3                    shared (cumul_sum, list, n) ordered
4        for (i = 1; i < n; i++)
5        {
6            /* other processing on list[i] if needed */
7
8            #pragma omp ordered
9            {
10               cumul_sum[i] = cumul_sum[i-1] + list[i];
11           }
12       }
```

∎

It is important to note that the ordered directive represents an ordered serialization point in the program. Only a single thread can enter an ordered block when all prior threads (as determined by loop indices) have exited. Therefore, if large portions of a loop are enclosed in ordered directives, corresponding speedups suffer. In the above example, the parallel formulation is expected to be no faster than the serial formulation unless there is significant processing associated with list[i] outside the ordered directive. A single for directive is constrained to have only one ordered block in it.

Memory Consistency: The flush Directive

The flush directive provides a mechanism for making memory consistent across threads. While it would appear that such a directive is superfluous for shared address space machines, it is important to note that variables may often be assigned to registers and register-allocated variables may be inconsistent. In such cases, the flush directive provides a memory fence by forcing a variable to be written to or read from the memory system. All write operations to shared variables must be committed to memory at a flush and all references to shared variables after a fence must be satisfied from the memory. Since private variables are relevant only to a single thread, the flush directive applies only to shared variables.

The syntax of the flush directive is as follows:

```
1   #pragma omp flush[(list)]
```

The optional list specifies the variables that need to be flushed. The default is that all shared variables are flushed.

Several OpenMP directives have an implicit flush. Specifically, a flush is implied at a barrier, at the entry and exit of critical, ordered, parallel, parallel for, and parallel sections blocks and at the exit of for, sections, and single blocks. A flush is not implied if a nowait clause is present. It is also not implied at the entry of for, sections, and single blocks and at entry or exit of a master block.

7.10.4   Data Handling in OpenMP

One of the critical factors influencing program performance is the manipulation of data by threads. We have briefly discussed OpenMP support for various data classes such as private, shared, firstprivate, and lastprivate. We now examine these in greater detail, with a view to understanding how these classes should be used. We identify the following heuristics to guide the process:

- If a thread initializes and uses a variable (such as loop indices) and no other thread accesses the data, then a local copy of the variable should be made for the thread. Such data should be specified as private.

- If a thread repeatedly reads a variable that has been initialized earlier in the program, it is beneficial to make a copy of the variable and inherit the value at the time of thread creation. This way, when a thread is scheduled on the processor, the data can reside at the same processor (in its cache if possible) and accesses will not result in interprocessor communication. Such data should be specified as firstprivate.

- If multiple threads manipulate a single piece of data, one must explore ways of breaking these manipulations into local operations followed by a single global operation. For example, if multiple threads keep a count of a certain event, it is beneficial to keep local counts and to subsequently accrue it using a single summation at the end of the parallel block. Such operations are supported by the reduction clause.

- If multiple threads manipulate different parts of a large data structure, the programmer should explore ways of breaking it into smaller data structures and making them private to the thread manipulating them.

- After all the above techniques have been explored and exhausted, remaining data items may be shared among various threads using the clause shared.

In addition to private, shared, firstprivate, and lastprivate, OpenMP supports one additional data class called threadprivate.

The threadprivate and copyin Directives   Often, it is useful to make a set of objects locally available to a thread in such a way that these objects persist through parallel and serial blocks provided the number of threads remains the same. In contrast to private variables, these variables are useful for maintaining persistent objects across parallel regions, which would otherwise have to be copied into the master thread's data space and reinitialized at the next parallel block. This class of variables is supported in OpenMP using the threadprivate directive. The syntax of the directive is as follows:

```
1   #pragma omp threadprivate(variable_list)
```

This directive implies that all variables in variable_list are local to each thread and are initialized once before they are accessed in a parallel region. Furthermore, these variables persist across different parallel regions provided dynamic adjustment of the number of threads is disabled and the number of threads is the same.

Similar to firstprivate, OpenMP provides a mechanism for assigning the same value to threadprivate variables across all threads in a parallel region. The syntax of the clause, which can be used with parallel directives, is copyin(variable_list).

7.10.5 OpenMP Library Functions

In addition to directives, OpenMP also supports a number of functions that allow a programmer to control the execution of threaded programs. As we shall notice, these functions are similar to corresponding Pthreads functions; however, they are generally at a higher level of abstraction, making them easier to use.

Controlling Number of Threads and Processors

The following OpenMP functions relate to the concurrency and number of processors used by a threaded program:

```
1   #include <omp.h>
2
3   void omp_set_num_threads (int num_threads);
4   int omp_get_num_threads ();
5   int omp_get_max_threads ();
6   int omp_get_thread_num ();
7   int omp_get_num_procs ();
8   int omp_in_parallel();
```

The function `omp_set_num_threads` sets the default number of threads that will be created on encountering the next `parallel` directive provided the `num_threads` clause is not used in the `parallel` directive. This function must be called outside the scope of a parallel region and dynamic adjustment of threads must be enabled (using either the `OMP_DYNAMIC` environment variable discussed in Section 7.10.6 or the `omp_set_dynamic` library function).

The `omp_get_num_threads` function returns the number of threads participating in a team. It binds to the closest parallel directive and in the absence of a parallel directive, returns 1 (for master thread). The `omp_get_max_threads` function returns the maximum number of threads that could possibly be created by a `parallel` directive encountered, which does not have a `num_threads` clause. The `omp_get_thread_num` returns a unique thread i.d. for each thread in a team. This integer lies between 0 (for the master thread) and `omp_get_num_threads()` `-1`. The `omp_get_num_procs` function returns the number of processors that are available to execute the threaded program at that point. Finally, the function `omp_in_parallel` returns a non-zero value if called from within the scope of a parallel region, and zero otherwise.

Controlling and Monitoring Thread Creation

The following OpenMP functions allow a programmer to set and monitor thread creation:

```
1    #include <omp.h>
2
3    void omp_set_dynamic (int dynamic_threads);
4    int omp_get_dynamic ();
5    void omp_set_nested (int nested);
6    int omp_get_nested ();
```

The `omp_set_dynamic` function allows the programmer to dynamically alter the number of threads created on encountering a parallel region. If the value `dynamic_threads` evaluates to zero, dynamic adjustment is disabled, otherwise it is enabled. The function must be called outside the scope of a parallel region. The corresponding state, i.e., whether dynamic adjustment is enabled or disabled, can be queried using the function `omp_get_dynamic`, which returns a non-zero value if dynamic adjustment is enabled, and zero otherwise.

The `omp_set_nested` enables nested parallelism if the value of its argument, `nested`, is non-zero, and disables it otherwise. When nested parallelism is disabled, any nested parallel regions subsequently encountered are serialized. The state of nested parallelism can be queried using the `omp_get_nested` function, which returns a non-zero value if nested parallelism is enabled, and zero otherwise.

Mutual Exclusion

While OpenMP provides support for critical sections and atomic updates, there are situations where it is more convenient to use an explicit lock. For such programs, OpenMP provides functions for initializing, locking, unlocking, and discarding locks. The lock data structure in OpenMP is of type omp_lock_t. The following functions are defined:

```
1   #include <omp.h>
2
3   void omp_init_lock (omp_lock_t *lock);
4   void omp_destroy_lock (omp_lock_t *lock);
5   void omp_set_lock (omp_lock_t *lock);
6   void omp_unset_lock (omp_lock_t *lock);
7   int omp_test_lock (omp_lock_t *lock);
```

Before a lock can be used, it must be initialized. This is done using the omp_init_lock function. When a lock is no longer needed, it must be discarded using the function omp_destroy_lock. It is illegal to initialize a previously initialized lock and destroy an uninitialized lock. Once a lock has been initialized, it can be locked and unlocked using the functions omp_set_lock and omp_unset_lock. On locking a previously unlocked lock, a thread gets exclusive access to the lock. All other threads must wait on this lock when they attempt an omp_set_lock. Only a thread owning a lock can unlock it. The result of a thread attempting to unlock a lock owned by another thread is undefined. Both of these operations are illegal prior to initialization or after the destruction of a lock. The function omp_test_lock can be used to attempt to set a lock. If the function returns a non-zero value, the lock has been successfully set, otherwise the lock is currently owned by another thread.

Similar to recursive mutexes in Pthreads, OpenMP also supports nestable locks that can be locked multiple times by the same thread. The lock object in this case is omp_nest_lock_t and the corresponding functions for handling a nested lock are:

```
1   #include <omp.h>
2
3   void omp_init_nest_lock (omp_nest_lock_t *lock);
4   void omp_destroy_nest_lock (omp_nest_lock_t *lock);
5   void omp_set_nest_lock (omp_nest_lock_t *lock);
6   void omp_unset_nest_lock (omp_nest_lock_t *lock);
7   int omp_test_nest_lock (omp_nest_lock_t *lock);
```

The semantics of these functions are similar to corresponding functions for simple locks. Notice that all of these functions have directly corresponding mutex calls in Pthreads.

7.10.6 Environment Variables in OpenMP

OpenMP provides additional environment variables that help control execution of parallel programs. These environment variables include the following.

OMP_NUM_THREADS This environment variable specifies the default number of threads created upon entering a parallel region. The number of threads can be changed using either the omp_set_num_threads function or the num_threads clause in the `parallel` directive. Note that the number of threads can be changed dynamically only if the variable OMP_SET_DYNAMIC is set to TRUE or if the function omp_set_dynamic has been called with a non-zero argument. For example, the following command, when typed into csh prior to execution of the program, sets the default number of threads to 8.

```
1   setenv OMP_NUM_THREADS 8
```

OMP_DYNAMIC   This variable, when set to TRUE, allows the number of threads to be controlled at runtime using the omp_set_num_threads function or the num_threads clause.   Dynamic control of number of threads can be disabled by calling the omp_set_dynamic function with a zero argument.

OMP_NESTED   This variable, when set to TRUE, enables nested parallelism, unless it is disabled by calling the omp_set_nested function with a zero argument.

OMP_SCHEDULE   This environment variable controls the assignment of iteration spaces associated with for directives that use the runtime scheduling class. The variable can take values static, dynamic, and guided along with optional chunk size. For example, the following assignment:

```
1   setenv OMP_SCHEDULE "static,4"
```

specifies that by default, all for directives use static scheduling with a chunk size of 4. Other examples of assignments include:

```
1   setenv OMP_SCHEDULE "dynamic"
2   setenv OMP_SCHEDULE "guided"
```

In each of these cases, a default chunk size of 1 is used.

7.10.7   Explicit Threads versus OpenMP Based Programming

OpenMP provides a layer on top of native threads to facilitate a variety of thread-related tasks. Using directives provided by OpenMP, a programmer is rid of the tasks of initializing attributes objects, setting up arguments to threads, partitioning iteration spaces, etc. This convenience is especially useful when the underlying problem has a static and/or regular task graph. The overheads associated with automated generation of threaded code from directives have been shown to be minimal in the context of a variety of applications.

However, there are some drawbacks to using directives as well. An artifact of explicit threading is that data exchange is more apparent. This helps in alleviating some of the overheads from data movement, false sharing, and contention. Explicit threading also provides a richer API in the form of condition waits, locks of different types, and increased flexibility for building composite synchronization operations as illustrated in Section 7.8. Finally, since explicit threading is used more widely than OpenMP, tools and support for Pthreads programs is easier to find.

A programmer must weigh all these considerations before deciding on an API for programming.

7.11   Bibliographic Remarks

A number of excellent references exist for both explicit thread-based and OpenMP-based programming. Lewis and Berg [LB97, LB95a] provide a detailed guide to programming with Pthreads. Kleiman, Shah, and Smaalders [KSS95] provide an excellent description of thread systems as well as programming using threads. Several other books have also addressed programming and system software issues related to multithreaded programming [NBF96, But97, Gal95, Lew91, RRRR96, ND96].

Many other thread APIs and systems have also been developed and are commonly used in a variety of applications. These include Java threads [Dra96, MK99, Hyd99, Lea99], Microsoft thread APIs [PG98, CWP98, Wil00, BW97], and the Solaris threads API [KSS95, Sun95]. Thread systems have a long and rich history of research dating back to the days of the HEP Denelcor [HLM84] from both the software as well as the hardware viewpoints. More recently, software systems such as Cilk [BJK+95, LRZ95], OxfordBSP [HDM97], Active Threads [Wei97], and Earth Manna [HMT+96] have been developed. Hardware support for multithreading has been explored in the Tera computer system [RS90a], MIT Alewife [ADJ+91], Horizon [KS88], simultaneous multithreading [TEL95, Tul96], multiscalar architecture [Fra93], and superthreaded architecture [TY96], among others.

The performance aspects of threads have also been explored. Early work on the performance tradeoffs of multithreaded processors was reported in [Aga89, SBCV90, Aga91, CGL92, LB95b]. Consistency models for shared memory have been extensively studied. Other areas of active research include runtime systems, compiler support, object-based extensions, performance evaluation, and software development tools. There have also been efforts aimed at supporting software shared memory across networks of workstations. All of these are only tangentially related to the issue of programming using threads.

Due to its relative youth, relatively few texts exist for programming in OpenMP [CDK+00]. The OpenMP standard and an extensive set of resources is available at http://www.openmp.org. A number of other articles (and special issues) have addressed issues relating to OpenMP performance, compilation, and interoperability [Bra97, CM98, DM98, LHZ98, Thr99].

Problems

7.1   Estimate the time taken for each of the following in Pthreads:

- Thread creation.
- Thread join.
- Successful lock.
- Successful unlock.
- Successful trylock.
- Unsuccessful trylock.

- Condition wait.

- Condition signal.

- Condition broadcast.

In each case, carefully document the method used to compute the time for each of these function calls. Also document the machine on which these observations were made.

7.2 Implement a multi-access threaded queue with multiple threads inserting and multiple threads extracting from the queue. Use mutex-locks to synchronize access to the queue. Document the time for 1000 insertions and 1000 extractions each by 64 insertion threads (producers) and 64 extraction threads (consumers).

7.3 Repeat Problem 7.2 using condition variables (in addition to mutex locks). Document the time for the same test case as above. Comment on the difference in the times.

7.4 A simple streaming media player consists of a thread monitoring a network port for arriving data, a decompressor thread for decompressing packets and generating frames in a video sequence, and a rendering thread that displays frames at programmed intervals. The three threads must communicate via shared buffers – an in-buffer between the network and decompressor, and an out-buffer between the decompressor and renderer. Implement this simple threaded framework. The network thread calls a dummy function listen_to_port to gather data from the network. For the sake of this program, this function generates a random string of bytes of desired length. The decompressor thread calls function decompress, which takes in data from the in-buffer and returns a frame of predetermined size. For this exercise, generate a frame with random bytes. Finally the render thread picks frames from the out buffer and calls the display function. This function takes a frame as an argument, and for this exercise, it does nothing. Implement this threaded framework using condition variables. Note that you can easily change the three dummy functions to make a meaningful streaming media decompressor.

7.5 Illustrate the use of recursive locks using a binary tree search algorithm. The program takes in a large list of numbers. The list is divided across multiple threads. Each thread tries to insert its elements into the tree by using a single lock associated with the tree. Show that the single lock becomes a bottleneck even for a moderate number of threads.

7.6 Improve the binary tree search program by associating a lock with each node in the tree (as opposed to a single lock with the entire tree). A thread locks a node when it reads or writes it. Examine the performance properties of this implementation.

7.7 Improve the binary tree search program further by using read-write locks. A thread read-locks a node before reading. It write-locks a node only when it needs to write into the tree node. Implement the program and document the range of program parameters where read-write locks actually yield performance improvements over regular locks.

7.8   Implement a threaded hash table in which collisions are resolved by chaining. Implement the hash table so that there is a single lock associated with a block of k hash-table entries. Threads attempting to read/write an element in a block must first lock the corresponding block. Examine the performance of your implementation as a function of k.

7.9   Change the locks to read-write locks in the hash table and use write locks only when inserting an entry into the linked list. Examine the performance of this program as a function of k. Compare the performance to that obtained using regular locks.

7.10   Write a threaded program for computing the Sieve of Eratosthenes. Think through the threading strategy carefully before implementing it. It is important to realize, for instance, that you cannot eliminate multiples of 6 from the sieve until you have eliminated multiples of 3 (at which point you would realize that you did not need to eliminate multiples of 6 in the first place). A pipelined (assembly line) strategy with the current smallest element forming the next station in the assembly line is one way to think about the problem.

7.11   Write a threaded program for solving a 15-puzzle. The program takes an initial position and keeps an open list of outstanding positions. This list is sorted on the "goodness" measure of the boards. A simple goodness measure is the Manhattan distance (i.e., the sum of x-displacement and y-displacement of every tile from where it needs to be). This open list is a work queue implemented as a heap. Each thread extracts work (a board) from the work queue, expands it to all possible successors, and inserts the successors into the work queue if it has not already been encountered. Use a hash table (from Problem 7.9) to keep track of entries that have been previously encountered. Plot the speedup of your program with the number of threads. You can compute the speedups for some reference board that is the same for various thread counts.

7.12   Modify the above program so that you now have multiple open lists (say k). Now each thread picks a random open list and tries to pick a board from the random list and expands and inserts it back into another, randomly selected list. Plot the speedup of your program with the number of threads. Compare your performance with the previous case. Make sure you use your locks and trylocks carefully to minimize serialization overheads.

7.13   Implement and test the OpenMP program for computing a matrix-matrix product in Example 7.14. Use the OMP_NUM_THREADS environment variable to control the number of threads and plot the performance with varying numbers of threads. Consider three cases in which (i) only the outermost loop is parallelized; (ii) the outer two loops are parallelized; and (iii) all three loops are parallelized. What is the observed result from these three cases?

7.14 Consider a simple loop that calls a function dummy containing a programmable delay. All invocations of the function are independent of the others. Partition this loop across four threads using static, dynamic, and guided scheduling. Use different parameters for static and guided scheduling. Document the result of this experiment as the delay within the dummy function becomes large.

7.15 Consider a sparse matrix stored in the compressed row format (you may find a description of this format on the web or any suitable text on sparse linear algebra). Write an OpenMP program for computing the product of this matrix with a vector. Download sample matrices from the Matrix Market (http://math.nist.gov/MatrixMarket/) and test the performance of your implementation as a function of matrix size and number of threads.

7.16 Implement a producer-consumer framework in OpenMP using sections to create a single producer task and a single consumer task. Ensure appropriate synchronization using locks. Test your program for a varying number of producers and consumers.

CHAPTER 8

Dense Matrix Algorithms

Algorithms involving matrices and vectors are applied in several numerical and non-numerical contexts. This chapter discusses some key algorithms for **dense** or **full matrices** that have no or few known usable zero entries. We deal specifically with square matrices for pedagogical reasons, but the algorithms in this chapter, wherever applicable, can easily be adapted for rectangular matrices as well.

Due to their regular structure, parallel computations involving matrices and vectors readily lend themselves to data-decomposition (Section 3.2.2). Depending on the computation at hand, the decomposition may be induced by partitioning the input, the output, or the intermediate data. Section 3.4.1 describes in detail the various schemes of partitioning matrices for parallel computation. The algorithms discussed in this chapter use one- and two-dimensional block, cyclic, and block-cyclic partitionings. For the sake of brevity, we will henceforth refer to one- and two-dimensional partitionings as 1-D and 2-D partitionings, respectively.

Another characteristic of most of the algorithms described in this chapter is that they use one task per process. As a result of a one-to-one mapping of tasks to processes, we do not usually refer to the tasks explicitly and decompose or partition the problem directly into processes.

8.1 Matrix-Vector Multiplication

This section addresses the problem of multiplying a dense $n \times n$ matrix A with an $n \times 1$ vector x to yield the $n \times 1$ result vector y. Algorithm 8.1 shows a serial algorithm for this problem. The sequential algorithm requires n^2 multiplications and additions. Assuming

---

```
1.      procedure MAT_VECT (A, x, y)
2.      begin
3.          for i := 0 to n − 1 do
4.          begin
5.              y[i] := 0;
6.              for j := 0 to n − 1 do
7.                  y[i] := y[i] + A[i, j] × x[j];
8.          endfor;
9.      end MAT_VECT
```

Algorithm 8.1   A serial algorithm for multiplying an $n \times n$ matrix A with an $n \times 1$ vector x to yield an $n \times 1$ product vector y.

that a multiplication and addition pair takes unit time, the sequential run time is

$$W = n^2. \tag{8.1}$$

At least three distinct parallel formulations of matrix-vector multiplication are possible, depending on whether rowwise 1-D, columnwise 1-D, or a 2-D partitioning is used.

8.1.1   Rowwise 1-D Partitioning

This section details the parallel algorithm for matrix-vector multiplication using rowwise block 1-D partitioning. The parallel algorithm for columnwise block 1-D partitioning is similar (Problem 8.2) and has a similar expression for parallel run time. Figure 8.1 describes the distribution and movement of data for matrix-vector multiplication with block 1-D partitioning.

One Row Per Process

First, consider the case in which the $n \times n$ matrix is partitioned among n processes so that each process stores one complete row of the matrix. The $n \times 1$ vector x is distributed such that each process owns one of its elements. The initial distribution of the matrix and the vector for rowwise block 1-D partitioning is shown in Figure 8.1(a). Process P_i initially owns $x[i]$ and $A[i, 0], A[i, 1], \ldots, A[i, n-1]$ and is responsible for computing $y[i]$. Vector x is multiplied with each row of the matrix (Algorithm 8.1); hence, every process needs the entire vector. Since each process starts with only one element of x, an all-to-all broadcast is required to distribute all the elements to all the processes. Figure 8.1(b) illustrates this communication step. After the vector x is distributed among the processes (Figure 8.1(c)), process P_i computes $y[i] = \sum_{j=0}^{n-1}(A[i, j] \times x[j])$ (lines 6 and 7 of Algorithm 8.1). As Figure 8.1(d) shows, the result vector y is stored exactly the way the starting vector x was stored.

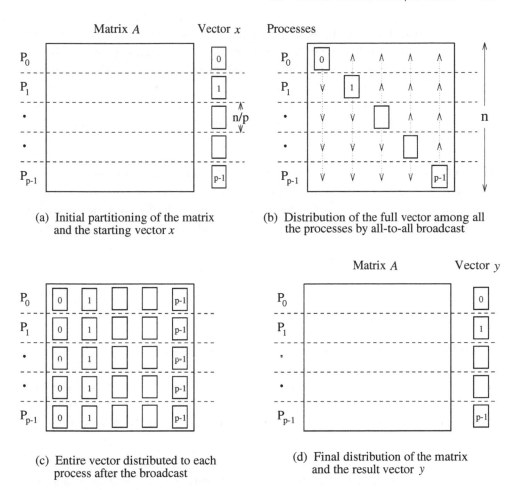

(a) Initial partitioning of the matrix
and the starting vector x

(b) Distribution of the full vector among all
the processes by all-to-all broadcast

(c) Entire vector distributed to each
process after the broadcast

(d) Final distribution of the matrix
and the result vector y

Figure 8.1   Multiplication of an $n \times n$ matrix with an $n \times 1$ vector using rowwise block 1-D partitioning. For the one-row-per-process case, $p = n$.

Parallel Run Time   Starting with one vector element per process, the all-to-all broadcast of the vector elements among n processes requires time $\Theta(n)$ on any architecture (Table 4.1). The multiplication of a single row of A with x is also performed by each process in time $\Theta(n)$. Thus, the entire procedure is completed by n processes in time $\Theta(n)$, resulting in a process-time product of $\Theta(n^2)$. The parallel algorithm is cost-optimal because the complexity of the serial algorithm is $\Theta(n^2)$.

Using Fewer than n Processes

Consider the case in which p processes are used such that $p < n$, and the matrix is partitioned among the processes by using block 1-D partitioning. Each process initially stores n/p complete rows of the matrix and a portion of the vector of size n/p. Since the vector

x must be multiplied with each row of the matrix, every process needs the entire vector (that is, all the portions belonging to separate processes). This again requires an all-to-all broadcast as shown in Figure 8.1(b) and (c). The all-to-all broadcast takes place among p processes and involves messages of size n/p. After this communication step, each process multiplies its n/p rows with the vector x to produce n/p elements of the result vector. Figure 8.1(d) shows that the result vector y is distributed in the same format as that of the starting vector x.

Parallel Run Time   According to Table 4.1, an all-to-all broadcast of messages of size n/p among p processes takes time $t_s \log p + t_w(n/p)(p-1)$. For large p, this can be approximated by $t_s \log p + t_w n$. After the communication, each process spends time n^2/p multiplying its n/p rows with the vector. Thus, the parallel run time of this procedure is

$$T_P = \frac{n^2}{p} + t_s \log p + t_w n. \tag{8.2}$$

The process-time product for this parallel formulation is $n^2 + t_s p \log p + t_w np$. The algorithm is cost-optimal for $p = O(n)$.

Scalability Analysis   We now derive the isoefficiency function for matrix-vector multiplication along the lines of the analysis in Section 5.4.2 by considering the terms of the overhead function one at a time. Consider the parallel run time given by Equation 8.2 for the hypercube architecture. The relation $T_o = pT_P - W$ gives the following expression for the overhead function of matrix-vector multiplication on a hypercube with block 1-D partitioning:

$$T_o = t_s p \log p + t_w np. \tag{8.3}$$

Recall from Chapter 5 that the central relation that determines the isoefficiency function of a parallel algorithm is $W = KT_o$ (Equation 5.14), where $K = E/(1-E)$ and E is the desired efficiency. Rewriting this relation for matrix-vector multiplication, first with only the t_s term of T_o,

$$W = Kt_s p \log p. \tag{8.4}$$

Equation 8.4 gives the isoefficiency term with respect to message startup time. Similarly, for the t_w term of the overhead function,

$$W = Kt_w np.$$

Since $W = n^2$ (Equation 8.1), we derive an expression for W in terms of p, K, and t_w (that is, the isoefficiency function due to t_w) as follows:

$$
\begin{aligned}
n^2 &= Kt_w np, \\
n &= Kt_w p, \\
n^2 &= K^2 t_w^2 p^2, \\
W &= K^2 t_w^2 p^2.
\end{aligned}
\tag{8.5}
$$

Now consider the degree of concurrency of this parallel algorithm. Using 1-D partitioning, a maximum of n processes can be used to multiply an $n \times n$ matrix with an $n \times 1$ vector. In other words, p is $O(n)$, which yields the following condition:

$$
\begin{aligned}
n &= \Omega(p), \\
n^2 &= \Omega(p^2), \\
W &= \Omega(p^2).
\end{aligned}
$$
(8.6)

The overall asymptotic isoefficiency function can be determined by comparing Equations 8.4, 8.5, and 8.6. Among the three, Equations 8.5 and 8.6 give the highest asymptotic rate at which the problem size must increase with the number of processes to maintain a fixed efficiency. This rate of $\Theta(p^2)$ is the asymptotic isoefficiency function of the parallel matrix-vector multiplication algorithm with 1-D partitioning.

8.1.2 2-D Partitioning

This section discusses parallel matrix-vector multiplication for the case in which the matrix is distributed among the processes using a block 2-D partitioning. Figure 8.2 shows the distribution of the matrix and the distribution and movement of vectors among the processes.

One Element Per Process

We start with the simple case in which an $n \times n$ matrix is partitioned among n^2 processes such that each process owns a single element. The $n \times 1$ vector x is distributed only in the last column of n processes, each of which owns one element of the vector. Since the algorithm multiplies the elements of the vector x with the corresponding elements in each row of the matrix, the vector must be distributed such that the ith element of the vector is available to the ith element of each row of the matrix. The communication steps for this are shown in Figure 8.2(a) and (b). Notice the similarity of Figure 8.2 to Figure 8.1. Before the multiplication, the elements of the matrix and the vector must be in the same relative locations as in Figure 8.1(c). However, the vector communication steps differ between various partitioning strategies. With 1-D partitioning, the elements of the vector cross only the horizontal partition-boundaries (Figure 8.1), but for 2-D partitioning, the vector elements cross both horizontal and vertical partition-boundaries (Figure 8.2).

As Figure 8.2(a) shows, the first communication step for the 2-D partitioning aligns the vector x along the principal diagonal of the matrix. Often, the vector is stored along the diagonal instead of the last column, in which case this step is not required. The second step copies the vector elements from each diagonal process to all the processes in the corresponding column. As Figure 8.2(b) shows, this step consists of n simultaneous one-to-all broadcast operations, one in each column of processes. After these two communication steps, each process multiplies its matrix element with the corresponding element of x. To

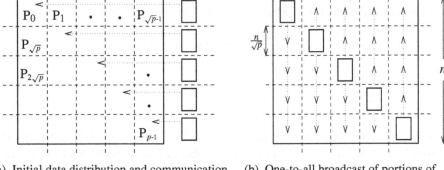

(a) Initial data distribution and communication
   steps to align the vector along the diagonal

(b) One-to-all broadcast of portions of
   the vector along process columns

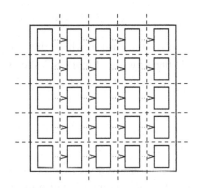

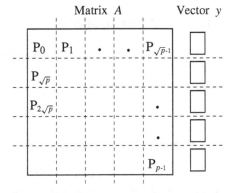

(c) All-to-one reduction of partial results

(d) Final distribution of the result vector

Figure 8.2 Matrix-vector multiplication with block 2-D partitioning. For the one-element-per-process case, $p = n^2$ if the matrix size is $n \times n$.

obtain the result vector y, the products computed for each row must be added, leaving the sums in the last column of processes. Figure 8.2(c) shows this step, which requires an all-to-one reduction (Section 4.1) in each row with the last process of the row as the destination. The parallel matrix-vector multiplication is complete after the reduction step.

Parallel Run Time Three basic communication operations are used in this algorithm: one-to-one communication to align the vector along the main diagonal, one-to-all broadcast of each vector element among the n processes of each column, and all-to-one reduction in each row. Each of these operations takes time $\Theta(\log n)$. Since each process performs a single multiplication in constant time, the overall parallel run time of this algorithm is $\Theta(n)$. The cost (process-time product) is $\Theta(n^2 \log n)$; hence, the algorithm is not cost-optimal.

Using Fewer than n^2 Processes

A cost-optimal parallel implementation of matrix-vector multiplication with block 2-D partitioning of the matrix can be obtained if the granularity of computation at each process is increased by using fewer than n^2 processes.

Consider a logical two-dimensional mesh of p processes in which each process owns an $(n/\sqrt{p}) \times (n/\sqrt{p})$ block of the matrix. The vector is distributed in portions of $n/\sqrt{p}$ elements in the last process-column only. Figure 8.2 also illustrates the initial data-mapping and the various communication steps for this case. The entire vector must be distributed on each row of processes before the multiplication can be performed. First, the vector is aligned along the main diagonal. For this, each process in the rightmost column sends its $n/\sqrt{p}$ vector elements to the diagonal process in its row. Then a columnwise one-to-all broadcast of these $n/\sqrt{p}$ elements takes place. Each process then performs n^2/p multiplications and locally adds the $n/\sqrt{p}$ sets of products. At the end of this step, as shown in Figure 8.2(c), each process has $n/\sqrt{p}$ partial sums that must be accumulated along each row to obtain the result vector. Hence, the last step of the algorithm is an all-to-one reduction of the $n/\sqrt{p}$ values in each row, with the rightmost process of the row as the destination.

Parallel Run Time   The first step of sending a message of size $n/\sqrt{p}$ from the rightmost process of a row to the diagonal process (Figure 8.2(a)) takes time $t_s + t_w n/\sqrt{p}$. We can perform the columnwise one-to-all broadcast in at most time $(t_s + t_w n/\sqrt{p}) \log(\sqrt{p})$ by using the procedure described in Section 4.1.3. Ignoring the time to perform additions, the final rowwise all-to-one reduction also takes the same amount of time. Assuming that a multiplication and addition pair takes unit time, each process spends approximately n^2/p time in computation. Thus, the parallel run time for this procedure is as follows:

$$
T_P = \overbrace{n^2/p}^{\text{computation}} + \overbrace{t_s + t_w n/\sqrt{p}}^{\text{aligning the vector}} + \underbrace{(t_s + t_w n/\sqrt{p}) \log(\sqrt{p})}_{\text{columnwise one-to-all broadcast}} + \overbrace{(t_s + t_w n/\sqrt{p}) \log(\sqrt{p})}^{\text{all-to-one reduction}}
$$

$$
\approx \frac{n^2}{p} + t_s \log p + t_w \frac{n}{\sqrt{p}} \log p \tag{8.7}
$$

Scalability Analysis   By using Equations 8.1 and 8.7, and applying the relation $T_o = pT_p - W$ (Equation 5.1), we get the following expression for the overhead function of this parallel algorithm:

$$
T_o = t_s p \log p + t_w n \sqrt{p} \log p. \tag{8.8}
$$

We now perform an approximate isoefficiency analysis along the lines of Section 5.4.2 by considering the terms of the overhead function one at a time (see Problem 8.4 for a more precise isoefficiency analysis). For the t_s term of the overhead function, Equation 5.14 yields

$$W = Kt_s p \log p. \tag{8.9}$$

Equation 8.9 gives the isoefficiency term with respect to the message startup time. We can obtain the isoefficiency function due to t_w by balancing the term $t_w n \sqrt{p} \log p$ with the problem size n^2. Using the isoefficiency relation of Equation 5.14, we get the following:

$$
\begin{aligned}
W = n^2 &= K t_w n \sqrt{p} \log p, \\
n &= K t_w \sqrt{p} \log p, \\
n^2 &= K^2 t_w^2 p \log^2 p, \\
W &= K^2 t_w^2 p \log^2 p.
\end{aligned}
\tag{8.10}
$$

Finally, considering that the degree of concurrency of 2-D partitioning is n^2 (that is, a maximum of n^2 processes can be used), we arrive at the following relation:

$$
\begin{aligned}
p &= O(n^2), \\
n^2 &= \Omega(p), \\
W &= \Omega(p).
\end{aligned}
\tag{8.11}
$$

Among Equations 8.9, 8.10, and 8.11, the one with the largest right-hand side expression determines the overall isoefficiency function of this parallel algorithm. To simplify the analysis, we ignore the impact of the constants and consider only the asymptotic rate of the growth of problem size that is necessary to maintain constant efficiency. The asymptotic isoefficiency term due to t_w (Equation 8.10) clearly dominates the ones due to t_s (Equation 8.9) and due to concurrency (Equation 8.11). Therefore, the overall asymptotic isoefficiency function is given by $\Theta(p \log^2 p)$.

The isoefficiency function also determines the criterion for cost-optimality (Section 5.4.3). With an isoefficiency function of $\Theta(p \log^2 p)$, the maximum number of processes that can be used cost-optimally for a given problem size W is determined by the following relations:

$$
\begin{aligned}
p \log^2 p &= O(n^2), \\
\log p + 2 \log \log p &= O(\log n).
\end{aligned}
\tag{8.12}
$$

Ignoring the lower-order terms,

$$\log p = O(\log n).$$

Substituting $\log n$ for $\log p$ in Equation 8.12,

$$
\begin{aligned}
p \log^2 n &= O(n^2), \\
p &= O\left(\frac{n^2}{\log^2 n}\right).
\end{aligned}
\tag{8.13}
$$

The right-hand side of Equation 8.13 gives an asymptotic upper bound on the number of processes that can be used cost-optimally for an $n \times n$ matrix-vector multiplication with a 2-D partitioning of the matrix.

Comparison of 1-D and 2-D Partitionings

A comparison of Equations 8.2 and 8.7 shows that matrix-vector multiplication is faster with block 2-D partitioning of the matrix than with block 1-D partitioning for the same number of processes. If the number of processes is greater than n, then the 1-D partitioning cannot be used. However, even if the number of processes is less than or equal to n, the analysis in this section suggests that 2-D partitioning is preferable.

Among the two partitioning schemes, 2-D partitioning has a better (smaller) asymptotic isoefficiency function. Thus, matrix-vector multiplication is more scalable with 2-D partitioning; that is, it can deliver the same efficiency on more processes with 2-D partitioning than with 1-D partitioning.

8.2 Matrix-Matrix Multiplication

This section discusses parallel algorithms for multiplying two $n \times n$ dense, square matrices A and B to yield the product matrix $C = A \times B$. All parallel matrix multiplication algorithms in this chapter are based on the conventional serial algorithm shown in Algorithm 8.2. If we assume that an addition and multiplication pair (line 8) takes unit time, then the sequential run time of this algorithm is n^3. Matrix multiplication algorithms with better asymptotic sequential complexities are available, for example Strassen's algorithm. However, for the sake of simplicity, in this book we assume that the conventional algorithm is the best available serial algorithm. Problem 8.5 explores the performance of parallel matrix multiplication regarding Strassen's method as the base algorithm.

```
1.     procedure MAT_MULT (A, B, C)
2.     begin
3.        for i := 0 to n − 1 do
4.           for j := 0 to n − 1 do
5.              begin
6.                 C[i, j] := 0;
7.                 for k := 0 to n − 1 do
8.                    C[i, j] := C[i, j] + A[i, k] × B[k, j];
9.              endfor;
10.    end MAT_MULT
```

Algorithm 8.2 The conventional serial algorithm for multiplication of two $n \times n$ matrices.

```
1.    procedure BLOCK_MAT_MULT (A, B, C)
2.    begin
3.       for i := 0 to q − 1 do
4.          for j := 0 to q − 1 do
5.             begin
6.                Initialize all elements of C_{i,j} to zero;
7.                for k := 0 to q − 1 do
8.                   C_{i,j} := C_{i,j} + A_{i,k} × B_{k,j};
9.             endfor;
10.   end BLOCK_MAT_MULT
```

Algorithm 8.3   The block matrix multiplication algorithm for $n \times n$ matrices with a block size of $(n/q) \times (n/q)$.

A concept that is useful in matrix multiplication as well as in a variety of other matrix algorithms is that of block matrix operations. We can often express a matrix computation involving scalar algebraic operations on all its elements in terms of identical matrix algebraic operations on blocks or submatrices of the original matrix. Such algebraic operations on the submatrices are called **block matrix operations**. For example, an $n \times n$ matrix A can be regarded as a $q \times q$ array of blocks $A_{i,j}$ $(0 \leq i, j < q)$ such that each block is an $(n/q) \times (n/q)$ submatrix. The matrix multiplication algorithm in Algorithm 8.2 can then be rewritten as Algorithm 8.3, in which the multiplication and addition operations on line 8 are matrix multiplication and matrix addition, respectively. Not only are the final results of Algorithm 8.2 and 8.3 identical, but so are the total numbers of scalar additions and multiplications performed by each. Algorithm 8.2 performs n^3 additions and multiplications, and Algorithm 8.3 performs q^3 matrix multiplications, each involving $(n/q) \times (n/q)$ matrices and requiring $(n/q)^3$ additions and multiplications. We can use p processes to implement the block version of matrix multiplication in parallel by choosing $q = \sqrt{p}$ and computing a distinct $C_{i,j}$ block at each process.

In the following sections, we describe a few ways of parallelizing Algorithm 8.3. Each of the following parallel matrix multiplication algorithms uses a block 2-D partitioning of the matrices.

8.2.1   A Simple Parallel Algorithm

Consider two $n \times n$ matrices A and B partitioned into p blocks $A_{i,j}$ and $B_{i,j}$ $(0 \leq i, j < \sqrt{p})$ of size $(n/\sqrt{p}) \times (n/\sqrt{p})$ each. These blocks are mapped onto a $\sqrt{p} \times \sqrt{p}$ logical mesh of processes. The processes are labeled from $P_{0,0}$ to $P_{\sqrt{p}-1,\sqrt{p}-1}$. Process $P_{i,j}$ initially stores $A_{i,j}$ and $B_{i,j}$ and computes block $C_{i,j}$ of the result matrix. Computing submatrix $C_{i,j}$ requires all submatrices $A_{i,k}$ and $B_{k,j}$ for $0 \leq k < \sqrt{p}$. To acquire all the required blocks, an all-to-all broadcast of matrix A's blocks is performed in each row of processes, and an all-to-all broadcast of matrix B's blocks is performed in each column.

After $P_{i,j}$ acquires $A_{i,0}, A_{i,1}, \ldots, A_{i,\sqrt{p}-1}$ and $B_{0,j}, B_{1,j}, \ldots, B_{\sqrt{p}-1,j}$, it performs the submatrix multiplication and addition step of lines 7 and 8 in Algorithm 8.3.

Performance and Scalability Analysis   The algorithm requires two all-to-all broadcast steps (each consisting of $\sqrt{p}$ concurrent broadcasts in all rows and columns of the process mesh) among groups of $\sqrt{p}$ processes. The messages consist of submatrices of n^2/p elements. From Table 4.1, the total communication time is $2(t_s \log(\sqrt{p}) + t_w(n^2/p)(\sqrt{p} - 1))$. After the communication step, each process computes a submatrix $C_{i,j}$, which requires $\sqrt{p}$ multiplications of $(n/\sqrt{p}) \times (n/\sqrt{p})$ submatrices (lines 7 and 8 of Algorithm 8.3 with $q = \sqrt{p}$). This takes a total of time $\sqrt{p} \times (n/\sqrt{p})^3 = n^3/p$. Thus, the parallel run time is approximately

$$T_P = \frac{n^3}{p} + t_s \log p + 2t_w \frac{n^2}{\sqrt{p}}. \tag{8.14}$$

The process-time product is $n^3 + t_s p \log p + 2t_w n^2 \sqrt{p}$, and the parallel algorithm is cost-optimal for $p = O(n^2)$.

The isoefficiency functions due to t_s and t_w are $t_s p \log p$ and $8(t_w)^3 p^{3/2}$, respectively. Hence, the overall isoefficiency function due to the communication overhead is $\Theta(p^{3/2})$. This algorithm can use a maximum of n^2 processes; hence, $p \leq n^2$ or $n^3 \geq p^{3/2}$. Therefore, the isoefficiency function due to concurrency is also $\Theta(p^{3/2})$.

A notable drawback of this algorithm is its excessive memory requirements. At the end of the communication phase, each process has $\sqrt{p}$ blocks of both matrices A and B. Since each block requires $\Theta(n^2/p)$ memory, each process requires $\Theta(n^2/\sqrt{p})$ memory. The total memory requirement over all the processes is $\Theta(n^2\sqrt{p})$, which is $\sqrt{p}$ times the memory requirement of the sequential algorithm.

8.2.2   Cannon's Algorithm

Cannon's algorithm is a memory-efficient version of the simple algorithm presented in Section 8.2.1. To study this algorithm, we again partition matrices A and B into p square blocks. We label the processes from $P_{0,0}$ to $P_{\sqrt{p}-1,\sqrt{p}-1}$, and initially assign submatrices $A_{i,j}$ and $B_{i,j}$ to process $P_{i,j}$. Although every process in the ith row requires all $\sqrt{p}$ submatrices $A_{i,k}$ ($0 \leq k < \sqrt{p}$), it is possible to schedule the computations of the $\sqrt{p}$ processes of the ith row such that, at any given time, each process is using a different $A_{i,k}$. These blocks can be systematically rotated among the processes after every submatrix multiplication so that every process gets a fresh $A_{i,k}$ after each rotation. If an identical schedule is applied to the columns, then no process holds more than one block of each matrix at any time, and the total memory requirement of the algorithm over all the processes is $\Theta(n^2)$. Cannon's algorithm is based on this idea. The scheduling for the multiplication of submatrices on separate processes in Cannon's algorithm is illustrated in Figure 8.3 for 16 processes.

The first communication step of the algorithm aligns the blocks of A and B in such a way that each process multiplies its local submatrices. As Figure 8.3(a) shows, this align-

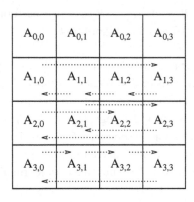

(a) Initial alignment of A

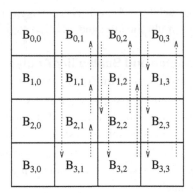

(b) Initial alignment of B

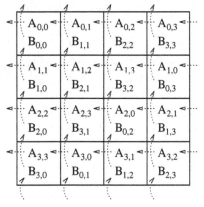

(c) A and B after initial alignment

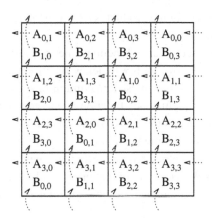

(d) Submatrix locations after first shift

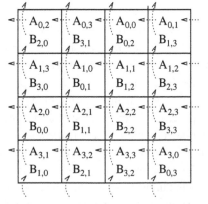

(e) Submatrix locations after second shift   (f) Submatrix locations after third shift

Figure 8.3   The communication steps in Cannon's algorithm on 16 processes.

ment is achieved for matrix A by shifting all submatrices $A_{i,j}$ to the left (with wraparound) by i steps. Similarly, as shown in Figure 8.3(b), all submatrices $B_{i,j}$ are shifted up (with wraparound) by j steps. These are circular shift operations (Section 4.6) in each row and column of processes, which leave process $P_{i,j}$ with submatrices $A_{i,(j+i)\bmod\sqrt{p}}$ and $B_{(i+j)\bmod\sqrt{p},j}$. Figure 8.3(c) shows the blocks of A and B after the initial alignment, when each process is ready for the first submatrix multiplication. After a submatrix multiplication step, each block of A moves one step left and each block of B moves one step up (again with wraparound), as shown in Figure 8.3(d). A sequence of $\sqrt{p}$ such submatrix multiplications and single-step shifts pairs up each $A_{i,k}$ and $B_{k,j}$ for k ($0 \le k < \sqrt{p}$) at $P_{i,j}$. This completes the multiplication of matrices A and B.

Performance Analysis The initial alignment of the two matrices (Figure 8.3(a) and (b)) involves a rowwise and a columnwise circular shift. In any of these shifts, the maximum distance over which a block shifts is $\sqrt{p} - 1$. The two shift operations require a total of time $2(t_s + t_w n^2/p)$ (Table 4.1). Each of the $\sqrt{p}$ single-step shifts in the compute-and-shift phase of the algorithm takes time $t_s + t_w n^2/p$. Thus, the total communication time (for both matrices) during this phase of the algorithm is $2(t_s + t_w n^2/p)\sqrt{p}$. For large enough p on a network with sufficient bandwidth, the communication time for the initial alignment can be disregarded in comparison with the time spent in communication during the compute-and-shift phase.

Each process performs $\sqrt{p}$ multiplications of $(n/\sqrt{p}) \times (n/\sqrt{p})$ submatrices. Assuming that a multiplication and addition pair takes unit time, the total time that each process spends in computation is n^3/p. Thus, the approximate overall parallel run time of this algorithm is

$$T_P = \frac{n^3}{p} + 2\sqrt{p}t_s + 2t_w \frac{n^2}{\sqrt{p}}. \tag{8.15}$$

The cost-optimality condition for Cannon's algorithm is identical to that for the simple algorithm presented in Section 8.2.1. As in the simple algorithm, the isoefficiency function of Cannon's algorithm is $\Theta(p^{3/2})$.

8.2.3 The DNS Algorithm

The matrix multiplication algorithms presented so far use block 2-D partitioning of the input and the output matrices and use a maximum of n^2 processes for $n \times n$ matrices. As a result, these algorithms have a parallel run time of $\Omega(n)$ because there are $\Theta(n^3)$ operations in the serial algorithm. We now present a parallel algorithm based on partitioning intermediate data that can use up to n^3 processes and that performs matrix multiplication in time $\Theta(\log n)$ by using $\Omega(n^3/\log n)$ processes. This algorithm is known as the DNS algorithm because it is due to Dekel, Nassimi, and Sahni.

We first introduce the basic idea, without concern for inter-process communication. Assume that n^3 processes are available for multiplying two $n \times n$ matrices. These processes are arranged in a three-dimensional $n \times n \times n$ logical array. Since the matrix multiplication

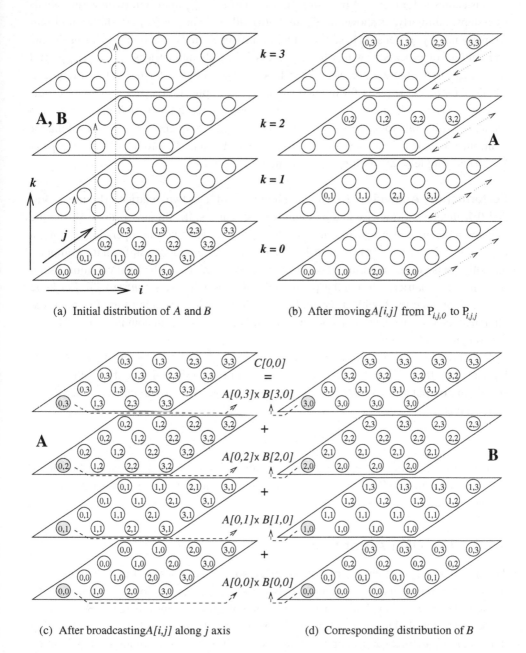

(a) Initial distribution of A and B (b) After moving $A[i,j]$ from $P_{i,j,0}$ to $P_{i,j,j}$

(c) After broadcasting $A[i,j]$ along j axis   (d) Corresponding distribution of B

Figure 8.4   The communication steps in the DNS algorithm while multiplying 4×4 matrices A and B on 64 processes. The shaded processes in part (c) store elements of the first row of A and the shaded processes in part (d) store elements of the first column of B.

algorithm performs n^3 scalar multiplications, each of the n^3 processes is assigned a single scalar multiplication. The processes are labeled according to their location in the array, and the multiplication $A[i, k] \times B[k, j]$ is assigned to process $P_{i,j,k}$ $(0 \le i, j, k < n)$. After each process performs a single multiplication, the contents of $P_{i,j,0}$, $P_{i,j,1}$, ..., $P_{i,j,n-1}$ are added to obtain $C[i, j]$. The additions for all $C[i, j]$ can be carried out simultaneously in $\log n$ steps each. Thus, it takes one step to multiply and $\log n$ steps to add; that is, it takes time $\Theta(\log n)$ to multiply the $n \times n$ matrices by this algorithm.

We now describe a practical parallel implementation of matrix multiplication based on this idea. As Figure 8.4 shows, the process arrangement can be visualized as n planes of $n \times n$ processes each. Each plane corresponds to a different value of k. Initially, as shown in Figure 8.4(a), the matrices are distributed among the n^2 processes of the plane corresponding to $k = 0$ at the base of the three-dimensional process array. Process $P_{i,j,0}$ initially owns $A[i, j]$ and $B[i, j]$.

The vertical column of processes $P_{i,j,*}$ computes the dot product of row $A[i, *]$ and column $B[*, j]$. Therefore, rows of A and columns of B need to be moved appropriately so that each vertical column of processes $P_{i,j,*}$ has row $A[i, *]$ and column $B[*, j]$. More precisely, process $P_{i,j,k}$ should have $A[i, k]$ and $B[k, j]$.

The communication pattern for distributing the elements of matrix A among the processes is shown in Figure 8.4(a)–(c). First, each column of A moves to a different plane such that the jth column occupies the same position in the plane corresponding to $k = j$ as it initially did in the plane corresponding to $k = 0$. The distribution of A after moving $A[i, j]$ from $P_{i,j,0}$ to $P_{i,j,j}$ is shown in Figure 8.4(b). Now all the columns of A are replicated n times in their respective planes by a parallel one-to-all broadcast along the j axis. The result of this step is shown in Figure 8.4(c), in which the n processes $P_{i,0,j}$, $P_{i,1,j}$, ..., $P_{i,n-1,j}$ receive a copy of $A[i, j]$ from $P_{i,j,j}$. At this point, each vertical column of processes $P_{i,j,*}$ has row $A[i, *]$. More precisely, process $P_{i,j,k}$ has $A[i, k]$.

For matrix B, the communication steps are similar, but the roles of i and j in process subscripts are switched. In the first one-to-one communication step, $B[i, j]$ is moved from $P_{i,j,0}$ to $P_{i,j,i}$. Then it is broadcast from $P_{i,j,i}$ among $P_{0,j,i}$, $P_{1,j,i}$, ..., $P_{n-1,j,i}$. The distribution of B after this one-to-all broadcast along the i axis is shown in Figure 8.4(d). At this point, each vertical column of processes $P_{i,j,*}$ has column $B[*, j]$. Now process $P_{i,j,k}$ has $B[k, j]$, in addition to $A[i, k]$.

After these communication steps, $A[i, k]$ and $B[k, j]$ are multiplied at $P_{i,j,k}$. Now each element $C[i, j]$ of the product matrix is obtained by an all-to-one reduction along the k axis. During this step, process $P_{i,j,0}$ accumulates the results of the multiplication from processes $P_{i,j,1}$, ..., $P_{i,j,n-1}$. Figure 8.4 shows this step for $C[0, 0]$.

The DNS algorithm has three main communication steps: (1) moving the columns of A and the rows of B to their respective planes, (2) performing one-to-all broadcast along the j axis for A and along the i axis for B, and (3) all-to-one reduction along the k axis. All these operations are performed within groups of n processes and take time $\Theta(\log n)$. Thus, the parallel run time for multiplying two $n \times n$ matrices using the DNS algorithm on n^3 processes is $\Theta(\log n)$.

DNS Algorithm with Fewer than n^3 Processes

The DNS algorithm is not cost-optimal for n^3 processes, since its process-time product of $\Theta(n^3 \log n)$ exceeds the $\Theta(n^3)$ sequential complexity of matrix multiplication. We now present a cost-optimal version of this algorithm that uses fewer than n^3 processes. Another variant of the DNS algorithm that uses fewer than n^3 processes is described in Problem 8.6.

Assume that the number of processes p is equal to q^3 for some $q < n$. To implement the DNS algorithm, the two matrices are partitioned into blocks of size $(n/q) \times (n/q)$. Each matrix can thus be regarded as a $q \times q$ two-dimensional square array of blocks. The implementation of this algorithm on q^3 processes is very similar to that on n^3 processes. The only difference is that now we operate on blocks rather than on individual elements. Since $1 \leq q \leq n$, the number of processes can vary between 1 and n^3.

Performance Analysis   The first one-to-one communication step is performed for both A and B, and takes time $t_s + t_w(n/q)^2$ for each matrix. The second step of one-to-all broadcast is also performed for both matrices and takes time $t_s \log q + t_w(n/q)^2 \log q$ for each matrix. The final all-to-one reduction is performed only once (for matrix C) and takes time $t_s \log q + t_w(n/q)^2 \log q$. The multiplication of $(n/q) \times (n/q)$ submatrices by each process takes time $(n/q)^3$. We can ignore the communication time for the first one-to-one communication step because it is much smaller than the communication time of one-to-all broadcasts and all-to-one reduction. We can also ignore the computation time for addition in the final reduction phase because it is of a smaller order of magnitude than the computation time for multiplying the submatrices. With these assumptions, we get the following approximate expression for the parallel run time of the DNS algorithm:

$$
T_P \approx \left(\frac{n}{q}\right)^3 + 3t_s \log q + 3t_w \left(\frac{n}{q}\right)^2 \log q
$$

Since $q = p^{1/3}$, we get

$$
T_P = \frac{n^3}{p} + t_s \log p + t_w \frac{n^2}{p^{2/3}} \log p. \tag{8.16}
$$

The total cost of this parallel algorithm is $n^3 + t_s p \log p + t_w n^2 p^{1/3} \log p$. The isoefficiency function is $\Theta(p(\log p)^3)$. The algorithm is cost-optimal for $n^3 = \Omega(p(\log p)^3)$, or $p = O(n^3/(\log n)^3)$.

8.3   Solving a System of Linear Equations

This section discusses the problem of solving a system of linear equations of the form

$$
\begin{array}{lllll}
a_{0,0}x_0 & + & a_{0,1}x_1 & + & \cdots + a_{0,n-1}x_{n-1} & = & b_0, \\
a_{1,0}x_0 & + & a_{1,1}x_1 & + & \cdots + a_{1,n-1}x_{n-1} & = & b_1,
\end{array}
$$

$$\vdots \qquad \vdots \qquad\qquad \vdots \qquad \vdots$$

$$a_{n-1,0}x_0 \quad + \quad a_{n-1,1}x_1 \quad + \quad \cdots \quad + \quad a_{n-1,n-1}x_{n-1} = \quad b_{n-1}.$$

In matrix notation, this system is written as $Ax = b$. Here A is a dense $n \times n$ matrix of coefficients such that $A[i, j] = a_{i,j}$, b is an $n \times 1$ vector $[b_0, b_1, \dots, b_{n-1}]^T$, and x is the desired solution vector $[x_0, x_1, \dots, x_{n-1}]^T$. We will make all subsequent references to $a_{i,j}$ by $A[i, j]$ and x_i by $x[i]$.

A system of equations $Ax = b$ is usually solved in two stages. First, through a series of algebraic manipulations, the original system of equations is reduced to an upper-triangular system of the form

$$x_0 \; + \; u_{0,1}x_1 \; + \; u_{0,2}x_2 \; + \quad \cdots \quad + \; u_{0,n-1}x_{n-1} \; = \; y_0,$$
$$x_1 \; + \; u_{1,2}x_2 \; + \quad \cdots \quad + \; u_{1,n-1}x_{n-1} \; = \; y_1,$$
$$\vdots \qquad\qquad \vdots$$
$$x_{n-1} \; = \; y_{n-1}.$$

We write this as $Ux = y$, where U is a unit upper-triangular matrix – one in which all subdiagonal entries are zero and all principal diagonal entries are equal to one. Formally, $U[i, j] = 0$ if $i > j$, otherwise $U[i, j] = u_{i,j}$. Furthermore, $U[i, i] = 1$ for $0 \le i < n$. In the second stage of solving a system of linear equations, the upper-triangular system is solved for the variables in reverse order from $x[n - 1]$ to $x[0]$ by a procedure known as **back-substitution** (Section 8.3.3).

We discuss parallel formulations of the classical Gaussian elimination method for upper-triangularization in Sections 8.3.1 and 8.3.2. In Section 8.3.1, we describe a straightforward Gaussian elimination algorithm assuming that the coefficient matrix is nonsingular, and its rows and columns are permuted in a way that the algorithm is numerically stable. Section 8.3.2 discusses the case in which a numerically stable solution of the system of equations requires permuting the columns of the matrix during the execution of the Gaussian elimination algorithm.

Although we discuss Gaussian elimination in the context of upper-triangularization, a similar procedure can be used to factorize matrix A as the product of a lower-triangular matrix L and a unit upper-triangular matrix U so that $A = L \times U$. This factorization is commonly referred to as **LU factorization**. Performing LU factorization (rather than upper-triangularization) is particularly useful if multiple systems of equations with the same left-hand side Ax need to be solved. Algorithm 3.3 gives a procedure for column-oriented LU factorization.

8.3.1 A Simple Gaussian Elimination Algorithm

The serial Gaussian elimination algorithm has three nested loops. Several variations of the algorithm exist, depending on the order in which the loops are arranged. Algorithm 8.4

```
1.    procedure GAUSSIAN_ELIMINATION (A, b, y)
2.    begin
3.        for k := 0 to n − 1 do              /* Outer loop */
4.        begin
5.            for j := k + 1 to n − 1 do
6.                A[k, j] := A[k, j]/A[k, k];   /* Division step */
7.                y[k] := b[k]/A[k, k];
8.                A[k, k] := 1;
9.                for i := k + 1 to n − 1 do
10.               begin
11.                   for j := k + 1 to n − 1 do
12.                       A[i, j] := A[i, j] − A[i, k] × A[k, j]; /* Elimination step */
13.                       b[i] := b[i] − A[i, k] × y[k];
14.                       A[i, k] := 0;
15.               endfor;              /* Line 9 */
16.           endfor;                  /* Line 3 */
17.   end GAUSSIAN_ELIMINATION
```

Algorithm 8.4   A serial Gaussian elimination algorithm that converts the system of linear equations $Ax = b$ to a unit upper-triangular system $Ux = y$. The matrix U occupies the upper-triangular locations of A. This algorithm assumes that $A[k, k] \neq 0$ when it is used as a divisor on lines 6 and 7.

shows one variation of Gaussian elimination, which we will adopt for parallel implementation in the remainder of this section. This program converts a system of linear equations $Ax = b$ to a unit upper-triangular system $Ux = y$. We assume that the matrix U shares storage with A and overwrites the upper-triangular portion of A. The element $A[k, j]$ computed on line 6 of Algorithm 8.4 is actually $U[k, j]$. Similarly, the element $A[k, k]$ equated to 1 on line 8 is $U[k, k]$. Algorithm 8.4 assumes that $A[k, k] \neq 0$ when it is used as a divisor on lines 6 and 7.

In this section, we will concentrate only on the operations on matrix A in Algorithm 8.4. The operations on vector b on lines 7 and 13 of the program are straightforward to implement. Hence, in the rest of the section, we will ignore these steps. If the steps on lines 7, 8, 13, and 14 are not performed, then Algorithm 8.4 leads to the LU factorization of A as a product $L \times U$. After the termination of the procedure, L is stored in the lower-triangular part of A, and U occupies the locations above the principal diagonal.

For k varying from 0 to $n − 1$, the Gaussian elimination procedure systematically eliminates variable $x[k]$ from equations $k + 1$ to $n − 1$ so that the matrix of coefficients becomes upper-triangular. As shown in Algorithm 8.4, in the kth iteration of the outer loop (starting on line 3), an appropriate multiple of the kth equation is subtracted from each of the equations $k + 1$ to $n − 1$ (loop starting on line 9). The multiples of the kth equation (or the kth row of matrix A) are chosen such that the kth coefficient becomes zero in equations $k + 1$

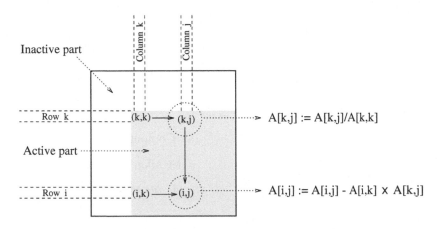

Figure 8.5   A typical computation in Gaussian elimination.

to $n - 1$ eliminating $x[k]$ from these equations. A typical computation of the Gaussian elimination procedure in the kth iteration of the outer loop is shown in Figure 8.5. The kth iteration of the outer loop does not involve any computation on rows 1 to $k - 1$ or columns 1 to $k - 1$. Thus, at this stage, only the lower-right $(n - k) \times (n - k)$ submatrix of A (the shaded portion in Figure 8.5) is computationally active.

Gaussian elimination involves approximately $n^2/2$ divisions (line 6) and approximately $(n^3/3) - (n^2/2)$ subtractions and multiplications (line 12). In this section, we assume that each scalar arithmetic operation takes unit time. With this assumption, the sequential run time of the procedure is approximately $2n^3/3$ (for large n); that is,

$$W = \frac{2}{3}n^3. \tag{8.17}$$

Parallel Implementation with 1-D Partitioning

We now consider a parallel implementation of Algorithm 8.4, in which the coefficient matrix is rowwise 1-D partitioned among the processes. A parallel implementation of this algorithm with columnwise 1-D partitioning is very similar, and its details can be worked out based on the implementation using rowwise 1-D partitioning (Problems 8.8 and 8.9).

We first consider the case in which one row is assigned to each process, and the $n \times n$ coefficient matrix A is partitioned along the rows among n processes labeled from P_0 to P_{n-1}. In this mapping, process P_i initially stores elements $A[i, j]$ for $0 \leq j < n$. Figure 8.6 illustrates this mapping of the matrix onto the processes for $n = 8$. The figure also illustrates the computation and communication that take place in the iteration of the outer loop when $k = 3$.

Algorithm 8.4 and Figure 8.5 show that $A[k, k + 1], A[k, k + 2], \ldots, A[k, n - 1]$ are divided by $A[k, k]$ (line 6) at the beginning of the kth iteration. All matrix elements participating in this operation (shown by the shaded portion of the matrix in Figure 8.6(a))

P_0	1	(0,1)	(0,2)	(0,3)	(0,4)	(0,5)	(0,6)	(0,7)
P_1	0	1	(1,2)	(1,3)	(1,4)	(1,5)	(1,6)	(1,7)
P_2	0	0	1	(2,3)	(2,4)	(2,5)	(2,6)	(2,7)
P_3	0	0	0	(3,3)	(3,4)	(3,5)	(3,6)	(3,7)
P_4	0	0	0	(4,3)	(4,4)	(4,5)	(4,6)	(4,7)
P_5	0	0	0	(5,3)	(5,4)	(5,5)	(5,6)	(5,7)
P_6	0	0	0	(6,3)	(6,4)	(6,5)	(6,6)	(6,7)
P_7	0	0	0	(7,3)	(7,4)	(7,5)	(7,6)	(7,7)

(a) Computation:

(i) $A[k,j] := A[k,j]/A[k,k]$ for $k < j <$

(ii) $A[k,k] := 1$

P_0	1	(0,1)	(0,2)	(0,3)	(0,4)	(0,5)	(0,6)	(0,7)
P_1	0	1	(1,2)	(1,3)	(1,4)	(1,5)	(1,6)	(1,7)
P_2	0	0	1	(2,3)	(2,4)	(2,5)	(2,6)	(2,7)
P_3	0	0	0	1	(3,4)	(3,5)	(3,6)	(3,7)
P_4	0	0	0	(4,3)	(4,4)	(4,5)	(4,6)	(4,7)
P_5	0	0	0	(5,3)	(5,4)	(5,5)	(5,6)	(5,7)
P_6	0	0	0	(6,3)	(6,4)	(6,5)	(6,6)	(6,7)
P_7	0	0	0	(7,3)	(7,4)	(7,5)	(7,6)	(7,7)

(b) Communication:

One–to–all broadcast of row $A[k,*]$

P_0	1	(0,1)	(0,2)	(0,3)	(0,4)	(0,5)	(0,6)	(0,7)
P_1	0	1	(1,2)	(1,3)	(1,4)	(1,5)	(1,6)	(1,7)
P_2	0	0	1	(2,3)	(2,4)	(2,5)	(2,6)	(2,7)
P_3	0	0	0	1	(3,4)	(3,5)	(3,6)	(3,7)
P_4	0	0	0	(4,3)	(4,4)	(4,5)	(4,6)	(4,7)
P_5	0	0	0	(5,3)	(5,4)	(5,5)	(5,6)	(5,7)
P_6	0	0	0	(6,3)	(6,4)	(6,5)	(6,6)	(6,7)
P_7	0	0	0	(7,3)	(7,4)	(7,5)	(7,6)	(7,7)

(c) Computation:

(i) $A[i,j] := A[i,j] - A[i,k] \times A[k,j]$
   for $k < i < n$ and $k < j < n$

(ii) $A[i,k] := 0$ for $k < i < n$

Figure 8.6 Gaussian elimination steps during the iteration corresponding to $k = 3$ for an 8×8 matrix partitioned rowwise among eight processes.

belong to the same process. So this step does not require any communication. In the second computation step of the algorithm (the elimination step of line 12), the modified (after division) elements of the kth row are used by all other rows of the active part of the matrix. As Figure 8.6(b) shows, this requires a one-to-all broadcast of the active part of the kth row to the processes storing rows $k + 1$ to $n - 1$. Finally, the computation $A[i, j] := A[i, j] - A[i, k] \times A[k, j]$ takes place in the remaining active portion of the matrix, which is shown shaded in Figure 8.6(c).

The computation step corresponding to Figure 8.6(a) in the kth iteration requires $n - k - 1$ divisions at process P_k. Similarly, the computation step of Figure 8.6(c) involves $n - k - 1$ multiplications and subtractions in the kth iteration at all processes P_i, such that $k < i < n$. Assuming a single arithmetic operation takes unit time, the total time spent in computation in the kth iteration is $3(n - k - 1)$. Note that when P_k is performing the divisions, the remaining $p - 1$ processes are idle, and while processes $P_{k+1}, \ldots, P_{n-1}$ are performing the elimination step, processes $P_0, \ldots, P_k$ are idle. Thus, the total time spent during the computation steps shown in Figures 8.6(a) and (c) in this parallel implementation of Gaussian elimination is $3\Sigma_{k=0}^{n-1}(n - k - 1)$, which is equal to $3n(n - 1)/2$.

The communication step of Figure 8.6(b) takes time $(t_s + t_w(n-k-1)) \log n$ (Table 4.1). Hence, the total communication time over all iterations is $\Sigma_{k=0}^{n-1}(t_s + t_w(n - k - 1)) \log n$, which is equal to $t_s n \log n + t_w(n(n - 1)/2) \log n$. The overall parallel run time of this algorithm is

$$T_P = \frac{3}{2}n(n - 1) + t_s n \log n + \frac{1}{2}t_w n(n - 1) \log n. \tag{8.18}$$

Since the number of processes is n, the cost, or the process-time product, is $\Theta(n^3 \log n)$ due to the term associated with t_w in Equation 8.18. This cost is asymptotically higher than the sequential run time of this algorithm (Equation 8.17). Hence, this parallel implementation is not cost-optimal.

Pipelined Communication and Computation   We now present a parallel implementation of Gaussian elimination that is cost-optimal on n processes.

In the parallel Gaussian elimination algorithm just presented, the n iterations of the outer loop of Algorithm 8.4 execute sequentially. At any given time, all processes work on the same iteration. The $(k + 1)$th iteration starts only after all the computation and communication for the kth iteration is complete. The performance of the algorithm can be improved substantially if the processes work asynchronously; that is, no process waits for the others to finish an iteration before starting the next one. We call this the *asynchronous* or *pipelined* version of Gaussian elimination. Figure 8.7 illustrates the pipelined Algorithm 8.4 for a 5×5 matrix partitioned along the rows onto a logical linear array of five processes.

During the kth iteration of Algorithm 8.4, process P_k broadcasts part of the kth row of the matrix to processes $P_{k+1}, \ldots, P_{n-1}$ (Figure 8.6(b)). Assuming that the processes form a logical linear array, and P_{k+1} is the first process to receive the kth row from process P_k. Then process P_{k+1} must forward this data to P_{k+2}. However, after forwarding the kth row

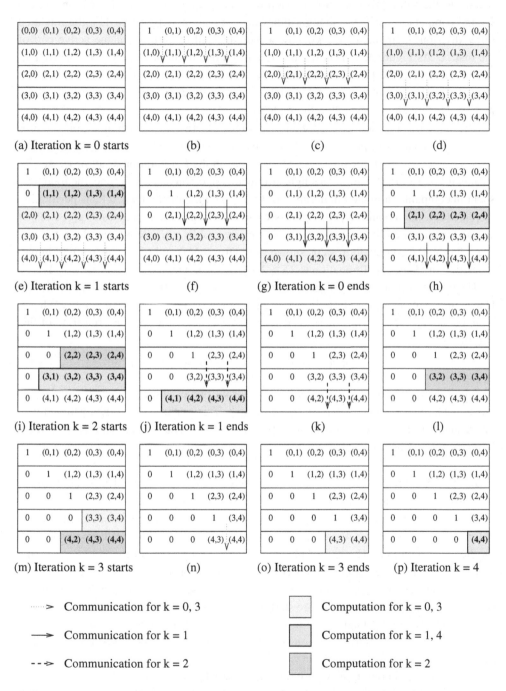

Figure 8.7   Pipelined Gaussian elimination on a 5 × 5 matrix partitioned with one row per process.

to P_{k+2}, process P_{k+1} need not wait to perform the elimination step (line 12) until all the processes up to P_{n-1} have received the kth row. Similarly, P_{k+2} can start its computation as soon as it has forwarded the kth row to P_{k+3}, and so on. Meanwhile, after completing the computation for the kth iteration, P_{k+1} can perform the division step (line 6), and start the broadcast of the $(k+1)$th row by sending it to P_{k+2}.

In pipelined Gaussian elimination, each process independently performs the following sequence of actions repeatedly until all n iterations are complete. For the sake of simplicity, we assume that steps (1) and (2) take the same amount of time (this assumption does not affect the analysis):

1. If a process has any data destined for other processes, it sends those data to the appropriate process.

2. If the process can perform some computation using the data it has, it does so.

3. Otherwise, the process waits to receive data to be used for one of the above actions.

Figure 8.7 shows the 16 steps in the pipelined parallel execution of Gaussian elimination for a 5×5 matrix partitioned along the rows among five processes. As Figure 8.7(a) shows, the first step is to perform the division on row 0 at process P_0. The modified row 0 is then sent to P_1 (Figure 8.7(b)), which forwards it to P_2 (Figure 8.7(c)). Now P_1 is free to perform the elimination step using row 0 (Figure 8.7(d)). In the next step (Figure 8.7(e)), P_2 performs the elimination step using row 0. In the same step, P_1, having finished its computation for iteration 0, starts the division step of iteration 1. At any given time, different stages of the same iteration can be active on different processes. For instance, in Figure 8.7(h), process P_2 performs the elimination step of iteration 1 while processes P_3 and P_4 are engaged in communication for the same iteration. Furthermore, more than one iteration may be active simultaneously on different processes. For instance, in Figure 8.7(i), process P_2 is performing the division step of iteration 2 while process P_3 is performing the elimination step of iteration 1.

We now show that, unlike the synchronous algorithm in which all processes work on the same iteration at a time, the pipelined or the asynchronous version of Gaussian elimination is cost-optimal. As Figure 8.7 shows, the initiation of consecutive iterations of the outer loop of Algorithm 8.4 is separated by a constant number of steps. A total of n such iterations are initiated. The last iteration modifies only the bottom-right corner element of the coefficient matrix; hence, it completes in a constant time after its initiation. Thus, the total number of steps in the entire pipelined procedure is $\Theta(n)$ (Problem 8.7). In any step, either $O(n)$ elements are communicated between directly-connected processes, or a division step is performed on $O(n)$ elements of a row, or an elimination step is performed on $O(n)$ elements of a row. Each of these operations take $O(n)$ time. Hence, the entire procedure consists of $\Theta(n)$ steps of $O(n)$ complexity each, and its parallel run time is $O(n^2)$. Since n processes are used, the cost is $O(n^3)$, which is of the same order as the sequential complexity of Gaussian elimination. Hence, the pipelined version of parallel Gaussian elimination with 1-D partitioning of the coefficient matrix is cost-optimal.

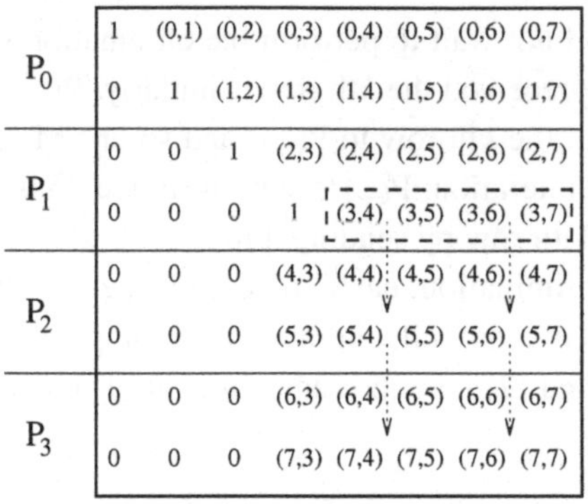

Figure 8.8   The communication in the Gaussian elimination iteration corresponding to $k = 3$ for an 8×8 matrix distributed among four processes using block 1-D partitioning.

Block 1-D Partitioning with Fewer than n Processes   The preceding pipelined implementation of parallel Gaussian elimination can be easily adapted for the case in which $n > p$. Consider an $n \times n$ matrix partitioned among p processes ($p < n$) such that each process is assigned n/p contiguous rows of the matrix. Figure 8.8 illustrates the communication steps in a typical iteration of Gaussian elimination with such a mapping. As the figure shows, the kth iteration of the algorithm requires that the active part of the kth row be sent to the processes storing rows $k + 1, k + 2, \dots, n - 1$.

Figure 8.9(a) shows that, with block 1-D partitioning, a process with all rows belonging to the active part of the matrix performs $(n - k - 1)n/p$ multiplications and subtractions during the elimination step of the kth iteration. Note that in the last $(n/p) - 1$ iterations, no process has all active rows, but we ignore this anomaly. If the pipelined version of

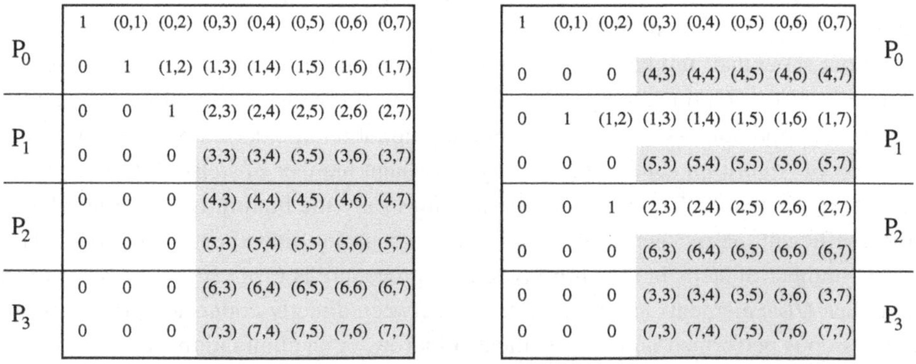

(a) Block 1-D mapping   (b) Cyclic 1-D mapping

Figure 8.9   Computation load on different processes in block and cyclic 1-D partitioning of an 8×8 matrix on four processes during the Gaussian elimination iteration corresponding to $k = 3$.

the algorithm is used, then the number of arithmetic operations on a maximally-loaded process in the kth iteration $(2(n - k - 1)n/p)$ is much higher than the number of words communicated $(n - k - 1)$ by a process in the same iteration. Thus, for sufficiently large values of n with respect to p, computation dominates communication in each iteration. Assuming that each scalar multiplication and subtraction pair takes unit time, the total parallel run time of this algorithm (ignoring communication overhead) is $2(n/p)\sum_{k=0}^{n-1}(n - k - 1)$, which is approximately equal to n^3/p.

The process-time product of this algorithm is n^3, even if the communication costs are ignored. Thus, the cost of the parallel algorithm is higher than the sequential run time (Equation 8.17) by a factor of 3/2. This inefficiency of Gaussian elimination with block 1-D partitioning is due to process idling resulting from an uneven load distribution. As Figure 8.9(a) shows for an 8×8 matrix and four processes, during the iteration corresponding to $k = 3$ (in the outer loop of Algorithm 8.4), one process is completely idle, one is partially loaded, and only two processes are fully active. By the time half of the iterations of the outer loop are over, only half the processes are active. The remaining idle processes make the parallel algorithm costlier than the sequential algorithm.

This problem can be alleviated if the matrix is partitioned among the processes using cyclic 1-D mapping as shown in Figure 8.9(b). With the cyclic 1-D partitioning, the difference between the computational loads of a maximally loaded process and the least loaded process in any iteration is of at most one row (that is, $O(n)$ arithmetic operations). Since there are n iterations, the cumulative overhead due to process idling is only $O(n^2p)$ with a cyclic mapping, compared to $\Theta(n^3)$ with a block mapping (Problem 8.12).

Parallel Implementation with 2-D Partitioning

We now describe a parallel implementation of Algorithm 8.4 in which the $n \times n$ matrix A is mapped onto an $n \times n$ mesh of processes such that process $P_{i,j}$ initially stores $A[i, j]$. The communication and computation steps in the iteration of the outer loop corresponding to $k = 3$ are illustrated in Figure 8.10 for $n = 8$. Algorithm 8.4 and Figures 8.5 and 8.10 show that in the kth iteration of the outer loop, $A[k, k]$ is required by processes $P_{k,k+1}$, $P_{k,k+2}, \ldots, P_{k,n-1}$ to divide $A[k, k+1]$, $A[k, k+2], \ldots, A[k, n-1]$, respectively. After the division on line 6, the modified elements of the kth row are used to perform the elimination step by all the other rows in the active part of the matrix. The modified (after the division on line 6) elements of the kth row are used by all other rows of the active part of the matrix. Similarly, the elements of the kth column are used by all other columns of the active part of the matrix for the elimination step. As Figure 8.10 shows, the communication in the kth iteration requires a one-to-all broadcast of $A[i, k]$ along the ith row (Figure 8.10(a)) for $k \leq i < n$, and a one-to-all broadcast of $A[k, j]$ along the jth column (Figure 8.10(c)) for $k < j < n$. Just like the 1-D partitioning case, a non-cost-optimal parallel formulation results if these broadcasts are performed synchronously on all processes (Problem 8.11).

Pipelined Communication and Computation   Based on our experience with Gaussian elimination using 1-D partitioning of the coefficient matrix, we develop a pipelined

1	(0,1)	(0,2)	(0,3)	(0,4)	(0,5)	(0,6)	(0,7)
0	1	(1,2)	(1,3)	(1,4)	(1,5)	(1,6)	(1,7)
0	0	1	(2,3)	(2,4)	(2,5)	(2,6)	(2,7)
0	0	0	(3,3)	(3,4)	(3,5)	(3,6)	(3,7)
0	0	0	(4,3)	(4,4)	(4,5)	(4,6)	(4,7)
0	0	0	(5,3)	(5,4)	(5,5)	(5,6)	(5,7)
0	0	0	(6,3)	(6,4)	(6,5)	(6,6)	(6,7)
0	0	0	(7,3)	(7,4)	(7,5)	(7,6)	(7,7)

(a) Rowwise broadcast of A[i,k]
for (k - 1) < i < n

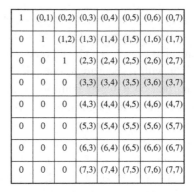

(b) A[k,j] := A[k,j]/A[k,k]
for k < j < n

1	(0,1)	(0,2)	(0,3)	(0,4)	(0,5)	(0,6)	(0,7)
0	1	(1,2)	(1,3)	(1,4)	(1,5)	(1,6)	(1,7)
0	0	1	(2,3)	(2,4)	(2,5)	(2,6)	(2,7)
0	0	0	1	(3,4)	(3,5)	(3,6)	(3,7)
0	0	0	(4,3)	(4,4)	(4,5)	(4,6)	(4,7)
0	0	0	(5,3)	(5,4)	(5,5)	(5,6)	(5,7)
0	0	0	(6,3)	(6,4)	(6,5)	(6,6)	(6,7)
0	0	0	(7,3)	(7,4)	(7,5)	(7,6)	(7,7)

(c) Columnwise broadcast of A[k,j]
for k < j < n

1	(0,1)	(0,2)	(0,3)	(0,4)	(0,5)	(0,6)	(0,7)
0	1	(1,2)	(1,3)	(1,4)	(1,5)	(1,6)	(1,7)
0	0	1	(2,3)	(2,4)	(2,5)	(2,6)	(2,7)
0	0	0	1	(3,4)	(3,5)	(3,6)	(3,7)
0	0	0	(4,3)	(4,4)	(4,5)	(4,6)	(4,7)
0	0	0	(5,3)	(5,4)	(5,5)	(5,6)	(5,7)
0	0	0	(6,3)	(6,4)	(6,5)	(6,6)	(6,7)
0	0	0	(7,3)	(7,4)	(7,5)	(7,6)	(7,7)

(d) A[i,j] := A[i,j]-A[i,k] × A[k,j]
for k < i < n and k < j < n

Figure 8.10 Various steps in the Gaussian elimination iteration corresponding to $k = 3$ for an 8 × 8 matrix on 64 processes arranged in a logical two-dimensional mesh.

version of the algorithm using 2-D partitioning.

As Figure 8.10 shows, in the kth iteration of the outer loop (lines 3–16 of Algorithm 8.4), $A[k, k]$ is sent to the right from $P_{k,k}$ to $P_{k,k+1}$ to $P_{k,k+2}$, and so on, until it reaches $P_{k,n-1}$. Process $P_{k,k+1}$ performs the division $A[k, k + 1]/A[k, k]$ as soon as it receives $A[k, k]$ from $P_{k,k}$. It does not have to wait for $A[k, k]$ to reach all the way up to $P_{k,n-1}$ before performing its local computation. Similarly, any subsequent process $P_{k,j}$ of the kth row can perform its division as soon as it receives $A[k, k]$. After performing the division, $A[k, j]$ is ready to be communicated downward in the jth column. As $A[k, j]$ moves down, each process it passes is free to use it for computation. Processes in the jth column need not wait until $A[k, j]$ reaches the last process of the column. Thus, $P_{i,j}$ performs the elimination step $A[i, j] := A[i, j] - A[i, k] \times A[k, j]$ as soon as $A[i, k]$ and $A[k, j]$ are available. Since some processes perform the computation for a given iteration earlier than other processes, they start working on subsequent iterations sooner.

The communication and computation can be pipelined in several ways. We present one such scheme in Figure 8.11. In Figure 8.11(a), the iteration of the outer loop for $k = 0$ starts at process $P_{0,0}$, when $P_{0,0}$ sends $A[0, 0]$ to $P_{0,1}$. Upon receiving $A[0, 0]$, $P_{0,1}$ computes $A[0, 1] := A[0, 1]/A[0, 0]$ (Figure 8.11(b)). Now $P_{0,1}$ forwards $A[0, 0]$ to $P_{0,2}$ and also sends the updated $A[0, 1]$ down to $P_{1,1}$ (Figure 8.11(c)). At the same time, $P_{1,0}$ sends $A[1, 0]$ to $P_{1,1}$. Having received $A[0, 1]$ and $A[1, 0]$, $P_{1,1}$ performs the elimination step $A[1, 1] := A[1, 1] - A[1, 0] \times A[0, 1]$, and having received $A[0, 0]$, $P_{0,2}$ performs the division step $A[0, 2] := A[0, 2]/A[0, 0]$ (Figure 8.11(d)). After this computation step, another set of processes (that is, processes $P_{0,2}$, $P_{1,1}$, and $P_{2,0}$) is ready to initiate communication (Figure 8.11(e)).

All processes performing communication or computation during a particular iteration lie along a diagonal in the bottom-left to top-right direction (for example, $P_{0,2}$, $P_{1,1}$, and $P_{2,0}$ performing communication in Figure 8.11(e) and $P_{0,3}$, $P_{1,2}$, and $P_{2,1}$ performing computation in Figure 8.11(f)). As the parallel algorithm progresses, this diagonal moves toward the bottom-right corner of the logical 2-D mesh. Thus, the computation and communication for each iteration moves through the mesh from top-left to bottom-right as a "front." After the front corresponding to a certain iteration passes through a process, the process is free to perform subsequent iterations. For instance, in Figure 8.11(g), after the front for $k = 0$ has passed $P_{1,1}$, it initiates the iteration for $k = 1$ by sending $A[1, 1]$ to $P_{1,2}$. This initiates a front for $k = 1$, which closely follows the front for $k = 0$. Similarly, a third front for $k = 2$ starts at $P_{2,2}$ (Figure 8.11(m)). Thus, multiple fronts that correspond to different iterations are active simultaneously.

Every step of an iteration, such as division, elimination, or transmitting a value to a neighboring process, is a constant-time operation. Therefore, a front moves a single step closer to the bottom-right corner of the matrix in constant time (equivalent to two steps of Figure 8.11). The front for $k = 0$ takes time $\Theta(n)$ to reach $P_{n-1,n-1}$ after its initiation at $P_{0,0}$. The algorithm initiates n fronts for the n iterations of the outer loop. Each front lags behind the previous one by a single step. Thus, the last front passes the bottom-right corner of the matrix $\Theta(n)$ steps after the first one. The total time elapsed between the first front starting at $P_{0,0}$ and the last one finishing is $\Theta(n)$. The procedure is complete after the last front passes the bottom-right corner of the matrix; hence, the total parallel run time is $\Theta(n)$. Since n^2 process are used, the cost of the pipelined version of Gaussian elimination is $\Theta(n^3)$, which is the same as the sequential run time of the algorithm. Hence, the pipelined version of Gaussian elimination with 2-D partitioning is cost-optimal.

2-D Partitioning with Fewer than n^2 Processes

Consider the case in which p processes are used so that $p < n^2$ and the matrix is mapped onto a $\sqrt{p} \times \sqrt{p}$ mesh by using block 2-D partitioning. Figure 8.12 illustrates that a typical parallel Gaussian iteration involves a rowwise and a columnwise communication of $n/\sqrt{p}$ values. Figure 8.13(a) illustrates the load distribution in block 2-D mapping for $n = 8$ and $p = 16$.

Figures 8.12 and 8.13(a) show that a process containing a completely active part of the

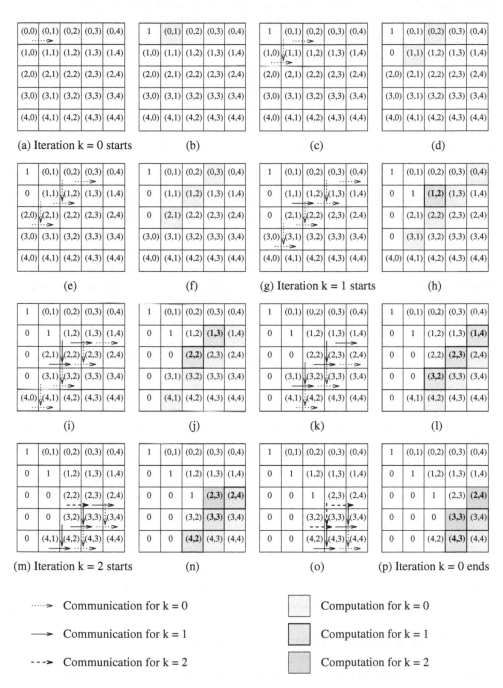

(a) Iteration k = 0 starts   (b)   (c)   (d)

(e)   (f)   (g) Iteration k = 1 starts   (h)

(i)   (j)   (k)   (l)

(m) Iteration k = 2 starts   (n)   (o)   (p) Iteration k = 0 ends

·····> Communication for k = 0   ☐ Computation for k = 0

——→ Communication for k = 1   ▨ Computation for k = 1

- - -> Communication for k = 2   ▨ Computation for k = 2

Figure 8.11   Pipelined Gaussian elimination for a 5 × 5 matrix with 25 processes.

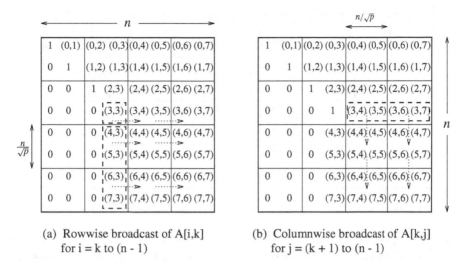

(a) Rowwise broadcast of A[i,k]
for i = k to (n - 1)

(b) Columnwise broadcast of A[k,j]
for j = (k + 1) to (n - 1)

Figure 8.12 The communication steps in the Gaussian elimination iteration corresponding to $k = 3$ for an 8×8 matrix on 16 processes of a two-dimensional mesh.

matrix performs n^2/p multiplications and subtractions, and communicates $n/\sqrt{p}$ words along its row and its column (ignoring the fact that in the last $(n/\sqrt{p}) - 1$ iterations, the active part of the matrix becomes smaller than the size of a block, and no process contains a completely active part of the matrix). If the pipelined version of the algorithm is used, the number of arithmetic operations per process $(2n^2/p)$ is an order of magnitude higher than the number of words communicated per process $(n/\sqrt{p})$ in each iteration. Thus, for sufficiently large values of n^2 with respect to p, the communication in each iteration is dominated by computation. Ignoring the communication cost and assuming that each scalar arithmetic operation takes unit time, the total parallel run time of this algorithm is $(2n^2/p) \times n$, which is equal to $2n^3/p$. The process-time product is $2n^3$, which is three times the cost of the serial algorithm (Equation 8.17). As a result, there is an upper bound of $1/3$ on the efficiency of the parallel algorithm.

As in the case of a block 1-D mapping, the inefficiency of Gaussian elimination with a block 2-D partitioning of the matrix is due to process idling resulting from an uneven load distribution. Figure 8.13(a) shows the active part of an 8×8 matrix of coefficients in the iteration of the outer loop for $k = 3$ when the matrix is block 2-D partitioned among 16 processes. As shown in the figure, seven out of 16 processes are fully idle, five are partially loaded, and only four are fully active. By the time half of the iterations of the outer loop have been completed, only one-fourth of the processes are active. The remaining idle processes make the parallel algorithm much costlier than the sequential algorithm.

This problem can be alleviated if the matrix is partitioned in a 2-D cyclic fashion as shown in Figure 8.13(b). With the cyclic 2-D partitioning, the maximum difference in computational load between any two processes in any iteration is that of one row and one column update. For example, in Figure 8.13(b), n^2/p matrix elements are active in the

1	(0,1)	(0,2)	(0,3)	(0,4)	(0,5)	(0,6)	(0,7)
0	1	(1,2)	(1,3)	(1,4)	(1,5)	(1,6)	(1,7)
0	0	1	(2,3)	(2,4)	(2,5)	(2,6)	(2,7)
0	0	0	(3,3)	(3,4)	(3,5)	(3,6)	(3,7)
0	0	0	(4,3)	(4,4)	(4,5)	(4,6)	(4,7)
0	0	0	(5,3)	(5,4)	(5,5)	(5,6)	(5,7)
0	0	0	(6,3)	(6,4)	(6,5)	(6,6)	(6,7)
0	0	0	(7,3)	(7,4)	(7,5)	(7,6)	(7,7)

(a) Block-checkerboard mapping

1	(0,4)	(0,1)	(0,5)	(0,2)	(0,6)	(0,3)	(0,7)
0	(4,4)	0	(4,5)	0	(4,6)	(4,3)	(4,7)
0	(1,4)	1	(1,5)	(1,2)	(1,6)	(1,3)	(1,7)
0	(5,4)	0	(5,5)	0	(5,6)	(5,3)	(5,7)
0	(2,4)	0	(2,5)	1	(2,6)	(2,3)	(2,7)
0	(6,4)	0	(6,5)	0	(6,6)	(6,3)	(6,7)
0	(3,4)	0	(3,5)	0	(3,6)	(3,3)	(3,7)
0	(7,4)	0	(7,5)	0	(7,6)	(7,3)	(7,7)

(b) Cyclic-checkerboard mapping

Figure 8.13 Computational load on different processes in block and cyclic 2-D mappings of an 8 × 8 matrix onto 16 processes during the Gaussian elimination iteration corresponding to $k = 3$.

bottom-right process, and $(n - 1)^2/p$ elements are active in the top-left process. The difference in workload between any two processes is at most $\Theta(n/\sqrt{p})$ in any iteration, which contributes $\Theta(n\sqrt{p})$ to the overhead function. Since there are n iterations, the cumulative overhead due to process idling is only $\Theta(n^2\sqrt{p})$ with cyclic mapping in contrast to $\Theta(n^3)$ with block mapping (Problem 8.12). In practical parallel implementations of Gaussian elimination and LU factorization, a block-cyclic mapping is used to reduce the overhead due to message startup time associated with a pure cyclic mapping and to obtain better serial CPU utilization by performing block-matrix operations (Problem 8.15).

From the discussion in this section, we conclude that pipelined parallel Gaussian elimination for an $n \times n$ matrix takes time $\Theta(n^3/p)$ on p processes with both 1-D and 2-D partitioning schemes. 2-D partitioning can use more processes ($O(n^2)$) than 1-D partitioning ($O(n)$) for an $n \times n$ coefficient matrix. Hence, an implementation with 2-D partitioning is more scalable.

8.3.2 Gaussian Elimination with Partial Pivoting

The Gaussian elimination algorithm in Algorithm 8.4 fails if any diagonal entry $A[k, k]$ of the matrix of coefficients is close or equal to zero. To avoid this problem and to ensure the numerical stability of the algorithm, a technique called *partial pivoting* is used. At the beginning of the outer loop in the kth iteration, this method selects a column i (called the *pivot* column) such that $A[k, i]$ is the largest in magnitude among all $A[k, j]$ such that $k \leq j < n$. It then exchanges the kth and the ith columns before starting the iteration. These columns can either be exchanged explicitly by physically moving them into each other's locations, or they can be exchanged implicitly by simply maintaining an $n \times 1$ permutation vector to keep track of the new indices of the columns of A. If partial pivoting is performed with an implicit exchange of column indices, then the factors L and U are not exactly triangular matrices, but columnwise permutations of triangular matrices.

Assuming that columns are exchanged explicitly, the value of $A[k, k]$ used as the divisor on line 6 of Algorithm 8.4 (after exchanging columns k and i) is greater than or equal to any $A[k, j]$ that it divides in the kth iteration. Partial pivoting in Algorithm 8.4 results in a unit upper-triangular matrix in which all elements above the principal diagonal have an absolute value of less than one.

1-D Partitioning

Performing partial pivoting is straightforward with rowwise partitioning as discussed in Section 8.3.1. Before performing the divide operation in the kth iteration, the process storing the kth row makes a comparison pass over the active portion of this row, and selects the element with the largest absolute value as the divisor. This element determines the pivot column, and all processes must know the index of this column. This information can be passed on to the rest of the processes along with the modified (after the division) elements of the kth row. The combined pivot-search and division step takes time $\Theta(n - k - 1)$ in the kth iteration, as in case of Gaussian elimination without pivoting. Thus, partial pivoting has no significant effect on the performance of Algorithm 8.4 if the coefficient matrix is partitioned along the rows.

Now consider a columnwise 1-D partitioning of the coefficient matrix. In the absence of pivoting, parallel implementations of Gaussian elimination with rowwise and columnwise 1-D partitioning are almost identical (Problem 8.9). However, the two are significantly different if partial pivoting is performed.

The first difference is that, unlike rowwise partitioning, the pivot search is distributed in columnwise partitioning. If the matrix size is $n \times n$ and the number of processes is p, then the pivot search in columnwise partitioning involves two steps. During pivot search for the kth iteration, first each process determines the maximum of the n/p (or fewer) elements of the kth row that it stores. The next step is to find the maximum of the resulting p (or fewer) values, and to distribute the maximum among all processes. Each pivot search takes time $\Theta(n/p) + \Theta(\log p)$. For sufficiently large values of n with respect to p, this is less than the time $\Theta(n)$ it takes to perform a pivot search with rowwise partitioning. This seems to suggest that a columnwise partitioning is better for partial pivoting that a rowwise partitioning. However, the following factors favor rowwise partitioning.

Figure 8.7 shows how communication and computation "fronts" move from top to bottom in the pipelined version of Gaussian elimination with rowwise 1-D partitioning. Similarly, the communication and computation fronts move from left to right in case of columnwise 1-D partitioning. This means that the $(k + 1)$th row is not ready for pivot search for the $(k + 1)$th iteration (that is, it is not fully updated) until the front corresponding to the kth iteration reaches the rightmost process. As a result, the $(k + 1)$th iteration cannot start until the entire kth iteration is complete. This effectively eliminates pipelining, and we are therefore forced to use the synchronous version with poor efficiency.

While performing partial pivoting, columns of the coefficient matrix may or may not be explicitly exchanged. In either case, the performance of Algorithm 8.4 is adversely affected with columnwise 1-D partitioning. Recall that cyclic or block-cyclic mappings result in a better load balance in Gaussian elimination than a block mapping. A cyclic mapping ensures that the active portion of the matrix is almost uniformly distributed among the processes at every stage of Gaussian elimination. If pivot columns are not exchanged explicitly, then this condition may cease to hold. After a pivot column is used, it no longer stays in the active portion of the matrix. As a result of pivoting without explicit exchange, columns are arbitrarily removed from the different processes' active portions of the matrix. This randomness may disturb the uniform distribution of the active portion. On the other hand, if columns belonging to different processes are exchanged explicitly, then this exchange requires communication between the processes. A rowwise 1-D partitioning neither requires communication for exchanging columns, nor does it lose the load-balance if columns are not exchanged explicitly.

2-D Partitioning

In the case of 2-D partitioning of the coefficient matrix, partial pivoting seriously restricts pipelining, although it does not completely eliminate it. Recall that in the pipelined version of Gaussian elimination with 2-D partitioning, fronts corresponding to various iterations move from top-left to bottom-right. The pivot search for the $(k + 1)$th iteration can commence as soon as the front corresponding to the kth iteration has moved past the diagonal of the active matrix joining its top-right and bottom-left corners.

Thus, partial pivoting may lead to considerable performance degradation in parallel Gaussian elimination with 2-D partitioning. If numerical considerations allow, it may be possible to reduce the performance loss due to partial pivoting. We can restrict the search for the pivot in the kth iteration to a band of q columns (instead of all $n - k$ columns). In this case, the ith column is selected as the pivot in the kth iteration if $A[k, i]$ is the largest element in a band of q elements of the active part of the ith row. This restricted partial pivoting not only reduces the communication cost, but also permits limited pipelining. By restricting the number of columns for pivot search to q, an iteration can start as soon as the previous iteration has updated the first $q + 1$ columns.

Another way to get around the loss of pipelining due to partial pivoting in Gaussian elimination with 2-D partitioning is to use fast algorithms for one-to-all broadcast, such as those described in Section 4.7.1. With 2-D partitioning of the $n \times n$ coefficient matrix on p processes, a process spends time $\Theta(n/\sqrt{p})$ in communication in each iteration of the pipelined version of Gaussian elimination. Disregarding the message startup time t_s, a non-pipelined version that performs explicit one-to-all broadcasts using the algorithm of Section 4.1 spends time $\Theta((n/\sqrt{p}) \log p)$ communicating in each iteration. This communication time is higher than that of the pipelined version. The one-to-all broadcast algorithms described in Section 4.7.1 take time $\Theta(n/\sqrt{p})$ in each iteration (disregarding the startup time). This time is asymptotically equal to the per-iteration communication time of the pipelined algorithm. Hence, using a smart algorithm to perform one-to-all broadcast, even non-pipelined parallel Gaussian elimination can attain performance comparable to that of the pipelined algorithm. However, the one-to-all broadcast algorithms described in Section 4.7.1 split a message into smaller parts and route them separately. For these algorithms to be effective, the sizes of the messages should be large enough; that is, n should be large compared to p.

Although pipelining and pivoting do not go together in Gaussian elimination with 2-D partitioning, the discussion of 2-D partitioning in this section is still useful. With some modification, it applies to the Cholesky factorization algorithm (Algorithm 8.6 in Problem 8.16), which does not require pivoting. Cholesky factorization applies only to symmetric, positive definite matrices. A real $n \times n$ matrix A is *positive definite* if $x^T A x > 0$ for any $n \times 1$ nonzero, real vector x. The communication pattern in Cholesky factorization is quite similar to that of Gaussian elimination (Problem 8.16), except that, due to symmetric lower and upper-triangular halves in the matrix, Cholesky factorization uses only one triangular half of the matrix.

8.3.3 Solving a Triangular System: Back-Substitution

We now briefly discuss the second stage of solving a system of linear equations. After the full matrix A has been reduced to an upper-triangular matrix U with ones along the principal diagonal, we perform back-substitution to determine the vector x. A sequential back-substitution algorithm for solving an upper-triangular system of equations $Ux = y$ is shown in Algorithm 8.5.

Starting with the last equation, each iteration of the main loop (lines 3–8) of Algorithm 8.5 computes the values of a variable and substitutes the variable's value back into the remaining equations. The program performs approximately $n^2/2$ multiplications and subtractions. Note that the number of arithmetic operations in back-substitution is less than that in Gaussian elimination by a factor of $\Theta(n)$. Hence, if back-substitution is used in conjunction with Gaussian elimination, it is best to use the matrix partitioning scheme that is the most efficient for parallel Gaussian elimination.

```
1.    procedure BACK_SUBSTITUTION (U, x, y)
2.    begin
3.        for k := n − 1 downto 0 do   /* Main loop */
4.            begin
5.                x[k] := y[k];
6.                for i := k − 1 downto 0 do
7.                    y[i] := y[i] − x[k] × U[i, k];
8.            endfor;
9.    end BACK_SUBSTITUTION
```

Algorithm 8.5   A serial algorithm for back-substitution. U is an upper-triangular matrix with all entries of the principal diagonal equal to one, and all subdiagonal entries equal to zero.

Consider a rowwise block 1-D mapping of the $n \times n$ matrix U onto p processes. Let the vector y be distributed uniformly among all the processes. The value of the variable solved in a typical iteration of the main loop (line 3) must be sent to all the processes with equations involving that variable. This communication can be pipelined (Problem 8.22). If so, the time to perform the computations of an iteration dominates the time that a process spends in communication in an iteration. In every iteration of a pipelined implementation, a process receives (or generates) the value of a variable and sends that value to another process. Using the value of the variable solved in the current iteration, a process also performs up to n/p multiplications and subtractions (lines 6 and 7). Hence, each step of a pipelined implementation requires a constant amount of time for communication and time $\Theta(n/p)$ for computation. The algorithm terminates in $\Theta(n)$ steps (Problem 8.22), and the parallel run time of the entire algorithm is $\Theta(n^2/p)$.

If the matrix is partitioned by using 2-D partitioning on a $\sqrt{p} \times \sqrt{p}$ logical mesh of processes, and the elements of the vector are distributed along one of the columns of the process mesh, then only the $\sqrt{p}$ processes containing the vector perform any computation. Using pipelining to communicate the appropriate elements of U to the process containing the corresponding elements of y for the substitution step (line 7), the algorithm can be executed in time $\Theta(n^2/\sqrt{p})$ (Problem 8.22). Thus, the cost of parallel back-substitution with 2-D mapping is $\Theta(n^2\sqrt{p})$. The algorithm is not cost-optimal because its sequential cost is only $\Theta(n^2)$. However, the entire process of solving the linear system, including upper-triangularization using Gaussian elimination, is still cost-optimal for $\sqrt{p} = O(n)$ because the sequential complexity of the entire process is $\Theta(n^3)$.

8.3.4 Numerical Considerations in Solving Systems of Linear Equations

A system of linear equations of the form $Ax = b$ can be solved by using a factorization algorithm to express A as the product of a lower-triangular matrix L, and a unit upper-triangular matrix U. The system of equations is then rewritten as $LUx = b$, and is solved in two steps. First, the lower-triangular system $Ly = b$ is solved for y. Second, the upper-triangular system $Ux = y$ is solved for x.

The Gaussian elimination algorithm given in Algorithm 8.4 effectively factorizes A into L and U. However, it also solves the lower-triangular system $Ly = b$ on the fly by means of steps on lines 7 and 13. Algorithm 8.4 gives what is called a ***row-oriented*** Gaussian elimination algorithm. In this algorithm, multiples of rows are subtracted from other rows. If partial pivoting, as described in Section 8.3.2, is incorporated into this algorithm, then the resulting upper-triangular matrix U has all its elements less than or equal to one in magnitude. The lower-triangular matrix L, whether implicit or explicit, may have elements with larger numerical values. While solving the system $Ax = b$, the triangular system $Ly = b$ is solved first. If L contains large elements, then rounding errors can occur while solving for y due to the finite precision of floating-point numbers in the computer. These errors in y are propagated through the solution of $Ux = y$.

An alternate form of Gaussian elimination is the **column-oriented** form that can be obtained from Algorithm 8.4 by reversing the roles of rows and columns. In the column-oriented algorithm, multiples of columns are subtracted from other columns, pivot search is also performed along the columns, and numerical stability is guaranteed by row interchanges, if needed. All elements of the lower-triangular matrix L generated by the column-oriented algorithm have a magnitude less than or equal to one. This minimizes numerical error while solving $Ly = b$, and results in a significantly smaller error in the overall solution than the row-oriented algorithm. Algorithm 3.3 gives a procedure for column-oriented LU factorization.

From a practical point of view, the column-oriented Gaussian elimination algorithm is more useful than the row-oriented algorithm. We have chosen to present the row-oriented algorithm in detail in this chapter because it is more intuitive. It is easy to see that the system of linear equations resulting from the subtraction of a multiple of an equation from other equations is equivalent to the original system. The entire discussion on the row-oriented algorithm of Algorithm 8.4 presented in this section applies to the column-oriented algorithm with the roles of rows and columns reversed. For example, columnwise 1-D partitioning is more suitable than rowwise 1-D partitioning for the column-oriented algorithm with partial pivoting.

8.4 Bibliographic Remarks

Matrix transposition with 1-D partitioning is essentially an all-to-all personalized communication problem [Ede89]. Hence, all the references in Chapter 4 for all-to-all personalized communication apply directly to matrix transposition. The recursive transposition algorithm, popularly known as RTA, was first reported by Eklundh [Ekl72]. Its adaptations for hypercubes have been described by Bertsekas and Tsitsiklis [BT97], Fox and Furmanski [FF86], Johnsson [Joh87], and McBryan and Van de Velde [MdV87] for one-port communication on each process. Johnsson [Joh87] also discusses parallel RTA for hypercubes that permit simultaneous communication on all channels. Further improvements on the hypercube RTA have been suggested by Ho and Raghunath [HR91], Johnsson and Ho [JH88], Johnsson [Joh90], and Stout and Wagar [SW87].

A number of sources of parallel dense linear algebra algorithms, including those for matrix-vector multiplication and matrix multiplication, are available [CAHH91, GPS90, GL96a, Joh87, Mod88, OS85]. Since dense matrix multiplication is highly computationally intensive, there has been a great deal of interest in developing parallel formulations of this algorithm and in testing its performance on various parallel architectures [Akl89, Ber89, CAHH91, Can69, Cha79, CS88, DNS81, dV89, FJL+88, FOH87, GK91, GL96a, Hip89, HJE91, Joh87, PV80, Tic88]. Some of the early parallel formulations of matrix multiplication were developed by Cannon [Can69], Dekel, Nassimi, and Sahni [DNS81], and Fox *et al.* [FOH87]. Variants and improvements of these algorithms have been presented by Berntsen [Ber89], and by Ho, Johnsson, and Edelman [HJE91]. In particular, Berntsen [Ber89] presents an algorithm that has strictly smaller communication overhead than Cannon's algorithm, but has a smaller degree of concurrency. Ho, Johnsson, and Edelman [HJE91] present another variant of Cannon's algorithm for a hypercube that permits communication on all channels simultaneously. This algorithm, while reducing communication, also reduces the degree of concurrency. Gupta and Kumar [GK91] present a detailed scalability analysis of several matrix multiplication algorithms. They present an analysis to determine the best algorithm to multiply two $n \times n$ matrices on a p-process hypercube for different ranges of n, p and the hardware-related constants. They also show that the improvements suggested by Berntsen and Ho et al. do not improve the overall scalability of matrix multiplication on a hypercube.

Parallel algorithms for LU factorization and solving dense systems of linear equations have been discussed by several researchers [Ber84, BT97, CG87, Cha87, Dav86, DHvdV93, FJL$^+$88, Gei85, GH86, GPS90, GR88, Joh87, LD90, Lei92, Mod88, Mol86, OR88, Ort88, OS86, PR85, Rob90, Saa86, Vav89]. Geist and Heath [GH85, GH86], and Heath [Hea85] specifically concentrate on parallel dense Cholesky factorization. Parallel algorithms for solving triangular systems have also been studied in detail [EHHR88, HR88, LC88, LC89, RO88, Rom87]. Demmel, Heath, and van der Vorst [DHvdV93] present a comprehensive survey of parallel matrix computations considering numerical implications in detail.

A portable software implementation of all matrix and vector operations discussed in this chapter, and many more, is available as PBLAS (parallel basic linear algebra subroutines) [C$^+$95]. The ScaLAPACK library [B$^+$97] uses PBLAS to implement a variety of linear algebra routines of practical importance, including procedures for various methods of matrix factorizations and solving systems of linear equations.

Problems

8.1   Consider the two algorithms for all-to-all personalized communication in Section 4.5.3. Which method would you use on a 64-node parallel computer with $\Theta(p)$ bisection width for transposing a 1024×1024 matrix with the 1-D partitioning if $t_s = 100\mu s$ and $t_w = 1\mu s$? Why?

8.2   Describe a parallel formulation of matrix-vector multiplication in which the matrix is 1-D block-partitioned along the columns and the vector is equally partitioned among all the processes. Show that the parallel run time is the same as in case of rowwise 1-D block partitioning.
   Hint: The basic communication operation used in the case of columnwise 1-D partitioning is all-to-all reduction, as opposed to all-to-all broadcast in the case of rowwise 1-D partitioning. Problem 4.8 describes all-to-all reduction.

8.3   Section 8.1.2 describes and analyzes matrix-vector multiplication with 2-D partitioning. If $n \gg \sqrt{p}$, then suggest ways of improving the parallel run time to $n^2/p + 2t_s \log p + 2t_w(n/\sqrt{p})$. Is the improved method more scalable than the one used in Section 8.1.2?

8.4 The overhead function for multiplying an $n \times n$ 2-D partitioned matrix with an $n \times 1$ vector using p processes is $t_s p \log p + t_w n \sqrt{p} \log p$ (Equation 8.8). Substituting this expression in Equation 5.14 yields a quadratic equation in n. Using this equation, determine the precise isoefficiency function for the parallel algorithm and compare it with Equations 8.9 and 8.10. Does this comparison alter the conclusion that the term associated with t_w is responsible for the overall isoefficiency function of this parallel algorithm?

8.5 Strassen's method [AHU74, CLR90] for matrix multiplication is an algorithm based on the divide-and-conquer technique. The sequential complexity of multiplying two $n \times n$ matrices using Strassen's algorithm is $\Theta(n^{2.81})$. Consider the simple matrix multiplication algorithm (Section 8.2.1) for multiplying two $n \times n$ matrices using p processes. Assume that the $n/\sqrt{p} \times n/\sqrt{p}$ submatrices are multiplied using Strassen's algorithm at each process. Derive an expression for the parallel run time of this algorithm. Is the parallel algorithm cost-optimal?

8.6 **(DNS algorithm with fewer than n^3 processes [DNS81])** Section 8.2.3 describes a parallel formulation of the DNS algorithm that uses fewer than n^3 processes. Another variation of this algorithm works with $p = n^2 q$ processes, where $1 \le q < n$. Here the process arrangement is regarded as a $q \times q \times q$ logical three-dimensional array of "superprocesses," in which each superprocess is an $(n/q) \times (n/q)$ mesh of processes. This variant can be viewed as identical to the block variant described in Section 8.2.3, except that the role of each process is now assumed by an $(n/q) \times (n/q)$ logical mesh of processes. This means that each block multiplication of $(n/q) \times (n/q)$ submatrices is performed in parallel by $(n/q)^2$ processes rather than by a single process. Any of the algorithms described in Sections 8.2.1 or 8.2.2 can be used to perform this multiplication.

Derive an expression for the parallel run time for this variant of the DNS algorithm in terms of n, p, t_s, and t_w. Compare the expression with Equation 8.16. Discuss the relative merits and drawbacks of the two variations of the DNS algorithm for fewer than n^3 processes.

8.7 Figure 8.7 shows that the pipelined version of Gaussian elimination requires 16 steps for a 5×5 matrix partitioned rowwise on five processes. Show that, in general, the algorithm illustrated in this figure completes in $4(n - 1)$ steps for an $n \times n$ matrix partitioned rowwise with one row assigned to each process.

8.8 Describe in detail a parallel implementation of the Gaussian elimination algorithm of Algorithm 8.4 without pivoting if the $n \times n$ coefficient matrix is partitioned columnwise among p processes. Consider both pipelined and non-pipelined implementations. Also consider the cases $p = n$ and $p < n$.

Hint: The parallel implementation of Gaussian elimination described in Section 8.3.1 shows horizontal and vertical communication on a logical two-dimensional mesh of processes (Figure 8.12). A rowwise partitioning requires only the vertical part of this communication. Similarly, columnwise partitioning performs only the horizontal part of this communication.

8.9 Derive expressions for the parallel run times of all the implementations in Problem 8.8. Is the run time of any of these parallel implementations significantly different from the corresponding implementation with rowwise 1-D partitioning?

8.10 Rework Problem 8.9 with partial pivoting. In which implementations are the parallel run times significantly different for rowwise and columnwise partitioning?

8.11 Show that Gaussian elimination on an $n \times n$ matrix 2-D partitioned on an $n \times n$ logical mesh of processes is not cost-optimal if the $2n$ one-to-all broadcasts are performed synchronously.

8.12 Show that the cumulative idle time over all the processes in the Gaussian elimination algorithm is $\Theta(n^3)$ for a block mapping, whether the $n \times n$ matrix is partitioned along one or both dimensions. Show that this idle time is reduced to $\Theta(n^2 p)$ for cyclic 1-D mapping and $\Theta(n^2 \sqrt{p})$ for cyclic 2-D mapping.

8.13 Prove that the isoefficiency function of the asynchronous version of the Gaussian elimination with 2-D mapping is $\Theta(p^{3/2})$ if pivoting is not performed.

8.14 Derive precise expressions for the parallel run time of Gaussian elimination with and without partial pivoting if the $n \times n$ matrix of coefficients is partitioned among p processes of a logical square two-dimensional mesh in the following formats:
(a) Rowwise block 1-D partitioning.
(b) Rowwise cyclic 1-D partitioning.
(c) Columnwise block 1-D partitioning.
(d) Columnwise cyclic 1-D partitioning.

8.15 Rewrite Algorithm 8.4 in terms of block matrix operations as discussed at the beginning of Section 8.2. Consider Gaussian elimination of an $n \times n$ matrix partitioned into a $q \times q$ array of submatrices, where each submatrix is of size of $n/q \times n/q$. This array of blocks is mapped onto a logical $\sqrt{p} \times \sqrt{p}$ mesh of processes in a cyclic manner, resulting in a 2-D block cyclic mapping of the original matrix onto the mesh. Assume that $n > q > \sqrt{p}$ and that n is divisible by q, which in turn is divisible by $\sqrt{p}$. Derive expressions for the parallel run time for both synchronous and pipelined versions of Gaussian elimination.
Hint: The division step $A[k, j] := A[k, j]/A[k, k]$ is replaced by submatrix operation $A_{k,j} := A_{k,k}^{-1} A_{k,j}$, where $A_{k,k}$ is the lower triangular part of the kth diagonal submatrix.

8.16 (**Cholesky factorization**) Algorithm 8.6 describes a row-oriented version of the Cholesky factorization algorithm for factorizing a symmetric positive definite matrix into the form $A = U^T U$. Cholesky factorization does not require pivoting. Describe a pipelined parallel formulation of this algorithm that uses 2-D partitioning of the matrix on a square mesh of processes. Draw a picture similar to Figure 8.11.

```
1.    procedure CHOLESKY (A)
2.    begin
3.        for k := 0 to n − 1 do
4.            begin
5.                A[k, k] := √A[k, k];
6.                for j := k + 1 to n − 1 do
7.                    A[k, j] := A[k, j]/A[k, k];
8.                for i := k + 1 to n − 1 do
9.                    for j := i to n − 1 do
10.                       A[i, j] := A[i, j] − A[k, i] × A[k, j];
11.           endfor;      /* Line 3 */
12.   end CHOLESKY
```

Algorithm 8.6   A row-oriented Cholesky factorization algorithm.

8.17 **(Scaled speedup)** Scaled speedup (Section 5.7) is defined as the speedup obtained when the problem size is increased linearly with the number of processes; that is, if W is chosen as a base problem size for a single process, then

$$Scaled\ speedup\ =\ \frac{Wp}{T_P(Wp,\ p)}. \tag{8.19}$$

For the simple matrix multiplication algorithm described in Section 8.2.1, plot the standard and scaled speedup curves for the base problem of multiplying 16×16 matrices. Use $p = 1, 4, 16, 64,$ and 256. Assume that $t_s = 10$ and $t_w = 1$ in Equation 8.14.

8.18 Plot a third speedup curve for Problem 8.17, in which the problem size is scaled up according to the isoefficiency function, which is $\Theta(p^{3/2})$. Use the same values of t_s and t_w.

Hint: The scaled speedup under this method of scaling is

$$Isoefficient\ scaled\ speedup\ =\ \frac{Wp^{3/2}}{T_P(Wp^{3/2},\ p)}.$$

8.19 Plot the efficiency curves for the simple matrix multiplication algorithm corresponding to the standard speedup curve (Problem 8.17), the scaled speedup curve (Problem 8.17), and the speedup curve when the problem size is increased according to the isoefficiency function (Problem 8.18).

8.20 A drawback of increasing the number of processes without increasing the total workload is that the speedup does not increase linearly with the number of processes, and the efficiency drops monotonically. Based on your experience with Problems 8.17 and 8.19, discuss whether using scaled speedup instead of standard speedup solves the problem in general. What can you say about the isoefficiency function of a parallel algorithm whose scaled speedup curve matches the speedup curve determined by increasing the problem size according to the isoefficiency function?

8.21 **(Time-constrained scaling)** Assume that $t_s = 10$ and $t_w = 1$ in the expression of parallel execution time (Equation 8.14) of the matrix-multiplication algorithm discussed in Section 8.2.1. For $p = 1, 4, 16, 64, 256, 1024$, and 4096, what is the largest problem that can be solved if the total run time is not to exceed 512 time units? In general, is it possible to solve an arbitrarily large problem in a fixed amount of time, provided that an unlimited number of processes is available? Give a brief explanation.

8.22 Describe a pipelined algorithm for performing back-substitution to solve a triangular system of equations of the form $Ux = y$, where the $n \times n$ unit upper-triangular matrix U is 2-D partitioned onto an $n \times n$ mesh of processes. Give an expression for the parallel run time of the algorithm. Modify the algorithm to work on fewer than n^2 processes, and derive an expression for the parallel execution time of the modified algorithm.

8.23 Consider the parallel algorithm given in Algorithm 8.7 for multiplying two $n \times n$ matrices A and B to obtain the product matrix C. Assume that it takes time t_{local} for a memory read or write operation on a matrix element and time t_c to add and multiply two numbers. Determine the parallel run time for this algorithm on an n^2-processor CREW PRAM. Is this parallel algorithm cost-optimal?

8.24 Assuming that concurrent read accesses to a memory location are serialized on an EREW PRAM, derive the parallel run time of the algorithm given in Algorithm 8.7 on an n^2-processor EREW PRAM. Is this algorithm cost-optimal on an EREW PRAM?

8.25 Consider a shared-address-space parallel computer with n^2 processors. Assume

---

```
1.    procedure MAT_MULT_CREW_PRAM (A, B, C, n)
2.    begin
3.        Organize the n² processes into a logical mesh of n × n;
4.        for each process Pᵢ,ⱼ do
5.        begin
6.            C[i, j] := 0;
7.            for k := 0 to n − 1 do
8.                C[i, j] := C[i, j] + A[i, k] × B[k, j];
9.        endfor;
10.   end MAT_MULT_CREW_PRAM
```

Algorithm 8.7   An algorithm for multiplying two $n \times n$ matrices A and B on a CREW PRAM, yielding matrix $C = A \times B$.

---

1.   **procedure** MAT_MULT_EREW_PRAM (A, B, C, n)
2.   **begin**
3.   Organize the n^2 processes into a logical mesh of $n \times n$;
4.   **for** each process $P_{i,j}$ **do**
5.   **begin**
6. $C[i, j] := 0$;
7.   **for** $k := 0$ **to** $n - 1$ **do**
8. $C[i, j] := C[i, j] +$
                              $A[i, (i + j + k) \bmod n] \times B[(i + j + k) \bmod n, j]$;
9.   **endfor**;
10.   **end** MAT_MULT_EREW_PRAM

Algorithm 8.8 An algorithm for multiplying two $n \times n$ matrices A and B on an EREW PRAM, yielding matrix $C = A \times B$.

that each processor has some local memory, and $A[i, j]$ and $B[i, j]$ are stored in the local memory of processor $P_{i,j}$. Furthermore, processor $P_{i,j}$ computes $C[i, j]$ in its local memory. Assume that it takes time $t_{local} + t_w$ to perform a read or write operation on nonlocal memory and time t_{local} on local memory. Derive an expression for the parallel run time of the algorithm in Algorithm 8.7 on this parallel computer.

8.26 Algorithm 8.7 can be modified so that the parallel run time on an EREW PRAM is less than that in Problem 8.24. The modified program is shown in Algorithm 8.8. What is the parallel run time of Algorithm 8.8 on an EREW PRAM and a shared-address-space parallel computer with memory access times as described in Problems 8.24 and 8.25? Is the algorithm cost-optimal on these architectures?

8.27 Consider an implementation of Algorithm 8.8 on a shared-address-space parallel computer with fewer than n^2 (say, p) processors and with memory access times as described in Problem 8.25. What is the parallel runtime?

8.28 Consider the implementation of the parallel matrix multiplication algorithm presented in Section 8.2.1 on a shared-address-space computer with memory access times as given in Problem 8.25. In this algorithm, each processor first receives all the data it needs into its local memory, and then performs the computation. Derive the parallel run time of this algorithm. Compare the performance of this algorithm with that in Problem 8.27.

8.29 Use the results of Problems 8.23–8.28 to comment on the viability of the PRAM model as a platform for parallel algorithm design. Also comment on the relevance of the message-passing model for shared-address-space computers.

CHAPTER 9

Sorting

Sorting is one of the most common operations performed by a computer. Because sorted data are easier to manipulate than randomly-ordered data, many algorithms require sorted data. Sorting is of additional importance to parallel computing because of its close relation to the task of routing data among processes, which is an essential part of many parallel algorithms. Many parallel sorting algorithms have been investigated for a variety of parallel computer architectures. This chapter presents several parallel sorting algorithms for PRAM, mesh, hypercube, and general shared-address-space and message-passing architectures.

Sorting is defined as the task of arranging an unordered collection of elements into monotonically increasing (or decreasing) order. Specifically, let $S = \langle a_1, a_2, \ldots, a_n \rangle$ be a sequence of n elements in arbitrary order; sorting transforms S into a monotonically increasing sequence $S' = \langle a'_1, a'_2, \ldots, a'_n \rangle$ such that $a'_i \leq a'_j$ for $1 \leq i \leq j \leq n$, and S' is a permutation of S.

Sorting algorithms are categorized as ***internal*** or ***external***. In internal sorting, the number of elements to be sorted is small enough to fit into the process's main memory. In contrast, external sorting algorithms use auxiliary storage (such as tapes and hard disks) for sorting because the number of elements to be sorted is too large to fit into memory. This chapter concentrates on internal sorting algorithms only.

Sorting algorithms can be categorized as ***comparison-based*** and ***noncomparison-based***. A comparison-based algorithm sorts an unordered sequence of elements by repeatedly comparing pairs of elements and, if they are out of order, exchanging them. This fundamental operation of comparison-based sorting is called ***compare-exchange***. The lower bound on the sequential complexity of any sorting algorithms that is comparison-based is $\Theta(n \log n)$, where n is the number of elements to be sorted. Noncomparison-based algorithms sort by using certain known properties of the elements (such as their binary representation or their distribution). The lower-bound complexity of these algorithms is

$\Theta(n)$. We concentrate on comparison-based sorting algorithms in this chapter, although we briefly discuss some noncomparison-based sorting algorithms in Section 9.6.

9.1   Issues in Sorting on Parallel Computers

Parallelizing a sequential sorting algorithm involves distributing the elements to be sorted onto the available processes. This process raises a number of issues that we must address in order to make the presentation of parallel sorting algorithms clearer.

9.1.1   Where the Input and Output Sequences are Stored

In sequential sorting algorithms, the input and the sorted sequences are stored in the process's memory. However, in parallel sorting there are two places where these sequences can reside. They may be stored on only one of the processes, or they may be distributed among the processes. The latter approach is particularly useful if sorting is an intermediate step in another algorithm. In this chapter, we assume that the input and sorted sequences are distributed among the processes.

Consider the precise distribution of the sorted output sequence among the processes. A general method of distribution is to enumerate the processes and use this enumeration to specify a global ordering for the sorted sequence. In other words, the sequence will be sorted with respect to this process enumeration. For instance, if P_i comes before P_j in the enumeration, all the elements stored in P_i will be smaller than those stored in P_j. We can enumerate the processes in many ways. For certain parallel algorithms and interconnection networks, some enumerations lead to more efficient parallel formulations than others.

9.1.2   How Comparisons are Performed

A sequential sorting algorithm can easily perform a compare-exchange on two elements because they are stored locally in the process's memory. In parallel sorting algorithms, this step is not so easy. If the elements reside on the same process, the comparison can be done easily. But if the elements reside on different processes, the situation becomes more complicated.

One Element Per Process

Consider the case in which each process holds only one element of the sequence to be sorted. At some point in the execution of the algorithm, a pair of processes (P_i, P_j) may need to compare their elements, a_i and a_j. After the comparison, P_i will hold the smaller and P_j the larger of $\{a_i, a_j\}$. We can perform comparison by having both processes send their elements to each other. Each process compares the received element with its own and retains the appropriate element. In our example, P_i will keep the smaller and P_j

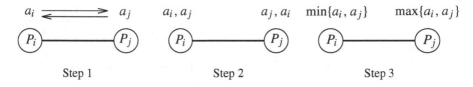

$a_i \rightleftharpoons a_j$ a_i, a_j a_j, a_i $\min\{a_i, a_j\}$ $\max\{a_i, a_j\}$

Step 1   Step 2   Step 3

Figure 9.1 A parallel compare-exchange operation. Processes P_i and P_j send their elements to each other. Process P_i keeps $\min\{a_i, a_j\}$, and P_j keeps $\max\{a_i, a_j\}$.

will keep the larger of $\{a_i, a_j\}$. As in the sequential case, we refer to this operation as *compare-exchange*. As Figure 9.1 illustrates, each compare-exchange operation requires one comparison step and one communication step.

If we assume that processes P_i and P_j are neighbors, and the communication channels are bidirectional, then the communication cost of a compare-exchange step is $(t_s + t_w)$, where t_s and t_w are message-startup time and per-word transfer time, respectively. In commercially available message-passing computers, t_s is significantly larger than t_w, so the communication time is dominated by t_s. Note that in today's parallel computers it takes more time to send an element from one process to another than it takes to compare the elements. Consequently, any parallel sorting formulation that uses as many processes as elements to be sorted will deliver very poor performance because the overall parallel run time will be dominated by interprocess communication.

More than One Element Per Process

A general-purpose parallel sorting algorithm must be able to sort a large sequence with a relatively small number of processes. Let p be the number of processes $P_0, P_1, \ldots, P_{p-1}$, and let n be the number of elements to be sorted. Each process is assigned a block of n/p elements, and all the processes cooperate to sort the sequence. Let $A_0, A_1, \ldots A_{p-1}$ be the blocks assigned to processes $P_0, P_1, \ldots P_{p-1}$, respectively. We say that $A_i \leq A_j$ if every element of A_i is less than or equal to every element in A_j. When the sorting algorithm finishes, each process P_i holds a set A_i' such that $A_i' \leq A_j'$ for $i \leq j$, and $\bigcup_{i=0}^{p-1} A_i = \bigcup_{i=0}^{p-1} A_i'$.

As in the one-element-per-process case, two processes P_i and P_j may have to redistribute their blocks of n/p elements so that one of them will get the smaller n/p elements and the other will get the larger n/p elements. Let A_i and A_j be the blocks stored in processes P_i and P_j. If the block of n/p elements at each process is already sorted, the redistribution can be done efficiently as follows. Each process sends its block to the other process. Now, each process merges the two sorted blocks and retains only the appropriate half of the merged block. We refer to this operation of comparing and splitting two sorted blocks as *compare-split*. The compare-split operation is illustrated in Figure 9.2.

If we assume that processes P_i and P_j are neighbors and that the communication channels are bidirectional, then the communication cost of a compare-split operation is

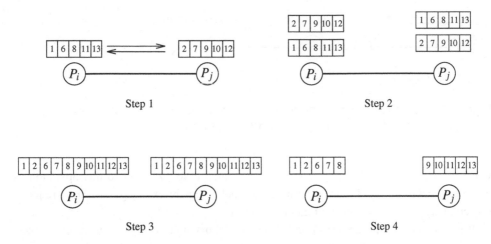

Figure 9.2   A compare-split operation. Each process sends its block of size n/p to the other process. Each process merges the received block with its own block and retains only the appropriate half of the merged block. In this example, process P_i retains the smaller elements and process P_j retains the larger elements.

$(t_s + t_w n/p)$. As the block size increases, the significance of t_s decreases, and for sufficiently large blocks it can be ignored. Thus, the time required to merge two sorted blocks of n/p elements is $\Theta(n/p)$.

9.2   Sorting Networks

In the quest for fast sorting methods, a number of networks have been designed that sort n elements in time significantly smaller than $\Theta(n \log n)$. These sorting networks are based on a comparison network model, in which many comparison operations are performed simultaneously.

The key component of these networks is a ***comparator***. A comparator is a device with two inputs x and y and two outputs x' and y'. For an ***increasing comparator***, $x' = \min\{x, y\}$ and $y' = \max\{x, y\}$; for a ***decreasing comparator*** $x' = \max\{x, y\}$ and $y' = \min\{x, y\}$. Figure 9.3 gives the schematic representation of the two types of comparators. As the two elements enter the input wires of the comparator, they are compared and, if necessary, exchanged before they go to the output wires. We denote an increasing comparator by $\oplus$ and a decreasing comparator by $\ominus$. A sorting network is usually made up of a series of columns, and each column contains a number of comparators connected in parallel. Each column of comparators performs a permutation, and the output obtained from the final column is sorted in increasing or decreasing order. Figure 9.4 illustrates a typical sorting network. The ***depth*** of a network is the number of columns it contains. Since the speed of a comparator is a technology-dependent constant, the speed of the network is proportional to its depth.

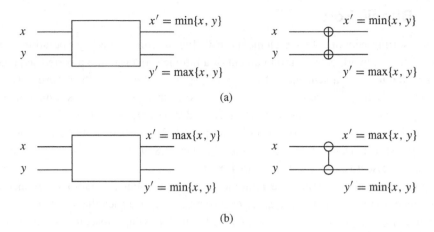

(a)

(b)

Figure 9.3 A schematic representation of comparators: (a) an increasing comparator, and (b) a decreasing comparator.

We can convert any sorting network into a sequential sorting algorithm by emulating the comparators in software and performing the comparisons of each column sequentially. The comparator is emulated by a compare-exchange operation, where x and y are compared and, if necessary, exchanged.

The following section describes a sorting network that sorts n elements in $\Theta(\log^2 n)$ time. To simplify the presentation, we assume that n is a power of two.

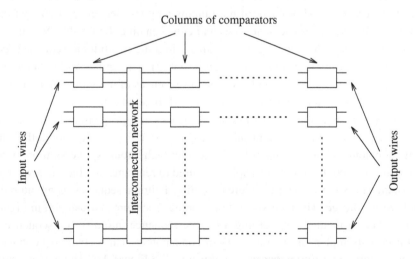

Figure 9.4 A typical sorting network. Every sorting network is made up of a series of columns, and each column contains a number of comparators connected in parallel.

9.2.1   Bitonic Sort

A bitonic sorting network sorts n elements in $\Theta(\log^2 n)$ time. The key operation of the bitonic sorting network is the rearrangement of a bitonic sequence into a sorted sequence. A **bitonic sequence** is a sequence of elements $\langle a_0, a_1, \ldots, a_{n-1} \rangle$ with the property that either (1) there exists an index i, $0 \leq i \leq n-1$, such that $\langle a_0, \ldots, a_i \rangle$ is monotonically increasing and $\langle a_{i+1}, \ldots, a_{n-1} \rangle$ is monotonically decreasing, or (2) there exists a cyclic shift of indices so that (1) is satisfied. For example, $\langle 1, 2, 4, 7, 6, 0 \rangle$ is a bitonic sequence, because it first increases and then decreases. Similarly, $\langle 8, 9, 2, 1, 0, 4 \rangle$ is another bitonic sequence, because it is a cyclic shift of $\langle 0, 4, 8, 9, 2, 1 \rangle$.

We present a method to rearrange a bitonic sequence to obtain a monotonically increasing sequence. Let $s = \langle a_0, a_1, \ldots, a_{n-1} \rangle$ be a bitonic sequence such that $a_0 \leq a_1 \leq \ldots \leq a_{n/2-1}$ and $a_{n/2} \geq a_{n/2+1} \geq \ldots \geq a_{n-1}$. Consider the following subsequences of s:

$$
\begin{aligned}
s_1 &= \langle \min\{a_0, a_{n/2}\}, \min\{a_1, a_{n/2+1}\}, \ldots, \min\{a_{n/2-1}, a_{n-1}\} \rangle \\
s_2 &= \langle \max\{a_0, a_{n/2}\}, \max\{a_1, a_{n/2+1}\}, \ldots, \max\{a_{n/2-1}, a_{n-1}\} \rangle
\end{aligned}
\tag{9.1}
$$

In sequence s_1, there is an element $b_i = \min\{a_i, a_{n/2+i}\}$ such that all the elements before b_i are from the increasing part of the original sequence and all the elements after b_i are from the decreasing part. Also, in sequence s_2, the element $b_i' = \max\{a_i, a_{n/2+i}\}$ is such that all the elements before b_i' are from the decreasing part of the original sequence and all the elements after b_i' are from the increasing part. Thus, the sequences s_1 and s_2 are bitonic sequences. Furthermore, every element of the first sequence is smaller than every element of the second sequence. The reason is that b_i is greater than or equal to all elements of s_1, b_i' is less than or equal to all elements of s_2, and b_i' is greater than or equal to b_i. Thus, we have reduced the initial problem of rearranging a bitonic sequence of size n to that of rearranging two smaller bitonic sequences and concatenating the results. We refer to the operation of splitting a bitonic sequence of size n into the two bitonic sequences defined by Equation 9.1 as a **bitonic split**. Although in obtaining s_1 and s_2 we assumed that the original sequence had increasing and decreasing sequences of the same length, the bitonic split operation also holds for any bitonic sequence (Problem 9.3).

We can recursively obtain shorter bitonic sequences using Equation 9.1 for each of the bitonic subsequences until we obtain subsequences of size one. At that point, the output is sorted in monotonically increasing order. Since after each bitonic split operation the size of the problem is halved, the number of splits required to rearrange the bitonic sequence into a sorted sequence is $\log n$. The procedure of sorting a bitonic sequence using bitonic splits is called **bitonic merge**. The recursive bitonic merge procedure is illustrated in Figure 9.5.

We now have a method for merging a bitonic sequence into a sorted sequence. This method is easy to implement on a network of comparators. This network of comparators, known as a **bitonic merging network**, it is illustrated in Figure 9.6. The network contains $\log n$ columns. Each column contains $n/2$ comparators and performs one step of the bitonic merge. This network takes as input the bitonic sequence and outputs the sequence in sorted order. We denote a bitonic merging network with n inputs by $\oplus$BM[n]. If we replace the

Original															
sequence	3	5	8	9	10	12	14	20	95	90	60	40	35	23	18	0
1st Split	3	5	8	9	10	12	14	0	95	90	60	40	35	23	18	20
2nd Split	3	5	8	0	10	12	14	9	35	23	18	20	95	90	60	40
3rd Split	3	0	8	5	10	9	14	12	18	20	35	23	60	40	95	90
4th Split	0	3	5	8	9	10	12	14	18	20	23	35	40	60	90	95

Figure 9.5 Merging a 16-element bitonic sequence through a series of $\log 16$ bitonic splits.

$\oplus$ comparators in Figure 9.6 by $\ominus$ comparators, the input will be sorted in monotonically decreasing order; such a network is denoted by $\ominus$BM[n].

Armed with the bitonic merging network, consider the task of sorting n unordered elements. This is done by repeatedly merging bitonic sequences of increasing length, as illustrated in Figure 9.7.

Let us now see how this method works. A sequence of two elements x and y forms a bitonic sequence, since either $x \leq y$, in which case the bitonic sequence has x and y in the increasing part and no elements in the decreasing part, or $x \geq y$, in which case the bitonic sequence has x and y in the decreasing part and no elements in the increasing part.

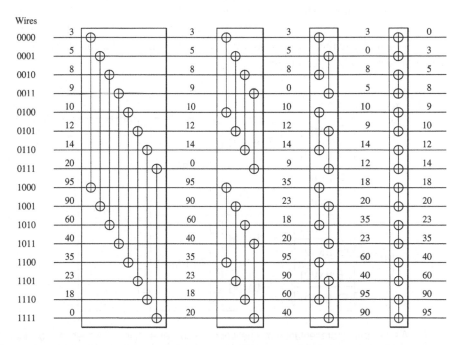

Figure 9.6 A bitonic merging network for $n = 16$. The input wires are numbered $0, 1 \ldots, n - 1$, and the binary representation of these numbers is shown. Each column of comparators is drawn separately; the entire figure represents a $\oplus$BM[16] bitonic merging network. The network takes a bitonic sequence and outputs it in sorted order.

Hence, any unsorted sequence of elements is a concatenation of bitonic sequences of size two. Each stage of the network shown in Figure 9.7 merges adjacent bitonic sequences in increasing and decreasing order. According to the definition of a bitonic sequence, the sequence obtained by concatenating the increasing and decreasing sequences is bitonic. Hence, the output of each stage in the network in Figure 9.7 is a concatenation of bitonic sequences that are twice as long as those at the input. By merging larger and larger bitonic sequences, we eventually obtain a bitonic sequence of size n. Merging this sequence sorts the input. We refer to the algorithm embodied in this method as ***bitonic sort*** and the network as a ***bitonic sorting network***. The first three stages of the network in Figure 9.7 are shown explicitly in Figure 9.8. The last stage of Figure 9.7 is shown explicitly in Figure 9.6.

The last stage of an n-element bitonic sorting network contains a bitonic merging network with n inputs. This has a depth of $\log n$. The other stages perform a complete sort of $n/2$ elements. Hence, the depth, $d(n)$, of the network in Figure 9.7 is given by the following recurrence relation:

$$d(n) = d(n/2) + \log n \tag{9.2}$$

Solving Equation 9.2, we obtain $d(n) = \sum_{i=1}^{\log n} i = (\log^2 n + \log n)/2 = \Theta(\log^2 n)$. This network can be implemented on a serial computer, yielding a $\Theta(n \log^2 n)$ sorting algorithm. The bitonic sorting network can also be adapted and used as a sorting algorithm for parallel computers. In the next section, we describe how this can be done for hypercube- and mesh-connected parallel computers.

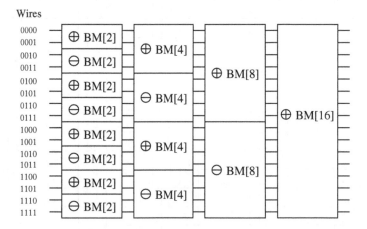

Figure 9.7   A schematic representation of a network that converts an input sequence into a bitonic sequence. In this example, ⊕BM[k] and ⊖BM[k] denote bitonic merging networks of input size k that use ⊕ and ⊖ comparators, respectively. The last merging network (⊕BM[16]) sorts the input. In this example, $n = 16$.

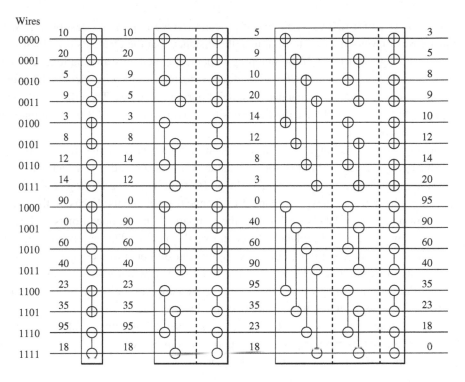

Figure 9.8 The comparator network that transforms an input sequence of 16 unordered numbers into a bitonic sequence. In contrast to Figure 9.6, the columns of comparators in each bitonic merging network are drawn in a single box, separated by a dashed line.

9.2.2 Mapping Bitonic Sort to a Hypercube and a Mesh

In this section we discuss how the bitonic sort algorithm can be mapped on general-purpose parallel computers. One of the key aspects of the bitonic algorithm is that it is communication intensive, and a proper mapping of the algorithm must take into account the topology of the underlying interconnection network. For this reason, we discuss how the bitonic sort algorithm can be mapped onto the interconnection network of a hypercube- and mesh-connected parallel computers.

The bitonic sorting network for sorting n elements contains $\log n$ stages, and stage i consists of i columns of $n/2$ comparators. As Figures 9.6 and 9.8 show, each column of comparators performs compare-exchange operations on n wires. On a parallel computer, the compare-exchange function is performed by a pair of processes.

One Element Per Process

In this mapping, each of the n processes contains one element of the input sequence. Graphically, each wire of the bitonic sorting network represents a distinct process. During each step of the algorithm, the compare-exchange operations performed by a column of comparators are performed by $n/2$ pairs of processes. One important question is how to map processes to wires in order to minimize the distance that the elements travel during a compare-exchange operation. If the mapping is poor, the elements travel a long distance before they can be compared, which will degrade performance. Ideally, wires that perform a compare-exchange should be mapped onto neighboring processes. Then the parallel formulation of bitonic sort will have the best possible performance over all the formulations that require n processes.

To obtain a good mapping, we must further investigate the way that input wires are paired during each stage of bitonic sort. Consider Figures 9.6 and 9.8, which show the full bitonic sorting network for $n = 16$. In each of the $(1 + \log 16)(\log 16)/2 = 10$ comparator columns, certain wires compare-exchange their elements. Focus on the binary representation of the wire labels. In any step, the compare-exchange operation is performed between two wires only if their labels differ in exactly one bit. During each of the four stages, wires whose labels differ in the least-significant bit perform a compare-exchange in the last step of each stage. During the last three stages, wires whose labels differ in the second-least-significant bit perform a compare-exchange in the second-to-last step of each stage. In general, wires whose labels differ in the ith least-significant bit perform a compare-exchange $(\log n - i + 1)$ times. This observation helps us efficiently map wires onto processes by mapping wires that perform compare-exchange operations more frequently to processes that are close to each other.

Hypercube   Mapping wires onto the processes of a hypercube-connected parallel computer is straightforward. Compare-exchange operations take place between wires whose labels differ in only one bit. In a hypercube, processes whose labels differ in only one bit are neighbors (Section 2.4.3). Thus, an optimal mapping of input wires to hypercube processes is the one that maps an input wire with label l to a process with label l where $l = 0, 1, \ldots, n - 1$.

Consider how processes are paired for their compare-exchange steps in a d-dimensional hypercube (that is, $p = 2^d$). In the final stage of bitonic sort, the input has been converted into a bitonic sequence. During the first step of this stage, processes that differ only in the dth bit of the binary representation of their labels (that is, the most significant bit) compare-exchange their elements. Thus, the compare-exchange operation takes place between processes along the dth dimension. Similarly, during the second step of the algorithm, the compare-exchange operation takes place among the processes along the $(d - 1)^{th}$ dimension. In general, during the ith step of the final stage, processes communicate along the $(d - (i - 1))^{th}$ dimension. Figure 9.9 illustrates the communication during the last stage of the bitonic sort algorithm.

A bitonic merge of sequences of size 2^k can be performed on a k-dimensional subcube, with each such sequence assigned to a different subcube (Problem 9.5). Furthermore, during the ith step of this bitonic merge, the processes that compare their elements are neighbors along the $(k - (i - 1))^{th}$ dimension. Figure 9.10 is a modification of Figure 9.7, showing the communication characteristics of the bitonic sort algorithm on a hypercube.

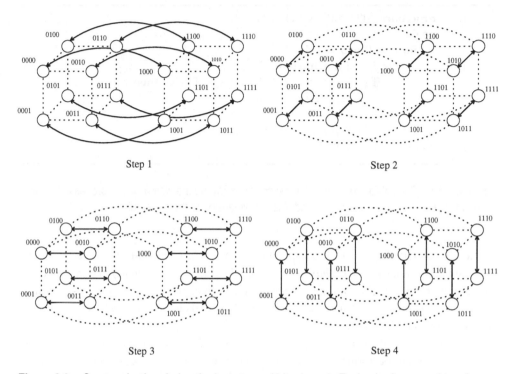

Figure 9.9 Communication during the last stage of bitonic sort. Each wire is mapped to a hypercube process; each connection represents a compare-exchange between processes.

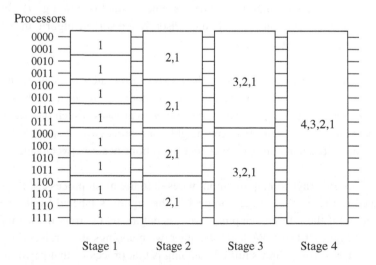

Figure 9.10 Communication characteristics of bitonic sort on a hypercube. During each stage of the algorithm, processes communicate along the dimensions shown.

```
1.    procedure BITONIC_SORT(label, d)
2.    begin
3.        for i := 0 to d − 1 do
4.            for j := i downto 0 do
5.                if (i + 1)ˢᵗ bit of label ≠ jᵗʰ bit of label then
6.                    comp_exchange_max(j);
7.                else
8.                    comp_exchange_min(j);
9.    end BITONIC_SORT
```

Algorithm 9.1   Parallel formulation of bitonic sort on a hypercube with $n = 2^d$ processes. In this algorithm, *label* is the process's label and d is the dimension of the hypercube.

The bitonic sort algorithm for a hypercube is shown in Algorithm 9.1. The algorithm relies on the functions *comp_exchange_max(i)* and *comp_exchange_min(i)*. These functions compare the local element with the element on the nearest process along the ith dimension and retain either the minimum or the maximum of the two elements. Problem 9.6 explores the correctness of Algorithm 9.1.

During each step of the algorithm, every process performs a compare-exchange operation. The algorithm performs a total of $(1 + \log n)(\log n)/2$ such steps; thus, the parallel run time is

$$T_P = \Theta(\log^2 n) \tag{9.3}$$

This parallel formulation of bitonic sort is cost optimal with respect to the sequential implementation of bitonic sort (that is, the process-time product is $\Theta(n \log^2 n)$), but it is not cost-optimal with respect to an optimal comparison-based sorting algorithm, which has a serial time complexity of $\Theta(n \log n)$.

Mesh   Consider how the input wires of the bitonic sorting network can be mapped efficiently onto an n-process mesh. Unfortunately, the connectivity of a mesh is lower than that of a hypercube, so it is impossible to map wires to processes such that each compare-exchange operation occurs only between neighboring processes. Instead, we map wires such that the most frequent compare-exchange operations occur between neighboring processes.

There are several ways to map the input wires onto the mesh processes. Some of these are illustrated in Figure 9.11. Each process in this figure is labeled by the wire that is mapped onto it. Of these three mappings, we concentrate on the row-major shuffled mapping, shown in Figure 9.11(c). We leave the other two mappings as exercises (Problem 9.7).

The advantage of row-major shuffled mapping is that processes that perform compare-exchange operations reside on square subsections of the mesh whose size is inversely related to the frequency of compare-exchanges. For example, processes that perform compare-exchange during every stage of bitonic sort (that is, those corresponding to wires

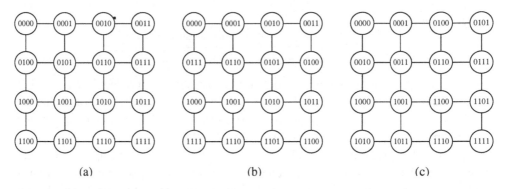

Figure 9.11 Different ways of mapping the input wires of the bitonic sorting network to a mesh of processes: (a) row-major mapping, (b) row-major snakelike mapping, and (c) row-major shuffled mapping.

that differ in the least-significant bit) are neighbors. In general, wires that differ in the ith least-significant bit are mapped onto mesh processes that are $2^{\lfloor (i-1)/2 \rfloor}$ communication links away. The compare-exchange steps of the last stage of bitonic sort for the row-major shuffled mapping are shown in Figure 9.12. Note that each earlier stage will have only some of these steps.

During the $(1 + \log n)(\log n)/2$ steps of the algorithm, processes that are a certain distance apart compare-exchange their elements. The distance between processes determines the communication overhead of the parallel formulation. The total amount of communication performed by each process is $\sum_{i=1}^{\log n} \sum_{j=1}^{i} 2^{\lfloor (j-1)/2 \rfloor} \approx 7\sqrt{n}$, which is $\Theta(\sqrt{n})$ (Problem 9.7). During each step of the algorithm, each process performs at most one comparison; thus, the total computation performed by each process is $\Theta(\log^2 n)$. This yields a

Stage 4

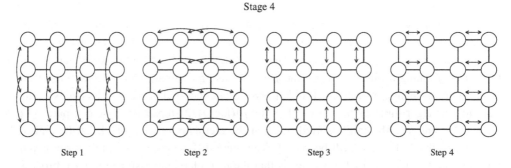

Step 1   Step 2   Step 3   Step 4

Figure 9.12 The last stage of the bitonic sort algorithm for $n = 16$ on a mesh, using the row-major shuffled mapping. During each step, process pairs compare-exchange their elements. Arrows indicate the pairs of processes that perform compare-exchange operations.

parallel run time of

$$T_P = \overbrace{\Theta(\log^2 n)}^{\text{comparisons}} + \overbrace{\Theta(\sqrt{n})}^{\text{communication}}.$$

This is not a cost-optimal formulation, because the process-time product is $\Theta(n^{1.5})$, but the sequential complexity of sorting is $\Theta(n \log n)$. Although the parallel formulation for a hypercube was optimal with respect to the sequential complexity of bitonic sort, the formulation for mesh is not. Can we do any better? No. When sorting n elements, one per mesh process, for certain inputs the element stored in the process at the upper-left corner will end up in the process at the lower-right corner. For this to happen, this element must travel along $2\sqrt{n} - 1$ communication links before reaching its destination. Thus, the run time of sorting on a mesh is bounded by $\Omega(\sqrt{n})$. Our parallel formulation achieves this lower bound; thus, it is asymptotically optimal for the mesh architecture.

A Block of Elements Per Process

In the parallel formulations of the bitonic sort algorithm presented so far, we assumed there were as many processes as elements to be sorted. Now we consider the case in which the number of elements to be sorted is greater than the number of processes.

Let p be the number of processes and n be the number of elements to be sorted, such that $p < n$. Each process is assigned a block of n/p elements and cooperates with the other processes to sort them. One way to obtain a parallel formulation with our new setup is to think of each process as consisting of n/p smaller processes. In other words, imagine emulating n/p processes by using a single process. The run time of this formulation will be greater by a factor of n/p because each process is doing the work of n/p processes. This virtual process approach (Section 5.3) leads to a poor parallel implementation of bitonic sort. To see this, consider the case of a hypercube with p processes. Its run time will be $\Theta((n \log^2 n)/p)$, which is not cost-optimal because the process-time product is $\Theta(n \log^2 n)$.

An alternate way of dealing with blocks of elements is to use the compare-split operation presented in Section 9.1. Think of the (n/p)-element blocks as elements to be sorted using compare-split operations. The problem of sorting the p blocks is identical to that of performing a bitonic sort on the p blocks using compare-split operations instead of compare-exchange operations (Problem 9.8). Since the total number of blocks is p, the bitonic sort algorithm has a total of $(1 + \log p)(\log p)/2$ steps. Because compare-split operations preserve the initial sorted order of the elements in each block, at the end of these steps the n elements will be sorted. The main difference between this formulation and the one that uses virtual processes is that the n/p elements assigned to each process are initially sorted locally, using a fast sequential sorting algorithm. This initial local sort makes the new formulation more efficient and cost-optimal.

Hypercube   The block-based algorithm for a hypercube with p processes is similar to the one-element-per-process case, but now we have p blocks of size n/p, instead of p

elements. Furthermore, the compare-exchange operations are replaced by compare-split operations, each taking $\Theta(n/p)$ computation time and $\Theta(n/p)$ communication time. Initially the processes sort their n/p elements (using merge sort) in time $\Theta((n/p)\log(n/p))$ and then perform $\Theta(\log^2 p)$ compare-split steps. The parallel run time of this formulation is

$$T_P = \overbrace{\Theta\left(\frac{n}{p}\log\frac{n}{p}\right)}^{\text{local sort}} + \overbrace{\Theta\left(\frac{n}{p}\log^2 p\right)}^{\text{comparisons}} + \overbrace{\Theta\left(\frac{n}{p}\log^2 p\right)}^{\text{communication}}.$$

Because the sequential complexity of the best sorting algorithm is $\Theta(n\log n)$, the speedup and efficiency are as follows:

$$S = \frac{\Theta(n\log n)}{\Theta((n/p)\log(n/p)) + \Theta((n/p)\log^2 p)}$$

$$E = \frac{1}{1 - \Theta((\log p)/(\log n)) + \Theta((\log^2 p)/(\log n))} \tag{9.4}$$

From Equation 9.4, for a cost-optimal formulation $(\log^2 p)/(\log n) = O(1)$. Thus, this algorithm can efficiently use up to $p = \Theta(2^{\sqrt{\log n}})$ processes. Also from Equation 9.4, the isoefficiency function due to both communication and extra work is $\Theta(p^{\log p}\log^2 p)$, which is worse than any polynomial isoefficiency function for sufficiently large p. Hence, this parallel formulation of bitonic sort has poor scalability.

Mesh The block-based mesh formulation is also similar to the one-element-per-process case. The parallel run time of this formulation is as follows:

$$T_P = \overbrace{\Theta\left(\frac{n}{p}\log\frac{n}{p}\right)}^{\text{local sort}} + \overbrace{\Theta\left(\frac{n}{p}\log^2 p\right)}^{\text{comparisons}} + \overbrace{\Theta\left(\frac{n}{\sqrt{p}}\right)}^{\text{communication}}$$

Note that comparing the communication overhead of this mesh-based parallel bitonic sort $(O(n/\sqrt{p}))$ to the communication overhead of the hypercube-based formulation $(O((n\log^2 p)/p))$, we can see that it is higher by a factor of $O(\sqrt{p}/\log^2 p)$. This factor is smaller than the $O(\sqrt{p})$ difference in the bisection bandwidth of these architectures. This illustrates that a proper mapping of the bitonic sort on the underlying mesh can achieve better performance than that achieved by simply mapping the hypercube algorithm on the mesh.

The speedup and efficiency are as follows:

$$S = \frac{\Theta(n\log n)}{\Theta((n/p)\log(n/p)) + \Theta((n/p)\log^2 p) + \Theta(n/\sqrt{p})}$$

$$E = \frac{1}{1 - \Theta((\log p)/(\log n)) + \Theta((\log^2 p)/(\log n)) + \Theta(\sqrt{p}/\log n)} \tag{9.5}$$

Table 9.1   The performance of parallel formulations of bitonic sort for n elements on p processes.

Architecture	Maximum Number of Processes for $E = \Theta(1)$	Corresponding Parallel Run Time	Isoefficiency Function
Hypercube	$\Theta(2^{\sqrt{\log n}})$	$\Theta(n/(2^{\sqrt{\log n}})\log n)$	$\Theta(p^{\log p}\log^2 p)$
Mesh	$\Theta(\log^2 n)$	$\Theta(n/\log n)$	$\Theta(2^{\sqrt{p}}\sqrt{p})$
Ring	$\Theta(\log n)$	$\Theta(n)$	$\Theta(2^p p)$

From Equation 9.5, for a cost-optimal formulation $\sqrt{p}/\log n = O(1)$. Thus, this formulation can efficiently use up to $p = \Theta(\log^2 n)$ processes. Also from Equation 9.5, the isoefficiency function $\Theta(2^{\sqrt{p}}\sqrt{p})$. The isoefficiency function of this formulation is exponential, and thus is even worse than that for the hypercube.

From the analysis for hypercube and mesh, we see that parallel formulations of bitonic sort are neither very efficient nor very scalable. This is primarily because the sequential algorithm is suboptimal. Good speedups are possible on a large number of processes only if the number of elements to be sorted is very large. In that case, the efficiency of the internal sorting outweighs the inefficiency of the bitonic sort. Table 9.1 summarizes the performance of bitonic sort on hypercube-, mesh-, and ring-connected parallel computer.

9.3   Bubble Sort and its Variants

The previous section presented a sorting network that could sort n elements in a time of $\Theta(\log^2 n)$. We now turn our attention to more traditional sorting algorithms. Since serial algorithms with $\Theta(n \log n)$ time complexity exist, we should be able to use $\Theta(n)$ processes to sort n elements in time $\Theta(\log n)$. As we will see, this is difficult to achieve. We can, however, easily parallelize many sequential sorting algorithms that have $\Theta(n^2)$ complexity. The algorithms we present are based on *bubble sort*.

The sequential bubble sort algorithm compares and exchanges adjacent elements in the sequence to be sorted. Given a sequence $\langle a_1, a_2, \ldots, a_n \rangle$, the algorithm first performs $n - 1$ compare-exchange operations in the following order: $(a_1, a_2), (a_2, a_3), \ldots, (a_{n-1}, a_n)$. This step moves the largest element to the end of the sequence. The last element in the transformed sequence is then ignored, and the sequence of compare-exchanges is applied to the resulting sequence $\langle a'_1, a'_2, \ldots, a'_{n-1} \rangle$. The sequence is sorted after $n - 1$ iterations. We can improve the performance of bubble sort by terminating when no exchanges take place during an iteration. The bubble sort algorithm is shown in Algorithm 9.2.

An iteration of the inner loop of bubble sort takes time $\Theta(n)$, and we perform a total of $\Theta(n)$ iterations; thus, the complexity of bubble sort is $\Theta(n^2)$. Bubble sort is difficult to parallelize. To see this, consider how compare-exchange operations are performed during each phase of the algorithm (lines 4 and 5 of Algorithm 9.2). Bubble sort compares all

---

1.   **procedure** BUBBLE_SORT(n)
2.   **begin**
3.   **for** $i := n - 1$ **downto** 1 **do**
4.   **for** $j := 1$ **to** i **do**
5.   *compare-exchange*(a_j, a_{j+1});
6.   **end** BUBBLE_SORT

Algorithm 9.2   Sequential bubble sort algorithm.

adjacent pairs in order; hence, it is inherently sequential. In the following two sections, we present two variants of bubble sort that are well suited to parallelization.

9.3.1 Odd-Even Transposition

The *odd-even transposition* algorithm sorts n elements in n phases (n is even), each of which requires $n/2$ compare-exchange operations. This algorithm alternates between two phases, called the odd and even phases. Let $\langle a_1, a_2, \ldots, a_n \rangle$ be the sequence to be sorted. During the odd phase, elements with odd indices are compared with their right neighbors, and if they are out of sequence they are exchanged; thus, the pairs $(a_1, a_2), (a_3, a_4), \ldots,$ (a_{n-1}, a_n) are compare-exchanged (assuming n is even). Similarly, during the even phase, elements with even indices are compared with their right neighbors, and if they are out of sequence they are exchanged; thus, the pairs $(a_2, a_3), (a_4, a_5), \ldots, (a_{n-2}, a_{n-1})$ are compare-exchanged. After n phases of odd-even exchanges, the sequence is sorted. Each phase of the algorithm (either odd or even) requires $\Theta(n)$ comparisons, and there are a total of n phases; thus, the sequential complexity is $\Theta(n^2)$. The odd-even transposition sort is shown in Algorithm 9.3 and is illustrated in Figure 9.13.

---

1.   **procedure** ODD-EVEN(n)
2.   **begin**
3.   **for** $i := 1$ **to** n **do**
4.   **begin**
5.   **if** i is odd **then**
6.   **for** $j := 0$ **to** $n/2 - 1$ **do**
7.   *compare-exchange*(a_{2j+1}, a_{2j+2});
8.   **if** i is even **then**
9.   **for** $j := 1$ **to** $n/2 - 1$ **do**
10.   *compare-exchange*(a_{2j}, a_{2j+1});
11.   **end for**
12.   **end** ODD-EVEN

Algorithm 9.3   Sequential odd-even transposition sort algorithm.

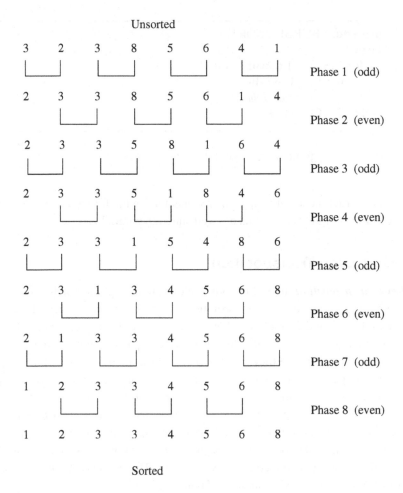

Figure 9.13   Sorting $n = 8$ elements, using the odd-even transposition sort algorithm. During each phase, $n = 8$ elements are compared.

Parallel Formulation

It is easy to parallelize odd-even transposition sort. During each phase of the algorithm, compare-exchange operations on pairs of elements are performed simultaneously. Consider the one-element-per-process case. Let n be the number of processes (also the number of elements to be sorted). Assume that the processes are arranged in a one-dimensional array. Element a_i initially resides on process P_i for $i = 1, 2, \ldots, n$. During the odd phase, each process that has an odd label compare-exchanges its element with the element residing on its right neighbor. Similarly, during the even phase, each process with an even label compare-exchanges its element with the element of its right neighbor. This parallel formulation is presented in Algorithm 9.4.

During each phase of the algorithm, the odd or even processes perform a compare-

---

```
1.     procedure ODD-EVEN_PAR(n)
2.     begin
3.        id := process's label
4.        for i := 1 to n do
5.        begin
6.           if i is odd then
7.              if id is odd then
8.                 compare-exchange_min(id + 1);
9.              else
10.                compare-exchange_max(id − 1);
11.          if i is even then
12.             if id is even then
13.                compare-exchange_min(id + 1);
14.             else
15.                compare-exchange_max(id − 1);
16.       end for
17.    end ODD-EVEN_PAR
```

Algorithm 9.4   The parallel formulation of odd-even transposition sort on an n-process ring.

exchange step with their right neighbors. As we know from Section 9.1, this requires time $\Theta(1)$. A total of n such phases are performed; thus, the parallel run time of this formulation is $\Theta(n)$. Since the sequential complexity of the best sorting algorithm for n elements is $\Theta(n \log n)$, this formulation of odd-even transposition sort is not cost-optimal, because its process-time product is $\Theta(n^2)$.

To obtain a cost-optimal parallel formulation, we use fewer processes. Let p be the number of processes, where $p < n$. Initially, each process is assigned a block of n/p elements, which it sorts internally (using merge sort or quicksort) in $\Theta((n/p) \log(n/p))$ time. After this, the processes execute p phases ($p/2$ odd and $p/2$ even), performing compare-split operations. At the end of these phases, the list is sorted (Problem 9.10). During each phase, $\Theta(n/p)$ comparisons are performed to merge two blocks, and time $\Theta(n/p)$ is spent communicating. Thus, the parallel run time of the formulation is

$$T_P = \Theta\left(\overbrace{\frac{n}{p} \log \frac{n}{p}}^{\text{local sort}}\right) + \overbrace{\Theta(n)}^{\text{comparisons}} + \overbrace{\Theta(n)}^{\text{communication}}.$$

Since the sequential complexity of sorting is $\Theta(n \log n)$, the speedup and efficiency of this formulation are as follows:

$$S = \frac{\Theta(n \log n)}{\Theta((n/p) \log(n/p)) + \Theta(n)}$$

$$E = \frac{1}{1 - \Theta((\log p)/(\log n)) + \Theta(p/\log n)} \tag{9.6}$$

From Equation 9.6, odd-even transposition sort is cost-optimal when $p = O(\log n)$. The isoefficiency function of this parallel formulation is $\Theta(p\, 2^p)$, which is exponential. Thus, it is poorly scalable and is suited to only a small number of processes.

9.3.2 Shellsort

The main limitation of odd-even transposition sort is that it moves elements only one position at a time. If a sequence has just a few elements out of order, and if they are $\Theta(n)$ distance from their proper positions, then the sequential algorithm still requires time $\Theta(n^2)$ to sort the sequence. To make a substantial improvement over odd-even transposition sort, we need an algorithm that moves elements long distances. Shellsort is one such serial sorting algorithm.

Let n be the number of elements to be sorted and p be the number of processes. To simplify the presentation we will assume that the number of processes is a power of two, that is, $p = 2^d$, but the algorithm can be easily extended to work for an arbitrary number of processes as well. Each process is assigned a block of n/p elements. The processes are considered to be arranged in a logical one-dimensional array, and the ordering of the processes in that array defines the global ordering of the sorted sequence. The algorithm consists of two phases. During the first phase, processes that are far away from each other in the array compare-split their elements. Elements thus move long distances to get close to their final destinations in a few steps. During the second phase, the algorithm switches to an odd-even transposition sort similar to the one described in the previous section. The only difference is that the odd and even phases are performed only as long as the blocks on the processes are changing. Because the first phase of the algorithm moves elements close to their final destinations, the number of odd and even phases performed by the second phase may be substantially smaller than p.

Initially, each process sorts its block of n/p elements internally in $\Theta(n/p \log(n/p))$ time. Then, each process is paired with its corresponding process in the reverse order of the array. That is, process P_i, where $i < p/2$, is paired with process P_{p-i-1}. Each pair of processes performs a compare-split operation. Next, the processes are partitioned into two groups; one group has the first $p/2$ processes and the other group has the last $p/2$ processes. Now, each group is treated as a separate set of $p/2$ processes and the above scheme of process-pairing is applied to determine which processes will perform the compare-split operation. This process continues for d steps, until each group contains only a single process. The compare-split operations of the first phase are illustrated in Figure 9.14 for $d = 3$. Note that it is not a direct parallel formulation of the sequential shellsort, but it relies on similar ideas.

In the first phase of the algorithm, each process performs $d = \log p$ compare-split operations. In each compare-split operation a total of $p/2$ pairs of processes need to exchange their locally stored n/p elements. The communication time required by these compare-split operations depend on the bisection bandwidth of the network. In the case in which the bisection bandwidth is $\Theta(p)$, the amount of time required by each operation is $\Theta(n/p)$.

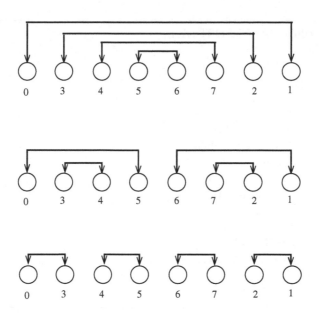

Figure 9.14 An example of the first phase of parallel shellsort on an eight-process array.

Thus, the complexity of this phase is $\Theta((n \log p)/p)$. In the second phase, l odd and even phases are performed, each requiring time $\Theta(n/p)$. Thus, the parallel run time of the algorithm is

$$
T_P = \overbrace{\Theta\left(\frac{n}{p} \log \frac{n}{p}\right)}^{\text{local sort}} + \overbrace{\Theta\left(\frac{n}{p} \log p\right)}^{\text{first phase}} + \overbrace{\Theta\left(l\frac{n}{p}\right)}^{\text{second phase}}. \tag{9.7}
$$

The performance of shellsort depends on the value of l. If l is small, then the algorithm performs significantly better than odd-even transposition sort; if l is $\Theta(p)$, then both algorithms perform similarly. Problem 9.13 investigates the worst-case value of l.

9.4 Quicksort

All the algorithms presented so far have worse sequential complexity than that of the lower bound for comparison-based sorting, $\Theta(n \log n)$. This section examines the *quicksort* algorithm, which has an average complexity of $\Theta(n \log n)$. Quicksort is one of the most common sorting algorithms for sequential computers because of its simplicity, low overhead, and optimal average complexity.

Quicksort is a divide-and-conquer algorithm that sorts a sequence by recursively dividing it into smaller subsequences. Assume that the n-element sequence to be sorted is stored in the array $A[1 \ldots n]$. Quicksort consists of two steps: divide and conquer. During the divide step, a sequence $A[q \ldots r]$ is partitioned (rearranged) into two nonempty subsequences $A[q \ldots s]$ and $A[s + 1 \ldots r]$ such that each element of the first subsequence is

---

```
1.    procedure QUICKSORT (A, q, r)
2.    begin
3.        if q < r then
4.        begin
5.            x := A[q];
6.            s := q;
7.            for i := q + 1 to r do
8.                if A[i] ≤ x then
9.                begin
10.                   s := s + 1;
11.                   swap(A[s], A[i]);
12.               end if
13.               swap(A[q], A[s]);
14.               QUICKSORT (A, q, s);
15.               QUICKSORT (A, s + 1, r);
16.       end if
17.   end QUICKSORT
```

Algorithm 9.5 The sequential quicksort algorithm.

smaller than or equal to each element of the second subsequence. During the conquer step, the subsequences are sorted by recursively applying quicksort. Since the subsequences $A[q \ldots s]$ and $A[s + 1 \ldots r]$ are sorted and the first subsequence has smaller elements than the second, the entire sequence is sorted.

How is the sequence $A[q \ldots r]$ partitioned into two parts – one with all elements smaller than the other? This is usually accomplished by selecting one element x from $A[q \ldots r]$ and using this element to partition the sequence $A[q \ldots r]$ into two parts – one with elements less than or equal to x and the other with elements greater than x. Element x is called the *pivot*. The quicksort algorithm is presented in Algorithm 9.5. This algorithm arbitrarily chooses the first element of the sequence $A[q \ldots r]$ as the pivot. The operation of quicksort is illustrated in Figure 9.15.

The complexity of partitioning a sequence of size k is $\Theta(k)$. Quicksort's performance is greatly affected by the way it partitions a sequence. Consider the case in which a sequence of size k is split poorly, into two subsequences of sizes 1 and $k - 1$. The run time in this case is given by the recurrence relation $T(n) = T(n - 1) + \Theta(n)$, whose solution is $T(n) = \Theta(n^2)$. Alternatively, consider the case in which the sequence is split well, into two roughly equal-size subsequences of $\lfloor k/2 \rfloor$ and $\lceil k/2 \rceil$ elements. In this case, the run time is given by the recurrence relation $T(n) = 2T(n/2) + \Theta(n)$, whose solution is $T(n) = \Theta(n \log n)$. The second split yields an optimal algorithm. Although quicksort can have $O(n^2)$ worst-case complexity, its average complexity is significantly better; the average number of compare-exchange operations needed by quicksort for sorting a randomly-ordered input sequence is $1.4n \log n$, which is asymptotically optimal. There are

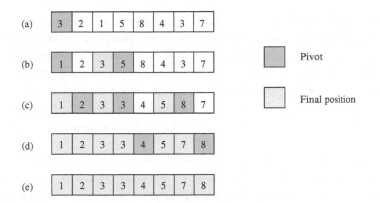

Figure 9.15   Example of the quicksort algorithm sorting a sequence of size $n = 8$.

several ways to select pivots. For example, the pivot can be the median of a small number of elements of the sequence, or it can be an element selected at random. Some pivot selection strategies have advantages over others for certain input sequences.

9.4.1 Parallelizing Quicksort

Quicksort can be parallelized in a variety of ways. First, consider a naive parallel formulation that was also discussed briefly in Section 3.2.1 in the context of recursive decomposition. Lines 14 and 15 of Algorithm 9.5 show that, during each call of QUICKSORT, the array is partitioned into two parts and each part is solved recursively. Sorting the smaller arrays represents two completely independent subproblems that can be solved in parallel. Therefore, one way to parallelize quicksort is to execute it initially on a single process; then, when the algorithm performs its recursive calls (lines 14 and 15), assign one of the subproblems to another process. Now each of these processes sorts its array by using quicksort and assigns one of its subproblems to other processes. The algorithm terminates when the arrays cannot be further partitioned. Upon termination, each process holds an element of the array, and the sorted order can be recovered by traversing the processes as we will describe later. This parallel formulation of quicksort uses n processes to sort n elements. Its major drawback is that partitioning the array $A[q \ldots r]$ into two smaller arrays, $A[q \ldots s]$ and $A[s + 1 \ldots r]$, is done by a single process. Since one process must partition the original array $A[1 \ldots n]$, the run time of this formulation is bounded below by $\Omega(n)$. This formulation is not cost-optimal, because its process-time product is $\Omega(n^2)$.

The main limitation of the previous parallel formulation is that it performs the partitioning step serially. As we will see in subsequent formulations, performing partitioning in parallel is essential in obtaining an efficient parallel quicksort. To see why, consider the recurrence equation $T(n) = 2T(n/2) + \Theta(n)$, which gives the complexity of quicksort for optimal pivot selection. The term $\Theta(n)$ is due to the partitioning of the array. Compare this complexity with the overall complexity of the algorithm, $\Theta(n \log n)$. From these two complexities, we can think of the quicksort algorithm as consisting of $\Theta(\log n)$ steps, each requiring time $\Theta(n)$ – that of splitting the array. Therefore, if the partitioning step is performed in time $\Theta(1)$, using $\Theta(n)$ processes, it is possible to obtain an overall parallel run time of $\Theta(\log n)$, which leads to a cost-optimal formulation. However, without parallelizing the partitioning step, the best we can do (while maintaining cost-optimality) is to use only $\Theta(\log n)$ processes to sort n elements in time $\Theta(n)$ (Problem 9.14). Hence, parallelizing the partitioning step has the potential to yield a significantly faster parallel formulation.

In the previous paragraph, we hinted that we could partition an array of size n into two smaller arrays in time $\Theta(1)$ by using $\Theta(n)$ processes. However, this is difficult for most parallel computing models. The only known algorithms are for the abstract PRAM models. Because of communication overhead, the partitioning step takes longer than $\Theta(1)$ on realistic shared-address-space and message-passing parallel computers. In the following sections we present three distinct parallel formulations: one for a CRCW PRAM, one for a shared-address-space architecture, and one for a message-passing platform. Each of these formulations parallelizes quicksort by performing the partitioning step in parallel.

9.4.2   Parallel Formulation for a CRCW PRAM

We will now present a parallel formulation of quicksort for sorting n elements on an n-process arbitrary CRCW PRAM. Recall from Section 2.4.1 that an arbitrary CRCW PRAM is a concurrent-read, concurrent-write parallel random-access machine in which write conflicts are resolved arbitrarily. In other words, when more than one process tries to write to the same memory location, only one arbitrarily chosen process is allowed to write, and the remaining writes are ignored.

Executing quicksort can be visualized as constructing a binary tree. In this tree, the pivot is the root; elements smaller than or equal to the pivot go to the left subtree, and elements larger than the pivot go to the right subtree. Figure 9.16 illustrates the binary tree constructed by the execution of the quicksort algorithm illustrated in Figure 9.15. The sorted sequence can be obtained from this tree by performing an in-order traversal. The PRAM formulation is based on this interpretation of quicksort.

The algorithm starts by selecting a pivot element and partitioning the array into two parts – one with elements smaller than the pivot and the other with elements larger than the pivot. Subsequent pivot elements, one for each new subarray, are then selected in parallel. This formulation does not rearrange elements; instead, since all the processes can read the pivot in constant time, they know which of the two subarrays (smaller or larger) the elements assigned to them belong to. Thus, they can proceed to the next iteration.

The algorithm that constructs the binary tree is shown in Algorithm 9.6. The array to be sorted is stored in $A[1 \ldots n]$ and process i is assigned element $A[i]$. The arrays *leftchild*$[1 \ldots n]$ and *rightchild*$[1 \ldots n]$ keep track of the children of a given pivot. For each process, the local variable *parent$_i$* stores the label of the process whose element is the pivot. Initially, all the processes write their process labels into the variable *root* in line 5.

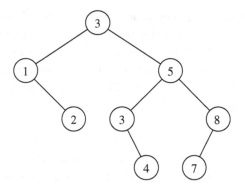

Figure 9.16 A binary tree generated by the execution of the quicksort algorithm. Each level of the tree represents a different array-partitioning iteration. If pivot selection is optimal, then the height of the tree is $\Theta(\log n)$, which is also the number of iterations.

```
1.    procedure BUILD_TREE (A[1 ... n])
2.    begin
3.        for each process i do
4.        begin
5.            root := i;
6.            parent_i := root;
7.            leftchild[i] := rightchild[i] := n + 1;
8.        end for
9.        repeat for each process i ≠ root do
10.       begin
11.           if (A[i] < A[parent_i]) or
                  (A[i] = A[parent_i] and i <parent_i) then
12.           begin
13.               leftchild[parent_i] := i;
14.               if i = leftchild[parent_i] then exit
15.               else parent_i := leftchild[parent_i];
16.           end for
17.           else
18.           begin
19.               rightchild[parent_i] := i;
20.               if i = rightchild[parent_i] then exit
21.               else parent_i := rightchild[parent_i];
22.           end else
23.       end repeat
24.   end BUILD_TREE
```

Algorithm 9.6 The binary tree construction procedure for the CRCW PRAM parallel quicksort formulation.

Because the concurrent write operation is arbitrary, only one of these labels will actually be written into *root*. The value $A[root]$ is used as the first pivot and *root* is copied into *parent$_i$* for each process i. Next, processes that have elements smaller than $A[parent_i]$ write their process labels into *leftchild[parent$_i$]*, and those with larger elements write their process label into *rightchild[parent$_i$]*. Thus, all processes whose elements belong in the smaller partition have written their labels into *leftchild[parent$_i$]*, and those with elements in the larger partition have written their labels into *rightchild[parent$_i$]*. Because of the arbitrary concurrent-write operations, only two values – one for *leftchild[parent$_i$]* and one for *rightchild[parent$_i$]* – are written into these locations. These two values become the labels of the processes that hold the pivot elements for the next iteration, in which two smaller arrays are being partitioned. The algorithm continues until n pivot elements are selected. A process exits when its element becomes a pivot. The construction of the binary tree is illustrated in Figure 9.17. During each iteration of the algorithm, a level of the tree is constructed in time $\Theta(1)$. Thus, the average complexity of the binary tree building algorithm is $\Theta(\log n)$ as the average height of the tree is $\Theta(\log n)$ (Problem 9.16).

After building the binary tree, the algorithm determines the position of each element in the sorted array. It traverses the tree and keeps a count of the number of elements in the left and right subtrees of any element. Finally, each element is placed in its proper position in time $\Theta(1)$, and the array is sorted. The algorithm that traverses the binary tree and computes the position of each element is left as an exercise (Problem 9.15). The average run time of this algorithm is $\Theta(\log n)$ on an n-process PRAM. Thus, its overall process-time product is $\Theta(n \log n)$, which is cost-optimal.

9.4.3   Parallel Formulation for Practical Architectures

We now turn our attention to a more realistic parallel architecture – that of a p-process system connected via an interconnection network. Initially, our discussion will focus on developing an algorithm for a shared-address-space system and then we will show how this algorithm can be adapted to message-passing systems.

Shared-Address-Space Parallel Formulation

The quicksort formulation for a shared-address-space system works as follows. Let A be an array of n elements that need to be sorted and p be the number of processes. Each process is assigned a consecutive block of n/p elements, and the labels of the processes define the global order of the sorted sequence. Let A_i be the block of elements assigned to process P_i.

The algorithm starts by selecting a pivot element, which is broadcast to all processes. Each process P_i, upon receiving the pivot, rearranges its assigned block of elements into two sub-blocks, one with elements smaller than the pivot S_i and one with elements larger than the pivot L_i. This *local* rearrangement is done in place using the *collapsing the loops* approach of quicksort. The next step of the algorithm is to rearrange the elements of the

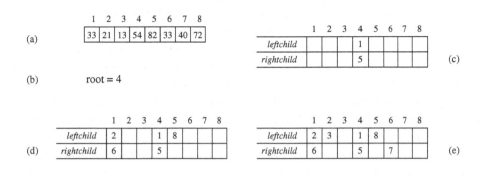

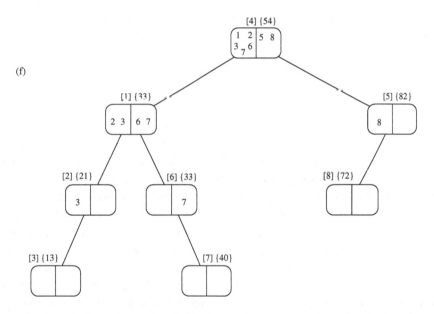

Figure 9.17 The execution of the PRAM algorithm on the array shown in (a). The arrays *leftchild* and *rightchild* are shown in (c), (d), and (e) as the algorithm progresses. Figure (f) shows the binary tree constructed by the algorithm. Each node is labeled by the process (in square brackets), and the element is stored at that process (in curly brackets). The element is the pivot. In each node, processes with smaller elements than the pivot are grouped on the left side of the node, and those with larger elements are grouped on the right side. These two groups form the two partitions of the original array. For each partition, a pivot element is selected at random from the two groups that form the children of the node.

original array A so that all the elements that are smaller than the pivot (i.e., $S = \bigcup_i S_i$) are stored at the beginning of the array, and all the elements that are larger than the pivot (i.e., $L = \bigcup_i L_i$) are stored at the end of the array.

Once this *global* rearrangement is done, then the algorithm proceeds to partition the processes into two groups, and assign to the first group the task of sorting the smaller elements S, and to the second group the task of sorting the larger elements L. Each of these steps is performed by recursively calling the parallel quicksort algorithm. Note that by simultaneously partitioning both the processes and the original array each group of processes can proceed independently. The recursion ends when a particular sub-block of elements is assigned to only a single process, in which case the process sorts the elements using a serial quicksort algorithm.

The partitioning of processes into two groups is done according to the relative sizes of the S and L blocks. In particular, the first $\lceil |S| p/n + 0.5 \rceil$ processes are assigned to sort the smaller elements S, and the rest of the processes are assigned to sort the larger elements L. Note that the 0.5 term in the above formula is to ensure that the processes are assigned in the most balanced fashion.

Example 9.1   Efficient parallel quicksort

Figure 9.18 illustrates this algorithm using an example of 20 integers and five processes. In the first step, each process locally rearranges the four elements that it is initially responsible for, around the pivot element (seven in this example), so that the elements smaller or equal to the pivot are moved to the beginning of the locally assigned portion of the array (and are shaded in the figure). Once this local rearrangement is done, the processes perform a global rearrangement to obtain the third array shown in the figure (how this is performed will be discussed shortly). In the second step, the processes are partitioned into two groups. The first contains $\{P_0, P_1\}$ and is responsible for sorting the elements that are smaller than or equal to seven, and the second group contains processes $\{P_2, P_3, P_4\}$ and is responsible for sorting the elements that are greater than seven. Note that the sizes of these process groups were created to match the relative size of the smaller than and larger than the pivot arrays. Now, the steps of pivot selection, local, and global rearrangement are recursively repeated for each process group and sub-array, until a sub-array is assigned to a single process, in which case it proceeds to sort it locally. Also note that these final local sub-arrays will in general be of different size, as they depend on the elements that were selected to act as pivots.   ∎

In order to globally rearrange the elements of A into the smaller and larger sub-arrays we need to know where each element of A will end up going at the end of that rearrangement. One way of doing this rearrangement is illustrated at the bottom of Figure 9.19. In this approach, S is obtained by concatenating the various S_i blocks over all the processes, in increasing order of process label. Similarly, L is obtained by concatenating the various L_i

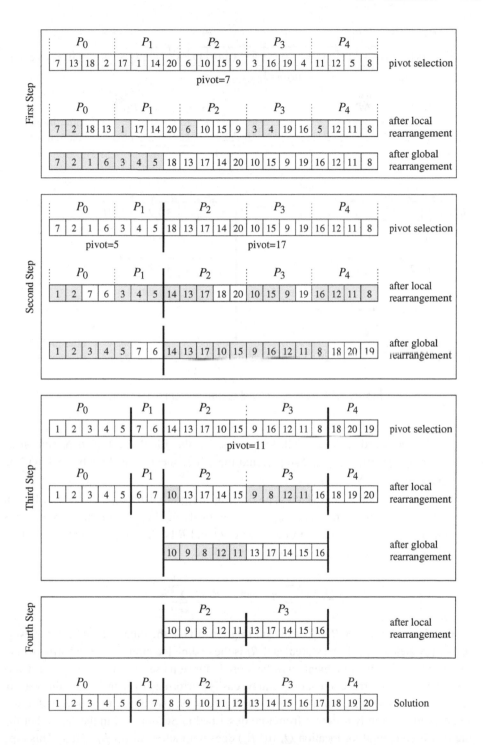

Figure 9.18 An example of the execution of an efficient shared-address-space quicksort algorithm.

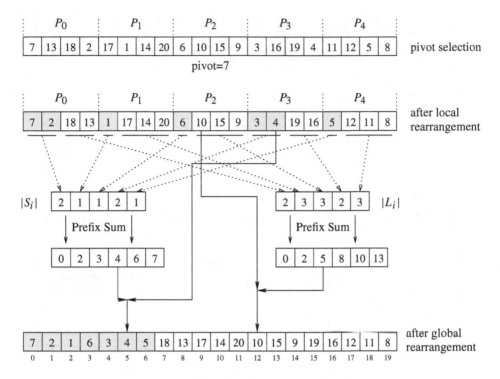

Figure 9.19 Efficient global rearrangement of the array.

blocks in the same order. As a result, for process P_i, the jth element of its S_i sub-block will be stored at location $\sum_{k=0}^{i-1} |S_k| + j$, and the jth element of its L_i sub-block will be stored at location $n - \sum_{k=i}^{p-1} |L_k| - j$.

These locations can be easily computed using the prefix-sum operation described in Section 4.3. Two prefix-sums are computed, one involving the sizes of the S_i sub-blocks and the other the sizes of the L_i sub-blocks. Let Q and R be the arrays of size p that store these prefix sums, respectively. Their elements will be

$$Q_i = \sum_{k=0}^{i-1} S_i, \quad \text{and} \quad R_i = \sum_{k=0}^{i-1} L_i.$$

Note that for each process P_i, Q_i is the starting location in the final array where its lower-than-the-pivot element will be stored, and R_i is the ending location in the final array where its greater-than-the-pivot elements will be stored. Once these locations have been determined, the overall rearrangement of A can be easily performed by using an auxiliary array A' of size n. These steps are illustrated in Figure 9.19. Note that the above definition of prefix-sum is slightly different from that described in Section 4.3, in the sense that the value that is computed for location Q_i (or R_i) does not include S_i (or L_i) itself. This type of prefix-sum is sometimes referred to as *non-inclusive* prefix-sum.

Analysis The complexity of the shared-address-space formulation of the quicksort algorithm depends on two things. The first is the amount of time it requires to split a particular array into the smaller-than- and the greater-than-the-pivot sub-arrays, and the second is the degree to which the various pivots being selected lead to balanced partitions. In this section, to simplify our analysis, we will assume that pivot selection always results in balanced partitions. However, the issue of proper pivot selection and its impact on the overall parallel performance is addressed in Section 9.4.4.

Given an array of n elements and p processes, the shared-address-space formulation of the quicksort algorithm needs to perform four steps: (i) determine and broadcast the pivot; (ii) locally rearrange the array assigned to each process; (iii) determine the locations in the globally rearranged array that the local elements will go to; and (iv) perform the global rearrangement. The first step can be performed in time $\Theta(\log p)$ using an efficient recursive doubling approach for shared-address-space broadcast. The second step can be done in time $\Theta(n/p)$ using the traditional quicksort algorithm for splitting around a pivot element. The third step can be done in $\Theta(\log p)$ using two prefix sum operations. Finally, the fourth step can be done in at least time $\Theta(n/p)$ as it requires us to copy the local elements to their final destination. Thus, the overall complexity of splitting an n-element array is $\Theta(n/p) + \Theta(\log p)$. This process is repeated for each of the two subarrays recursively on half the processes, until the array is split into p parts, at which point each process sorts the elements of the array assigned to it using the serial quicksort algorithm. Thus, the overall complexity of the parallel algorithm is:

$$T_P = \overbrace{\Theta\left(\frac{n}{p}\log\frac{n}{p}\right)}^{\text{local sort}} + \overbrace{\Theta\left(\frac{n}{p}\log p\right) + \Theta(\log^2 p)}^{\text{array splits}}. \tag{9.8}$$

The communication overhead in the above formulation is reflected in the $\Theta(\log^2 p)$ term, which leads to an overall isoefficiency of $\Theta(p\log^2 p)$. It is interesting to note that the overall scalability of the algorithm is determined by the amount of time required to perform the pivot broadcast and the prefix sum operations.

Message-Passing Parallel Formulation

The quicksort formulation for message-passing systems follows the general structure of the shared-address-space formulation. However, unlike the shared-address-space case in which array A and the globally rearranged array A' are stored in shared memory and can be accessed by all the processes, these arrays are now explicitly distributed among the processes. This makes the task of splitting A somewhat more involved.

In particular, in the message-passing version of the parallel quicksort, each process stores n/p elements of array A. This array is also partitioned around a particular pivot element using a two-phase approach. In the first phase (which is similar to the shared-address-space formulation), the locally stored array A_i at process P_i is partitioned into the smaller-than- and larger-than-the-pivot sub-arrays S_i and L_i locally. In the next phase, the algorithm first determines which processes will be responsible for recursively sorting the smaller-than-the-pivot sub-arrays (i.e., $S = \bigcup_i S_i$) and which process will be responsible for recursively sorting the larger-than-the-pivot sub-arrays (i.e., $L = \bigcup_i L_i$). Once this is done, then the processes send their S_i and L_i arrays to the corresponding processes. After that, the processes are partitioned into the two groups, one for S and one for L, and the algorithm proceeds recursively. The recursion terminates when each sub-array is assigned to a single process, at which point it is sorted locally.

The method used to determine which processes will be responsible for sorting S and L is identical to that for the shared-address-space formulation, which tries to partition the processes to match the relative size of the two sub-arrays. Let p_S and p_L be the number of processes assigned to sort S and L, respectively. Each one of the p_S processes will end up storing $|S|/p_S$ elements of the smaller-than-the-pivot sub-array, and each one of the p_L processes will end up storing $|L|/p_L$ elements of the larger-than-the-pivot sub-array. The method used to determine where each process P_i will send its S_i and L_i elements follows the same overall strategy as the shared-address-space formulation. That is, the various S_i (or L_i) sub-arrays will be stored in consecutive locations in S (or L) based on the process number. The actual processes that will be responsible for these elements are determined by the partition of S (or L) into p_S (or p_L) equal-size segments, and can be computed using a prefix-sum operation. Note that each process P_i may need to split its S_i (or L_i) sub-arrays into multiple segments and send each one to different processes. This can happen because its elements may be assigned to locations in S (or L) that span more than one process. In general, each process may have to send its elements to two different processes; however, there may be cases in which more than two partitions are required.

Analysis   Our analysis of the message-passing formulation of quicksort will mirror the corresponding analysis of the shared-address-space formulation.

Consider a message-passing parallel computer with p processes and $O(p)$ bisection bandwidth. The amount of time required to split an array of size n is $\Theta(\log p)$ for broadcasting the pivot element, $\Theta(n/p)$ for splitting the locally assigned portion of the array, $\Theta(\log p)$ for performing the prefix sums to determine the process partition sizes and the destinations of the various S_i and L_i sub-arrays, and the amount of time required for sending and receiving the various arrays. This last step depends on how the processes are mapped on the underlying architecture and on the maximum number of processes that each process needs to communicate with. In general, this communication step involves all-to-all personalized communication (because a particular process may end-up receiving elements from all other processes), whose complexity has a lower bound of $\Theta(n/p)$. Thus, the overall complexity for the split is $\Theta(n/p) + \Theta(\log p)$, which is asymptotically similar to that of the shared-address-space formulation. As a result, the overall runtime is also the same as in Equation 9.8, and the algorithm has a similar isoefficiency function of $\Theta(p \log^2 p)$.

9.4.4 Pivot Selection

In the parallel quicksort algorithm, we glossed over pivot selection. Pivot selection is particularly difficult, and it significantly affects the algorithm's performance. Consider the case in which the first pivot happens to be the largest element in the sequence. In this case, after the first split, one of the processes will be assigned only one element, and the remaining $p - 1$ processes will be assigned $n - 1$ elements. Hence, we are faced with a problem whose size has been reduced only by one element but only $p - 1$ processes will participate in the sorting operation. Although this is a contrived example, it illustrates a significant problem with parallelizing the quicksort algorithm. Ideally, the split should be done such that each partition has a non-trivial fraction of the original array.

One way to select pivots is to choose them at random as follows. During the ith split, one process in each of the process groups randomly selects one of its elements to be the pivot for this partition. This is analogous to the random pivot selection in the sequential quicksort algorithm. Although this method seems to work for sequential quicksort, it is not well suited to the parallel formulation. To see this, consider the case in which a bad pivot is selected at some point. In sequential quicksort, this leads to a partitioning in which one subsequence is significantly larger than the other. If all subsequent pivot selections are good, one poor pivot will increase the overall work by at most an amount equal to the length of the subsequence; thus, it will not significantly degrade the performance of sequential quicksort. In the parallel formulation, however, one poor pivot may lead to a partitioning in which a process becomes idle, and that will persist throughout the execution of the algorithm.

If the initial distribution of elements in each process is uniform, then a better pivot selection method can be derived. In this case, the n/p elements initially stored at each process form a representative sample of all n elements. In other words, the median of each n/p-element subsequence is very close to the median of the entire n-element sequence. Why is this a good pivot selection scheme under the assumption of identical initial distributions? Since the distribution of elements on each process is the same as the overall distribution of the n elements, the median selected to be the pivot during the first step is a good approximation of the overall median. Since the selected pivot is very close to the overall median, roughly half of the elements in each process are smaller and the other half larger than the pivot. Therefore, the first split leads to two partitions, such that each of them has roughly $n/2$ elements. Similarly, the elements assigned to each process of the group that is responsible for sorting the smaller-than-the-pivot elements (and the group responsible for sorting the larger-than-the-pivot elements) have the same distribution as the $n/2$ smaller (or larger) elements of the original list. Thus, the split not only maintains load balance but also preserves the assumption of uniform element distribution in the process group. Therefore, the application of the same pivot selection scheme to the sub-groups of processes continues to yield good pivot selection.

Can we really assume that the n/p elements in each process have the same distribution as the overall sequence? The answer depends on the application. In some applications, either the random or the median pivot selection scheme works well, but in others neither scheme delivers good performance. Two additional pivot selection schemes are examined in Problems 9.20 and 9.21.

9.5 Bucket and Sample Sort

A popular serial algorithm for sorting an array of n elements whose values are uniformly distributed over an interval $[a, b]$ is the *bucket sort* algorithm. In this algorithm, the interval $[a, b]$ is divided into m equal-sized subintervals referred to as *buckets*, and each element is placed in the appropriate bucket. Since the n elements are uniformly distributed over the interval $[a, b]$, the number of elements in each bucket is roughly n/m. The algorithm then sorts the elements in each bucket, yielding a sorted sequence. The run time of this algorithm is $\Theta(n \log(n/m))$. For $m = \Theta(n)$, it exhibits linear run time, $\Theta(n)$. Note that the reason that bucket sort can achieve such a low complexity is because it assumes that the n elements to be sorted are uniformly distributed over an interval $[a, b]$.

Parallelizing bucket sort is straightforward. Let n be the number of elements to be sorted and p be the number of processes. Initially, each process is assigned a block of n/p elements, and the number of buckets is selected to be $m = p$. The parallel formulation of bucket sort consists of three steps. In the first step, each process partitions its block of n/p elements into p sub-blocks, one for each of the p buckets. This is possible because each process knows the interval $[a, b)$ and thus the interval for each bucket. In the second step, each process sends sub-blocks to the appropriate processes. After this step, each process has only the elements belonging to the bucket assigned to it. In the third step, each process sorts its bucket internally by using an optimal sequential sorting algorithm.

Unfortunately, the assumption that the input elements are uniformly distributed over an interval $[a, b]$ is not realistic. In most cases, the actual input may not have such a distribution or its distribution may be unknown. Thus, using bucket sort may result in buckets that have a significantly different number of elements, thereby degrading performance. In such situations an algorithm called *sample sort* will yield significantly better performance. The idea behind sample sort is simple. A sample of size s is selected from the n-element sequence, and the range of the buckets is determined by sorting the sample and choosing $m - 1$ elements from the result. These elements (called *splitters*) divide the sample into m equal-sized buckets. After defining the buckets, the algorithm proceeds in the same way as bucket sort. The performance of sample sort depends on the sample size s and the way it is selected from the n-element sequence.

Consider a splitter selection scheme that guarantees that the number of elements ending up in each bucket is roughly the same for all buckets. Let n be the number of elements to be sorted and m be the number of buckets. The scheme works as follows. It divides the n elements into m blocks of size n/m each, and sorts each block by using quicksort. From each sorted block it chooses $m - 1$ evenly spaced elements. The $m(m - 1)$ elements selected from all the blocks represent the sample used to determine the buckets. This

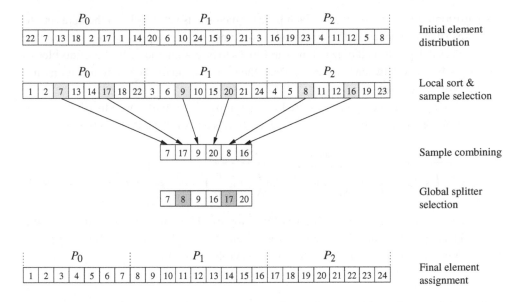

Figure 9.20 An example of the execution of sample sort on an array with 24 elements on three processes.

scheme guarantees that the number of elements ending up in each bucket is less than $2n/m$ (Problem 9.28).

How can we parallelize the splitter selection scheme? Let p be the number of processes. As in bucket sort, set $m = p$; thus, at the end of the algorithm, each process contains only the elements belonging to a single bucket. Each process is assigned a block of n/p elements, which it sorts sequentially. It then chooses $p - 1$ evenly spaced elements from the sorted block. Each process sends its $p - 1$ sample elements to one process – say P_0. Process P_0 then sequentially sorts the $p(p - 1)$ sample elements and selects the $p - 1$ splitters. Finally, process P_0 broadcasts the $p - 1$ splitters to all the other processes. Now the algorithm proceeds in a manner identical to that of bucket sort. This algorithm is illustrated in Figure 9.20.

Analysis We now analyze the complexity of sample sort on a message-passing computer with p processes and $O(p)$ bisection bandwidth.

The internal sort of n/p elements requires time $\Theta((n/p)\log(n/p))$, and the selection of $p - 1$ sample elements requires time $\Theta(p)$. Sending $p - 1$ elements to process P_0 is similar to a gather operation (Section 4.4); the time required is $\Theta(p^2)$. The time to internally sort the $p(p - 1)$ sample elements at P_0 is $\Theta(p^2 \log p)$, and the time to select $p - 1$ splitters is $\Theta(p)$. The $p - 1$ splitters are sent to all the other processes by using one-to-all broadcast (Section 4.1), which requires time $\Theta(p \log p)$. Each process can *insert* these $p - 1$ splitters in its local sorted block of size n/p by performing $p - 1$ binary searches. Each process thus partitions its block into p sub-blocks, one for each bucket. The time required for this partitioning is $\Theta(p \log(n/p))$. Each process then sends sub-blocks to the appropriate processes (that is, buckets). The communication time for this step is difficult to compute precisely, as it depends on the size of the sub-blocks to be communicated. These sub-blocks can vary arbitrarily between 0 and n/p. Thus, the upper bound on the communication time is $O(n) + O(p \log p)$.

If we assume that the elements stored in each process are uniformly distributed, then each sub-block has roughly $\Theta(n/p^2)$ elements. In this case, the parallel run time is

$$T_P = \overbrace{\Theta\left(\frac{n}{p} \log \frac{n}{p}\right)}^{\text{local sort}} + \overbrace{\Theta\left(p^2 \log p\right)}^{\text{sort sample}} + \overbrace{\Theta\left(p \log \frac{n}{p}\right)}^{\text{block partition}} + \overbrace{\Theta(n/p) + O(p \log p)}^{\text{communication}}. \quad (9.9)$$

In this case, the isoefficiency function is $\Theta(p^3 \log p)$. If bitonic sort is used to sort the $p(p-1)$ sample elements, then the time for sorting the sample would be $\Theta(p \log p)$, and the isoefficiency will be reduced to $\Theta(p^2 \log p)$ (Problem 9.30).

9.6   Other Sorting Algorithms

As mentioned in the introduction to this chapter, there are many sorting algorithms, and we cannot explore them all in this chapter. However, in this section we briefly present two additional sorting algorithms that are important both practically and theoretically. Our discussion of these schemes will be brief. Refer to the bibliographic remarks (Section 9.7) for references on these and other algorithms.

9.6.1   Enumeration Sort

All the sorting algorithms presented so far are based on compare-exchange operations. This section considers an algorithm based on *enumeration sort*, which does not use compare-exchange. The basic idea behind enumeration sort is to determine the rank of each element. The *rank* of an element a_i is the number of elements smaller than a_i in the sequence to be sorted. The rank of a_i can be used to place it in its correct position in the sorted sequence. Several parallel algorithms are based on enumeration sort. Here we present one such algorithm that is suited to the CRCW PRAM model. This formulation sorts n elements by using n^2 processes in time $\Theta(1)$.

Assume that concurrent writes to the same memory location of the CRCW PRAM result in the sum of all the values written being stored at that location (Section 2.4.1). Consider the n^2 processes as being arranged in a two-dimensional grid. The algorithm consists of two steps. During the first step, each column j of processes computes the number of elements smaller than a_j. During the second step, each process $P_{1,j}$ of the first row places a_j in its proper position as determined by its rank. The algorithm is shown in Algorithm 9.7. It uses an auxiliary array $C[1 \ldots n]$ to store the rank of each element. The crucial steps of this algorithm are lines 7 and 9. There, each process $P_{i,j}$, writes 1 in $C[j]$

```
1.      procedure ENUM_SORT (n)
2.      begin
3.          for each process P₁,ⱼ do
4.              C[j] := 0;
5.          for each process Pᵢ,ⱼ do
6.              if (A[i] < A[j]) or (A[i] = A[j] and i < j) then
7.                  C[j] := 1;
8.              else
9.                  C[j] := 0;
10.         for each process P₁,ⱼ do
11.             A[C[j]] := A[j];
12.     end ENUM_SORT
```

Algorithm 9.7   Enumeration sort on a CRCW PRAM with additive-write conflict resolution.

if the element $A[i]$ is smaller than $A[j]$ and writes 0 otherwise. Because of the additive-write conflict resolution scheme, the effect of these instructions is to count the number of elements smaller than $A[j]$ and thus compute its rank. The run time of this algorithm is $\Theta(1)$. Modifications of this algorithm for various parallel architectures are discussed in Problem 9.26.

9.6.2   Radix Sort

The *radix sort* algorithm relies on the binary representation of the elements to be sorted. Let b be the number of bits in the binary representation of an element. The radix sort algorithm examines the elements to be sorted r bits at a time, where $r < b$. Radix sort requires b/r iterations. During iteration i, it sorts the elements according to their i^{th} least significant block of r bits. For radix sort to work properly, each of the b/r sorts must be stable. A sorting algorithm is **stable** if its output preserves the order of input elements with the same value. Radix sort is stable if it preserves the input order of any two r-bit blocks when these blocks are equal. The most common implementation of the intermediate b/r radix-2^r sorts uses enumeration sort (Section 9.6.1) because the range of possible values $[0 \ldots 2^r - 1]$ is small. For such cases, enumeration sort significantly outperforms any comparison-based sorting algorithm.

Consider a parallel formulation of radix sort for n elements on a message-passing computer with n processes. The parallel radix sort algorithm is shown in Algorithm 9.8. The main loop of the algorithm (lines 3–17) performs the b/r enumeration sorts of the r-bit blocks. The enumeration sort is performed by using the *prefix_sum()* and *parallel_sum()* functions. These functions are similar to those described in Sections 4.1 and 4.3. During each iteration of the inner loop (lines 6–15), radix sort determines the position of the elements with an r-bit value of j. It does this by summing all the elements with the same value and then assigning them to processes. The variable *rank* holds the position of each

```
1.      procedure RADIX_SORT(A, r)
2.      begin
3.          for i := 0 to b/r − 1 do
4.          begin
5.              offset := 0;
6.              for j := 0 to 2^r − 1 do
7.              begin
8.                  flag := 0;
9.                  if the i^th least significant r-bit block of A[P_k] = j then
10.                     flag := 1;
11.                 index := prefix_sum(flag)
12.                 if flag = 1 then
13.                     rank := offset + index;
14.                 offset := parallel_sum(flag);
15.             endfor
16.             each process P_k send its element A[P_k] to process P_rank;
17.         endfor
18.     end RADIX_SORT
```

Algorithm 9.8   A parallel radix sort algorithm, in which each element of the array $A[1 \ldots n]$ to be sorted is assigned to one process. The function *prefix_sum()* computes the prefix sum of the *flag* variable, and the function *parallel_sum()* returns the total sum of the *flag* variable.

clement. At the end of the loop (line 16), each process sends its element to the appropriate process. Process labels determine the global order of sorted elements.

As shown in Sections 4.1 and 4.3, the complexity of both the *parallel_sum()* and *prefix_sum()* operations is $\Theta(\log n)$ on a message-passing computer with n processes. The complexity of the communication step on line 16 is $\Theta(n)$. Thus, the parallel run time of this algorithm is

$$T_P = \frac{b}{r} 2^r (\Theta(\log n) + \Theta(n))$$

9.7   Bibliographic Remarks

Knuth [Knu73] discusses sorting networks and their history. The question of whether a sorting network could sort n elements in time $O(\log n)$ remained open for a long time. In 1983, Ajtai, Komlos, and Szemeredi [AKS83] discovered a sorting network that could sort n elements in time $O(\log n)$ by using $O(n \log n)$ comparators. Unfortunately, the constant of their sorting network is quite large (many thousands), and thus is not practical. The bitonic sorting network was discovered by Batcher [Bat68], who also discovered the network for odd-even sort. These were the first networks capable of sorting n elements in time $O(\log^2 n)$. Stone [Sto71] maps the bitonic sort onto a perfect-shuffle interconnection network, sorting n elements by using n processes in time $O(\log^2 n)$. Siegel [Sie77] shows that bitonic sort can also be performed on the hypercube in time $O(\log^2 n)$. The block-based hypercube formulation of bitonic sort is discussed in Johnsson [Joh84] and Fox et al. [FJL$^+$88]. Algorithm 9.1 is adopted from [FJL$^+$88]. The shuffled row-major indexing formulation of bitonic sort on a mesh-connected computer is presented by Thompson and Kung [TK77]. They also show how the odd-even merge sort can be used with snake-like row-major indexing. Nassimi and Sahni [NS79] present a row-major indexed bitonic sort formulation for a mesh with the same performance as shuffled row-major indexing. An improved version of the mesh odd-even merge is proposed by Kumar and Hirschberg [KH83]. The compare-split operation can be implemented in many ways. Baudet and Stevenson [BS78] describe one way to perform this operation. An alternative way of performing a compare-split operation based on a bitonic sort (Problem 9.1) that requires no additional memory was discovered by Hsiao and Menon [HM80].

The odd-even transposition sort is described by Knuth [Knu73]. Several early references to parallel sorting by odd-even transposition are given by Knuth [Knu73] and Kung [Kun80]. The block-based extension of the algorithm is due to Baudet and Stevenson [BS78]. Another variation of block-based odd-even transposition sort that uses bitonic merge-split is described by DeWitt, Friedland, Hsiao, and Menon [DFHM82]. Their algorithm uses p processes and runs in time $O(n + n \log(n/p))$. In contrast to the algorithm of Baudet and Stevenson [BS78], which is faster but requires $4n/p$ storage locations in each process, the algorithm of DeWitt et al. requires only $(n/p) + 1$ storage locations to perform the compare-split operation.

The shellsort algorithm described in Section 9.3.2 is due to Fox et al. [FJL$^+$88]. They show that, as n increases, the probability that the final odd-even transposition will exhibit worst-case performance (in other words, will require p phases) diminishes. A different shellsort algorithm based on the original sequential algorithm [She59] is described by Quinn [Qui88].

The sequential quicksort algorithm is due to Hoare [Hoa62]. Sedgewick [Sed78] provides a good reference on the details of the implementation and how they affect its performance. The random pivot-selection scheme is described and analyzed by Robin [Rob75]. The algorithm for sequence partitioning on a single process was suggested by Sedgewick [Sed78] and used in parallel formulations by Raskin [Ras78], Deminet [Dem82], and Quinn [Qui88]. The CRCW PRAM algorithm (Section 9.4.2) is due to Chlebus and Vrto [CV91]. Many other quicksort-based algorithms for PRAM and shared-address-space parallel computers have been developed that can sort n elements in time $\Theta(\log n)$ by using $\Theta(n)$ processes. Martel and Gusfield [MG89] developed a quicksort algorithm for a CRCW PRAM that requires space $O(n^3)$ on the average. An algorithm suited to shared-address-space parallel computers with fetch-and-add capabilities was discovered by Heidelberger, Norton, and Robinson [HNR90]. Their algorithm runs in time $\Theta(\log n)$ on the average and can be adapted for commercially available shared-address-space computers. The hypercube formulation of quicksort described in Problem 9.17 is due to Wagar [Wag87]. His hyperquicksort algorithm uses the median-based pivot-selection scheme and assumes that the elements in each process have the same distribution. His experimental results show that hyperquicksort is faster than bitonic sort on a hypercube. An alternate pivot-selection scheme (Problem 9.20) was implemented by Fox *et al.* [FJL$^+$88]. This scheme significantly improves the performance of hyperquicksort when the elements are not evenly distributed in each process. Plaxton [Pla89] describes a quicksort algorithm on a p-process hypercube that sorts n elements in time $O((n \log n)/p + (n \log^{3/2} p)/p + \log^3 p \log(n/p))$. This algorithm uses a time $O((n/p) \log \log p + \log^2 p \log(n/p))$ parallel selection algorithm to determine the perfect pivot selection. The mesh formulation of quicksort (Problem 9.24) is due to Singh, Kumar, Agha, and Tomlinson [SKAT91a]. They also describe a modification to the algorithm that reduces the complexity of each step by a factor of $\Theta(\log p)$.

The sequential bucket sort algorithm was first proposed by Isaac and Singleton in 1956. Hirschberg [Hir78] proposed a bucket sort algorithm for the EREW PRAM model. This algorithm sorts n elements in the range $[0 \ldots n - 1]$ in time $\Theta(\log n)$ by using n processes. A side effect of this algorithm is that duplicate elements are eliminated. Their algorithm requires space $\Theta(n^2)$. Hirschberg [Hir78] generalizes this algorithm so that duplicate elements remain in the sorted array. The generalized algorithm sorts n elements in time $\Theta(k \log n)$ by using $n^{1+1/k}$ processes, where k is an arbitrary integer.

The sequential sample sort algorithm was discovered by Frazer and McKellar [FM70]. The parallel sample sort algorithm (Section 9.5) was discovered by Shi and Schaeffer [SS90]. Several parallel formulations of sample sort for different parallel architectures have been proposed. Abali, Ozguner, and Bataineh [AOB93] presented a splitter selection scheme that guarantees that the number of elements ending up in each bucket is n/p. Their algorithm requires time $O((n \log n)/p + p \log^2 n)$, on average, to sort n elements on a p-process hypercube. Reif and Valiant [RV87] present a sample sort algorithm that sorts n elements on an n-process hypercube-connected computer in time $O(\log n)$ with high probability. Won and Sahni [WS88] and Seidel and George [SG88] present parallel formulations of a variation of sample sort called **bin sort** [FKO86].

Many other parallel sorting algorithms have been proposed. Various parallel sorting algorithms can be efficiently implemented on a PRAM model or on shared-address-space computers. Akl [Akl85], Borodin and Hopcroft [BH82], Shiloach and Vishkin [SV81], and Bitton, DeWitt, Hsiao, and Menon [BDHM84] provide a good survey of the subject. Valiant [Val75] proposed a sorting algorithm for a shared-address-space SIMD computer that sorts by merging. It sorts n elements in time $O(\log n \log \log n)$ by using $n/2$ processes. Reischuk [Rei81] was the first to develop an algorithm that sorted n elements in time $\Theta(\log n)$ for an n-process PRAM. Cole [Col88] developed a parallel merge-sort algorithm that sorts n elements in time $\Theta(\log n)$ on an EREW PRAM. Natvig [Nat90] has shown that the constants hidden behind the asymptotic notation are very large. In fact, the $\Theta(\log^2 n)$ bitonic sort outperforms the $\Theta(\log n)$ merge sort as long as n is smaller than 7.6×10^{22}! Plaxton [Pla89] has developed a hypercube sorting algorithm, called **smooth-sort**, that runs asymptotically faster than any previously known algorithm for that architecture. Leighton [Lei85a] proposed a sorting algorithm, called **columnsort**, that consists of a sequence of sorts followed by elementary matrix operations. Columnsort is a generalization of Batcher's odd-even sort. Nigam and Sahni [NS93] presented an algorithm based on Leighton's columnsort for reconfigurable meshes with buses that sorts n elements on an n^2-process mesh in time $O(1)$.

Problems

9.1 Consider the following technique for performing the compare-split operation. Let $x_1, x_2, \ldots, x_k$ be the elements stored at process P_i in increasing order, and let $y_1, y_2, \ldots, y_k$ be the elements stored at process P_j in decreasing order. Process P_i sends x_1 to P_j. Process P_j compares x_1 with y_1 and then sends the larger element back to process P_i and keeps the smaller element for itself. The same procedure is repeated for pairs $(x_2, y_2), (x_3, y_3), \ldots, (x_k, y_k)$. If for any pair (x_l, y_l) for $1 \le l \le k$, $x_l \ge y_l$, then no more exchanges are needed. Finally, each process sorts its elements. Show that this method correctly performs a compare-split operation. Analyze its run time, and compare the relative merits of this method to those of the method presented in the text. Is this method better suited for MIMD or SIMD parallel computers?

9.2 Show that the $\le$ relation, as defined in Section 9.1 for blocks of elements, is a partial ordering relation.
Hint: A relation is a *partial ordering* if it is reflexive, antisymmetric, and transitive.

9.3 Consider the sequence $s = \{a_0, a_1, \ldots, a_{n-1}\}$, where n is a power of 2. In the following cases, prove that the sequences s_1 and s_2 obtained by performing the bitonic split operation described in Section 9.2.1, on the sequence s, satisfy the properties that (1) s_1 and s_2 are bitonic sequences, and (2) the elements of s_1 are smaller than the elements of s_2:

(a) s is a bitonic sequence such that $a_0 \le a_1 \le \cdots \le a_{n/2-1}$ and $a_{n/2} \ge a_{n/2+1} \ge \cdots \ge a_{n-1}$.

(b) s is a bitonic sequence such that $a_0 \le a_1 \le \cdots \le a_i$ and $a_{i+1} \ge a_{i+2} \ge \cdots \ge a_{n-1}$ for some i, $0 \le i \le n - 1$.

(c) s is a bitonic sequence that becomes increasing-decreasing after shifting its elements.

9.4 In the parallel formulations of bitonic sort, we assumed that we had n processes available to sort n items. Show how the algorithm needs to be modified when only $n/2$ processes are available.

9.5 Show that, in the hypercube formulation of bitonic sort, each bitonic merge of sequences of size 2^k is performed on a k-dimensional hypercube and each sequence is assigned to a separate hypercube.

9.6   Show that the parallel formulation of bitonic sort shown in Algorithm 9.1 is correct. In particular, show that the algorithm correctly compare-exchanges elements and that the elements end up in the appropriate processes.

9.7   Consider the parallel formulation of bitonic sort for a mesh-connected parallel computer. Compute the exact parallel run time of the following formulations:

(a)   One that uses the row-major mapping shown in Figure 9.11(a) for a mesh with store-and-forward routing.

(b)   One that uses the row-major snakelike mapping shown in Figure 9.11(b) for a mesh with store-and-forward routing.

(c)   One that uses the row-major shuffled mapping shown in Figure 9.11(c) for a mesh with store-and-forward routing.

Also, determine how the above run times change when cut-through routing is used.

9.8   Show that the block-based bitonic sort algorithm that uses compare-split operations is correct.

9.9   Consider a ring-connected parallel computer with n processes. Show how to map the input wires of the bitonic sorting network onto the ring so that the communication cost is minimized. Analyze the performance of your mapping. Consider the case in which only p processes are available. Analyze the performance of your parallel formulation for this case. What is the largest number of processes that can be used while maintaining a cost-optimal parallel formulation? What is the isoefficiency function of your scheme?

9.10   Prove that the block-based odd-even transposition sort yields a correct algorithm. *Hint:* This problem is similar to Problem 9.8.

9.11   Show how to apply the idea of the shellsort algorithm (Section 9.3.2) to a p-process mesh-connected computer. Your algorithm does not need to be an exact copy of the hypercube formulation.

9.12   Show how to parallelize the sequential shellsort algorithm for a p-process hypercube. Note that the shellsort algorithm presented in Section 9.3.2 is not an exact parallelization of the sequential algorithm.

9.13   Consider the shellsort algorithm presented in Section 9.3.2. Its performance depends on the value of l, which is the number of odd and even phases performed during the second phase of the algorithm. Describe a worst-case initial key distribution that will require $l = \Theta(p)$ phases. What is the probability of this worst-case scenario?

9.14   In Section 9.4.1 we discussed a parallel formulation of quicksort for a CREW PRAM that is based on assigning each subproblem to a separate process. This formulation uses n processes to sort n elements. Based on this approach, derive a parallel formulation that uses p processes, where $(p < n)$. Derive expressions for the parallel run time, efficiency, and isoefficiency function. What is the maximum number of processes that your parallel formulation can use and still remain cost-optimal?

9.15 Derive an algorithm that traverses the binary search tree constructed by the algorithm in Algorithm 9.6 and determines the position of each element in the sorted array. Your algorithm should use n processes and solve the problem in time $\Theta(\log n)$ on an arbitrary CRCW PRAM.

9.16 Consider the PRAM formulation of the quicksort algorithm (Section 9.4.2). Compute the average height of the binary tree generated by the algorithm.

9.17 Consider the following parallel quicksort algorithm that takes advantage of the topology of a p-process hypercube connected parallel computer. Let n be the number of elements to be sorted and $p = 2^d$ be the number of processes in a d-dimensional hypercube. Each process is assigned a block of n/p elements, and the labels of the processes define the global order of the sorted sequence. The algorithm starts by selecting a pivot element, which is broadcast to all processes. Each process, upon receiving the pivot, partitions its local elements into two blocks, one with elements smaller than the pivot and one with elements larger than the pivot. Then the processes connected along the dth communication link exchange appropriate blocks so that one retains elements smaller than the pivot and the other retains elements larger than the pivot. Specifically, each process with a 0 in the dth bit (the most significant bit) position of the binary representation of its process label retains the smaller elements, and each process with a 1 in the dth bit retains the larger elements. After this step, each process in the $(d-1)$-dimensional hypercube whose d^{th} label bit is 0 will have elements smaller than the pivot, and each process in the other $(d-1)$-dimensional hypercube will have elements larger than the pivot. This procedure is performed recursively in each subcube, splitting the subsequences further. After d such splits – one along each dimension – the sequence is sorted with respect to the global ordering imposed on the processes. This does not mean that the elements at each process are sorted. Therefore, each process sorts its local elements by using sequential quicksort. This hypercube formulation of quicksort is shown in Algorithm 9.9. The execution of the algorithm is illustrated in Figure 9.21.

Analyze the complexity of this hypercube-based parallel quicksort algorithm. Derive expressions for the parallel runtime, speedup, and efficiency. Perform this analysis assuming that the elements that were initially assigned at each process are distributed uniformly.

9.18 Consider the parallel formulation of quicksort for a d-dimensional hypercube described in Problem 9.17. Show that after d splits – one along each communication link – the elements are sorted according to the global order defined by the process's labels.

9.19 Consider the parallel formulation of quicksort for a d-dimensional hypercube described in Problem 9.17. Compare this algorithm against the message-passing

---

```
    1.        procedure HYPERCUBE_QUICKSORT (B, n)
    2.     begin
    3.          id := process's label;
    4.          for i := 1 to d do
    5.          begin
    6.              x := pivot;
    7.              partition B into B₁ and B₂ such that B₁ ≤ x < B₂;
    8.              if iᵗʰ bit is 0 then
    9.              begin
   10.                  send B₂ to the process along the iᵗʰ communication link;
   11.                  C := subsequence received along the iᵗʰ communication link;
   12.                  B := B₁ ∪ C;
   13.              endif
   14.              else
   15.                  send B₁ to the process along the iᵗʰ communication link;
   16.                  C := subsequence received along the iᵗʰ communication link;
   17.                  B := B₂ ∪ C;
   18.              endelse
   19.          endfor
   20.          sort B using sequential quicksort;
   21.     end HYPERCUBE_QUICKSORT
```

Algorithm 9.9   A parallel formulation of quicksort on a d-dimensional hypercube. B is the n/p-element subsequence assigned to each process.

quicksort algorithm described in Section 9.4.3. Which algorithm is more scalable? Which algorithm is more sensitive on poor selection of pivot elements?

9.20   An alternative way of selecting pivots in the parallel formulation of quicksort for a d-dimensional hypercube (Problem 9.17) is to select all the $2^d - 1$ pivots at once as follows:

(a)   Each process picks a sample of l elements at random.

(b)   All processes together sort the sample of $l \times 2^d$ items by using the shellsort algorithm (Section 9.3.2).

(c)   Choose $2^d - 1$ equally distanced pivots from this list.

(d)   Broadcast pivots so that all the processes know the pivots.

How does the quality of this pivot selection scheme depend on l? Do you think l should be a function of n? Under what assumptions will this scheme select good pivots? Do you think this scheme works when the elements are not identically distributed on each process? Analyze the complexity of this scheme.

9.21   Another pivot selection scheme for parallel quicksort for hypercube (Section 9.17) is as follows. During the split along the ith dimension, 2^{i-1} pairs of processes ex-

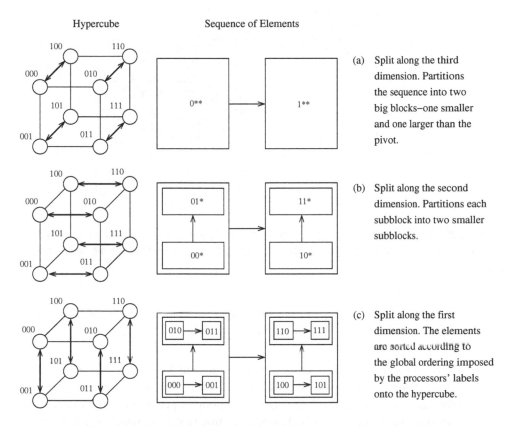

Figure 9.21 The execution of the hypercube formulation of quicksort for $d = 3$. The three splits – one along each communication link – are shown in (a), (b), and (c). The second column represents the partitioning of the n-element sequence into subcubes. The arrows between subcubes indicate the movement of larger elements. Each box is marked by the binary representation of the process labels in that subcube. A $*$ denotes that all the binary combinations are included.

change elements. The pivot is selected in two steps. In the first step, each of the 2^{i-1} pairs of processes compute the median of their combined sequences. In the second step, the median of the 2^{i-1} medians is computed. This median of medians becomes the pivot for the split along the ith communication link. Subsequent pivots are selected in the same way among the participating subcubes. Under what assumptions will this scheme yield good pivot selections? Is this better than the median scheme described in the text? Analyze the complexity of selecting the pivot.

Hint: If A and B are two sorted sequences, each having n elements, then we can find the median of $A \cup B$ in time $\Theta(\log n)$.

9.22 In the parallel formulation of the quicksort algorithm on shared-address-space and message-passing architectures (Section 9.4.3) each iteration is followed by a bar-

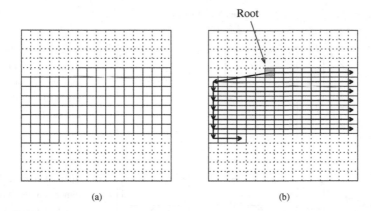

Figure 9.22 (a) An arbitrary portion of a mesh that holds part of the sequence to be sorted at some point during the execution of quicksort, and (b) a binary tree embedded into the same portion of the mesh.

rier synchronization. Is barrier synchronization necessary to ensure the correctness of the algorithm? If not, then how does the performance change in the absence of barrier synchronization?

9.23 Consider the message-passing formulation of the quicksort algorithm presented in Section 9.4.3. Compute the exact (that is, using t_s, t_w, and t_c) parallel run time and efficiency of the algorithm under the assumption of perfect pivots. Compute the various components of the isoefficiency function of your formulation when

    (a) $t_c = 1, t_w = 1, t_s = 1$

    (b) $t_c = 1, t_w = 1, t_s = 10$

    (c) $t_c = 1, t_w = 10, t_s = 100$

for cases in which the desired efficiency is $0.50, 0.75$, and 0.95. Does the scalability of this formulation depend on the desired efficiency and the architectural characteristics of the machine?

9.24 Consider the following parallel formulation of quicksort for a mesh-connected message-passing parallel computer. Assume that one element is assigned to each process. The recursive partitioning step consists of selecting the pivot and then rearranging the elements in the mesh so that those smaller than the pivot are in one part of the mesh and those larger than the pivot are in the other. We assume that the processes in the mesh are numbered in row-major order. At the end of the quicksort algorithm, elements are sorted with respect to this order.

Consider the partitioning step for an arbitrary subsequence illustrated in Figure 9.22(a). Let k be the length of this sequence, and let $P_m, P_{m+1}, \ldots, P_{m+k}$ be the mesh processes storing it. Partitioning consists of the following four steps:

    1. A pivot is selected at random and sent to process P_m. Process P_m broad-

casts this pivot to all k processes by using an embedded tree, as shown in Figure 9.22(b). The root (P_m) transmits the pivot toward the leaves. The tree embedding is also used in the following steps.

2. Information is gathered at each process and passed up the tree. In particular, each process counts the number of elements smaller and larger than the pivot in both its left and right subtrees. Each process knows the pivot value and therefore can determine if its element is smaller or larger. Each process propagates two values to its parent: the number of elements smaller than the pivot and the number of elements larger than the pivot in the process's subtree. Because the tree embedded in the mesh is not complete, some nodes will not have left or right subtrees. At the end of this step, process P_m knows how many of the k elements are smaller and larger than the pivot. If s is the number of the elements smaller than the pivot, then the position of the pivot in the sorted sequence is P_{m+s}.

3. Information is propagated down the tree to enable each element to be moved to its proper position in the smaller or larger partitions. Each process in the tree receives from its parent the next empty position in the smaller and larger partitions. Depending on whether the element stored at each process is smaller or larger than the pivot, the process propagates the proper information down to its subtrees. Initially, the position for elements smaller than the pivot is P_m and the position for elements larger than the pivot is P_{m+s+1}.

4. The processes perform a permutation, and each element moves to the proper position in the smaller or larger partition.

This algorithm is illustrated in Figure 9.23.

Analyze the complexity of this mesh-based parallel quicksort algorithm. Derive expressions for the parallel runtime, speedup, and efficiency. Perform this analysis assuming that the elements that were initially assigned at each process are distributed uniformly.

9.25 Consider the quicksort formulation for a mesh described in Problem 9.24. Describe a scaled-down formulation that uses $p < n$ processes. Analyze its parallel run time, speedup, and isoefficiency function.

9.26 Consider the enumeration sort algorithm presented in Section 9.6.1. Show how the algorithm can be implemented on each of the following:

(a)   a CREW PRAM

(b)   a EREW PRAM

(c)   a hypercube-connected parallel computer

(d)   a mesh-connected parallel computer.

Analyze the performance of your formulations. Furthermore, show how you can extend this enumeration sort to a hypercube to sort n elements using p processes.

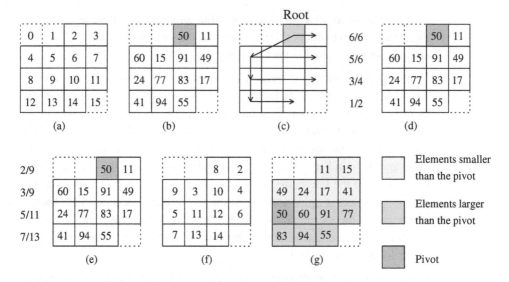

Figure 9.23   Partitioning a sequence of 13 elements on a 4 × 4 mesh: (a) row-major numbering of the mesh processes, (b) the elements stored in each process (the shaded element is the pivot), (c) the tree embedded on a portion of the mesh, (d) the number of smaller or larger elements in the process of the first column after the execution of the second step, (e) the destination of the smaller or larger elements propagated down to the processes in the first column during the third step, (f) the destination of the elements at the end of the third step, and (g) the locations of the elements after one-to-one personalized communication.

9.27   Derive expressions for the speedup, efficiency, and isoefficiency function of the bucket sort parallel formulation presented in Section 9.5. Compare these expressions with the expressions for the other sorting algorithms presented in this chapter. Which parallel formulations perform better than bucket sort, and which perform worse?

9.28   Show that the splitter selection scheme described in Section 9.5 guarantees that the number of elements in each of the m buckets is less than $2n/m$.

9.29   Derive expressions for the speedup, efficiency, and isoefficiency function of the sample sort parallel formulation presented in Section 9.5. Derive these metrics under each of the following conditions: (1) the p sub-blocks at each process are of equal size, and (2) the size of the p sub-blocks at each process can vary by a factor of $\log p$.

9.30   In the sample sort algorithm presented in Section 9.5, all processes send $p - 1$ elements to process P_0, which sorts the $p(p - 1)$ elements and distributes splitters to all the processes. Modify the algorithm so that the processes sort the $p(p - 1)$ elements in parallel using bitonic sort. How will you choose the splitters? Compute the parallel run time, speedup, and efficiency of your formulation.

9.31 How does the performance of radix sort (Section 9.6.2) depend on the value of r? Compute the value of r that minimizes the run time of the algorithm.

9.32 Extend the radix sort algorithm presented in Section 9.6.2 to the case in which p processes ($p < n$) are used to sort n elements. Derive expressions for the speedup, efficiency, and isoefficiency function for this parallel formulation. Can you devise a better ranking mechanism?

CHAPTER 10

Graph Algorithms

Graph theory plays an important role in computer science because it provides an easy and systematic way to model many problems. Many problems can be expressed in terms of graphs, and can be solved using standard graph algorithms. This chapter presents parallel formulations of some important and fundamental graph algorithms.

10.1   Definitions and Representation

An *undirected graph* G is a pair (V, E), where V is a finite set of points called *vertices* and E is a finite set of *edges*. An edge $e \in E$ is an unordered pair (u, v), where $u, v \in V$. An edge (u, v) indicates that vertices u and v are connected. Similarly, a *directed graph* G, is a pair (V, E), where V is the set of vertices as we just defined, but an edge $(u, v) \in E$ is an ordered pair; that is, it indicates that there is a connection from u to v. Figure 10.1 illustrates an undirected and a directed graph. We use the term *graph* to refer to both directed and undirected graphs.

Many definitions are common to directed and undirected graphs, although certain terms have slightly different meanings for each. If (u, v) is an edge in an undirected graph, (u, v) is *incident on* vertices u and v. However, if a graph is directed, then edge (u, v) is *incident from* vertex u and is *incident to* vertex v. For example, in Figure 10.1(a), edge e is incident on vertices 5 and 4, but in Figure 10.1(b), edge f is incident from vertex 5 and incident to vertex 2. If (u, v) is an edge in a undirected graph $G = (V, E)$, vertices u and v are said to be *adjacent* to each other. If the graph is directed, vertex v is said to be *adjacent to* vertex u.

A *path* from a vertex v to a vertex u is a sequence $\langle v_0, v_1, v_2, \ldots, v_k \rangle$ of vertices where $v_0 = v$, $v_k = u$, and $(v_i, v_{i+1}) \in E$ for $i = 0, 1, \ldots, k - 1$. The length of a path is defined as the number of edges in the path. If there exists a path from v to u, then u is *reachable* from v. A path is *simple* if all of its vertices are distinct. A path forms a

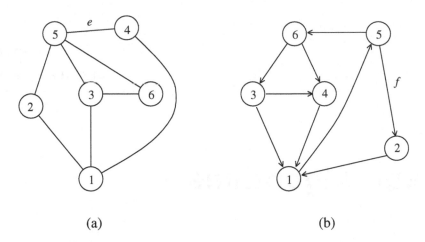

Figure 10.1   (a) An undirected graph and (b) a directed graph.

cycle if its starting and ending vertices are the same – that is, $v_0 = v_k$. A graph with
no cycles is called *acyclic*. A cycle is *simple* if all the intermediate vertices are distinct.
For example, in Figure 10.1(a), the sequence $\langle 3, 6, 5, 4 \rangle$ is a path from vertex 3 to vertex
4, and in Figure 10.1(b) there is a directed simple cycle $\langle 1, 5, 6, 4, 1 \rangle$. Additionally, in
Figure 10.1(a), the sequence $\langle 1, 2, 5, 3, 6, 5, 4, 1 \rangle$ is an undirected cycle that is not simple
because it contains the loop $\langle 5, 3, 6, 5 \rangle$.

An undirected graph is *connected* if every pair of vertices is connected by a path. We
say that a graph $G' = (V', E')$ is a *subgraph* of $G = (V, E)$ if $V' \subseteq V$ and $E' \subseteq E$.
Given a set $V' \subseteq V$, the subgraph of G *induced* by V' is the graph $G' = (V', E')$, where
$E' = \{(u, v) \in E | u, v \in V'\}$. A *complete graph* is a graph in which each pair of vertices
is adjacent. A *forest* is an acyclic graph, and a *tree* is a connected acyclic graph. Note that
if $G = (V, E)$ is a tree, then $|E| = |V| - 1$.

Sometimes weights are associated with each edge in E. Weights are usually real numbers representing the cost or benefit of traversing the associated edge. For example, in an
electronic circuit a resistor can be represented by an edge whose weight is its resistance. A
graph that has weights associated with each edge is called a *weighted graph* and is denoted
by $G = (V, E, w)$, where V and E are as we just defined and $w : E \to \Re$ is a real-valued
function defined on E. The weight of a graph is defined as the sum of the weights of its
edges. The weight of a path is the sum of the weights of its edges.

There are two standard methods for representing a graph in a computer program. The
first method is to use a matrix, and the second method is to use a linked list.

Consider a graph $G = (V, E)$ with n vertices numbered $1, 2, \ldots, n$. The *adjacency
matrix* of this graph is an $n \times n$ array $A = (a_{i,j})$, which is defined as follows:

$$a_{i,j} = \begin{cases} 1 & \text{if } (v_i, v_j) \in E \\ 0 & \text{otherwise} \end{cases}$$

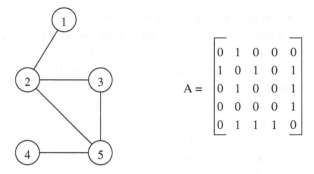

$$A = \begin{bmatrix} 0 & 1 & 0 & 0 & 0 \\ 1 & 0 & 1 & 0 & 1 \\ 0 & 1 & 0 & 0 & 1 \\ 0 & 0 & 0 & 0 & 1 \\ 0 & 1 & 1 & 1 & 0 \end{bmatrix}$$

Figure 10.2 An undirected graph and its adjacency matrix representation.

Figure 10.2 illustrates an adjacency matrix representation of an undirected graph. Note that the adjacency matrix of an undirected graph is symmetric. The adjacency matrix representation can be modified to facilitate weighted graphs. In this case, $A = (a_{i,j})$ is defined as follows:

$$a_{i,j} = \begin{cases} w(v_i, v_j) & \text{if } (v_i, v_j) \in E \\ 0 & \text{if } i = j \\ \infty & \text{otherwise} \end{cases}$$

We refer to this modified adjacency matrix as the **weighted adjacency matrix**. The space required to store the adjacency matrix of a graph with n vertices is $\Theta(n^2)$.

The **adjacency list** representation of a graph $G = (V, E)$ consists of an array $Adj[1..|V|]$ of lists. For each $v \in V$, $Adj[v]$ is a linked list of all vertices u such that G contains an edge $(v, u) \in E$. In other words, $Adj[v]$ is a list of all vertices adjacent to v. Figure 10.3 shows an example of the adjacency list representation. The adjacency list representation can be modified to accommodate weighted graphs by storing the weight of each edge $(v, u) \in E$ in the adjacency list of vertex v. The space required to store the adjacency list is $\Theta(|E|)$.

The nature of the graph determines which representation should be used. A graph $G = (V, E)$ is **sparse** if $|E|$ is much smaller than $O(|V|^2)$; otherwise it is **dense**. The adjacency

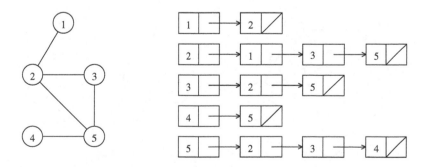

Figure 10.3 An undirected graph and its adjacency list representation.

matrix representation is useful for dense graphs, and the adjacency list representation is often more efficient for sparse graphs. Note that the sequential run time of an algorithm using an adjacency matrix and needing to traverse all the edges of the graph is bounded below by $\Omega(|V|^2)$ because the entire array must be accessed. However, if the adjacency list representation is used, the run time is bounded below by $\Omega(|V| + |E|)$ for the same reason. Thus, if the graph is sparse ($|E|$ is much smaller than $|V|^2$), the adjacency list representation is better than the adjacency matrix representation.

The rest of this chapter presents several graph algorithms. The first four sections present algorithms for dense graphs, and the last section discusses algorithms for sparse graphs. We assume that dense graphs are represented by an adjacency matrix, and sparse graphs by an adjacency list. Throughout this chapter, n denotes the number of vertices in the graph.

10.2   Minimum Spanning Tree: Prim's Algorithm

A *spanning tree* of an undirected graph G is a subgraph of G that is a tree containing all the vertices of G. In a weighted graph, the weight of a subgraph is the sum of the weights of the edges in the subgraph. A *minimum spanning tree* (MST) for a weighted undirected graph is a spanning tree with minimum weight. Many problems require finding an MST of an undirected graph. For example, the minimum length of cable necessary to connect a set of computers in a network can be determined by finding the MST of the undirected graph containing all the possible connections. Figure 10.4 shows an MST of an undirected graph.

If G is not connected, it cannot have a spanning tree. Instead, it has a *spanning forest*. For simplicity in describing the MST algorithm, we assume that G is connected. If G is not connected, we can find its connected components (Section 10.6) and apply the MST algorithm on each of them. Alternatively, we can modify the MST algorithm to output a minimum spanning forest.

Prim's algorithm for finding an MST is a greedy algorithm. The algorithm begins by selecting an arbitrary starting vertex. It then grows the minimum spanning tree by choosing

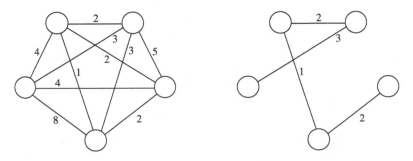

Figure 10.4   An undirected graph and its minimum spanning tree.

1.　　**procedure** PRIM_MST(V, E, w, r)
2.　　**begin**
3.　　　　$V_T := \{r\}$;
4.　　　　$d[r] := 0$;
5.　　　　**for** all $v \in (V - V_T)$ **do**
6.　　　　　　**if** edge (r, v) exists set $d[v] := w(r, v)$;
7.　　　　　　**else** set $d[v] := \infty$;
8.　　　　**while** $V_T \neq V$ **do**
9.　　　　**begin**
10.　　　　　　find a vertex u such that $d[u] := \min\{d[v] | v \in (V - V_T)\}$;
11.　　　　　　$V_T := V_T \cup \{u\}$;
12.　　　　　　**for** all $v \in (V - V_T)$ **do**
13.　　　　　　　　$d[v] := \min\{d[v], w(u, v)\}$;
14.　　　　**endwhile**
15.　　**end** PRIM_MST

Algorithm 10.1　Prim's sequential minimum spanning tree algorithm.

a new vertex and edge that are guaranteed to be in a spanning tree of minimum cost. The algorithm continues until all the vertices have been selected.

Let $G = (V, E, w)$ be the weighted undirected graph for which the minimum spanning tree is to be found, and let $A = (a_{i,j})$ be its weighted adjacency matrix. Prim's algorithm is shown in Algorithm 10.1. The algorithm uses the set V_T to hold the vertices of the minimum spanning tree during its construction. It also uses an array $d[1..n]$ in which, for each vertex $v \in (V - V_T)$, $d[v]$ holds the weight of the edge with the least weight from any vertex in V_T to vertex v. Initially, V_T contains an arbitrary vertex r that becomes the root of the MST. Furthermore, $d[r] = 0$, and for all v such that $v \in (V - V_T)$, $d[v] = w(r, v)$ if such an edge exists; otherwise $d[v] = \infty$. During each iteration of the algorithm, a new vertex u is added to V_T such that $d[u] = \min\{d[v] | v \in (V - V_T)\}$. After this vertex is added, all values of $d[v]$ such that $v \in (V - V_T)$ are updated because there may now be an edge with a smaller weight between vertex v and the newly added vertex u. The algorithm terminates when $V_T = V$. Figure 10.5 illustrates the algorithm. Upon termination of Prim's algorithm, the cost of the minimum spanning tree is $\sum_{v \in V} d[v]$. Algorithm 10.1 can be easily modified to store the edges that belong in the minimum spanning tree.

In Algorithm 10.1, the body of the **while** loop (lines 10–13) is executed $n-1$ times. Both the computation of $\min\{d[v] | v \in (V - V_T)\}$ (line 10), and the **for** loop (lines 12 and 13) execute in $O(n)$ steps. Thus, the overall complexity of Prim's algorithm is $\Theta(n^2)$.

Parallel Formulation

Prim's algorithm is iterative. Each iteration adds a new vertex to the minimum spanning tree. Since the value of $d[v]$ for a vertex v may change every time a new vertex u is added

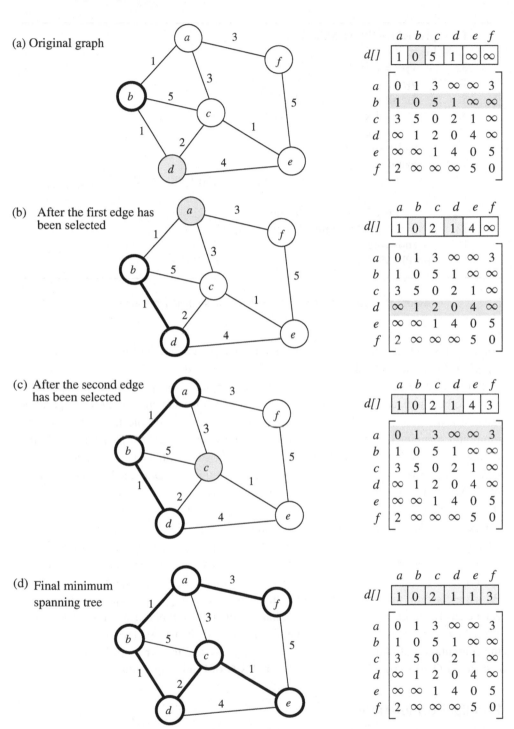

Figure 10.5 Prim's minimum spanning tree algorithm. The MST is rooted at vertex b. For each iteration, vertices in V_T as well as the edges selected so far are shown in bold. The array $d[v]$ shows the values of the vertices in $V - V_T$ after they have been updated.

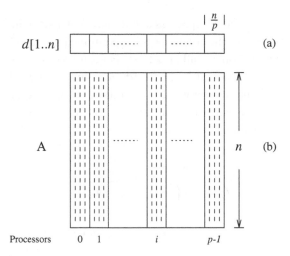

Figure 10.6 The partitioning of the distance array d and the adjacency matrix A among p processes.

in V_T, it is hard to select more than one vertex to include in the minimum spanning tree. For example, in the graph of Figure 10.5, after selecting vertex b, if both vertices d and c are selected, the MST will not be found. That is because, after selecting vertex d, the value of $d[c]$ is updated from 5 to 2. Thus, it is not easy to perform different iterations of the **while** loop in parallel. However, each iteration can be performed in parallel as follows.

Let p be the number of processes, and let n be the number of vertices in the graph. The set V is partitioned into p subsets using the 1-D block mapping (Section 3.4.1). Each subset has n/p consecutive vertices, and the work associated with each subset is assigned to a different process. Let V_i be the subset of vertices assigned to process P_i for $i = 0, 1, \ldots, p - 1$. Each process P_i stores the part of the array d that corresponds to V_i (that is, process P_i stores $d[v]$ such that $v \in V_i$). Figure 10.6(a) illustrates the partitioning. Each process P_i computes $d_i[u] = \min\{d_i[v]|v \in (V - V_T) \cap V_i\}$ during each iteration of the **while** loop. The global minimum is then obtained over all $d_i[u]$ by using the all-to-one reduction operation (Section 4.1) and is stored in process P_0. Process P_0 now holds the new vertex u, which will be inserted into V_T. Process P_0 broadcasts u to all processes by using one-to-all broadcast (Section 4.1). The process P_i responsible for vertex u marks u as belonging to set V_T. Finally, each process updates the values of $d[v]$ for its local vertices.

When a new vertex u is inserted into V_T, the values of $d[v]$ for $v \in (V - V_T)$ must be updated. The process responsible for v must know the weight of the edge (u, v). Hence, each process P_i needs to store the columns of the weighted adjacency matrix corresponding to set V_i of vertices assigned to it. This corresponds to 1-D block mapping of the matrix (Section 3.4.1). The space to store the required part of the adjacency matrix at each process is $\Theta(n^2/p)$. Figure 10.6(b) illustrates the partitioning of the weighted adjacency matrix.

The computation performed by a process to minimize and update the values of $d[v]$ during each iteration is $\Theta(n/p)$. The communication performed in each iteration is due to the all-to-one reduction and the one-to-all broadcast. For a p-process message-passing parallel computer, a one-to-all broadcast of one word takes time $(t_s + t_w) \log p$ (Section 4.1). Finding the global minimum of one word at each process takes the same amount of time (Section 4.1). Thus, the total communication cost of each iteration is $\Theta(\log p)$. The parallel run time of this formulation is given by

$$T_P = \overbrace{\Theta\left(\frac{n^2}{p}\right)}^{\text{computation}} + \overbrace{\Theta(n \log p)}^{\text{communication}}.$$

Since the sequential run time is $W = \Theta(n^2)$, the speedup and efficiency are as follows:

$$S = \frac{\Theta(n^2)}{\Theta(n^2/p) + \Theta(n \log p)}$$

$$E = \frac{1}{1 + \Theta((p \log p)/n)} \tag{10.1}$$

From Equation 10.1 we see that for a cost-optimal parallel formulation $(p \log p)/n = O(1)$. Thus, this formulation of Prim's algorithm can use only $p = O(n/\log n)$ processes. Furthermore, from Equation 10.1, the isoefficiency function due to communication is $\Theta(p^2 \log^2 p)$. Since n must grow at least as fast as p in this formulation, the isoefficiency function due to concurrency is $\Theta(p^2)$. Thus, the overall isoefficiency of this formulation is $\Theta(p^2 \log^2 p)$.

10.3   Single-Source Shortest Paths: Dijkstra's Algorithm

For a weighted graph $G = (V, E, w)$, the ***single-source shortest paths*** problem is to find the shortest paths from a vertex $v \in V$ to all other vertices in V. A ***shortest path*** from u to v is a minimum-weight path. Depending on the application, edge weights may represent time, cost, penalty, loss, or any other quantity that accumulates additively along a path and is to be minimized. In the following section, we present Dijkstra's algorithm, which solves the single-source shortest-paths problem on both directed and undirected graphs with non-negative weights.

Dijkstra's algorithm, which finds the shortest paths from a single vertex s, is similar to Prim's minimum spanning tree algorithm. Like Prim's algorithm, it incrementally finds the shortest paths from s to the other vertices of G. It is also greedy; that is, it always chooses an edge to a vertex that appears closest. Algorithm 10.2 shows Dijkstra's algorithm. Comparing this algorithm with Prim's minimum spanning tree algorithm, we see that the two are almost identical. The main difference is that, for each vertex $u \in (V - V_T)$, Dijkstra's

```
1.    procedure DIJKSTRA_SINGLE_SOURCE_SP(V, E, w, s)
2.    begin
3.        V_T := {s};
4.        for all v ∈ (V − V_T) do
5.            if (s, v) exists set l[v] := w(s, v);
6.            else set l[v] := ∞;
7.        while V_T ≠ V do
8.        begin
9.            find a vertex u such that l[u] := min{l[v]|v ∈ (V − V_T)};
10.           V_T := V_T ∪ {u};
11.           for all v ∈ (V − V_T) do
12.               l[v] := min{l[v], l[u] + w(u, v)};
13.       endwhile
14.   end  DIJKSTRA_SINGLE_SOURCE_SP
```

Algorithm 10.2   Dijkstra's sequential single-source shortest paths algorithm.

algorithm stores $l[u]$, the minimum cost to reach vertex u from vertex s by means of vertices in V_T; Prim's algorithm stores $d[u]$, the cost of the minimum-cost edge connecting a vertex in V_T to u. The run time of Dijkstra's algorithm is $\Theta(n^2)$.

Parallel Formulation

The parallel formulation of Dijkstra's single-source shortest path algorithm is very similar to the parallel formulation of Prim's algorithm for minimum spanning trees (Section 10.2). The weighted adjacency matrix is partitioned using the 1-D block mapping (Section 3.4.1). Each of the p processes is assigned n/p consecutive columns of the weighted adjacency matrix, and computes n/p values of the array l. During each iteration, all processes perform computation and communication similar to that performed by the parallel formulation of Prim's algorithm. Consequently, the parallel performance and scalability of Dijkstra's single-source shortest path algorithm is identical to that of Prim's minimum spanning tree algorithm.

10.4   All-Pairs Shortest Paths

Instead of finding the shortest paths from a single vertex v to every other vertex, we are sometimes interested in finding the shortest paths between all pairs of vertices. Formally, given a weighted graph $G(V, E, w)$, the ***all-pairs shortest paths*** problem is to find the shortest paths between all pairs of vertices $v_i, v_j \in V$ such that $i \neq j$. For a graph with n vertices, the output of an all-pairs shortest paths algorithm is an $n \times n$ matrix $D = (d_{i,j})$ such that $d_{i,j}$ is the cost of the shortest path from vertex v_i to vertex v_j.

The following sections present two algorithms to solve the all-pairs shortest paths problem. The first algorithm uses Dijkstra's single-source shortest paths algorithm, and the second uses Floyd's algorithm. Dijkstra's algorithm requires non-negative edge weights (Problem 10.4), whereas Floyd's algorithm works with graphs having negative-weight edges provided they contain no negative-weight cycles.

10.4.1   Dijkstra's Algorithm

In Section 10.3 we presented Dijkstra's algorithm for finding the shortest paths from a vertex v to all the other vertices in a graph. This algorithm can also be used to solve the all-pairs shortest paths problem by executing the single-source algorithm on each process, for each vertex v. We refer to this algorithm as Dijkstra's all-pairs shortest paths algorithm. Since the complexity of Dijkstra's single-source algorithm is $\Theta(n^2)$, the complexity of the all-pairs algorithm is $\Theta(n^3)$.

Parallel Formulations

Dijkstra's all-pairs shortest paths problem can be parallelized in two distinct ways. One approach partitions the vertices among different processes and has each process compute the single-source shortest paths for all vertices assigned to it. We refer to this approach as the *source-partitioned formulation*. Another approach assigns each vertex to a set of processes and uses the parallel formulation of the single-source algorithm (Section 10.3) to solve the problem on each set of processes. We refer to this approach as the *source-parallel formulation*. The following sections discuss and analyze these two approaches.

Source-Partitioned Formulation   The source-partitioned parallel formulation of Dijkstra's algorithm uses n processes. Each process P_i finds the shortest paths from vertex v_i to all other vertices by executing Dijkstra's sequential single-source shortest paths algorithm. It requires no interprocess communication (provided that the adjacency matrix is replicated at all processes). Thus, the parallel run time of this formulation is given by

$$T_P = \Theta(n^2).$$

Since the sequential run time is $W = \Theta(n^3)$, the speedup and efficiency are as follows:

$$S = \frac{\Theta(n^3)}{\Theta(n^2)}$$
$$E = \Theta(1) \tag{10.2}$$

It might seem that, due to the absence of communication, this is an excellent parallel formulation. However, that is not entirely true. The algorithm can use at most n processes. Therefore, the isoefficiency function due to concurrency is $\Theta(p^3)$, which is the overall isoefficiency function of the algorithm. If the number of processes available for solving the problem is small (that is, $n = \Theta(p)$), then this algorithm has good performance. However, if the number of processes is greater than n, other algorithms will eventually outperform this algorithm because of its poor scalability.

Source-Parallel Formulation The major problem with the source-partitioned parallel formulation is that it can keep only n processes busy doing useful work. Performance can be improved if the parallel formulation of Dijkstra's single-source algorithm (Section 10.3) is used to solve the problem for each vertex v. The source-parallel formulation is similar to the source-partitioned formulation, except that the single-source algorithm runs on disjoint subsets of processes.

Specifically, p processes are divided into n partitions, each with p/n processes (this formulation is of interest only if $p > n$). Each of the n single-source shortest paths problems is solved by one of the n partitions. In other words, we first parallelize the all-pairs shortest paths problem by assigning each vertex to a separate set of processes, and then parallelize the single-source algorithm by using the set of p/n processes to solve it. The total number of processes that can be used efficiently by this formulation is $O(n^2)$.

The analysis presented in Section 10.3 can be used to derive the performance of this formulation of Dijkstra's all-pairs algorithm. Assume that we have a p-process message-passing computer such that p is a multiple of n. The p processes are partitioned into n groups of size p/n each. If the single-source algorithm is executed on each p/n process group, the parallel run time is

$$T_P = \Theta \overbrace{\left(\frac{n^3}{p} \right)}^{\text{computation}} + \overbrace{\Theta(n \log p)}^{\text{communication}}. \tag{10.3}$$

Notice the similarities between Equations 10.3 and 10.2. These similarities are not surprising because each set of p/n processes forms a different group and carries out the computation independently. Thus, the time required by each set of p/n processes to solve the single-source problem determines the overall run time. Since the sequential run time is $W = \Theta(n^3)$, the speedup and efficiency are as follows:

$$S = \frac{\Theta(n^3)}{\Theta(n^3/p) + \Theta(n \log p)}$$

$$E = \frac{1}{1 + \Theta((p \log p)/n^2)} \tag{10.4}$$

From Equation 10.4 we see that for a cost-optimal formulation $p \log p/n^2 = O(1)$. Hence, this formulation can use up to $O(n^2/\log n)$ processes efficiently. Equation 10.4 also shows that the isoefficiency function due to communication is $\Theta((p \log p)^{1.5})$. The isoefficiency function due to concurrency is $\Theta(p^{1.5})$. Thus, the overall isoefficiency function is $\Theta((p \log p)^{1.5})$.

Comparing the two parallel formulations of Dijkstra's all-pairs algorithm, we see that the source-partitioned formulation performs no communication, can use no more than n processes, and solves the problem in time $\Theta(n^2)$. In contrast, the source-parallel formulation uses up to $n^2/\log n$ processes, has some communication overhead, and solves the problem in time $\Theta(n \log n)$ when $n^2/\log n$ processes are used. Thus, the source-parallel formulation exploits more parallelism than does the source-partitioned formulation.

10.4.2 Floyd's Algorithm

Floyd's algorithm for solving the all-pairs shortest paths problem is based on the following observation. Let $G = (V, E, w)$ be the weighted graph, and let $V = \{v_1, v_2, \ldots, v_n\}$ be the vertices of G. Consider a subset $\{v_1, v_2, \ldots, v_k\}$ of vertices for some k where $k \leq n$. For any pair of vertices $v_i, v_j \in V$, consider all paths from v_i to v_j whose intermediate vertices belong to the set $\{v_1, v_2, \ldots, v_k\}$. Let $p_{i,j}^{(k)}$ be the minimum-weight path among them, and let $d_{i,j}^{(k)}$ be the weight of $p_{i,j}^{(k)}$. If vertex v_k is not in the shortest path from v_i to v_j, then $p_{i,j}^{(k)}$ is the same as $p_{i,j}^{(k-1)}$. However, if v_k is in $p_{i,j}^{(k)}$, then we can break $p_{i,j}^{(k)}$ into two paths – one from v_i to v_k and one from v_k to v_j. Each of these paths uses vertices from $\{v_1, v_2, \ldots, v_{k-1}\}$. Thus, $d_{i,j}^{(k)} = d_{i,k}^{(k-1)} + d_{k,j}^{(k-1)}$. These observations are expressed in the following recurrence equation:

$$d_{i,j}^{(k)} = \begin{cases} w(v_i, v_j) & \text{if } k = 0 \\ \min\left\{d_{i,j}^{(k-1)}, d_{i,k}^{(k-1)} + d_{k,j}^{(k-1)}\right\} & \text{if } k \geq 1 \end{cases} \tag{10.5}$$

The length of the shortest path from v_i to v_j is given by $d_{i,j}^{(n)}$. In general, the solution is a matrix $D^{(n)} = (d_{i,j}^{(n)})$.

Floyd's algorithm solves Equation 10.5 bottom-up in the order of increasing values of k. Algorithm 10.3 shows Floyd's all-pairs algorithm. The run time of Floyd's algorithm is determined by the triple-nested **for** loops in lines 4–7. Each execution of line 7 takes time $\Theta(1)$; thus, the complexity of the algorithm is $\Theta(n^3)$. Algorithm 10.3 seems to imply that we must store n matrices of size $n \times n$. However, when computing matrix $D^{(k)}$, only matrix $D^{(k-1)}$ is needed. Consequently, at most two $n \times n$ matrices must be stored. Therefore, the overall space complexity is $\Theta(n^2)$. Furthermore, the algorithm works correctly even when only one copy of D is used (Problem 10.6).

---

1.   **procedure** FLOYD_ALL_PAIRS_SP(A)
2.   **begin**
3. $D^{(0)} = A$;
4.   **for** $k := 1$ **to** n **do**
5.   **for** $i := 1$ **to** n **do**
6.   **for** $j := 1$ **to** n **do**
7. $d_{i,j}^{(k)} := \min\left(d_{i,j}^{(k-1)}, d_{i,k}^{(k-1)} + d_{k,j}^{(k-1)}\right)$;
8.   **end** FLOYD_ALL_PAIRS_SP

Algorithm 10.3 Floyd's all-pairs shortest paths algorithm. This program computes the all-pairs shortest paths of the graph $G = (V, E)$ with adjacency matrix A.

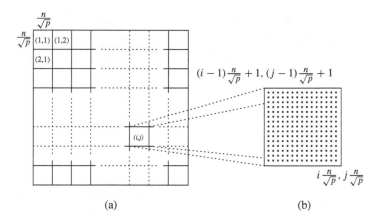

Figure 10.7 (a) Matrix $D^{(k)}$ distributed by 2-D block mapping into $\sqrt{p} \times \sqrt{p}$ subblocks, and (b) the subblock of $D^{(k)}$ assigned to process $P_{i,j}$.

Parallel Formulation

A generic parallel formulation of Floyd's algorithm assigns the task of computing matrix $D^{(k)}$ for each value of k to a set of processes. Let p be the number of processes available. Matrix $D^{(k)}$ is partitioned into p parts, and each part is assigned to a process. Each process computes the $D^{(k)}$ values of its partition. To accomplish this, a process must access the corresponding segments of the kth row and column of matrix $D^{(k-1)}$. The following section describes one technique for partitioning matrix $D^{(k)}$. Another technique is considered in Problem 10.8.

2-D Block Mapping One way to partition matrix $D^{(k)}$ is to use the 2-D block mapping (Section 3.4.1). Specifically, matrix $D^{(k)}$ is divided into p blocks of size $(n/\sqrt{p}) \times (n/\sqrt{p})$, and each block is assigned to one of the p processes. It is helpful to think of the p processes as arranged in a logical grid of size $\sqrt{p} \times \sqrt{p}$. Note that this is only a conceptual layout and does not necessarily reflect the actual interconnection network. We refer to the process on the ith row and j^{th} column as $P_{i,j}$. Process $P_{i,j}$ is assigned a subblock of $D^{(k)}$ whose upper-left corner is $((i-1)n/\sqrt{p}+1, (j-1)n/\sqrt{p}+1)$ and whose lower-right corner is $(in/\sqrt{p}, jn/\sqrt{p})$. Each process updates its part of the matrix during each iteration. Figure 10.7(a) illustrates the 2-D block mapping technique.

During the kth iteration of the algorithm, each process $P_{i,j}$ needs certain segments of the kth row and k^{th} column of the $D^{(k-1)}$ matrix. For example, to compute $d_{l,r}^{(k)}$ it must get $d_{l,k}^{(k-1)}$ and $d_{k,r}^{(k-1)}$. As Figure 10.8 illustrates, $d_{l,k}^{(k-1)}$ resides on a process along the same row, and element $d_{k,r}^{(k-1)}$ resides on a process along the same column as $P_{i,j}$. Segments are transferred as follows. During the kth iteration of the algorithm, each of the $\sqrt{p}$ processes containing part of the kth row sends it to the $\sqrt{p}-1$ processes in the same column. Similarly, each of the $\sqrt{p}$ processes containing part of the kth column sends it to the $\sqrt{p}-1$ processes in the same row.

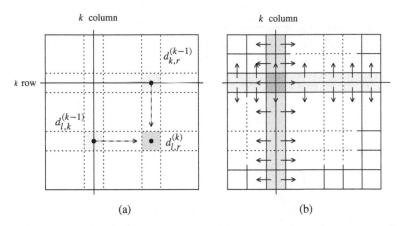

Figure 10.8   (a) Communication patterns used in the 2-D block mapping. When computing $d_{i,j}^{(k)}$, information must be sent to the highlighted process from two other processes along the same row and column. (b) The row and column of $\sqrt{p}$ processes that contain the kth row and column send them along process columns and rows.

Algorithm 10.4 shows the parallel formulation of Floyd's algorithm using the 2-D block mapping. We analyze the performance of this algorithm on a p-process message-passing computer with a cross-bisection bandwidth of $\Theta(p)$. During each iteration of the algorithm, the kth row and k^{th} column of processes perform a one-to-all broadcast along a row or a column of $\sqrt{p}$ processes. Each such process has $n/\sqrt{p}$ elements of the kth row or column, so it sends $n/\sqrt{p}$ elements. This broadcast requires time $\Theta((n \log p)/\sqrt{p})$. The synchronization step on line 7 requires time $\Theta(\log p)$. Since each process is assigned n^2/p elements of the $D^{(k)}$ matrix, the time to compute corresponding $D^{(k)}$ values is $\Theta(n^2/p)$. Therefore, the parallel run time of the 2-D block mapping formulation of Floyd's algorithm is

$$T_P = \overbrace{\Theta\left(\frac{n^3}{p}\right)}^{\text{computation}} + \overbrace{\Theta\left(\frac{n^2}{\sqrt{p}} \log p\right)}^{\text{communication}}.$$

Since the sequential run time is $W = \Theta(n^3)$, the speedup and efficiency are as follows:

$$S = \frac{\Theta(n^3)}{\Theta(n^3/p) + \Theta((n^2 \log p)/\sqrt{p})}$$

$$E = \frac{1}{1 + \Theta((\sqrt{p} \log p)/n)} \tag{10.6}$$

From Equation 10.6 we see that for a cost-optimal formulation $(\sqrt{p} \log p)/n = O(1)$; thus, 2-D block mapping can efficiently use up to $O(n^2/\log^2 n)$ processes. Equation 10.6 can also be used to derive the isoefficiency function due to communication, which is $\Theta(p^{1.5} \log^3 p)$. The isoefficiency function due to concurrency is $\Theta(p^{1.5})$. Thus, the overall isoefficiency function is $\Theta(p^{1.5} \log^3 p)$.

---

1.   **procedure** FLOYD_2DBLOCK($D^{(0)}$)
2.   **begin**
3.   **for** $k := 1$ **to** n **do**
4.   **begin**
5.   each process $P_{i,j}$ that has a segment of the kth row of $D^{(k-1)}$;
                 broadcasts it to the $P_{*,j}$ processes;
6.   each process $P_{i,j}$ that has a segment of the kth column of $D^{(k-1)}$;
                 broadcasts it to the $P_{i,*}$ processes;
7.   each process waits to receive the needed segments;
8.   each process $P_{i,j}$ computes its part of the $D^{(k)}$ matrix;
9.   **end**
10. **end** FLOYD_2DBLOCK

Algorithm 10.4   Floyd's parallel formulation using the 2-D block mapping. $P_{*,j}$ denotes all the processes in the jth column, and $P_{i,*}$ denotes all the processes in the ith row. The matrix $D^{(0)}$ is the adjacency matrix.

Speeding Things Up   In the 2-D block mapping formulation of Floyd's algorithm, a synchronization step ensures that all processes have the appropriate segments of matrix $D^{(k-1)}$ before computing elements of matrix $D^{(k)}$ (line 7 in Algorithm 10.4). In other words, the kth iteration starts only when the $(k-1)^{\text{th}}$ iteration has completed and the relevant parts of matrix $D^{(k-1)}$ have been transmitted to all processes. The synchronization step can be removed without affecting the correctness of the algorithm. To accomplish this, a process starts working on the kth iteration as soon as it has computed the $(k-1)^{\text{th}}$ iteration and has the relevant parts of the $D^{(k-1)}$ matrix. This formulation is called *pipelined 2-D block mapping*. A similar technique is used in Section 8.3 to improve the performance of Gaussian elimination.

Consider a p-process system arranged in a two-dimensional topology. Assume that process $P_{i,j}$ starts working on the kth iteration as soon as it has finished the $(k-1)^{\text{th}}$ iteration and has received the relevant parts of the $D^{(k-1)}$ matrix. When process $P_{i,j}$ has elements of the kth row and has finished the $(k-1)^{\text{th}}$ iteration, it sends the part of matrix $D^{(k-1)}$ stored locally to processes $P_{i,j-1}$ and $P_{i,j+1}$. It does this because that part of the $D^{(k-1)}$ matrix is used to compute the $D^{(k)}$ matrix. Similarly, when process $P_{i,j}$ has elements of the kth column and has finished the $(k-1)^{\text{th}}$ iteration, it sends the part of matrix $D^{(k-1)}$ stored locally to processes $P_{i-1,j}$ and $P_{i+1,j}$. When process $P_{i,j}$ receives elements of matrix $D^{(k)}$ from a process along its row in the logical mesh, it stores them locally and forwards them to the process on the side opposite from where it received them. The columns follow a similar communication protocol. Elements of matrix $D^{(k)}$ are not forwarded when they reach a mesh boundary. Figure 10.9 illustrates this communication and termination protocol for processes within a row (or a column).

Consider the movement of values in the first iteration. In each step, $n/\sqrt{p}$ elements of

Time

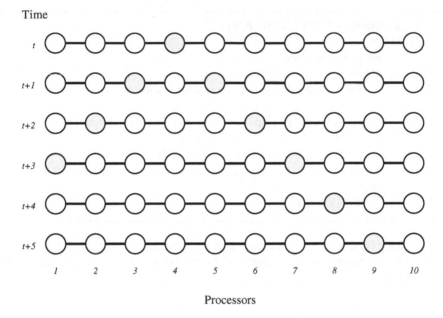

Processors

Figure 10.9   Communication protocol followed in the pipelined 2-D block mapping formulation of Floyd's algorithm. Assume that process 4 at time t has just computed a segment of the kth column of the $D^{(k-1)}$ matrix. It sends the segment to processes 3 and 5. These processes receive the segment at time $t + 1$ (where the time unit is the time it takes for a matrix segment to travel over the communication link between adjacent processes). Similarly, processes farther away from process 4 receive the segment later. Process 1 (at the boundary) does not forward the segment after receiving it.

the first row are sent from process $P_{i,j}$ to $P_{i+1,j}$. Similarly, elements of the first column are sent from process $P_{i,j}$ to process $P_{i,j+1}$. Each such step takes time $\Theta(n/\sqrt{p})$. After $\Theta(\sqrt{p})$ steps, process $P_{\sqrt{p},\sqrt{p}}$ gets the relevant elements of the first row and first column in time $\Theta(n)$. The values of successive rows and columns follow after time $\Theta(n^2/p)$ in a pipelined mode. Hence, process $P_{\sqrt{p},\sqrt{p}}$ finishes its share of the shortest path computation in time $\Theta(n^3/p) + \Theta(n)$. When process $P_{\sqrt{p},\sqrt{p}}$ has finished the $(n-1)^{th}$ iteration, it sends the relevant values of the nth row and column to the other processes. These values reach process $P_{1,1}$ in time $\Theta(n)$. The overall parallel run time of this formulation is

$$T_P = \overbrace{\Theta\left(\frac{n^3}{p}\right)}^{\text{computation}} + \overbrace{\Theta(n).}^{\text{communication}}$$

Since the sequential run time is $W = \Theta(n^3)$, the speedup and efficiency are as follows:

$$S = \frac{\Theta(n^3)}{\Theta(n^3/p) + \Theta(n)}$$

Table 10.1 The performance and scalability of the all-pairs shortest paths algorithms on various architectures with $O(p)$ bisection bandwidth. Similar run times apply to all $k-d$ cube architectures, provided that processes are properly mapped to the underlying processors.

	Maximum Number of Processes for $E = \Theta(1)$	Corresponding Parallel Run Time	Isoefficiency Function
Dijkstra source-partitioned	$\Theta(n)$	$\Theta(n^2)$	$\Theta(p^3)$
Dijkstra source-parallel	$\Theta(n^2/\log n)$	$\Theta(n \log n)$	$\Theta((p \log p)^{1.5})$
Floyd 1-D block	$\Theta(n/\log n)$	$\Theta(n^2 \log n)$	$\Theta((p \log p)^3)$
Floyd 2-D block	$\Theta(n^2/\log^2 n)$	$\Theta(n \log^2 n)$	$\Theta(p^{1.5} \log^3 p)$
Floyd pipelined 2-D block	$\Theta(n^2)$	$\Theta(n)$	$\Theta(p^{1.5})$

$$E = \frac{1}{1 + \Theta(p/n^2)} \tag{10.7}$$

From Equation 10.7 we see that for a cost-optimal formulation $p/n^2 = O(1)$. Thus, the pipelined formulation of Floyd's algorithm uses up to $O(n^2)$ processes efficiently. Also from Equation 10.7, we can derive the isoefficiency function due to communication, which is $\Theta(p^{1.5})$. This is the overall isoefficiency function as well. Comparing the pipelined formulation to the synchronized 2-D block mapping formulation, we see that the former is significantly faster.

10.4.3 Performance Comparisons

The performance of the all-pairs shortest paths algorithms previously presented is summarized in Table 10.1 for a parallel architecture with $O(p)$ bisection bandwidth. Floyd's pipelined formulation is the most scalable and can use up to $\Theta(n^2)$ processes to solve the problem in time $\Theta(n)$. Moreover, this parallel formulation performs equally well even on architectures with bisection bandwidth $O(\sqrt{p})$, such as a mesh-connected computer. Furthermore, its performance is independent of the type of routing (store-and-forward or cut-through).

10.5 Transitive Closure

In many applications we wish to determine if any two vertices in a graph are connected. This is usually done by finding the transitive closure of a graph. Formally, if $G = (V, E)$ is a graph, then the **transitive closure** of G is defined as the graph $G^* = (V, E^*)$, where $E^* = \{(v_i, v_j)|$ there is a path from v_i to v_j in $G\}$. We compute the transitive closure of a graph by computing the connectivity matrix A^*. The **connectivity matrix** of G is a matrix

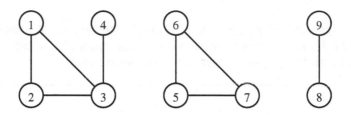

Figure 10.10   A graph with three connected components: $\{1, 2, 3, 4\}$, $\{5, 6, 7\}$, and $\{8, 9\}$.

$A^* = (a^*_{i,j})$ such that $a^*_{i,j} = 1$ if there is a path from v_i to v_j or $i = j$, and $a^*_{i,j} = \infty$ otherwise.

To compute A^* we assign a weight of 1 to each edge of E and use any of the all-pairs shortest paths algorithms on this weighted graph. Matrix A^* can be obtained from matrix D, where D is the solution to the all-pairs shortest paths problem, as follows:

$$a^*_{i,j} = \begin{cases} \infty & \text{if } d_{i,j} = \infty \\ 1 & \text{if } d_{i,j} > 0 \text{ or } i = j \end{cases}$$

Another method for computing A^* is to use Floyd's algorithm on the adjacency matrix of G, replacing the *min* and $+$ operations in line 7 of Algorithm 10.3 by logical **or** and logical **and** operations. In this case, we initially set $a_{i,j} = 1$ if $i = j$ or $(v_i, v_j) \in E$, and $a_{i,j} = 0$ otherwise. Matrix A^* is obtained by setting $a^*_{i,j} = \infty$ if $d_{i,j} = 0$ and $a^*_{i,j} = 1$ otherwise. The complexity of computing the transitive closure is $\Theta(n^3)$.

10.6   Connected Components

The ***connected components*** of an undirected graph $G = (V, E)$ are the maximal disjoint sets $C_1, C_2, \ldots, C_k$ such that $V = C_1 \cup C_2 \cup \ldots \cup C_k$, and $u, v \in C_i$ if and only if u is reachable from v and v is reachable from u. The connected components of an undirected graph are the equivalence classes of vertices under the "is reachable from" relation. For example, Figure 10.10 shows a graph with three connected components.

10.6.1   A Depth-First Search Based Algorithm

We can find the connected components of a graph by performing a depth-first traversal on the graph. The outcome of this depth-first traversal is a forest of depth-first trees. Each tree in the forest contains vertices that belong to a different connected component. Figure 10.11 illustrates this algorithm. The correctness of this algorithm follows directly from the definition of a spanning tree (that is, a depth-first tree is also a spanning tree of a graph induced by the set of vertices in the depth-first tree) and from the fact that G is undirected. Assuming that the graph is stored using a sparse representation, the run time of this algorithm is $\Theta(|E|)$ because the depth-first traversal algorithm traverses all the edges in G.

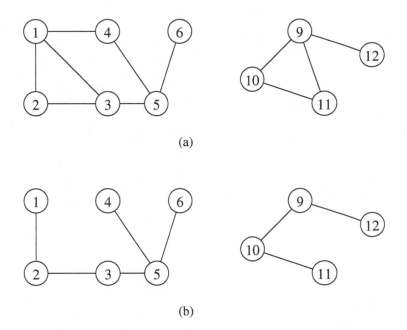

(a)

(b)

Figure 10.11   Part (b) is a depth-first forest obtained from depth-first traversal of the graph in part (a). Each of these trees is a connected component of the graph in part (a).

Parallel Formulation

The connected-component algorithm can be parallelized by partitioning the adjacency matrix of G into p parts and assigning each part to one of p processes. Each process P_i has a subgraph G_i of G, where $G_i = (V, E_i)$ and E_i are the edges that correspond to the portion of the adjacency matrix assigned to this process. In the first step of this parallel formulation, each process P_i computes the depth-first spanning forest of the graph G_i. At the end of this step, p spanning forests have been constructed. During the second step, spanning forests are merged pairwise until only one spanning forest remains. The remaining spanning forest has the property that two vertices are in the same connected component of G if they are in the same tree. Figure 10.12 illustrates this algorithm.

To merge pairs of spanning forests efficiently, the algorithm uses disjoint sets of edges. Assume that each tree in the spanning forest of a subgraph of G is represented by a set. The sets for different trees are pairwise disjoint. The following operations are defined on the disjoint sets:

find(x) returns a pointer to the representative element of the set containing x. Each set has its own unique representative.

union(x, y) unites the sets containing the elements x and y. The two sets are assumed to be disjoint prior to the operation.

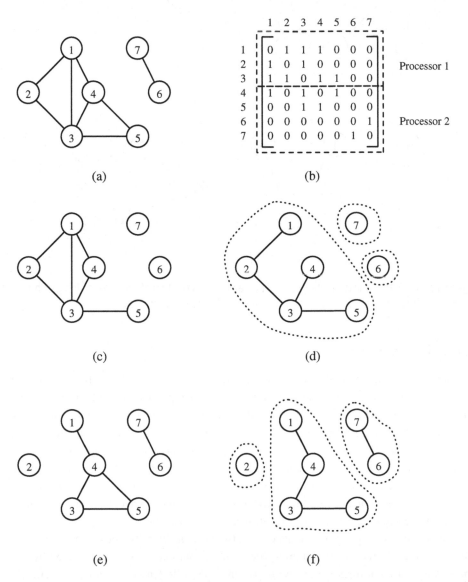

(a)

(b)

(c)

(d)

(e)

(f)

Figure 10.12 Computing connected components in parallel. The adjacency matrix of the graph G in (a) is partitioned into two parts as shown in (b). Next, each process gets a subgraph of G as shown in (c) and (e). Each process then computes the spanning forest of the subgraph, as shown in (d) and (f). Finally, the two spanning trees are merged to form the solution.

The spanning forests are merged as follows. Let A and B be the two spanning forests to be merged. At most $n - 1$ edges (since A and B are forests) of one are merged with the edges of the other. Suppose we want to merge forest A into forest B. For each edge (u, v) of A, a find operation is performed for each vertex to determine if the two vertices are already in the same tree of B. If not, then the two trees (sets) of B containing u and v are united by a union operation. Otherwise, no union operation is necessary. Hence, merging A and B requires at most $2(n - 1)$ find operations and $(n - 1)$ union operations. We can implement the disjoint-set data structure by using disjoint-set forests with ranking and path compression. Using this implementation, the cost of performing $2(n - 1)$ finds and $(n - 1)$ unions is $O(n)$. A detailed description of the disjoint-set forest is beyond the scope of this book. Refer to the bibliographic remarks (Section 10.8) for references.

Having discussed how to efficiently merge two spanning forests, we now concentrate on how to partition the adjacency matrix of G and distribute it among p processes. The next section discusses a formulation that uses 1-D block mapping. An alternative partitioning scheme is discussed in Problem 10.12.

1-D Block Mapping   The $n \times n$ adjacency matrix is partitioned into p stripes (Section 3.4.1). Each stripe is composed of n/p consecutive rows and is assigned to one of the p processes. To compute the connected components, each process first computes a spanning forest for the n-vertex graph represented by the n/p rows of the adjacency matrix assigned to it.

Consider a p-process message-passing computer. Computing the spanning forest based on the $(n/p) \times n$ adjacency matrix assigned to each process requires time $\Theta(n^2/p)$. The second step of the algorithm–the pairwise merging of spanning forests – is performed by embedding a virtual tree on the processes. There are $\log p$ merging stages, and each takes time $\Theta(n)$. Thus, the cost due to merging is $\Theta(n \log p)$. Finally, during each merging stage, spanning forests are sent between nearest neighbors. Recall that $\Theta(n)$ edges of the spanning forest are transmitted. Thus, the communication cost is $\Theta(n \log p)$. The parallel run time of the connected-component algorithm is

$$T_P = \overbrace{\Theta\left(\frac{n^2}{p}\right)}^{\text{local computation}} + \overbrace{\Theta(n \log p)}^{\text{forest merging}}.$$

Since the sequential complexity is $W = \Theta(n^2)$, the speedup and efficiency are as follows:

$$S = \frac{\Theta(n^2)}{\Theta(n^2/p) + \Theta(n \log p)}$$

$$E = \frac{1}{1 + \Theta((p \log p)/n)} \tag{10.8}$$

From Equation 10.8 we see that for a cost-optimal formulation $p = O(n/\log n)$. Also from Equation 10.8, we derive the isoefficiency function, which is $\Theta(p^2 \log^2 p)$. This is the isoefficiency function due to communication and due to the extra computations performed in the merging stage. The isoefficiency function due to concurrency is $\Theta(p^2)$; thus, the overall isoefficiency function is $\Theta(p^2 \log^2 p)$. The performance of this parallel formulation is similar to that of Prim's minimum spanning tree algorithm and Dijkstra's single-source shortest paths algorithm on a message-passing computer.

10.7   Algorithms for Sparse Graphs

The parallel algorithms in the previous sections are based on the best-known algorithms for dense-graph problems. However, we have yet to address parallel algorithms for sparse graphs. Recall that a graph $G = (V, E)$ is sparse if $|E|$ is much smaller than $|V|^2$. Figure 10.13 shows some examples of sparse graphs.

Any dense-graph algorithm works correctly on sparse graphs as well. However, if the sparseness of the graph is taken into account, it is usually possible to obtain significantly

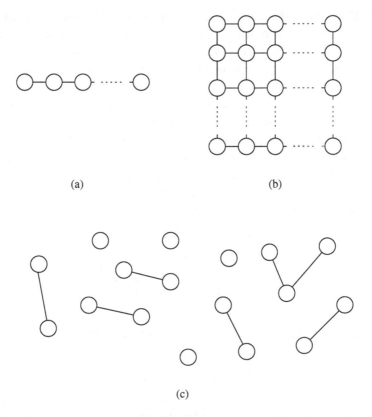

(a)   (b)

(c)

Figure 10.13   Examples of sparse graphs: (a) a linear graph, in which each vertex has two incident edges; (b) a grid graph, in which each vertex has four incident vertices; and (c) a random sparse graph.

better performance. For example, the run time of Prim's minimum spanning tree algorithm (Section 10.2) is $\Theta(n^2)$ regardless of the number of edges in the graph. By modifying Prim's algorithm to use adjacency lists and a binary heap, the complexity of the algorithm reduces to $\Theta(|E| \log n)$. This modified algorithm outperforms the original algorithm as long as $|E| = O(n^2/\log n)$. An important step in developing sparse-graph algorithms is to use an adjacency list instead of an adjacency matrix. This change in representation is crucial, since the complexity of adjacency-matrix-based algorithms is usually $\Omega(n^2)$, and is independent of the number of edges. Conversely, the complexity of adjacency-list-based algorithms is usually $\Omega(n + |E|)$, which depends on the sparseness of the graph.

In the parallel formulations of sequential algorithms for dense graphs, we obtained good performance by partitioning the adjacency matrix of a graph so that each process performed roughly an equal amount of work and communication was localized. We were able to achieve this largely because the graph was dense. For example, consider Floyd's all-pairs shortest paths algorithm. By assigning equal-sized blocks from the adjacency matrix to all processes, the work was uniformly distributed. Moreover, since each block consisted of consecutive rows and columns, the communication overhead was limited.

However, it is difficult to achieve even work distribution and low communication overhead for sparse graphs. Consider the problem of partitioning the adjacency list of a graph. One possible partition assigns an equal number of vertices and their adjacency lists to each process. However, the number of edges incident on a given vertex may vary. Hence, some processes may be assigned a large number of edges while others receive very few, leading to a significant work imbalance among the processes. Alternately, we can assign an equal number of edges to each process. This may require splitting the adjacency list of a vertex among processes. As a result, the time spent communicating information among processes that store separate parts of the adjacency list may increase dramatically. Thus, it is hard to derive efficient parallel formulations for general sparse graphs (Problems 10.14 and 10.15). However, we can often derive efficient parallel formulations if the sparse graph has a certain structure. For example, consider the street map shown in Figure 10.14. The graph corresponding to the map is sparse: the number of edges incident on any vertex is at most four. We refer to such graphs as **grid graphs**. Other types of sparse graphs for which an efficient parallel formulation can be developed are those corresponding to well-shaped finite element meshes, and graphs whose vertices have similar degrees. The next two sections present efficient algorithms for finding a maximal independent set of vertices, and for computing single-source shortest paths for these types of graphs.

10.7.1 Finding a Maximal Independent Set

Consider the problem of finding a maximal independent set (MIS) of vertices of a graph. We are given a sparse undirected graph $G = (V, E)$. A set of vertices $I \subset V$ is called **independent** if no pair of vertices in I is connected via an edge in G. An independent set is called **maximal** if by including any other vertex not in I, the independence property is violated. These definitions are illustrated in Figure 10.15. Note that as the example

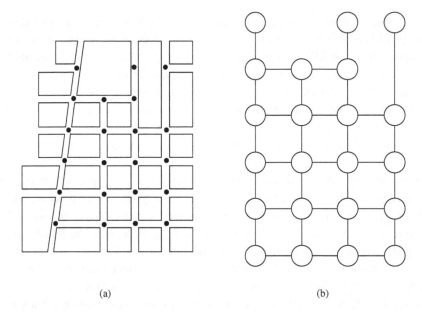

Figure 10.14 A street map (a) can be represented by a graph (b). In the graph shown in (b), each street intersection is a vertex and each edge is a street segment. The vertices of (b) are the intersections of (a) marked by dots.

illustrates, maximal independent sets are not unique. Maximal independent sets of vertices can be used to determine which computations can be done in parallel in certain types of task graphs. For example, maximal independent sets can be used to determine the sets of rows that can be factored concurrently in parallel incomplete factorization algorithms, and to compute a coloring of a graph in parallel.

Many algorithms have been proposed for computing a maximal independent set of vertices. The simplest class of algorithms starts by initially setting I to be empty, and assigning all vertices to a set C that acts as the *candidate* set of vertices for inclusion in I. Then

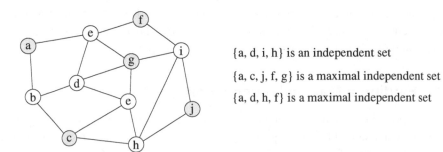

Figure 10.15   Examples of independent and maximal independent sets.

the algorithm proceeds by repeatedly moving a vertex v from C into I and removing all vertices adjacent to v from C. This process terminates when C becomes empty, in which case I is a maximal independent set. The resulting set I will contain an independent set of vertices, because every time we add a vertex into I we remove from C all the vertices whose subsequent inclusion will violate the independence condition. Also, the resulting set is maximal, because any other vertex that is not already in I is adjacent to at least one of the vertices in I.

Even though the above algorithm is very simple, it is not well suited for parallel processing, as it is serial in nature. For this reason parallel MIS algorithms are usually based on the randomized algorithm originally developed by Luby for computing a coloring of a graph. Using Luby's algorithm, a maximal independent set I of vertices V a graph is computed in an incremental fashion as follows. The set I is initially set to be empty, and the set of candidate vertices, C, is set to be equal to V. A unique random number is assigned to each vertex in C, and if a vertex has a random number that is smaller than all of the random numbers of the adjacent vertices, it is included in I. The set C is updated so that all the vertices that were selected for inclusion in I and their adjacent vertices are removed from it. Note that the vertices that are selected for inclusion in I are indeed independent (i.e., not directly connected via an edge). This is because, if v was inserted in I, then the random number assigned to v is the smallest among the random numbers assigned to its adjacent vertices; thus, no other vertex u adjacent to v will have been selected for inclusion. Now the above steps of random number assignment and vertex selection are repeated for the vertices left in C, and I is augmented similarly. This incremental augmentation of I ends when C becomes empty. On the average, this algorithm converges after $O(\log |V|)$ such augmentation steps. The execution of the algorithm for a small graph is illustrated in Figure 10.16. In the rest of this section we describe a shared-address-space parallel formulation of Luby's algorithm. A message-passing adaption of this algorithm is described in the message-passing chapter.

Shared-Address-Space Parallel Formulation

A parallel formulation of Luby's MIS algorithm for a shared-address-space parallel computer is as follows. Let I be an array of size $|V|$. At the termination of the algorithm, $I[i]$ will store one, if vertex v_i is part of the MIS, or zero otherwise. Initially, all the elements in I are set to zero, and during each iteration of Luby's algorithm, some of the entries of that array will be changed to one. Let C be an array of size $|V|$. During the course of the algorithm, $C[i]$ is one if vertex v_i is part of the candidate set, or zero otherwise. Initially, all the elements in C are set to one. Finally, let R be an array of size $|V|$ that stores the random numbers assigned to each vertex.

During each iteration, the set C is logically partitioned among the p processes. Each process generates a random number for its assigned vertices from C. When all the processes finish generating these random numbers, they proceed to determine which vertices can be included in I. In particular, for each vertex assigned to them, they check to see if

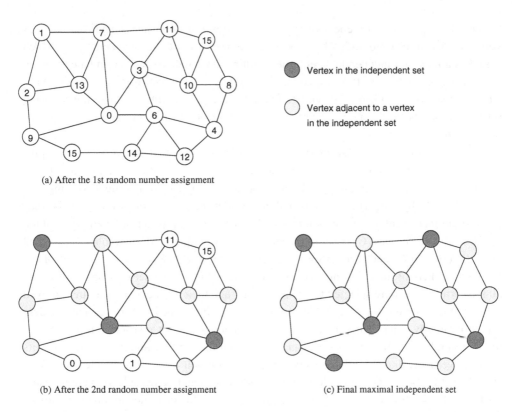

(a) After the 1st random number assignment

Vertex in the independent set

Vertex adjacent to a vertex
in the independent set

(b) After the 2nd random number assignment

(c) Final maximal independent set

Figure 10.16   The different augmentation steps of Luby's randomized maximal independent set algorithm. The numbers inside each vertex correspond to the random number assigned to the vertex.

the random number assigned to it is smaller than the random numbers assigned to all of its adjacent vertices. If it is true, they set the corresponding entry in I to one. Because R is shared and can be accessed by all the processes, determining whether or not a particular vertex can be included in I is quite straightforward.

Array C can also be updated in a straightforward fashion as follows. Each process, as soon as it determines that a particular vertex v will be part of I, will set to zero the entries of C corresponding to its adjacent vertices. Note that even though more than one process may be setting to zero the same entry of C (because it may be adjacent to more than one vertex that was inserted in I), such concurrent writes will not affect the correctness of the results, because the value that gets concurrently written is the same.

The complexity of each iteration of Luby's algorithm is similar to that of the serial algorithm, with the extra cost of the global synchronization after each random number assignment. The detailed analysis of Luby's algorithm is left as an exercise (Problem 10.16).

```
1.    procedure JOHNSON_SINGLE_SOURCE_SP(V, E, s)
2.    begin
3.        Q := V;
4.        for all v ∈ Q do
5.            l[v] := ∞;
6.        l[s] := 0;
7.        while Q ≠ ∅ do
8.        begin
9.            u := extract_min(Q);
10.           for each v ∈ Adj[u] do
11.               if v ∈ Q and l[u] + w(u, v) < l[v] then
12.                   l[v] := l[u] + w(u, v);
13.           endwhile
14.   end JOHNSON_SINGLE_SOURCE_SP
```

Algorithm 10.5   Johnson's sequential single-source shortest paths algorithm.

10.7.2   Single-Source Shortest Paths

It is easy to modify Dijkstra's single-source shortest paths algorithm so that it finds the shortest paths for sparse graphs efficiently. The modified algorithm is known as Johnson's algorithm. Recall that Dijkstra's algorithm performs the following two steps in each iteration. First, it extracts a vertex $u \in (V - V_T)$ such that $l[u] = \min\{l[v]|v \in (V - V_T)\}$ and inserts it into set V_T. Second, for each vertex $v \subset (V - V_T)$, it computes $l[v] = \min\{l[v], l[u] + w(u, v)\}$. Note that, during the second step, only the vertices in the adjacency list of vertex u need to be considered. Since the graph is sparse, the number of vertices adjacent to vertex u is considerably smaller than $\Theta(n)$; thus, using the adjacency-list representation improves performance.

Johnson's algorithm uses a priority queue Q to store the value $l[v]$ for each vertex $v \in (V - V_T)$. The priority queue is constructed so that the vertex with the smallest value in l is always at the front of the queue. A common way to implement a priority queue is as a binary min-heap. A binary min-heap allows us to update the value $l[v]$ for each vertex v in time $O(\log n)$. Algorithm 10.5 shows Johnson's algorithm. Initially, for each vertex v other than the source, it inserts $l[v] = \infty$ in the priority queue. For the source vertex s it inserts $l[s] = 0$. At each step of the algorithm, the vertex $u \in (V - V_T)$ with the minimum value in l is removed from the priority queue. The adjacency list for u is traversed, and for each edge (u, v) the distance $l[v]$ to vertex v is updated in the heap. Updating vertices in the heap dominates the overall run time of the algorithm. The total number of updates is equal to the number of edges; thus, the overall complexity of Johnson's algorithm is $\Theta(|E| \log n)$.

Parallelization Strategy

An efficient parallel formulation of Johnson's algorithm must maintain the priority queue Q efficiently. A simple strategy is for a single process, for example, P_0, to maintain Q. All other processes will then compute new values of $l[v]$ for $v \in (V - V_T)$, and give them to P_0 to update the priority queue. There are two main limitation of this scheme. First, because a single process is responsible for maintaining the priority queue, the overall parallel run time is $O(|E| \log n)$ (there are $O(|E|)$ queue updates and each update takes time $O(\log n)$). This leads to a parallel formulation with no asymptotic speedup, since $O(|E| \log n)$ is the same as the sequential run time. Second, during each iteration, the algorithm updates roughly $|E|/|V|$ vertices. As a result, no more than $|E|/|V|$ processes can be kept busy at any given time, which is very small for most of the interesting classes of sparse graphs, and to a large extent, independent of the size of the graphs.

The first limitation can be alleviated by distributing the maintainance of the priority queue to multiple processes. This is a non-trivial task, and can only be done effectively on architectures with low latency, such as shared-address-space computers. However, even in the best case, when each priority queue update takes only time $O(1)$, the maximum speedup that can be achieved is $O(\log n)$, which is quite small. The second limitation can be alleviated by recognizing the fact that depending on the l value of the vertices at the top of the priority queue, more than one vertex can be extracted at the same time. In particular, if v is the vertex at the top of the priority queue, all vertices u such that $l[u] = l[v]$ can also be extracted, and their adjacency lists processed concurrently. This is because the vertices that are at the same minimum distance from the source can be processed in any order. Note that in order for this approach to work, all the vertices that are at the same minimum distance must be processed in lock-step. An additional degree of concurrency can be extracted if we know that the minimum weight over all the edges in the graph is m. In that case, all vertices u such that $l[u] \leq l[v] + m$ can be processed concurrently (and in lock-step). We will refer to these as the *safe* vertices. However, this additional concurrency can lead to asymptotically better speedup than $O(\log n)$ only if more than one update operation of the priority queue can proceed concurrently, substantially complicating the parallel algorithm for maintaining the single priority queue.

Our discussion thus far was focused on developing a parallel formulation of Johnson's algorithm that finds the shortest paths to the vertices in the same order as the serial algorithm, and explores concurrently only safe vertices. However, as we have seen, such an approach leads to complicated algorithms and limited concurrency. An alternate approach is to develop a parallel algorithm that processes both safe and *unsafe* vertices concurrently, as long as these unsafe vertices can be reached from the source via a path involving vertices whose shortest paths have already been computed (i.e., their corresponding l-value in the priority queue is not infinite). In particular, in this algorithm, each one of the p processes extracts one of the p top vertices and proceeds to update the l values of the vertices adjacent to it. Of course, the problem with this approach is that it does not ensure that the l values of the vertices extracted from the priority queue correspond to the cost

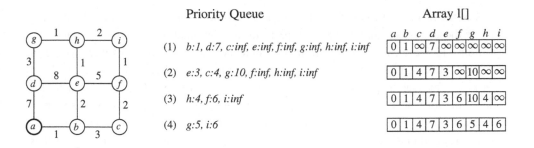

	Priority Queue	Array l[]

Figure 10.17 An example of the modified Johnson's algorithm for processing unsafe vertices concurrently.

of the shortest path. For example, consider two vertices v and u that are at the top of the priority queue, with $l[v] < l[u]$. According to Johnson's algorithm, at the point a vertex is extracted from the priority queue, its l value is the cost of the shortest path from the source to that vertex. Now, if there is an edge connecting v and u, such that $l[v] + w(v, u) < l[u]$, then the correct value of the shortest path to u is $l[v] + w(v, u)$, and not $l[u]$. However, the correctness of the results can be ensured by detecting when we have incorrectly computed the shortest path to a particular vertex, and inserting it back into the priority queue with the updated l value. We can detect such instances as follows. Consider a vertex v that has just been extracted from the queue, and let u be a vertex adjacent to v that has already been extracted from the queue. If $l[v] + w(v, u)$ is smaller than $l[u]$, then the shortest path to u has been incorrectly computed, and u needs to be inserted back into the priority queue with $l[u] = l[v] + w(v, u)$.

To see how this approach works, consider the example grid graph shown in Figure 10.17. In this example, there are three processes and we want to find the shortest path from vertex a. After initialization of the priority queue, vertices b and d will be reachable from the source. In the first step, process P_0 and P_1 extract vertices b and d and proceed to update the l values of the vertices adjacent to b and d. In the second step, processes P_0, P_1, and P_2 extract e, c, and g, and proceed to update the l values of the vertices adjacent to them. Note that when processing vertex e, process P_0 checks to see if $l[e] + w(e, d)$ is smaller or greater than $l[d]$. In this particular example, $l[e] + w(e, d) > l[d]$, indicating that the previously computed value of the shortest path to d does not change when e is considered, and all computations so far are correct. In the third step, processes P_0 and P_1 work on h and f, respectively. Now, when process P_0 compares $l[h] + w(h, g) = 5$ against the value of $l[g] = 10$ that was extracted in the previous iteration, it finds it to be smaller. As a result, it inserts back into the priority queue vertex g with the updated $l[g]$ value. Finally, in the fourth and last step, the remaining two vertices are extracted from the priority queue, and all single-source shortest paths have been computed.

This approach for parallelizing Johnson's algorithm falls into the category of speculative decomposition discussed in Section 3.2.4. Essentially, the algorithm assumes that the $l[]$

values of the top p vertices in the priority queue will not change as a result of processing some of these vertices, and proceeds to perform the computations required by Johnson's algorithm. However, if at some later point it detects that its assumptions were wrong, it goes back and essentially recomputes the shortest paths of the affected vertices.

In order for such a speculative decomposition approach to be effective, we must also remove the bottleneck of working with a single priority queue. In the rest of this section we present a message-passing algorithm that uses speculative decomposition to extract concurrency and in which there is no single priority queue. Instead, each process maintains its own priority queue for the vertices that it is assigned to. Problem 10.13 discusses another approach.

Distributed Memory Formulation

Let p be the number of processes, and let $G = (V, E)$ be a sparse graph. We partition the set of vertices V into p disjoint sets $V_1, V_2, \ldots, V_p$, and assign each set of vertices and its associated adjacency lists to one of the p processes. Each process maintains a priority queue for the vertices assigned to it, and computes the shortest paths from the source to these vertices. Thus, the priority queue Q is partitioned into p disjoint priority queues $Q_1, Q_2, \ldots, Q_p$, each assigned to a separate process. In addition to the priority queue, each process P_i also maintains an array sp such that $sp[v]$ stores the cost of the shortest path from the source vertex to v for each vertex $v \in V_i$. The cost $sp[v]$ is updated to $l[v]$ each time vertex v is extracted from the priority queue. Initially, $sp[v] = \infty$ for every vertex v other than the source, and we insert $l[s]$ into the appropriate priority queue for the source vertex s. Each process executes Johnson's algorithm on its local priority queue. At the end of the algorithm, $sp[v]$ stores the length of the shortest path from source to vertex v.

When process P_i extracts the vertex $u \in V_i$ with the smallest value $l[u]$ from Q_i, the l values of vertices assigned to processes other than P_i may need to be updated. Process P_i sends a message to processes that store vertices adjacent to u, notifying them of the new values. Upon receiving these values, processes update the values of l. For example, assume that there is an edge (u, v) such that $u \in V_i$ and $v \in V_j$, and that process P_i has just extracted vertex u from its priority queue. Process P_i then sends a message to P_j containing the potential new value of $l[v]$, which is $l[u] + w(u, v)$. Process P_j, upon receiving this message, sets the value of $l[v]$ stored in its priority queue to $\min\{l[v], l[u] + w(u, v)\}$.

Since both processes P_i and P_j execute Johnson's algorithm, it is possible that process P_j has already extracted vertex v from its priority queue. This means that process P_j might have already computed the shortest path $sp[v]$ from the source to vertex v. Then there are two possible cases: either $sp[v] \leq l[u] + w(u, v)$, or $sp[v] > l[u] + w(u, v)$. The first case means that there is a longer path to vertex v passing through vertex u, and the second case means that there is a shorter path to vertex v passing through vertex u. For the first case, process P_j needs to do nothing, since the shortest path to v does not change. For

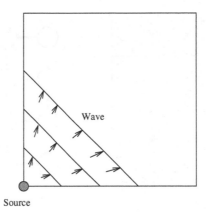

Figure 10.18 The wave of activity in the priority queues.

the second case, process P_j must update the cost of the shortest path to vertex v. This is done by inserting the vertex v back into the priority queue with $l[v] = l[u] + w(u, v)$ and disregarding the value of $sp[v]$. Since a vertex v can be reinserted into the priority queue, the algorithm terminates only when all the queues become empty.

Initially, only the priority queue of the process with the source vertex is non-empty. After that, the priority queues of other processes become populated as messages containing new l values are created and sent to adjacent processes. When processes receive new l values, they insert them into their priority queues and perform computations. Consider the problem of computing the single-source shortest paths in a grid graph where the source is located at the bottom-left corner. The computations propagate across the grid graph in the form of a wave. A process is idle before the wave arrives, and becomes idle again after the wave has passed. This process is illustrated in Figure 10.18. At any time during the execution of the algorithm, only the processes along the wave are busy. The other processes have either finished their computations or have not yet started them. The next sections discuss three mappings of grid graphs onto a p-process mesh.

2-D Block Mapping One way to map an $n \times n$ grid graph onto p processors is to use the 2-D block mapping (Section 3.4.1). Specifically, we can view the p processes as a logical mesh and assign a different block of $n/\sqrt{p} \times n/\sqrt{p}$ vertices to each process. Figure 10.19 illustrates this mapping.

At any time, the number of busy processes is equal to the number of processes intersected by the wave. Since the wave moves diagonally, no more than $O(\sqrt{p})$ processes are busy at any time. Let W be the overall work performed by the sequential algorithm. If we assume that, at any time, $\sqrt{p}$ processes are performing computations, and if we ignore the overhead due to inter-process communication and extra work, then the maximum speedup

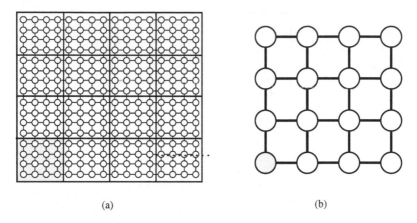

(a)   (b)

Figure 10.19   Mapping the grid graph (a) onto a mesh, and (b) by using the 2-D block mapping. In this example, $n = 16$ and $\sqrt{p} = 4$. The shaded vertices are mapped onto the shaded process.

and efficiency are as follows:

$$S = \frac{W}{W/\sqrt{p}} = \sqrt{p}$$

$$E = \frac{1}{\sqrt{p}}$$

The efficiency of this mapping is poor and becomes worse as the number of processes increases.

2-D Cyclic Mapping   The main limitation of the 2-D block mapping is that each process is responsible for only a small, confined area of the grid. Alternatively, we can make each process responsible for scattered areas of the grid by using the 2-D cyclic mapping (Section 3.4.1). This increases the time during which a process stays busy. In 2-D cyclic mapping, the $n \times n$ grid graph is divided into n^2/p blocks, each of size $\sqrt{p} \times \sqrt{p}$. Each block is mapped onto the $\sqrt{p} \times \sqrt{p}$ process mesh. Figure 10.20 illustrates this mapping. Each process contains a block of n^2/p vertices. These vertices belong to diagonals of the graph that are $\sqrt{p}$ vertices apart. Each process is assigned roughly $2n/\sqrt{p}$ such diagonals.

Now each process is responsible for vertices that belong to different parts of the grid graph. As the wave propagates through the graph, the wave intersects some of the vertices on each process. Thus, processes remain busy for most of the algorithm. The 2-D cyclic mapping, though, incurs a higher communication overhead than does the 2-D block mapping. Since adjacent vertices reside on separate processes, every time a process extracts a vertex u from its priority queue it must notify other processes of the new value of $l[u]$. The analysis of this mapping is left as an exercise (Problem 10.17).

1-D Block Mapping   The two mappings discussed so far have limitations. The 2-D block mapping fails to keep more than $O(\sqrt{p})$ processes busy at any time, and the 2-D

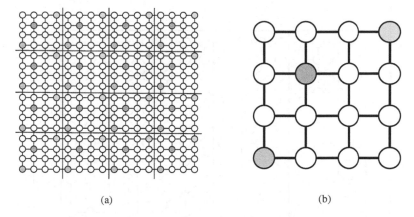

(a)   (b)

Figure 10.20   Mapping the grid graph (a) onto a mesh, and (b) by using the 2-D cyclic mapping. In this example, $n = 16$ and $\sqrt{p} = 4$. The shaded graph vertices are mapped onto the correspondingly shaded mesh processes.

cyclic mapping has high communication overhead. Another mapping treats the p processes as a linear array and assigns n/p stripes of the grid graph to each processor by using the 1-D block mapping. Figure 10.21 illustrates this mapping.

Initially, the wave intersects only one process. As computation progresses, the wave spills over to the second process so that two processes are busy. As the algorithm continues, the wave intersects more processes, which become busy. This process continues until all p processes are busy (that is, until they all have been intersected by the wave). After this point, the number of busy processes decreases. Figure 10.22 illustrates the propagation of the wave. If we assume that the wave propagates at a constant rate, then $p/2$ processes (on

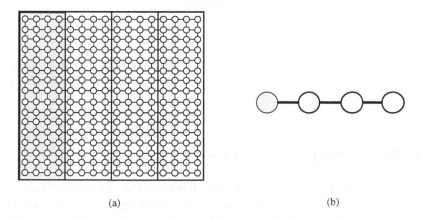

(a)   (b)

Figure 10.21   Mapping the grid graph (a) onto a linear array of processes (b). In this example, $n = 16$ and $p = 4$. The shaded vertices are mapped onto the shaded process.

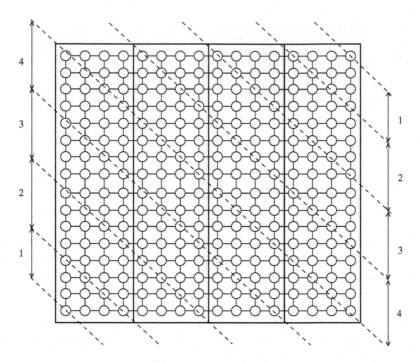

Figure 10.22   The number of busy processes as the computational wave propagates across the grid graph.

the average) are busy. Ignoring any overhead, the speedup and efficiency of this mapping are as follows:

$$S = \frac{W}{W/(p/2)} = \frac{p}{2}$$

$$E = \frac{1}{2}$$

Thus, the efficiency of this mapping is at most 50 percent. The 1-D block mapping is substantially better than the 2-D block mapping but cannot use more than $O(n)$ processes.

10.8   Bibliographic Remarks

Detailed discussions of graph theory and graph algorithms can be found in numerous texts. Gibbons [Gib85] provides a good reference to the algorithms presented in this chapter. Aho, Hopcroft, and Ullman [AHU74], and Cormen, Leiserson, and Rivest [CLR90] provide a detailed description of various graph algorithms and issues related to their efficient implementation on sequential computers.

The sequential minimum spanning tree algorithm described in Section 10.2 is due to Prim [Pri57]. Bentley [Ben80] and Deo and Yoo [DY81] present parallel formulations of Prim's MST algorithm. Deo and Yoo's algorithm is suited to a shared-address-space computer. It finds the MST in $\Theta(n^{1.5})$ using $\Theta(n^{0.5})$ processes. Bentley's algorithm works on a tree-connected systolic array and finds the MST in time $\Theta(n \log n)$ using $n/\log n$ processes. The hypercube formulation of Prim's MST algorithm in Section 10.2 is similar to Bentley's algorithm.

The MST of a graph can be also computed by using either Kruskal's [Kru56] or Sollin's [Sol77] sequential algorithms. The complexity of Sollin's algorithm (Problem 10.21) is $\Theta(n^2 \log n)$. Savage and Jaja [SJ81] have developed a formulation of Sollin's algorithm for the CREW PRAM. Their algorithm uses n^2 processes and solves the problem in time $\Theta(\log^2 n)$. Chin, Lam, and Chen [CLC82] have developed a formulation of Sollin's algorithm for a CREW PRAM that uses $n\lceil n/\log n \rceil$ processes and finds the MST in time $\Theta(\log^2 n)$. Awerbuch and Shiloach [AS87] present a formulation of Sollin's algorithm for the shuffle-exchange network that uses $\Theta(n^2)$ processes and runs in time $\Theta(\log^2 n)$. Doshi and Varman [DV87] present a $\Theta(n^2/p)$ time algorithm for a p-process ring-connected computer for Sollin's algorithm. Leighton [Lei83] and Nath, Maheshwari, and Bhatt [NMB83] present parallel formulations of Sollin's algorithm for a mesh of trees network. The first algorithm runs in $\Theta(\log^2 n)$ and the second algorithm runs in $O(\log^4 n)$ for an $n \times n$ mesh of trees. Huang [Hua85] describes a formulation of Sollin's algorithm that runs in $\Theta(n^2/p)$ on a $\sqrt{p} \times \sqrt{p}$ mesh of trees.

The single-source shortest paths algorithm in Section 10.3 was discovered by Dijkstra [Dij59]. Due to the similarity between Dijkstra's algorithm and Prim's MST algorithm, all the parallel formulations of Prim's algorithm discussed in the previous paragraph can also be applied to the single-source shortest paths problem. Bellman [Bel58] and Ford [FR62] independently developed a single-source shortest paths algorithm that operates on graphs with negative weights but without negative-weight cycles. The Bellman-Ford single-source algorithm has a sequential complexity of $O(|V||E|)$. Paige and Kruskal [PK89] present parallel formulations of both the Dijkstra and Bellman-Ford single-source shortest paths algorithm. Their formulation of Dijkstra's algorithm runs on an EREW PRAM of $\Theta(n)$ processes and runs in time $\Theta(n \log n)$. Their formulation of Bellman-Ford's algorithm runs in time $\Theta(n|E|/p + n \log p)$ on a p-process EREW PRAM where $p \le |E|$. They also present algorithms for the CRCW PRAM [PK89].

Significant work has been done on the all-pairs shortest paths problem. The source-partitioning formulation of Dijkstra's all-pairs shortest paths is discussed by Jenq and Sahni [JS87] and Kumar and Singh [KS91b]. The source parallel formulation of Dijkstra's all-pairs shortest paths algorithm is discussed by Paige and Kruskal [PK89] and Kumar and Singh [KS91b]. The Floyd's all-pairs shortest paths algorithm discussed in Section 10.4.2 is due to Floyd [Flo62]. The 1-D and 2-D block mappings (Problem 10.8) are presented by Jenq and Sahni [JS87], and the pipelined version of Floyd's algorithm is presented by Bertsekas and Tsitsiklis [BT89] and Kumar and Singh [KS91b]. Kumar and Singh [KS91b] present isoefficiency analysis and performance comparison of different parallel formulations for the all-pairs shortest paths on hypercube- and mesh-connected computers. The discussion in Section 10.4.3 is based upon the work of Kumar and Singh [KS91b] and of Jenq and Sahni [JS87]. In particular, Algorithm 10.4 is adopted from the paper by Jenq and Sahni [JS87]. Levitt and Kautz [LK72] present a formulation of Floyd's algorithm for two-dimensional cellular arrays that uses n^2 processes and runs in time $\Theta(n)$. Deo, Pank, and Lord have developed a parallel formulation of Floyd's algorithm for the CREW PRAM model that has complexity $\Theta(n)$ on n^2 processes. Chandy and Misra [CM82] present a distributed all-pairs shortest-path algorithm based on diffusing computation.

The connected-components algorithm discussed in Section 10.6 was discovered by Woo and Sahni [WS89]. Cormen, Leiserson, and Rivest [CLR90] discusses ways to efficiently implement disjoint-set data structures with ranking and path compression. Several algorithms exist for computing the connected components; many of them are based on the technique of vertex collapsing, similar to Sollin's algorithm for the minimum spanning tree. Most of the parallel formulations of Sollin's algorithm can also find the connected components. Hirschberg [Hir76] and Hirschberg, Chandra, and Sarwate [HCS79] developed formulations of the connected-components algorithm based on vertex collapsing. The former has a complexity of $\Theta(\log^2 n)$ on a CREW PRAM with n^2 processes, and the latter has similar complexity and uses $n\lceil n/\log n \rceil$ processes. Chin, Lam, and Chen [CLC81] made the vertex collapse algorithm more efficient by reducing the number of processes to $n\lceil n/\log^2 n \rceil$ for a CREW PRAM, while keeping the run time at $\Theta(\log^2 n)$. Nassimi and Sahni [NS80] used the vertex collapsing technique to develop a formulation for a mesh-connected computer that finds the connected components in time $\Theta(n)$ by using n^2 processes.

The single-source shortest paths algorithm for sparse graphs, discussed in Section 10.7.2, was discovered by Johnson [Joh77]. Paige and Kruskal [PK89] discuss the possibility of maintaining the queue Q in parallel. Rao and Kumar [RK88a] presented techniques to perform concurrent insertions and deletions in a priority queue. The 2-D block mapping, 2-D block-cyclic mapping, and 1-D block mapping formulation of Johnson's algorithm (Section 10.7.2) are due to Wada and Ichiyoshi [WI89]. They also presented theoretical and experimental evaluation of these schemes on a mesh-connected parallel computer.

The serial maximal independent set algorithm described in Section 10.7.1 was developed by Luby [Lub86] and its parallel formulation on shared-address-space architectures was motivated by the algorithm described by Karypis and Kumar [KK99]. Jones and Plassman [JP93] have developed an asynchronous variation of Luby's algorithm that is particularly suited for distributed memory parallel computers. In their algorithm, each vertex is assigned a single random number, and after a communication step, each vertex determines the number of its adjacent vertices that have smaller and greater random numbers. At this point each vertex gets into a loop waiting to receive the color values of its adjacent vertices that have smaller random numbers. Once all these colors have been received, the vertex selects a consistent color, and sends it to all of its adjacent vertices with greater random numbers. The algorithm terminates when all vertices have been colored. Note that besides the initial communication step to determine the number of smaller and greater adjacent vertices, this algorithm proceeds asynchronously.

Other parallel graph algorithms have been proposed. Shiloach and Vishkin [SV82] presented an algorithm for finding the maximum flow in a directed flow network with n vertices that runs in time $O(n^2 \log n)$ on an n-process EREW PRAM. Goldberg and Tarjan [GT88] presented a different maximum-flow algorithm that runs in time $O(n^2 \log n)$ on an n-process EREW PRAM but requires less space. Atallah and Kosaraju [AK84] proposed a number of algorithms for a mesh-connected parallel computer. The algorithms they considered are for finding the bridges and articulation points of an undirected graph, finding the length of the shortest cycle, finding an MST, finding the cyclic index, and testing if a graph is bipartite. Tarjan and Vishkin [TV85] presented algorithms for computing the biconnected components of a graph. Their CRCW PRAM formulation runs in time $\Theta(\log n)$ by using $\Theta(|E| + |V|)$ processes, and their CREW PRAM formulation runs in time $\Theta(\log^2 n)$ by using $\Theta(n^2/\log^2 n)$ processes.

Problems

10.1 In the parallel formulation of Prim's minimum spanning tree algorithm (Section 10.2), the maximum number of processes that can be used efficiently on a hypercube is $\Theta(n/\log n)$. By using $\Theta(n/\log n)$ processes the run time is $\Theta(n \log n)$. What is the run time if you use $\Theta(n)$ processes? What is the minimum parallel run time that can be obtained on a message-passing parallel computer? How does this time compare with the run time obtained when you use $\Theta(n/\log n)$ processes?

10.2 Show how Dijkstra's single-source algorithm and its parallel formulation (Section 10.3) need to be modified in order to output the shortest paths instead of the cost. Analyze the run time of your sequential and parallel formulations.

10.3 Given a graph $G = (V, E)$, the breadth-first ranking of vertices of G are the values assigned to the vertices of V in a breadth-first traversal of G from a node v. Show how the breadth-first ranking of vertices of G can be performed on a p-process mesh.

10.4 Dijkstra's single-source shortest paths algorithm (Section 10.3) requires nonnegative edge weights. Show how Dijkstra's algorithm can be modified to work on graphs with negative weights but no negative cycles in time $\Theta(|E||V|)$. Analyze the performance of the parallel formulation of the modified algorithm on a p-process message-passing architecture.

10.5 Compute the total amount of memory required by the different parallel formulations of the all-pairs shortest paths problem described in Section 10.4.

10.6 Show that Floyd's algorithm in Section 10.4.2 is correct if we replace line 7 of Algorithm 10.3 by the following line:

$$d_{i,j} = \min\{d_{i,j}, (d_{i,k} + d_{k,j})\}$$

10.7 Compute the parallel run time, speedup, and efficiency of Floyd's all-pairs shortest paths algorithm using 2-D block mapping on a p-process mesh with store-and-forward routing and a p-process hypercube and a p-process mesh with cut-through routing.

10.8 An alternative way of partitioning the matrix $D^{(k)}$ in Floyd's all-pairs shortest paths algorithm is to use the 1-D block mapping (Section 3.4.1). Each of the p processes is assigned n/p consecutive columns of the $D^{(k)}$ matrix.

   (a) Compute the parallel run time, speedup, and efficiency of 1-D block mapping on a hypercube-connected parallel computer. What are the advantages and disadvantages of this partitioning over the 2-D block mapping presented in Section 10.4.2?

   (b) Compute the parallel run time, speedup, and efficiency of 1-D block mapping on a p-process mesh with store-and-forward routing, a p-process mesh with cut-through routing, and a p-process ring.

10.9 Describe and analyze the performance of a parallel formulation of Floyd's algorithm that uses 1-D block mapping and the pipelining technique described in Section 10.4.2.

10.10 Compute the exact parallel run time, speedup, and efficiency of Floyd's pipelined formulation (Section 10.4.2).

10.11 Compute the parallel run time, the speedup, and the efficiency of the parallel formulation of the connected-component algorithm presented in Section 10.6 for a p-process mesh with store-and-forward routing and with cut-through routing. Comment on the difference in the performance of the two architectures.

10.12 The parallel formulation for the connected-component problem presented in Section 10.6 uses 1-D block mapping to partition the matrix among processes. Consider an alternative parallel formulation in which 2-D block mapping is used instead. Describe this formulation and analyze its performance and scalability on a hypercube, a mesh with SF-routing, and a mesh with CT-routing. How does this scheme compare with 1-D block mapping?

10.13 Consider the problem of parallelizing Johnson's single-source shortest paths algorithm for sparse graphs (Section 10.7.2). One way of parallelizing it is to use p_1 processes to maintain the priority queue and p_2 processes to perform the computations of the new l values. How many processes can be efficiently used to maintain the priority queue (in other words, what is the maximum value for p_1)? How many processes can be used to update the l values? Is the parallel formulation that is obtained by using the $p_1 + p_2$ processes cost-optimal? Describe an algorithm that uses p_1 processes to maintain the priority queue.

10.14 Consider Dijkstra's single-source shortest paths algorithm for sparse graphs (Section 10.7). We can parallelize this algorithm on a p-process hypercube by splitting the n adjacency lists among the processes horizontally; that is, each process gets

n/p lists. What is the parallel run time of this formulation? Alternatively, we can partition the adjacency list vertically among the processes; that is, each process gets a fraction of each adjacency list. If an adjacency list contains m elements, then each process contains a sublist of m/p elements. The last element in each sublist has a pointer to the element in the next process. What is the parallel run time and speedup of this formulation? What is the maximum number of processes that it can use?

10.15 Repeat Problem 10.14 for Floyd's all-pairs shortest paths algorithm.

10.16 Analyze the performance of Luby's shared-address-space algorithm for finding a maximal independent set of vertices on sparse graphs described in Section 10.7.1. What is the parallel run time and speedup of this formulation?

10.17 Compute the parallel run time, speedup, and efficiency of the 2-D cyclic mapping of the sparse graph single-source shortest paths algorithm (Section 10.7.2) for a mesh-connected computer. You may ignore the overhead due to extra work, but you should take into account the overhead due to communication.

10.18 Analyze the performance of the single-source shortest paths algorithm for sparse graphs (Section 10.7.2) when the 2-D block-cyclic mapping is used (Section 3.4.1). Compare it with the performance of the 2-D cyclic mapping computed in Problem 10.17. As in Problem 10.17, ignore extra computation but include communication overhead.

10.19 Consider the 1-D block-cyclic mapping described in Section 3.4.1. Describe how you will apply this mapping to the single-source shortest paths problem for sparse graphs. Compute the parallel run time, speedup, and efficiency of this mapping. In your analysis, include the communication overhead but not the overhead due to extra work.

10.20 Of the mapping schemes presented in Section 10.7.2 and in Problems 10.18 and 10.19, which one has the smallest overhead due to extra computation?

10.21 Sollin's algorithm (Section 10.8) starts with a forest of n isolated vertices. In each iteration, the algorithm simultaneously determines, for each tree in the forest, the smallest edge joining any vertex in that tree to a vertex in another tree. All such edges are added to the forest. Furthermore, two trees are never joined by more than one edge. This process continues until there is only one tree in the forest – the minimum spanning tree. Since the number of trees is reduced by a factor of at least two in each iteration, this algorithm requires at most $\log n$ iterations to find the MST. Each iteration requires at most $O(n^2)$ comparisons to find the smallest edge incident on each vertex; thus, its sequential complexity is $\Theta(n^2 \log n)$.
Develop a parallel formulation of Sollin's algorithm on an n-process hypercube-connected parallel computer. What is the run time of your formulation? Is it cost optimal?

CHAPTER 11

Search Algorithms for Discrete Optimization Problems

Search algorithms can be used to solve discrete optimization problems (DOPs), a class of computationally expensive problems with significant theoretical and practical interest. Search algorithms solve DOPs by evaluating candidate solutions from a finite or countably infinite set of possible solutions to find one that satisfies a problem-specific criterion. DOPs are also referred to as combinatorial problems.

11.1 Definitions and Examples

A *discrete optimization problem* can be expressed as a tuple (S, f). The set S is a finite or countably infinite set of all solutions that satisfy specified constraints. This set is called the set of *feasible solutions*. The function f is the cost function that maps each element in set S onto the set of real numbers R.

$$f : S \rightarrow R$$

The objective of a DOP is to find a feasible solution x_{opt}, such that $f(x_{opt}) \leq f(x)$ for all $x \in S$.

Problems from various domains can be formulated as DOPs. Some examples are planning and scheduling, the optimal layout of VLSI chips, robot motion planning, test-pattern generation for digital circuits, and logistics and control.

Example 11.1 The 0/1 integer-linear-programming problem
In the 0/1 integer-linear-programming problem, we are given an $m \times n$ matrix A,

an $m \times 1$ vector b, and an $n \times 1$ vector c. The objective is to determine an $n \times 1$ vector $\overline{x}$ whose elements can take on only the value 0 or 1. The vector must satisfy the constraint

$$A\overline{x} \geq b$$

and the function

$$f(\overline{x}) = c^T \overline{x}$$

must be minimized. For this problem, the set S is the set of all values of the vector $\overline{x}$ that satisfy the equation $A\overline{x} \geq b$.   ∎

Example 11.2   The 8-puzzle problem

The 8-puzzle problem consists of a 3×3 grid containing eight tiles, numbered one through eight. One of the grid segments (called the "blank") is empty. A tile can be moved into the blank position from a position adjacent to it, thus creating a blank in the tile's original position. Depending on the configuration of the grid, up to four moves are possible: up, down, left, and right. The initial and final configurations of the tiles are specified. The objective is to determine a shortest sequence of moves that transforms the initial configuration to the final configuration. Figure 11.1 illustrates sample initial and final configurations and a sequence of moves leading from the initial configuration to the final configuration.

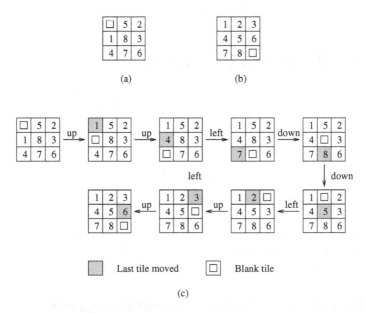

Figure 11.1   An 8-puzzle problem instance: (a) initial configuration; (b) final configuration; and (c) a sequence of moves leading from the initial to the final configuration.

The set S for this problem is the set of all sequences of moves that lead from the initial to the final configurations. The cost function f of an element in S is defined as the number of moves in the sequence. ∎

In most problems of practical interest, the solution set S is quite large. Consequently, it is not feasible to exhaustively enumerate the elements in S to determine the optimal element x_{opt}. Instead, a DOP can be reformulated as the problem of finding a minimum-cost path in a graph from a designated initial node to one of several possible goal nodes. Each element x in S can be viewed as a path from the initial node to one of the goal nodes. There is a cost associated with each edge of the graph, and a cost function f is defined in terms of these edge costs. For many problems, the cost of a path is the sum of the edge costs. Such a graph is called a **state space**, and the nodes of the graph are called **states**. A **terminal node** is one that has no successors. All other nodes are called **nonterminal nodes**. The 8-puzzle problem can be naturally formulated as a graph search problem. In particular, the initial configuration is the initial node, and the final configuration is the goal node. Example 11.3 illustrates the process of reformulating the 0/1 integer-linear-programming problem as a graph search problem.

Example 11.3 The 0/1 integer-linear-programming problem revisited
Consider an instance of the 0/1 integer-linear-programming problem defined in Example 11.1. Let the values of A, b, and c be given by

$$A = \begin{bmatrix} 5 & 2 & 1 & 2 \\ 1 & -1 & -1 & 2 \\ 3 & 1 & 1 & 3 \end{bmatrix}, \quad b = \begin{bmatrix} 8 \\ 2 \\ 5 \end{bmatrix}, \quad c = \begin{bmatrix} 2 \\ 1 \\ -1 \\ -2 \end{bmatrix}.$$

The constraints corresponding to A, b, and c are as follows:

$$5x_1 + 2x_2 + x_3 + 2x_4 \geq 8$$
$$x_1 - x_2 - x_3 + 2x_4 \geq 2$$
$$3x_1 + x_2 + x_3 + 3x_4 \geq 5$$

and the function $f(x)$ to be minimized is

$$f(x) = 2x_1 + x_2 - x_3 - 2x_4.$$

Each of the four elements of vector $\bar{x}$ can take the value 0 or 1. There are $2^4 = 16$ possible values for x. However, many of these values do not satisfy the problem's constraints.

The problem can be reformulated as a graph-search problem. The initial node represents the state in which none of the elements of vector x have been assigned values. In this example, we assign values to vector elements in subscript order; that

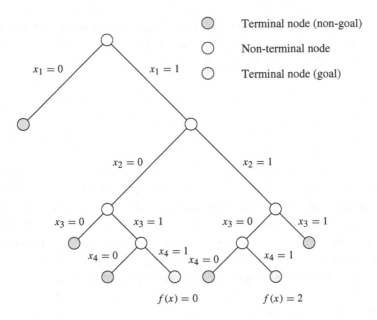

Figure 11.2 The graph corresponding to the 0/1 integer-linear-programming problem.

is, first x_1, then x_2, and so on. The initial node generates two nodes corresponding to $x_1 = 0$ and $x_1 = 1$. After a variable x_i has been assigned a value, it is called a *fixed variable*. All variables that are not fixed are called *free variables*.

After instantiating a variable to 0 or 1, it is possible to check whether an instantiation of the remaining free variables can lead to a feasible solution. We do this by using the following condition:

$$\sum_{x_j \text{ is free}} \max\{A[i, j], 0\} + \sum_{x_j \text{ is fixed}} A[i, j]x_j \geq b_i, \quad i = 1, \ldots, m \qquad (11.1)$$

The left side of Equation 11.1 is the maximum value of $\sum_{k=1}^{n} A[i, k]x_k$ that can be obtained by instantiating the free variables to either 0 or 1. If this value is greater than or equal to b_i, for $i = 1, 2, \ldots, m$, then the node may lead to a feasible solution.

For each of the nodes corresponding to $x_1 = 0$ and $x_1 = 1$, the next variable (x_2) is selected and assigned a value. The nodes are then checked for feasibility. This process continues until all the variables have been assigned and the feasible set has been generated. Figure 11.2 illustrates this process.

Function $f(x)$ is evaluated for each of the feasible solutions; the solution with the minimum value is the desired solution. Note that it is unnecessary to generate the entire feasible set to determine the solution. Several search algorithms can determine an optimal solution by searching only a portion of the graph.   ∎

For some problems, it is possible to estimate the cost to reach the goal state from an intermediate state. This cost is called a ***heuristic estimate***. Let $h(x)$ denote the heuristic estimate of reaching the goal state from state x and $g(x)$ denote the cost of reaching state x from initial state s along the current path. The function h is called a ***heuristic function***. If $h(x)$ is a lower bound on the cost of reaching the goal state from state x for all x, then h is called ***admissible***. We define function $l(x)$ as the sum $h(x) + g(x)$. If h is admissible, then $l(x)$ is a lower bound on the cost of the path to a goal state that can be obtained by extending the current path between s and x. In subsequent examples we will see how an admissible heuristic can be used to determine the least-cost sequence of moves from the initial state to a goal state.

Example 11.4 An admissible heuristic function for the 8-puzzle

Assume that each position in the 8-puzzle grid is represented as a pair. The pair $(1, 1)$ represents the top-left grid position and the pair $(3, 3)$ represents the bottom-right position. The distance between positions (i, j) and (k, l) is defined as $|i - k| + |j - l|$. This distance is called the ***Manhattan distance***. The sum of the Manhattan distances between the initial and final positions of all tiles is an estimate of the number of moves required to transform the current configuration into the final configuration. This estimate is called the ***Manhattan heuristic***. Note that if $h(x)$ is the Manhattan distance between configuration x and the final configuration, then $h(x)$ is also a lower bound on the number of moves from configuration x to the final configuration. Hence the Manhattan heuristic is admissible. ∎

Once a DOP has been formulated as a graph search problem, it can be solved by algorithms such as branch-and-bound search and heuristic search. These techniques use heuristics and the structure of the search space to solve DOPs without searching the set S exhaustively.

DOPs belong to the class of NP-hard problems. One may argue that it is pointless to apply parallel processing to these problems, since we can never reduce their worst-case run time to a polynomial without using exponentially many processors. However, the average-time complexity of heuristic search algorithms for many problems is polynomial. Furthermore, there are heuristic search algorithms that find suboptimal solutions for specific problems in polynomial time. In such cases, bigger problem instances can be solved using parallel computers. Many DOPs (such as robot motion planning, speech understanding, and task scheduling) require real-time solutions. For these applications, parallel processing may be the only way to obtain acceptable performance. Other problems, for which optimal solutions are highly desirable, can be solved for moderate-sized instances in a reasonable amount of time by using parallel search techniques (for example, VLSI floor-plan optimization, and computer-aided design).

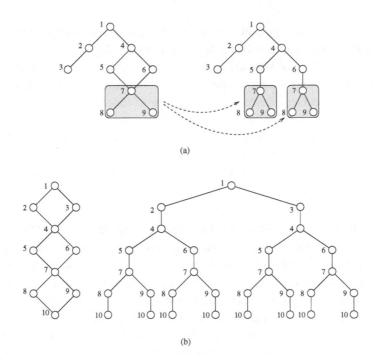

Figure 11.3   Two examples of unfolding a graph into a tree.

11.2   Sequential Search Algorithms

The most suitable sequential search algorithm to apply to a state space depends on whether the space forms a graph or a tree. In a tree, each new successor leads to an unexplored part of the search space. An example of this is the 0/1 integer-programming problem. In a graph, however, a state can be reached along multiple paths. An example of such a problem is the 8-puzzle. For such problems, whenever a state is generated, it is necessary to check if the state has already been generated. If this check is not performed, then effectively the search graph is unfolded into a tree in which a state is repeated for every path that leads to it (Figure 11.3).

For many problems (for example, the 8-puzzle), unfolding increases the size of the search space by a small factor. For some problems, however, unfolded graphs are much larger than the original graphs. Figure 11.3(b) illustrates a graph whose corresponding tree has an exponentially higher number of states. In this section, we present an overview of various sequential algorithms used to solve DOPs that are formulated as tree or graph search problems.

11.2.1   Depth-First Search Algorithms

Depth-first search (DFS) algorithms solve DOPs that can be formulated as tree-search problems. DFS begins by expanding the initial node and generating its successors. In each subsequent step, DFS expands one of the most recently generated nodes. If this node has no successors (or cannot lead to any solutions), then DFS backtracks and expands a different node. In some DFS algorithms, successors of a node are expanded in an order determined by their heuristic values. A major advantage of DFS is that its storage requirement is linear in the depth of the state space being searched. The following sections discuss three algorithms based on depth-first search.

Simple Backtracking

Simple backtracking is a depth-first search method that terminates upon finding the first solution. Thus, it is not guaranteed to find a minimum-cost solution. Simple backtracking uses no heuristic information to order the successors of an expanded node. A variant, *ordered backtracking*, does use heuristics to order the successors of an expanded node.

Depth-First Branch-and-Bound

Depth-first branch-and-bound (DFBB) exhaustively searches the state space; that is, it continues to search even after finding a solution path. Whenever it finds a new solution path, it updates the current best solution path. DFBB discards inferior partial solution paths (that is, partial solution paths whose extensions are guaranteed to be worse than the current best solution path). Upon termination, the current best solution is a globally optimal solution.

Iterative Deepening A*

Trees corresponding to DOPs can be very deep. Thus, a DFS algorithm may get stuck searching a deep part of the search space when a solution exists higher up on another branch. For such trees, we impose a bound on the depth to which the DFS algorithm searches. If the node to be expanded is beyond the depth bound, then the node is not expanded and the algorithm backtracks. If a solution is not found, then the entire state space is searched again using a larger depth bound. This technique is called *iterative deepening depth-first search* (ID-DFS). Note that this method is guaranteed to find a solution path with the fewest edges. However, it is not guaranteed to find a least-cost path.

Iterative deepening A* (IDA*) is a variant of ID-DFS. IDA* uses the l-values of nodes to bound depth (recall from Section 11.1 that for node x, $l(x) = g(x) + h(x)$). IDA* repeatedly performs cost-bounded DFS over the search space. In each iteration, IDA* expands nodes depth-first. If the l-value of the node to be expanded is greater than the cost bound, then IDA* backtracks. If a solution is not found within the current cost bound, then IDA* repeats the entire depth-first search using a higher cost bound. In the first iteration, the cost bound is set to the l-value of the initial state s. Note that since $g(s)$ is zero, $l(s)$ is equal to $h(s)$. In each subsequent iteration, the cost bound is increased. The new

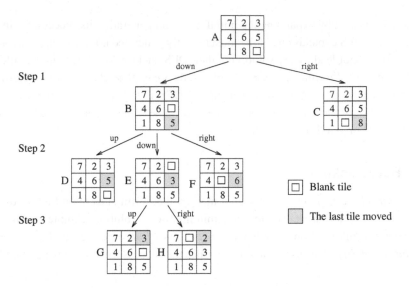

Figure 11.4   States resulting from the first three steps of depth-first search applied to an instance of the 8-puzzle.

cost bound is equal to the minimum l-value of the nodes that were generated but could not be expanded in the previous iteration. The algorithm terminates when a goal node is expanded. IDA* is guaranteed to find an optimal solution if the heuristic function is admissible. It may appear that IDA* performs a lot of redundant work across iterations. However, for many problems the redundant work performed by IDA* is minimal, because most of the work is done deep in the search space.

Example 11.5   Depth-first search: the 8-puzzle

Figure 11.4 shows the execution of depth-first search for solving the 8-puzzle problem. The search starts at the initial configuration. Successors of this state are generated by applying possible moves. During each step of the search algorithm a new state is selected, and its successors are generated. The DFS algorithm expands the deepest node in the tree. In step 1, the initial state A generates states B and C. One of these is selected according to a predetermined criterion. In the example, we order successors by applicable moves as follows: up, down, left, and right. In step 2, the DFS algorithm selects state B and generates states D, E, and F. Note that the state D can be discarded, as it is a duplicate of the parent of B. In step 3, state E is expanded to generate states G and H. Again G can be discarded because it is a duplicate of B. The search proceeds in this way until the algorithm backtracks or the final configuration is generated.   ∎

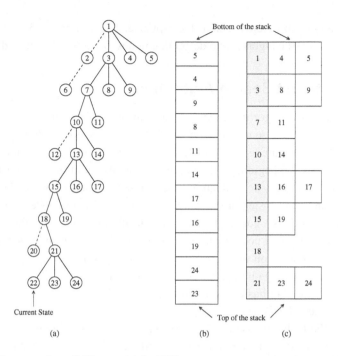

Figure 11.5   Representing a DFS tree: (a) the DFS tree; successor nodes shown with dashed lines have already been explored; (b) the stack storing untried alternatives only; and (c) the stack storing untried alternatives along with their parent. The shaded blocks represent the parent state and the block to the right represents successor states that have not been explored.

In each step of the DFS algorithm, untried alternatives must be stored. For example, in the 8-puzzle problem, up to three untried alternatives are stored at each step. In general, if m is the amount of storage required to store a state, and d is the maximum depth, then the total space requirement of the DFS algorithm is $O(md)$. The state-space tree searched by parallel DFS can be efficiently represented as a stack. Since the depth of the stack increases linearly with the depth of the tree, the memory requirements of a stack representation are low.

There are two ways of storing untried alternatives using a stack. In the first representation, untried alternates are pushed on the stack at each step. The ancestors of a state are not represented on the stack. Figure 11.5(b) illustrates this representation for the tree shown in Figure 11.5(a). In the second representation, shown in Figure 11.5(c), untried alternatives are stored along with their parent state. It is necessary to use the second representation if the sequence of transformations from the initial state to the goal state is required as a part of the solution. Furthermore, if the state space is a graph in which it is possible to generate an ancestor state by applying a sequence of transformations to the current state, then it is desirable to use the second representation, because it allows us to check for duplication of ancestor states and thus remove any cycles from the state-space graph. The second representation is useful for problems such as the 8-puzzle. In Example 11.5, using the second representation allows the algorithm to detect that nodes D and G should be discarded.

11.2.2 Best-First Search Algorithms

Best-first search (BFS) algorithms can search both graphs and trees. These algorithms use heuristics to direct the search to portions of the search space likely to yield solutions. Smaller heuristic values are assigned to more promising nodes. BFS maintains two lists: *open* and *closed*. At the beginning, the initial node is placed on the *open* list. This list is sorted according to a heuristic evaluation function that measures how likely each node is to yield a solution. In each step of the search, the most promising node from the *open* list is removed. If this node is a goal node, then the algorithm terminates. Otherwise, the node is expanded. The expanded node is placed on the *closed* list. The successors of the newly expanded node are placed on the *open* list under one of the following circumstances: (1) the successor is not already on the *open* or *closed* lists, and (2) the successor is already on the *open* or *closed* list but has a lower heuristic value. In the second case, the node with the higher heuristic value is deleted.

A common BFS technique is the *A* algorithm*. The A* algorithm uses the lower bound function l as a heuristic evaluation function. Recall from Section 11.1 that for each node x, $l(x)$ is the sum of $g(x)$ and $h(x)$. Nodes in the *open* list are ordered according to the value of the l function. At each step, the node with the smallest l-value (that is, the best node) is removed from the *open* list and expanded. Its successors are inserted into the *open* list at the proper positions and the node itself is inserted into the *closed* list. For an admissible heuristic function, A* finds an optimal solution.

The main drawback of any BFS algorithm is that its memory requirement is linear in the size of the search space explored. For many problems, the size of the search space is exponential in the depth of the tree expanded. For problems with large search spaces, memory becomes a limitation.

> **Example 11.6**   Best-first search: the 8-puzzle
> Consider the 8-puzzle problem from Examples 11.2 and 11.4. Figure 11.6 illustrates four steps of best-first search on the 8-puzzle. At each step, a state x with the minimum l-value ($l(x) = g(x) + h(x)$) is selected for expansion. Ties are broken arbitrarily. BFS can check for a duplicate nodes, since all previously generated nodes are kept on either the *open* or *closed* list. ∎

11.3   Search Overhead Factor

Parallel search algorithms incur overhead from several sources. These include communication overhead, idle time due to load imbalance, and contention for shared data structures. Thus, if both the sequential and parallel formulations of an algorithm do the same amount

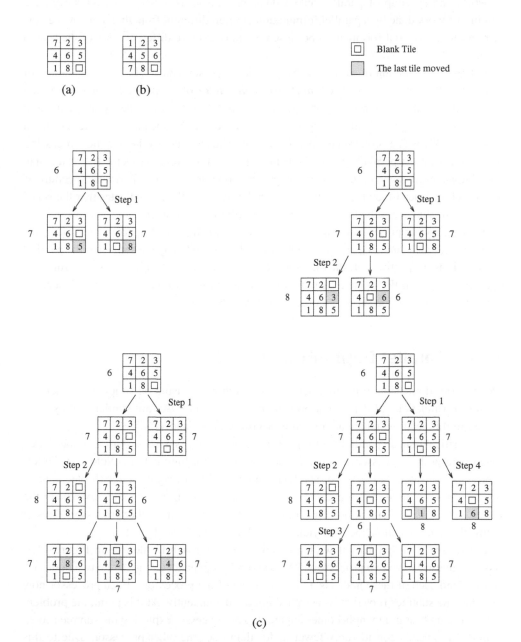

Figure 11.6 Applying best-first search to the 8-puzzle: (a) initial configuration; (b) final configuration; and (c) states resulting from the first four steps of best-first search. Each state is labeled with its h-value (that is, the Manhattan distance from the state to the final state).

of work, the speedup of parallel search on p processors is less than p. However, the amount of work done by a parallel formulation is often different from that done by the corresponding sequential formulation because they may explore different parts of the search space.

Let W be the amount of work done by a single processor, and W_p be the total amount of work done by p processors. The **search overhead factor** of the parallel system is defined as the ratio of the work done by the parallel formulation to that done by the sequential formulation, or W_p/W. Thus, the upper bound on speedup for the parallel system is given by $p \times (W/W_p)$. The actual speedup, however, may be less due to other parallel processing overhead. In most parallel search algorithms, the search overhead factor is greater than one. However, in some cases, it may be less than one, leading to superlinear speedup. If the search overhead factor is less than one on the average, then it indicates that the serial search algorithm is not the fastest algorithm for solving the problem.

To simplify our presentation and analysis, we assume that the time to expand each node is the same, and W and W_p are the number of nodes expanded by the serial and the parallel formulations, respectively. If the time for each expansion is t_c, then the sequential run time is given by $T_S = t_c W$. In the remainder of the chapter, we assume that $t_c = 1$. Hence, the problem size W and the serial run time T_S become the same.

11.4   Parallel Depth-First Search

We start our discussion of parallel depth-first search by focusing on simple backtracking. Parallel formulations of depth-first branch-and-bound and IDA* are similar to those discussed in this section and are addressed in Sections 11.4.6 and 11.4.7.

The critical issue in parallel depth-first search algorithms is the distribution of the search space among the processors. Consider the tree shown in Figure 11.7. Note that the left subtree (rooted at node A) can be searched in parallel with the right subtree (rooted at node B). By statically assigning a node in the tree to a processor, it is possible to expand the whole subtree rooted at that node without communicating with another processor. Thus, it seems that such a static allocation yields a good parallel search algorithm.

Let us see what happens if we try to apply this approach to the tree in Figure 11.7. Assume that we have two processors. The root node is expanded to generate two nodes (A and B), and each of these nodes is assigned to one of the processors. Each processor now searches the subtrees rooted at its assigned node independently. At this point, the problem with static node assignment becomes apparent. The processor exploring the subtree rooted at node A expands considerably fewer nodes than does the other processor. Due to this imbalance in the workload, one processor is idle for a significant amount of time, reducing efficiency. Using a larger number of processors worsens the imbalance. Consider the partitioning of the tree for four processors. Nodes A and B are expanded to generate nodes C, D, E, and F. Assume that each of these nodes is assigned to one of the four processors. Now the processor searching the subtree rooted at node E does most of the work, and those

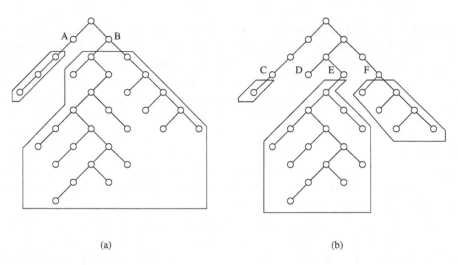

(a)   (b)

Figure 11.7 The unstructured nature of tree search and the imbalance resulting from static partitioning.

searching the subtrees rooted at nodes C and D spend most of their time idle. The static partitioning of unstructured trees yields poor performance because of substantial variation in the size of partitions of the search space rooted at different nodes. Furthermore, since the search space is usually generated dynamically, it is difficult to get a good estimate of the size of the search space beforehand. Therefore, it is necessary to balance the search space among processors dynamically.

In *dynamic load balancing*, when a processor runs out of work, it gets more work from another processor that has work. Consider the two-processor partitioning of the tree in Figure 11.7(a). Assume that nodes A and B are assigned to the two processors as we just described. In this case when the processor searching the subtree rooted at node A runs out of work, it requests work from the other processor. Although the dynamic distribution of work results in communication overhead for work requests and work transfers, it reduces load imbalance among processors. This section explores several schemes for dynamically balancing the load between processors.

A parallel formulation of DFS based on dynamic load balancing is as follows. Each processor performs DFS on a disjoint part of the search space. When a processor finishes searching its part of the search space, it requests an unsearched part from other processors. This takes the form of work request and response messages in message passing architectures, and locking and extracting work in shared address space machines. Whenever a processor finds a goal node, all the processors terminate. If the search space is finite and the problem has no solutions, then all the processors eventually run out of work, and the algorithm terminates.

Since each processor searches the state space depth-first, unexplored states can be conveniently stored as a stack. Each processor maintains its own local stack on which it executes DFS. When a processor's local stack is empty, it requests (either via explicit messages or by locking) untried alternatives from another processor's stack. In the beginning, the entire search space is assigned to one processor, and other processors are assigned null search spaces (that is, empty stacks). The search space is distributed among the processors as they request work. We refer to the processor that sends work as the ***donor*** processor and to the processor that requests and receives work as the ***recipient*** processor.

As illustrated in Figure 11.8, each processor can be in one of two states: *active* (that is, it has work) or *idle* (that is, it is trying to get work). In message passing architectures, an idle processor selects a donor processor and sends it a work request. If the idle processor receives work (part of the state space to be searched) from the donor processor, it becomes active. If it receives a *reject* message (because the donor has no work), it selects another donor and sends a work request to that donor. This process repeats until the processor gets work or all the processors become idle. When a processor is idle and it receives a work request, that processor returns a *reject* message. The same process can be implemented on shared address space machines by locking another processors' stack, examining it to see if it has work, extracting work, and unlocking the stack.

On message passing architectures, in the active state, a processor does a fixed amount of work (expands a fixed number of nodes) and then checks for pending work requests. When a work request is received, the processor partitions its work into two parts and sends one part to the requesting processor. When a processor has exhausted its own search space, it becomes idle. This process continues until a solution is found or until the entire space has been searched. If a solution is found, a message is broadcast to all processors to stop searching. A termination detection algorithm is used to detect whether all processors have become idle without finding a solution (Section 11.4.4).

11.4.1   Important Parameters of Parallel DFS

Two characteristics of parallel DFS are critical to determining its performance. First is the method for splitting work at a processor, and the second is the scheme to determine the donor processor when a processor becomes idle.

Work-Splitting Strategies

When work is transferred, the donor's stack is split into two stacks, one of which is sent to the recipient. In other words, some of the nodes (that is, alternatives) are removed from the donor's stack and added to the recipient's stack. If too little work is sent, the recipient quickly becomes idle; if too much, the donor becomes idle. Ideally, the stack is split into two equal pieces such that the size of the search space represented by each stack is the same. Such a split is called a ***half-split***. It is difficult to get a good estimate of the size of the tree rooted at an unexpanded alternative in the stack. However, the alternatives near the bottom of the stack (that is, close to the initial node) tend to have bigger trees rooted at them, and alternatives near the top of the stack tend to have small trees rooted at them. To

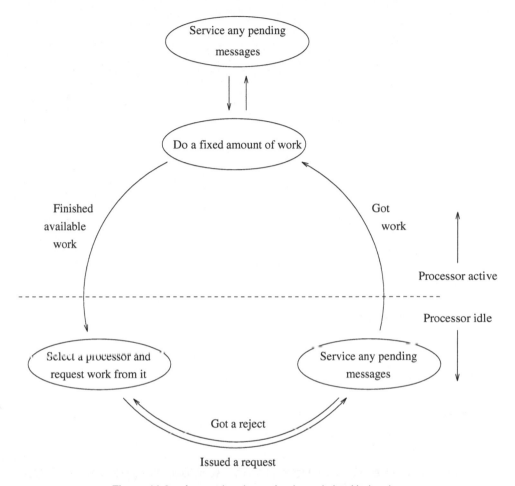

Figure 11.8 A generic scheme for dynamic load balancing.

avoid sending very small amounts of work, nodes beyond a specified stack depth are not given away. This depth is called the *cutoff depth*.

Some possible strategies for splitting the search space are (1) send nodes near the bottom of the stack, (2) send nodes near the cutoff depth, and (3) send half the nodes between the bottom of the stack and the cutoff depth. The suitability of a splitting strategy depends on the nature of the search space. If the search space is uniform, both strategies 1 and 3 work well. If the search space is highly irregular, strategy 3 usually works well. If a strong heuristic is available (to order successors so that goal nodes move to the left of the state-space tree), strategy 2 is likely to perform better, since it tries to distribute those parts of the search space likely to contain a solution. The cost of splitting also becomes important if the stacks are deep. For such stacks, strategy 1 has lower cost than strategies 2 and 3.

Figure 11.9 shows the partitioning of the DFS tree of Figure 11.5(a) into two subtrees using strategy 3. Note that the states beyond the cutoff depth are not partitioned. Figure

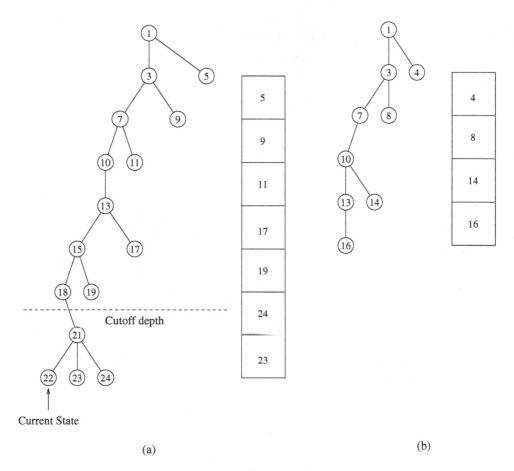

Figure 11.9   Splitting the DFS tree in Figure 11.5. The two subtrees along with their stack representations are shown in (a) and (b).

11.9 also shows the representation of the stack corresponding to the two subtrees. The stack representation used in the figure stores only the unexplored alternatives.

Load-Balancing Schemes

This section discusses three dynamic load-balancing schemes: asynchronous round robin, global round robin, and random polling. Each of these schemes can be coded for message passing as well as shared address space machines.

Asynchronous Round Robin   In asynchronous round robin (ARR), each processor maintains an independent variable, *target*. Whenever a processor runs out of work, it uses *target* as the label of a donor processor and attempts to get work from it. The value of *target* is incremented (modulo p) each time a work request is sent. The initial value of *target* at each processor is set to $((label + 1)$ modulo $p)$ where *label* is the local processor label. Note that work requests are generated independently by each processor. However, it is possible for two or more processors to request work from the same donor at nearly the same time.

Global Round Robin   Global round robin (GRR) uses a single global variable called *target*. This variable can be stored in a globally accessible space in shared address space machines or at a designated processor in message passing machines. Whenever a processor needs work, it requests and receives the value of *target*, either by locking, reading, and unlocking on shared address space machines or by sending a message requesting the designated processor (say P_0). The value of *target* is incremented (modulo p) before responding to the next request. The recipient processor then attempts to get work from a donor processor whose label is the value of *target*. GRR ensures that successive work requests are distributed evenly over all processors. A drawback of this scheme is the contention for access to *target*.

Random Polling   Random polling (RP) is the simplest load-balancing scheme. When a processor becomes idle, it randomly selects a donor. Each processor is selected as a donor with equal probability, ensuring that work requests are evenly distributed.

11.4.2   A General Framework for Analysis of Parallel DFS

To analyze the performance and scalability of parallel DFS algorithms for any load-balancing scheme, we must compute the overhead T_o of the algorithm. Overhead in any load-balancing scheme is due to communication (requesting and sending work), idle time (waiting for work), termination detection, and contention for shared resources. If the search overhead factor is greater than one (i.e., if parallel search does more work than serial search), this will add another term to T_o. In this section we assume that the search overhead factor is one, i.e., the serial and parallel versions of the algorithm perform the same amount of computation. We analyze the case in which the search overhead factor is other than one in Section 11.6.1.

For the load-balancing schemes discussed in Section 11.4.1, idle time is subsumed by communication overhead due to work requests and transfers. When a processor becomes idle, it immediately selects a donor processor and sends it a work request. The total time for which the processor remains idle is equal to the time for the request to reach the donor and for the reply to arrive. At that point, the idle processor either becomes busy or generates another work request. Therefore, the time spent in communication subsumes the time for which a processor is idle. Since communication overhead is the dominant overhead in parallel DFS, we now consider a method to compute the communication overhead for each load-balancing scheme.

It is difficult to derive a precise expression for the communication overhead of the load-balancing schemes for DFS because they are dynamic. This section describes a technique that provides an upper bound on this overhead. We make the following assumptions in the analysis.

1. The work at any processor can be partitioned into independent pieces as long as its size exceeds a threshold ϵ.

2. A reasonable work-splitting mechanism is available. Assume that work w at one processor is partitioned into two parts: ψw and $(1 - \psi)w$ for $0 \leq \psi \leq 1$. Then there exists an arbitrarily small constant α $(0 < \alpha \leq 0.5)$, such that $\psi w > \alpha w$ and $(1 - \psi)w > \alpha w$. We call such a splitting mechanism α-splitting. The constant α sets a lower bound on the load imbalance that results from work splitting: both partitions of w have at least αw work.

The first assumption is satisfied by most depth-first search algorithms. The third work-splitting strategy described in Section 11.4.1 results in α-splitting even for highly irregular search spaces.

In the load-balancing schemes to be analyzed, the total work is dynamically partitioned among the processors. Processors work on disjoint parts of the search space independently. An idle processor polls for work. When it finds a donor processor with work, the work is split and a part of it is transferred to the idle processor. If the donor has work w_i, and it is split into two pieces of size w_j and w_k, then assumption 2 states that there is a constant α such that $w_j > \alpha w_i$ and $w_k > \alpha w_i$. Note that α is less than 0.5. Therefore, after a work transfer, neither processor (donor and recipient) has more than $(1 - \alpha)w_i$ work. Suppose there are p pieces of work whose sizes are $w_0, w_1, \ldots, w_{p-1}$. Assume that the size of the largest piece is w. If all of these pieces are split, the splitting strategy yields $2p$ pieces of work whose sizes are given by $\psi_0 w_0, \psi_1 w_1, \ldots, \psi_{p-1} w_{p-1}, (1 - \psi_0)w_0, (1 - \psi_1)w_1, \ldots, (1 - \psi_{p-1})w_{p-1}$. Among them, the size of the largest piece is given by $(1 - \alpha)w$.

Assume that there are p processors and a single piece of work is assigned to each processor. If every processor receives a work request at least once, then each of these p pieces has been split at least once. Thus, the maximum work at any of the processors has been reduced by a factor of $(1 - \alpha)$. We define $V(p)$ such that, after every $V(p)$ work requests, each processor receives at least one work request. Note that $V(p) \geq p$. In general, $V(p)$ depends on the load-balancing algorithm. Initially, processor P_0 has W units of work, and all other processors have no work. After $V(p)$ requests, the maximum work remaining at any processor is less than $(1-\alpha)W$; after $2V(p)$ requests, the maximum work remaining at any processor is less than $(1-\alpha)^2 W$. Similarly, after $(\log_{1/(1-\alpha)}(W/\epsilon))V(p)$ requests, the maximum work remaining at any processor is below a threshold value ϵ. Hence, the total number of work requests is $O(V(p) \log W)$.

Communication overhead is caused by work requests and work transfers. The total number of work transfers cannot exceed the total number of work requests. Therefore, the total number of work requests, weighted by the total communication cost of one work request and a corresponding work transfer, gives an upper bound on the total communication overhead. For simplicity, we assume the amount of data associated with a work request and work transfer is a constant. In general, the size of the stack should grow logarithmically with respect to the size of the search space. The analysis for this case can be done similarly (Problem 11.3).

If t_{comm} is the time required to communicate a piece of work, then the communication overhead T_o is given by

$$T_o = t_{comm} V(p) \log W \qquad (11.2)$$

The corresponding efficiency E is given by

$$E = \frac{1}{1 + T_o/W}$$

$$= \frac{1}{1 + (t_{comm} V(p) \log W)/W}$$

In Section 5.4.2 we showed that the isoefficiency function can be derived by balancing the problem size W and the overhead function T_o. As shown by Equation 11.2, T_o depends on two values: t_{comm} and $V(p)$. The value of t_{comm} is determined by the underlying architecture, and the function $V(p)$ is determined by the load-balancing scheme. In the following subsections, we derive $V(p)$ for each scheme introduced in Section 11.4.1. We subsequently use these values of $V(p)$ to derive the scalability of various schemes on message-passing and shared-address-space machines.

Computation of V(p) for Various Load-Balancing Schemes

Equation 11.2 shows that $V(p)$ is an important component of the total communication overhead. In this section, we compute the value of $V(p)$ for different load-balancing schemes.

Asynchronous Round Robin   The worst case value of $V(p)$ for ARR occurs when all processors issue work requests at the same time to the same processor. This case is illustrated in the following scenario. Assume that processor $p - 1$ had all the work and that the local counters of all the other processors (0 to $p - 2$) were pointing to processor zero. In this case, for processor $p - 1$ to receive a work request, one processor must issue $p - 1$ requests while each of the remaining $p - 2$ processors generates up to $p - 2$ work requests (to all processors except processor $p - 1$ and itself). Thus, $V(p)$ has an upper bound of $(p - 1) + (p - 2)(p - 2)$; that is, $V(p) = O(p^2)$. Note that the actual value of $V(p)$ is between p and p^2.

Global Round Robin   In GRR, all processors receive requests in sequence. After p requests, each processor has received one request. Therefore, $V(p)$ is p.

Random Polling   For RR, the worst-case value of $V(p)$ is unbounded. Hence, we compute the average-case value of $V(p)$.

Consider a collection of p boxes. In each trial, a box is chosen at random and marked. We are interested in the mean number of trials required to mark all the boxes. In our algorithm, each trial corresponds to a processor sending another randomly selected processor a request for work.

Let $F(i, p)$ represent a state in which i of the p boxes have been marked, and $p - i$ boxes have not been marked. Since the next box to be marked is picked at random, there is i/p probability that it will be a marked box and $(p - i)/p$ probability that it will be an unmarked box. Hence the system remains in state $F(i, p)$ with a probability of i/p and transits to state $F(i + 1, p)$ with a probability of $(p - i)/p$. Let $f(i, p)$ denote the average number of trials needed to change from state $F(i, p)$ to $F(p, p)$. Then, $V(p) = f(0, p)$. We have

$$f(i, p) = \frac{i}{p}(1 + f(i, p)) + \frac{p - i}{p}(1 + f(i + 1, p)),$$

$$\frac{p - i}{p} f(i, p) = 1 + \frac{p - i}{p} f(i + 1, p),$$

$$f(i, p) = \frac{p}{p - i} + f(i + 1, p).$$

Hence,

$$f(0, p) = p \times \sum_{i=0}^{p-1} \frac{1}{p - i},$$

$$= p \times \sum_{i=1}^{p} \frac{1}{i},$$

$$= p \times H_p,$$

where H_p is a harmonic number. It can be shown that, as p becomes large, $H_p \simeq 1.69 \ln p$ (where $\ln p$ denotes the natural logarithm of p). Thus, $V(p) = O(p \log p)$.

11.4.3 Analysis of Load-Balancing Schemes

This section analyzes the performance of the load-balancing schemes introduced in Section 11.4.1. In each case, we assume that work is transferred in fixed-size messages (the effect of relaxing this assumption is explored in Problem 11.3).

Recall that the cost of communicating an m-word message in the simplified cost model is $t_{comm} = t_s + t_w m$. Since the message size m is assumed to be a constant, $t_{comm} = O(1)$ if there is no congestion on the interconnection network. The communication overhead T_o (Equation 11.2) reduces to

$$T_o = O(V(p) \log W). \tag{11.3}$$

We balance this overhead with problem size W for each load-balancing scheme to derive the isoefficiency function due to communication.

Asynchronous Round Robin As discussed in Section 11.4.2, $V(p)$ for ARR is $O(p^2)$. Substituting into Equation 11.3, communication overhead T_o is given by $O(p^2 \log W)$. Balancing communication overhead against problem size W, we have

$$W = O(p^2 \log W).$$

Substituting W into the right-hand side of the same equation and simplifying,

$$\begin{aligned} W &= O(p^2 \log(p^2 \log W)), \\ &= O(p^2 \log p + p^2 \log \log W). \end{aligned}$$

The double-log term ($\log \log W$) is asymptotically smaller than the first term, provided p grows no slower than $\log W$, and can be ignored. The isoefficiency function for this scheme is therefore given by $O(p^2 \log p)$.

Global Round Robin From Section 11.4.2, $V(p) = O(p)$ for GRR. Substituting into Equation 11.3, this yields a communication overhead T_o of $O(p \log W)$. Simplifying as for ARR, the isoefficiency function for this scheme due to communication overhead is $O(p \log p)$.

In this scheme, however, the global variable *target* is accessed repeatedly, possibly causing contention. The number of times this variable is accessed is equal to the total number of work requests, $O(p \log W)$. If the processors are used efficiently, the total execution time is $O(W/p)$. Assume that there is no contention for *target* while solving a problem of size W on p processors. Then, W/p is larger than the total time during which the shared variable is accessed. As the number of processors increases, the execution time (W/p) decreases, but the number of times the shared variable is accessed increases. Thus, there is a crossover point beyond which the shared variable becomes a bottleneck, prohibiting further reduction in run time. This bottleneck can be eliminated by increasing W at a rate such that the ratio between W/p and $O(p \log W)$ remains constant. This requires W to grow with respect to p as follows:

$$\frac{W}{p} = O(p \log W) \tag{11.4}$$

We can simplify Equation 11.4 to express W in terms of p. This yields an isoefficiency term of $O(p^2 \log p)$.

Since the isoefficiency function due to contention asymptotically dominates the isoefficiency function due to communication, the overall isoefficiency function is given by $O(p^2 \log p)$. Note that although it is difficult to estimate the actual overhead due to contention for the shared variable, we are able to determine the resulting isoefficiency function.

Random Polling We saw in Section 11.4.2 that $V(p) = O(p \log p)$ for RP. Substituting this value into Equation 11.3, the communication overhead T_o is $O(p \log p \log W)$. Equating T_o with the problem size W and simplifying as before, we derive the isoefficiency function due to communication overhead as $O(p \log^2 p)$. Since there is no contention in RP, this function also gives its overall isoefficiency function.

11.4.4   Termination Detection

One aspect of parallel DFS that has not been addressed thus far is termination detection. In this section, we present two schemes for termination detection that can be used with the load-balancing algorithms discussed in Section 11.4.1.

Dijkstra's Token Termination Detection Algorithm

Consider a simplified scenario in which once a processor goes idle, it never receives more work. Visualize the p processors as being connected in a logical ring (note that a logical ring can be easily mapped to underlying physical topologies). Processor P_0 initiates a token when it becomes idle. This token is sent to the next processor in the ring, P_1. At any stage in the computation, if a processor receives a token, the token is held at the processor until the computation assigned to the processor is complete. On completion, the token is passed to the next processor in the ring. If the processor was already idle, the token is passed to the next processor. Note that if at any time the token is passed to processor P_i, then all processors $P_0, \ldots, P_{i-1}$ have completed their computation. Processor P_{p-1} passes its token to processor P_0; when it receives the token, processor P_0 knows that all processors have completed their computation and the algorithm can terminate.

Such a simple scheme cannot be applied to the search algorithms described in this chapter, because after a processor goes idle, it may receive more work from other processors. The token termination detection scheme thus must be modified.

In the modified scheme, the processors are also organized into a ring. A processor can be in one of two states: *black* or *white*. Initially, all processors are in state *white*. As before, the token travels in the sequence $P_0, P_1, \ldots, P_{p-1}, P_0$. If the only work transfers allowed in the system are from processor P_i to P_j such that $i < j$, then the simple termination scheme is still adequate. However, if processor P_j sends work to processor P_i, the token must traverse the ring again. In this case processor P_j is marked *black* since it causes the token to go around the ring again. Processor P_0 must be able to tell by looking at the token it receives whether it should be propagated around the ring again. Therefore the token itself is of two types: a *white* (or valid) token, which when received by processor P_0 implies termination; and a *black* (or invalid) token, which implies that the token must traverse the ring again. The modified termination algorithm works as follows:

1. When it becomes idle, processor P_0 initiates termination detection by making itself *white* and sending a *white* token to processor P_1.

2. If processor P_j sends work to processor P_i and $j > i$ then processor P_j becomes *black*.

3. If processor P_i has the token and P_i is idle, then it passes the token to P_{i+1}. If P_i is *black*, then the color of the token is set to *black* before it is sent to P_{i+1}. If P_i is *white*, the token is passed unchanged.

4. After P_i passes the token to P_{i+1}, P_i becomes *white*.

The algorithm terminates when processor P_0 receives a *white* token and is itself idle. The algorithm correctly detects termination by accounting for the possibility of a processor receiving work after it has already been accounted for by the token.

The run time of this algorithm is $O(P)$ with a small constant. For a small number of processors, this scheme can be used without a significant impact on the overall performance. For a large number of processors, this algorithm can cause the overall isoefficiency function of the load-balancing scheme to be at least $O(p^2)$ (Problem 11.4).

Tree-Based Termination Detection

Tree-based termination detection associates weights with individual work pieces. Initially processor P_0 has all the work and a weight of one is associated with it. When its work is partitioned and sent to another processor, processor P_0 retains half of the weight and gives half of it to the processor receiving the work. If P_i is the recipient processor and w_i is the weight at processor P_i, then after the first work transfer, both w_0 and w_i are 0.5. Each time the work at a processor is partitioned, the weight is halved. When a processor completes its computation, it returns its weight to the processor from which it received work. Termination is signaled when the weight w_0 at processor P_0 becomes one and processor P_0 has finished its work.

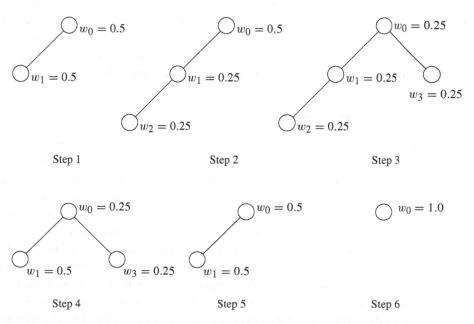

Figure 11.10 Tree-based termination detection. Steps 1–6 illustrate the weights at various processors after each work transfer.

Example 11.7   Tree-based termination detection

Figure 11.10 illustrates tree-based termination detection for four processors. Initially, processor P_0 has all the weight ($w_0 = 1$), and the weight at the remaining processors is 0 ($w_1 = w_2 = w_3 = 0$). In step 1, processor P_0 partitions its work and gives part of it to processor P_1. After this step, w_0 and w_1 are 0.5 and w_2 and w_3 are 0. In step 2, processor P_1 gives half of its work to processor P_2. The weights w_1 and w_2 after this work transfer are 0.25 and the weights w_0 and w_3 remain unchanged. In step 3, processor P_3 gets work from processor P_1 and the weights of all processors become 0.25. In step 4, processor P_2 completes its work and sends its weight to processor P_1. The weight w_1 of processor P_1 becomes 0.5. As processors complete their work, weights are propagated up the tree until the weight w_0 at processor P_0 becomes 1. At this point, all work has been completed and termination can be signaled.   ∎

This termination detection algorithm has a significant drawback. Due to the finite precision of computers, recursive halving of the weight may make the weight so small that it becomes 0. In this case, weight will be lost and termination will never be signaled. This condition can be alleviated by using the inverse of the weights. If processor P_i has weight w_i, instead of manipulating the weight itself, it manipulates $1/w_i$. The details of this algorithm are considered in Problem 11.5.

The tree-based termination detection algorithm does not change the overall isoefficiency function of any of the search schemes we have considered. This follows from the fact that there are exactly two weight transfers associated with each work transfer. Therefore, the algorithm has the effect of increasing the communication overhead by a constant factor. In asymptotic terms, this change does not alter the isoefficiency function.

11.4.5   Experimental Results

In this section, we demonstrate the validity of scalability analysis for various parallel DFS algorithms. The satisfiability problem tests the validity of boolean formulae. Such problems arise in areas such as VLSI design and theorem proving. The *satisfiability problem* can be stated as follows: given a boolean formula containing binary variables in conjunctive normal form, determine if it is unsatisfiable. A boolean formula is unsatisfiable if there exists no assignment of truth values to variables for which the formula is true.

The Davis-Putnam algorithm is a fast and efficient way to solve this problem. The algorithm works by performing a depth-first search of the binary tree formed by true or false assignments to the literals in the boolean expression. Let n be the number of literals. Then the maximum depth of the tree cannot exceed n. If, after a partial assignment of values to literals, the formula becomes false, then the algorithm backtracks. The formula is unsatisfiable if depth-first search fails to find an assignment to variables for which the formula is true.

Even if a formula is unsatisfiable, only a small subset of the 2^n possible combinations

Table 11.1   Average speedups for various load-balancing schemes.

Scheme	Number of processors							
	8	16	32	64	128	256	512	1024
ARR	7.506	14.936	29.664	57.721	103.738	178.92	259.372	284.425
GRR	7.384	14.734	29.291	57.729	110.754	184.828	155.051	
RP	7.524	15.000	29.814	58.857	114.645	218.255	397.585	660.582

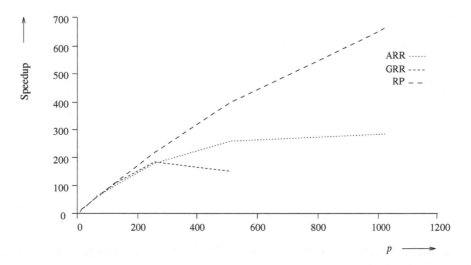

Figure 11.11   Speedups of parallel DFS using ARR, GRR and RP load-balancing schemes.

will actually be explored. For example, for a 65-variable problem, the total number of possible combinations is 2^{65} (approximately 3.7×10^{19}), but only about 10^7 nodes are actually expanded in a specific problem instance. The search tree for this problem is pruned in a highly nonuniform fashion and any attempt to partition the tree statically results in an extremely poor load balance.

The satisfiability problem is used to test the load-balancing schemes on a message passing parallel computer for up to 1024 processors. We implemented the Davis-Putnam algorithm, and incorporated the load-balancing algorithms discussed in Section 11.4.1. This program was run on several unsatisfiable formulae. By choosing unsatisfiable instances, we ensured that the number of nodes expanded by the parallel formulation is the same as the number expanded by the sequential one; any speedup loss was due only to the overhead of load balancing.

In the problem instances on which the program was tested, the total number of nodes in the tree varied between approximately 10^5 and 10^7. The depth of the trees (which is equal to the number of variables in the formula) varied between 35 and 65. Speedup was calculated with respect to the optimum sequential execution time for the same problem.

Table 11.2   Number of requests generated for GRR and RP.

Scheme	Number of processors							
	8	16	32	64	128	256	512	1024
GRR	260	661	1572	3445	8557	17088	41382	72874
RP	562	2013	5106	15060	46056	136457	382695	885872

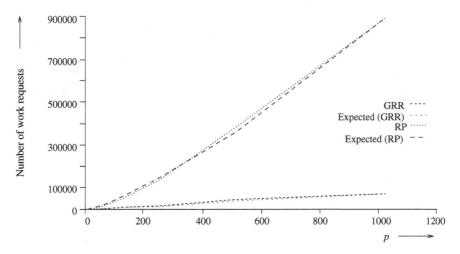

Figure 11.12   Number of work requests generated for RP and GRR and their expected values ($O(p \log^2 p)$ and $O(p \log p)$ respectively).

Average speedup was calculated by taking the ratio of the cumulative time to solve all the problems in parallel using a given number of processors to the corresponding cumulative sequential time. On a given number of processors, the speedup and efficiency were largely determined by the tree size (which is roughly proportional to the sequential run time). Thus, speedup on similar-sized problems was quite similar.

All schemes were tested on a sample set of five problem instances. Table 11.1 shows the average speedup obtained by parallel algorithms using different load-balancing techniques. Figure 11.11 is a graph of the speedups obtained. Table 11.2 presents the total number of work requests made by RP and GRR for one problem instance. Figure 11.12 shows the corresponding graph and compares the number of messages generated with the expected values $O(p \log^2 p)$ and $O(p \log p)$ for RP and GRR, respectively.

The isoefficiency function of GRR is $O(p^2 \log p)$ which is much worse than the isoefficiency function of RP. This is reflected in the performance of our implementation. From Figure 11.11, we see that the performance of GRR deteriorates very rapidly for more than 256 processors. Good speedups can be obtained for $p > 256$ only for very large problem instances. Experimental results also show that ARR is more scalable than GRR, but sig-

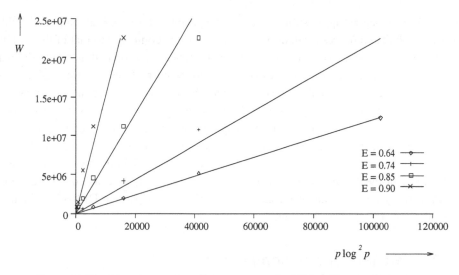

Figure 11.13 Experimental isoefficiency curves for RP for different efficiencies.

nificantly less scalable than RP. Although the isoefficiency functions of ARR and GRR are both $O(p^2 \log p)$, ARR performs better than GRR. The reason for this is that $p^2 \log p$ is an upper bound, derived using $V(p) = O(p^2)$. This value of $V(p)$ is only a loose upper bound for ARR. In contrast, the value of $V(p)$ used for GRR ($O(p)$) is a tight bound.

To determine the accuracy of the isoefficiency functions of various schemes, we experimentally verified the isoefficiency curves for the RP technique (the selection of this technique was arbitrary). We ran 30 different problem instances varying in size from 10^5 nodes to 10^7 nodes on a varying number of processors. Speedup and efficiency were computed for each of these. Data points with the same efficiency for different problem sizes and number of processors were then grouped. Where identical efficiency points were not available, the problem size was computed by averaging over points with efficiencies in the neighborhood of the required value. These data are presented in Figure 11.13, which plots the problem size W against $p \log^2 p$ for values of efficiency equal to 0.9, 0.85, 0.74, and 0.64. We expect points corresponding to the same efficiency to be collinear. We can see from Figure 11.13 that the points are reasonably collinear, which shows that the experimental isoefficiency function of RP is close to the theoretically derived isoefficiency function.

11.4.6 Parallel Formulations of Depth-First Branch-and-Bound Search

Parallel formulations of depth-first branch-and-bound search (DFBB) are similar to those of DFS. The preceding formulations of DFS can be applied to DFBB with one minor modification: all processors are kept informed of the current best solution path. The current best solution path for many problems can be represented by a small data structure. For shared address space computers, this data structure can be stored in a globally accessible memory. Each time a processor finds a solution, its cost is compared to that of the current best solution path. If the cost is lower, then the current best solution path is replaced. On a message-passing computer, each processor maintains the current best solution path known to it. Whenever a processor finds a solution path better than the current best known, it broadcasts its cost to all other processors, which update (if necessary) their current best solution cost. Since the cost of a solution is captured by a single number and solutions are found infrequently, the overhead of communicating this value is fairly small. Note that, if a processor's current best solution path is worse than the globally best solution path, the efficiency of the search is affected but not its correctness. Because of DFBB's low communication overhead, the performance and scalability of parallel DFBB is similar to that of parallel DFS discussed earlier.

11.4.7   Parallel Formulations of IDA*

Since IDA* explores the search tree iteratively with successively increasing cost bounds, it is natural to conceive a parallel formulation in which separate processors explore separate parts of the search space independently. Processors may be exploring the tree using different cost bounds. This approach suffers from two drawbacks.

1. It is unclear how to select a threshold for a particular processor. If the threshold chosen for a processor happens to be higher than the global minimum threshold, then the processor will explore portions of the tree that are not explored by sequential IDA*.

2. This approach may not find an optimal solution. A solution found by one processor in a particular iteration is not provably optimal until all the other processors have also exhausted the search space associated with thresholds lower than the cost of the solution found.

A more effective approach executes each iteration of IDA* by using parallel DFS (Section 11.4). All processors use the same cost bound; each processor stores the bound locally and performs DFS on its own search space. After each iteration of parallel IDA*, a designated processor determines the cost bound for the next iteration and restarts parallel DFS with the new bound. The search terminates when a processor finds a goal node and informs all the other processors. The performance and scalability of this parallel formulation of IDA* are similar to those of the parallel DFS algorithm.

11.5   Parallel Best-First Search

Recall from Section 11.2.2 that an important component of best-first search (BFS) algorithms is the *open* list. It maintains the unexpanded nodes in the search graph, ordered

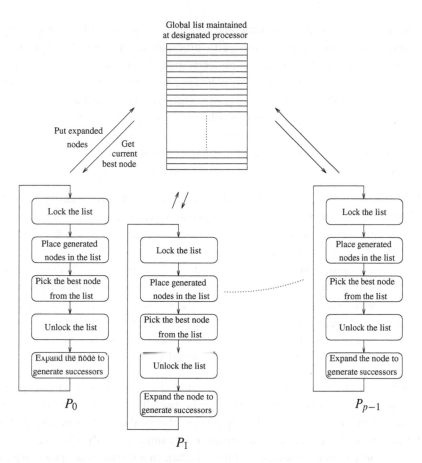

Figure 11.14 A general schematic for parallel best-first search using a centralized strategy. The locking operation is used here to serialize queue access by various processors.

according to their l-value. In the sequential algorithm, the most promising node from the *open* list is removed and expanded, and newly generated nodes are added to the *open* list.

In most parallel formulations of BFS, different processors concurrently expand different nodes from the *open* list. These formulations differ according to the data structures they use to implement the *open* list. Given p processors, the simplest strategy assigns each processor to work on one of the current best nodes on the *open* list. This is called the **centralized strategy** because each processor gets work from a single global *open* list. Since this formulation of parallel BFS expands more than one node at a time, it may expand nodes that would not be expanded by a sequential algorithm. Consider the case in which the first node on the *open* list is a solution. The parallel formulation still expands the first p nodes on the *open* list. However, since it always picks the best p nodes, the amount of extra work is limited. Figure 11.14 illustrates this strategy. There are two problems with this approach:

1. The termination criterion of sequential BFS fails for parallel BFS. Since at any moment, p nodes from the *open* list are being expanded, it is possible that one of the nodes may be a solution that does not correspond to the best goal node (or the path found is not the shortest path). This is because the remaining $p - 1$ nodes may lead to search spaces containing better goal nodes. Therefore, if the cost of a solution found by a processor is c, then this solution is not guaranteed to correspond to the best goal node until the cost of nodes being searched at other processors is known to be at least c. The termination criterion must be modified to ensure that termination occurs only after the best solution has been found.

2. Since the *open* list is accessed for each node expansion, it must be easily accessible to all processors, which can severely limit performance. Even on shared-address-space architectures, contention for the *open* list limits speedup. Let t_{exp} be the average time to expand a single node, and t_{access} be the average time to access the *open* list for a single-node expansion. If there are n nodes to be expanded by both the sequential and parallel formulations (assuming that they do an equal amount of work), then the sequential run time is given by $n(t_{access} + t_{exp})$. Assume that it is impossible to parallelize the expansion of individual nodes. Then the parallel run time will be at least nt_{access}, because the *open* list must be accessed at least once for each node expanded. Hence, an upper bound on the speedup is $(t_{access} + t_{exp})/t_{access}$.

One way to avoid the contention due to a centralized *open* list is to let each processor have a local *open* list. Initially, the search space is statically divided among the processors by expanding some nodes and distributing them to the local *open* lists of various processors. All the processors then select and expand nodes simultaneously. Consider a scenario where processors do not communicate with each other. In this case, some processors might explore parts of the search space that would not be explored by the sequential algorithm. This leads to a high search overhead factor and poor speedup. Consequently, the processors must communicate among themselves to minimize unnecessary search. The use of a distributed *open* list trades-off communication and computation: decreasing communication between distributed *open* lists increases search overhead factor, and decreasing search overhead factor with increased communication increases communication overhead.

The best choice of communication strategy for parallel BFS depends on whether the search space is a tree or a graph. Searching a graph incurs the additional overhead of checking for duplicate nodes on the closed list. We discuss some communication strategies for tree and graph search separately.

Communication Strategies for Parallel Best-First Tree Search

A communication strategy allows state-space nodes to be exchanged between *open* lists on different processors. The objective of a communication strategy is to ensure that nodes with good l-values are distributed evenly among processors. In this section we discuss three such strategies, as follows.

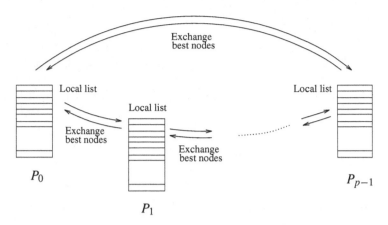

Figure 11.15   A message-passing implementation of parallel best-first search using the ring communication strategy.

1. In the ***random communication strategy***, each processor periodically sends some of its best nodes to the *open* list of a randomly selected processor. This strategy ensures that, if a processor stores a good part of the search space, the others get part of it. If nodes are transferred frequently, the search overhead factor can be made very small; otherwise it can become quite large. The communication cost determines the best node transfer frequency. If the communication cost is low, it is best to communicate after every node expansion.

2. In the ***ring communication strategy***, the processors are mapped in a virtual ring. Each processor periodically exchanges some of its best nodes with the *open* lists of its neighbors in the ring. This strategy can be implemented on message passing as well as shared address space machines with the processors organized into a logical ring. As before, the cost of communication determines the node transfer frequency. Figure 11.15 illustrates the ring communication strategy.

   Unless the search space is highly uniform, the search overhead factor of this scheme is very high. The reason is that this scheme takes a long time to distribute good nodes from one processor to all other processors.

3. In the ***blackboard communication strategy***, there is a shared blackboard through which nodes are switched among processors as follows. After selecting the best node from its local *open* list, a processor expands the node only if its l-value is within a tolerable limit of the best node on the blackboard. If the selected node is much better than the best node on the blackboard, the processor sends some of its best nodes to the blackboard before expanding the current node. If the selected node is much worse than the best node on the blackboard, the processor retrieves some good nodes from the blackboard and reselects a node for expansion. Figure 11.16 illustrates the blackboard communication strategy. The blackboard strategy is suited

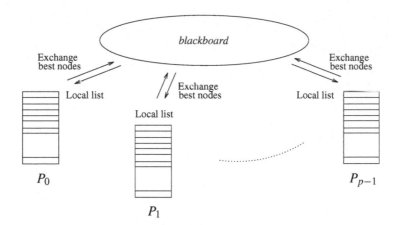

Figure 11.16 An implementation of parallel best-first search using the blackboard communication strategy.

only to shared-address-space computers, because the value of the best node in the blackboard has to be checked after each node expansion.

Communication Strategies for Parallel Best-First Graph Search

While searching graphs, an algorithm must check for node replication. This task is distributed among processors. One way to check for replication is to map each node to a specific processor. Subsequently, whenever a node is generated, it is mapped to the same processor, which checks for replication locally. This technique can be implemented using a hash function that takes a node as input and returns a processor label. When a node is generated, it is sent to the processor whose label is returned by the hash function for that node. Upon receiving the node, a processor checks whether it already exists in the local *open* or *closed* lists. If not, the node is inserted in the *open* list. If the node already exists, and if the new node has a better cost associated with it, then the previous version of the node is replaced by the new node on the *open* list.

For a random hash function, the load-balancing property of this distribution strategy is similar to the random-distribution technique discussed in the previous section. This result follows from the fact that each processor is equally likely to be assigned a part of the search space that would also be explored by a sequential formulation. This method ensures an even distribution of nodes with good heuristic values among all the processors (Problem 11.10). However, hashing techniques degrade performance because each node generation results in communication (Problem 11.11).

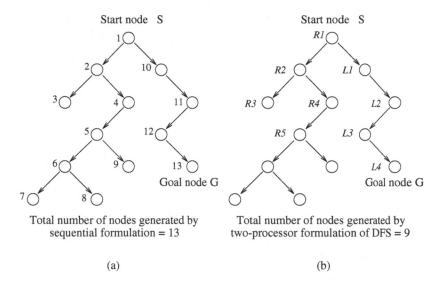

Figure 11.17(a): Total number of nodes generated by sequential formulation = 13

Figure 11.17(b): Total number of nodes generated by two-processor formulation of DFS = 9

(a)   (b)

Figure 11.17 The difference in number of nodes searched by sequential and parallel formulations of DFS. For this example, parallel DFS reaches a goal node after searching fewer nodes than sequential DFS.

11.6 Speedup Anomalies in Parallel Search Algorithms

In parallel search algorithms, speedup can vary greatly from one execution to another because the portions of the search space examined by various processors are determined dynamically and can differ for each execution. Consider the case of sequential and parallel DFS performed on the tree illustrated in Figure 11.17. Figure 11.17(a) illustrates sequential DFS search. The order of node expansions is indicated by node labels. The sequential formulation generates 13 nodes before reaching the goal node G.

Now consider the parallel formulation of DFS illustrated for the same tree in Figure 11.17(b) for two processors. The nodes expanded by the processors are labeled R and L. The parallel formulation reaches the goal node after generating only nine nodes. That is, the parallel formulation arrives at the goal node after searching fewer nodes than its sequential counterpart. In this case, the search overhead factor is 9/13 (less than one), and if communication overhead is not too large, the speedup will be superlinear.

Finally, consider the situation in Figure 11.18. The sequential formulation (Figure 11.18(a)) generates seven nodes before reaching the goal node, but the parallel formulation generates 12 nodes. In this case, the search overhead factor is greater than one, resulting in sublinear speedup.

In summary, for some executions, the parallel version finds a solution after generating fewer nodes than the sequential version, making it possible to obtain superlinear speedup. For other executions, the parallel version finds a solution after generating more nodes,

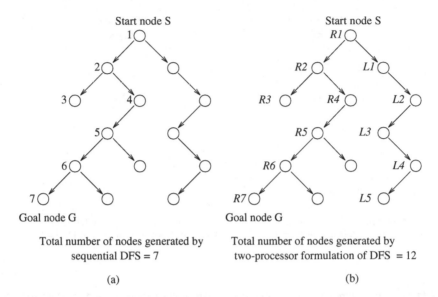

Figure 11.18 A parallel DFS formulation that searches more nodes than its sequential counterpart.

resulting in sublinear speedup. Executions yielding speedups greater than p by using p processors are referred to as ***acceleration anomalies***. Speedups of less than p using p processors are called ***deceleration anomalies***.

Speedup anomalies also manifest themselves in best-first search algorithms. Here, anomalies are caused by nodes on the *open* list that have identical heuristic values but require vastly different amounts of search to detect a solution. Assume that two such nodes exist; node A leads rapidly to the goal node, and node B leads nowhere after extensive work. In parallel BFS, both nodes are chosen for expansion by different processors. Consider the relative performance of parallel and sequential BFS. If the sequential algorithm picks node A to expand, it arrives quickly at a goal. However, the parallel algorithm wastes time expanding node B, leading to a deceleration anomaly. In contrast, if the sequential algorithm expands node B, it wastes substantial time before abandoning it in favor of node A. However, the parallel algorithm does not waste as much time on node B, because node A yields a solution quickly, leading to an acceleration anomaly.

11.6.1 Analysis of Average Speedup in Parallel DFS

In isolated executions of parallel search algorithms, the search overhead factor may be equal to one, less than one, or greater than one. It is interesting to know the average value of the search overhead factor. If it is less than one, this implies that the sequential search algorithm is not optimal. In this case, the parallel search algorithm running on a sequential processor (by emulating a parallel processor by using time-slicing) would expand fewer nodes than the sequential algorithm on the average. In this section, we show that for a certain type of search space, the average value of the search overhead factor in parallel

DFS is less than one. Hence, if the communication overhead is not too large, then on the average, parallel DFS will provide superlinear speedup for this type of search space.

Assumptions

We make the following assumptions for analyzing speedup anomalies:

1. The state-space tree has M leaf nodes. Solutions occur only at leaf nodes. The amount of computation needed to generate each leaf node is the same. The number of nodes generated in the tree is proportional to the number of leaf nodes generated. This is a reasonable assumption for search trees in which each node has more than one successor on the average.

2. Both sequential and parallel DFS stop after finding one solution.

3. In parallel DFS, the state-space tree is equally partitioned among p processors; thus, each processor gets a subtree with M/p leaf nodes.

4. There is at least one solution in the entire tree. (Otherwise, both parallel search and sequential search generate the entire tree without finding a solution, resulting in linear speedup.)

5. There is no information to order the search of the state-space tree; hence, the density of solutions across the unexplored nodes is independent of the order of the search.

6. The solution density ρ is defined as the probability of the leaf node being a solution. We assume a Bernoulli distribution of solutions; that is, the event of a leaf node being a solution is independent of any other leaf node being a solution. We also assume that $\rho \ll 1$.

7. The total number of leaf nodes generated by p processors before one of the processors finds a solution is denoted by W_p. The average number of leaf nodes generated by sequential DFS before a solution is found is given by W. Both W and W_p are less than or equal to M.

Analysis of the Search Overhead Factor

Consider the scenario in which the M leaf nodes are statically divided into p regions, each with $K = M/p$ leaves. Let the density of solutions among the leaves in the ith region be ρ_i. In the parallel algorithm, each processor P_i searches region i independently until a processor finds a solution. In the sequential algorithm, the regions are searched in random order.

Theorem 11.6.1 *Let ρ be the solution density in a region; and assume that the number of leaves K in the region is large. Then, if $\rho > 0$, the mean number of leaves generated by a single processor searching the region is $1/\rho$.*

Proof: Since we have a Bernoulli distribution, the mean number of trials is given by

$$
\begin{aligned}
\rho + 2\rho(1-\rho) + \cdots + K\rho(1-\rho)^{K-1} &= \frac{1-(1-\rho)^{K+1}}{\rho} - (K+1)(1-\rho)^K, \\
&= \frac{1}{\rho} - (1-\rho)^K \left(\frac{1}{\rho} + K \right). \quad (11.5)
\end{aligned}
$$

For a fixed value of ρ and a large value of K, the second term in Equation 11.5 becomes small; hence, the mean number of trials is approximately equal to $1/\rho$.   □

Sequential DFS selects any one of the p regions with probability $1/p$ and searches it to find a solution. Hence, the average number of leaf nodes expanded by sequential DFS is

$$
W \simeq \frac{1}{p} \left(\frac{1}{\rho_1} + \frac{1}{\rho_2} + \cdots + \frac{1}{\rho_p} \right).
$$

This expression assumes that a solution is always found in the selected region; thus, only one region must be searched. However, the probability of region i not having any solutions is $(1 - \rho_i)^K$. In this case, another region must be searched. Taking this into account makes the expression for W more precise and increases the average value of W somewhat. The overall results of the analysis will not change.

In each step of parallel DFS, one node from each of the p regions is explored simultaneously. Hence the probability of success in a step of the parallel algorithm is $1 - \prod_{i=1}^{p}(1 - \rho_i)$. This is approximately $\rho_1 + \rho_2 + \cdots + \rho_p$ (neglecting the second-order terms, since each ρ_i are assumed to be small). Hence,

$$
W_p \simeq \frac{p}{\rho_1 + \rho_2 + \cdots + \rho_p}.
$$

Inspecting the above equations, we see that $W = 1/HM$ and $W_p = 1/AM$, where HM is the harmonic mean of $\rho_1, \rho_2, \ldots, \rho_p$, and AM is their arithmetic mean. Since the arithmetic mean (AM) and the harmonic mean (HM) satisfy the relation $AM \geq HM$, we have $W \geq W_p$. In particular:

- When $\rho_1 = \rho_2 = \cdots = \rho_p$, $AM = HM$, therefore $W \simeq W_p$. When solutions are uniformly distributed, the average search overhead factor for parallel DFS is one.

- When each ρ_i is different, $AM > HM$, therefore $W > W_p$. When solution densities in various regions are nonuniform, the average search overhead factor for parallel DFS is less than one, making it possible to obtain superlinear speedups.

The assumption that each node can be a solution independent of the other nodes being solutions is false for most practical problems. Still, the preceding analysis suggests that parallel DFS obtains higher efficiency than sequential DFS provided that the solutions are not distributed uniformly in the search space and that no information about solution density in various regions is available. This characteristic applies to a variety of problem spaces searched by simple backtracking. The result that the search overhead factor for parallel DFS is at least one on the average is important, since DFS is currently the best known and most practical sequential algorithm used to solve many important problems.

11.7 Bibliographic Remarks

Extensive literature is available on search algorithms for discrete optimization techniques such as branch-and-bound and heuristic search [KK88a, LW66, Pea84]. The relationship between branch-and-bound search, dynamic programming, and heuristic search techniques in artificial intelligence is explored by Kumar and Kanal [KK83, KK88b]. The average time complexity of heuristic search algorithms for many problems is shown to be polynomial by Smith [Smi84] and Wilf [Wil86]. Extensive work has been done on parallel formulations of search algorithms. We briefly outline some of these contributions.

Parallel Depth-First Search Algorithms

Many parallel algorithms for DFS have been formulated [AJM88, FM87, KK94, KGR94, KR87b, MV87, Ran91, Rao90, SK90, SK89, Vor87a]. Load balancing is the central issue in parallel DFS. In this chapter, distribution of work in parallel DFS was done using stack splitting [KGR94, KR87b]. An alternative scheme for work-distribution is node splitting, in which only a single node is given out [FK88, FTI90, Ran91]

This chapter discussed formulations of state-space search in which a processor requests work when it goes idle. Such load-balancing schemes are called *receiver-initiated* schemes. In other load-balancing schemes, a processor that has work gives away part of its work to another processor (with or without receiving a request). These schemes are called *sender-initiated* schemes.

Several researchers have used receiver-initiated load-balancing schemes in parallel DFS [FM87, KR87b, KGR94]. Kumar *et al.* [KGR94] analyze these load-balancing schemes including global round robin, random polling, asynchronous round robin, and nearest neighbor. The description and analysis of these schemes in Section 11.4 is based on the papers by Kumar *et al.* [KGR94, KR87b].

Parallel DFS using sender-initiated load balancing has been proposed by some researchers [FK88, FTI90, PFK90, Ran91, SK89]. Furuichi *et al.* propose the single-level and multilevel sender-based schemes [FTI90]. Kimura and Nobuyuki [KN91] presented the scalability analysis of these schemes. Ferguson and Korf [FK88, PFK90] present a load-balancing scheme called *distributed tree search* (DTS).

Other techniques using randomized allocation have been presented for parallel DFS of state-space trees [KP92, Ran91, SK89, SK90]. Issues relating to granularity control in parallel DFS have also been explored [RK87, SK89].

Saletore and Kale [SK90] present a formulation of parallel DFS in which nodes are assigned priorities and are expanded accordingly. They show that the search overhead factor of this prioritized DFS formulation is very close to one, allowing it to yield consistently increasing speedups with an increasing number of processors for sufficiently large problems.

In some parallel formulations of depth-first search, the state space is searched independently in a random order by different processors [JAM87, JAM88]. Challou *et al.* [CGK93] and Ertel [Ert92] show that such methods are useful for solving robot motion planning and theorem proving problems, respectively.

Most generic DFS formulations apply to depth-first branch-and-bound and IDA*. Some researchers have specifically studied parallel formulations of depth-first branch-and-bound [AKR89, AKR90, EDH80]. Many parallel formulations of IDA* have been proposed [RK87, RKR87, KS91a, PKF92, MD92].

Most of the parallel DFS formulations are suited only for MIMD computers. Due to the nature of the search problem, SIMD computers were considered inherently unsuitable for parallel search. However, work by Frye and Myczkowski [FM92], Powley *et al.* [PKF92], and Mahanti and Daniels [MD92] showed that parallel depth-first search techniques can be developed even for SIMD computers. Karypis and Kumar [KK94] presented parallel DFS schemes for SIMD computers that are as scalable as the schemes for MIMD computers.

Several researchers have experimentally evaluated parallel DFS. Finkel and Manber [FM87] present performance results for problems such as the traveling salesman problem and the knight's tour for the Crystal multicomputer developed at the University of Wisconsin. Monien and Vornberger [MV87] show linear speedups on a network of transputers for a variety of combinatorial problems. Kumar *et al.* [AKR89, AKR90, AKRS91, KGR94] show linear speedups for problems such as the 15-puzzle, tautology verification, and automatic test pattern generation for various architectures such as a 128-processor BBN Butterfly, a 128-processor Intel iPSC, a 1024-processor nCUBE 2, and a 128-processor Symult 2010. Kumar, Grama, and Rao [GKR91, KGR94, KR87b, RK87] have investigated the scalability and performance of many of these schemes for hypercubes, meshes, and networks of workstations. Experimental results in Section 11.4.5 are taken from the paper by Kumar, Grama, and Rao [KGR94].

Parallel formulations of DFBB have also been investigated by several researchers. Many of these formulations are based on maintaining a current best solution, which is used as a global bound. It has been shown that the overhead for maintaining the current best solution tends to be a small fraction of the overhead for dynamic load balancing. Parallel formulations of DFBB have been shown to yield near linear speedups for many problems and architectures [ST95, LM97, Eck97, Eck94, AKR89].

Many researchers have proposed termination detection algorithms for use in parallel search. Dijkstra [DSG83] proposed the ring termination detection algorithm. The termination detection algorithm based on weights, discussed in Section 11.4.4, is similar to the one proposed by Rokusawa *et al.* [RICN88]. Dutt and Mahapatra [DM93] discuss the termination detection algorithm based on minimum spanning trees.

Parallel Formulations of Alpha-Beta Search

Alpha-beta search is essentially a depth-first branch-and-bound search technique that finds an optimal solution tree of an AND/OR graph [KK83, KK88b]. Many researchers have developed parallel formulations of alpha-beta search [ABJ82, Bau78, FK88, FF82, HB88, Lin83, MC82, MFMV90, MP85, PFK90]. Some of these methods have shown reasonable speedups on dozens of processors [FK88, MFMV90, PFK90].

The utility of parallel processing has been demonstrated in the context of a number of games, and in particular, chess. Work on large scale parallel $\alpha - \beta$ search led to the development of Deep Thought [Hsu90] in 1990. This program was capable of playing chess at grandmaster level. Subsequent advances in the use of dedicated hardware, parallel processing, and algorithms resulted in the development of IBM's Deep Blue [HCH95, HG97] that beat the reigning world champion Gary Kasparov. Feldmann *et al.* [FMM94] developed a distributed chess program that is acknowledged to be one of the best computer chess players based entirely on general purpose hardware.

Parallel Best-First Search

Many researchers have investigated parallel formulations of A* and branch-and-bound algorithms [KK84, KRR88, LK85, MV87, Qui89, HD89a, Vor86, WM84, Rao90, GKP92, AM88, CJP83, KB57, LP92, Rou87, PC89, PR89, PR90, PRV88, Ten90, MRSR92, Vor87b, Moh83, MV85, HD87]. All these formulations use different data structures to store the *open* list. Some formulations use the centralized strategy [Moh83, HD87]; some use distributed strategies such as the random communication strategy [Vor87b, Dal87, KRR88], the ring communication strategy [Vor86, WM84]; and the blackboard communication strategy [KRR88]. Kumar *et al.* [KRR88] experimentally evaluated the centralized strategy and some distributed strategies in the context of the traveling salesman problem, the vertex cover problem and the 15-puzzle. Dutt and Mahapatra [DM93, MD93] have proposed and evaluated a number of other communication strategies.

Manzini analyzed the hashing technique for distributing nodes in parallel graph search [MS90]. Evett *et al.* [EHMN90] proposed parallel retracting A* (PRA*), which operates under limited-memory conditions. In this formulation, each node is hashed to a unique processor. If a processor receives more nodes than it can store locally, it retracts nodes with poorer heuristic values. These retracted nodes are reexpanded when more promising nodes fail to yield a solution.

Karp and Zhang [KZ88] analyze the performance of parallel best-first branch-and-bound (that is, A*) by using a random distribution of nodes for a specific model of search trees. Renolet *et al.* [RDK89] use Monte Carlo simulations to model the performance of parallel best-first search. Wah and Yu [WY85] present stochastic models to analyze the performance of parallel formulations of depth-first branch-and-bound and best-first branch-and-bound search.

Bixby [Bix91] presents a parallel branch-and-cut algorithm to solve the symmetric traveling salesman problem. He also presents solutions of the LP relaxations of airline crew-scheduling models. Miller *et al.* [Mil91] present parallel formulations of the best-first branch-and-bound technique for solving the asymmetric traveling salesman problem on heterogeneous network computer architectures. Roucairol [Rou91] presents parallel best-first branch-and-bound formulations for shared-address-space computers and uses them to solve the multiknapsack and quadratic-assignment problems.

Speedup Anomalies in Parallel Formulations of Search Algorithms

Many researchers have analyzed speedup anomalies in parallel search algorithms [IYF79, LS84, Kor81, LW86, MVS86, RKR87]. Lai and Sahni [LS84] present early work quantifying speedup anomalies in best-first search. Lai and Sprague [LS86] present enhancements and extensions to this work. Lai and Sprague [LS85] also present an analytical model and derive characteristics of the lower-bound function for which anomalies are guaranteed not to occur as the number of processors is increased. Li and Wah [LW84, LW86] and Wah *et al.* [WLY84] investigate dominance relations and heuristic functions and their effect on detrimental (speedup of < 1 using p processors) and acceleration anomalies. Quinn and Deo [QD86] derive an upper bound on the speedup attainable by any parallel formulation of the branch-and-bound algorithm using the best-bound search strategy. Rao and Kumar [RK88b, RK93] analyze the average speedup in parallel DFS for two separate models with and without heuristic ordering information. They show that the search overhead factor in these cases is at most one. Section 11.6.1 is based on the results of Rao and Kumar [RK93].

Finally, many programming environments have been developed for implementing parallel search. Some examples are DIB [FM87], Chare-Kernel [SK89], MANIP [WM84], and PICOS [RDK89].

Role of Heuristics

Heuristics form the most important component of search techniques, and parallel formulations of search algorithms must be viewed in the context of these heuristics. In BFS techniques, heuristics focus search by lowering the effective branching factor. In DFBB methods, heuristics provide better bounds, and thus serve to prune the search space.

Often, there is a tradeoff between the strength of the heuristic and the effective size of search space. Better heuristics result in smaller search spaces but are also more expensive to compute. For example, an important application of strong heuristics is in the computation of bounds for mixed integer programming (MIP). Mixed integer programming has seen significant advances over the years [JNS97]. Whereas 15 years back, MIP problems with 100 integer variables were considered challenging, today, many problems with up to 1000 integer variables can be solved on workstation class machines using branch-and-cut methods. The largest known instances of TSPs and QAPs have been solved using branch-and-bound with powerful heuristics [BMCP98, MP93]. The presence of effective heuristics may prune the search space considerably. For example, when Padberg and Rinaldi introduced the branch-and-cut algorithm in 1987, they used it to solve a 532 city

TSP, which was the largest TSP solved optimally at that time. Subsequent improvements to the method led to the solution of a a 2392 city problem [PR91]. More recently, using cutting planes, problems with over 7000 cities have been solved [JNS97] on serial machines. However, for many problems of interest, the reduced search space still requires the use of parallelism [BMCP98, MP93, Rou87, MMR95]. Use of powerful heuristics combined with effective parallel processing has enabled the solution of extremely large problems [MP93]. For example, QAP problems from the Nugent and Eschermann test suites with up to 4.8×10^{10} nodes (Nugent22 with Gilmore-Lawler bound) were solved on a NEC Cenju-3 parallel computer in under nine days [BMCP98]. Another dazzling demonstration of this was presented by the IBM Deep Blue. Deep blue used a combination of dedicated hardware for generating and evaluating board positions and parallel search of the game tree using an IBM SP2 to beat the current world chess champion, Gary Kasparov [HCH95, HG97].

Heuristics have several important implications for exploiting parallelism. Strong heuristics narrow the state space and thus reduce the concurrency available in the search space. Use of powerful heuristics poses other computational challenges for parallel processing as well. For example, in branch-and-cut methods, a cut generated at a certain state may be required by other states. Therefore, in addition to balancing load, the parallel branch-and-cut formulation must also partition cuts among processors so that processors working in certain LP domains have access to the desired cuts [BCCL95, LM97, Eck97].

In addition to inter-node parallelism that has been discussed up to this point, intra-node parallelism can become a viable option if the heuristic is computationally expensive. For example, the assignment heuristic of Pekny *et al.* has been effectively parallelized for solving large instances of TSPs [MP93]. If the degree of inter-node parallelism is small, this form of parallelism provides a desirable alternative. Another example of this is in the solution of MIP problems using branch-and-cut methods. Branch-and-cut methods rely on LP relaxation for generating lower bounds of partially instantiated solutions followed by generation of valid inequalities [JNS97]. These LP relaxations constitute a major part of the overall computation time. Many of the industrial codes rely on Simplex to solve the LP problem since it can adapt the solution to added rows and columns. While interior point methods are better suited to parallelism, they tend to be less efficient for reoptimizing LP solutions with added rows and columns (in branch-and-cut methods). LP relaxation using Simplex has been shown to parallelize well on small numbers of processors but efforts to scale to larger numbers of processors have not been successful. LP based branch and bound methods have also been used for solving quadratic assignment problems using iterative solvers such as preconditioned Conjugate Gradient to approximately compute the interior point directions [PLRR94]. These methods have been used to compute lower bounds using linear programs with over 150,000 constraints and 300,000 variables for solving QAPs. These and other iterative solvers parallelize very effectively to a large number of processors. A general parallel framework for computing heuristic solutions to problems is presented by Pramanick and Kuhl [PK95].

Problems

11.1 **[KGR94]** In Section 11.4.1, we identified access to the global pointer, *target*, as a bottleneck in the GRR load-balancing scheme. Consider a modification of this scheme in which it is augmented with message combining. This scheme works as follows. All the requests to read the value of the global pointer *target* at processor zero are combined at intermediate processors. Thus, the total number of requests handled by processor zero is greatly reduced. This technique is essentially a software implementation of the fetch-and-add operation. This scheme is called GRR-M (GRR with message combining).

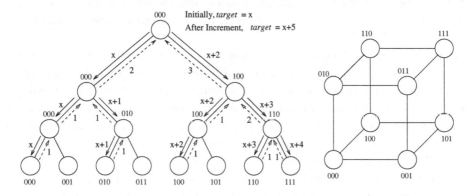

Figure 11.19 Message combining and a sample implementation on an eight-processor hypercube.

An implementation of this scheme is illustrated in Figure 11.19. Each processor is at a leaf node in a complete (logical) binary tree. Note that such a logical tree can be easily mapped on to a physical topology. When a processor wants to atomically read and increment *target*, it sends a request up the tree toward processor zero. An internal node of the tree holds a request from one of its children for at most time δ, then forwards the message to its parent. If a request comes from the node's other child within time δ, the two requests are combined and sent up as a single request. If i is the total number of increment requests that have been combined, the resulting increment of *target* is i.

The returned value at each processor is equal to what it would have been if all the requests to *target* had been serialized. This is done as follows: each combined message is stored in a table at each processor until the request is granted. When the value of *target* is sent back to an internal node, two values are sent down to the left and right children if both requested a value of *target*. The two values are determined from the entries in the table corresponding to increment requests by the two children. The scheme is illustrated by Figure 11.19, in which the original value of *target* is x, and processors P_0, P_2, P_4, P_6 and P_7 issue requests. The total requested increment is five. After the messages are combined and processed, the value of *target* received at these processors is $x, x + 1, x + 2, x + 3$ and $x + 4$, respectively.

Analyze the performance and scalability of this scheme for a message passing architecture.

11.2 **[Lin92]** Consider another load-balancing strategy. Assume that each processor maintains a variable called *counter*. Initially, each processor initializes its local copy of *counter* to zero. Whenever a processor goes idle, it searches for two processors P_i and P_{i+1} in a logical ring embedded into any architecture, such that the value of *counter* at P_i is greater than that at P_{i+1}. The idle processor then sends a work request to processor P_{i+1}. If no such pair of processors exists, the request is sent to processor zero. On receiving a work request, a processor increments its local value of *counter*.

Devise algorithms to detect the pairs P_i and P_{i+1}. Analyze the scalability of this load-balancing scheme based on your algorithm to detect the pairs P_i and P_{i+1} for a message passing architecture.

Hint: The upper bound on the number of work transfers for this scheme is similar to that for GRR.

11.3 In the analysis of various load-balancing schemes presented in Section 11 4 2, we assumed that the cost of transferring work is independent of the amount of work transferred. However, there are problems for which the work-transfer cost is a function of the amount of work transferred. Examples of such problems are found in tree-search applications for domains in which strong heuristics are available. For such applications, the size of the stack used to represent the search tree can vary significantly with the number of nodes in the search tree.

Consider a case in which the size of the stack for representing a search space of w nodes varies as $\sqrt{w}$. Assume that the load-balancing scheme used is GRR. Analyze the performance of this scheme for a message passing architecture.

11.4 Consider Dijkstra's token termination detection scheme described in Section 11.4.4. Show that the contribution of termination detection using this scheme to the overall isoefficiency function is $O(p^2)$. Comment on the value of the constants associated with this isoefficiency term.

11.5 Consider the tree-based termination detection scheme in Section 11.4.4. In this algorithm, the weights may become very small and may eventually become zero due to the finite precision of computers. In such cases, termination is never signaled. The algorithm can be modified by manipulating the reciprocal of the weight instead of the weight itself. Write the modified termination algorithm and show that it is capable of detecting termination correctly.

11.6 **[DM93]** Consider a termination detection algorithm in which a spanning tree of minimum diameter is mapped onto the architecture of the given parallel computer. The **center** of such a tree is a vertex with the minimum distance to the vertex farthest from it. The center of a spanning tree is considered to be its root.

While executing parallel search, a processor can be either *idle* or *busy*. The termination detection algorithm requires all work transfers in the system to be acknowledged by an *ack* message. A processor is busy if it has work, or if it has sent work to another processor and the corresponding *ack* message has not been received; otherwise the processor is idle. Processors at the leaves of the spanning tree send *stop* messages to their parent when they become idle. Processors at intermediate levels in the tree pass the *stop* message on to their parents when they have received *stop* messages from all their children and they themselves become idle. When the root processor receives *stop* messages from all its children and becomes idle, termination is signaled.

Since it is possible for a processor to receive work after it has sent a *stop* message to its parent, a processor signals that it has received work by sending a *resume* message to its parent. The *resume* message moves up the tree until it meets the previously issued *stop* message. On meeting the *stop* message, the *resume* message nullifies the *stop* message. An *ack* message is then sent to the processor that transferred part of its work.

Show using examples that this termination detection technique correctly signals termination. Determine the isoefficiency term due to this termination detection scheme for a spanning tree of depth log p.

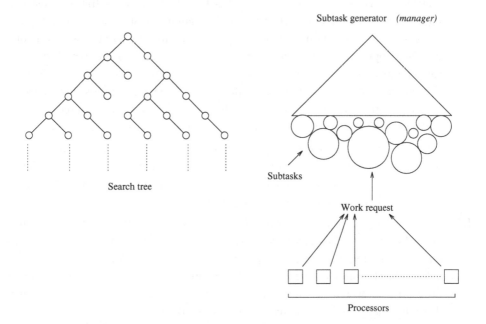

Figure 11.20   The single-level work-distribution scheme for tree search.

11.7   **[FTI90, KN91]** Consider the single-level load-balancing scheme which works as follows: a designated processor called *manager* generates many subtasks and gives them one-by-one to the requesting processors on demand. The *manager* traverses the search tree depth-first to a predetermined cutoff depth and distributes nodes at that depth as subtasks. Increasing the cutoff depth increases the number of subtasks, but makes them smaller. The processors request another subtask from the manager only after finishing the previous one. Hence, if a processor gets subtasks corresponding to large subtrees, it will send fewer requests to the *manager*. If the cutoff depth is large enough, this scheme results in good load balance among the processors. However, if the cutoff depth is too large, the subtasks given out to the processors become small and the processors send more frequent requests to the *manager*. In this case, the *manager* becomes a bottleneck. Hence, this scheme has a poor scalability. Figure 11.20 illustrates the single-level work-distribution scheme.

Assume that the cost of communicating a piece of work between any two processors is negligible. Derive analytical expressions for the scalability of the single-level load-balancing scheme.

11.8 **[FTI90, KN91]** Consider the multilevel work-distribution scheme that circumvents the subtask generation bottleneck of the single-level scheme through multiple-level subtask generation. In this scheme, processors are arranged in an m-ary tree of depth d. The task of top-level subtask generation is given to the root processor. It divides the task into super-subtasks and distributes them to its successor processors on demand. These processors subdivide the super-subtasks into subtasks and distribute them to successor processors on request. The leaf processors repeatedly request work from their parents as soon as they have finished their previous work. A leaf processor is allocated to another subtask generator when its designated subtask generator runs out of work. For $d = 1$, the multi- and single-level schemes are identical. Comment on the performance and scalability of this scheme.

11.9 **[FK88]** Consider the ***distributed tree search*** scheme in which processors are allocated to separate parts of the search tree dynamically. Initially, all the processors are assigned to the root. When the root node is expanded (by one of the processors assigned to it), disjoint subsets of processors at the root are assigned to each successor, in accordance with a selected processor-allocation strategy. One possible processor-allocation strategy is to divide the processors equally among ancestor nodes. This process continues until there is only one processor assigned to a node. At this time, the processor searches the tree rooted at the node sequentially. If a processor finishes searching the search tree rooted at the node, it is reassigned to its parent node. If the parent node has other successor nodes still being explored, then this processor is allocated to one of them. Otherwise, the processor is assigned to its parent. This process continues until the entire tree is searched. Comment on the performance and scalability of this scheme.

11.10 Consider a parallel formulation of best-first search of a graph that uses a hash function to distribute nodes to processors (Section 11.5). The performance of this scheme is influenced by two factors: the communication cost and the number of "good" nodes expanded (a "good" node is one that would also be expanded by the sequential algorithm). These two factors can be analyzed independently of each other.

Assuming a completely random hash function (one in which each node has a probability of being hashed to a processor equal to $1/p$), show that the expected number of nodes expanded by this parallel formulation differs from the optimal number by a constant factor (that is, independent of p). Assuming that the cost of communicating a node from one processor to another is $O(1)$, derive the isoefficiency function of this scheme.

11.11 For the parallel formulation in Problem 11.10, assume that the number of nodes expanded by the sequential and parallel formulations are the same. Analyze the communication overhead of this formulation for a message passing architecture. Is the formulation scalable? If so, what is the isoefficiency function? If not, for what interconnection network would the formulation be scalable?

Hint: Note that a fully random hash function corresponds to an all-to-all personalized communication operation, which is bandwidth sensitive.

CHAPTER 12

Dynamic Programming

Dynamic programming (DP) is a commonly used technique for solving a wide variety of discrete optimization problems such as scheduling, string-editing, packaging, and inventory management. More recently, it has found applications in bioinformatics in matching sequences of amino-acids and nucleotides (the Smith-Waterman algorithm). DP views a problem as a set of interdependent subproblems. It solves subproblems and uses the results to solve larger subproblems until the entire problem is solved. In contrast to divide-and-conquer, where the solution to a problem depends only on the solution to its subproblems, in DP there may be interrelationships across subproblems. In DP, the solution to a subproblem is expressed as a function of solutions to one or more subproblems at the preceding levels.

12.1 Overview of Dynamic Programming

We start our discussion with a simple DP algorithm for computing shortest paths in a graph.

Example 12.1 The shortest-path problem
Consider a DP formulation for the problem of finding a shortest (least-cost) path between a pair of vertices in an acyclic graph. (Refer to Section 10.1 for an introduction to graph terminology.) An edge connecting node i to node j has cost $c(i, j)$. If two vertices i and j are not connected then $c(i, j) = \infty$. The graph contains n nodes numbered $0, 1, \ldots, n - 1$, and has an edge from node i to node j only if $i < j$. The shortest-path problem is to find a least-cost path between nodes 0 and $n - 1$. Let $f(x)$ denote the cost of the least-cost path from node 0 to node x. Thus, $f(0)$ is zero, and finding $f(n - 1)$ solves the problem. The DP formulation for this problem yields the following recursive equations for $f(x)$:

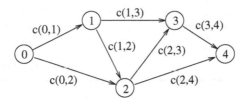

Figure 12.1 A graph for which the shortest path between nodes 0 and 4 is to be computed.

$$f(x) = \begin{cases} 0 & x = 0 \\ \min_{0 \le j < x} \{f(j) + c(j, x)\} & 1 \le x \le n - 1 \end{cases} \quad (12.1)$$

As an instance of this algorithm, consider the five-node acyclic graph shown in Figure 12.1. The problem is to find $f(4)$. It can be computed given $f(3)$ and $f(2)$. More precisely,

$$f(4) = \min\{f(3) + c(3, 4), f(2) + c(2, 4)\}.$$

Therefore, $f(2)$ and $f(3)$ are elements of the set of subproblems on which $f(4)$ depends. Similarly, $f(3)$ depends on $f(1)$ and $f(2)$, and $f(1)$ and $f(2)$ depend on $f(0)$. Since $f(0)$ is known, it is used to solve $f(1)$ and $f(2)$, which are used to solve $f(3)$. ∎

In general, the solution to a DP problem is expressed as a minimum (or maximum) of possible alternate solutions. Each of these alternate solutions is constructed by composing one or more subproblems. If r represents the cost of a solution composed of subproblems $x_1, x_2, \ldots, x_l$, then r can be written as

$$r = g(f(x_1), f(x_2), \ldots, f(x_l)).$$

The function g is called the ***composition function***, and its nature depends on the problem. If the optimal solution to each problem is determined by composing optimal solutions to the subproblems and selecting the minimum (or maximum), the formulation is said to be a DP formulation. Figure 12.2 illustrates an instance of composition and minimization of solutions. The solution to problem x_8 is the minimum of the three possible solutions having costs r_1, r_2, and r_3. The cost of the first solution is determined by composing solutions to subproblems x_1 and x_3, the second solution by composing solutions to subproblems x_4 and x_5, and the third solution by composing solutions to subproblems x_2, x_6, and x_7.

DP represents the solution to an optimization problem as a recursive equation whose left side is an unknown quantity and whose right side is a minimization (or maximization) expression. Such an equation is called a ***functional equation*** or an ***optimization equation***. In Equation 12.1, the composition function g is given by $f(j) + c(j, x)$. This function

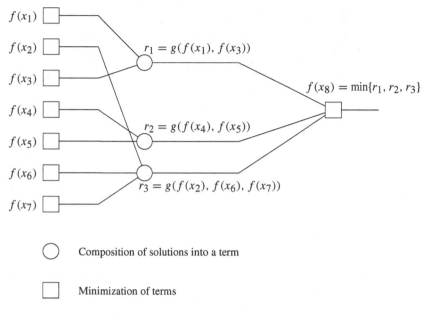

Figure 12.2   The computation and composition of subproblem solutions to solve problem $f(x_8)$

is additive, since it is the sum of two terms. In a general DP formulation, the cost function need not be additive. A functional equation that contains a single recursive term (for example, $f(j)$) yields a *monadic* DP formulation. For an arbitrary DP formulation, the cost function may contain multiple recursive terms. DP formulations whose cost function contains multiple recursive terms are called *polyadic* formulations.

The dependencies between subproblems in a DP formulation can be represented by a directed graph. Each node in the graph represents a subproblem. A directed edge from node i to node j indicates that the solution to the subproblem represented by node i is used to compute the solution to the subproblem represented by node j. If the graph is acyclic, then the nodes of the graph can be organized into levels such that subproblems at a particular level depend only on subproblems at previous levels. In this case, the DP formulation can be categorized as follows. If subproblems at all levels depend only on the results at the immediately preceding levels, the formulation is called a *serial* DP formulation; otherwise, it is called a *nonserial* DP formulation.

Based on the preceding classification criteria, we define four classes of DP formulations: *serial monadic*, *serial polyadic*, *nonserial monadic*, and *nonserial polyadic*. These classes, however, are not exhaustive; some DP formulations cannot be classified into any of these categories.

Due to the wide variety of problems solved using DP, it is difficult to develop generic parallel algorithms for them. However, parallel formulations of the problems in each of the four DP categories have certain similarities. In this chapter, we discuss parallel DP formulations for sample problems in each class. These samples suggest parallel algorithms

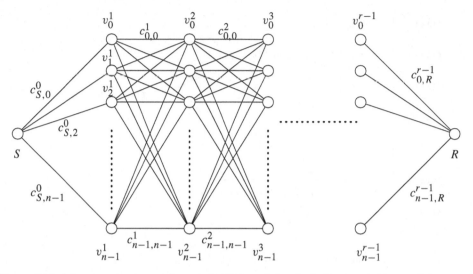

Figure 12.3   An example of a serial monadic DP formulation for finding the shortest path in a graph whose nodes can be organized into levels.

for other problems in the same class. Note, however, that not all DP problems can be parallelized as illustrated in these examples.

12.2   Serial Monadic DP Formulations

We can solve many problems by using serial monadic DP formulations. This section discusses the shortest-path problem for a multistage graph and the 0/1 knapsack problem. We present parallel algorithms for both and point out the specific properties that influence these parallel formulations.

12.2.1   The Shortest-Path Problem

Consider a weighted multistage graph of $r + 1$ levels, as shown in Figure 12.3. Each node at level i is connected to every node at level $i + 1$. Levels zero and r contain only one node, and every other level contains n nodes. We refer to the node at level zero as the starting node S and the node at level r as the terminating node R. The objective of this problem is to find the shortest path from S to R. The ith node at level l in the graph is labeled v_i^l. The cost of an edge connecting v_i^l to node v_j^{l+1} is labeled $c_{i,j}^l$. The cost of reaching the goal node R from any node v_i^l is represented by C_i^l. If there are n nodes at level l, the vector $[C_0^l, C_1^l, \ldots, C_{n-1}^l]^T$ is referred to as C^l. The shortest-path problem reduces to computing C^0. Since the graph has only one starting node, $C^0 = [C_0^0]$. The structure of the graph is such that any path from v_i^l to R includes a node v_j^{l+1} ($0 \leq j \leq n - 1$). The cost of any such path is the sum of the cost of the edge between v_i^l and v_j^{l+1} and the cost of the shortest path between v_j^{l+1} and R (which is given by C_j^{l+1}). Thus, C_i^l, the cost of the shortest path between v_i^l and R, is equal to the minimum cost over all paths through each node in level $l + 1$. Therefore,

$$C_i^l = \min \left\{ (c_{i,j}^l + C_j^{l+1}) | j \text{ is a node at level } l + 1 \right\}. \tag{12.2}$$

Since all nodes v_j^{r-1} have only one edge connecting them to the goal node R at level r, the cost C_j^{r-1} is equal to $c_{j,R}^{r-1}$. Hence,

$$C^{r-1} = [c_{0,R}^{r-1}, c_{1,R}^{r-1}, \ldots, c_{n-1,R}^{r-1}]. \tag{12.3}$$

Because Equation 12.2 contains only one recursive term in its right-hand side, it is a monadic formulation. Note that the solution to a subproblem requires solutions to subproblems only at the immediately preceding level. Consequently, this is a serial monadic formulation.

Using this recursive formulation of the shortest-path problem, the cost of reaching the goal node R from any node at level l $(0 < l < r - 1)$ is

$$
\begin{aligned}
C_0^l &= \min\{(c_{0,0}^l + C_0^{l+1}), (c_{0,1}^l + C_1^{l+1}), \ldots, (c_{0,n-1}^l + C_{n-1}^{l+1})\}, \\
C_1^l &= \min\{(c_{1,0}^l + C_0^{l+1}), (c_{1,1}^l + C_1^{l+1}), \ldots, (c_{1,n-1}^l + C_{n-1}^{l+1})\}, \\
&\vdots \\
C_{n-1}^l &= \min\{(c_{n-1,0}^l + C_0^{l+1}), (c_{n-1,1}^l + C_1^{l+1}), \ldots, (c_{n-1,n-1}^l + C_{n-1}^{l+1})\}.
\end{aligned}
$$

Now consider the operation of multiplying a matrix with a vector. In the matrix-vector product, if the addition operation is replaced by minimization and the multiplication operation is replaced by addition, the preceding set of equations is equivalent to

$$C^l = M_{l,l+1} \times C^{l+1}, \tag{12.4}$$

where C^l and C^{l+1} are $n \times 1$ vectors representing the cost of reaching the goal node from each node at levels l and $l + 1$, and $M_{l,l+1}$ is an $n \times n$ matrix in which entry (i, j) stores the cost of the edge connecting node i at level l to node j at level $l + 1$. This matrix is

$$
M_{l,l+1} = \begin{bmatrix}
c_{0,0}^l & c_{0,1}^l & \cdots & c_{0,n-1}^l \\
c_{1,0}^l & c_{1,1}^l & \cdots & c_{1,n-1}^l \\
\vdots & \vdots & & \vdots \\
c_{n-1,0}^l & c_{n-1,1}^l & \cdots & c_{n-1,n-1}^l
\end{bmatrix}.
$$

The shortest-path problem has thus been reformulated as a sequence of matrix-vector multiplications. On a sequential computer, the DP formulation starts by computing C^{r-1}

from Equation 12.3, and then computes C^{r-k-1} for $k = 1, 2, \ldots, r-2$ using Equation 12.4. Finally, C^0 is computed using Equation 12.2.

Since there are n nodes at each level, the cost of computing each vector C^l is $\Theta(n^2)$. The parallel algorithm for this problem can be derived using the parallel algorithms for the matrix-vector product discussed in Section 8.1. For example, $\Theta(n)$ processing elements can compute each vector C^l in time $\Theta(n)$ and solve the entire problem in time $\Theta(rn)$. Recall that r is the number of levels in the graph.

Many serial monadic DP formulations with dependency graphs identical to the one considered here can be parallelized using a similar parallel algorithm. For certain dependency graphs, however, this formulation is unsuitable. Consider a graph in which each node at a level can be reached from only a small fraction of nodes at the previous level. Then matrix $M_{l,l+1}$ contains many elements with value ∞. In this case, matrix M is considered to be a sparse matrix for the minimization and addition operations. This is because, for all x, $x + \infty = \infty$, and $\min\{x, \infty\} = x$. Therefore, the addition and minimization operations need not be performed for entries whose value is ∞. If we use a regular dense matrix-vector multiplication algorithm, the computational complexity of each matrix-vector multiplication becomes significantly higher than that of the corresponding sparse matrix-vector multiplication. Consequently, we must use a sparse matrix-vector multiplication algorithm to compute each vector.

12.2.2 The 0/1 Knapsack Problem

A one-dimensional 0/1 knapsack problem is defined as follows. We are given a knapsack of capacity c and a set of n objects numbered $1, 2, \ldots, n$. Each object i has weight w_i and profit p_i. Object profits and weights are integers. Let $v = [v_1, v_2, \ldots, v_n]$ be a solution vector in which $v_i = 0$ if object i is not in the knapsack, and $v_i = 1$ if it is in the knapsack. The goal is to find a subset of objects to put into the knapsack so that

$$\sum_{i=1}^{n} w_i v_i \leq c$$

(that is, the objects fit into the knapsack) and

$$\sum_{i=1}^{n} p_i v_i$$

is maximized (that is, the profit is maximized).

A straightforward method to solve this problem is to consider all 2^n possible subsets of the n objects and choose the one that fits into the knapsack and maximizes the profit. Here we provide a DP formulation that is faster than the simple method when $c = O(2^n/n)$. Let $F[i, x]$ be the maximum profit for a knapsack of capacity x using only objects $\{1, 2, \ldots, i\}$. Then $F[n, c]$ is the solution to the problem. The DP formulation for this problem is as follows:

$$F[i, x] = \begin{cases} 0 & x \geq 0, i = 0 \\ -\infty & x < 0, i = 0 \\ \max\{F[i-1, x], (F[i-1, x-w_i] + p_i)\} & 1 \leq i \leq n \end{cases}$$

This recursive equation yields a knapsack of maximum profit. When the current capacity of the knapsack is x, the decision to include object i can lead to one of two situations: (i) the object is not included, knapsack capacity remains x, and profit is unchanged; (ii) the object is included, knapsack capacity becomes $x - w_i$, and profit increases by p_i. The DP algorithm decides whether or not to include an object based on which choice leads to maximum profit.

The sequential algorithm for this DP formulation maintains a table F of size $n \times c$. The table is constructed in row-major order. The algorithm first determines the maximum profit by using only the first object with knapsacks of different capacities. This corresponds to filling the first row of the table. Filling entries in subsequent rows requires two entries from the previous row: one from the same column and one from the column offset by the weight of the object. Thus, the computation of an arbitrary entry $F[i, j]$ requires $F[i-1, j]$ and $F[i-1, j-w_i]$. This is illustrated in Figure 12.4. Computing each entry takes constant time; the sequential run time of this algorithm is $\Theta(nc)$.

This formulation is a serial monadic formulation. The subproblems $F[i, x]$ are organized into n levels for $i = 1, 2, \ldots, n$. Computation of problems in level i depends only on the subproblems at level $i - 1$. Hence the formulation is serial. The formulation is monadic because each of the two alternate solutions of $F[i, x]$ depends on only one subproblem. Furthermore, dependencies between levels are sparse because a problem at one level depends only on two subproblems from previous level.

Consider a parallel formulation of this algorithm on a CREW PRAM with c processing elements labeled P_0 to P_{c-1}. Processing element P_{r-1} computes the rth column of matrix F. When computing $F[j, r]$ during iteration j, processing element P_{r-1} requires the values $F[j-1, r]$ and $F[j-1, r-w_j]$. Processing element P_{r-1} can read any element of matrix F in constant time, so computing $F[j, r]$ also requires constant time. Therefore, each iteration takes constant time. Since there are n iterations, the parallel run time is $\Theta(n)$. The formulation uses c processing elements, hence its processor-time product is $\Theta(nc)$. Therefore, the algorithm is cost-optimal.

Let us now consider its formulation on a distributed memory machine with c-processing elements. Table F is distributed among the processing elements so that each processing element is responsible for one column. This is illustrated in Figure 12.4. Each processing element locally stores the weights and profits of all objects. In the jth iteration, for computing $F[j, r]$ at processing element P_{r-1}, $F[j-1, r]$ is available locally but $F[j-1, r-w_j]$ must be fetched from another processing element. This corresponds to the circular w_j-shift operation described in Section 4.6. The time taken by this circular shift operation on p processing elements is bounded by $(t_s + t_w m) \log p$ for a message of size m on a network with adequate bandwidth. Since the size of the message is one word and we have $p = c$, this

Table F

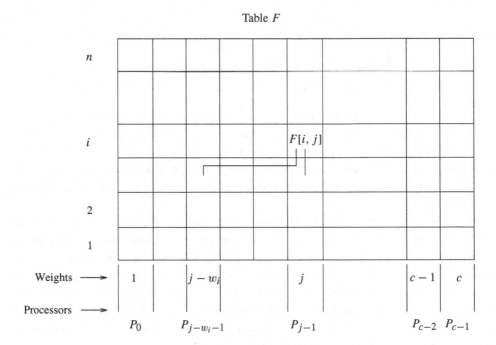

Figure 12.4 Computing entries of table F for the 0/1 knapsack problem. The computation of entry $F[i, j]$ requires communication with processing elements containing entries $F[i - 1, j]$ and $F[i - 1, j - w_i]$.

time is given by $(t_s + t_w) \log c$. If the sum and maximization operations take time t_c, then each iteration takes time $t_c + (t_s + t_w) \log c$. Since there are n such iterations, the total time is given by $O(n \log c)$. The processor-time product for this formulation is $O(nc \log c)$; therefore, the algorithm is not cost-optimal.

Let us see what happens to this formulation as we increase the number of elements per processor. Using p-processing elements, each processing element computes c/p elements of the table in each iteration. In the jth iteration, processing element P_0 computes the values of elements $F[j, 1], \ldots, F[j, c/p]$, processing element P_1 computes values of elements $F[j, c/p + 1], \ldots, F[j, 2c/p]$, and so on. Computing the value of $F[j, k]$, for any k, requires values $F[j - 1, k]$ and $F[j - 1, k - w_j]$. Required values of the F table can be fetched from remote processing elements by performing a circular shift. Depending on the values of w_j and p, the required nonlocal values may be available from one or two processing elements. Note that the total number of words communicated via these messages is c/p irrespective of whether they come from one or two processing elements. The time for this operation is at most $(2t_s + t_w c/p)$ assuming that c/p is large and the network has enough bandwidth (Section 4.6). Since each processing element computes c/p such elements, the total time for each iteration is $t_c c/p + 2t_s + t_w c/p$. Therefore, the parallel run time of the algorithm for n iterations is $n(t_c c/p + 2t_s + t_w c/p)$. In asymptotic terms, this algorithm's parallel run time is $O(nc/p)$. Its processor-time product is $O(nc)$, which is cost-optimal.

There is an upper bound on the efficiency of this formulation because the amount of data that needs to be communicated is of the same order as the amount of computation. This upper bound is determined by the values of t_w and t_c (Problem 12.1).

12.3 Nonserial Monadic DP Formulations

The DP algorithm for determining the longest common subsequence of two given sequences can be formulated as a nonserial monadic DP formulation.

12.3.1 The Longest-Common-Subsequence Problem

Given a sequence $A = \langle a_1, a_2, \ldots, a_n \rangle$, a subsequence of A can be formed by deleting some entries from A. For example, $\langle a, b, z \rangle$ is a subsequence of $\langle c, a, d, b, r, z \rangle$, but $\langle a, c, z \rangle$ and $\langle a, d, l \rangle$ are not. The **longest-common-subsequence** (LCS) problem can be stated as follows. Given two sequences $A = \langle a_1, a_2, \ldots, a_n \rangle$ and $B = \langle b_1, b_2, \ldots, b_m \rangle$, find the longest sequence that is a subsequence of both A and B. For example, if $A = \langle c, a, d, b, r, z \rangle$ and $B = \langle a, s, b, z \rangle$, the longest common subsequence of A and B is $\langle a, b, z \rangle$.

Let $F[i, j]$ denote the length of the longest common subsequence of the first i elements of A and the first j elements of B. The objective of the LCS problem is to determine $F[n, m]$. The DP formulation for this problem expresses $F[i, j]$ in terms of $F[i - 1, j - 1]$, $F[i, j - 1]$, and $F[i - 1, j]$ as follows:

$$F[i, j] = \begin{cases} 0 & \text{if } i = 0 \text{ or } j = 0 \\ F[i - 1, j - 1] + 1 & \text{if } i, j > 0 \text{ and } x_i = y_j \\ \max \{F[i, j - 1], F[i - 1, j]\} & \text{if } i, j > 0 \text{ and } x_i \neq y_j \end{cases}$$

Given sequences A and B, consider two pointers pointing to the start of the sequences. If the entries pointed to by the two pointers are identical, then they form components of the longest common subsequence. Therefore, both pointers can be advanced to the next entry of the respective sequences and the length of the longest common subsequence can be incremented by one. If the entries are not identical then two situations arise: the longest common subsequence may be obtained from the longest subsequence of A and the sequence obtained by advancing the pointer to the next entry of B; or the longest subsequence may be obtained from the longest subsequence of B and the sequence obtained by advancing the pointer to the next entry of A. Since we want to determine the longest subsequence, the maximum of these two must be selected.

The sequential implementation of this DP formulation computes the values in table F in row-major order. Since there is a constant amount of computation at each entry in the table, the overall complexity of this algorithm is $\Theta(nm)$. This DP formulation is nonserial

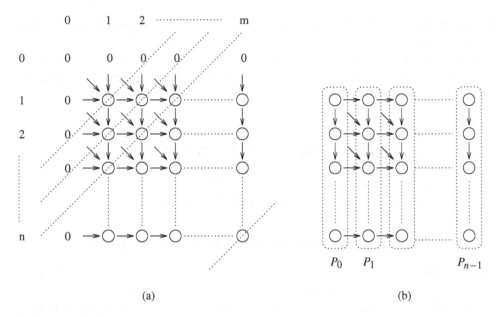

Figure 12.5   (a) Computing entries of table F for the longest-common-subsequence problem. Computation proceeds along the dotted diagonal lines. (b) Mapping elements of the table to processing elements.

monadic, as illustrated in Figure 12.5(a). Treating nodes along a diagonal as belonging to one level, each node depends on two subproblems at the preceding level and one subproblem two levels earlier. The formulation is monadic because a solution to any subproblem at a level is a function of only one of the solutions at preceding levels. (Note that, for the third case in Equation 12.5, both $F[i, j - 1]$ and $F[i - 1, j]$ are possible solutions to $F[i, j]$, and the optimal solution to $F[i, j]$ is the maximum of the two.) Figure 12.5 shows that this problem has a very regular structure.

Example 12.2   Computing LCS of two amino-acid sequences
Let us consider the LCS of two amino-acid sequences H E A G A W G H E E and P A W H E A E. For the interested reader, the names of the corresponding amino-acids are A: Alanine, E: Glutamic acid, G: Glycine, H: Histidine, P: Proline, and W: Tryptophan. The table of F entries for these two sequences is shown in Figure 12.6. The LCS of the two sequences, as determined by tracing back from the maximum score and enumerating all the matches, is A W H E E.
∎

To simplify the discussion, we discuss parallel formulation only for the case in which $n = m$. Consider a parallel formulation of this algorithm on a CREW PRAM with n processing elements. Each processing element P_i computes the ith column of table F.

	H	E	A	G	A	W	G	H	E	E
	0	0	0	0	0	0	0	0	0	0	0
P	0	0	0	0	0	0	0	0	0	0	0
A	0	0	0	1	1	1	1	1	1	1	1
W	0	0	0	1	1	1	2	2	2	2	2
H	0	1	1	1	1	1	2	2	3	3	3
E	0	1	2	2	2	2	2	2	3	4	4
A	0	1	2	3	3	3	3	3	3	4	4
E	0	1	2	3	3	3	3	3	3	4	5

Figure 12.6 The F table for computing the LCS of sequences H E A G A W G H E E and P A W H E A E.

Table entries are computed in a diagonal sweep from the top-left to the bottom-right corner. Since there are n processing elements, and each processing element can access any entry in table F, the elements of each diagonal are computed in constant time (the diagonal can contain at most n elements). Since there are $2n - 1$ such diagonals, the algorithm requires $\Theta(n)$ iterations. Thus, the parallel run time is $\Theta(n)$. The algorithm is cost-optimal, since its $\Theta(n^2)$ processor-time product equals the sequential complexity.

This algorithm can be adapted to run on a logical linear array of n processing elements by distributing table F among different processing elements. Note that this logical topology can be mapped to a variety of physical architectures using embedding techniques in Section 2.7.1. Processing element P_i stores the $(i + 1)$th column of the table. Entries in table F are assigned to processing elements as illustrated in Figure 12.5(b). When computing the value of $F[i, j]$, processing element P_{j-1} may need either the value of $F[i - 1, j - 1]$ or the value of $F[i, j - 1]$ from the processing element to its left. It takes time $t_s + t_w$ to communicate a single word from a neighboring processing element. To compute each entry in the table, a processing element needs a single value from its immediate neighbor, followed by the actual computation, which takes time t_c. Since each processing element computes a single entry on the diagonal, each iteration takes time $(t_s + t_w + t_c)$. The algorithm makes $(2n - 1)$ diagonal sweeps (iterations) across the table; thus, the total parallel run time is

$$T_P = (2n - 1)(t_s + t_w + t_c).$$

Since the sequential run time is $n^2 t_c$, the efficiency of this algorithm is

$$E = \frac{n^2 t_c}{n(2n-1)(t_s + t_w + t_c)}.$$

A careful examination of this expression reveals that it is not possible to obtain efficiencies above a certain threshold. To compute this threshold, assume it is possible to communicate values between processing elements instantaneously; that is, $t_s = t_w = 0$. In this case, the efficiency of the parallel algorithm is

$$E_{max} = \frac{1}{2 - 1/n}. \tag{12.5}$$

Thus, the efficiency is bounded above by 0.5. This upper bound holds even if multiple columns are mapped to a processing element. Higher efficiencies are possible using alternate mappings (Problem 12.3).

Note that the basic characteristic that allows efficient parallel formulations of this algorithm is that table F can be partitioned so computing each element requires data only from neighboring processing elements. In other words, the algorithm exhibits locality of data access.

12.4   Serial Polyadic DP Formulations

Floyd's algorithm for determining the shortest paths between all pairs of nodes in a graph can be reformulated as a serial polyadic DP formulation.

12.4.1   Floyd's All-Pairs Shortest-Paths Algorithm

Consider a weighted graph G, which consists of a set of nodes V and a set of edges E. An edge from node i to node j in E has a weight $c_{i,j}$. Floyd's algorithm determines the cost $d_{i,j}$ of the shortest path between each pair of nodes (i, j) in V (Section 10.4.2). The cost of a path is the sum of the weights of the edges in the path.

Let $d_{i,j}^k$ be the minimum cost of a path from node i to node j, using only nodes $v_0, v_1, \ldots, v_{k-1}$. The functional equation of the DP formulation for this problem is

$$d_{i,j}^k = \begin{cases} c_{i,j} & k = 0 \\ \min \{d_{i,j}^{k-1}, (d_{i,k}^{k-1} + d_{k,j}^{k-1})\} & 0 \leq k \leq n-1 \end{cases}. \tag{12.6}$$

Since $d_{i,j}^n$ is the shortest path from node i to node j using all n nodes, it is also the cost of the overall shortest path between nodes i and j. The sequential formulation of this algorithm requires n iterations, and each iteration requires time $\Theta(n^2)$. Thus, the overall run time of the sequential algorithm is $\Theta(n^3)$.

Equation 12.6 is a serial polyadic formulation. Nodes $d_{i,j}^k$ can be partitioned into n levels, one for each value of k. Elements at level $k+1$ depend only on elements at level

k. Hence, the formulation is serial. The formulation is polyadic since one of the solutions to $d_{i,j}^k$ requires a composition of solutions to two subproblems $d_{i,k}^{k-1}$ and $d_{k,j}^{k-1}$ from the previous level. Furthermore, the dependencies between levels are sparse because the computation of each element in $d_{i,j}^{k+1}$ requires only three results from the preceding level (out of n^2).

A simple CREW PRAM formulation of this algorithm uses n^2 processing elements. Processing elements are organized into a logical two-dimensional array in which processing element $P_{i,j}$ computes the value of $d_{i,j}^k$ for $k = 1, 2, \ldots, n$. In each iteration k, processing element $P_{i,j}$ requires the values $d_{i,j}^{k-1}$, $d_{i,k}^{k-1}$, and $d_{k,j}^{k-1}$. Given these values, it computes the value of $d_{i,j}^k$ in constant time. Therefore, the PRAM formulation has a parallel run time of $\Theta(n)$. This formulation is cost-optimal because its processor-time product is the same as the sequential run time of $\Theta(n^3)$. This algorithm can be adapted to various practical architectures to yield efficient parallel formulations (Section 10.4.2).

As with serial monadic formulations, data locality is of prime importance in serial polyadic formulations since many such formulations have sparse connectivity between levels.

12.5 Nonserial Polyadic DP Formulations

In nonserial polyadic DP formulations, in addition to processing subproblems at a level in parallel, computation can also be pipelined to increase efficiency. We illustrate this with the optimal matrix-parenthesization problem.

12.5.1 The Optimal Matrix-Parenthesization Problem

Consider the problem of multiplying n matrices, $A_1, A_2, \ldots, A_n$, where each A_i is a matrix with r_{i-1} rows and r_i columns. The order in which the matrices are multiplied has a significant impact on the total number of operations required to evaluate the product.

Example 12.3 Optimal matrix parenthesization
Consider three matrices A_1, A_2, and A_3 of dimensions 10×20, 20×30, and 30×40, respectively. The product of these matrices can be computed as $(A_1 \times A_2) \times A_3$ or as $A_1 \times (A_2 \times A_3)$. In $(A_1 \times A_2) \times A_3$, computing $(A_1 \times A_2)$ requires $10 \times 20 \times 30$ operations and yields a matrix of dimensions 10×30. Multiplying this by A_3 requires $10 \times 30 \times 40$ additional operations. Therefore the total number of operations is $10 \times 20 \times 30 + 10 \times 30 \times 40 = 18000$. Similarly, computing $A_1 \times (A_2 \times A_3)$ requires $20 \times 30 \times 40 + 10 \times 20 \times 40 = 32000$ operations. Clearly, the first parenthesization is desirable. ∎

The objective of the parenthesization problem is to determine a parenthesization that minimizes the number of operations. Enumerating all possible parenthesizations is not

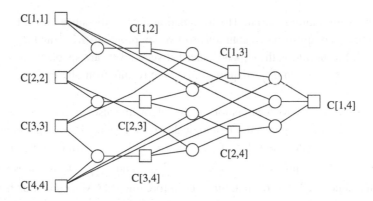

Figure 12.7 A nonserial polyadic DP formulation for finding an optimal matrix parenthesization for a chain of four matrices. A square node represents the optimal cost of multiplying a matrix chain. A circle node represents a possible parenthesization.

feasible since there are exponentially many of them.

Let $C[i, j]$ be the optimal cost of multiplying the matrices $A_i, \ldots, A_j$. This chain of matrices can be expressed as a product of two smaller chains, $A_i, A_{i+1}, \ldots, A_k$ and $A_{k+1}, \ldots, A_j$. The chain $A_i, A_{i+1}, \ldots, A_k$ results in a matrix of dimensions $r_{i-1} \times r_k$, and the chain $A_{k+1}, \ldots, A_j$ results in a matrix of dimensions $r_k \times r_j$. The cost of multiplying these two matrices is $r_{i-1} r_k r_j$. Hence, the cost of the parenthesization $(A_i, A_{i+1}, \ldots, A_k)(A_{k+1}, \ldots, A_j)$ is given by $C[i, k] + C[k + 1, j] + r_{i-1} r_k r_j$. This gives rise to the following recurrence relation for the parenthesization problem:

$$C[i, j] = \begin{cases} \min_{i \le k < j} \{C[i, k] + C[k + 1, j] + r_{i-1} r_k r_j\} & 1 \le i < j \le n \\ 0 & j = i, 0 < i \le n \end{cases} \tag{12.7}$$

Given Equation 12.7, the problem reduces to finding the value of $C[1, n]$. The composition of costs of matrix chains is shown in Figure 12.7. Equation 12.7 can be solved if we use a bottom-up approach for constructing the table C that stores the values $C[i, j]$. The algorithm fills table C in an order corresponding to solving the parenthesization problem on matrix chains of increasing length. Visualize this by thinking of filling in the table diagonally (Figure 12.8). Entries in diagonal l corresponds to the cost of multiplying matrix chains of length $l+1$. From Equation 12.7, we can see that the value of $C[i, j]$ is computed as $\min\{C[i, k] + C[k+1, j] + r_{i-1} r_k r_j\}$, where k can take values from i to $j-1$. Therefore, computing $C[i, j]$ requires that we evaluate $(j - i)$ terms and select their minimum. The computation of each term takes time t_c, and the computation of $C[i, j]$ takes time $(j - i)t_c$. Thus, each entry in diagonal l can be computed in time lt_c.

In computing the cost of the optimal parenthesization sequence, the algorithm computes $(n - 1)$ chains of length two. This takes time $(n-1)t_c$. Similarly, computing $(n-2)$ chains of length three takes time $(n - 2)2t_c$. In the final step, the algorithm computes one chain

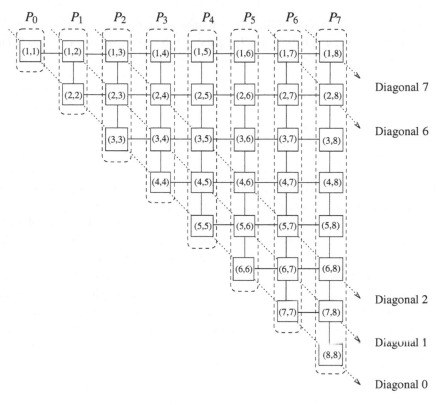

Figure 12.8 The diagonal order of computation for the optimal matrix-parenthesization problem.

of length n. This takes time $(n-1)t_c$. Thus, the sequential run time of this algorithm is

$$
\begin{aligned}
T_S &= (n-1)t_c + (n-2)2t_c + \cdots + 1(n-1)t_c, \\
&= \sum_{i=1}^{n-1}(n-i)it_c, \\
&\simeq (n^3/6)t_c.
\end{aligned}
\tag{12.8}
$$

The sequential complexity of the algorithm is $\Theta(n^3)$.

Consider the parallel formulation of this algorithm on a logical ring of n processing elements. In step l, each processing element computes a single element belonging to the lth diagonal. Processing element P_i computes the $(i+1)$th column of Table C. Figure 12.8 illustrates the partitioning of the table among different processing elements. After computing the assigned value of the element in table C, each processing element sends its value to all other processing elements using an all-to-all broadcast (Section 4.2). Therefore, the assigned value in the next iteration can be computed locally. Computing an entry in table C during iteration l takes time lt_c because it corresponds to the cost of multiplying a chain of length $l+1$. An all-to-all broadcast of a single word on n processing elements takes time $t_s \log n + t_w(n-1)$ (Section 4.2). The total time required to compute the entries along diagonal l is $lt_c + t_s \log n + t_w(n-1)$. The parallel run time is the sum of the time taken over computation of $n-1$ diagonals.

$$
\begin{aligned}
T_P &= \sum_{l=1}^{n-1} (lt_c + t_s \log n + t_w(n-1)), \\
&= \frac{(n-1)(n)}{2} t_c + t_s(n-1)\log n + t_w(n-1)^2.
\end{aligned}
$$

The parallel run time of this algorithm is $\Theta(n^2)$. Since the processor-time product is $\Theta(n^3)$, which is the same as the sequential complexity, this algorithm is cost-optimal.

When using p processing elements ($1 \leq p \leq n$) organized in a logical ring, if there are n nodes in a diagonal, each processing element stores n/p nodes. Each processing element computes the cost $C[i, j]$ of the entries assigned to it. After computation, an all-to-all broadcast sends the solution costs of the subproblems for the most recently computed diagonal to all the other processing elements. Because each processing element has complete information about subproblem costs at preceding diagonals, no other communication is required. The time taken for all-to-all broadcast of n/p words is $t_s \log p + t_w n(p-1)/p \approx t_s \log p + t_w n$. The time to compute n/p entries of the table in the lth diagonal is $lt_c n/p$. The parallel run time is

$$
\begin{aligned}
T_P &= \sum_{l=1}^{n-1} (lt_c n/p + t_s \log p + t_w n), \\
&= \frac{n^2(n-1)}{2p} t_c + t_s(n-1)\log p + t_w n(n-1).
\end{aligned}
$$

In order terms, $T_P = \Theta(n^3/p) + \Theta(n^2)$. Here, $\Theta(n^3/p)$ is the computation time, and $\Theta(n^2)$ the communication time. If n is sufficiently large with respect to p, communication time can be made an arbitrarily small fraction of computation time, yielding linear speedup.

This formulation can use at most $\Theta(n)$ processing elements to accomplish the task in time $\Theta(n^2)$. This time can be improved by pipelining the computation of the cost $C[i, j]$ on $n(n+1)/2$ processing elements. Each processing element computes a single entry $c(i, j)$ of matrix C. Pipelining works due to the nonserial nature of the problem. Computation of an entry on a diagonal t does not depend only on the entries on diagonal $t-1$ but also on all the earlier diagonals. Hence work on diagonal t can start even before work on diagonal $t-1$ is completed.

12.6 Summary and Discussion

This chapter provides a framework for deriving parallel algorithms that use dynamic programming. It identifies possible sources of parallelism, and indicates under what conditions they can be utilized effectively.

By representing computation as a graph, we identify three sources of parallelism. First, the computation of the cost of a single subproblem (a node in a level) can be parallelized. For example, for computing the shortest path in the multistage graph shown in Figure 12.3, node computation can be parallelized because the complexity of node computation is itself $\Theta(n)$. For many problems, however, node computation complexity is lower, limiting available parallelism.

Second, subproblems at each level can be solved in parallel. This provides a viable method for extracting parallelism from a large class of problems (including all the problems in this chapter).

The first two sources of parallelism are available to both serial and nonserial formulations. Nonserial formulations allow a third source of parallelism: pipelining of computations among different levels. Pipelining makes it possible to start solving a problem as soon as the subproblems it depends on are solved. This form of parallelism is used in the parenthesization problem.

Note that pipelining was also applied to the parallel formulation of Floyd's all-pairs shortest-paths algorithm in Section 10.4.2. As discussed in Section 12.4, this algorithm corresponds to a serial DP formulation. The nature of pipelining in this algorithm is different from the one in nonserial DP formulation. In the pipelined version of Floyd's algorithm, computation in a stage is pipelined with the communication among earlier stages. If communication cost is zero (as in a PRAM), then Floyd's algorithm does not benefit from pipelining.

Throughout the chapter, we have seen the importance of data locality. If the solution to a problem requires results from other subproblems, the cost of communicating those results must be less than the cost of solving the problem. In some problems (the 0/1 knapsack problem, for example) the degree of locality is much smaller than in other problems such as the longest-common-subsequence problem and Floyd's all-pairs shortest-paths algorithm.

12.7 Bibliographic Remarks

Dynamic programming was originally presented by Bellman [Bel57] for solving multistage decision problems. Various formal models have since been developed for DP [KH67, MM73, KK88b]. Several textbooks and articles present sequential DP formulations of the longest-common-subsequence problem, the matrix chain multiplication problem, the 0/1 knapsack problem, and the shortest-path problem [CLR90, HS78, PS82, Bro79].

Li and Wah [LW85, WL88] show that monadic serial DP formulations can be solved in parallel on systolic arrays as matrix-vector products. They further present a more concurrent but non-cost-optimal formulation by formulating the problem as a matrix-matrix product. Ranka and Sahni [RS90b] present a polyadic serial formulation for the string editing problem and derive a parallel formulation based on a checkerboard partitioning.

The DP formulation of a large class of optimization problems is similar to that of the optimal matrix-parenthesization problem. Some examples of these problems are optimal triangularization of polygons, optimal binary search trees [CLR90], and CYK parsing [AU72]. The serial complexity of the standard DP formulation for all these problems is $\Theta(n^3)$. Several parallel formulations have been proposed by Ibarra *et al.* [IPS91] that use $\Theta(n)$ processing elements on a hypercube and that solve the problem in time $\Theta(n^2)$. Guibas, Kung, and Thompson [GKT79] present a systolic algorithm that uses $\Theta(n^2)$ processing cells and solves the problem in time $\Theta(n)$. Karypis and Kumar [KK93] analyze three distinct mappings of the systolic algorithm presented by Guibas *et al.* [GKT79] and experimentally evaluate them by using the matrix-multiplication parenthesization problem. They show that a straightforward mapping of this algorithm to a mesh architecture has an upper bound on efficiency of 1/12. They also present a better mapping without this drawback, and show near-linear speedup on a mesh embedded into a 256-processor hypercube for the optimal matrix-parenthesization problem.

Many faster parallel algorithms for solving the parenthesization problem have been proposed, but they are not cost-optimal and are applicable only to theoretical models such as the PRAM. For example, a generalized method for parallelizing such programs is described by Valiant *et al.* [VSBR83] that leads directly to formulations that run in time $O(\log^2 n)$ on $O(n^9)$ processing elements. Rytter [Ryt88] uses the parallel pebble game on trees to reduce the number of processing elements to $O(n^6/\log n)$ for a CREW PRAM and $O(n^6)$ for a hypercube, yet solves this problem in time $O(\log^2 n)$. Huang *et al.* [HLV90] present a similar algorithm for CREW PRAM models that run in time $O(\sqrt{n}\log n)$ on $O(n^{3.5}\log n)$ processing elements. DeMello *et al.* [DCG90] use vectorized formulations of DP for the Cray to solve optimal control problems.

As we have seen, the serial polyadic formulation of the 0/1 knapsack problem is difficult to parallelize due to lack of communication locality. Lee *et al.* [LSS88] use specific characteristics of the knapsack problem and derive a divide-and-conquer strategy for parallelizing the DP algorithm for the 0/1 knapsack problem on a MIMD message-passing computer (Problem 12.2). Lee *et al.* demonstrate experimentally that it is possible to obtain linear speedup for large instances of the problem on a hypercube.

Problems

12.1   Consider the parallel algorithm for solving the 0/1 knapsack problem in Section 12.2.2. Derive the speedup and efficiency for this algorithm. Show that the efficiency of this algorithm cannot be increased beyond a certain value by increasing the problem size for a fixed number of processing elements. What is the upper bound on efficiency for this formulation as a function of t_w and t_c?

12.2   [LSS88] In the parallel formulation of the 0/1 knapsack problem presented in Section 12.2.2, the degree of concurrency is proportional to c, the knapsack capacity. Also this algorithm has limited data locality, as the amount of data to be communicated is of the same order of magnitude as the computation at each processing element. Lee *et al.* present another formulation in which the degree of concurrency is proportional to n, the number of weights. This formulation also has much more data locality. In this formulation, the set of weights is partitioned among processing elements. Each processing element computes the maximum profit it can achieve from its local weights for knapsacks of various sizes up to c. This information is expressed as lists that are merged to yield the global solution.

Compute the parallel run time, speedup, and efficiency of this formulation. Compare the performance of this algorithm with that in Section 12.2.2.

12.3 We noticed that the parallel formulation of the longest-common-subsequence problem has an upper bound of 0.5 on its efficiency. It is possible to use an alternate mapping to achieve higher efficiency for this problem. Derive a formulation that does not suffer from this upper bound, and give the run time of this formulation. *Hint:* Consider the blocked-cyclic mapping discussed in Section 3.4.1.

12.4 **[HS78]** The traveling salesman problem (TSP) is defined as follows: Given a set of cities and the distance between each pair of cities, determine a tour through all cities of minimum length. A tour of all cities is a trip visiting each city once and returning to the starting point. Its length is the sum of distances traveled.

This problem can be solved using a DP formulation. View the cities as vertices in a graph $G(V, E)$. Let the set of cities V be represented by $\{v_1, v_2, \ldots, v_n\}$ and let $S \subseteq \{v_2, v_3, \ldots, v_n\}$. Furthermore, let $c_{i,j}$ be the distance between cities i and j. If $f(S, k)$ represents the cost of starting at city v_1, passing through all the cities in set S, and terminating in city k, then the following recursive equations can be used to compute $f(S, k)$:

$$f(S, k) = \begin{cases} c_{1,k} & S = \{k\} \\ \min_{m \in S - \{k\}} \{f(S - \{k\}), m\} + c_{m,k} & S \neq \{k\} \end{cases} \quad (12.9)$$

Based on Equation 12.9, derive a parallel formulation. Compute the parallel run time and the speedup. Is this parallel formulation cost-optimal?

12.5 **[HS78]** Consider the problem of merging two sorted files containing $O(n)$ and $O(m)$ records. These files can be merged into a sorted file in time $O(m + n)$. Given r such files, the problem of merging them into a single file can be formulated as a sequence of merge operations performed on pairs of files. The overall cost of the merge operation is a function of the sequence in which they are merged. The optimal merge order can be formulated as a greedy problem and its parallel formulations derived using principles illustrated in this chapter.

Write down the recursive equations for this problem. Derive a parallel formulation for merging files using p processing elements. Compute the parallel run time and speedup, and determine whether your parallel formulation is cost-optimal.

12.6 **[HS78]** Consider the problem of designing a fault-tolerant circuit containing n devices connected in series, as shown in Figure 12.9(a). If the probability of failure of each of these devices is given by f_i, the overall probability of failure of the

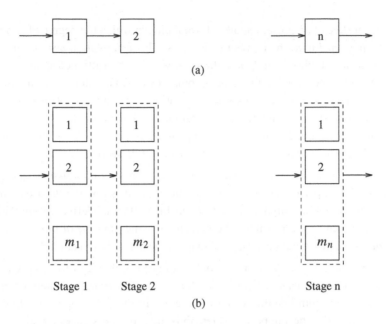

(a)

Stage 1   Stage 2   Stage n

(b)

Figure 12.9   (a) n devices connected in a series within a circuit. (b) Each stage in the circuit now has m_i functional units. There are n such stages connected in the series.

circuit is given by $1 - \prod(1 - f_i)$. Here, $\prod$ represents a product of specified terms. The reliability of this circuit can be improved by connecting multiple functional devices in parallel at each stage, as shown in Figure 12.9(b). If stage i in the circuit has r_i duplicate functional units, each with a probability of failure given by f_i, then the overall probability of failure of this stage is reduced to $r_i^{m_i}$ and the overall probability of failure of the circuit is given by $1 - \prod(1 - r_i^{m_i})$. In general, for physical reasons, the probability of failure at a particular level may not be $r_i^{m_i}$, but some function $\phi_i(r_i, m_i)$. The objective of the problem is to minimize the overall probability of failure of the circuit, $1 - \prod(1 - \phi_i(r_i, m_i))$.

Construction cost adds a new dimension to this problem. If each of the functional units used at stage i costs c_i then due to cost constraints, the overall cost $\sum c_i m_i$ should be less than a fixed quantity c.

The problem can be formally defined as

Minimize $1 - \prod(1 - \phi_i(r_i, m_i))$, such that $\sum c_i m_i < c$

where $m_i > 0$ and $0 < i \leq n$.

Let $f_i(x)$ represent the reliability of a system with i stages of cost x. The optimal solution is given by $f_n(c)$. The recursive equation for $f_i(x)$ is as follows:

$$f_i(x) = \begin{cases} 1 & i = 0 \\ \max_{i \leq m_i \leq u_i} \{\phi_i(m_i) f_{i-1}(c - c_i m_i)\} & i \geq 1 \end{cases} \qquad (12.10)$$

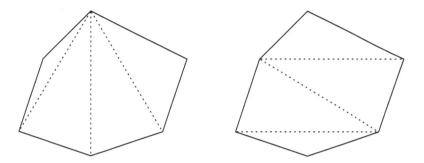

Figure 12.10   Two possible triangulations of a regular polygon.

Classify this formulation into one of the four DP categories, and derive a parallel formulation for this algorithm. Determine its parallel run time, speedup, and isoefficiency function.

12.7   **[CLR90]** Consider the simplified optimal polygon-triangulation problem. This problem can be defined as follows. Given a simple polygon, break the polygon into a set of triangles by connecting nodes of the polygon with chords. This process is illustrated in Figure 12.10. The cost of constructing a triangle with nodes v_i, v_j, and v_k is defined by a function $f(v_i, v_j, v_k)$. For this problem, let the cost be the total length of the edges of the triangle (using Euclidean distance). The optimal polygon-triangulation problem breaks up a polygon into a set of triangles such that the total length of each triangle (the sum of the individual lengths) is minimized.

Give a DP formulation for this problem. Classify it into one of the four categories and derive a parallel formulation for p processing elements. Determine its parallel run time, speedup, and isoefficiency function.

Hint: This problem is similar to the optimal matrix-parenthesization problem.

CHAPTER 13

Fast Fourier Transform

The discrete Fourier transform (DFT) plays an important role in many scientific and technical applications, including time series and waveform analysis, solutions to linear partial differential equations, convolution, digital signal processing, and image filtering. The DFT is a linear transformation that maps n regularly sampled points from a cycle of a periodic signal, like a sinc wave, onto an equal number of points representing the frequency spectrum of the signal. In 1965, Cooley and Tukey devised an algorithm to compute the DFT of an n-point series in $\Theta(n \log n)$ operations. Their new algorithm was a significant improvement over previously known methods for computing the DFT, which required $\Theta(n^2)$ operations. The revolutionary algorithm by Cooley and Tukey and its variations are referred to as the *fast Fourier transform* (FFT). Due to its wide application in scientific and engineering fields, there has been a lot of interest in implementing FFT on parallel computers.

Several different forms of the FFT algorithm exist. This chapter discusses its simplest form, the one-dimensional, unordered, radix-2 FFT. Parallel formulations of higher-radix and multidimensional FFTs are similar to the simple algorithm discussed in this chapter because the underlying ideas behind all sequential FFT algorithms are the same. An ordered FFT is obtained by performing bit reversal (Section 13.4) on the output sequence of an unordered FFT. Bit reversal does not affect the overall complexity of a parallel implementation of FFT.

In this chapter we discuss two parallel formulations of the basic algorithm: the *binary-exchange algorithm* and the *transpose algorithm*. Depending on the size of the input n, the number of processes p, and the memory or network bandwidth, one of these may run faster than the other.

13.1   The Serial Algorithm

Consider a sequence $X = \langle X[0], X[1], \ldots, X[n-1] \rangle$ of length n. The discrete Fourier transform of the sequence X is the sequence $Y = \langle Y[0], Y[1], \ldots, Y[n-1] \rangle$, where

$$Y[i] = \sum_{k=0}^{n-1} X[k]\omega^{ki}, \quad 0 \le i < n. \tag{13.1}$$

In Equation 13.1, ω is the primitive nth root of unity in the complex plane; that is, $\omega = e^{2\pi\sqrt{-1}/n}$, where e is the base of natural logarithms. More generally, the powers of ω in the equation can be thought of as elements of the finite commutative ring of integers modulo n. The powers of ω used in an FFT computation are also known as **twiddle factors**.

The computation of each $Y[i]$ according to Equation 13.1 requires n complex multiplications. Therefore, the sequential complexity of computing the entire sequence Y of length n is $\Theta(n^2)$. The fast Fourier transform algorithm described below reduces this complexity to $\Theta(n \log n)$.

Assume that n is a power of two. The FFT algorithm is based on the following step that permits an n-point DFT computation to be split into two $(n/2)$-point DFT computations:

$$
\begin{aligned}
Y[i] &= \sum_{k=0}^{(n/2)-1} X[2k]\omega^{2ki} + \sum_{k=0}^{(n/2)-1} X[2k+1]\omega^{(2k+1)i} \\
&= \sum_{k=0}^{(n/2)-1} X[2k]e^{2(2\pi\sqrt{-1}/n)ki} + \sum_{k=0}^{(n/2)-1} X[2k+1]\omega^i e^{2(2\pi\sqrt{-1}/n)ki} \\
&= \sum_{k=0}^{(n/2)-1} X[2k]e^{2\pi\sqrt{-1}ki/(n/2)} + \omega^i \sum_{k=0}^{(n/2)-1} X[2k+1]e^{2\pi\sqrt{-1}ki/(n/2)}
\end{aligned}
$$

$$\tag{13.2}$$

Let $\tilde{\omega} = e^{2\pi\sqrt{-1}/(n/2)} = \omega^2$; that is, $\tilde{\omega}$ is the primitive $(n/2)$th root of unity. Then, we can

---

```
1.    procedure R_FFT(X, Y, n, ω)
2.    if (n = 1) then Y[0] := X[0] else
3.    begin
4.        R_FFT(⟨X[0], X[2], ..., X[n − 2]⟩, ⟨Q[0], Q[1], ..., Q[n/2]⟩, n/2, ω²);
5.        R_FFT(⟨X[1], X[3], ..., X[n − 1]⟩, ⟨T[0], T[1], ..., T[n/2]⟩, n/2, ω²);
6.        for i := 0 to n − 1 do
7.            Y[i] := Q[i mod (n/2)] + ωⁱ T[i mod (n/2)];
8.    end R_FFT
```

Algorithm 13.1   The recursive, one-dimensional, unordered, radix-2 FFT algorithm. Here $\omega = e^{2\pi\sqrt{-1}/n}$.

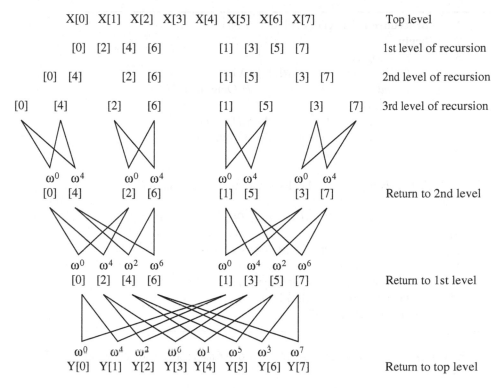

X[0] X[1] X[2] X[3] X[4] X[5] X[6] X[7]   Top level

[0] [2] [4] [6]   [1] [3] [5] [7]   1st level of recursion

[0] [4]   [2] [6]   [1] [5]   [3] [7]   2nd level of recursion

[0]   [4]   [2]   [6]   [1]   [5]   [3]   [7]   3rd level of recursion

ω^0 ω^4 ω^0 ω^4 ω^0 ω^4 ω^0 ω^4
[0] [4]   [2] [6]   [1] [5]   [3] [7]   Return to 2nd level

ω^0 ω^4 ω^2 ω^6 ω^0 ω^4 ω^2 ω^6
[0] [2] [4] [6]   [1] [3] [5] [7]   Return to 1st level

ω^0 ω^4 ω^2 ω^6 ω^1 ω^5 ω^3 ω^7
Y[0] Y[1] Y[2] Y[3] Y[4] Y[5] Y[6] Y[7]   Return to top level

Figure 13.1   A recursive 8-point unordered FFT computation.

rewrite Equation 13.2 as follows:

$$Y[i] = \sum_{k=0}^{(n/2)-1} X[2k]\tilde{\omega}^{ki} + \omega^i \sum_{k=0}^{(n/2)-1} X[2k+1]\tilde{\omega}^{ki} \tag{13.3}$$

In Equation 13.3, each of the two summations on the right-hand side is an $(n/2)$-point DFT computation. If n is a power of two, each of these DFT computations can be divided similarly into smaller computations in a recursive manner. This leads to the recursive FFT algorithm given in Algorithm 13.1. This FFT algorithm is called the radix-2 algorithm because at each level of recursion, the input sequence is split into two equal halves.

Figure 13.1 illustrates how the recursive algorithm works on an 8-point sequence. As the figure shows, the first set of computations corresponding to line 7 of Algorithm 13.1 takes place at the deepest level of recursion. At this level, the elements of the sequence whose indices differ by $n/2$ are used in the computation. In each subsequent level, the difference between the indices of the elements used together in a computation decreases by a factor of two. The figure also shows the powers of ω used in each computation.

The size of the input sequence over which an FFT is computed recursively decreases by a factor of two at each level of recursion (lines 4 and 5 of Algorithm 13.1). Hence, the maximum number of levels of recursion is $\log n$ for an initial sequence of length n. At the

---

```
1.      procedure ITERATIVE_FFT(X, Y, n)
2.      begin
3.          r := log n;
4.          for i := 0 to n − 1 do R[i] := X[i];
5.          for m := 0 to r − 1 do        /* Outer loop */
6.              begin
7.                  for i := 0 to n − 1 do S[i] := R[i];
8.                  for i := 0 to n − 1 do  /* Inner loop */
9.                      begin
```

/* Let $(b_0 b_1 \cdots b_{r-1})$ be the binary representation of i */

```
10.                         j := (b_0 ... b_{m-1} 0 b_{m+1} \cdots b_{r-1});
11.                         k := (b_0 ... b_{m-1} 1 b_{m+1} \cdots b_{r-1});
12.                         R[i] := S[j] + S[k] × ω^{(b_m b_{m-1} \cdots b_0 0 \cdots 0)};
13.                     endfor;  /* Inner loop */
14.             endfor;         /* Outer loop */
15.         for i := 0 to n − 1 do Y[i] := R[i];
16.     end ITERATIVE_FFT
```

Algorithm 13.2   The Cooley-Tukey algorithm for one-dimensional, unordered, radix-2 FFT. Here $\omega = e^{2\pi \sqrt{-1}/n}$.

mth level of recursion, 2^m FFTs of size $n/2^m$ each are computed. Thus, the total number of arithmetic operations (line 7) at each level is $\Theta(n)$ and the overall sequential complexity of Algorithm 13.1 is $\Theta(n \log n)$.

The serial FFT algorithm can also be cast in an iterative form. The parallel implementations of the iterative form are easier to illustrate. Therefore, before describing parallel FFT algorithms, we give the iterative form of the serial algorithm. An iterative FFT algorithm is derived by casting each level of recursion, starting with the deepest level, as an iteration. Algorithm 13.2 gives the classic iterative Cooley-Tukey algorithm for an n-point, one-dimensional, unordered, radix-2 FFT. The program performs $\log n$ iterations of the outer loop starting on line 5. The value of the loop index m in the iterative version of the algorithm corresponds to the $(\log n − m)$th level of recursion in the recursive version (Figure 13.1). Just as in each level of recursion, each iteration performs n complex multiplications and additions.

Algorithm 13.2 has two main loops. The outer loop starting at line 5 is executed $\log n$ times for an n-point FFT, and the inner loop starting at line 8 is executed n times during each iteration of the outer loop. All operations of the inner loop are constant-time arithmetic operations. Thus, the sequential time complexity of the algorithm is $\Theta(n \log n)$. In every iteration of the outer loop, the sequence R is updated using the elements that were stored in the sequence S during the previous iteration. For the first iteration, the input sequence X serves as the initial sequence R. The updated sequence X from the final iteration is the desired Fourier transform and is copied to the output sequence Y.

Line 12 in Algorithm 13.2 performs a crucial step in the FFT algorithm. This step updates $R[i]$ by using $S[j]$ and $S[k]$. The indices j and k are derived from the index i as follows. Assume that $n = 2^r$. Since $0 \leq i < n$, the binary representation of i contains r bits. Let $(b_0 b_1 \cdots b_{r-1})$ be the binary representation of index i. In the mth iteration of the outer loop ($0 \leq m < r$), index j is derived by forcing the mth most significant bit of i (that is, b_m) to zero. Index k is derived by forcing b_m to 1. Thus, the binary representations of j and k differ only in their mth most significant bits. In the binary representation of i, b_m is either 0 or 1. Hence, of the two indices j and k, one is the same as index i, depending on whether $b_m = 0$ or $b_m = 1$. In the mth iteration of the outer loop, for each i between 0 and $n - 1$, $R[i]$ is generated by executing line 12 of Algorithm 13.2 on $S[i]$ and on another element of S whose index differs from i only in the mth most significant bit. Figure 13.2 shows the pattern in which these elements are paired for the case in which $n = 16$.

13.2 The Binary-Exchange Algorithm

This section discusses the *binary-exchange algorithm* for performing FFT on a parallel computer. First, a decomposition is induced by partitioning the input or the output vector. Therefore, each task starts with one element of the input vector and computes the corresponding element of the output. If each task is assigned the same label as the index of its input or output element, then in each of the $\log n$ iterations of the algorithm, exchange of data takes place between pairs of tasks with labels differing in one bit position.

13.2.1 A Full Bandwidth Network

In this subsection, we describe the implementation of the binary-exchange algorithm on a parallel computer on which a bisection width (Section 2.4.4) of $\Theta(p)$ is available to p parallel processes. Since the pattern of interaction among the tasks of parallel FFT matches that of a hypercube network, we describe the algorithm assuming such an interconnection network. However, the performance and scalability analysis would be valid for any parallel computer with an overall simultaneous data-transfer capacity of $O(p)$.

One Task Per Process

We first consider a simple mapping in which one task is assigned to each process. Figure 13.3 illustrates the interaction pattern induced by this mapping of the binary-exchange algorithm for $n = 16$. As the figure shows, process i ($0 \leq i < n$) initially stores $X[i]$ and finally generates $Y[i]$. In each of the $\log n$ iterations of the outer loop, process P_i updates the value of $R[i]$ by executing line 12 of Algorithm 13.2. All n updates are performed in parallel.

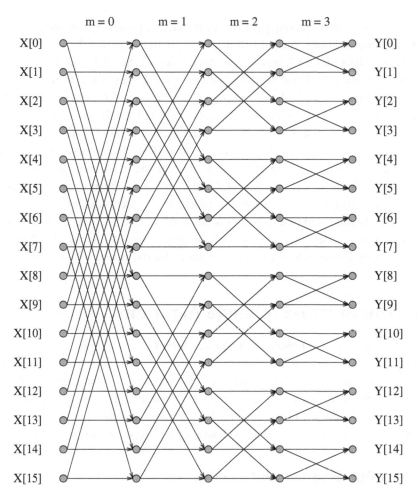

Figure 13.2 The pattern of combination of elements of the input and the intermediate sequences during a 16-point unordered FFT computation.

To perform the updates, process P_i requires an element of S from a process whose label differs from i at only one bit. Recall that in a hypercube, a node is connected to all those nodes whose labels differ from its own at only one bit position. Thus, the parallel FFT computation maps naturally onto a hypercube with a one-to-one mapping of processes to nodes. In the first iteration of the outer loop, the labels of each pair of communicating processes differ only at their most significant bits. For instance, processes P_0 to P_7 communicate with P_8 to P_{15}, respectively. Similarly, in the second iteration, the labels of processes communicating with each other differ at the second most significant bit, and so on.

In each of the $\log n$ iterations of this algorithm, every process performs one complex multiplication and addition, and exchanges one complex number with another process. Thus, there is a constant amount of work per iteration. Hence, it takes time $\Theta(\log n)$

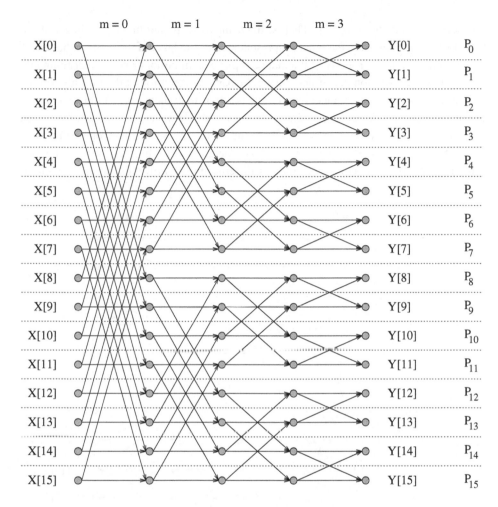

Figure 13.3 A 16-point unordered FFT on 16 processes. P_i denotes the process labeled i.

to execute the algorithm in parallel by using a hypercube with n nodes. This hypercube formulation of FFT is cost-optimal because its process-time product is $\Theta(n \log n)$, the same as the complexity of a serial n-point FFT.

Multiple Tasks Per Process

We now consider a mapping in which the n tasks of an n-point FFT are mapped onto p processes, where $n > p$. For the sake of simplicity, let us assume that both n and p are powers of two, i.e., $n = 2^r$ and $p = 2^d$. As Figure 13.4 shows, we partition the sequences into blocks of n/p contiguous elements and assign one block to each process.

An interesting property of the mapping shown in Figure 13.4 is that, if $(b_0 b_1 \cdots b_{r-1})$ is the binary representation of any i, such that $0 \le i < n$, then $R[i]$ and $S[i]$ are mapped onto the process labeled $(b_0 \cdots b_{d-1})$. That is, the d most significant bits of the index of any element of the sequence are the binary representation of the label of the process that the element belongs to. This property of the mapping plays an important role in determining the amount of communication performed during the parallel execution of the FFT algorithm.

Figure 13.4 shows that elements with indices differing at their d $(= 2)$ most significant bits are mapped onto different processes. However, all elements with indices having the same d most significant bits are mapped onto the same process. Recall from the previous section that an n-point FFT requires $r = \log n$ iterations of the outer loop. In the mth iteration of the loop, elements with indices differing in the mth most significant bit are

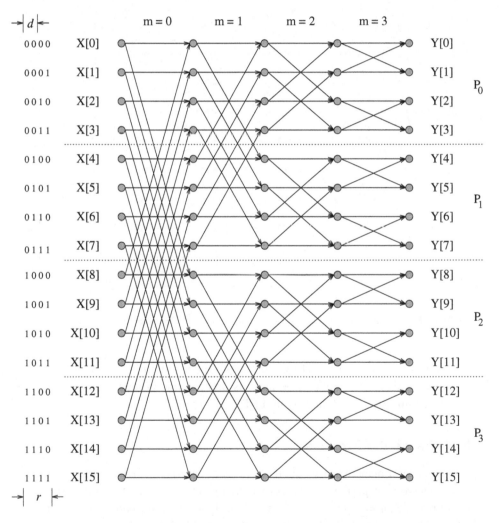

Figure 13.4   A 16-point FFT on four processes. P_i denotes the process labeled i. In general, the number of processes is $p = 2^d$ and the length of the input sequence is $n = 2^r$.

combined. As a result, elements combined during the first d iterations belong to different processes, and pairs of elements combined during the last $(r - d)$ iterations belong to the same processes. Hence, this parallel FFT algorithm requires interprocess interaction only during the first $d = \log p$ of the $\log n$ iterations. There is no interaction during the last $r - d$ iterations. Furthermore, in the ith of the first d iterations, all the elements that a process requires come from exactly one other process – the one whose label is different at the ith most significant bit.

Each interaction operation exchanges n/p words of data. Therefore, the time spent in communication in the entire algorithm is $t_s \log p + t_w(n/p) \log p$. A process updates n/p elements of R during each of the $\log n$ iterations. If a complex multiplication and addition pair takes time t_c, then the parallel run time of the binary-exchange algorithm for n-point FFT on a p-node hypercube network is

$$T_P = t_c \frac{n}{p} \log n + t_s \log p + t_w \frac{n}{p} \log p. \tag{13.4}$$

The process-time product is $t_c n \log n + t_s p \log p + t_w n \log p$. For the parallel system to be cost-optimal, this product should be $O(n \log n)$ – the sequential time complexity of the FFT algorithm. This is true for $p \le n$.

The expressions for speedup and efficiency are given by the following equations:

$$
\begin{aligned}
S &= \frac{t_c n \log n}{T_P} \\
&= \frac{p n \log n}{n \log n + (t_s/t_c) p \log p + (t_w/t_c) n \log p} \\
E &= \frac{1}{1 + (t_s p \log p)/(t_c n \log n) + (t_w \log p)/(t_c \log n)}
\end{aligned}
\tag{13.5}
$$

Scalability Analysis

From Section 13.1, we know that the problem size W for an n-point FFT is

$$W = n \log n. \tag{13.6}$$

Since an n-point FFT can utilize a maximum of n processes with the mapping of Figure 13.3, $n \ge p$ or $n \log n \ge p \log p$ to keep p processes busy. Thus, the isoefficiency function of this parallel FFT algorithm is $\Omega(p \log p)$ due to concurrency. We now derive the isoefficiency function for the binary exchange algorithm due to the different communication-related terms. We can rewrite Equation 13.5 as

$$\frac{t_s p \log p}{t_c n \log n} + \frac{t_w \log p}{t_c \log n} = \frac{1 - E}{E}.$$

In order to maintain a fixed efficiency E, the expression $(t_s p \log p)/(t_c n \log n) + (t_w \log p)/(t_c \log n)$ should be equal to a constant $1/K$, where $K = E/(1 - E)$. We have defined the constant K in this manner to keep the terminology consistent with Chapter 5.

As proposed in Section 5.4.2, we use an approximation to obtain closed expressions for the isoefficiency function. We first determine the rate of growth of the problem size with respect to p that would keep the terms due to t_s constant. To do this, we assume $t_w = 0$. Now the condition for maintaining constant efficiency E is as follows:

$$\frac{t_s p \log p}{t_c n \log n} = \frac{1}{K}$$

$$n \log n = K \frac{t_s}{t_c} p \log p$$

$$W = K \frac{t_s}{t_c} p \log p \tag{13.7}$$

Equation 13.7 gives the isoefficiency function due to the overhead resulting from interaction latency or the message startup time.

Similarly, we derive the isoefficiency function due to the overhead resulting from t_w. We assume that $t_s = 0$; hence, a fixed efficiency E requires that the following relation be maintained:

$$\frac{t_w \log p}{t_c \log n} = \frac{1}{K}$$

$$\log n = K \frac{t_w}{t_c} \log p$$

$$n = p^{K t_w / t_c}$$

$$n \log n = K \frac{t_w}{t_c} p^{K t_w / t_c} \log p$$

$$W = K \frac{t_w}{t_c} p^{K t_w / t_c} \log p \tag{13.8}$$

If the term $K t_w / t_c$ is less than one, then the rate of growth of the problem size required by Equation 13.8 is less than $\Theta(p \log p)$. In this case, Equation 13.7 determines the overall isoefficiency function of this parallel system. However, if $K t_w / t_c$ exceeds one, then Equation 13.8 determines the overall isoefficiency function, which is now greater than the isoefficiency function of $\Theta(p \log p)$ given by Equation 13.7.

For this algorithm, the asymptotic isoefficiency function depends on the relative values of K, t_w, and t_c. Here, K is an increasing function of the efficiency E to be maintained, t_w depends on the communication bandwidth of the parallel computer, and t_c depends on the speed of the computation speed of the processors. The FFT algorithm is unique in that the order of the isoefficiency function depends on the desired efficiency and hardware-dependent parameters. In fact, the efficiency corresponding to $K t_w / t_c = 1$ (i.e., $1/(1 - E) = t_c / t_w$, or $E = t_c / (t_c + t_w)$) acts as a kind of threshold. For a fixed t_c and t_w, efficiencies up to the threshold can be obtained easily. For $E \leq t_c / (t_c + t_w)$, the asymptotic isoefficiency function is $\Theta(p \log p)$. Efficiencies much higher than the threshold $t_c / (t_c + t_w)$ can be obtained only if the problem size is extremely large. The reason is that for these efficiencies, the asymptotic isoefficiency function is $\Theta(p^{K t_w / t_c} \log p)$. The following examples illustrate the effect of the value of $K t_w / t_c$ on the isoefficiency function.

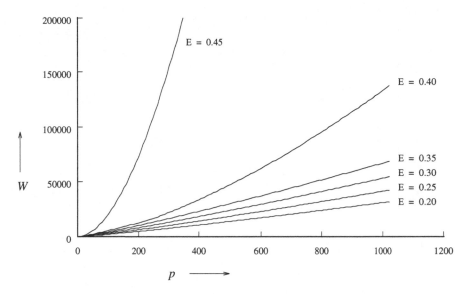

Figure 13.5 Isoefficiency functions of the binary-exchange algorithm on a hypercube with $t_c = 2$, $t_w = 4$, and $t_s = 25$ for various values of E.

Example 13.1 Threshold effect in the binary-exchange algorithm

Consider a hypothetical hypercube for which the relative values of the hardware parameters are given by $t_c = 2$, $t_w = 4$, and $t_s = 25$. With these values, the threshold efficiency $t_c/(t_c + t_w)$ is 0.33.

Now we study the isoefficiency functions of the binary-exchange algorithm on a hypercube for maintaining efficiencies below and above the threshold. The isoefficiency function of this algorithm due to concurrency is $p \log p$. From Equations 13.7 and 13.8, the isoefficiency functions due to the t_s and t_w terms in the overhead function are $K(t_s/t_c) p \log p$ and $K(t_w/t_c) p^{K t_w/t_c} \log p$, respectively. To maintain a given efficiency E (that is, for a given K), the overall isoefficiency function is given by:

$$W = \max\{p \log p, \; K \frac{t_s}{t_c} p \log p, \; K \frac{t_w}{t_c} p^{K t_w/t_c} \log p\}$$

Figure 13.5 shows the isoefficiency curves given by this function for $E = 0.20$, 0.25, 0.30, 0.35, 0.40, and 0.45. Notice that the various isoefficiency curves are regularly spaced for efficiencies up to the threshold. However, the problem sizes required to maintain efficiencies above the threshold are much larger. The asymptotic isoefficiency functions for $E = 0.20$, 0.25, and 0.30 are $\Theta(p \log p)$. The isoefficiency function for $E = 0.40$ is $\Theta(p^{1.33} \log p)$, and that for $E = 0.45$ is $\Theta(p^{1.64} \log p)$.

Figure 13.6 shows the efficiency curve of n-point FFTs on a 256-node hypercube with the same hardware parameters. The efficiency E is computed by using Equation 13.5 for various values of n, when p is equal to 256. The figure shows

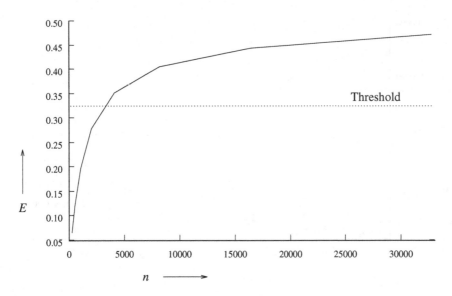

Figure 13.6 The efficiency of the binary-exchange algorithm as a function of n on a 256-node hypercube with $t_c = 2$, $t_w = 4$, and $t_s = 25$.

that the efficiency initially increases rapidly with the problem size, but the efficiency curve flattens out beyond the threshold. ∎

Example 13.1 shows that there is a limit on the efficiency that can be obtained for reasonable problem sizes, and that the limit is determined by the ratio between the CPU speed and the communication bandwidth of the parallel computer being used. This limit can be raised by increasing the bandwidth of the communication channels. However, making the CPUs faster without increasing the communication bandwidth lowers the limit. Hence, the binary-exchange algorithm performs poorly on a parallel computer whose communication and computation speeds are not balanced. If the hardware is balanced with respect to its communication and computation speeds, then the binary-exchange algorithm is fairly scalable, and reasonable efficiencies can be maintained while increasing the problem size at the rate of $\Theta(p \log p)$.

13.2.2 Limited Bandwidth Network

Now we consider the implementation of the binary-exchange algorithm on a parallel computer whose cross-section bandwidth is less than $\Theta(p)$. We choose a mesh interconnection network to illustrate the algorithm and its performance characteristics. Assume that n tasks are mapped onto p processes running on a mesh with $\sqrt{p}$ rows and $\sqrt{p}$ columns, and that $\sqrt{p}$ is a power of two. Let $n = 2^r$ and $p = 2^d$. Also assume that the processes are labeled in a row-major fashion and that the data are distributed in the same manner as for the hypercube; that is, an element with index $(b_0 b_1 \cdots b_{r-1})$ is mapped onto the process labeled

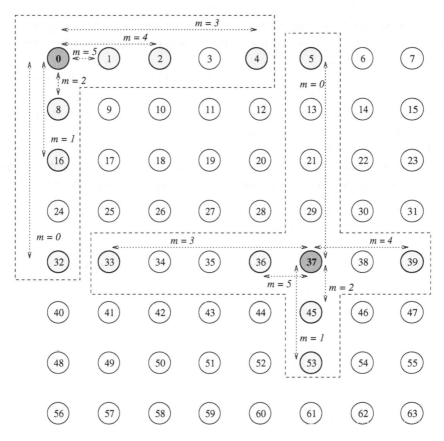

Figure 13.7 Data communication during an FFT computation on a logical square mesh of 64 processes. The figure shows all the processes with which the processes labeled 0 and 37 exchange data.

$(b_0 \cdots b_{d-1})$.

As in case of the hypercube, communication takes place only during the first $\log p$ iterations between processes whose labels differ at one bit. However, unlike the hypercube, the communicating processes are not directly linked in a mesh. Consequently, messages travel over multiple links and there is overlap among messages sharing the same links. Figure 13.7 shows the messages sent and received by processes 0 and 37 during an FFT computation on a 64-node mesh. As the figure shows, process 0 communicates with processes 1, 2, 4, 8, 16, and 32. Note that all these processes lie in the same row or column of the mesh as that of process 0. Processes 1, 2, and 4 lie in the same row as process 0 at distances of 1, 2, and 4 links, respectively. Processes 8, 16, and 32 lie in the same column, again at distances of 1, 2, and 4 links. More precisely, in $\log \sqrt{p}$ of the $\log p$ steps that require communication, the communicating processes are in the same row, and in the remaining $\log \sqrt{p}$ steps, they are in the same column. The number of messages that share at least one link is equal to the number of links that each message traverses (Problem 13.9) because, during a given FFT iteration, all pairs of nodes exchange messages that traverse the same number of links.

The distance between the communicating processes in a row or a column grows from one link to $\sqrt{p}/2$ links, doubling in each of the $\log \sqrt{p}$ iterations. This is true for any process in the mesh, such as process 37 shown in Figure 13.7. Thus, the total time spent in performing rowwise communication is $\Sigma_{m=0}^{d/2-1}(t_s + t_w(n/p)2^m)$. An equal amount of time is spent in columnwise communication. Recall that we assumed that a complex multiplication and addition pair takes time t_c. Since a process performs n/p such calculations in each of the $\log n$ iterations, the overall parallel run time is given by the following equation:

$$
\begin{aligned}
T_P &= t_c \frac{n}{p} \log n + 2 \sum_{m=0}^{d/2-1} \left(t_s + t_w \frac{n}{p} 2^m \right) \\
&= t_c \frac{n}{p} \log n + 2 \left(t_s \log \sqrt{p} + t_w \frac{n}{p} (\sqrt{p} - 1) \right) \\
&\approx t_c \frac{n}{p} \log n + t_s \log p + 2 t_w \frac{n}{\sqrt{p}} \qquad (13.9)
\end{aligned}
$$

The speedup and efficiency are given by the following equations:

$$
\begin{aligned}
S &= \frac{t_c n \log n}{T_P} \\
&= \frac{pn \log n}{n \log n + (t_s/t_c)p \log p + 2(t_w/t_c)n\sqrt{p}} \\
E &= \frac{1}{1 + (t_s p \log p)/(t_c n \log n) + 2(t_w \sqrt{p})/(t_c \log n)} \qquad (13.10)
\end{aligned}
$$

The process-time product of this parallel system is $t_c n \log n + t_s p \log p + 2 t_w n \sqrt{p}$. The process-time product should be $O(n \log n)$ for cost-optimality, which is obtained when $\sqrt{p} = O(\log n)$, or $p = O(\log^2 n)$. Since the communication term due to t_s in Equation 13.9 is the same as for the hypercube, the corresponding isoefficiency function is again $\Theta(p \log p)$ as given by Equation 13.7. By performing isoefficiency analysis along the same lines as in Section 13.2.1, we can show that the isoefficiency function due to the t_w term is $2K(t_w/t_c)2^{2K(t_w/t_c)\sqrt{p}}\sqrt{p}$ (Problem 13.4). Given this isoefficiency function, the problem size must grow exponentially with the number of processes to maintain constant efficiency. Hence, the binary-exchange FFT algorithm is not very scalable on a mesh.

The communication overhead of the binary-exchange algorithm on a mesh cannot be reduced by using a different mapping of the sequences onto the processes. In any mapping, there is at least one iteration in which pairs of processes that communicate with each other are at least $\sqrt{p}/2$ links apart (Problem 13.2). The algorithm inherently requires $\Theta(p)$ bisection bandwidth on a p-node ensemble, and on an architecture like a 2-D mesh with $\Theta(\sqrt{p})$ bisection bandwidth, the communication time cannot be asymptotically better than $t_s \log p + 2(n/\sqrt{p})t_w$ as discussed above.

13.2.3   Extra Computations in Parallel FFT

So far, we have described a parallel formulation of the FFT algorithm on a hypercube and a mesh, and have discussed its performance and scalability in the presence of communication overhead on both architectures. In this section, we discuss another source of overhead that can be present in a parallel FFT implementation.

Recall from Algorithm 13.2 that the computation step of line 12 multiplies a power of ω (a twiddle factor) with an element of S. For an n-point FFT, line 12 executes $n \log n$ times in the sequential algorithm. However, only n distinct powers of ω (that is, ω^0, ω^1, ω^2, ..., ω^{n-1}) are used in the entire algorithm. So some of the twiddle factors are used repeatedly. In a serial implementation, it is useful to precompute and store all n twiddle factors before starting the main algorithm. That way, the computation of twiddle factors requires only $\Theta(n)$ complex operations rather than the $\Theta(n \log n)$ operations needed to compute all twiddle factors in each iteration of line 12.

In a parallel implementation, the total work required to compute the twiddle factors cannot be reduced to $\Theta(n)$. The reason is that, even if a certain twiddle factor is used more than once, it might be used on different processes at different times. If FFTs of the same size are computed on the same number of processes, every process needs the same set of twiddle factors for each computation. In this case, the twiddle factors can be precomputed and stored, and the cost of their computation can be amortized over the execution of all instances of FFTs of the same size. However, if we consider only one instance of FFT, then twiddle factor computation gives rise to additional overhead in a parallel implementation, because it performs more overall operations than the sequential implementation.

As an example, consider the various powers of ω used in the three iterations of an 8-point FFT. In the mth iteration of the loop starting on line 5 of the algorithm, ω^l is computed for all i ($0 \le i < n$), such that l is the integer obtained by reversing the order of the $m + 1$ most significant bits of i and then padding them by $\log n - (m + 1)$ zeros to the right (refer to Figure 13.1 and Algorithm 13.2 to see how l is derived). Table 13.1 shows the binary representation of the powers of ω required for all values of i and m for an 8-point FFT.

If eight processes are used, then each process computes and uses one column of Table 13.1. Process 0 computes just one twiddle factor for all its iterations, but some pro-

Table 13.1   The binary representation of the various powers of ω calculated in different iterations of an 8-point FFT (also see Figure 13.1). The value of m refers to the iteration number of the outer loop, and i is the index of the inner loop of Algorithm 13.2.

	i							
	0	1	2	3	4	5	6	7
$m = 0$	000	000	000	000	100	100	100	100
$m = 1$	000	000	100	100	010	010	110	110
$m = 2$	000	100	010	110	001	101	011	111

Table 13.2   The maximum number of new powers of ω used by any process in each iteration of an 8-point FFT computation.

	$p = 1$	$p = 2$	$p = 4$	$p = 8$
$m = 0$	2	1	1	1
$m = 1$	2	2	1	1
$m = 2$	4	4	2	1
Total $= h(8,p)$	8	7	4	3

cesses (in this case, all other processes 2–7) compute a new twiddle factor in each of the three iterations. If $p = n/2 = 4$, then each process computes two consecutive columns of the table. In this case, the last process computes the twiddle factors in the last two columns of the table. Hence, the last process computes a total of four different powers – one each for $m = 0$ (100) and $m = 1$ (110), and two for $m = 2$ (011 and 111). Although different processes may compute a different number of twiddle factors, the total overhead due to the extra work is proportional to p times the maximum number of twiddle factors that any single process computes. Let $h(n, p)$ be the maximum number of twiddle factors that any of the p processes computes during an n-point FFT. Table 13.2 shows the values of $h(8,p)$ for $p = 1, 2, 4$, and 8. The table also shows the maximum number of new twiddle factors that any single process computes in each iteration.

The function h is defined by the following recurrence relation (Problem 13.5):

$$h(n, 1) = n$$
$$h(p, p) = \log p \qquad\qquad (p \neq 1)$$
$$h(n, p) = h(n, 2p) + n/p - 1 \quad (p \neq 1, n > p)$$

The solution to this recurrence relation for $p > 1$ and $n \geq p$ is

$$h(n, p) = 2\left(\frac{n}{p} - 1\right) + \log p.$$

Thus, if it takes time t'_c to compute one twiddle factor, then at least one process spends time $t'_c 2(n/p - 1) + t'_c \log p$ computing twiddle factors. The total cost of twiddle factor computation, summed over all processes, is $2t'_c(n - p) + t'_c p \log p$. Since even a serial implementation incurs a cost of $t'_c n$ in computing twiddle factors, the total parallel overhead due to extra work ($T_o^{extra\_work}$) is given by the following equation:

$$
\begin{aligned}
T_o^{extra\_work} &= (2t'_c(n - p) + t'_c p \log p) - t'_c n \\
&= t'_c(n + p(\log p - 2)) \\
&= \Theta(n) + \Theta(p \log p)
\end{aligned}
$$

This overhead is independent of the architecture of the parallel computer used for the FFT computation. The isoefficiency function due to $T_o^{extra\_work}$ is $\Theta(p \log p)$. Since this term is of the same order as the isoefficiency terms due to message startup time and concurrency, the extra computations do not affect the overall scalability of parallel FFT.

13.3 The Transpose Algorithm

The binary-exchange algorithm yields good performance on parallel computers with sufficiently high communication bandwidth with respect to the processing speed of the CPUs. Efficiencies below a certain threshold can be maintained while increasing the problem size at a moderate rate with an increasing number of processes. However, this threshold is very low if the communication bandwidth of the parallel computer is low compared to the speed of its processors. In this section, we describe a different parallel formulation of FFT that trades off some efficiency for a more consistent level of parallel performance. This parallel algorithm involves matrix transposition, and hence is called the ***transpose algorithm***.

The performance of the transpose algorithm is worse than that of the binary-exchange algorithm for efficiencies below the threshold. However, it is much easier to obtain efficiencies above the binary-exchange algorithm's threshold using the transpose algorithm. Thus, the transpose algorithm is particularly useful when the ratio of communication bandwidth to CPU speed is low and high efficiencies are desired. On a hypercube or a p-node network with $\Theta(p)$ bisection width, the transpose algorithm has a fixed asymptotic isoefficiency function of $\Theta(p^2 \log p)$. That is, the order of this isoefficiency function is independent of the ratio of the speed of point-to-point communication and the computation.

13.3.1 Two-Dimensional Transpose Algorithm

The simplest transpose algorithm requires a single transpose operation over a two-dimensional array; hence, we call this algorithm the ***two-dimensional transpose algorithm***.

Assume that $\sqrt{n}$ is a power of 2, and that the sequences of size n used in Algorithm 13.2 are arranged in a $\sqrt{n} \times \sqrt{n}$ two-dimensional square array, as shown in Figure 13.8 for $n = 16$. Recall that computing the FFT of a sequence of n points requires $\log n$ iterations of the outer loop of Algorithm 13.2. If the data are arranged as shown in Figure 13.8, then the FFT computation in each column can proceed independently for $\log \sqrt{n}$ iterations without any column requiring data from any other column. Similarly, in the remaining $\log \sqrt{n}$ iterations, computation proceeds independently in each row without any row requiring data from any other row. Figure 13.8 shows the pattern of combination of the elements for a 16-point FFT. The figure illustrates that if data of size n are arranged in a $\sqrt{n} \times \sqrt{n}$ array, then an n-point FFT computation is equivalent to independent $\sqrt{n}$-point FFT computations in the columns of the array, followed by independent $\sqrt{n}$-point FFT computations in the rows.

If the $\sqrt{n} \times \sqrt{n}$ array of data is transposed after computing the $\sqrt{n}$-point column FFTs, then the remaining part of the problem is to compute the $\sqrt{n}$-point columnwise FFTs of the transposed matrix. The transpose algorithm uses this property to compute the FFT in

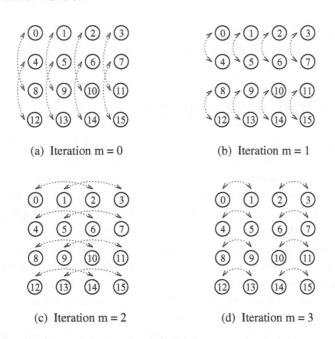

(a) Iteration m = 0   (b) Iteration m = 1

(c) Iteration m = 2   (d) Iteration m = 3

Figure 13.8   The pattern of combination of elements in a 16-point FFT when the data are arranged in a 4 × 4 two-dimensional square array.

parallel by using a columnwise striped partitioning to distribute the $\sqrt{n} \times \sqrt{n}$ array of data among the processes. For instance, consider the computation of the 16-point FFT shown in Figure 13.9, where the 4 × 4 array of data is distributed among four processes such that each process stores one column of the array. In general, the two-dimensional transpose algorithm works in three phases. In the first phase, a $\sqrt{n}$-point FFT is computed for each column. In the second phase, the array of data is transposed. The third and final phase is identical to the first phase, and involves the computation of $\sqrt{n}$-point FFTs for each column of the transposed array. Figure 13.9 shows that the first and third phases of the algorithm do not require any interprocess communication. In both these phases, all $\sqrt{n}$ points for each columnwise FFT computation are available on the same process. Only the second phase requires communication for transposing the $\sqrt{n} \times \sqrt{n}$ matrix.

In the transpose algorithm shown in Figure 13.9, one column of the data array is assigned to one process. Before analyzing the transpose algorithm further, consider the more general case in which p processes are used and $1 \leq p \leq \sqrt{n}$. The $\sqrt{n} \times \sqrt{n}$ array of data is striped into blocks, and one block of $\sqrt{n}/p$ rows is assigned to each process. In the first and third phases of the algorithm, each process computes $\sqrt{n}/p$ FFTs of size $\sqrt{n}$ each. The second phase transposes the $\sqrt{n} \times \sqrt{n}$ matrix, which is distributed among p processes with a one-dimensional partitioning. Recall from Section 4.5 that such a transpose requires an all-to-all personalized communication.

Now we derive an expression for the parallel run time of the two-dimensional transpose

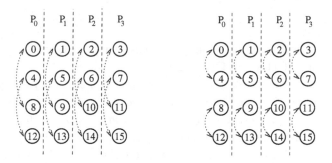

(a) Steps in phase 1 of the transpose algorithm (before transpose)

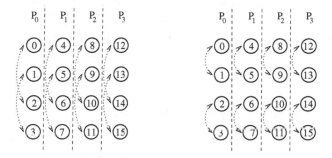

(b) Steps in phase 3 of the transpose algorithm (after transpose)

Figure 13.9   The two-dimensional transpose algorithm for a 16-point FFT on four processes.

algorithm. The only inter-process interaction in this algorithm occurs when the $\sqrt{n} \times \sqrt{n}$ array of data partitioned along columns or rows and mapped onto p processes is transposed. Replacing the message size m by n/p – the amount of data owned by each process – in the expression for all-to-all personalized communication in Table 4.1 yields $t_s(p-1)+t_w n/p$ as the time spent in the second phase of the algorithm. The first and third phases each take time $t_c \times \sqrt{n}/p \times \sqrt{n} \log \sqrt{n}$. Thus, the parallel run time of the transpose algorithm on a hypercube or any $\Theta(p)$ bisection width network is given by the following equation:

$$
\begin{aligned}
T_P &= 2t_c \frac{\sqrt{n}}{p}\sqrt{n}\log\sqrt{n}+t_s(p-1)+t_w\frac{n}{p} \\
&= t_c\frac{n}{p}\log n + t_s(p-1)+t_w\frac{n}{p} \quad\quad (13.11)
\end{aligned}
$$

The expressions for speedup and efficiency are as follows:

$$
S \approx \frac{pn\log n}{n\log n + (t_s/t_c)p^2 + (t_w/t_c)n}
$$

$$
E \approx \frac{1}{1 + (t_s p^2)/(t_c n\log n) + t_w/(t_c\log n)}
$$

$$(13.12)$$

The process-time product of this parallel system is $t_c n \log n + t_s p^2 + t_w n$. This parallel system is cost-optimal if $n \log n = \Omega(p^2 \log p)$.

Note that the term associated with t_w in the expression for efficiency in Equation 13.12 is independent of the number of processes. The degree of concurrency of this algorithm requires that $\sqrt{n} = \Omega(p)$ because at most $\sqrt{n}$ processes can be used to partition the $\sqrt{n} \times \sqrt{n}$ array of data in a striped manner. As a result, $n = \Omega(p^2)$, or $n \log n = \Omega(p^2 \log p)$. Thus, the problem size must increase at least as fast as $\Theta(p^2 \log p)$ with respect to the number of processes to use all of them efficiently. The overall isoefficiency function of the two-dimensional transpose algorithm is $\Theta(p^2 \log p)$ on a hypercube or another interconnection network with bisection width $\Theta(p)$. This isoefficiency function is independent of the ratio of t_w for point-to-point communication and t_c. On a network whose cross-section bandwidth b is less than $\Theta(p)$ for p nodes, the t_w term must be multiplied by an appropriate expression of $\Theta(p/b)$ in order to derive T_P, S, E, and the isoefficiency function (Problem 13.6).

Comparison with the Binary-Exchange Algorithm

A comparison of Equations 13.4 and 13.11 shows that the transpose algorithm has a much higher overhead than the binary-exchange algorithm due to the message startup time t_s, but has a lower overhead due to per-word transfer time t_w. As a result, either of the two algorithms may be faster depending on the relative values of t_s and t_w. If the latency t_s is very low, then the transpose algorithm may be the algorithm of choice. On the other hand, the binary-exchange algorithm may perform better on a parallel computer with a high communication bandwidth but a significant startup time.

Recall from Section 13.2.1 that an overall isoefficiency function of $\Theta(p \log p)$ can be realized by using the binary-exchange algorithm if the efficiency is such that $K t_w / t_c \leq 1$, where $K = E/(1 - E)$. If the desired efficiency is such that $K t_w / t_c = 2$, then the overall isoefficiency function of both the binary-exchange and the two-dimensional transpose algorithms is $\Theta(p^2 \log p)$. When $K t_w / t_c > 2$, the two-dimensional transpose algorithm is more scalable than the binary-exchange algorithm; hence, the former should be the algorithm of choice, provided that $n \geq p^2$. Note, however, that the transpose algorithm yields a performance benefit over the binary-exchange algorithm only if the target architecture has a cross-section bandwidth of $\Theta(p)$ for p nodes (Problem 13.6).

13.3.2 The Generalized Transpose Algorithm

In the two-dimensional transpose algorithm, the input of size n is arranged in a $\sqrt{n} \times \sqrt{n}$ two-dimensional array that is partitioned along one dimension on p processes. These processes, irrespective of the underlying architecture of the parallel computer, can be regarded as arranged in a logical one-dimensional linear array. As an extension of this scheme,

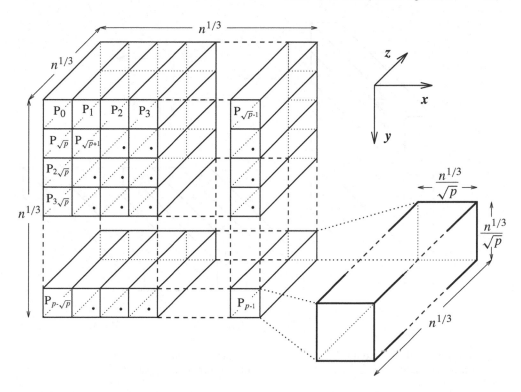

Figure 13.10 Data distribution in the three-dimensional transpose algorithm for an n-point FFT on p processes ($\sqrt{p} \leq n^{1/3}$).

consider the n data points to be arranged in an $n^{1/3} \times n^{1/3} \times n^{1/3}$ three-dimensional array mapped onto a logical $\sqrt{p} \times \sqrt{p}$ two-dimensional mesh of processes. Figure 13.10 illustrates this mapping. To simplify the algorithm description, we label the three axes of the three-dimensional array of data as x, y, and z. In this mapping, the x-y plane of the array is checkerboarded into $\sqrt{p} \times \sqrt{p}$ parts. As the figure shows, each process stores $(n^{1/3}/\sqrt{p}) \times (n^{1/3}/\sqrt{p})$ columns of data, and the length of each column (along the z-axis) is $n^{1/3}$. Thus, each process has $(n^{1/3}/\sqrt{p}) \times (n^{1/3}/\sqrt{p}) \times n^{1/3} = n/p$ elements of data.

Recall from Section 13.3.1 that the FFT of a two-dimensionally arranged input of size $\sqrt{n} \times \sqrt{n}$ can be computed by first computing the $\sqrt{n}$-point one-dimensional FFTs of all the columns of the data and then computing the $\sqrt{n}$-point one-dimensional FFTs of all the rows. If the data are arranged in an $n^{1/3} \times n^{1/3} \times n^{1/3}$ three-dimensional array, the entire n-point FFT can be computed similarly. In this case, $n^{1/3}$-point FFTs are computed over the elements of the columns of the array in all three dimensions, choosing one dimension at a time. We call this algorithm the ***three-dimensional transpose algorithm***. This algorithm can be divided into the following five phases:

1. In the first phase, $n^{1/3}$-point FFTs are computed on all the rows along the z-axis.

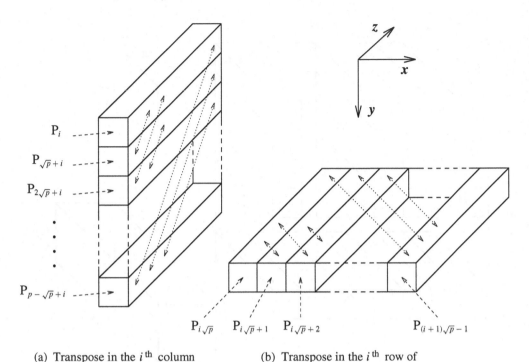

(a) Transpose in the ith column
    of processors during phase 2

(b) Transpose in the ith row of
    processors during phase 4

Figure 13.11   The communication (transposition) phases in the three-dimensional transpose algorithm for an n-point FFT on p processes.

2. In the second phase, all the $n^{1/3}$ cross-sections of size $n^{1/3} \times n^{1/3}$ along the y-z plane are transposed.

3. In the third phase, $n^{1/3}$-point FFTs are computed on all the rows of the modified array along the z-axis.

4. In the fourth phase, each of the $n^{1/3} \times n^{1/3}$ cross-sections along the x-z plane is transposed.

5. In the fifth and final phase, $n^{1/3}$-point FFTs of all the rows along the z-axis are computed again.

For the data distribution shown in Figure 13.10, in the first, third, and fifth phases of the algorithm, all processes perform $(n^{1/3}/\sqrt{p}) \times (n^{1/3}/\sqrt{p})$ FFT computations, each of size $n^{1/3}$. Since all the data for performing these computations are locally available on each process, no interprocess communication is involved in these three odd-numbered phases. The time spent by a process in each of these phases is $t_c n^{1/3} \log(n^{1/3}) \times (n^{1/3}/\sqrt{p}) \times (n^{1/3}/\sqrt{p})$. Thus, the total time that a process spends in computation is $t_c(n/p) \log n$.

Figure 13.11 illustrates the second and fourth phases of the three-dimensional transpose algorithm. As Figure 13.11(a) shows, the second phase of the algorithm requires transposing square cross-sections of size $n^{1/3} \times n^{1/3}$ along the y-z plane. Each column of $\sqrt{p}$ processes performs the transposition of $(n^{1/3}/\sqrt{p})$ such cross-sections. This transposition involves all-to-all personalized communications among groups of $\sqrt{p}$ processes with individual messages of size $n/p^{3/2}$. If a p-node network with bisection width $\Theta(p)$ is used, this phase takes time $t_s(\sqrt{p} - 1) + t_w n/p$. The fourth phase, shown in Figure 13.11(b), is similar. Here each row of $\sqrt{p}$ processes performs the transpose of $(n^{1/3}/\sqrt{p})$ cross-sections along the x-z plane. Again, each cross-section consists of $n^{1/3} \times n^{1/3}$ data elements. The communication time of this phase is the same as that of the second phase. The total parallel run time of the three-dimensional transpose algorithm for an n-point FFT is

$$T_P = t_c \frac{n}{p} \log n + 2t_s(\sqrt{p} - 1) + 2t_w \frac{n}{p}. \tag{13.13}$$

Having studied the two- and three-dimensional transpose algorithms, we can derive a more general q-dimensional transpose algorithm similarly. Let the n-point input be arranged in a logical q-dimensional array of size $n^{1/q} \times n^{1/q} \times \cdots \times n^{1/q}$ (a total of q terms). Now the entire n-point FFT computation can be viewed as q subcomputations. Each of the q subcomputations along a different dimension consists of $n^{(q-1)/q}$ FFTs over $n^{1/q}$ data points. We map the array of data onto a logical $(q - 1)$-dimensional array of p processes, where $p \le n^{(q-1)/q}$, and $p = 2^{(q-1)s}$ for some integer s. The FFT of the entire data is now computed in $(2q - 1)$ phases (recall that there are three phases in the two-dimensional transpose algorithm and five phases in the three-dimensional transpose algorithm). In the q odd-numbered phases, each process performs $n^{(q-1)/q}/p$ of the required $n^{1/q}$-point FFTs. The total computation time for each process over all q computation phases is the product of q (the number of computation phases), $n^{(q-1)/q}/p$ (the number of $n^{1/q}$-point FFTs computed by each process in each computation phase), and $t_c n^{1/q} \log(n^{1/q})$ (the time to compute a single $n^{1/q}$-point FFT). Multiplying these terms gives a total computation time of $t_c(n/p) \log n$.

In each of the $(q - 1)$ even-numbered phases, sub-arrays of size $n^{1/q} \times n^{1/q}$ are transposed on rows of the q-dimensional logical array of processes. Each such row contains $p^{1/(q-1)}$ processes. One such transpose is performed along every dimension of the $(q - 1)$-dimensional process array in each of the $(q - 1)$ communication phases. The time spent in communication in each transposition is $t_s(p^{1/(q-1)} - 1) + t_w n/p$. Thus, the total parallel run time of the q-dimensional transpose algorithm for an n-point FFT on a p-node network with bisection width $\Theta(p)$ is

$$T_P = t_c \frac{n}{p} \log n + (q - 1)t_s(p^{1/(q-1)} - 1) + (q - 1)t_w \frac{n}{p}. \tag{13.14}$$

Equation 13.14 can be verified by replacing q with 2 and 3, and comparing the result with Equations 13.11 and 13.13, respectively.

A comparison of Equations 13.11, 13.13, 13.14, and 13.4 shows an interesting trend. As the dimension q of the transpose algorithm increases, the communication overhead due to t_w increases, but that due to t_s decreases. The binary-exchange algorithm and the two-dimensional transpose algorithms can be regarded as two extremes. The former minimizes the overhead due to t_s but has the largest overhead due to t_w. The latter minimizes the overhead due to t_w but has the largest overhead due to t_s. The variations of the transpose algorithm for $2 < q < \log p$ lie between these two extremes. For a given parallel computer, the specific values of t_c, t_s, and t_w determine which of these algorithms has the optimal parallel run time (Problem 13.8).

Note that, from a practical point of view, only the binary-exchange algorithm and the two- and three-dimensional transpose algorithms are feasible. Higher-dimensional transpose algorithms are very complicated to code. Moreover, restrictions on n and p limit their applicability. These restrictions for a q-dimensional transpose algorithm are that n must be a power of two that is a multiple of q, and that p must be a power of 2 that is a multiple of $(q - 1)$. In other words, $n = 2^{qr}$, and $p = 2^{(q-1)s}$, where q, r, and s are integers.

Example 13.2   A comparison of binary-exchange, 2-D transpose, and 3-D transpose algorithms

This example shows that either the binary-exchange algorithm or any of the transpose algorithms may be the algorithm of choice for a given parallel computer, depending on the size of the FFT. Consider a 64-node version of the hypercube described in Example 13.1 with $t_c = 2$, $t_s = 25$, and $t_w = 4$. Figure 13.12 shows speedups attained by the binary-exchange algorithm, the 2-D transpose algorithm, and the 3-D transpose algorithm for different problem sizes. The speedups are based on the parallel run times given by Equations 13.4, 13.11, and 13.13, respectively. The figure shows that for different ranges of n, a different algorithm provides the highest speedup for an n-point FFT. For the given values of the hardware parameters, the binary-exchange algorithm is best suited for very low granularity FFT computations, the 2-D transpose algorithm is best for very high granularity computations, and the 3-D transpose algorithm's speedup is the maximum for intermediate granularities. ∎

13.4   Bibliographic Remarks

Due to the important role of Fourier transform in scientific and technical computations, there has been great interest in implementing FFT on parallel computers and on studying its performance. Swarztrauber [Swa87] describes many implementations of the FFT algorithm on vector and parallel computers. Cvetanovic [Cve87] and Norton and Silberger [NS87] give a comprehensive performance analysis of the FFT algorithm on pseudo-shared-memory architectures such as the IBM RP-3. They consider various partitionings of data among memory blocks and, in each case, obtain expressions for communication overhead and speedup in terms of problem size, number of processes, memory latency, CPU speed, and speed of communication. Aggarwal, Chandra, and Snir [ACS89c] analyze the performance of FFT and other algorithms on LPRAM – a new model for parallel

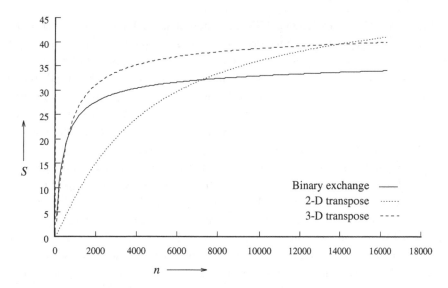

Figure 13.12 A comparison of the speedups obtained by the binary-exchange, 2-D transpose, and 3-D transpose algorithms on a 64-node hypercube with $t_c = 2$, $t_w = 4$, and $t_s = 25$.

computation. This model differs from the standard PRAM model in that remote accesses are more expensive than local accesses in an LPRAM. Parallel FFT algorithms and their implementation and experimental evaluation on various architectures have been pursued by many other researchers [AGGM90, Bai90, BCJ90, BKH89, DT89, GK93b, JKFM89, KA88, Loa92].

The basic FFT algorithm whose parallel formulations are discussed in this chapter is called the unordered FFT because the elements of the output sequence are stored in bit-reversed index order. In other words, the frequency spectrum of the input signal is obtained by reordering the elements of the output sequence Y produced by Algorithm 13.2 in such a way that for all i, $Y[i]$ is replaced by $Y[j]$, where j is obtained by reversing the bits in the binary representation of i. This is a permutation operation (Section 4.6) and is known as **bit reversal**. Norton and Silberger [NS87] show that an ordered transform can be obtained with at most $2d + 1$ communication steps, where $d = \log p$. Since the unordered FFT computation requires only d communication steps, the total communication overhead in the case of ordered FFT is roughly double of that for unordered FFT. Clearly, an unordered transform is preferred where applicable. The output sequence need not be ordered when the transform is used as a part of a larger computation and as such remains invisible to the user [Swa87]. In many practical applications of FFT, such as convolution and solution of the discrete Poisson equation, bit reversal can be avoided [Loa92]. If required, bit reversal can be performed by using an algorithm described by Van Loan [Loa92] for a distributed-memory parallel computer. The asymptotic communication complexity of this algorithm is the same as that of the binary-exchange algorithm on a hypercube.

Several variations of the simple FFT algorithm presented here have been suggested in the literature. Gupta and Kumar [GK93b] show that the total communication over-head for mesh and hypercube architectures is the same for the one- and two-dimensional FFTs. Certain schemes for computing the DFT have been suggested that involve fewer arithmetic operations on a serial computer than the simple Cooley-Tukey FFT algorithm requires [Nus82, RB76, Win77]. Notable among these are computing one-dimensional FFTs with radix greater than two and computing multidimensional FFTs by transforming them into a set of one-dimensional FFTs by using the polynomial transform method. A radix-q FFT is computed by splitting the input sequence of size n into q sequences of size n/q each, computing the q smaller FFTs, and then combining the result. For example, in a radix-4 FFT, each step computes four outputs from four inputs, and the total number of iterations is $\log_4 n$ rather than $\log_2 n$. The input length should, of course, be a power of four. Despite the reduction in the number of iterations, the aggregate communication time for a radix-q FFT remains the same as that for radix-2. For example, for a radix-4 algo-rithm on a hypercube, each communication step now involves four processes distributed in two dimensions rather than two processes in one dimension. In contrast, the number of multiplications in a radix-4 FFT is 25% fewer than in a radix-2 FFT [Nus82]. This number can be marginally improved by using higher radices, but the amount of communication remains unchanged.

Problems

13.1 Let the serial run time of an n-point FFT computation be $t_c n \log n$. Consider its implementation on an architecture on which the parallel run time is $(t_c n \log n)/p + (t_w n \log p)/p$. Assume that $t_c = 1$ and $t_w = 0.2$.

1. Write expressions for the speedup and efficiency.

2. What is the isoefficiency function if an efficiency of 0.6 is desired?

3. How will the isoefficiency function change (if at all) if an efficiency of 0.4 is desired?

4. Repeat parts 1 and 2 for the case in which $t_w = 1$ and everything else is the same.

13.2 **[Tho83]** Show that, while performing FFT on a square mesh of p processes by using any mapping of data onto the processes, there is at least one iteration in which the pairs of processes that need to communicate are at least $\sqrt{p}/2$ links apart.

13.3 Describe the communication pattern of the binary-exchange algorithm on a linear array of p processes. What are the parallel run time, speedup, efficiency, and isoefficiency function of the binary-exchange algorithm on a linear array?

13.4 Show that, if $t_s = 0$, the isoefficiency function of the binary-exchange algorithm on a mesh is given by $W = 2K(t_w/t_c)2^{2K(t_w/t_c)\sqrt{p}}\sqrt{p}$.
     Hint: Use Equation 13.10.

13.5 Prove that the maximum number of twiddle factors computed by any process in the parallel implementation of an n-point FFT using p processes is given by the recurrence relation given in Section 13.2.3.

13.6 Derive expressions for the parallel run time, speedup, and efficiency of the two-dimensional transpose algorithm described in Section 13.3.1 for an n-point FFT on a p-node two-dimensional mesh and a linear array of p nodes.

13.7 Ignoring t_s, by what factor should the communication bandwidth of a p-node mesh be increased so that it yields the same performance on the two-dimensional transpose algorithm for an n-point FFT on a p-node hypercube?

13.8 You are given the following sets of communication-related constants for a hypercube network: (i) $t_s = 250$, $t_w = 1$, (ii) $t_s = 50$, $t_w = 1$, (iii) $t_s = 10$, $t_w = 1$, (iv) $t_s = 2$, $t_w = 1$, and (v) $t_s = 0$, $t_w = 1$.

    1. Given a choice among the binary-exchange algorithm and the two-, three-, four-, and five-dimensional transpose algorithms, which one would you use for $n = 2^{15}$ and $p = 2^{12}$ for each of the preceding sets of values of t_s and t_w?

    2. Repeat part 1 for (a) $n = 2^{12}$, $p = 2^6$, and (b) $n = 2^{20}$, $p = 2^{12}$.

13.9 [GK93b] Consider computing an n-point FFT on a $\sqrt{p} \times \sqrt{p}$ mesh. If the channel bandwidth grows at a rate of $\Theta(p^x)$ $(x > 0)$ with the number of nodes p in the mesh, show that the isoefficiency function due to communication overhead is $\Theta(p^{0.5-x}2^{2(t_w/t_c)p^{0.5-x}})$ and that due to concurrency is $\Theta(p^{1+x} \log p)$. Also show that the best possible isoefficiency for FFT on a mesh is $\Theta(p^{1.5} \log p)$, even if the channel bandwidth increases arbitrarily with the number of nodes in the network.

Complexity of Functions and Order Analysis

Order analysis and the asymptotic complexity of functions are used extensively in this book to analyze the performance of algorithms.

A.1 Complexity of Functions

When analyzing parallel algorithms in this book, we use the following three types of functions:

1. **Exponential functions:** A function f from reals to reals is called an ***exponential*** function in x if it can be expressed in the form $f(x) = a^x$ for $x, a \in \Re$ (the set of real numbers) and $a > 1$. Examples of exponential functions are 2^x, 1.5^{x+2}, and $3^{1.5x}$.

2. **Polynomial functions:** A function f from reals to reals is called a ***polynomial*** function of ***degree*** b in x if it can be expressed in the form $f(x) = x^b$ for $x, b \in \Re$ and $b > 0$. A ***linear*** function is a polynomial function of degree one and a ***quadratic*** function is a polynomial function of degree two. Examples of polynomial functions are 2, $5x$, and $5.5x^{2.3}$.

   A function f that is a sum of two polynomial functions g and h is also a polynomial function whose degree is equal to the maximum of the degrees of g and h. For example, $2x + x^2$ is a polynomial function of degree two.

3. **Logarithmic functions:** A function f from reals to reals that can be expressed in the form $f(x) = \log_b x$ for $b \in \Re$ and $b > 1$ is **logarithmic** in x. In this expression, b is called the **base** of the logarithm. Examples of logarithmic functions are $\log_{1.5} x$ and $\log_2 x$. Unless stated otherwise, all logarithms in this book are of base two. We use $\log x$ to denote $\log_2 x$, and $\log^2 x$ to denote $(\log_2 x)^2$.

Most functions in this book can be expressed as sums of two or more functions. A function f is said to **dominate** a function g if $f(x)$ grows at a faster rate than $g(x)$. Thus, function f dominates function g if and only if $f(x)/g(x)$ is a monotonically increasing function in x. In other words, f dominates g if and only if for any constant $c > 0$, there exists a value x_0 such that $f(x) > cg(x)$ for $x > x_0$. An exponential function dominates a polynomial function and a polynomial function dominates a logarithmic function. The relation *dominates* is transitive. If function f dominates function g, and function g dominates function h, then function f also dominates function h. Thus, an exponential function also dominates a logarithmic function.

A.2   Order Analysis of Functions

In the analysis of algorithms, it is often cumbersome or impossible to derive exact expressions for parameters such as run time, speedup, and efficiency. In many cases, an approximation of the exact expression is adequate. The approximation may indeed be more illustrative of the behavior of the function because it focuses on the critical factors influencing the parameter.

Example A.1   Distances traveled by three cars
Consider three cars A, B, and C. Assume that we start monitoring the cars at time $t = 0$. At $t = 0$, car A is moving at a velocity of 1000 feet per second and maintains a constant velocity. At $t = 0$, car B's velocity is 100 feet per second and it is accelerating at a rate of 20 feet per second per second. Car C starts from a standstill at $t = 0$ and accelerates at a rate of 25 feet per second per second. Let $D_A(t)$, $D_B(t)$, and $D_C(t)$ represent the distances traveled in t seconds by cars A, B, and C. From elementary physics, we know that

$$\begin{aligned} D_A(t) &= 1000t, \\ D_B(t) &= 100t + 20t^2, \\ D_C(t) &= 25t^2. \end{aligned}$$

Now, we compare the cars according to the distance they travel in a given time. For $t > 45$ seconds, car B outperforms car A. Similarly, for $t > 20$ seconds, car C outperforms car B, and for $t > 40$ seconds, car C outperforms car A. Furthermore, $D_C(t) < 1.25D_B(t)$ and $D_B(t) < D_C(t)$ for $t > 20$, which implies that after a certain time, the difference in the performance of cars B and C is bounded by the

other scaled by a constant multiplicative factor. All these facts can be captured by
the order analysis of the expressions. ∎

The Θ Notation: From Example A.1, $D_C(t) < 1.25 D_B(t)$ and $D_B(t) < D_C(t)$ for
$t > 20$; that is, the difference in the performance of cars B and C after $t = 0$ is bounded by
the other scaled by a constant multiplicative factor. Such an equivalence in performance
is often significant when analyzing performance. The Θ notation captures the relationship between these two functions. The functions $D_C(t)$ and $D_B(t)$ can be expressed by
using the Θ notation as $D_C(t) = \Theta(D_B(t))$ and $D_B(t) = \Theta(D_C(t))$. Furthermore, both
functions are equal to $\Theta(t^2)$.

Formally, the Θ notation is defined as follows: given a function $g(x)$, $f(x) = \Theta(g(x))$
if and only if for any constants $c_1, c_2 > 0$, there exists an $x_0 \geq 0$ such that $c_1 g(x) \leq
f(x) \leq c_2 g(x)$ for all $x \geq x_0$.

The O Notation: Often, we would like to bound the growth of a particular parameter
by a simpler function. From Example A.1 we have seen that for $t > 45$, $D_B(t)$ is always
greater than $D_A(t)$. This relation between $D_A(t)$ and $D_B(t)$ is expressed using the O
(big-oh) notation as $D_A(t) = O(D_B(t))$.

Formally, the O notation is defined as follows: given a function $g(x)$, $f(x) = O(g(x))$
if and only if for any constant $c > 0$, their exists an $x_0 \geq 0$ such that $f(x) \leq c g(x)$ for
all $x \geq x_0$. From this definition we deduce that $D_A(t) = O(t^2)$ and $D_B(t) = O(t^2)$.
Furthermore, $D_A(t) = O(t)$ also satisfies the conditions of the O notation.

The Ω Notation: The O notation sets an upper bound on the rate of growth of a function. The Ω notation is the converse of the O notation; that is, it sets a lower bound on
the rate of growth of a function. From Example A.1, $D_A(t) < D_C(t)$ for $t > 40$. This
relationship can be expressed using the Ω notation as $D_C(t) = \Omega(D_A(t))$.

Formally, given a function $g(x)$, $f(x) = \Omega(g(x))$ if and only if for any constant $c > 0$,
there exists an $x_0 \geq 0$ such that $f(x) \geq c g(x)$ for all $x \geq x_0$.

Properties of Functions Expressed in Order Notation

The order notations for expressions have a number of properties that are useful when analyzing the performance of algorithms. Some of the important properties are as follows:

1. $x^a = O(x^b)$ if and only if $a \leq b$.

2. $\log_a(x) = \Theta(\log_b(x))$ for all a and b.

3. $a^x = O(b^x)$ if and only if $a \leq b$.

4. For any constant c, $c = O(1)$.

5. If $f = O(g)$ then $f + g = O(g)$.

6. If $f = \Theta(g)$ then $f + g = \Theta(g) = \Theta(f)$.

7. $f = O(g)$ if and only if $g = \Omega(f)$.

8. $f = \Theta(g)$ if and only if $f = \Omega(g)$ and $f = O(g)$.

Bibliography

[ABJ82]   S. G. Akl, D. T. Bernard, and R. J. Jordan. Design and implementation of a parallel tree search algorithm. *IEEE Transactions on Pattern Analysis and Machine Intelligence*, PAMI-4:192–203, 1982.

[ACM91]   ACM. *Resources in Parallel and Concurrent Systems*. ACM Press, New York, NY, 1991.

[ACS89a]   A. Aggarwal, A. K. Chandra, and M. Snir. A model for hierarchical memory. Technical Report RC 15118 (No. 67337), IBM T. J. Watson Research Center, Yorktown Heights, NY, 1989.

[ACS89b]   A. Aggarwal, A. K. Chandra, and M. Snir. On communication latency in PRAM computations. Technical Report RC 14973 (No. 66882), IBM T. J. Watson Research Center, Yorktown Heights, NY, 1989.

[ACS89c]   A. Aggarwal, A. K. Chandra, and M. Snir. Communication complexity of PRAMs. Technical Report RC 14998 (64644), IBM T. J. Watson Research Center, Yorktown Heights, NY, 1989.

[ADJ⁺91]   A. Agarwal, G. D'Souza, K. Johnson, D. Kranz, J. Kubiatowicz, K. Kurihara, B.-H. Lim, G. Maa, D. Nussbaum, M. Parkin, and D. Yeung. The MIT alewife machine : A large-scale distributed-memory multiprocessor. In *Proceedings of Workshop on Scalable Shared Memory Multiprocessors*. Kluwer Academic, 1991.

[AFKW90]   I. Angus, G. C. Fox, J. Kim, and D. W. Walker. *Solving Problems on Concurrent Processors: Software for Concurrent Processors: Volume II*. Prentice-Hall, Englewood Cliffs, NJ, 1990.

[AG94]   G. S. Almasi and A. Gottlieb. *Highly Parallel Computing*. Benjamin/Cummings, Redwood City, CA, 1994. (Second Edition).

[Aga89]   A. Agarwal. Performance tradeoffs in multithreaded processors. Technical Report 89-566, Massachusetts Institute of Technology, Microsystems Program Office, Cambridge, MA, 1989.

[Aga91]   A. Agarwal. Performance tradeoffs in multithreaded processors. Technical report MIT/LCS/TR 501; VLSI memo no. 89-566, Laboratory for Computer Science, Massachusetts Institute of Technology, Cambridge, MA, 1991.

[AGGM90] A. Averbuch, E. Gabber, B. Gordissky, and Y. Medan. A parallel FFT on an MIMD machine. *Parallel Computing*, 15:61–74, 1990.

[Agh86]   G. Agha. *Actors: A Model of Concurrent Computation in Distributed Systems*. MIT Press, Cambridge, MA, 1986.

[AHMP87] H. Alt, T. Hagerup, K. Mehlhorn, and F. P. Preparata. Deterministic simulation of idealized parallel computers on more realistic ones. *SIAM Journal of Computing*, 16(5):808–835, October 1987.

[AHU74]   A. V. Aho, J. E. Hopcroft, and J. D. Ullman. *The Design and Analysis of Computer Algorithms*. Addison-Wesley, Reading, MA, 1974.

[AJM88]   D. P. Agrawal, V. K. Janakiram, and R. Mehrotra. A randomized parallel branch-and-bound algorithm. In *Proceedings of the 1988 International Conference on Parallel Processing*, 1988.

[AK84]   M. J. Atallah and S. R. Kosaraju. Graph problems on a mesh-connected processor array. *Journal of ACM*, 31(3):649–667, July 1984.

[Akl85]   S. G. Akl. *Parallel Sorting Algorithms*. Academic Press, San Diego, CA, 1985.

[Akl89]   S. G. Akl. *The Design and Analysis of Parallel Algorithms*. Prentice-Hall, Englewood Cliffs, NJ, 1989.

[Akl97]   S. G. Akl. *Parallel Computation Models and Methods*. Prentice-Hall, Englewood Cliffs, NJ, 1997.

[AKR89]   S. Arvindam, V. Kumar, and V. N. Rao. Floorplan optimization on multiprocessors. In *Proceedings of the 1989 International Conference on Computer Design*, 1989. Also published as Technical Report ACT-OODS-241-89, Microelectronics and Computer Corporation, Austin, TX.

[AKR90]   S. Arvindam, V. Kumar, and V. N. Rao. Efficient parallel algorithms for search problems: Applications in VLSI CAD. In *Proceedings of the Third Symposium on the Frontiers of Massively Parallel Computation*, 1990.

[AKRS91]   S. Arvindam, V. Kumar, V. N. Rao, and V. Singh. Automatic test pattern generation on multiprocessors. *Parallel Computing*, 17, number 12:1323–1342, December 1991.

[AKS83]   M. Ajtai, J. Komlos, and E. Szemeredi. An $O(n \log n)$ sorting network. In *Proceedings of the 15th Annual ACM Symposium on Theory of Computing*, 1–9, 1983.

[AL93]   S. G. Akl and K. A. Lyons. *Parallel Computational Geometry*. Prentice-Hall, Englewood Cliffs, NJ, 1993.

[AM88]   T. S. Abdelrahman and T. N. Mudge. Parallel branch-and-bound algorithms on hypercube multiprocessors. In *Proceedings of the Third Conference on Hypercubes, Concurrent Computers, and Applications*, 1492–1499, New York, NY, 1988. ACM Press.

[Amd67]   G. M. Amdahl. Validity of the single processor approach to achieving large scale computing capabilities. In *AFIPS Conference Proceedings*, 483–485, 1967.

[And91]   G. R. Andrews. *Concurrent Programming: Principles and Practice*. Benjamin/Cummings, Redwood City, CA, 1991.

[AOB93]   B. Abali, F. Ozguner, and A. Bataineh. Balanced parallel sort on hypercube multiprocessors. *IEEE Transactions on Parallel and Distributed Systems*, 4(5):572–581, May 1993.

[AS87]   B. Awerbuch and Y. Shiloach. New connectivity and MSF algorithms for shuffle-exchange network and PRAM. *IEEE Transactions on Computers*, C–36(10):1258–1263, October 1987.

[AU72]   A. V. Aho and J. D. Ullman. *The Theory of Parsing, Translation and Compiling: Volume 1, Parsing*. Prentice-Hall, Englewood Cliffs, NJ, 1972.

[B+97]   L. S. Blackford *et al. ScaLAPACK Users' Guide*. SIAM, 1997.

[BA82]   M. Ben-Ari. *Principles of Concurrent Programming*. Prentice-Hall, Englewood Cliffs, NJ, 1982.

[Bab88]   R. G. Babb. *Programming Parallel Processors*. Addison-Wesley, Reading, MA, 1988.

[Bai90]   D. H. Bailey. FFTs in external or hierarchical memory. *Journal of Supercomputing*, 4:23–35, 1990.

[Bar68]   G. H. Barnes. The ILLIAC IV computer. *IEEE Transactions on Computers*, C-17(8):746–757, 1968.

[Bat68]   K. E. Batcher. Sorting networks and their applications. In *Proceedings of the 1968 Spring Joint Computer Conference*, 307–314, 1968.

[Bat76]   K. E. Batcher. The Flip network in STARAN. In *Proceedings of International Conference on Parallel Processing*, 65–71, 1976.

[Bat80]   K. E. Batcher. Design of a massively parallel processor. *IEEE Transactions on Computers*, 836–840, September 1980.

[Bau78]   G. M. Baudet. *The Design and Analysis of Algorithms for Asynchronous Multiprocessors*. Ph.D. Thesis, Carnegie-Mellon University, Pittsburgh, PA, 1978.

[BB90]   K. P. Belkhale and P. Banerjee. Approximate algorithms for the partitionable independent task scheduling problem. In *Proceedings of the 1990 International Conference on Parallel Processing*, I72–I75, 1990.

[BBN89]   BBN Advanced Computers Inc. *TC-2000 Technical Product Summary*. Cambridge, MA. 1989.

[BCCL95]   R. E. Bixby, W. Cook, A. Cox, and E. K. Lee. Parallel mixed integer programming. Technical Report CRPC TR 95554, Center for Research on Parallel Computation, Research Monograph, 1995.

[BCJ90]   E. C. Bronson, T. L. Casavant, and L. H. Jamieson. Experimental application-driven architecture analysis of an SIMD/MIMD parallel processing system. *IEEE Transactions on Parallel and Distributed Systems*, 1(2):195–205, 1990.

[BDHM84]   D. Bitton, D. J. DeWitt, D. K. Hsiao, and M. J. Mcnon. A taxonomy of parallel sorting. *Computing Surveys*, 16(3):287–318, September 1984.

[Bel57]   R. Bellman. *Dynamic Programming*. Princeton University Press, Princeton, NJ, 1957.

[Bel58]   R. Bellman. On a routing problem. *Quarterly of Applied Mathematics*, 16(1):87–90, 1958.

[Ben80]   J. L. Bentley. A parallel algorithm for constructing minimum spanning trees. *Journal of the ACM*, 27(1):51–59, March 1980.

[Ber84]   S. Berkowitz. On computing the determinant in small parallel time using a small number of processors. *Information Processing Letters*, 18(3):147–150, March 1984.

[Ber89]   J. Berntsen. Communication efficient matrix multiplication on hypercubes. *Parallel Computing*, 12:335–342, 1989.

[BH82]   A. Borodin and J. E. Hopcroft. Routing merging and sorting on parallel models of computation. In *Proceedings of the 14th Annual ACM Symposium on Theory of Computing*, 338–344, May 1982.

[Bix91]   R. E. Bixby. Two applications of linear programming. In *Proceedings of the Workshop on Parallel Computing of Discrete Optimization Problems*, 1991.

[BJK$^+$95] R. Blumofe, C. Joerg, B. Kuszmaul, C. Leiserson, K. Randall, and Y. Zhou. Cilk: An efficient multithreaded runtime system. In *Proceedings of the 5th Symposium on Principles and Practice of Parallel Programming*, 1995.

[BKH89]   S. Bershader, T. Kraay, and J. Holland. The giant-Fourier-transform. In *Proceedings of the Fourth Conference on Hypercubes, Concurrent Computers, and Applications: Volume I*, 387–389, 1989.

[Ble90]   G. E. Blelloch. *Vector Models for Data-Parallel Computing*. MIT Press, Cambridge, MA, 1990.

[BMCP98]   A. Brungger, A. Marzetta, J. Clausen, and M. Perregaard. Solving large-scale qap problems in parallel with the search library zram. *Journal of Parallel and Distributed Computing*, 50:157–169, 1998.

[BNK92]   A. Bar-Noy and S. Kipnis. Designing broadcasting algorithms in the postal model for message-passing systems. In *Proceedings of 4th ACM Symposium on Parallel Algorithms and Architectures*, 13–22, 1992.

[BOS$^+$91] D. P. Bertsekas, C. Ozveren, G. D. Stamoulis, P. Tseng, and J. N. Tsitsiklis. Optimal communication algorithms for hypercubes. *Journal of Parallel and Distributed Computing*, 11:263–275, 1991.

[BR90]   R. Boppana and C. S. Raghavendra. On optimal and practical routing methods for a massive data movement operation on hypercubes. Technical report, University of Southern California, Los Angeles, CA, 1990.

[Bra97]   R. Bramley. Technology news & reviews: Chemkin software; OpenMP Fortran Standard; ODE toolbox for Matlab; Java products; Scientific WorkPlace 3.0. *IEEE Computational Science and Engineering*, 4(4):75–78, October/December 1997.

[Bro79]   K. Brown. Dynamic programming in computer science. Technical Report CMU-CS-79-106, Carnegie Mellon University, Pittsburgh, PA, 1979.

[BS78]   G. M. Baudet and D. Stevenson. Optimal sorting algorithms for parallel computers. *IEEE Transactions on Computers*, C–27(1):84–87, January 1978.

[BT89]   D. P. Bertsekas and J. N. Tsitsiklis. *Parallel and Distributed Computation: Numerical Methods*. Prentice-Hall, NJ, 1989.

[BT97]   D. P. Bertsekas and J. N. Tsitsiklis. *Parallel and Distributed Computation: Numerical Methods*. Athena Scientific, 1997.

[But97]   D. R. Butenhof. *Programming with POSIX Threads*. Addison-Wesley, Reading, MA, 1997.

[Buy99]   R. Buyya, editor. *High Performance Cluster Computing: Architectures and Systems*. Prentice Hall, 1999.

[BW89]   M. L. Barton and G. R. Withers. Computing performance as a function of the speed, quantity, and the cost of processors. In *Supercomputing '89 Proceedings*, 759–764, 1989.

[BW97]   J. Beveridge and R. Wiener. *Multithreading Applications in Win32: the Complete Guide to Threads*. Addison-Wesley Developers Press, Reading, MA, 1997.

[C$^+$95]   J. Choi *et al*. A proposal for a set of Parallel Basic Linear Algebra Subprograms. Technical Report CS-95-292, Computer Science Department, University of Tennessee, 1995.

[CAHH91]   N. P. Chrisopchoides, M. Aboelaze, E. N. Houstis, and C. E. Houstis. The parallelization of some level 2 and 3 BLAS operations on distributed-memory machines. In *Proceedings of the First International Conference of the Austrian Center of Parallel Computation*. Springer-Verlag Series Lecture Notes in Computer Science, 1991.

[Can69]   L. E. Cannon. *A cellular computer to implement the Kalman Filter Algorithm*. Ph.D. Thesis, Montana State University, Bozman, MT, 1969.

[Car89]   G. F. Carey, editor. *Parallel Supercomputing: Methods, Algorithms and Applications*. Wiley, New York, NY, 1989.

[CD87]   S. Chandran and L. S. Davis. An approach to parallel vision algorithms. In R. Porth, editor, *Parallel Processing*. SIAM, Philadelphia, PA, 1987.

[CDK$^+$00]   R. Chandra, L. Dagum, D. Kohr, D. Maydan, J. McDonald, and R. M. (editors). *Parallel Programming in OpenMP*. Morgan Kaufmann Publishers, 2000.

[CG87]   E. Chu and A. George. Gaussian elimination with partial pivoting and load balancing on a multiprocessor. *Parallel Computing*, 5:65–74, 1987.

[CGK93]   D. Challou, M. Gini, and V. Kumar. Parallel search algorithms for robot motion planning. In *Proceedings of the IEEE Conference on Robotics and Automation*, 46–51, 1993.

[CGL92]   D. E. Culler, M. Gunter, and J. C. Lee. Analysis of multithreaded microprocessors under multiprogramming. Report UCB/CSD 92/687, University of California, Berkeley, Computer Science Division, Berkeley, CA, May 1992.

[Cha79]   A. K. Chandra. Maximal parallelism in matrix multiplication. Technical Report RC-6193, IBM T. J. Watson Research Center, Yorktown Heights, NY, 1979.

[Cha87]   R. Chamberlain. An alternate view of LU factorization on a hypercube multiprocessor. In M. T. Heath, editor, *Hypercube Multiprocessors 1987*, 569–575. SIAM, Philadelphia, PA, 1987.

[CJP83]   H. Crowder, E. L. Johnson, and M. Padberg. Solving large-scale zero-one linear programming problem. *Operations Research*, 2:803–834, 1983.

[CKP+93a] D. Culler, R. Karp, D. Patterson, A. Sahay, K. Schauser, E. Santos, R. Subramonian, and T. von Eicken. LogP: Towards a realistic model of parallel computation. In *Proceedings of the Fourth ACM SIGPLAN Symposium on Principles and Practices of Parallel Programming*, 1–12, 1993.

[CKP+93b] D. E. Culler, R. Karp, D. A. Patterson, *et al*. Logp: Towards a realistic model of parallel computation. In *Principles and Practices of Parallel Programming*, May 1993.

[CL93]   B. Codenotti and M. Leoncini. *Introduction to Parallel Processing*. Addison-Wesley, 1993.

[CLC81]   F. Y. Chin, J. Lam, and I. Chen. Optimal parallel algorithms for the connected component problem. In *Proceedings of the 1981 International Conference on Parallel Processing*, 170–175, 1981.

[CLC82]   F. Y. Chin, J. Lam, and I. Chen. Efficient parallel algorithms for some graph problems. *Communications of the ACM*, 25(9):659–665, September 1982.

[CLR90]   T. H. Cormen, C. E. Leiserson, and R. L. Rivest. *Introduction to Algorithms*. MIT Press, McGraw-Hill, New York, NY, 1990.

[CM82]   K. M. Chandy and J. Misra. Distributed computation on graphs: Shortest path algorithms. *Communications of the ACM*, 25(11):833–837, November 1982.

[CM98]   B. Chapman and P. Mehrotra. OpenMP and HPF: Integrating two paradigms. *Lecture Notes in Computer Science*, 1470, 1998.

[Col88]   R. Cole. Parallel merge sort. *SIAM Journal on Computing*, 17(4):770–785, August 1988.

[Col89]   M. Cole. *Algorithmic Skeletons: Structured Management of Parallel Computation*. MIT Press, Cambridge, MA, 1989.

[Con89]   T. Conlon. *Programming in PARLOG*. Addison-Wesley, Reading, MA, 1989.

[CR89]   E. A. Carmona and M. D. Rice. A model of parallel performance. Technical Report AFWL-TR-89-01, Air Force Weapons Laboratory, 1989.

[CR91]   E. A. Carmona and M. D. Rice. Modeling the serial and parallel fractions of a parallel algorithm. *Journal of Parallel and Distributed Computing*, 1991.

[CS88]   B. V. Cherkassky and R. Smith. Efficient mapping and implementations of matrix algorithms on a hypercube. *Journal of Supercomputing*, 2:7–27, 1988.

[CSG98]   D. E. Culler, J. P. Singh, and A. Gupta. *Parallel Computer Architecture: A Hardware/Software Approach*. Morgan Kaufmann, 1998.

[CT92]   K. M. Chandy and S. Taylor. *An Introduction to Parallel Programming*. Jones and Bartlett, Austin, TX, 1992.

[CV91]   B. S. Chlebus and I. Vrto. Parallel quicksort. *Journal of Parallel and Distributed Processing*, 1991.

[Cve87]   Z. Cvetanovic. Performance analysis of the FFT algorithm on a shared-memory parallel architecture. *IBM Journal of Research and Development*, 31(4):435–451, 1987.

[CWP98]   A. Cohen, M. Woodring, and R. Petrusha. *Win32 Multithreaded Programming*. O'Reilly & Associates, 1998.

[D⁺92]   W. J. Dally *et al*. The message-driven processor. *IEEE Micro*, 12(2):23–39, 1992.

[Dal87]   W. J. Dally. *A VLSI Architecture for Concurrent Data Structures*. Kluwer Academic Publishers, Boston, MA, 1987.

[Dal90a]   W. J. Dally. Analysis of k-ary n-cube interconnection networks. *IEEE Transactions on Computers*, 39(6), June 1990.

[Dal90b]   W. J. Dally. Network and processor architecture for message-driven computers. In R. Sauya and G. Birtwistle, editors, *VLSI and Parallel Computation*. Morgan Kaufmann, San Mateo, CA, 1990.

[Dav86]   G. J. Davis. Column LU factorization with pivoting on a hypercube multiprocessor. *SIAM Journal on Algebraic and Discrete Methods*, 7:538–550, 1986. Also available as Technical Report ORNL-6219, Oak Ridge National Laboratory, Oak Ridge, TN, 1985.

[DCG90]   J. D. DeMello, J. L. Calvet, and J. M. Garcia. Vectorization and multitasking of dynamic programming in control: experiments on a CRAY-2. *Parallel Computing*, 13:261–269, 1990.

[DDSV99]   J. Dongarra, I. S. Duff, D. Sorensen, and H. V. Vorst. *Numerical Linear Algebra for High Performance Computers (Software, Environments, Tools)*. SIAM, 1999.

[DeC89]   A. L. DeCegama. *The Technology of Parallel Processing: Parallel Processing Architectures and VLSI Hardware: Volume 1*. Prentice-Hall, Englewood Cliffs, NJ, 1989.

[DEH89]   P. M. Dew, R. A. Earnshaw, and T. R. Heywood. *Parallel Processing for Computer Vision and Display*. Addison-Wesley, Reading, MA, 1989.

[Dem82]   J. Deminet. Experiences with multiprocessor algorithms. *IEEE Transactions on Computers*, C-31(4):278–288, 1982.

[DFHM82]   D. J. DeWitt, D. B. Friedland, D. K. Hsiao, and M. J. Menon. A taxonomy of parallel sorting algorithms. Technical Report TR-482, Computer Sciences Department, University of Wisconsin, Madison, WI, 1982.

[DFRC96]   F. Dehne, A. Fabri, and A. Rau-Chaplin. Scalable parallel computational geometry for coarse grained multicomputers. *International Journal on Computational Geometry*, 6(3):379–400, 1996.

[DHvdV93]   J. W. Demmel, M. T. Heath, and H. A. van der Vorst. Parallel numerical linear algebra. *Acta Numerica*, 111–197, 1993.

[Dij59]   E. W. Dijkstra. A note on two problems in connection with graphs. *Numerische Mathematik*, 1:269–271, 1959.

[DM93]   S. Dutt and N. R. Mahapatra. Parallel A* algorithms and their performance on hypercube multiprocessors. In *Proceedings of the Seventh International Parallel Processing Symposium*, 797–803, 1993.

[DM98]   L. Dagum and R. Menon. OpenMP: An industry-standard API for shared-memory programming. *IEEE Computational Science and Engineering*, 5(1):46–55, January/March 1998.

[DNS81]   E. Dekel, D. Nassimi, and S. Sahni. Parallel matrix and graph algorithms. *SIAM Journal on Computing*, 10:657–673, 1981.

[Dra96]   D. G. Drake. Introduction to Java threads. *JavaWorld: IDG's magazine for the Java community*, 1(2), April 1996.

[DRGNP]   F. Darema-Rogers, D. George, V. Norton, and G. Pfister. VM parallel environment. In *Proceedings of the IBM Kingston Parallel Processing Symposium*.

[DS86]   W. J. Dally and C. L. Seitz. The torus routing chip. *Journal of Distributed Computing*, 1(3):187–196, 1986.

[DS87]   W. J. Dally and C. L. Seitz. Deadlock-free message routing in multiprocessor interconnection networks. *IEEE Transactions on Computers*, C-36(5):547–553, 1987.

[DSG83]   E. W. Dijkstra, W. H. Seijen, and A. J. M. V. Gasteren. Derivation of a termination detection algorithm for a distributed computation. *Information Processing Letters*, 16(5):217–219, 1983.

[DT89]   L. Desbat and D. Trystram. Implementing the discrete Fourier transform on a hypercube vector-parallel computer. In *Proceedings of the Fourth Conference on Hypercubes, Concurrent Computers, and Applications: Volume I*, 407–410, 1989.

[DV87]   K. A. Doshi and P. J. Varman. Optimal graph algorithms on a fixed-size linear array. *IEEE Transactions on Computers*, C–36(4):460–470, April 1987.

[dV89]   E. F. V. de Velde. Multicomputer matrix computations: Theory and practice. In *Proceedings of the Fourth Conference on Hypercubes, Concurrent Computers, and Applications*, 1303–1308, 1989.

[DY81]   N. Deo and Y. B. Yoo. Parallel algorithms for the minimum spanning tree problem. In *Proceedings of the 1981 International Conference on Parallel Processing*, 188–189, 1981.

[Eck94]   J. Eckstein. Parallel branch-and-bound methods for mixed-integer programming on the cm-5. *SIAM Journal on Optimization*, 4(4):794–814, 1994.

[Eck97]   J. Eckstein. Distributed versus centralized storage and control for parallel branch and bound: Mixed integer programming on the cm-5. *Computational Optimization and Applications*, 7(2):199–220, 1997.

[Ede89]   A. Edelman. Optimal matrix transposition and bit-reversal on hypercubes: Node address–memory address exchanges. Technical report, Thinking Machines Corporation, Cambridge, MA, 1989.

[EDH80]   O. I. El-Dessouki and W. H. Huen. Distributed enumeration on network computers. *IEEE Transactions on Computers*, C-29:818–825, September 1980.

[EHHR88] S. C. Eisenstat, M. T. Heath, C. S. Henkel, and C. H. Romine. Modified cyclic algorithms for solving triangular systems on distributed-memory multiprocessors. *SIAM Journal on Scientific and Statistical Computing*, 9(3):589–600, 1988.

[EHMN90] M. Evett, J. Hendler, A. Mahanti, and D. Nau. PRA*: A memory-limited heuristic search procedure for the connection machine. In *Proceedings of the Third Symposium on the Frontiers of Massively Parallel Computation*, 145–149, 1990.

[Ekl72]   J. O. Eklundh. A fast computer method for matrix transposing. *IEEE Transactions on Computers*, 21(7):801–803, 1972.

[Ert92]   W. Ertel.   OR—parallel theorem proving with random competition.   In A. Voronokov, editor, *LPAR '92: Logic Programming and Automated Reasoning*, 226–237. Springer-Verlag, New York, NY, 1992.

[EZL89]   D. L. Eager, J. Zahorjan, and E. D. Lazowska. Speedup versus efficiency in parallel systems. *IEEE Transactions on Computers*, 38(3):408–423, 1989.

[Fen81]   T. Y. Feng. A survey of interconnection networks. *IEEE Computer*, 12–27, December 1981.

[FF82]   R. A. Finkel and J. P. Fishburn. Parallelism in alpha-beta search. *Artificial Intelligence*, 19:89–106, 1982.

[FF86]   G. C. Fox and W. Furmanski.   Optimal communication algorithms on hypercube.   Technical Report CCCP-314, California Institute of Technology, Pasadena, CA, 1986.

[FJDS96]   L. Fosdick, E. Jessup, G. Domik, and C. Schauble. *Introduction to High-Performance Scientific Computing*. MIT Press, 1996.

[FJL⁺88]   G. C. Fox, M. Johnson, G. Lyzenga, S. W. Otto, J. Salmon, and D. Walker. *Solving Problems on Concurrent Processors: Volume 1*. Prentice-Hall, Englewood Cliffs, NJ, 1988.

[FK88]   C. Ferguson and R. Korf. Distributed tree search and its application to alpha-beta pruning. In *Proceedings of the 1988 National Conference on Artificial Intelligence*, 1988.

[FK89]   H. P. Flatt and K. Kennedy. Performance of parallel processors. *Parallel Computing*, 12:1–20, 1989.

[FKO86]   E. Felten, S. Karlin, and S. W. Otto. Sorting on a hypercube. *Caltech/JPL*, 1986. Hm 244.

[Fla90]   H. P. Flatt. Further applications of the overhead model for parallel systems. Technical Report G320-3540, IBM Corporation, Palo Alto Scientific Center, Palo Alto, CA, 1990.

[Flo62]   R. W. Floyd. Algorithm 97: Shortest path. *Communications of the ACM*, 5(6):345, June 1962.

[Fly72]   M. J. Flynn. Some computer organizations and their effectiveness. *IEEE Transactions on Computers*, C-21(9):948–960, 1972.

[Fly95]   M. J. Flynn. *Computer Architecture: Pipelined and Parallel Processor Design.* Jones and Bartlett, 1995.

[FM70]   W. D. Frazer and A. C. McKellar. Samplesort: A sampling approach to minimal storage tree sorting. *Journal of the ACM*, 17(3):496–507, July 1970.

[FM87]   R. A. Finkel and U. Manber. DIB—a distributed implementation of backtracking. *ACM Transactions on Programming Languages and Systems*, 9(2):235–256, April 1987.

[FM92]   R. Frye and J. Myczkowski. Load balancing algorithms on the connection machine and their use in Monte-Carlo methods. In *Proceedings of the Unstructured Scientific Computation on Multiprocessors Conference*, 1992.

[FMM94]   R. Feldmann, P. Mysliwietz, and B. Monien. Studying overheads in massively parallel min/max-tree evaluation. In *Proc. of the 6th ACM Symposium on Parallel Algorithms and Architectures*, 94–103, 1994.

[FOH87]   G. C. Fox, S. W. Otto, and A. J. G. Hey. Matrix algorithms on a hypercube I: Matrix multiplication. *Parallel Computing*, 4:17–31, 1987.

[Fos95]   I. Foster. *Designing and Building Parallel Programs: Concepts and Tools for Parallel Software Engineering.* Addison-Wesley, 1995.

[Fou94]   T. J. Fountain. *Parallel Computing: Principles and Practice.* Cambridge University Press, 1994.

[FR62]   L. R. Ford and R. L. Rivest. *Flows in Networks.* Princeton University Press, Princeton, NJ, 1962.

[Fra93]   M. Franklin. The multiscalar architecture. Technical Report CS-TR-1993-1196, University of Wisconsin, 1993.

[FTI90]   M. Furuichi, K. Taki, and N. Ichiyoshi. A multi-level load balancing scheme for OR-parallel exhaustive search programs on the Multi-PSI. In *Proceedings of the Second ACM SIGPLAN Symposium on Principles and Practice of Parallel Programming*, 50–59, 1990.

[FW78]   S. Fortune and J. Wyllie. Parallelism in random access machines. In *Proceedings of ACM Symposium on Theory of Computing*, 114–118, 1978.

[Gal95]   B. O. Gallmeister. *Posix. 4 : Programming for the Real World.* O'Reilly & Associates, 1995.

[GBD+94]   G. A. Geist, A. Beguelin, J. Dongarra, W. Jiang, R. Manchek, and V. Sunderam. *PVM: Parallel Virtual Machine.* MIT Press, Cambridge, MA, 1994.

[Gei85]   G. A. Geist. Efficient parallel LU factorization with pivoting on a hypercube multiprocessor. Technical Report ORNL-6211, Oak Ridge National Laboratory, Oak Ridge, TN, 1985.

[GGK+83] A. Gottlieb, R. Grishman, C. P. Kruskal, K. P. McAuliffe, L. Rudolph, and M. Snir. The NYU Ultracomputer—designing a MIMD, shared memory parallel computer. *IEEE Transactions on Computers*, C–32(2):175–189, February 1983.

[GGK93]   A. Y. Grama, A. Gupta, and V. Kumar. Isoefficiency: Measuring the scalability of parallel algorithms and architectures. *IEEE Parallel and Distributed Technology*, 1(3):12–21, August 1993.

[GH85]   G. A. Geist and M. T. Heath. Parallel Cholesky factorization on a hypercube multiprocessor. Technical Report ORNL-6190, Oak Ridge National Laboratory, Oak Ridge, TN, 1985.

[GH86]   G. A. Geist and M. T. Heath. Matrix factorization on a hypercube multiprocessor. In M. T. Heath, editor, *Hypercube Multiprocessors 1986*, 161–180. SIAM, Philadelphia, PA, 1986.

[GH01]   S. Goedecker and A. Hoisie. *Performance Optimization of Numerically Intensive Codes*. SIAM, 2001.

[Gib85]   A. Gibbons. *Algorithmic Graph Theory*. Cambridge University Press, Cambridge, 1985.

[Gib89]   P. B. Gibbons. A more practical PRAM model. In *Proceedings of the 1989 ACM Symposium on Parallel Algorithms and Architectures*, 158–168, 1989.

[GK91]   A. Gupta and V. Kumar. The scalability of matrix multiplication algorithms on parallel computers. Technical Report TR 91-54, Department of Computer Science, University of Minnesota, Minneapolis, MN, 1991. A short version appears in *Proceedings of 1993 International Conference on Parallel Processing*, pages III-115–III-119, 1993.

[GK93a]   A. Gupta and V. Kumar. Performance properties of large scale parallel systems. *Journal of Parallel and Distributed Computing*, 19:234–244, 1993. Also available as Technical Report TR 92-32, Department of Computer Science, University of Minnesota, Minneapolis, MN.

[GK93b]   A. Gupta and V. Kumar. The scalability of FFT on parallel computers. *IEEE Transactions on Parallel and Distributed Systems*, 4(8):922–932, August 1993. A detailed version is available as Technical Report TR 90-53, Department of Computer Science, University of Minnesota, Minneapolis, MN.

[GKP92]   A. Grama, V. Kumar, and P. M. Pardalos. Parallel processing of discrete optimization problems. In *Encyclopaedia of Microcomputers*. Marcel Dekker Inc., New York, 1992.

[GKR91]   A. Y. Grama, V. Kumar, and V. N. Rao. Experimental evaluation of load balancing techniques for the hypercube. In *Proceedings of the Parallel Computing '91 Conference*, 497–514, 1991.

[GKRS96]   A. Grama, V. Kumar, S. Ranka, and V. Singh. A^3: A simple and asymptotically accurate model for parallel computation. In *Proceedings of the Sixth Symposium on Frontiers of Massively Parallel Computing*, Annapolis, MD, 1996.

[GKS92]   A. Gupta, V. Kumar, and A. H. Sameh. Performance and scalability of preconditioned conjugate gradient methods on parallel computers. Technical Report TR 92-64, Department of Computer Science, University of Minnesota, Minneapolis, MN, 1992. A short version appears in *Proceedings of the Sixth SIAM Conference on Parallel Processing for Scientific Computing*, pages 664–674, 1993.

[GKT79]   L. J. Guibas, H. T. Kung, and C. D. Thompson. Direct VLSI Implementation of Combinatorial Algorithms. In *Proceedings of Conference on Very Large Scale Integration, California Institute of Technology*, 509–525, 1979.

[GL96a]   G. H. Golub and C. V. Loan. *Matrix Computations*. The Johns Hopkins University Press, Baltimore, MD, 1996.

[GL96b]   W. D. Gropp and E. Lusk. *User's Guide for mpich, a Portable Implementation of MPI*. Mathematics and Computer Science Division, Argonne National Laboratory. ANL-96/6. 1996.

[GLDS96]   W. Gropp, E. Lusk, N. Doss, and A. Skjellum. A high-performance, portable implementation of the MPI message passing interface standard. *Parallel Computing*, 22(6):789–828, September 1996.

[GLS99]   W. Gropp, E. Lusk, and A. Skjellum. *Using MPI*. MIT Press, 1999. 2nd Edition.

[GMB88]   J. L. Gustafson, G. R. Montry, and R. E. Benner. Development of parallel methods for a 1024-processor hypercube. *SIAM Journal on Scientific and Statistical Computing*, 9(4):609–638, 1988.

[GO93]   G. H. Golub and J. M. Ortega. *Scientific Computing: An Introduction with Parallel Computing*. Academic Press, 1993.

[GPS90]   K. A. Gallivan, R. J. Plemmons, and A. H. Sameh. Parallel algorithms for dense linear algebra computations. *SIAM Review*, 32(1):54–135, March 1990. Also appears in K. A. Gallivan *et al*. *Parallel Algorithms for Matrix Computations*. SIAM, Philadelphia, PA, 1990.

[GR88]   G. A. Geist and C. H. Romine. LU factorization algorithms on distributed-memory multiprocessor architectures. *SIAM Journal on Scientific and Statistical Computing*, 9(4):639–649, 1988. Also available as Technical Report ORNL/TM-10383, Oak Ridge National Laboratory, Oak Ridge, TN, 1987.

[GR90]   A. Gibbons and W. Rytter. *Efficient Parallel Algorithms*. Cambridge University Press, Cambridge, UK, 1990.

[Gre91]   S. Green. *Parallel Processing for Computer Graphics*. MIT Press, Cambridge, MA, 1991.

[GSNL98]   W. Gropp, M. Snir, W. Nitzberg, and E. Lusk. *MPI: The Complete Reference*. MIT Press, 1998.

[GT88]   A. V. Goldberg and R. E. Tarjan. A new approach to the maximum-flow problem. *Journal of the ACM*, 35(4):921–940, October 1988.

[Gup87]   A. Gupta. *Parallelism in Production Systems*. Morgan Kaufmann, Los Altos, CA, 1987.

[Gus88]   J. L. Gustafson. Reevaluating Amdahl's law. *Communications of the ACM*, 31(5):532–533, 1988.

[Gus92]   J. L. Gustafson. The consequences of fixed time performance measurement. In *Proceedings of the 25th Hawaii International Conference on System Sciences: Volume III*, 113–124, 1992.

[HB84]   K. Hwang and F. A. Briggs. *Computer Architecture and Parallel Processing*. McGraw-Hill, New York, NY, 1984.

[HB88]   M. M. Huntbach and F. W. Burton. Alpha-beta search on virtual tree machines. *Information Science*, 44:3–17, 1988.

[HCH95]   F.-H. Hsu, M. S. Campbell, and A. J. Hoane. Deep Blue system overview. In *Proceedings of the 1995 International Conference on Supercomputing, Barcelona, Spain*, 240–244, 1995.

[HCS79]   D. S. Hirschberg, A. K. Chandra, and D. V. Sarwate. Computing connected components on parallel computers. *Communications of the ACM*, 22(8):461–464, August 1979.

[HD87]   S.-R. Huang and L. S. Davis. A tight upper bound for the speedup of parallel best-first branch-and-bound algorithms. Technical report, Center for Automation Research, University of Maryland, College Park, MD, 1987.

[HD89a]   S. R. Huang and L. S. Davis. Parallel iterative a* search: An admissible distributed heuristic search algorithm. In *Proceedings of the Eleventh International Joint Conference on Artificial Intelligence*, 23–29, 1989.

[HD89b]   K. Hwang and D. DeGroot. *Parallel Processing for Supercomputers and Artificial Intelligence*. McGraw-Hill, New York, NY, 1989.

[HDM97]   J. Hill, S. Donaldson, and A. McEwan. Installation and user guide for the oxford bsp toolset: User guide for the oxford bsp toolset (v1.3) implementation of bsplib. Technical report, Oxford University Computing Laboratory, 1997.

[Hea85]   M. T. Heath. Parallel Cholesky factorization in message-passing multiprocessor environments. Technical Report ORNL-6150, Oak Ridge National Laboratory, Oak Ridge, TN, 1985.

[HG97]   S. Hamilton and L. Garber. Deep Blue's hardware-software synergy. *IEEE Computer*, 30(10):29–35, October 1997.

[Hil85]   W. D. Hillis. *The Connection Machine*. MIT Press, Cambridge, MA, 1985.

[Hil90]   M. D. Hill. What is scalability? *Computer Architecture News*, 18(4), 1990.

[Hip89]   P. G. Hipes. Matrix multiplication on the JPL/Caltech Mark IIIfp hypercube. Technical Report C3P 746, Concurrent Computation Program, California Institute of Technology, Pasadena, CA, 1989.

[Hir76]   D. S. Hirschberg. Parallel algorithms for the transitive closure and connected component problem. In *Proceedings of the 8th Annual ACM Symposium on the Theory of Computing*, 55–57, 1976.

[Hir78]   D. S. Hirschberg. Fast parallel sorting algorithms. *Communications of the ACM*, 21(8):657–666, August 1978.

[HJ87]   C.-T. Ho and S. L. Johnsson. Spanning balanced trees in Boolean cubes. Technical Report YALEU/DCS/RR-508, Department of Computer Science, Yale University, New Haven, CT, 1987.

[HJE91]   C.-T. Ho, S. L. Johnsson, and A. Edelman. Matrix multiplication on hypercubes using full bandwidth and constant storage. In *Proceedings of the 1991 International Conference on Parallel Processing*, 447–451, 1991.

[HK96]   S. Hambrusch and A. Khokhar. C^3: A parallel model for coarse-grained machines. *Journal of Parallel and Distributed Computing*, 32(2):139–154, February 1996.

[HLM84]   R. E. Hiromoto, O. M. Lubeck, and J. Moore. Experiences with the Denelcor HEP. *Parallel Computing*, 1(3–4):197–206, 1984.

[HLV90]   S. H. S. Huang, H. Liu, and V. Vishwanathan. A sub-linear parallel algorithm for some dynamic programming problems. In *Proceedings of the 1990 International Conference on Parallel Processing*, III–261–III–264, 1990.

[HM80]   D. K. Hsiao and M. J. Menon. Parallel record-sorting methods for hardware realization. Osu-cisrc-tr-80-7, Computer Science Information Department, Ohio State University, Columbus, OH, 1980.

[HMT$^+$96]   H. Hum, O. Maquelin, K. Theobald, X. Tian, and G. Gao. A study of the earth-manna multithreaded system. *Intl. J. of Par. Prog.*, 24:319–347, 1996.

[HNR90]   P. Heidelberger, A. Norton, and J. T. Robinson. Parallel quicksort using fetch-and-add. *IEEE Transactions on Computers*, C-39(1):133–138, January 1990.

[Hoa62]   C. A. R. Hoare. Quicksort. *Computer Journal*, 5:10–15, 1962.

[HP89]   S. W. Hornick and F. P. Preparata. Deterministic PRAM simulation with constant redundancy. In *Proceedings of the 1989 ACM Symposium on Parallel Algorithms and Architectures*, 103–109, 1989.

[HQ91]   P. J. Hatcher and M. J. Quinn. *Data Parallel Programming*. MIT Press, Cambridge, MA, 1991.

[HR88]   M. T. Heath and C. H. Romine. Parallel solution of triangular systems on distributed-memory multiprocessors. *SIAM Journal on Scientific and Statistical Computing*, 9(3):558–588, 1988.

[HR91]   C.-T. Ho and M. T. Raghunath. Efficient communication primitives on circuit-switched hypercubes. In *Sixth Distributed Memory Computing Conference Proceedings*, 390–397, 1991.

[HS78]   E. Horowitz and S. Sahni. *Fundamentals of Computer Algorithms*. Computer Science Press, Rockville, MD, 1978.

[HS86]   W. D. Hillis and G. L. Steele. Data parallel algorithms. *Communications of the ACM*, 29(12):1170–1183, 1986.

[Hsu90]   F.-H. Hsu. Large scale parallelization of alpha-beta search: An algorithmic and architectural study with computer chess. Technical report, Carnegie Mellon University, Pittsburgh, PA, 1990. Ph.D. Thesis.

[Hua85]   M. A. Huang. Solving some graph problems with optimal or near-optimal speedup on mesh-of-trees networks. In *Proceedings of the 26th Annual IEEE Symposium on Foundations of Computer Science*, 232–340, 1985.

[HX98]   K. Hwang and Z. Xu. *Scalable Parallel Computing*. McGraw-Hill, New York, NY, 1998.

[Hyd99]   P. Hyde. *Java Thread Programming*. Sams, 1999.

[IPS91]   O. H. Ibarra, T. C. Pong, and S. M. Sohn. Parallel recognition and parsing on the hypercube. *IEEE Transactions on Computers*, 40(6):764–770, June 1991.

[IYF79]   M. Imai, Y. Yoshida, and T. Fukumura. A parallel searching scheme for multi-processor systems and its application to combinatorial problems. In *Proceedings of the International Joint Conference on Artificial Intelligence*, 416–418, 1979.

[Jaj92]   J. Jaja. *An Introduction to Parallel Algorithms*. Addison-Wesley, Reading, MA, 1992.

[JAM87]   V. K. Janakiram, D. P. Agrawal, and R. Mehrotra. Randomized parallel algorithms for Prolog programs and backtracking applications. In *Proceedings of the 1987 International Conference on Parallel Processing*, 278–281, 1987.

[JAM88]   V. K. Janakiram, D. P. Agrawal, and R. Mehrotra. A randomized parallel backtracking algorithm. *IEEE Transactions on Computers*, C-37(12), 1988.

[JGD87]   L. H. Jamieson, D. B. Gannon, and R. J. Douglass, editors. *The Characteristics of Parallel Algorithms*. MIT Press, Cambridge, MA, 1987.

[JH88]   S. L. Johnsson and C.-T. Ho. Matrix transposition on Boolean n-cube configured ensemble architectures. *SIAM Journal on Matrix Analysis and Applications*, 9(3):419–454, July 1988.

[JH89]   S. L. Johnsson and C.-T. Ho. Optimum broadcasting and personalized communication in hypercubes. *IEEE Transactions on Computers*, 38(9):1249–1268, September 1989.

[JH91]   S. L. Johnsson and C.-T. Ho. Optimal all-to-all personalized communication with minimum span on Boolean cubes. In *Sixth Distributed Memory Computing Conference Proceedings*, 299–304, 1991.

[JKFM89]   S. L. Johnsson, R. Krawitz, R. Frye, and D. McDonald. A radix-2 FFT on the connection machine. Technical report, Thinking Machines Corporation, Cambridge, MA, 1989.

[JNS97]   L. Johnson, G. Nemhauser, and M. Savelsbergh. Progress in integer programming: An exposition. Technical report, School of Industrial and Systems Engineering, Georgia Institute of Technology, 1997. Available from `http://akula.isye.gatech.edu/ mwps/mwps.html`.

[Joh77]   D. B. Johnson. Efficient algorithms for shortest paths in sparse networks. *Journal of the ACM*, 24(1):1–13, March 1977.

[Joh84]   S. L. Johnsson. Combining parallel and sequential sorting on a boolean *n*-cube. In *Proceedings of International Conference on Parallel Processing*, 1984.

[Joh87]   S. L. Johnsson. Communication efficient basic linear algebra computations on hypercube architectures. *Journal of Parallel and Distributed Computing*, 4(2):133–172, April 1987.

[Joh90]   S. L. Johnsson. Communication in network architectures. In R. Suaya and G. Birtwistle, editors, *VLSI and Parallel Computation*, 223–389. Morgan Kaufmann, San Mateo, CA, 1990.

[JP93]   M. T. Jones and P. E. Plassmann. A parallel graph coloring heuristic. *SIAM Journal on Scientific Computing*, 14:654–669, 1993.

[JS87]   J.-F. Jenq and S. Sahni. All pairs shortest paths on a hypercube multiprocessor. In *Proceedings of the 1987 International Conference on Parallel Processing*, 713–716, 1987.

[KA88]   R. A. Kamin and G. B. Adams. Fast Fourier transform algorithm design and tradeoffs. Technical Report RIACS TR 88.18, NASA Ames Research Center, Moffet Field, CA, 1988.

[KA99a]   Y.-K. Kwok and I. Ahmad. Benchmarking and comparison of the task graph scheduling algorithms. *Journal of Parallel and Distributed Computing*, 59:381–422, 1999.

[KA99b]   Y.-K. Kwok and I. Ahmad. Static scheduling algorithms for allocating directed task graphs to multiprocessors. *ACM Computing Surveys*, 31(4):406–471, 1999.

[KB57]   T. C. Koopmans and M. J. Beckmann. Assignment problems and the location of economic activities. *Econometrica*, 25:53–76, 1957.

[Ken90]   Kendall Square Research Corporation. *KSR-1 Overview*. Waltham, MA. 1990.

[KF90]   A. H. Karp and H. P. Flatt. Measuring parallel processor performance. *Communications of the ACM*, 33(5):539–543, 1990.

[KG94]   V. Kumar and A. Gupta. Analyzing scalability of parallel algorithms and architectures. *Journal of Parallel and Distributed Computing*, 22(3):379–391, 1994. Also available as Technical Report TR 91-18, Department of Computer Science Department, University of Minnesota, Minneapolis, MN.

[KGK90]   V. Kumar, P. S. Gopalakrishnan, and L. N. Kanal, editors. *Parallel Algorithms for Machine Intelligence and Vision*. Springer-Verlag, New York, NY, 1990.

[KGR94]   V. Kumar, A. Grama, and V. N. Rao. Scalable load balancing techniques for parallel computers. *Journal of Parallel and Distributed Computing*, 22(1):60–79, July 1994.

[KH67]   R. M. Karp and M. H. Held. Finite state processes and dynamic programming. *SIAM Journal of Applied Math*, 15:693–718, 1967.

[KH83]   M. Kumar and D. S. Hirschberg. An efficient implementation of Batcher's odd-even merge algorithm and its application in parallel sorting schemes. *IEEE Transactions on Computers*, C–32, March 1983.

[KK79]   P. Kermani and L. Kleinrock. Virtual cut-through: A new communication switching technique. *Computer Networks*, 3(4):267–286, 1979.

[KK83]   V. Kumar and L. N. Kanal. A general branch-and-bound formulation for understanding and synthesizing and/or tree search procedures. *Artificial Intelligence*, 21:179–198, 1983.

[KK84]   V. Kumar and L. N. Kanal. Parallel branch-and-bound formulations for and/or tree search. *IEEE Transactions on Pattern Analysis and Machine Intelligence*, PAMI–6:768–778, 1984.

[KK88a]   L. N. Kanal and V. Kumar. *Search in Artificial Intelligence*. Springer-Verlag, New York, NY, 1988.

[KK88b]   V. Kumar and L. N. Kanal. The CDP: A unifying formulation for heuristic search, dynamic programming, and branch-and-bound. In L. N. Kanal and V. Kumar, editors, *Search in Artificial Intelligence*, 1–27. Springer-Verlag, New York, NY, 1988.

[KK93]   G. Karypis and V. Kumar. Efficient Parallel Mappings of a Dynamic Programming Algorithm. In *Proceedings of 7th International Parallel Processing Symposium*, number 563–568, 1993.

[KK94]   G. Karypis and V. Kumar. Unstructured tree search on simd parallel computers. *Journal of Parallel and Distributed Computing*, 22(3):379–391, September 1994.

[KK99]   G. Karypis and V. Kumar. Parallel multilevel k-way partitioning for irregular graphs. *SIAM Review*, 41(2):278–300, 1999.

[KKKS94]   L. N. Kanal, V. Kumar, H. Kitano, and C. Suttner, editors. *Parallel Processing for Artificial Intelligence*. North-Holland, Amsterdam, The Netherlands, 1994.

[KN91]   K. Kimura and I. Nobuyuki. Probabilistic analysis of the efficiency of the dynamic load distribution. In *Sixth Distributed Memory Computing Conference Proceedings*, 1991.

[Knu73]   D. E. Knuth. *The Art of Computer Programming: Sorting and Searching*. Addison-Wesley, Reading, MA, 1973.

[Kor81]   W. Kornfeld. The use of parallelism to implement a heuristic search. In *Proceedings of the International Joint Conference on Artificial Intelligence*, 575–580, 1981.

[Kow88]   J. S. Kowalik. *Parallel Computation and Computers for Artificial Intelligence*. Kluwer Academic Publishers, Boston, MA, 1988.

[KP92]   C. Kaklamanis and G. Persiano. Branch-and-bound and backtrack search on mesh-connected arrays of processors. In *Proceedings of Fourth Annual Symposium on Parallel Algorithms and Architectures*, 118–126, 1992.

[KR87a]   V. K. P. Kumar and C. S. Raghavendra. Array processor with multiple broadcasting. *Journal of Parallel and Distributed Computing*, 173–190, 1987.

[KR87b]   V. Kumar and V. N. Rao. Parallel depth-first search, part II: Analysis. *International Journal of Parallel Programming*, 16(6):501–519, 1987.

[KR88]   R. M. Karp and V. Ramachandran. A survey of complexity of algorithms for shared-memory machines. Technical Report 408, University of California, Berkeley, 1988.

[KR89]   V. Kumar and V. N. Rao. Load balancing on the hypercube architecture. In *Proceedings of the Fourth Conference on Hypercubes, Concurrent Computers, and Applications*, 603–608, 1989.

[KRR88]   V. Kumar, K. Ramesh, and V. N. Rao. Parallel best-first search of state-space graphs: A summary of results. In *Proceedings of the 1988 National Conference on Artificial Intelligence*, 122–126, 1988.

[KRS88]   C. P. Kruskal, L. Rudolph, and M. Snir. A complexity theory of efficient parallel algorithms. Technical Report RC13572, IBM T. J. Watson Research Center, Yorktown Heights, NY, 1988.

[Kru56]   J. B. Kruskal. On the shortest spanning subtree of a graph and the traveling salesman problem. In *Proceedings of the AMS*, volume 7, 48–50, 1956.

[KS88]   J. Kuehn and B. Smith. The horizon supercomputing system: architecture and software. In *Proceedings of Supercomputing Conference*, 28–34, 1988.

[KS91a]   L. V. Kale and V. Saletore. Efficient parallel execution of IDA* on shared and distributed-memory multiprocessors. In *Sixth Distributed Memory Computing Conference Proceedings*, 1991.

[KS91b]   V. Kumar and V. Singh. Scalability of parallel algorithms for the all-pairs shortest path problem. *Journal of Parallel and Distributed Computing*, 13(2):124–138, October 1991. A short version appears in the *Proceedings of the International Conference on Parallel Processing*, 1990.

[KSS95]   S. Kleiman, D. Shah, and B. Smaalders. *Programming with Threads*. SunSoft Press, Mountainview, CA, 1995.

[KU86]   A. R. Karlin and E. Upfal. Parallel hashing – an efficient implementation of shared memory. In *Proceedings of 18th ACM Conference on Theory of Computing*, 160–168, 1986.

[Kun80]   J. T. Kung. The structure of parallel algorithms. In M. Yovits, editor, *Advances in Computing*, 73–74. Academic Press, San Diego, CA, 1980.

[Kun86]   H. T. Kung. Memory requirements for balanced computer architectures. In *Proceedings of the 1986 IEEE Symposium on Computer Architecture*, 49–54, 1986.

[KV92]   K. Kreeger and N. R. Vempaty. Comparison of meshes vs. hypercubes for data rearrangement. Technical Report UCF-CS-92-28, Department of Computer Science, University of Central Florida, Orlando, FL, 1992.

[KZ88]   R. M. Karp and Y. Zhang. A randomized parallel branch-and-bound procedure. In *Proceedings of the ACM Annual Symposium on Theory of Computing*, 290–300, 1988.

[Law75]   D. H. Lawrie. Access and alignment of data in an array processor. *IEEE Transactions on Computers*, C-24(1):1145–1155, 1975.

[LB95a]   B. Lewis and D. J. Berg. *Threads Primer: A Guide to Multithreaded Programming*. Prentice Hall PTR/Sun Microsystems Press, 1995.

[LB95b]   B.-H. Lim and R. Bianchini. Limits on the performance benefits of multithreading and prefetching. Research report RC 20238 (89547), IBM T. J. Watson Research Center, Yorktown Heights, NY, October 1995.

[LB97]   B. Lewis and D. J. Berg. *Multithreaded Programming with Pthreads*. Prentice Hall PTR/Sun Microsystems Press, 1997.

[LB98]   T. G. Lewis and D. Berg. *Multithreaded Programming with PThreads*. Sun Microsystems Press / Prentice Hall, 1998.

[LC88]   G.-J. Li and T. Coleman. A parallel triangular solver for a hypercube multi-processor. *SIAM Journal on Scientific and Statistical Computing*, 9:485–502, 1988.

[LC89]   G.-J. Li and T. Coleman. A new method for solving triangular systems on distributed memory message passing multiprocessors. *SIAM Journal on Scientific and Statistical Computing*, 10:382–396, 1989.

[LD90]   S. Lakshmivarahan and S. K. Dhall. *Analysis and Design of Parallel Algorithms: Arithmetic and Matrix Problems*. McGraw-Hill, New York, NY, 1990.

[LDP89]   M. R. Leuze, L. W. Dowdy, and K. H. Park. Multiprogramming a distributed-memory multiprocessor. *Concurrency: Practice and Experience*, 1(1):19–33, September 1989.

[Lea99]   D. Lea. *Concurrent Programming in Java, Second Edition: Design Principles and Patterns*. Addison-Wesley, 1999.

[Lei83]   F. T. Leighton. Parallel computation using mesh of trees. In *Proceedings of International Workshop on Graph-Theoretic Concepts in Computer Science*, 1983.

[Lei85a]   F. T. Leighton. Tight bounds on the complexity of parallel sorting. *IEEE Transactions on Computers*, C–34(4):344–354, April 1985.

[Lei85b]   C. E. Leiserson. Fat-trees: Universal networks for hardware efficient super-computing. In *Proceedings of the 1985 International Conference on Parallel Processing*, 393–402, 1985.

[Lei92]   F. T. Leighton. *Introduction to Parallel Algorithms and Architectures*. Morgan Kaufmann, San Mateo, CA, 1992.

[LER92]   T. G. Lewis and H. El-Rewini. *Introduction to Parallel Computing*. Prentice-Hall, Englewood Cliffs, NJ, 1992.

[Les93]   B. P. Lester. *The Art of Parallel Programming*. Prentice-Hall, Englewood Cliffs, NJ, 1993.

[Lev87]   S. P. Levitan. Measuring communications structures in parallel architectures and algorithms. In L. H. Jamieson, D. B. Gannon, and R. J. Douglass, editors, *The Characteristics of Parallel Algorithms*. MIT Press, Cambridge, MA, 1987.

[Lew91]   D. A. Lewine. *Posix Programmer's Guide: Writing Portable Unix Programs with the Posix. 1 Standard*. O'Reilly & Associates, 1991.

[LHZ98]   H. Lu, C. Hu, and W. Zwaenepoel. OpenMP on networks of workstations. In *SC '98, High Performance Networking and Computing Conference*, Orlando, Florida, 1998.

[Lil92]   D. J. Lilja. *Architectural Alternatives for Exploiting Parallelism*. IEEE Computer Society Press, Los Alamitos, CA, 1992.

[Lin83]   G. Lindstrom. The key node method: A highly parallel alpha-beta algorithm. Technical Report 83-101, Computer Science Department, University of Utah, Salt Lake City, UT, 1983.

[Lin92]   Z. Lin. A distributed fair polling scheme applied to or-parallel logic programming. *International Journal of Parallel Programming*, 20(4), August 1992.

[LK72]   K. N. Levitt and W. T. Kautz. Cellular arrays for the solution of graph problems. *Communications of the ACM*, 15(9):789–801, September 1972.

[LK85]   D. B. Leifker and L. N. Kanal. A hybrid SSS*/alpha-beta algorithm for parallel search of game trees. In *Proceedings of the International Joint Conference on Artificial Intelligence*, 1044–1046, 1985.

[LLG$^+$92]   D. Lenoski, J. Laudon, K. Gharachorloo, W. D. Weber, A. Gupta, J. L. Hennessy, M. Horowitz, and M. Lam. The Stanford dash multiprocessor. *IEEE Computer*, 63–79, March 1992.

[LM97]   E. K. Lee and J. E. Mitchell. Computational experience of an interior-point algorithm in a parallel branch-and-cut framework. In *Proceedings for SIAM Conference on Parallel Processing for Scientific Computing*, 1997.

[LMR88]   F. T. Leighton, B. Maggs, and S. K. Rao. Universal packet routing algorithms. In *29th Annual Symposium on Foundations of Computer Science*, 256–271, 1988.

[Loa92]   C. V. Loan. *Computational Frameworks for the Fast Fourier Transform*. SIAM, Philadelphia, PA, 1992.

[LP92]   Y. Li and P. M. Pardalos. Parallel algorithms for the quadratic assignment problem. In P. M. Pardalos, editor, *Advances in Optimization and Parallel Computing*, 177–189. North-Holland, Amsterdam, The Netherlands, 1992.

[LPP88]   F. Luccio, A. Pietracaprina, and G. Pucci. A probabilistic simulation of PRAMs on a bounded degree network. *Information Processing Letters*, 28:141–147, July 1988.

[LPP89]   F. Luccio, A. Pietracaprina, and G. Pucci. A new scheme for deterministic simulation of PRAMs in VLSI. *SIAM Journal of Computing*, 1989.

[LRZ95]   C. Leiserson, K. Randall, and Y. Zhou. Cilk: An efficient multithreaded runtime system. In *Proceedings of the Fifth ACM SIGPLAN Symposium on Principles and Practice of Parallel Programming (PPoPP)*, Santa Barbara, CA, 1995.

[LS84]   T. H. Lai and S. Sahni. Anomalies in parallel branch and bound algorithms. *Communications of the ACM*, 594–602, 1984.

[LS85]   T. H. Lai and A. Sprague. Performance of parallel branch-and-bound algorithms. *IEEE Transactions on Computers*, C-34(10), October 1985.

[LS86]   T. H. Lai and A. Sprague. A note on anomalies in parallel branch-and-bound algorithms with one-to-one bounding functions. *Information Processing Letters*, 23:119–122, October 1986.

[LSS88]   J. Lee, E. Shragowitz, and S. Sahni. A hypercube algorithm for the 0/1 knapsack problem. *Journal of Parallel and Distributed Computing*, (5):438–456, 1988.

[Lub86]   M. Luby. A simple parallel algorithm for the maximal independent set problem. *SIAM Journal on Computing*, 15(4):1036–1053, 1986.

[LW66]   E. L. Lawler and D. Woods. Branch-and-bound methods: A survey. *Operations Research*, 14, 1966.

[LW84]   G.-J. Li and B. W. Wah. Computational efficiency of parallel approximate branch-and-bound algorithms. In *Proceedings of the 1984 International Conference on Parallel Processing*, 473–480, 1984.

[LW85]   G.-J. Li and B. W. Wah. Parallel processing of serial dynamic programming problems. In *Proceedings of COMPSAC 85*, 81–89, 1985.

[LW86]   G.-J. Li and B. W. Wah. Coping with anomalies in parallel branch-and-bound algorithms. *IEEE Transactions on Computers*, C-35, June 1986.

[LW95]   D. Lenoski and W. D. Weber. *Scalable Shared-Memory Multiprocessing*. Morgan Kaufmann, San Mateo, CA, 1995.

[LY86]   M. Li and Y. Yesha. New lower bounds for parallel computations. In *Proceedings of 18th ACM Conference on Theory of Computing*, 177–187, 1986.

[MC82]   T. A. Marsland and M. S. Campbell. Parallel search of strongly ordered game trees. *Computing Surveys*, 14:533–551, 1982.

[MD92]   A. Mahanti and C. Daniels. SIMD parallel heuristic search. *Artificial Intelligence*, 1992.

[MD93]   N. R. Mahapatra and S. Dutt. Scalable duplicate pruning strategies for parallel A* graph search. In *Proceedings of the Fifth IEEE Symposium on Parallel and Distributed Processing*, 1993.

[MdV87]   O. A. McBryan and E. F. V. de Velde. Hypercube algorithms and implementations. *SIAM Journal on Scientific and Statistical Computing*, 8(2):s227–s287, March 1987.

[Mes94]   Message Passing Interface Forum. *MPI: A Message-Passing Interface Standard*. Available at http://www.mpi-forum.org. May 1994.

[Mes97]   Message Passing Interface Forum. *MPI-2: Extensions to the Message-Passing Interface*. Available at http://www.mpi-forum.org. July 1997.

[MFMV90]   B. Monien, R. Feldmann, P. Mysliwietz, and O. Vornberger. Parallel game tree search by dynamic tree decomposition. In V. Kumar, P. S. Gopalakrishnan, and L. N. Kanal, editors, *Parallel Algorithms for Machine Intelligence and Vision*. Springer-Verlag, New York, NY, 1990.

[MG89]   C. U. Martel and D. Q. Gusfield. A fast parallel quicksort algorithm. *Information Processing Letters*, 30:97–102, 1989.

[Mil91]   D. Miller. Exact distributed algorithms for travelling salesman problem. In *Proceedings of the Workshop on Parallel Computing of Discrete Optimization Problems*, 1991.

[MK99]   J. Magee and J. Kramer. *Concurrency: State Models and Java Programs*. John Wiley & Sons, 1999.

[MKRS88]   R. Miller, V. K. P. Kumar, D. I. Reisis, and Q. F. Stout. Meshes with reconfigurable buses. In *Proceedings of MIT Conference on Advanced Research in VLSI*, 163–178, 1988.

[MM73]   A. Martelli and U. Montanari. From dynamic programming to search algorithms with functional costs. In *Proceedings of the International Joint Conference on Artifi cial Intelligence*, 345–349, 1973.

[MM91]   P. Messina and A. Murli, editors. *Practical Parallel Computing: Status and Prospects*. Wiley, Chichester, UK, 1991.

[MMR95]   B. Mans, T. Mautor, and C. Roucairol. A parallel depth first search branch and bound for the quadratic assignment problem. *European Journal of Operational Research*, 81(3):617–628, 1995.

[Mod88]   J. J. Modi. *Parallel Algorithms and Matrix Computation*. Oxford University Press, Oxford, UK, 1988.

[Moh83]   J. Mohan. Experience with two parallel programs solving the traveling salesman problem. In *Proceedings of the 1983 International Conference on Parallel Processing*, 191–193, 1983.

[Mol86]   C. B. Moler. Matrix computation on distributed-memory multiprocessors.
In M. T. Heath, editor, *Hypercube Multiprocessors 1986*, 181–195. SIAM,
Philadelphia, PA, 1986.

[Mol87]   C. B. Moler. Another look at Amdahl's law. Technical Report TN-02-0587-
0288, Intel Scientific Computers, 1987.

[Mol93]   D. I. Moldovan. *Parallel Processing: From Applications to Systems*. Morgan
Kaufmann, San Mateo, CA, 1993.

[MP85]   T. A. Marsland and F. Popowich. Parallel game tree search. *IEEE Transactions on Pattern Analysis and Machine Intelligence*, PAMI-7(4):442–452,
July 1985.

[MP93]   D. L. Miller and J. F. Pekny. The role of performance metrics for parallel
mathematical programming algorithms. *ORSA Journal on Computing*, 5(1),
1993.

[MR]   D. C. Marinescu and J. R. Rice. On high level characterization of parallelism.
Technical Report CSD-TR-1011, CAPO Report CER-90-32, Computer Sci-
ence Department, Purdue University, West Lafayette, IN. Also published in
Journal of Parallel and Distributed Computing, 1993.

[MRSR92] G. P. McKeown, V. J. Rayward-Smith, and S. A. Rush. *Parallel Branch-and-
Bound*, 111–150. Advanced Topics in Computer Science. Blackwell Scientific Publications, Oxford, UK, 1992.

[MS88]   Y. W. E. Ma and D. G. Shea. Downward scalability of parallel architectures. In *Proceedings of the 1988 International Conference on Supercomputing*, 109–120, 1988.

[MS90]   G. Manzini and M. Somalvico. Probabilistic performance analysis of heuristic search using parallel hash tables. In *Proceedings of the International Symposium on Artificial Intelligence and Mathematics*, 1990.

[MS96]   R. Miller and Q. F. Stout. *Parallel Algorithms for Regular Architectures*. MIT
Press, Cambridge, MA, 1996.

[MV84]   K. Mehlhorn and U. Vishkin. Randomized and deterministic simulations of
PRAMs by parallel machines with restricted granularity of parallel memories.
Acta Informatica, 21(4):339–374, November 1984.

[MV85]   B. Monien and O. Vornberger. The ring machine. Technical report, University of Paderborn, Germany, 1985. Also in *Computers and Artificial Intelligence*, 3(1987).

[MV87]   B. Monien and O. Vornberger. Parallel processing of combinatorial search trees. In *Proceedings of International Workshop on Parallel Algorithms and Architectures*, 1987.

[MVS86]   B. Monien, O. Vornberger, and E. Spekenmeyer. Superlinear speedup for parallel backtracking. Technical Report 30, University of Paderborn, Germany, 1986.

[NA91]   D. Nussbaum and A. Agarwal. Scalability of parallel machines. *Communications of the ACM*, 34(3):57–61, 1991.

[Nat90]   L. Natvig. Investigating the practical value of Cole's $O(\log n)$ time crew pram merge sort algorithm. In *5th International Symposium on Computing and Information Sciences*, October 1990.

[NBF96]   B. Nichols, B. Buttlar, and J. P. Farrell. *Pthreads Programming*. O'Reilly & Associates, Newton, MA 02164, 1996.

[nCU90]   nCUBE Corporation. *nCUBE 6400 Processor Manual*. Beaverton, OR, 1990.

[ND96]   S. J. Norton and M. D. DiPasquale. *Thread time: the multithreaded programming guide*. Hewlett-Packard professional books. Prentice-Hall, Englewood Cliffs, NJ 07632, 1996.

[Ni91]   L. M. Ni. A layered classification of parallel computers. In *Proceedings of 1991 International Conference for Young Computer Scientists*, 28–33, 1991.

[Nic90]   J. R. Nickolls. The design of the MasPar MP-1: A cost-effective massively parallel computer. In *IEEE Digest of Papers—Comcom*, 25–28. IEEE Computer Society Press, Los Alamitos, CA, 1990.

[NM93]   L. M. Ni and McKinley. A survey of wormhole routing techniques in direct connect networks. *IEEE Computer*, 26(2), February 1993.

[NMB83]   D. Nath, S. N. Maheshwari, and P. C. P. Bhatt. Efficient VLSI networks for parallel processing based on orthogonal trees. *IEEE Transactions on Computers*, C–32:21–23, June 1983.

[NS79]   D. Nassimi and S. Sahni. Bitonic sort on a mesh connected parallel computer. *IEEE Transactions on Computers*, C–28(1), January 1979.

[NS80]   D. Nassimi and S. Sahni. Finding connected components and connected ones on a mesh-connected computer. *SIAM Journal of Computing*, 9(4):744–757, November 1980.

[NS87]   A. Norton and A. J. Silberger. Parallelization and performance analysis of the Cooley-Tukey FFT algorithm for shared memory architectures. *IEEE Transactions on Computers*, C-36(5):581–591, 1987.

[NS93]   M. Nigam and S. Sahni. Sorting *n* numbers on *n* × *n* reconfigurable meshes with buses. In *7th International Parallel Processing Symposium*, 174–181, 1993.

[NSF91]   *Grand Challenges: High Performance Computing and Communications.* A Report by the Committee on Physical, Mathematical and Engineering Sciences, NSF/CISE, 1800 G Street NW, Washington, DC, 20550, 1991.

[Nug88]   S. F. Nugent. The iPSC/2 direct-connect communications technology. In *Proceedings of the Third Conference on Hypercubes, Concurrent Computers, and Applications*, 51–60, 1988.

[Nus82]   H. J. Nussbaumer. *Fast Fourier Transform and Convolution Algorithms.* Springer-Verlag, New York, NY, 1982.

[NW88]   D. M. Nicol and F. H. Willard. Problem size, parallel architecture, and optimal speedup. *Journal of Parallel and Distributed Computing*, 5:404–420, 1988.

[GOV99]   *Funding a Revolution: Government Support for Computing Research.* Committee on Innovations in Computing and Communications. National Academy Press, 1999.

[OR88]   J. M. Ortega and C. H. Romine. The *ijk* forms of factorization methods II: Parallel systems. *Parallel Computing*, 7:149–162, 1988.

[Ort88]   J. M. Ortega. *Introduction to Parallel and Vector Solution of Linear Systems.* Plenum Press, New York, NY, 1988.

[OS85]   D. P. O'Leary and G. W. Stewart. Data-flow algorithms for parallel matrix computations. *Communications of the ACM*, 28:840–853, 1985.

[OS86]   D. P. O'Leary and G. W. Stewart. Assignment and scheduling in parallel matrix factorization. *Linear Algebra and its Applications*, 77:275–299, 1986.

[Pac98]   P. Pacheco. *Parallel Programming with MPI.* Morgan Kaufmann, 1998.

[PBG+85]   G. F. Pfister, W. C. Brantley, D. A. George, S. L. Harvey, W. J. Kleinfelder, K. P. McAuliffe, E. A. Melton, V. A. Norlton, and J. Weiss. The IBM research parallel processor prototype (RP3): Introduction and architecture. In *Proceedings of 1985 International Conference on Parallel Processing*, 764–771, 1985.

[PC89]   P. M. Pardalos and J. Crouse. A parallel algorithm for the quadratic assignment problem. In *Supercomputing '89 Proceedings*, 351–360. ACM Press, New York, NY, 1989.

[PD89]   K. H. Park and L. W. Dowdy. Dynamic partitioning of multiprocessor systems. *International Journal of Parallel Processing*, 18(2):91–120, 1989.

[Pea84]   J. Pearl. *Heuristics—Intelligent Search Strategies for Computer Problem Solving*. Addison-Wesley, Reading, MA, 1984.

[Per87]   R. Perrott. *Parallel Programming*. Addison-Wesley, Reading, MA, 1987.

[Pfi98]   G. F. Pfister. *In Search of Clusters*. Prentice Hall, Englewood Cliffs, NJ, 1998. 2nd Edition.

[PFK90]   C. Powley, C. Ferguson, and R. Korf. Parallel heuristic search: Two approaches. In V. Kumar, P. S. Gopalakrishnan, and L. N. Kanal, editors, *Parallel Algorithms for Machine Intelligence and Vision*. Springer-Verlag, New York, NY, 1990.

[PG98]   T. Q. Pham and P. K. Garg. *Multithreaded Programming with Win32*. Prentice Hall, 1998.

[PH90]   D. A. Patterson and J. L. Hennessy. *Computer Architecture: A Quantitative Approach*. Morgan Kaufmann, San Mateo, CA, 1990.

[PH96]   D. A. Patterson and J. L. Hennessy. *Computer Architecture: A Quantitative Approach, 2nd edition*. Morgan Kaufmann, San Mateo, CA, 1996.

[PK89]   R. C. Paige and C. P. Kruskal. Parallel algorithms for shortest path problems. In *Proceedings of 1989 International Conference on Parallel Processing*, 14–19, 1989.

[PK95]   I. Pramanick and J. G. Kuhl. An inherently parallel method for heuristic problem-solving: Part I – general framework. *IEEE Transactions on Parallel and Distributed Systems*, 6(10), October 1995.

[PKF92]   C. Powley, R. Korf, and C. Ferguson. IDA* on the connection machine. *Artificial Intelligence*, 1992.

[Pla89]   C. C. Plaxton. Load balancing, selection and sorting on the hypercube. In *Proceedings of the 1989 ACM Symposium on Parallel Algorithms and Architectures*, 64–73, 1989.

[PLRR94]   P. M. Pardalos, Y. Li, K. Ramakrishna, and M. Resende. Lower bounds for the quadratic assignment problem. *Annals of Operations Research*, 50:387–411, 1994. Special Volume on Applications of Combinatorial Optimization.

[PR85]   V. Pan and J. H. Reif. Efficient parallel solution of linear systems. In *17th Annual ACM Symposium on Theory of Computing*, 143–152, 1985.

[PR89]   P. M. Pardalos and G. P. Rodgers. Parallel branch-and-bound algorithms for unconstrainted quadratic zero-one programming. In R. Sharda *et al.*, editors, *Impacts of Recent Computer Advances on Operations Research*, 131–143. North-Holland, Amsterdam, The Netherlands, 1989.

[PR90]   P. M. Pardalos and G. P. Rodgers. Parallel branch-and-bound algorithms for quadratic zero-one programming on a hypercube architecture. *Annals of Operations Research*, 22:271–292, 1990.

[PR91]   M. Padberg and G. Rinaldi. A branch-and-cut algorithm for the resolution of large-scale symmetric traveling salesman problems. *SIAM Review*, 33:60–100, 1991.

[Pri57] R. C. Prim. Shortest connection network and some generalizations. *Bell Systems Technical Journal*, 36:1389–1401, 1957.

[PRV88] G. Plateau, C. Roucairol, and I. Valabregue. Algorithm PR2 for the parallel size reduction of the 0/1 multiknapsack problem. In *INRIA Rapports de Recherche*, number 811, 1988.

[PS82]   C. H. Papadimitriou and K. Steiglitz. *Combinatorial Optimization: Algorithms and Complexity*. Prentice-Hall, Englewood Cliffs, NJ, 1982.

[PV80]   F. P. Preparata and J. Vuillemin. Area-time optimal VLSI networks for matrix multiplication. In *Proceedings of the 14th Princeton Conference on Information Science and Systems*, 300–309, 1980.

[PY88]   C. H. Papadimitriou and M. Yannakakis. Towards an architecture independent analysis of parallel algorithms. In *Proceedings of 20th ACM Symposium on Theory of Computing*, 510–513, 1988.

[QD86]   M. J. Quinn and N. Deo. An upper bound for the speedup of parallel branch-and-bound algorithms. *BIT*, 26(1), March 1986.

[Qui88] M. J. Quinn. Parallel sorting algorithms for tightly coupled multiprocessors. *Parallel Computing*, 6:349–357, 1988.

[Qui89] M. J. Quinn. Analysis and implementation of branch-and-bound algorithms on a hypercube multicomputer. *IEEE Transactions on Computers*, 1989.

[Qui94] M. J. Quinn. *Parallel Computing: Theory and Practice*. McGraw-Hill, New York, NY, 1994.

[Ram97]   V. Ramachandran. Qsm: A general purpose shared-memory model for parallel computation. In *Foundations of Software Technology and Theoretical Computer Science*, 1–5, 1997.

[Ran89]   A. G. Ranade. *Fluent Parallel Computation*. Ph.D. Thesis, Department of Computer Science, Yale University, New Haven, CT, 1989.

[Ran91]   A. G. Ranade. Optimal speedup for backtrack search on a butterfly network. In *Proceedings of the Third ACM Symposium on Parallel Algorithms and Architectures*, 1991.

[Rao90]   V. N. Rao. *Parallel Processing of Heuristic Search*. Ph.D. Thesis, University of Texas, Austin, TX, 1990.

[Ras78]   L. Raskin. *Performance Evaluation of Multiple Processor Systems*. Ph.D. Thesis, Carnegie-Mellon University, Pittsburgh, PA, 1978.

[RB76]   C. M. Rader and N. M. Brenner. A new principle for Fast fourier transform. *IEEE Transactions on Acoustics, Speech and Signal Processing*, 24:264–265, 1976.

[RDK89]   C. Renolet, M. Diamond, and J. Kimbel. Analytical and heuristic modeling of distributed algorithms. Technical Report E3646, FMC Corporation, Advanced Systems Center, Minneapolis, MN, 1989.

[Rei81]   R. Reischuk. Probabilistic algorithms for sorting and selection. *SIAM Journal of Computing*, 396–409, 1981.

[RF89]   D. A. Reed and R. M. Fujimoto. *Multicomputer Networks: Message-Based Parallel Processing*. MIT Press, Cambridge, MA, 1989.

[RICN88]   K. Rokusawa, N. Ichiyoshi, T. Chikayama, and H. Nakashima. An efficient termination detection and abortion algorithm for distributed processing systems. In *Proceedings of 1988 International Conference on Parallel Processing: Vol. I*, 18–22, 1988.

[RK87]   V. N. Rao and V. Kumar. Parallel depth-first search, part I: Implementation. *International Journal of Parallel Programming*, 16(6):479–499, 1987.

[RK88a]   V. N. Rao and V. Kumar. Concurrent access of priority queues. *IEEE Transactions on Computers*, C–37 (12), 1988.

[RK88b]   V. N. Rao and V. Kumar. Superlinear speedup in state-space search. In *Proceedings of the 1988 Foundation of Software Technology and Theoretical Computer Science*, number 338, 161–174. Springer-Verlag Series Lecture Notes in Computer Science, 1988.

[RK93]   V. N. Rao and V. Kumar. On the efficicency of parallel backtracking. *IEEE Transactions on Parallel and Distributed Systems*, 4(4):427–437, April 1993. available as a technical report TR 90-55, Computer Science Department, University of Minnesota.

[RKR87]   V. N. Rao, V. Kumar, and K. Ramesh. A parallel implementation of iterative-deepening-A*. In *Proceedings of the National Conference on Artificial Intelligence (AAAI-87)*, 878–882, 1987.

[RND77]   E. M. Reingold, J. Nievergelt, and N. Deo. *Combinatorial Algorithms: Theory and Practice*. Prentice-Hall, Englewood Cliffs, NJ, 1977.

[RO88]   C. H. Romine and J. M. Ortega. Parallel solution of triangular systems of equations. *Parallel Computing*, 6:109–114, 1988.

[Rob75]   M. O. Robin. Probabilistic algorithms. In J. Traub, editor, *Algorithms and Complexity: New Directions and Recent Results*, 21–39. Academic Press, San Diego, CA, 1975.

[Rob90]   Y. Robert. *The Impact of Vector and Parallel Architectures on Gaussian Elimination*. John Wiley and Sons, New York, NY, 1990.

[Rom87]   C. H. Romine. The parallel solution of triangular systems on a hypercube. In M. T. Heath, editor, *Hypercube Multiprocessors 1987*, 552–559. SIAM, Philadelphia, PA, 1987.

[Rou87]   C. Roucairol. A parallel branch-and-bound algorithm for the quadratic assignment problem. *Discrete Applied Mathematics*, 18:211–225, 1987.

[Rou91]   C. Roucairol. Parallel branch-and-bound on shared-memory multiprocessors. In *Proceedings of the Workshop On Parallel Computing of Discrete Optimization Problems*, 1991.

[RRRR96]   K. A. Robbins, S. Robbins, K. R. Robbins, and S. Robbins. *Practical UNIX Programming: A Guide to Concurrency, Communication, and Multithreading*. Prentice Hall, 1996.

[RS90a]   A. P. R. Alverson, D. Callahan, D. Cummings, B. Koblenz and B. Smith. The tera computer system. In *International Conference on Supercomputing*, 1–6, 1990.

[RS90b]   S. Ranka and S. Sahni. *Hypercube Algorithms for Image Processing and Pattern Recognition*. Springer-Verlag, New York, NY, 1990.

[RV87]   J. H. Reif and L. G. Valiant. A logarithmic time sort for linear size networks. *Journal of the ACM*, 34(1):60–76, January 1987.

[Ryt88]   W. Rytter. Efficient parallel computations for dynamic programming. *Theoretical Computer Science*, 59:297–307, 1988.

[RZ89]   M. Reeve and S. E. Zenith, editors. *Parallel Processing and Artificial Intelligence*. Wiley, Chichester, UK, 1989.

[Saa86]   Y. Saad. Communication complexity of the Gaussian elimination algorithm on multiprocessors. *Linear Algebra and its Applications*, 77:315–340, 1986.

[SB77]   H. Sullivan and T. R. Bashkow. A large scale, homogeneous, fully distributed parallel machine. In *Proceedings of Fourth Symposium on Computer Architecture*, 105–124, March 1977.

[SBCV90]   R. H. Saavedra-Barrera, D. E. Culler, and T. Von Eiken. Analysis of multithreaded architectures for parallel computing. Report UCB/CSD 90/569, University of California, Berkeley, Computer Science Division, Berkeley, CA, April 1990.

[Sch80]   J. T. Schwartz. Ultracomputers. *ACM Transactions on Programming Languages and Systems*, 2:484–521, October 1980.

[Sed78]   R. Sedgewick. Implementing quicksort programs. *Communications of the ACM*, 21(10):847–857, 1978.

[Sei85]   C. L. Seitz. The cosmic cube. *Communications of the ACM*, 28(1):22–33, 1985.

[Sei89]   S. R. Seidel. Circuit-switched vs. store-and-forward solutions to symmetric communication problems. In *Proceedings of the Fourth Conference on Hypercubes, Concurrent Computers, and Applications*, 253–255, 1989.

[Sei92]   C. L. Seitz. Mosaic C: An experimental fine-grain multicomputer. Technical report, California Institute of Technology, Pasadena, CA, 1992.

[SG88]   S. R. Seidel and W. L. George. Binsorting on hypercube with d-port communication. In *Proceedings of the Third Conference on Hypercube Concurrent Computers*, 1455–1461, January 1988.

[SG91]   X.-H. Sun and J. L. Gustafson. Toward a better parallel performance metric. *Parallel Computing*, 17:1093–1109, December 1991. Also available as Technical Report IS-5053, UC-32, Ames Laboratory, Iowa State University, Ames, IA.

[Sha85]   J. A. Sharp. *Data-Flow Computing*. Ellis Horwood, Chichester, UK, 1985.

[She59]   D. L. Shell. A high-speed sorting procedure. *Communications of the ACM*, 2(7):30–32, July 1959.

[SHG93]   J. P. Singh, J. L. Hennessy, and A. Gupta. Scaling parallel programs for multiprocessors: Methodology and examples. *IEEE Computer*, 26(7):42–50, 1993.

[Sie77]   H. J. Siegel. The universality of various types of SIMD machine interconnection networks. In *Proceedings of the 4th Annual Symposium on Computer Architecture*, 23–25, 1977.

[Sie85]   H. J. Siegel. *Interconnection Networks for Large-Scale Parallel Processing*. D. C. Heath, Lexington, MA, 1985.

[SJ81]   C. Savage and J. Jaja. Fast, efficient parallel algorithms for some graph problems. *SIAM Journal of Computing*, 10(4):682–690, November 1981.

[SK89]   W. Shu and L. V. Kale. A dynamic scheduling strategy for the chare-kernel system. In *Proceedings of Supercomputing Conference*, 389–398, 1989.

[SK90]   V. Saletore and L. V. Kale. Consistent linear speedup to a first solution in parallel state-space search. In *Proceedings of the 1990 National Conference on Artificial Intelligence*, 227–233, August 1990.

[SKAT91a]   V. Singh, V. Kumar, G. Agha, and C. Tomlinson. Efficient algorithms for parallel sorting on mesh multicomputers. *International Journal of Parallel Programming*, 20(2):95–131, 1991.

[SKAT91b]   V. Singh, V. Kumar, G. Agha, and C. Tomlinson. Scalability of parallel sorting on mesh multicomputers. *International Journal of Parallel Programming*, 20(2), 1991.

[SM86]   S. J. Stolfo and D. P. Miranker. The DADO production system machine. *Journal of Parallel and Distributed Computing*, 3:269–296, June 1986.

[Smi84]   D. R. Smith. Random trees and the analysis of branch and bound procedures. *Journal of the ACM*, 31(1), 1984.

[SN90]   X.-H. Sun and L. M. Ni. Another view of parallel speedup. In *Supercomputing '90 Proceedings*, 324–333, 1990.

[SN93]   X.-H. Sun and L. M. Ni. Scalable problems and memory-bounded speedup. *Journal of Parallel and Distributed Computing*, 19:27–37, September 1993.

[Sni82]   M. Snir. On parallel search. In *Proceedings of Principles of Distributed Computing*, 242–253, 1982.

[Sni85]   M. Snir. On parallel searching. *SIAM Journal of Computing*, 14(3):688–708, August 1985.

[Sny86]   L. Snyder. Type architectures, shared-memory and the corollary of modest potential. *Annual Review of Computer Science*, 1:289–317, 1986.

[SOHL⁺96] M. Snir, S. W. Otto, S. Huss-Lederman, D. W. Walker, and J. Dongarra. *MPI: The Complete Reference*. MIT Press, Cambridge, MA, 1996.

[Sol77]   M. Sollin. An algorithm attributed to Sollin. In S. Goodman and S. Hedetniemi, editors, *Introduction to The Design and Analysis of Algorithms*. McGraw-Hill, Cambridge, MA, 1977.

[SR91]   X.-H. Sun and D. T. Rover. Scalability of parallel algorithm-machine combinations. Technical Report IS-5057, Ames Laboratory, Iowa State University, Ames, IA, 1991. Also published in *IEEE Transactions on Parallel and Distributed Systems*.

[SS88]   Y. Saad and M. H. Schultz. Topological properties of hypercubes. *IEEE Transactions on Computers*, 37:867–872, 1988.

[SS89a]   Y. Saad and M. H. Schultz. Data communication in hypercubes. *Journal of Parallel and Distributed Computing*, 6:115–135, 1989. Also available as Technical Report YALEU/DCS/RR-428 from the Department of Computer Science, Yale University, New Haven, CT.

[SS89b]   Y. Saad and M. H. Schultz. Data communication in parallel architectures. *Parallel Computing*, 11:131–150, 1989.

[SS90]   H. Shi and J. Schaeffer. Parallel sorting by regular sampling. *Journal of Parallel and Distributed Computing*, 14:361–372, 1990.

[ST95]   B. M. S. Tschvke, R. Lling. Solving the traveling salesman problem with a distributed branch-and-bound algorithm on a 1024 processor network. In *Proceedings of the 9th International Parallel Processing Symposium*, 182–189, Santa Barbara, CA, April 1995.

[Sto71]   H. S. Stone. Parallel processing with the perfect shuffle. *IEEE Transactions on Computers*, C-20(2):153–161, 1971.

[Sto93]   H. S. Stone. *High-Performance Computer Architecture: Third Edition*. Addison-Wesley, Reading, MA, 1993.

[Sun95]   SunSoft. *Solaris multithreaded programming guide*. SunSoft Press, Mountainview, CA, 1995.

[Sup91]   Supercomputer Systems Division, Intel Corporation. *Paragon XP/S Product Overview*. Beaverton, OR, 1991.

[SV81]   Y. Shiloach and U. Vishkin. Finding the maximum, merging and sorting in a parallel computation model. *Journal of Algorithms*, 88–102, 1981.

[SV82]   Y. Shiloach and U. Vishkin. An $O(n^2 \log n)$ parallel max-flow algorithm. *Journal of Algorithms*, 3:128–146, 1982.

[SW87]   Q. F. Stout and B. A. Wagar. Passing messages in link-bound hypercubes. In M. T. Heath, editor, *Hypercube Multiprocessors 1987*, 251–257. SIAM, Philadelphia, PA, 1987.

[Swa87]   P. N. Swarztrauber. Multiprocessor FFTs. *Parallel Computing*, 5:197–210, 1987.

[SZ96]   X.-H. Sun and J. P. Zhu. Performance considerations of shared virtual memory machines. *IEEE Trans. on Parallel and Distributed Systems*, 6(11):1185–1194, 1996.

[Tab90]   D. Tabak. *Multiprocessors*. Prentice-Hall, Englewood Cliffs, NJ, 1990.

[Tab91]   D. Tabak. *Advanced Multiprocessors*. McGraw-Hill, New York, NY, 1991.

[Tak87]   R. Take. An optimal routing method of all-to-all communication on hypercube networks. In *35th Information Processing Society of Japan*, 1987.

[TEL95]   D. M. Tullsen, S. Eggers, and H. M. Levy. Simultaneous multithreading: Maximizing on-chip parallelism. In *Proceedings of the 22nd Annual International Symposium on Computer Architecture*, 1995.

[Ten90]   S. Teng. Adaptive parallel algorithms for integral knapsack problems. *Journal of Parallel and Distributed Computing*, 8:400–406, 1990.

[Thi90]   Thinking Machines Corporation. *The CM-2 Technical Summary*. Cambridge, MA. 1990.

[Thi91]   Thinking Machines Corporation. *The CM-5 Technical Summary*. Cambridge, MA. 1991.

[Tho83]   C. D. Thompson. Fourier transforms in VLSI. *IBM Journal of Research and Development*, C-32(11):1047–1057, 1983.

[Thr99]   J. Throop. Standards: OpenMP: Shared-memory parallelism from the ashes. *Computer*, 32(5):108–109, May 1999.

[Tic88]   W. F. Tichy. Parallel matrix multiplication on the connection machine. Technical Report RIACS TR 88.41, Research Institute for Advanced Computer Science, NASA Ames Research Center, Moffet Field, CA, 1988.

[TK77]   C. D. Thompson and H. T. Kung. Sorting on a mesh-connected parallel computer. *Communications of the ACM*, 21:263–271, 1977.

[TL90]   Z. Tang and G.-J. Li. Optimal granularity of grid iteration problems. In *Proceedings of the 1990 International Conference on Parallel Processing*, I111–I118, 1990.

[Tul96]   D. M. Tullsen. *Simultaneous multithreading*. Ph.D. Thesis, University of Washington, Seattle, WA, 1996.

[TV85]   R. E. Tarjan and U. Vishkin. An efficient parallel biconnectivity algorithm. *SIAM Journal on Computing*, 14(4):862–874, November 1985.

[TY96]   J.-Y. Tsai and P.-C. Yew. The superthreaded architecture: Thread pipelining with run-time data dependence checking and control speculation. In *Proceedings of the International Conference on Parallel Architectures and Compilation Techniques*, 35–46, 1996.

[Upf84]   E. Upfal. A probabilistic relation between desirable and feasible models of parallel computation. In *Proceedings of the 16th ACM Conference on Theory of Computing*, 258–265, 1984.

[UW84]   E. Upfal and A. Widgerson. How to share memory in a distributed system. In *Proceedings of the 25th Annual Symposium on the Foundation of Computer Science*, 171–180, 1984.

[Val75]   L. G. Valiant. Parallelism in comparison problems. *SIAM Journal of Computing*, 4(3):348–355, September 1975.

[Val82]   L. G. Valiant. A scheme for fast parallel communication. *SIAM Journal on Computing*, 11:350–361, 1982.

[Val90a]   L. G. Valiant. A bridging model for parallel computation. *Communications of the ACM*, 33(8), 1990.

[Val90b]   L. G. Valiant. General purpose parallel architectures. *Handbook of Theoretical Computer Science*, 1990.

[Vav89]   S. A. Vavasis. Gaussian elimination with pivoting is P-complete. *SIAM Journal on Discrete Mathematics*, 2:413–423, 1989.

[VB81]   L. G. Valiant and G. J. Brebner. Universal schemes for parallel communication. In *Proceedings of the 13th ACM Symposium on Theory of Computation*, 263–277, 1981.

[VC89]   F. A. Van-Catledge. Towards a general model for evaluating the relative performance of computer systems. *International Journal of Supercomputer Applications*, 3(2):100–108, 1989.

[Vor86]   O. Vornberger. Implementing branch-and-bound in a ring of processors. Technical Report 29, University of Paderborn, Germany, 1986.

[Vor87a]   O. Vornberger. The personal supercomputer: A network of transputers. In *Proceedings of the 1987 International Conference on Supercomputing*, 1987.

[Vor87b]   O. Vornberger. Load balancing in a network of transputers. In *Proceedings of the Second International Workshop on Distributed Parallel Algorithms*, 1987.

[VS86]   J. S. Vitter and R. A. Simmons. New classes for parallel complexity: A study of unification and other complete problems for P. *IEEE Transactions on Computers*, May 1986.

[VSBR83]   L. G. Valiant, S. Skyum, S. Berkowitz, and C. Rackoff. Fast parallel computation of polynomials using few processors. *SIAM Journal of Computing*, 12(4):641–644, 1983.

[WA98]   B. Wilkinson and C. M. Allen. *Parallel Programming: Techniques and Applications Using Networked Workstations and Parallel Computers*. Prentice Hall, 1998.

[WA99]   B. Wilkinson and M. Allen. *Parallel Programming*. Prentice-Hall, NJ, 1999.

[Wag87]   B. A. Wagar. Hyperquicksort: A fast sorting algorithm for hypercubes. In *Proceedings of the Second Conference on Hypercube Multiprocessors*, 292–299, 1987.

[Wal91]   Y. Wallach. *Parallel Processing and Ada*. Prentice-Hall, Englewood Cliffs, NJ, 1991.

[WB72]   W. A. Wulf and C. G. Bell. C.mmp—a multimicroprocessor. In *Proceedings of AFIPS Conference*, 765–777, 1972.

[Wei97]   B. Weissman. *Active threads manual*. Technical Report TR-97-037, International Computer Science Institute, Berkeley, CA 94704, 1997.

[WF80]   C. L. Wu and T. Y. Feng. On a class of multistage interconnection networks. *IEEE Transactions on Computers*, 669–702, August 1980.

[WF84]   C. L. Wu and T. Y. Feng. *Interconnection Networks for Parallel and Distributed Processing*. IEEE Computer Society Press, Washington, DC, 1984.

[WI89]   K. Wada and N. Ichiyoshi. A distributed shortest path algorithm and its mapping on the Multi-PSI. In *Proceedings of International Conference of Parallel Processing*, 1989.

[Wil86]   H. S. Wilf. *Algorithms and Complexity*. Prentice-Hall, NJ, 1986.

[Wil95]   G. V. Wilson. *Practical Parallel Programming*. MIT Press, Cambridge, MA, 1995.

[Wil00]   A. Williams. *Windows 2000 Systems Programming Black Book*. The Coriolis Group, 2000.

[Win77]   S. Winograd. A new method for computing DFT. In *IEEE International Conference on Acoustics, Speech and Signal Processing*, 366–368, 1977.

[WL88]   B. W. Wah and G.-J. Li. Systolic processing for dynamic programming problems. *Circuits, Systems, and Signal Processing*, 7(2):119–149, 1988.

[WLY84]   B. W. Wah, G.-J. Li, and C. F. Yu. The status of MANIP—a multicomputer architecture for solving combinatorial extremum-search problems. In *Proceedings of 11th Annual International Symposium on Computer Architecture*, 56–63, 1984.

[WM84]   B. W. Wah and Y. W. E. Ma. MANIP—a multicomputer architecture for solving combinatorial extremum-search problems. *IEEE Transactions on Computers*, C–33, May 1984.

[Woo86]   J. V. Woods, editor. *Fifth Generation Computer Architectures*. North-Holland, Amsterdam, The Netherlands, 1986.

[Wor88]   P. H. Worley. *Information Requirements and the Implications for Parallel Computation*. Ph.D. Thesis, Stanford University, Department of Computer Science, Palo Alto, CA, 1988.

[Wor90]   P. H. Worley. The effect of time constraints on scaled speedup. *SIAM Journal on Scientific and Statistical Computing*, 11(5):838–858, 1990.

[Wor91]   P. H. Worley. Limits on parallelism in the numerical solution of linear PDEs. *SIAM Journal on Scientific and Statistical Computing*, 12:1–35, January 1991.

[WS88]   Y. Won and S. Sahni. A balanced bin sort for hypercube multiprocessors. *Journal of Supercomputing*, 2:435–448, 1988.

[WS89]   J. Woo and S. Sahni. Hypercube computing: Connected components. *Journal of Supercomputing*, 3:209–234, 1989.

[WS91]   J. Woo and S. Sahni. Computing biconnected components on a hypercube. *Journal of Supercomputing*, June 1991. Also available as Technical Report TR 89-7 from the Department of Computer Science, University of Minnesota, Minneapolis, MN.

[WY85]   B. W. Wah and C. F. Yu. Stochastic modeling of branch-and-bound algorithms with best-first search. *IEEE Transactions on Software Engineering*, SE-11, September 1985.

[Zho89]   X. Zhou. Bridging the gap between Amdahl's law and Sandia laboratory's result. *Communications of the ACM*, 32(8):1014–5, 1989.

[Zom96]   A. Zomaya, editor. *Parallel and Distributed Computing Handbook*. McGraw-Hill, 1996.

[ZRV89]   J. R. Zorbas, D. J. Reble, and R. E. VanKooten. Measuring the scalability of parallel computer systems. In *Supercomputing '89 Proceedings*, 832–841, 1989.

Author Index

Subject Index